Understanding Data Communications and Networks

Second Edition

UNDERSTANDING DATA COMMUNICATIONS AND NETWORKS

SECOND EDITION

WILLIAM A. SHAY

University of Wisconsin–Green Bay

An Imprint of Brooks/Cole Publishing Company

I(T)P® An International Thomson Publishing Company

Pacific Grove • Albany • Belmont • Bonn • Boston • Cincinnati • Detroit • Johannesburg • London •
Madrid • Melbourne • Mexico City • New York • Paris • Singapore • Tokyo • Toronto • Washington

Sponsoring Editor: *Mike Sugarman*
Marketing Team: *Michele Mootz*
Editorial Associate: *Kathryn Schooling*
Production Editor: *Marlene Thom*
Production: *Argosy*
Manuscript Editor: *Cindy Kogut*

Manufacturing Buyer: *Vena Dyer*
Interior Design and Illustration: *Argosy*
Cover Design: *Lisa Henry*
Cover Photo: *Bruce Bishop/The Photo File*
Typesetting: *Argosy*
Printing and Binding: *R.R. Donnelley & Sons, Crawfordsville*

For more information, contact PWS Publishing at Brooks/Cole Publishing Company:

BROOKS/COLE PUBLISHING COMPANY
511 Forest Lodge Road
Pacific Grove, CA 93950
USA

International Thomson Editores
Seneca 53
Col. Polanco
11560 México, D.F., México

International Thomson Publishing Europe
Berkshire House 168-173
High Holborn
London WC1V 7AA
England

International Thomson Publishing GmbH
Königswinterer Strasse 418
53227 Bonn
Germany

Nelson ITP
102 Dodds Street
South Melbourne, 3205
Victoria, Australia

International Thomson Publishing Asia
221 Henderson Road
#05-10 Henderson Building
Singapore 0315

Nelson Canada
1120 Birchmount Road
Scarborough, Ontario
Canada M1K 5G4

International Thomson Publishing Japan
Hirakawacho Kyowa Building, 3F
2-2-1 Hirakawacho
Chiyoda-ku, Tokyo 102
Japan

Printed in the United States of America

10   9   8   7   6   5   4   3   2   1

Trademark Notice

Library of Congress Cataloging-in-Publication Data

Shay, William A.
    Understanding data communications and networks / William A. Shay.
    — 2nd ed.
        p.   cm.
    Includes index.
    ISBN 0-534-95054-X
    1. Data transmission systems.   2. Computer networks.   I. Title.
TK5105.S49 1998
004.6—dc21
                                        98-29402
                                        CIP

TO JUDY—MY WIFE AND BEST FRIEND, ALWAYS

Contents

PREFACE

PURPOSE

The first edition of this book first appeared four years ago; much in the fields of data communications and computer networks has changed since then. Probably most visible is the emergence of the World Wide Web (WWW) and the many applications it supports. Perhaps less visible is the impact the Web has had on underlying network protocols to support these applications and the increased importance of issues involving privacy and security. In just a few years the scope of network users has changed forever. Not long ago most network users were primarily professionals, who might use email occasionally to talk to colleagues or request some vital information. Now network users number in the tens of millions and their uses range from professional needs to purely recreational activities.

Although much of this book's content has changed, its purpose is still fundamentally the same. It is designed for junior-level students in a computer science program who have a minimum of two semesters of programming and a knowledge of precalculus and discrete mathematics. It covers standard topics found in a typical introductory course in data communications and computer networks, such as transmission media, analog and digital signals, data transmissions, compression and encryption methods, network topologies, data security, Ethernets and token ring protocols, wide area network protocols, and World Wide Web applications. This book is designed to help the reader understand

- The differences, advantages, and disadvantages of different transmission media

- Analog and digital signals, modulation and demodulation techniques, and how modems work

- The effect of noise on transmissions and the need for error detection and correction, the mechanisms used, and their advantages and disadvantages

- Standards such as RS-232, RS-449, HDLC, SDLC, DES, X.25, OSI, SNA, IEEE 802.3, IEEE 802.4, IEEE 802.5, ATM, JPEG, MPEG, and TCP/IP, standards organizations, and why standards are needed
- The need for data compression techniques and a comparison of the different methods used.
- Worms and viruses and how they can affect a system
- The need for security, and various encryption techniques
- Differences between public and private key encryption systems
- The need for flow control and various ways of implementing it
- Local area network protocols and contention strategies for shared transmission media
- Methods of connecting local area networks
- Packet-switched networks and routing strategies
- The need for protocols to support real-time video applications and the emergence of ATM
- How to design and set up working client/server applications
- How increased Web use and the proliferation of multimedia applications have affected existing protocols and what is being done to deal with it
- How to incorporate client/server programming techniques into Web page development

Major changes have been made to the first edition, some based on comments I received from its readers and the rest based on the evolution of technology. Many involve clarification of figures or an improved description of protocols. However, the most significant changes from the first edition include the following:

- Improved coverage of wireless communications, especially satellite transmission, and a discussion of low earth orbit satellites.
- Update of the modulation/demodulation standards used in modem technology.
- New section on cable modems.
- Expanded coverage of Lempel-Ziv compression techniques.
- New sections on both JPEG and MPEG compression techniques for graphic and multimedia transmissions.
- Increased coverage of encryption methods, including new sections on the clipper chip and the Diffie-Hellman key exchange method.
- Increased coverage of public key encryption, including new material on authentication using hash-based schemes.
- Update of the section on viruses to include virus evolution and polymorphic viruses.
- Updated coverage of local area network standards to include 100 Mbps technologies.

- Revised discussion of Novell NetWare to include NetWare 4.0.

- Expanded discussion of routing techniques to include additional protocols such as link state routing and the Border Gateway Protocol.

- Expanded and revised discussion of the Internet protocol to include descriptions of the Domain Name System (DNS) and Internet protocol version 6.

- Revised coverage of TCP, including congestion control.

- New section on socket programming to include coverage of the client/server paradigm and the inclusion of a working client/server model that implements a file transfer protocol using socket connections.

- A new section on the World Wide Web with a focus on the use of client/server programming in the development of Web pages. Again, working models of client-side JavaScript programming and server-side CGI programming in C are presented.

- A new section on the Asynchronous Transfer Mode (ATM) protocol.

Although it would be difficult (almost certainly impossible) to cover all these subjects in a one-semester course, the range of topics allows instructors flexibility in choosing the topics best suited for their students.

An *Instructor's Solutions Manual,* with answers to review questions and exercises, is available from the publisher. Also, Web page support for this text is accessible via the URL http://www.pws.com/compsci/authors/shayw.

ORGANIZATION AND OUTLINE

This text offers a mix of theory and application. The theory provides a solid foundation for further study and the application brings students closer to the realities of communications systems and networks. It also gives them valuable experience. All students should benefit from the applications, and the more theoretical material will challenge the more ambitious students. In addition, the last two chapters present actual models of working client and server programs on which the student can build.

Each chapter serves as a base on which to build the next. For example, when studying multiplexing, contention, or compression, students should have an understanding of how signals propagate through different media. When studying local area networks, they should understand problems of contention on multiple-access lines, noisy channels, and flow control. When studying wide area network protocols, they should understand local area network protocols and why these are not suitable for larger networks. Essentially, the text uses a bottom-up approach.

Chapter 1 provides an introduction to the field, touching on current issues and applications in the field of communications and networks. It describes the needs for standards and lists relevant standards organizations, and then summarizes a long-standing protocol model, the Open System Interconnect.

Chapters 2 and 3 deal mainly with kinds of transmission media, signal types, and data transmission, including modulation techniques and modems, interface standards, multiplexing, contention, and data compression. Chapter 4 covers the security and integrity of transmitted data. It deals with methods used to detect or even correct transmission errors. It also covers different ways of encrypting data and authenticating its sender. This chapter concludes with a section on viruses and how they have evolved over the years. Together these chapters form the "data communications" part of the text.

Chapter 5 begins the "computer networks" part by discussing general protocols that regulate the flow of information between stations. It also presents some of the standard protocols used in local area networks. Chapter 6 covers local area networks (LANs), discussing the standards that define Ethernets and token ring and token bus networks. It then addresses the issues of connecting multiple LANs and the problem of ensuring that information gets to its intended destination and closes with a discussion of Novell NetWare, one of the most popular LAN managers.

Chapter 7 covers wide area networks (WANs) and the need for protocols different from LAN protocols. It describes different ways of routing information within a network and outlines some different methods for dealing with congestion. It also gives significant attention to four important protocols: the X.25 packet-switched network interface, both the old and new versions of the Internet Protocol (IP), and the Transmission Control Protocol (TCP). Chapter 7 finishes with a development of a working client/server model that uses UNIX socket connections to transfer a file between two computers connected to the Internet. Finally, Chapter 8 covers applications and additional protocols such as TCP/IP applications, WWW, X.400 email standards, ISDN (a worldwide digital network standard), Asynchronous Transfer Mode (ATM), and IBM's System Network Architecture (SNA). The section on the Web also contains a discussion of developing a Web page and supporting its use with client-side programs written in JavaScript and server-side programs written in C.

The questions at the end of each chapter are divided into two groups. The first group, Review Questions, contains questions for which answers can be obtained directly from the corresponding chapter. These questions encourage the reader to go back through the text and pick out what the author or instructor believes is important. I believe this method to be better pedagogically than simply listing important topics at the end, which encourages students to read textbooks as they would a novel—linearly. Learning complex material, however, often requires reading, rereading, and going back through the text to sort out and understand different concepts. A colleague related a conversation she had with a student having some difficulty with course work. The student had a part-time job during which he had some free time. Rather than fight boredom he decided to bring his textbook to work and read when he had the opportunity. Later in the semester his performance improved, and he related to the instructor that after reading the material four or five times, it actually began to make sense.

Review questions are not enough though. The second group, Exercises, contains questions that challenge readers to apply what they have learned and to compare, make logical deductions, and consider alternatives. The answers are not always simply stated and may be more elusive but that's typical of real problems.

ACKNOWLEDGMENTS

An undertaking such as writing a text is rarely, if ever, an individual effort. Many people have contributed and have given me valuable ideas, information, and support during this project. I especially would like to recognize the following people, who provided valuable advice during the writing of the first edition.

Abdullah Abonamah
University of Akron

George W. Ball
Alfred University

Mehran Basiratmand
Florida International University

Ron Bates
DeAnza College

Bruce Derr

Mohammad El-Soussi
Santa Barbara City College

James E. Holden
Clarion University

David Kieper
University of Wisconsin – Green Bay

Lance Leventhal

Judith Molka
University of Pittsburgh

Dan O'Connell
Fredonia College-SUNY

Jon L. Spear
Syracuse University

Janet M. Urlaub
Sinclair Community College

David Whitney
San Francisco State University

I took all of your comments and suggestions seriously and incorporated many into the final manuscript.

To those who took the time to review the manuscript for the second edition or provided me with useful suggestions on how to improve the first edition, many thanks.

Dr. George W. Ball
Alfred University

Dr. J. Archer Harris
James Madison University

Dr. Paul N. Higbee
University of North Florida

Dr. Gene Hill Price
Old Dominion University

Dr. J. Mark Pullen
George Mason University

Dr. Sub Ramakrishnan
Bowling Green State University

Dr. Seyed H. Roosta
Mount Mercy College

Dr. Brit Williams
Kennesaw State University

Stan Wine
*Hunter College and
New Era of Networks, Inc.*

My thanks also to

All the people at PWS and Brooks/Cole, including Mary Thomas Stone, Elise Kaiser, Mike Sugarman, and Marlene Thom: Your contributions and efforts helped make a manuscript into a book.

My family, Judy, Dan, and Tim: You made sacrifices so that I could use my "free time" to prepare the manuscript. We will make up for it; I promise.

Finally, to those who will eventually read this text, I would very much appreciate your opinion. Please feel free to send any comments to William Shay, Department of Information and Computing Sciences, University of Wisconsin-Green Bay, Green Bay, WI 54311-7001, or via email at shayw@uwgb.edu.

William A. Shay

UNDERSTANDING DATA COMMUNICATIONS AND NETWORKS

CHAPTER 1

INTRODUCTION TO COMMUNICATIONS, STANDARDS, AND PROTOCOLS

The love of learning, the sequestered nooks, And all the sweet serenity of books.
—**Henry Wadsworth Longfellow** (1807–1882), U.S. poet

1.1 WHY STUDY COMMUNICATIONS?

Why should we study computer and data communications? The many reasons range from "It is an absolutely fascinating field" to "I have to know how to connect my PC to the company's network." But one of the most compelling reasons is that communication technology has invaded virtually every aspect of daily life, from professional and educational uses to purely recreational ones. It has become so pervasive that we either take it for granted or are simply not aware of its applications.

A BRIEF HISTORY

The field of communications is certainly not new: People have been communicating since early humans grunted and scratched pictures on cave walls. For thousands of years people communicated using little more than words, parchments, stone tablets, and smoke signals. The primary forms of sending information were based on the auditory and visual senses. You either heard someone speaking or saw the letters and symbols that defined a message.

Communications changed drastically in 1837, when Samuel Morse invented the telegraph. This invention made it possible to send information using electrical impulses over a copper wire. Messages were sent by translating each character into a sequence of long or short electrical impulses (or in less technical terms, dots and dashes) and transmitting them. This association of characters with electrical impulses was called the **Morse code.** The ability to send information with no obvious verbal or visual medium began a sequence of events that forever changed the way people communicate.

In 1876 Alexander Graham Bell took the telegraph one step further. Rather than converting a message into a sequence of dots and dashes, he showed that a voice could be converted directly to electrical energy and transmitted over a wire using continuously varying voltages. At the wire's other end the electrical signals were converted back to sound. The result was that a person's voice could be transmitted electronically between two points as long as a physical connection existed between them. To most people whose lives were based on only what they could see and hear, this invention was absolutely incredible and seemed magical.

The earliest telephones required a different pair of wires for each phone to which you wished to connect. To place a call, a person had to first connect the telephone to the correct wires and then hope the person on the other end was there listening. There were no bells or signaling devices to interrupt dinner. That changed with the invention of the switchboard (Figure 1.1), a switching device that connected lines between two telephones. Callers simply picked up the phone and recited the number of the person they wished to call. Telephones had not yet evolved to the point where people had to perform manual activities such as dialing numbers or pushing buttons. Establishing connections was voice activated. That is, an operator heard the number and then used a switchboard to connect one person's phone lines with another person's lines.

During the next 70 years the telephone system grew to the point where the telephone became a common device in a home. Most of us do not even think about how the telephone system works. We know we can dial a number and be connected to just about anywhere in the world.

Figure 1.1   Early Switchboards

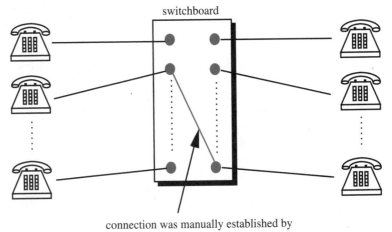

connection was manually established by
a switchboard operator

Another event important to communications occurred in 1945 with the invention of the first electronic computer, ENIAC (Electronic Numerical Integrator and Calculator). Designed for computing ballistics tables for World War II, it was the first device that could actually process information electronically. Although ENIAC played no direct role in data or computer communications, it did show that calculations and decision making could be done electronically, an important ability in today's communications systems.

The relation between computers and communications began to emerge after the invention of the transistor in 1947 allowed smaller and cheaper computers to be built. The new generation of computers that emerged during the 1960s made new applications such as processing and routing telephone calls economically feasible. In addition, more businesses were buying computers and developing applications, and the need to transfer information between them began to grow.

The first communication system between computers was simple but reliable. Basically, it involved writing information from one computer onto a magnetic tape, throwing the tape into the back of the car, then transporting the tape to another computer. (People today still do the same thing, although the tape has been replaced by disks and CD-ROMs.) Once there, the other computer could read the information on the tape. This was a very reliable form of communication, assuming the person driving the car didn't get into an accident or leave the windows open while driving through a car wash.

Another milestone in electronic communications occurred with the development of the personal computer (PC). The ability to have computing power on a desk generated an entirely new way of storing and retrieving information. The 1980s saw the infusion of millions of PCs into virtually every business, company, school, and organization and into many homes as well. The fact that so many people now had computers generated the need to make information even more easily accessible.

The 1990s saw the emergence of the **World Wide Web,** an application that makes information from around the world easily accessible from one's desk. With the click of a mouse button, computer users can access files, programs, video clips, and sound bites. Online services such as America Online and CompuServe provide a wealth of services to their users, such as chat rooms, bulletin boards, airline reservation systems, and more. Computers and communications have progressed to the point where most businesses or schools can no longer function without them. Our almost total dependence on them demands that we understand them and their abilities and limitations.

APPLICATIONS

Transferring data between computers is just one area of communications. For example, most people are aware that a television uses an antenna or cable to bring signals into a home. But that is the last step in a worldwide communication system that began in 1962 with Telstar, a communications satellite designed to transfer telephone and television signals between the United States and Europe. Telstar showed that transmitting information between continents was both technologically and economically feasible.

Many communications satellites transmit television signals today. Figure 1.2 shows a common system. A transmitter in one part of the world sends a signal to an orbiting satellite, which relays the signal to receivers in other parts. Signals from the receiver are sent to broadcast towers and are transmitted locally using a frequency approved by the Federal Communications Commission (FCC). An antenna receives the signals and relays them to the television set in your home.

Television antennas are not the only way to receive signals. Many homes subscribe to a cable television service that brings signals into the home using optical fibers and coaxial cable. In addition, many people purchase their own receiving dishes and receive satellite signals directly.

Other communications applications are **local area networks (LANs)** and **wide area networks (WANs),** systems that allow multiple computers to communicate over short (LAN) or long (WAN) distances. Once connected, users can send or receive data files, log in to remote computers, send mail (**email,** or electronic mail), or connect to the World Wide Web. With email, a person can send personal or business messages from one computer to another. The email system stores messages on a computer disk where someone else can read them.

The phenomenal growth of email, which sends and receives messages electronically, has caused some people to predict it will eventually replace postal service.

Figure 1.2   Television Reception

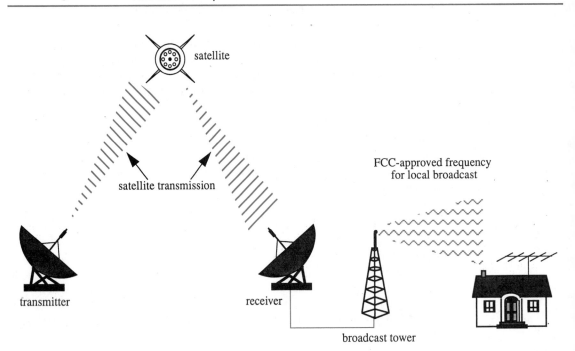

satellite

satellite transmission

FCC-approved frequency
for local broadcast

transmitter

receiver

broadcast tower

This is not likely to happen in the foreseeable future, but email is used extensively by many professionals and, with the emergence of the World Wide Web, by individuals for personal reasons as well.

With email, it is possible to send a message to remote locations from the privacy of your own home; Figure 1.3 shows how. A person with a PC and modem at home can access his or her company's or Internet Service provider's computer. This computer is connected to a local area network that allows a message to be sent to any person connected to it. The local area network also connects to a wide area network that allows a message to be sent across the country or to other countries. Local area networks at the other end can route a transmitted message to any connected PC. An individual on that end with a PC and modem can receive the message at home.

The following additional applications are described only briefly here. We will discuss some of these topics more fully in later chapters.

- **Facsimile machines (fax).** A fax machine creates an electronic equivalent of an image on a sheet of paper and then sends the image over telephone lines. A fax machine at the other end recreates the original paper's image. The fax is widely used to send letters, charts, and diagrams in minutes.

- **Voice and video communications.** LANs, used to connect PCs and other devices, transfer data primarily. Communications systems can also transmit voice and video images. Many companies often manage their own telephone systems or private branch exchanges (PBX) (discussed further in Section 2.2). Video communications can be used to play a tape or receive a video transmission from outside and relay the signals throughout a company or organization. Video communication has special needs because it typically requires the sending of 30 images per second, and each image requires a large amount of information to maintain crisp pictures with true color.

Figure 1.3   Electronic Mail Connections

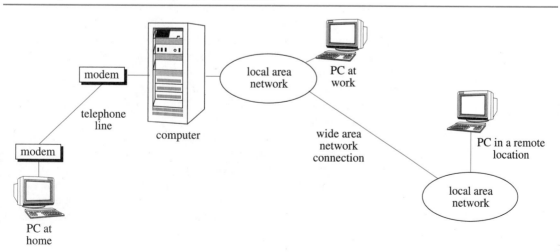

- **Teleconferencing.** Many people are no doubt painfully aware of the number of business meetings or conferences that occur each day. One of the most difficult aspects of planning such meetings is making sure everyone who needs to be present can attend. When the necessary people are in different parts of the country, they must make arrangements to travel to the meeting site. Tele-conferencing involves setting up video cameras and televisions at different locations so that people at each location can see and hear each other. In effect, they "attend" meetings or conferences without leaving their individual locations. Figures and charts needed for presentations also can be broadcast for all to see.

- **Cellular telephones.** The telephone system is certainly the most extensive communications system. Until the 1960s, however, the two communicating sites had to be connected physically. At that time, the telephone system started to use satellite and microwave towers to send signals. Still, for a while those making and receiving the calls had to use a telephone that was connected physically to a local office. That changed with the invention of the cellular telephone, a device that connects to the telephone system using radio waves. It allows people to make telephone calls from their cars, the office picnic, or the ballpark—any place that has sending and receiving towers nearby. Section 2.2 discusses cellular telephones further.

- **Information services.** Those with a PC and modem can subscribe to many different information services. Bulletin boards (data banks) allow the free exchange of some software, files, or other information. Other services allow users to get stock quotations and make transactions electronically or to examine airline schedules and make reservations. World Wide Web search engines search databases for documents based on keywords or topics. They then return links to sites that the user can access with the click of a mouse button.

ISSUES

These new technological developments have created many issues of concern. For example, we have used the word *connect* and its various forms many times in the previous discussion. But how do we connect? What do we use to make a connection? Do we use wire, cable, or optical fiber? Can we connect without them? Chapter 2 discusses many options.

Communications technology is like traffic planning in a large city. Roads allow you to get where you want to go, but they must be able to handle large amounts of traffic, especially in a large city. Designers must strike a balance between flow and cost. A 10-lane highway circling the city will provide better traffic flow than a 6-lane highway, but are more lanes worth the extra cost? The answer probably is yes in the largest cities but no in the smaller ones. Communications systems are similar. They must allow a certain amount of information to be transmitted, but just how much depends on the applications. The amount of information we need to send will affect how devices are connected. Chapters 6 and 7 discuss different ways of connecting devices.

Once we decide how to connect, we must establish some rules for communication. City streets are of little use without traffic signals or laws to control traffic. The same is true for communications systems. Whether the primary medium is a cable or through the air, we need to know that many sources will want to send information. We need some rules to prevent messages from colliding or to specify what to do when they do collide. Chapters 3, 5, 6, and 7 discuss ways of providing orderly communications.

Ease of use is another concern. Most people will not use a technology if it is difficult to use. For example, most people who purchased VCRs never learned to program them, at least until "VCR plus" was available. For a communication system or network to be viable, the information must be readily accessible. But how accessible do we want it? Should anyone be able to look at it? If it's an online library catalog, yes. If it's financial information for your retirement or investment account, no.

Communications systems must be secure. We must realize that the easy exchange of information invites unauthorized and illegal use of it. How can we make information accessible to those who need it yet prevent anyone else from seeing it? This is especially tough when the unauthorized people have many resources and make concerted efforts to break security measures. As the sensitivity of the information increases, security measures become more sophisticated. No system, however, is perfectly safe. Consequently, laws that provide for severe penalties were passed to help deter such activities. Chapter 4 deals with security.

Even if we deal with all the issues and manage to connect computers to provide the most efficient, cost-effective, secure, and easy transfer of information, one problem remains: Many computers are incompatible. In some cases transferring information from one computer to another is like moving a transmission from one car to another. If both cars are Ford Escorts built in the same year you can do it, but if one is an Escort and the other is a Grand Prix you will have some problems.

One heavily researched area today is the development of open systems. If fully implemented, an **open system** would allow any two computers to exchange information provided they are connected. Given the diversity among computer systems, this is a very ambitious goal. Section 1.4 describes open systems and a popular open-system model.

Finally, we return to the opening question: Why study data communications? Simply, it's a field that is experiencing and will experience tremendous growth. There is a desperate need for people who understand it and can help shape its future.

1.2   COMPUTER NETWORKS

During the 1950s, most computers were similar in one respect. They had a main memory, a central processing unit (CPU), and peripherals (Figure 1.4). The memory and CPU were central to the system. Since then a new generation of computing has emerged in which computation and data storage need not be centralized. A user may retrieve a program from one place, run it on any of a variety of processors, and send the result to a third location.

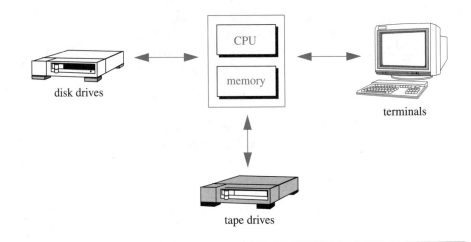

disk drives

terminals

tape drives

Figure 1.4   Communicating Devices in a Computer System

A system connecting different devices such as PCs, printers, and disk drives is a **network.** Typically, each device in a network serves a specific purpose for one or more individuals. For example, a PC may sit on your desk providing access to information or software you need. A PC may also be devoted to managing a disk drive containing shared files. We call it a *file server.* Often a network covers a small geographic area and connects devices in a single building or group of buildings. Such a network is a **local area network (LAN).** A network that covers a larger area such as a municipality, state, country, or the world is called a **wide area network (WAN).**

To illustrate a network's use, suppose a small business has connected several devices as shown in Figure 1.5. A company executive is planning a presentation to the board of directors that includes an analysis of last month's sales. The data reside in a file server, the statistical software to analyze sales runs on a PC, and a program forecasting future sales runs only on the mainframe. The executive can transfer the sales figures from the file server to a PC (Step 1 in Figure 1.5). She can then run the statistical software, send the results to the mainframe, and run the forecasting software (Step 2). When the results are generated, she can transfer them back to the PC (Step 3), where she can format the data for presentation. Finally, she can print her charts on a laser printer (Step 4).

The arrangement in Figure 1.5 is a simple scheme that works for one person. Most networks, however, involve many people using many PCs, each of which can access any of many printers or servers. With all these people accessing information, their requests inevitably will conflict. Consequently, the devices must be connected in a way that permits an orderly transfer of information for all concerned. A good analogy is a street layout in a large city. With only one person driving it matters little where the streets are, which ones are one-way, where the traffic signals are, or how they are synchronized. But with thousands of cars on the streets during the morning rush hour, a bad layout will create congestion that causes major delays. The same is true of computer networks. They must be connected in a way that allows data to

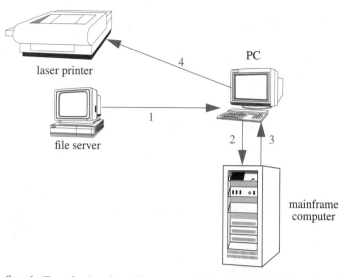

Step 1: Transfer data from file server to PC and run statistical software.
Step 2: Transfer results from Step 1 to mainframe and run forecasting program.
Step 3: Transfer results from Step 2 back to PC for printer formatting.
Step 4: Send results to laser printer.

Figure 1.5   Variety of Connected Computing Devices

travel among many users with little or no delay. We call the connection strategy the **network topology**. The best topology depends on the types of devices and user needs. What works well for one group may perform dismally for another.

COMMON BUS TOPOLOGY

Figure 1.6 shows a **common bus topology** (or simply **bus topology**) connecting devices such as workstations, mainframes, and file servers. They communicate through a single bus (a collection of parallel lines). A common approach gives each device an interface that listens to the bus and examines its data traffic. If an interface determines that data are destined for the device it serves, it reads the data from the bus and transfers it to the device. Similarly, if a device wants to transmit data, the interface circuits sense when the bus is empty and then transmit data. This is not unlike waiting on a freeway entrance ramp during rush hour. You sense an opening and either quickly dart to it or muscle your way through, depending on whether you're driving a subcompact or a large truck.

Sometimes, two devices try to transmit simultaneously. Each one detects an absence of traffic and begins transmitting before becoming aware of the other device's transmission. The result is a collision of signals. As the devices transmit they continue to listen to the bus and detect the noise resulting from the collision. When a device detects a collision it stops transmitting, waits a random period of

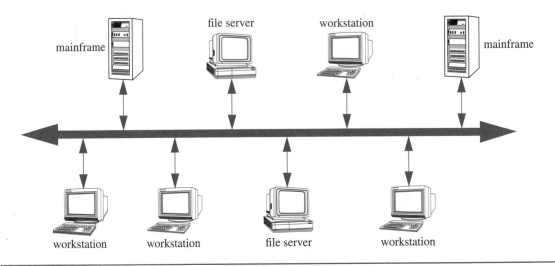

Figure 1.6   Common Bus Topology

time, and tries again. This process, called **Carrier Sense, Multiple Access with Collision Detection (CSMA/CD)** is discussed along with other ways of accessing common media in Sections 3.4 and 6.2.

One popular common bus network is an **Ethernet.** Its common bus typically is Ethernet cable, which consists of copper, optical fiber, or combinations of both (although recent developments allow connections using microwave and infrared technology). Its design allows terminals, PCs, disk storage systems, and office machines to communicate. A major advantage of an Ethernet is the ability to add new devices to the network easily.

STAR TOPOLOGY

Another common connecting arrangement is the **star topology** (Figure 1.7). It uses a central computer that communicates with other devices in the network. Control is centralized; if a device wants to communicate, it does so only through the central computer. The computer, in turn, routes the data to its destination. Centralization provides a focal point for responsibility, an advantage of the star topology. The bus topology, however, has some advantages over a star topology. The lack of central control makes adding new devices easy because no device needs to be aware of others. In addition, the failure or removal of a device in a bus network does not cause the network to fail. In a star topology, the failure of the central computer brings down the entire network.

Star topologies often involve a single mainframe computer that services many terminals and secondary storage devices. With appropriate terminal emulation software, PCs can communicate with the mainframe. Data transfers between terminals or between terminals and storage devices occur only through the main computer.

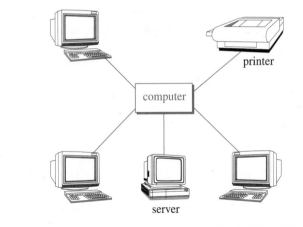

Figure 1.7   Star Topology

RING TOPOLOGY

In a **ring topology** (Figure 1.8), devices are connected circularly. Each one can communicate directly with either or both of its neighbors but nobody else. If it wants to communicate with a device farther away, it sends a message that passes through each device in between.

A ring network may be either unidirectional or bidirectional. **Unidirectional** means that all transmissions travel in the same direction. Thus, each device can

Figure 1.8   Ring Topology

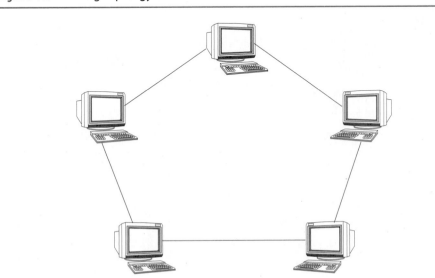

communicate with only one neighbor. **Bidirectional** means that data transmissions travel in either direction, and a device can communicate with both neighbors.

Ring topologies such as IBM's **token ring network** often connect PCs in a single office or department. Applications from one PC thus can access data stored on others without requiring a mainframe to coordinate communications. Instead, communications are coordinated by passing a **token** (a predefined sequence of bits) among all the stations in the ring. A station can send something only when it receives the token.

A disadvantage of the ring topology is that when one station sends to another, all stations in between are involved. More time is spent relaying messages meant for others than in, for example, a bus topology. Moreover, the failure of one station causes a break in the ring that affects communications among all the stations. Ways of dealing with such problems and other aspects of token rings are discussed further in Sections 3.4 and 6.3.

FULLY CONNECTED TOPOLOGY

The **fully connected topology** (Figure 1.9) has a direct connection between every pair of devices in the network. This is an extreme design. Communication becomes very simple because there is no competition for common lines. If two devices want to communicate, they do so directly without involving other devices. The cost of direct connections between every pair of devices is high, however. Furthermore, many connections may be vastly underutilized. If two devices rarely communicate, the physical connection between them is seldom used. In such cases, a more eco-

Figure 1.9   Fully Connected Topology

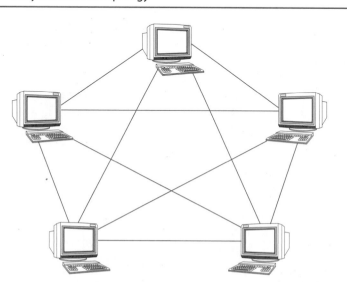

nomical approach is for the two to communicate indirectly, eliminating the underused line.

COMBINED TOPOLOGIES

Many computer networks use combinations of the various topologies. Figure 1.10 shows a possible combination. It has a common bus, sometimes called the **backbone,** which allows users to access mainframes and high-volume or frequently accessed storage. Groups of users such as research scientists, accountants, or sales personnel, however, may have specialized needs and use a LAN most of the time. Periodically, they may want to access high-volume storage or the computing power of a mainframe, but the requirements are not frequent enough to justify connecting each PC to the backbone.

Figure 1.10   Combined Topology

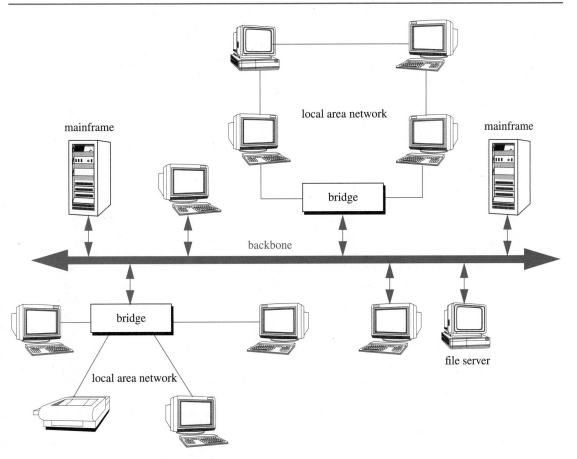

A compromise design identifies several LANs connecting PCs and other devices in a ring, star, or bus topology. Devices within a LAN communicate according to the rules defined by its topology. If a PC must communicate with a device in another LAN, it can do so using a bridge that connects the two LANs. As we will see in Chapter 6, different LANs use different rules to communicate, and the bridge is needed to convert between them.

1.3   STANDARDS AND STANDARDS ORGANIZATIONS

THE NEED FOR STANDARDS

You might think that the primary problem in establishing communications between two computers is simply making sure that the data bits get from one computer to the other. However, because computers are often very different from one another, the transfer process is actually much more complex, like moving an automobile transmission from a Cadillac to a Toyota. All automobiles are based on the same principles, but different models have unique features appealing to a different style and market; the same is true of computers, except the user may be a little more fanatical (PC users hate Macs, and Mac users hate PCs). Companies design and manufacture computers in different styles and for different applications. Most follow the same general principles, but specifics reflect the thinking and philosophy of many people. Computers have different architectures, understand different languages, store data in different formats, and communicate at different rates. Consequently, there is much incompatibility, and communication is difficult.

This incompatibility raises a basic question: How can computers communicate at all? They communicate the same way trade representatives from different countries do. Each person speaks a different language, so they need translators. Furthermore, they need to observe a **protocol** that defines the rules and the manner in which they begin and proceed with discussions. If all involved do not agree to a protocol, the discussions become chaotic. An orderly discussion occurs only if the participants follow the rules. Similarly, if computers are to communicate, they need protocols to determine which one "speaks" and translators to account for different languages. The next step is to define the protocols. Here lies another problem: Protocols are great, but if the principal parties involved follow different protocols, they might as well follow none. If the necessary people could agree on a common protocol, it would become a standard protocol and everyone could use it. Unfortunately, this is a lot like getting everyone to agree on a computer architecture, which we know didn't happen. Getting a diverse group of people to agree on anything is difficult. Different groups have different goals and ideas about which protocol best meets those goals. Consequently, many different standards have evolved and been used over the years.

There are two types of standards. **De facto standards** are those that exist by virtue of their widespread use. That is, they have become so common that vendors know that producing products consistent with them will have a large market. Many

IBM products have become de facto standards. The second type of standard is one that is formally recognized and adopted by an agency that has achieved national or worldwide recognition. Those who wish to see their work become a standard write a proposal and submit it to an agency for consideration. Typically, if the proposal has merit and widespread acceptance, the agency will make suggestions and send it back to its originators for modifications. After several rounds of suggestions and modifications, the proposal will be adopted or refused. If approved, the standard gives vendors a model on which to design new products.

AGENCIES

The use of agencies certainly puts some order in the rapidly expanding field of communications. Hundreds of standards are approved for different aspects of communications, however, making incompatibility among different types of devices an ongoing problem. For example, many PC users purchase a modem (a device allowing a computer to send and receive signals over a telephone line) to connect to a company or university computer or to an Internet service provider. If the wrong modem is used, however, communication will not happen. More than a dozen standards describe different ways of sending and receiving signals over the telephone, and if the two modems use different standards there will be no connection. Chapter 2 discusses this problem fully.

The following agencies are important to the field of computer networks and data communications:

- **American National Standards Institute (ANSI).** ANSI is a private, nongovernmental agency whose members are manufacturers, users, and other interested companies. It has nearly 1000 members and is itself a member of the International Organization for Standardization, or ISO (described in this list). ANSI standards are common in many fields. In Chapter 6 we discuss the Fiber Distributed Data Interface (FDDI), a standard for local area networks using optical fiber. Another standard (discussed in Chapter 2) is the American Standard Code for Information Interchange (ASCII), used by many computers for storing information.

- **International Electrotechnical Commission (IEC).** A nongovernmental agency devising standards for data processing and interconnections and safety in office equipment. They were involved in the development of the Joint Photographic Experts Group (JPEG), a group that devised a compression standard for images.

- **International Telecommunications Union (ITU),** formerly called **Comité Consultatif International de Télégraphique et Téléphonique (CCITT).** The English equivalent is the International Consultative Committee for Telephony and Telegraphy. ITU is an agency of the United Nations and has three sectors. ITU-R deals with radio communications; ITU-D is a development sector; and the one relevant to this book, ITU-T, deals with telecommunications. ITU members include various scientific and industrial organizations, telecommunications agencies, telephone authorities, and the ISO. ITU has produced numerous standards dealing with network and telephone communications. Two well-known sets of standards are the V series and X series. The V series deals with telephone communications. Chapter 2 discusses some V standards that describe how a modem generates and interprets analog telephone signals. The X series deals with network interfaces and public networks. Examples include the X.25 standard for interfacing to a packet-switched network (discussed in Chapter 7) and the X.400 standard for electronic mail systems (discussed in Chapter 8). There are many other X and V standards; Reference [Sh90] provides an extensive list.

- **Electronic Industries Association (EIA).** The members of EIA include electronics firms and manufacturers of telecommunications equipment. It is also a member of ANSI. The EIA's primary activities deal with electrical connections and the physical transfer of data between devices. Their most well-known standard is the RS-232 (also called EIA-232) standard, which most PCs use for communicating with other devices such as modems or printers. The EIA-232 standard is discussed in Chapter 3.

- **Internet Engineering Task Force (IETF).** IETF is an international community whose members include network designers, vendors, and researchers, all of whom have an interest in the stable operation of the Internet and in its evolution. It is divided into work groups that handle various technical aspects of the Internet such as applications, operations and management, routing, security, and transport services. These working groups have been charged with the responsibility of developing and reviewing specifications intended as Internet standards. An important result of IETF's work is the next-generation Internet protocol that is presented in Chapter 7.

- **Institute of Electrical and Electronic Engineers (IEEE).** The IEEE is the largest professional organization in the world and consists of computing and engineering professionals. It publishes many different journals, runs conferences, and has a group that develops standards. Perhaps its best-known work in the communications field is its Project 802 LAN standards. Discussed in Chapter 6, the 802 standards define the communication protocols for bus and ring networks.

- **International Organization for Standardization (ISO).** The ISO is a worldwide organization consisting of standards bodies from many countries, such as ANSI from the United States. One of ISO's most significant activities is its work on open systems, which define the protocols that would allow any two computers to communicate independent of their architecture. One well-known model is the Open Systems Interconnect (OSI), a seven-layer organization of protocols. Some once believed OSI would be the model used for all future communications. With the explosion of the Internet and WWW applications that is unlikely. However it is often studied as a model for layering protocols. We will discuss the OSI model in the next section.

- **National Institute of Standards and Technology (NIST).** Formerly the **National Bureau of Standards (NBS)**, the NIST is an agency of the United

States Department of Commerce. It issues standards the federal government uses for equipment purchases. It also develops standards for many physical quantities such as time, length, temperature, radioactivity, and radio frequencies. One important standard with security applications is the Data Encryption Standard (DES), a method of encrypting or changing information into a form that cannot be understood. The DES standard has been manufactured in chips used in communications devices. The standard, discussed in Chapter 4, is complex as well as controversial (some believe the National Security Agency purposely weakened it to prevent encryption techniques that it could not solve).

*   **International Business Machines (IBM).** Although not a standards agency, IBM should be listed because so much of its work has become de facto standards. Notable examples include its Systems Network Architecture (SNA) and the Extended Binary-Coded Decimal Interchange Code (EBCDIC). SNA is a protocol model designed to allow IBM computers and equipment to communicate. We will discuss it in Chapter 8, but in many ways it is similar to the OSI model. The EBCDIC code (discussed in Chapter 2) is an alternative to ASCII for storing data and is commonly used on IBM mainframes (although its PCs commonly use the ASCII code).

These agencies are by no means the only standards bodies, but they are the ones most pertinent to data communications and networks. Reference [Qu90] contains a much larger list of standards bodies.

1.4   OPEN SYSTEMS AND THE OSI MODEL

We have stated that protocols allow otherwise incompatible systems to communicate. Given two specific systems, the definition of a protocol is fairly straightforward. The problem becomes bigger and more difficult as the number of different types of systems increases. A set of protocols that would allow any two different systems to communicate regardless of their underlying architecture is called an **open system.** The ISO has addressed the problem of allowing many devices to communicate and has developed its **Open Systems Interconnect (OSI)** model. If fully developed, it would allow any two computers to communicate provided they are connected.

The OSI model is a seven-layer model (Figure 1.11). Each layer performs specific functions and communicates with the layers directly above and below it. Higher layers deal more with user services, applications, and activities, and the lower layers deal more with the actual transmission of information.

The purpose of layering the protocol is to separate specific functions and to make their implementation transparent to other components. This layering allows independent design and testing of each component. For example, the data link layer and physical layer perform separate functions. The physical layer performs a service to the data link layer. The data link layer does not care how the service is performed, just that it is done. Thus, if changes occur in how the physical layer is implemented,

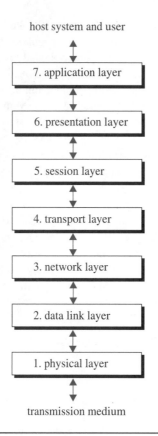

host system and user

7. application layer

6. presentation layer

5. session layer

4. transport layer

3. network layer

2. data link layer

1. physical layer

transmission medium

Figure 1.11   ISO's OSI Layered Protocol Model

the data link layer (and all higher layers) is unaffected. This approach applies to any two consecutive layers and is the same concept as that behind the modular programming (or top-down design) style that you may have learned in your first programming class.

Compare the process to a meeting among several heads of state. Each leader needs to make his or her thoughts known, but the ideas often must be recast in appropriate diplomatic language to avoid offending someone. Furthermore, if they all speak a different language, one language must be chosen as the primary form of communication. Figure 1.12 illustrates a possible three-layer protocol involving a crisis that two of the leaders are trying to resolve. One leader adamantly states that he is not going to tolerate the situation. The diplomat recasts the message into a less-threatening tenor, and a translator translates the message to the chosen language. On the other side, another translator translates back to a specific language. The diplomat receives the message and tells the head of state what it really means.

In a sense, the two leaders are communicating directly, even though the message actually passes through other individuals. The OSI model works similarly. The

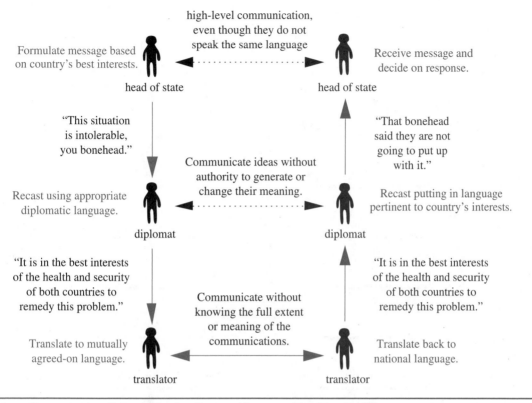

Figure 1.12 Communication Protocol between Two Heads of State

lowest level, the physical layer, deals with actual data transmission. The highest level deals with the computer system connected to the network. Each layer in between corresponds to a different level of abstraction in data communications and defines certain functions and protocols.

Two otherwise incompatible sites, each running the OSI model, can communicate with each other (Figure 1.13). Logically, each layer communicates directly with its counterpart at the other site. Physically, each layer communicates with the layers immediately above and below it. When a process wants to send information, it starts by handing it over to the application layer. That layer performs its functions and sends the data to the presentation layer. It, in turn, performs its functions and gives the data to the session layer. This process continues until the physical layer receives the data and actually transmits it.

On the receiving end, the process works in reverse. The physical layer receives the bit stream and gives it to the data link layer. The data link layer performs certain functions and sends the data to the network layer. This process continues until the application eventually receives the information and gives it to the receiving process. The two processes appear to communicate directly, with each layer appearing to

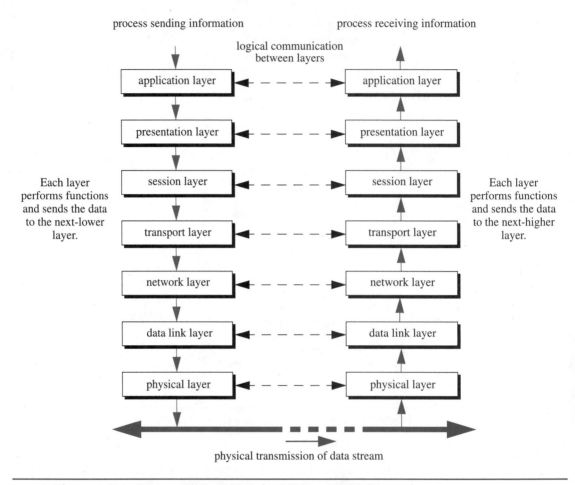

Figure 1.13   Communication Using the OSI Seven-Layer Protocol

communicate directly with its counterpart at another network node. In reality, all data are broken into a bit stream and transmitted between physical layers.

This process is a bit like sending a letter, where you communicate with the letter's recipient by addressing the envelope and dropping it in a mailbox. As far as you are concerned, the activity is then complete: The communication is independent of how the letter is eventually routed or whether it goes by truck, plane, train, boat, or carrier pigeon. You know the letter will arrive and you can simply wait for a response.

OVERVIEW OF THE MODEL

The highest layer, the **application layer,** works directly with the user or application programs. Note that it is not the same as an application program. The application layer provides user services such as electronic mail, file transfers, remote job entry, and resource allocation. For example, the application layer on one end should appear to send a file directly to the application layer on the other end independent of the underlying network or computer architectures.

The application layer also defines the protocols that allow access to a full screen text editor from different types of terminals. The reason is that different types of terminals use different control sequences for cursor control. For example, just moving the cursor may involve arrow keys or special key combinations. Ideally, we would like to make such differences transparent to the user.

The **presentation layer** is responsible for presenting data in a format its user can understand. For example, suppose two different computers use different numeric and character formats. The presentation layer translates data from one representation to another and insulates the user from such differences. In effect, the presentation layer determines the difference between data and information. After all, networks exist so users can exchange information, not raw bit streams. Users do not want to be concerned with different formats; they would prefer to concentrate on the informational content and what it means to them.

The presentation layer can also provide security measures. It may encrypt data before handing it to the lower layers for transfer. The presentation layer at the other end would decrypt the data after receiving it. The user need never know the data had been altered. This is especially important in wide area networks (ones that span large geographic distances), where unauthorized access is a serious problem.

The **session layer** allows applications on two different computers to establish a **session,** or logical connection. For example, a user may log on to a remote system and may communicate by alternately sending and receiving messages. The session layer helps coordinate the process by informing each end when it can send or must listen. This is a form of synchronization.

The session layer also handles error recovery. For example, suppose a user is sending the contents of a large file over a network that suddenly fails. When it is operational again, must the user start retransmitting from the beginning of the file? The answer is no, because the session layer lets the user insert checkpoints in a long stream. If a network crashes, only the data transmitted since the last checkpoint are lost.

The session layer also brackets operations that must appear to the user as a single transaction. A common example is the deletion of a record from a database. Although the user sees the deletion as a single operation, it actually may involve several. The record must be found and subsequently deleted by altering pointers and addresses and perhaps entries in an index or hash table. If a user is accessing a database through a network, the session layer makes sure that all low-level operations are received before the deletion actually begins. If the database operations were applied one at a time as they were received, a network failure could compromise the database's integrity by changing some pointers but not others (you may recall your introductory data structures class, where incorrect programs did not change all your pointers) or by deleting a record but not a reference to it.

The fourth layer is the **transport layer.** It is the lowest layer that deals primarily with end-to-end communications (the lower layers deal with the network itself). The transport layer may determine which network to use for communication. A computer may be connected to several networks that may differ in speed, cost, and type of communication, the choice often depending on many factors. For example, does the information consist of a long continuous stream of data? Or does it consist of many intermittent transfers? The telephone network is appropriate for long, continuous data transfers. Once a connection has been established, it is maintained until the transfer is complete.

Another approach divides the data into small **packets** (subsets of the data) and transfers them intermittently. In such cases, a constant connection between two points is unnecessary. Instead, each packet may be transmitted independently through the network. Consequently, when the packets arrive at the other end they must be reassembled before their contents are passed to the layer above. One problem is that if the packets follow different routes there is no guarantee that they will arrive in the order in which they were sent (just as there is no guarantee that a letter mailed on Monday will arrive before one mailed on Tuesday) or that they will all arrive. Not only must the receiver determine the correct order of incoming packets, it also must verify it got them all.

The **network layer** deals with routing strategies. For example, in a bidirectional ring network, there are two paths between any two points. A more complex topology may have many routes from which to choose. Which ones are fastest, cheapest, or safest? Which ones are open or uncongested? Should an entire message follow the same route, or should parts of it be transferred independently?

The network layer controls the **communications subnet,** the collection of transmission media and switching elements required for routing and data transmission. The network layer is the highest layer in the subnet. This layer may also contain accounting software for customer billing. Remember, networks exist to allow users to communicate. As with most services, someone must pay. The fee depends on the amount of data transmitted and possibly the time of day. The network layer can maintain such information and handle billing.

The **data link layer** supervises the flow of information between adjacent network nodes. It uses error detection or correction techniques to ensure that a transmission contains no errors. If the data link detects an error, it can either request a new transmission or, depending on the implementation, correct the error. It also controls how much information is sent at a time: Too much and the network becomes congested; too little and the sending and receiving ends experience excessive waits.

The data link layer also recognizes a format. Data are often transmitted in **frames,** which consist of a group of bytes organized according to a specified format. The data link layer marks the beginning and end of each outgoing frame with unique bit patterns and recognizes these patterns to define an incoming frame. It then sends error-free frames to the previous layer, the network layer.

Finally, the **physical layer** transmits data bits over a network. It is concerned with the physical or electrical aspects of data communications. For example, is the medium copper cable, optical fiber, or satellite communications? How can data be transferred physically from point A to point B? The physical layer transmits data bits received from the data link layer in streams without regard to their meaning or format. Similarly, it receives bits without analyzing them and gives them to the data link layer.

In summary, the lowest three layers deal primarily with the details of network communications. Together, they provide a service to the upper layers. The upper layers deal with end-to-end communications. They define the communication protocols between two users but are not concerned with the low-level details of data transmission. Some network implementations may not use all seven layers or may combine some of the functions from different layers. Try to remember that OSI is just a model (albeit an important one), and many network protocols are not OSI compliant. However, it is an important place to begin because it helps us understand where many network functions belong within a protocol. Table 1.1 contains a summary of the functions we have discussed so far.

PHYSICAL LAYER

The physical layer has two primary aspects: transmission media and connection strategies. The transmission media define how signals are sent. Typical options are twisted-pair wire, coaxial cable, optical fiber, satellites, microwave towers, and radio waves. Each option has different electrical or electromagnetic properties that make it suitable for different situations. A full description of transmission media requires discussions of analog and digital transmissions, bandwidth, signal-to-noise ratios, broadband, baseband, voice grade transmissions, and even Fourier analysis. They warrant their own chapter and are covered in Chapter 2.

To some extent the physical layer also covers the connection strategy. We know that two computers must be connected to communicate. How they are connected is a design issue. For example, consider the network in Figure 1.14. The connection strategy of the physical layer answers the question, If node *A* wants to communicate with node *F*, how do we connect them? Take care to distinguish this problem from determining the route, or network path. If the lines represent physical connections, there are four routes along which data may travel from node *A* to node *F*. (Can you list them?) The network layer will determine which one is best, but the issue here is how the two endpoints are actually connected via the chosen route.

Table 1.1   Summary of OSI Layers

LAYER	FUNCTIONS
7. Application	Provides electronic mail, file transfers, and other user services.
6. Presentation	Translates data formats, encrypts and decrypts data.
5. Session	Synchronizes communicating users, recovers from errors, and brackets operations.
4. Transport	Determines network, may assemble and reassemble packets.
3. Network	Determines routes, manages billing information.
2. Data link	Detects or corrects errors, defines frames.
1. Physical	Transmits physical data.

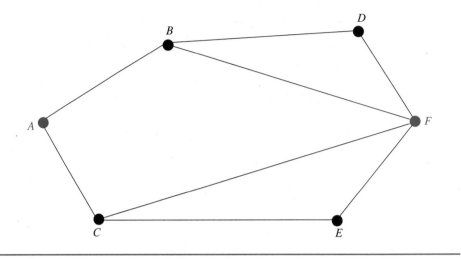

Figure 1.14   Sample Computer Network

There are three connection strategies: circuit switching, message switching, and packet-switching. In **circuit switching,** once a connection is made between two nodes, it is maintained until one of them terminates it. In other words, the connection is dedicated to the communication between the two parties. Circuit switching is common in the telephone system (Figure 1.15) because the channel allocated to one telephone connection cannot be used by another.

How does it work? A person at node *A* wants to talk to someone at node *F.* The person at *A* requests a connection to *F.* In a telephone network, dialing a number makes the connection. In a computer network, the user enters appropriate com-

Figure 1.15   Dedicated Circuit Connecting *A* and *F*

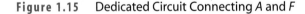

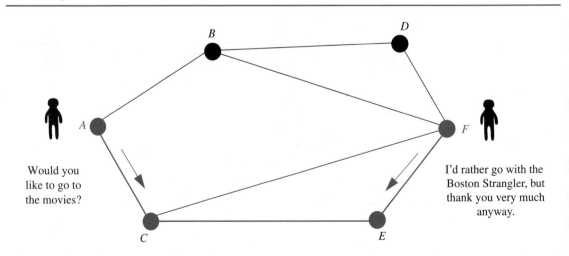

mands to connect to a specified location. Either way, logic at node *A* must determine the next node in a route that leads to *F*. This process involves factors such as the cost of the connection and the availability of different paths. For example, a telephone call from San Francisco to Los Angeles is not normally routed through Miami. However, if the lines between the two cities are congested, the connection may be indirect; for example, through Sacramento.

In Figure 1.15, node *A* has determined that *C* is a better choice than *B* in the route from *A* to *F*. Thus, node *A* connects to node *C*. Node *C*, in turn, proceeds similarly. It might choose node *F*, or it might decide to go through node *E*. Again, cost and existing connections affect the choice. In this case, node *C* connects to node *E*. Finally, *E* connects to *F*. The connection is made, and node *F* may be willing to accept it. In the telephone system, you accept a connection by picking up the receiver and saying "Hello." In a computer network, appropriate commands are used to accept connections. If node *F* does not respond (e.g., busy signal or no answer), node *A* terminates the request.

If node *F* accepts the connection, information may be exchanged. The person at node *A* asks, "Do you want to go to the movies?" The person at node *F* responds by saying, "I'd really love to go with you, but my canary just died and I'm in mourning. Ask me some other time when I'm out of town."

Circuit switching requires that the route be determined and the connection made before any information is transmitted. Also, the network maintains the connection until a node terminates it. This type of connection is most useful when the communications between the two nodes are continuous, that is, when node *A* "says" something and node *F* "hears" almost immediately, with virtually no transmission delay. This approach is not always the best way to communicate, however. First of all, if node *A* calls node *F*, *F* must answer. Otherwise, *A* cannot send any information. Second, suppose nodes *A* and *F* exchange information infrequently. (Did you ever experience long periods of silence during a telephone conversation?) In that case, the connection is underused.

Message switching is an alternative to circuit switching. A network uses message switching to establish a route when a message (a unit of information) is sent. For example, suppose node *A* sends the message "Will you go to the movies with me?" to node *F*. Node *A* attaches the location or address of *F* to the message and looks for the first node in the route. As Figure 1.16, shows, node *A* chooses node *C*. As before, the choice depends on cost and the availability of connections. Node *A* sends the message (along with the address of *F*) to *C*. The message is stored there temporarily, while logic looks for another node. It sends the message to node *E*, where it is again stored temporarily. Finally, logic at *E* locates node *F* and sends the message to its final destination. Because the message is stored in its entirety at each node, networks that use this method are also called **store-and-forward networks**.

How are message switching and circuit switching different?

- In message switching, the message is stored temporarily at each node. In circuit switching, the node simply acts as a switching device to route the data. For example, your telephone conversations are not stored at intermediate locations (unless someone is listening and recording your conversation!). The transmission delays resulting from message switching make this connection strategy

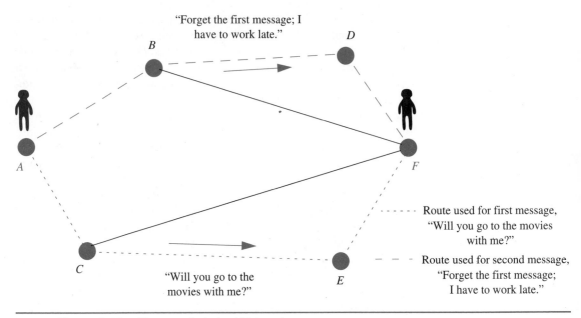

Figure 1.16   Message-Switched Network

unsuitable for telephone networks. Delays in voice transmission would make conversations very difficult.

- In circuit switching, a single route is dedicated to the exchange of all messages between two nodes. In message switching, different messages may travel over different routes. Suppose node *A* wanted to send a second message, "Forget the first message; I have to work late," to node *F*. Because routing is often time dependent, *A* might choose *B* for the first node in the route. The message then goes to nodes *D* and *F*. Different messages thus can share common connections over time, providing a higher utilization.

- Circuit switching requires that both parties be ready when data is sent. Message switching does not. The message may be sent and stored for later retrieval.

The third connection strategy, **packet-switching,** minimizes the effects of problems caused by long messages on message-switched networks. Long messages may exceed the buffering capacity at a node, or connections between adjacent nodes may be tied up for long periods. A failure in a connection may mean the loss of the entire message. Consequently, message-switched networks are no longer common and have given way to the more efficient packet-switched networks. Let's see how they work.

Suppose a user at node *A* wants to send a message to node *F*. If the message is long, it is divided into smaller units called **packets.** Their size is design dependent. Each packet contains its destination address or some other designator indicating where it should go and is routed there by network protocols. When the packets all arrive, they are reassembled. Like message switching, a physical connection between the two endpoints is not maintained. The smaller size of the packets facilitates the necessary buffering at intermediate network nodes.

The two common routing methods in packet-switched networks are the datagram and the virtual circuit. In the **datagram** approach, each packet is transmitted independently. That is, network protocols route each one as though it were a separate message. This allows routing strategies to consider the changing conditions within the network. Congestion on certain routes may cause rerouting. (Chapter 7 discusses routing strategies in more detail.)

In the **virtual circuit** approach, network protocols establish a route (virtual circuit) before sending any packets. The delivery of the packets using the same route ensures that the packets arrive in order and without error. The process is similar to circuit switching, with one important difference: The route is not dedicated. That is, different virtual circuits may share a common network connection. Logic at each node must store received packets and schedule them for transmission.

Datagrams have a disadvantage when the message consists of many packets, because independent routing represents a lot of overhead. In such cases, a virtual circuit may be more efficient. Another disadvantage of datagrams is that packets may not arrive in the order in which they were sent. Consider the network shown in Figure 1.17. Suppose the user at node A wants to send a message consisting of three packets to node F. Logic at node A decides to route packets P_1 and P_2 to node C. However, as it examines possible routes for P_3, it determines that the route through C has become congested. Therefore, it sends P_3 to node B. Packets P_1 and P_2 then travel to nodes E and F while packet P_3 goes directly from B to F. Depending on network traffic, F could receive the packets in the order P_1, P_3, P_2 and must reassemble them in the correct order.

Figure 1.17   Packet-Switched Network

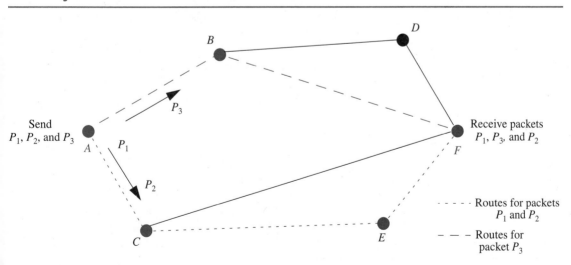

On the other hand, the sensitivity to changing conditions may be an advantage. Routing P_3 differently made the packets arrive out of order, but P_3 may have arrived much sooner than it would have otherwise. In networks with a lot of traffic, a good route may turn bad quickly if every node begins to send over it—just as a major expressway from the suburbs to the center of a large city is a good route at 5:00 A.M. but very congested at 7:00 A.M.

We will discuss routing strategies and protocols for packet-switched networks more fully in Chapter 7. For now, Table 1.2 provides a comparison among the three connection strategies we have presented.

DATA LINK LAYER

While the physical layer sends and receives data, the data link layer sits above it and makes sure that it works correctly. For example, what happens if two nodes simultaneously try to transmit data along the same line (contention)? How does a node

Table 1.2   Comparison of Connection Strategies

STRATEGY	ADVANTAGES	DISADVANTAGES
Circuit switching	Speed. It is appropriate when transmission delays are unacceptable.	Because network connections are dedicated, all other routes must avoid them. Both users must be present during communications, such as during a telephone conversation.
Message switching	Routes are not dedicated and may be reused immediately after the transmission of a message. The recipient need not accept the message immediately.	Messages generally take longer to reach their destination. Problems also can occur with long messages, as they must be buffered at intermediate nodes. The end of a message travels a route chosen earlier based on conditions that may no longer be true.
Packet-switching	If congestion develops, the datagram approach to packet-switching may choose alternate routes for parts of the message. Thus, network routes are utilized better.	More overhead because each packet is routed separately. Routing decisions must be made for each packet. Packets may arrive out of order in the datagram approach.

know the data it has received are correct (error detection and correction)? Could electrical interference such as that caused by an electrical storm or voltage fluctuations have changed some bits? If the interference changed a packet's destination, how does a node know it did not receive something it should have?

Contention occurs when two or more nodes want to transmit over the same medium at the same time. There are several ways of handling it. Some bus networks use a method called **collision detection.** Collision detection does not prevent multiple nodes from transmitting simultaneously over a common bus. Rather, it is a response to simultaneous transmissions, or collisions. Typically, if a device sends something that collides with another transmission, sensing circuits detect the collision, and the device tries to send again later.

Sometimes a device tries to avoid collisions by listening to the bus activity. If the bus is busy, the device does not transmit. If the circuits detect no activity on the bus, the device goes ahead and transmits. If two devices both sense no activity on the bus and transmit simultaneously, a collision occurs. We call this method of resolving contention **Carrier Sense Multiple Access with Collision Detection (CSMA/CD).** In effect, it reduces the number of collisions but does not eliminate them. Section 3.4 discusses this approach in detail, and Section 6.2 discusses it as it relates to the Ethernet LAN standard.

Token passing is another contention scheme that prevents collisions. Here, a unique bit stream, called a **token,** circulates among all network nodes. If a node wants to transmit, it must wait until it receives the token and must append the token to the end of the message. It also changes token control bits to indicate that the token is in use. The message is sent to its destination, and the receiving node now has the token. Depending on the protocol, that station may seize the token and send a message if it has one, or it may send the token to the next node.

Ring networks often use token passing, as shown in Figure 1.18. The token circulates clockwise around the ring. Node *E* currently has the token; therefore, only it can send a message. Because the token is unique, collisions cannot occur. Drawbacks do exist, however: A token may get lost or duplicated or may be hogged by a node. Chapter 6 discusses ways of dealing with such events.

Token passing is not limited to rings. It can be used with any network topology by numbering the nodes and circulating the token among them in numerical order. Device numbering is easiest to do in ring or linear networks, however. Section 3.4 discusses token passing and some of its variations, and Sections 6.3 and 6.4 discuss it as it relates to the token ring and token bus LAN standards.

The physical layer sends bit streams across the network. But how does the receiver know whether it has received the correct data? Bad connections, faulty lines, or electrical interference all can affect transmissions. The data link layer executes error detection and correction algorithms. With **error detection** the receiving data link layer determines whether an error has occurred and, if so, typically requests that the information be retransmitted. With **error correction** the data link layer has the ability to set the damaged bits to their correct value.

Perhaps the simplest detection method uses a **parity bit,** an extra bit attached to each sequence of data bits, or frame. For example, an **even parity** makes the total

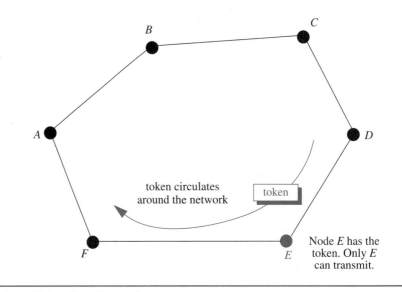

Figure 1.18   Token Ring Network

number of 1 bits (including itself) even. That is, if the frame has an odd number of 1 bits, the parity bit is 1. If it has an even number, the parity bit is 0. (There is an analogous definition for odd parity.) Consider the frames in Figure 1.19. The first frame has four 1 bits. Therefore, its even parity bit is 0. The second frame has five 1 bits, so its even parity bit is 1. The parity bit is transmitted with the frame and the receiver checks the parity. If it finds an odd number of 1 bits, an error has occurred.

The problem with parity bits is that errors can go undetected. For example, if two bits change during transmission, the number of 1 bits remains even. Thus, parity bits can detect single but not double errors. More sophisticated techniques exist that deal with multiple-bit errors. Sections 4.2 to 4.4 discuss several of them in greater detail.

NETWORK LAYER

The network layer provides the transport layer with the ability to establish end-to-end communications. This ability allows the transport layer to do its tasks without

Figure 1.19   Parity Bits

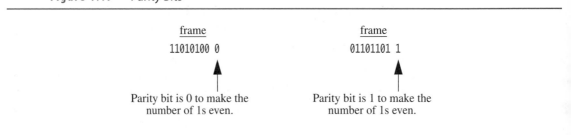

frame	frame
11010100 0	01101101 1

Parity bit is 0 to make the number of 1s even.   Parity bit is 1 to make the number of 1s even.

worrying about the details of sending information back and forth between the two stations. It is a lot like making a telephone call without worrying about the details of telephone switching equipment. This process, which often requires communication across multiple intermediate nodes, can be quite difficult. There are several common protocols, but they are too complex to discuss here, and we delay them to later chapters. For example, Section 7.3 discusses packet-switched networks and the X.25 protocol, and Section 7.4 discusses the Internet Protocol.

The network layer contains algorithms designed to find the best route between two points. We mentioned route determination when we described switching techniques. We indicated that route determination considers factors such as connection costs and availability of lines as it tries to find the quickest and cheapest route to a particular node. For example, Figure 1.20 shows a network containing several routes from A to F. Each line connecting two nodes represents the cost, indicated by the numbers on the lines. Going from A to F through B and D results in a total cost of 16. Going through B and E instead results in a cost of only 12. In general, the network layer determines which route is best. Perhaps more accurately, network-layer protocols running at network nodes collectively determine which route is best. There are many different ways to approach routing. Section 7.2 discusses several of them, and Section 6.5 discusses routing as it applies to LAN interconnections. References [Ta96] and [Sp91] also discuss many approaches.

Successful routing is often more difficult than it seems at first. Courses in discrete mathematics and data structures typically cover algorithms designed to find the best or cheapest routes through a graph. They make assumptions that are often not true in real networks, however. They assume that a graph's nodes and the costs of edges connecting them do not change. In dynamic environments both assumptions are often false. New stations and nodes can enter the network regularly and affect

Figure 1.20   Route Costs

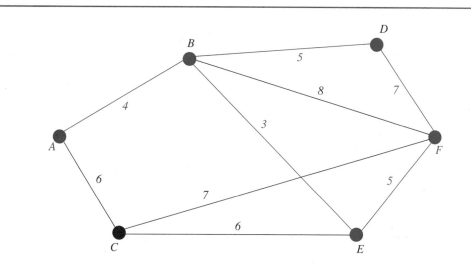

both existing routes and their costs. Algorithms must be robust enough to respond to changing conditions.

Even when they do respond, other problems occur. A good route may attract a lot of traffic and overload the computers on it. The resulting congestion often results in some of the traffic being eliminated. This seems severe, but when a network node has too much information to handle, it often has little choice. In this case, the network-layer protocol must be able to inform the sender when part of a message is lost.

Other problems can occur when information traveling one route is detoured because changing conditions generated a new best route. The information then may travel that route, only to be detoured again. In an extreme case, information can be detoured continually, causing an endless flow of information throughout the network to bounce from node to node. It is the electronic equivalent of a panhandler looking for a place to call home.

TRANSPORT LAYER

The transport layer represents a transitional layer. The three layers below transport deal primarily with network communications (Figure 1.21). Each node between a sending and a receiving node executes its protocols to ensure the information is being transmitted correctly and efficiently. The transport layer and the three layers

Figure 1.21   End-to-End Connection with Intermediate Nodes

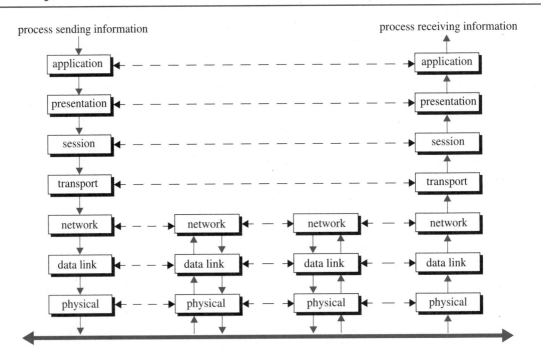

above it provide user services. They execute primarily at the sending and receiving nodes to ensure information arrives at the destination and to acknowledge its arrival to the sending node.

One of the transport layer's functions is to provide a reliable and efficient network connection. It allows the three layers above it to perform their tasks independent of a specific network architecture. At the same time, it relies on the lower three layers to control actual network operations. It makes sure information gets from the source to the eventual destination. The major responsibility of this layer is to provide the session layer with a network connection, or transport connection. Most important, the transport layer provides reliable and efficient communications. In practice, networks are sometimes unreliable; that is, there is no guarantee that the connections will not fail. What happens if a data packet is lost? What if a packet is significantly delayed? How do these problems affect users? The transport layer insulates the session layer from many details of the network. We discuss the specifics of a common transport protocol, TCP (Transmission Control Protocol), in Chapter 7.

Transport functions include multiplexing, buffering, and connnection management. The transport layer can establish multiple connections (**multiplexing**) to the network. Data are divided and parts of it are sent to separate network nodes, a process called **downward multiplexing** (Figure 1.22). Why transport data this way? Suppose someone wants to transfer a large file. Network connections limit the amount of data that can be sent through a single node. The transport layer, however, can establish connections to multiple nodes and thus increase the overall transmission rate.

Figure 1.22   Downward Multiplexing

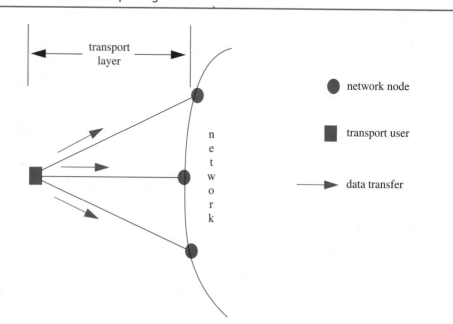

In **upward multiplexing** (Figure 1.23), several transport users share a single node. This method applies when a user wants a constant connection to the network but cannot afford it. The sharing may cause a delay, but it has little effect if network accesses are infrequent.

The transport layer also handles **buffering** at network nodes. An interesting aspect here is that buffering may occur at either the destination or the source node. When a sending transport layer receives data from the session layer for transmission, it divides it into units called **transport protocol data units** (TPDUs). The transport protocol sends them to the receiving transport layer (via the lower layers), where they eventually are routed to the receiving session layer.

A transport protocol typically requires the acknowledgment of each received TPDU. This acknowledgment is especially useful in packet-switching networks, in which packets may be delayed or even lost because of a network failure. Suppose transport user *A* wants to send several TPDUs to user *B*. In some cases, the TPDUs are buffered at the source and queued for transmission by the lower layers. The transport layer waits for an acknowledgment for each TPDU but does not remove them from the buffer. If the protocol requires an acknowledgment for each TPDU, the sending transport layer waits for it. If it does not occur within a set period of time, the sender retransmits the TPDU, which is possible only if it is still in the buffer.

When a receiving transport layer receives a TPDU, it holds the TPDU until the session layer is ready for it. Keep in mind that there is no guarantee the session layer will accept it immediately. If the receiver knows the sender is buffering all TPDUs, it may elect to use a single buffer to save space. The disadvantage of this choice is

Figure 1.23   Upward Multiplexing

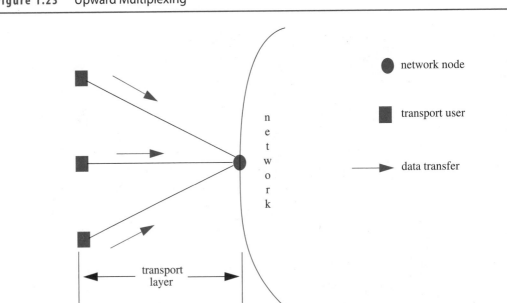

that the receiver may have no room for subsequent TPDUs until the one being held is delivered to the session layer. In this case, the receiver ignores the TPDUs and refuses to acknowledge their reception. The sender receives no acknowledgment and eventually retransmits the TPDUs.

If the network is reliable (that is, errors are few), the TPDUs may instead be buffered at the destination. If the sender knows the receiver is buffering the data, the sender need not do so. It reasons that there is little need to hold on to something once it is sent. After all, the chances of it arriving quickly and safely are high. It's a bit like not keeping a copy of every letter you mail because you are afraid the post office will lose it and you will have to remail it.

Connection management is the protocol by which the transport layer establishes and releases connections between two nodes. At first glance, making and releasing connections may seem easy, but it is deceptively tricky. For example, suppose the transport layer is trying to establish a connection between users A and B. You might think the connection is as simple as (1) user A requesting a connection to user B and (2) user B indicating readiness for a connection, after which (3) a connection occurs (Figure 1.24). This is a **two-way handshake protocol** for establishing a connection. The problem is that it does not always work because of potential delays in either A's request or B's response.

For example, consider the timing shown in Figure 1.25. Note that requests and acknowledgments are made by transmitting special TPDUs. At time t_1, user A requests a connection. However, for some reason, perhaps network congestion or a problem at an intermediate site, the request is delayed. User A, thinking the message is lost, makes another connection request at time t_2. User B receives the second request at time t_3 and promptly acknowledges it. User A receives the acknowledgment at time t_4, and the connection is made. No problem so far.

Users A and B do whatever they are supposed to do and eventually disconnect. However, the first connection request is still floating around somewhere. Suppose it finally arrives at user B at time t_5. User B thinks it is another request and acknowledges it. As far as B is concerned there is another connection, but this time it is unintentional. Worse yet, consider what could happen if user A sent a data TPDU during the first connection that was seriously delayed. Not receiving an acknowledgment, user A would have retransmitted it. But the first request is still somewhere in the network. What happens if B finally gets it after time t_5? User B thinks it is another

Figure 1.24   Two-Way Handshake Protocol to Establish a Connection

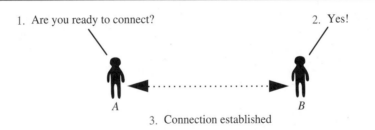

1. Are you ready to connect?   2. Yes!

A B

3. Connection established

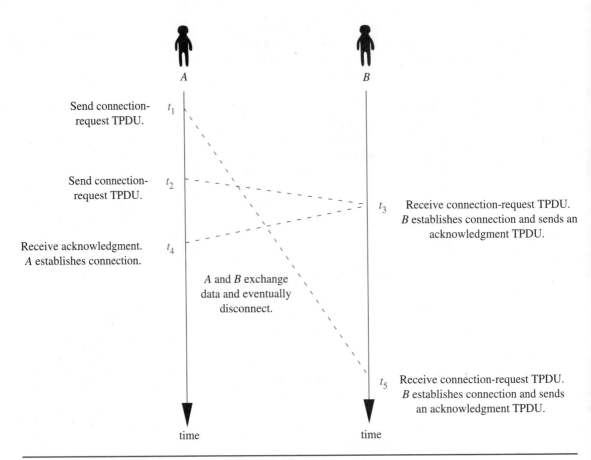

Figure 1.25   Failure of a Two-Way Handshake Protocol

TPDU and responds to it. How serious is this problem? Imagine if the connections were private ones to Swiss banks, and the data packets requested deposits of $5 million. Bank officials will not be happy paying interest on a bogus $5 million deposit.

The problem may be solved in two ways. The first is to send a sequence number with every TPDU. It may be based on a counter or clock that increases each time. The second is to use a **three-way handshake** protocol, designed by Tomlinson (Ref. [To75]). It works as follows:

1. User A transmits a TPDU requesting a connection. Its sequence number is x.

2. User B transmits a TPDU acknowledging both the request and sequence number. Its sequence number is y.

3. User A acknowledges the acknowledgment by including sequence numbers x and y in its first data TPDU.

Let's see how this works in a case similar to that of Figure 1.25. Figure 1.26 shows the details. At time t_1, user A sends TPDU x requesting a connection. How-

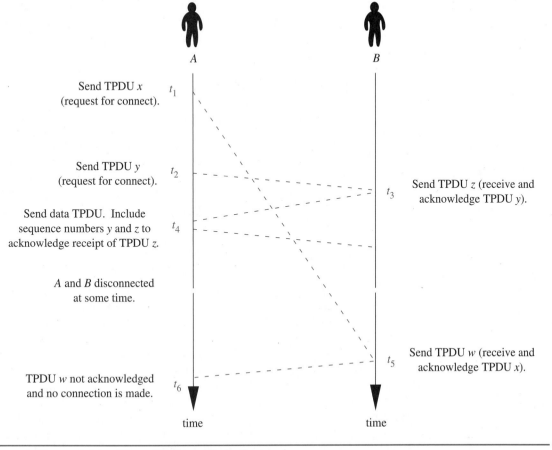

Send TPDU x
(request for connect). t_1

Send TPDU y
(request for connect). t_2

Send TPDU z (receive and
acknowledge TPDU y). t_3

Send data TPDU. Include
sequence numbers y and z to
acknowledge receipt of TPDU z. t_4

A and B disconnected
at some time.

Send TPDU w (receive and
acknowledge TPDU x). t_5

TPDU w not acknowledged
and no connection is made. t_6

time   time

Figure 1.26   Three-Way Handshake Protocol

ever, as before, the TPDU is delayed. User A, receiving no acknowledgment, sends another TPDU at time t_2. This is TPDU y. User B receives TPDU y at time t_3. It acknowledges by sending TPDU z, which contains sequence number y. User A receives TPDU z at time t_4. It acknowledges sequence numbers y and z by including them in its first data TPDU. Everything works so far.

Suppose, as before, users A and B disconnect, and TPDU x arrives at user B at time t_5. User B thinks it is another request and acknowledges it by sending TPDU w, which contains sequence number x. When user A receives this TPDU, it realizes something is wrong because it has not requested a connection. Even if it had requested a second connection, the acknowledged sequence number would not match the one used with the connection request. Either way, A does not acknowledge. Meanwhile, user B is waiting for the acknowledgment. Suppose B subsequently receives a delayed data TPDU from a previous connection. The TPDU will not contain the sequence number w that B sent previously. Consequently, B ignores it and no connection is made.

Terminating connections also can be a problem because of delayed or lost TPDUs. Basically, both parties must agree to disconnect before doing so. A similar three-way handshake protocol is used. In theory, it works as follows:

1. User *A* requests a disconnect.
2. User *B* acknowledges the request.
3. User *A* acknowledges the acknowledgment and disconnects.
4. When user *B* receives the acknowledgment, it disconnects.

As before, problems can occur if a request or acknowledgment is lost. In part, this is handled by having *A* and *B* set timers. If either *A*'s request or *B*'s acknowledgment is lost, *A* will retransmit the request after the timer expires. If *A*'s acknowledgment is lost, *B* will disconnect when its timer expires. We will discuss a specific transport protocol (Transmission Control Protocol, or TCP) in Chapter 7. References [Ta96] and [St97] are also good sources for transport protocols.

SESSION LAYER

The next three layers deal primarily with user services and functions. (The previous four layers focused on communications.) The session layer contains the protocols necessary for establishing and maintaining a connection, or session, between two end users. The difference between the transport and session layers is often unclear at first. The transport layer provides the session layer with a connection between two nodes, and we just stated that the session provides a connection between users. What is the difference? Figure 1.27 shows an analogy that should help clear up any confusion.

In the figure, an executive is asking her secretary to call a customer. The executive is analogous to the session layer and the secretary to the transport layer. Thus, the request in (a) is similar to requesting a session. The executive requests the connection but does not get involved with technical details such as looking up the phone number or dialing it. In (b), the secretary makes the call and thus initiates procedures to establish the transport connection. The process of dialing and initiating the connection is independent of the way the telephone company's switching circuits actually route the call. But again, transport layers don't care about such details. When the call is completed in (c), the transport connection is made. However, the session is not established until the executive finally gets on the phone in (d).

Figure 1.28 shows another example related to computer communications. A large company with offices all over the world has all its essential data and software on a mainframe computer at a central location. Each office (airline reservation systems, major brokerage companies, banks, and so on) has its own front-end processor that communicates with the company's mainframe over a network. Through the processor, regional office employees frequently access the mainframe for short periods. These are the sessions that the session layer provides. Because of the frequent access, the transport layer maintains a single transport connection between the minicomputer and mainframe. Each session uses the same transport connection, a system

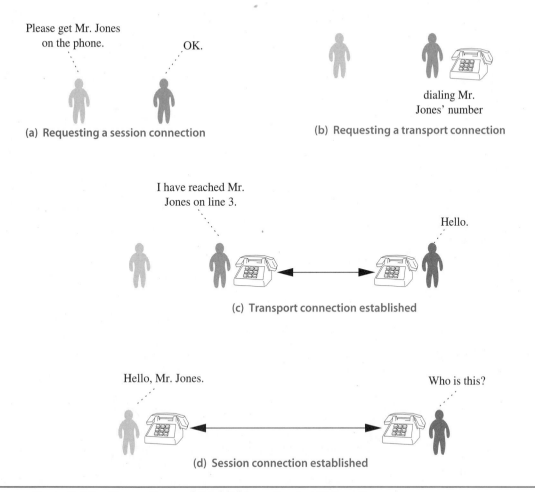

Please get Mr. Jones
on the phone.

OK.

(a) Requesting a session connection

dialing Mr.
Jones' number

(b) Requesting a transport connection

I have reached Mr.
Jones on line 3.

Hello.

(c) Transport connection established

Hello, Mr. Jones.

Who is this?

(d) Session connection established

Figure 1.27   Requesting and Establishing a Session Connection

that is more efficient than negotiating a new connection every time a user wants to access the mainframe.

Don't interpret Figure 1.28 as a form of multiplexing. A transport connection services only one session at a time. A second session can use the transport connection only when the first session is finished.

If the transport connection is disrupted because of a network failure, the session layer can request another transport connection without disrupting the session. This recovery is analogous to the executive in Figure 1.27 being disconnected from her client and then waiting on the telephone while the secretary calls a second time.

Three operations promote orderly communications and allow the session layer to define logical units of information: dialog management, synchronization points, and activities.

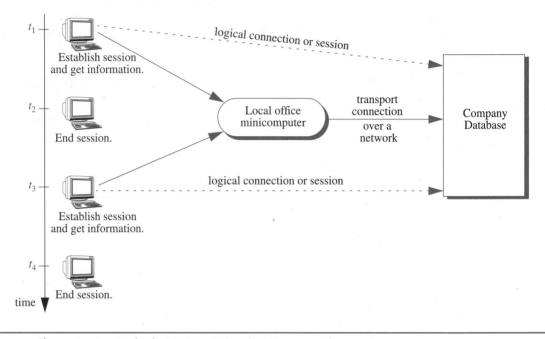

Figure 1.28   Multiple Sessions Using One Transport Connection

Dialog management: Most communications are **full duplex;** that is, data transmissions can go in two directions at the same time. In **half-duplex** communications, data can go in either direction, but transmissions must alternate. This is the common personal communication protocol: You normally take turns talking (unless the conversation is between two politicians, neither of whom ever bothers to listen).

If desired, the session layer can manage half-duplex communications. Through the exchange of a data token, it will coordinate conversations (or data exchanges) so that only one user can send at a time. Only the user with the token can send data. When the session layer establishes a session, one user initially gets the token. He or she is the sender, and the other is the receiver. As long as the sender has the token, he or she can send data. If the receiver wants to transmit data, he or she can request the token. The sender decides when to give it up. On acquiring the token, the receiver becomes the sender.

Synchronization points: In many cases, a session allows a user to transmit large amounts of data. Some questions you might ask are, What happens if an error occurs after much of the data have been transmitted? Is everything lost? Must I start over from the beginning? The lower layers handle some of the problems of lost packets, but received packets still must percolate up through the OSI layers. What happens if an error occurs there? For example, a file might be transmitted successfully and then be lost because of a disk error when the receiving user is writing it. This error has nothing to do with network communication per se, and the lower layers cannot deal with it.

The session-layer user can prevent large losses by defining synchronization points within the data stream. These points divide the data into distinct dialog units. More important, they also define recovery points in case an error occurs. There are two types of synchronization points: major and minor. Figure 1.29 shows major synchronization points that define separate dialog units.

At each **major synchronization point,** the receiving session layer must acknowledge that the dialog unit has been received successfully by the intended user. This assures the sender that the dialog unit has arrived where it is finally supposed to be. If an error occurs before acknowledgment, the sender may resynchronize or retransmit data starting from the most recent synchronization point. Retaining copies of the dialog unit is the sender's responsibility. However, once a dialog unit has been acknowledged, the sender may delete it and free the buffer space.

Minor synchronization points are similar to major ones. The sender may refine the dialog unit by inserting them. Figure 1.30 shows the placement of minor synchronization points. The user may resynchronize to a minor synchronization point within the current dialog unit. Minor synchronization points are not acknowledged, which reduces overhead. On the other hand, the sender cannot free the space used to buffer the dialog units. (Can you guess why?)

Figure 1.29 Major Synchronization Points Defining Dialog Units

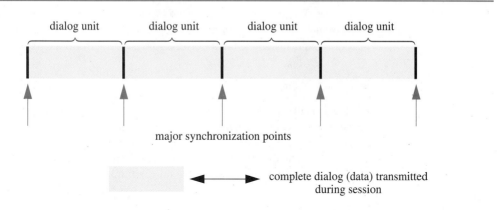

Figure 1.30 Minor Synchronization Points within a Dialog Unit

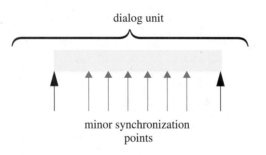

Activities: The user may place another structure on the data by defining a unit of work called an **activity.** Figure 1.31 shows that an activity consists of one or more dialog units. Activities are separate, independent units much like the dialogs and, as with dialog units, must be defined.

One way to think of an activity is as a series of requests that must be processed on an all-or-nothing basis. For example, suppose you work in the catalog order department of a retail store. When a customer calls in an order, the information you enter from a PC is transmitted across a network to the company's main computer. Suppose you have just entered the customer's account number. Because many databases lock records during accesses, the customer's account is now locked. Now suppose the PC stops working, perhaps because someone accidentally unplugs it. When it is running again, you try to resume by accessing the customer's account, but you get a message stating the account is locked. (It is like locking yourself out of the house and leaving your keys inside.)

To avoid such an occurrence, the session-layer user can request the quarantining of a series of commands or messages transmitted on a network. The receiving session layer puts them all in a buffer before processing any of them. Because the messages are not processed immediately, the scenario just described does not occur. When you enter the account number, the session layer saves it. The customer's account is not accessed and hence not locked.

The sending session layer marks the beginning and end of an activity with special commands. When the receiving session layer detects the start of an activity, it buffers all incoming commands until it sees the end of the activity. Then and only then will it pass the commands to the higher layers, where they perform the required task.

PRESENTATION LAYER

Computer networking would be much simpler if all computers spoke the same language. We are not talking here about languages such as Pascal, C, Ada, or COBOL. We are referring to the way in which a computer represents the entity we call information.

We must distinguish between information and data, as the difference is important. When we speak of **data,** we conjure up images of hoards of numbers, hexa-

Figure 1.31 Session Activity

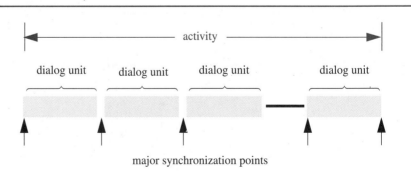

major synchronization points

decimal dumps, or pages of letters and special symbols. In short, a computer does not store information, it stores data. **Information** is a meaning we attach to the data. At the most basic level, data are an assortment of bits and bytes and other unmentionable things. Information is a human interpretation of it. A problem exists because different computers have different ways of representing the same information. Thus, it is not enough to define effective data communications. We must define effective communication of information. The presentation layer does this.

For example, consider a network that transmits data between two computers (Figure 1.32). One stores information using ASCII and the other uses EBCDIC, which represent two different ways of storing data (Chapter 2 discusses ASCII and EBCDIC further). When the ASCII-based computer says "HELLO," the network transmits the ASCII message. The EBCDIC-based computer receives and stores the data. Unfortunately, anyone interpreting it will see it as " <<!" because of the different interpretation placed on the bits received.

What we really want is communication of information, as shown in Figure 1.33. The ASCII version of "HELLO" is transmitted. Because the receiver uses EBCDIC, the data must be converted. In this case, the hexadecimal characters 48 45 4C 4C 4F are transmitted, but C8 C5 D3 D3 D6 are received. The two computers have not exchanged data; instead, and more important, they have exchanged information in the form of the word "HELLO."

The problem involves more than just code conversion. We may also have problems transmitting numbers. For example, computers may store integers using either

Figure 1.32 Data Exchange between Two Computers

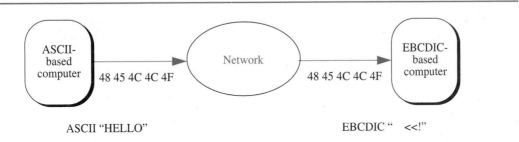

ASCII "HELLO"   EBCDIC " <<!"

Figure 1.33 Information Exchange between Two Computers

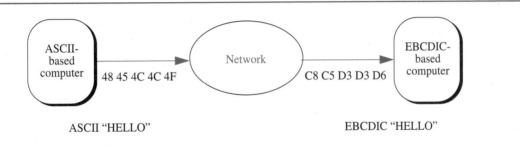

ASCII "HELLO"   EBCDIC "HELLO"

a two's complement or a one's complement format. The difference is minor, but it must be considered. In addition, the number of bits used to represent an integer varies. Common formats use 16, 32, 64, or 80 bits. Bits must be added or removed to allow for the different sizes. Sometimes a translation is impossible. For example, the maximum integer in a 16-bit format is 32,767. What happens if a computer that uses 32-bit integers tries to transfer 50,000 to a computer limited to 16-bit integers?

Floating-point numbers also present problems. Figure 1.34 shows a common format, although many variations exist. The number of bits used for the mantissa and exponent vary. The number of bits may even vary within a machine, because numbers may be either single or double precision. The exponent may also be interpreted in different ways. Sometimes it is a power of 2; in other cases, it is a power of 16. Sometimes the mantissa is not stored in contiguous bits. When one considers the range of differences, it is amazing that computers can share numeric information at all.

The problem increases with more sophisticated data structures such as arrays, records, and linked lists. The presentation layer must consider how the fields of a record are stored. For example, does each one begin on a word boundary or a byte boundary? Where are link fields stored? How many bytes do they occupy? Is a multidimensional array stored by row or by column?

The presentation layer must know the system it serves. It must also know the format of data it receives from other sources. It must ensure the proper transfer of information throughout the network.

Another function of the presentation layer is **data compression,** * which is a way of reducing the number of bits while retaining their meaning. If transmission is expensive, compression can lower costs significantly and increase the amount of information that can be sent per unit of time. For example, suppose the data in a large file consist entirely of strings of capital letters. For example, it might be a list of keywords or employees' last names. How many data bits must be transferred? If the characters are EBCDIC, the number is $8n$, where n is the number of characters. If the presentation layer redefined the code assigning 0 to A, 1 to B, and so on up to 25 to Z, each character of the alphabet can be represented using 5 bits (the fewest number of bits required to store numbers up to 25). Thus, about 38% fewer bits are actually sent. There are many other methods for data compression, and Section 3.5 discusses them in more detail.

Figure 1.34   Generic Format for Floating-Point Numbers

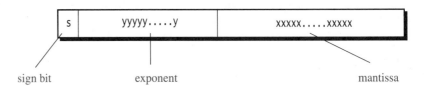

---

*The most effective data compression can be done at this level because the most knowledge of the data and their usage is available. However, compression often is done at lower levels instead of or in addition to this level.

Security is another reason to change the bits (or encrypt them) before sending them. If an unauthorized person intercepts the transmitted message, its encrypted form makes the message unintelligible. To understand its meaning, the data must be decrypted. Chapter 4 deals with the important issue of encryption in detail.

APPLICATION LAYER

The application layer, the highest layer in the OSI model, communicates with the user and the application programs. It is called the application layer because it contains network applications, which differ from user applications such as payroll or accounting programs, graphic design packages, language translators, or database programs. Typical network applications include World Wide Web applications, electronic mail, file transfer, and virtual terminal protocols (all discussed in Chapter 8) and distributed systems.

Most colleges and major organizations are connected to the Internet, which allows the exchange of personal or professional messages by electronic mail. As an example, many of the comments the author and editor exchanged during production of this book were done by email. The lower layers of the model provide the means of expressing the message and getting it to its destination. The **email protocol** in the application layer defines the architecture of an electronic mail system. It stores mail in a mailbox (really a file) from which users can organize and read their messages and provide responses.

A **file transfer protocol** also allows users to exchange information, but in a different way. It typically allows a user to connect to a remote system, examine some of its directories and files, and copy them to the user's system. To the user it is almost that simple, except for a few problems. One is file structure. Some files consist of a simple sequence of bytes; others are flat files consisting of a linear sequence of records. Hashed files allow random access to a record through a key field value. Hierarchical files[*] may organize all occurrences of a key field in a tree structure. These differences pose a problem when transferring files.

The **World Wide Web** allows users to view documents stored at computers in other locations. It also allows the user to follow a link stored on one document to another document at another site. By following links, the user can hop from one location to another with a simple click of a mouse button. Common jargon for this is **Web browsing** or **Web surfing.** We'll discuss the Web more fully in Chapter 8.

A **virtual terminal protocol** allows a user at a terminal to connect to a remote computer across a computer network. Once connected, the user interacts as though the computer were on-site. Allowing access to different computers from different terminals presents problems because of the variety of equipment and software. One problem is that software often is written with specific equipment in mind. Full-screen text editors are examples. The editor displays text on a screen and allows the user to move the cursor and make changes. The displayed number of rows and columns,

---

[*]Be sure to distinguish between a file's structure and its implementation. For example, a file may be hierarchical, but there are many implementations of a hierarchical structure.

however, varies from one terminal to another. Commands to move the cursor and delete or insert text require control sequences that also vary by terminal. Perhaps you have noticed that different terminals have different keyboards. Other examples include software that depends on screen formats for input. Often layouts provide a simple uncluttered view of a user's options. Spacing, tabs, and highlighting help the user work with the software. Again, such features are terminal dependent.

Distributed systems are another growing application of computer networks. A **distributed system** allows many devices to run the same software and to access common resources. Example resources include workstations, file servers, mainframes, and printers (Figure 1.35). In a true distributed system, a user logs on and has no knowledge of the underlying structure. The user requests a particular resource and gets it without knowing or caring where it came from or what kind of workstation he or she is using to get it. The distributed system hides the details.

Distributed systems present many challenges. Suppose a user requests a file by name. A problem is that different systems use different rules for naming files. How can we make these rules transparent to the user and still adhere to what a particular computer requires? Often the files exist on different computers. How does the distributed system know where to look for a requested file? Because different computers are used, how does the distributed system handle the problem of duplicate file names? The problems of a true distributed system are many; References [Sa90], [Ch90], [Ta90], and [Le90] address some of them.

SUMMARY

This section has described each of the seven layers of the OSI protocol model. Each layer defines communication protocols of computer networks and insulates the layer above from the details of the one below. Together, they insulate the user from bit-

Figure 1.35   Distributed System

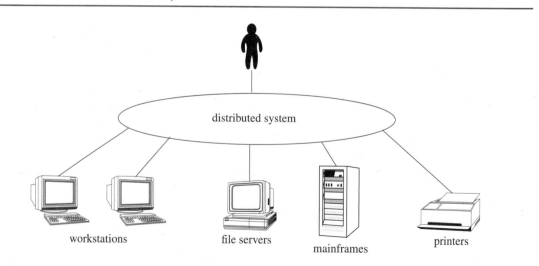

workstations   file servers   mainframes   printers

level details of data communications. If fully implemented, they also allow communication between incompatible devices.

The lowest three layers deal primarily with network communications. The physical layer sends and receives bit streams without regard to meaning. It does not know what the data mean or even if they are correct. The physical layer also contains connection strategies. Circuit switching creates and maintains dedicated lines between nodes. Message switching routes messages through the network. There are no dedicated lines connecting nodes. Packet-switching divides a message into packets for independent routing.

The data link layer provides error detection for the physical layer. Error detection techniques include parity bits and other detection or correction codes. Some can detect single-bit errors only; others can detect when noise destroys many bits. The data link layer also contains contention strategies. Collision detection allows simultaneous transmission by multiple devices but detects any resulting collision. Each device then waits a random amount of time before retransmitting. With token passing, a token moves among the network nodes. A node can transmit only when it has the token.

The highest of the bottom three layers is the network layer. It contains routing strategies. Algorithms can determine the cheapest route between two nodes, and each node knows its successor on a route. But because the cheapest route may vary with time as network conditions change, adaptive routing strategies may be used to detect changes in the network and alter routes accordingly.

The top four layers service the user. The lowest one is the transport layer. It provides buffering, multiplexing, and connection management. Connection management ensures that delayed messages do not compromise requests to establish or release connections.

The session layer manages dialogs between users. In half-duplex communication, the session layer keeps track of who can speak and who must listen. It also allows the definition of synchronization points that protect against a failure at a higher layer. Data between major synchronization points must be buffered to permit recovery. This layer also allows the quarantining of requests when a sequence of requests must be processed on an all-or-nothing basis.

The presentation layer accounts for differences in data representation. It allows two systems to exchange information even though they may have different ways of storing it. It can also compress data to decrease the number of transmitted bits. The presentation layer also implements encryption and decryption.

The last and highest layer is the application layer, which contains user services such as electronic mail, file transfer software, and virtual terminals. It communicates directly with the user or application program.

1.5   THE FUTURE OF DATA COMMUNICATIONS

We have invested time discussing the history of communications and current technologies and models. The next logical question is, Where do we go from here? In other words, what can we expect to see in the future? Exotic and fantastic predictions are being made, but they probably are no more fantastic than today's realities appeared to people a few decades ago. To them, the concept of spacecraft circling the earth transmitting television pictures and telephone conversations was science fiction. The prospect that light could be used to transmit picture and sound was fantasy. Certainly the very idea that computers could actually "talk" to one another was absurd and maybe a little scary to people who saw too many movies about computers taking control of the world.

The fact is that much of what we will see in the future already exists. It's just that many products that are technologically feasible are not always economically feasible on a large scale. So we return to the question: What can we look forward to? Here are some possibilities.

- **Electronic telephone directories:** The telephone will be replaced by a communications terminal. France already has done so, as have a few test cities in the United States. One of the terminal's functions will be the same as the telephone. Another function will allow callers to access telephone databases. They will enter someone's name and address, and the terminal will display the phone number for that person. Callers also will be able to enter a product or service and get a list of businesses that provide it—electronic yellow pages.

    The terminal also will transmit and receive video images. The main obstacle to this technology has been the tremendous amount of information that transmitting a quality image requires. With the increasing capacities of optical fibers and satellites, we now have the ability to do this. Bringing it into everyone's home, however, is not yet economically feasible.

- **Portable telephones:** Bring your telephone with you wherever you go. This idea is not futuristic, as cellular telephones are already quite common. Many people use them for business or status reasons, and an increasing number of people are finding other good reasons to have them. Imagine having your car break down at 2:00 A.M. on a deserted highway 10 miles from the nearest telephone booth. Eventually, telephone booths may be seen only in the Smithsonian. Portable telephones allow portable fax machines. If you are late for a business meeting because you are stuck in rush-hour traffic, you can fax your notes or sales charts to your office from your car. (Better yet, have a passenger who is not driving do it—another good reason for carpooling.)

- **Electronic mail:** The Internet already allows electronic mail (email) to be exchanged worldwide. In the past, this technology was used primarily by companies, government agencies, and universities. However, many people at home now have this ability if they have a computer, modem, and a connection to a company computer or an Internet service provider such as America Online or CompuServe. Still, there are many people who probably don't care to use such services or do not want to change lifelong habits of writing letters by hand. To them, sending greeting cards, anniversary cards, or sympathy cards electronically would not carry the same emotional content as a Hallmark card.

- **All-digital telephone system:** This concept is a little tough to describe without getting into the differences between analog and digital signals, as Chapter 2 does. For now, just think of it as communicating using the same signal types a computer uses. Most people do not care whether their phone calls are carried by an analog or digital signal. If someone calls and tells me I won the lottery, I am not going to ask whether the phone call is analog or digital. (In fact, except for the signals that go directly into and out of a home, the telephone system is already all-digital.)

All-digital systems have definitely affected communications. For example, digital signals can carry information to the destination telephone. An increasingly common feature of the telephone system is caller ID. As your telephone rings, the telephone number of the caller is displayed on a device. You can use this information to decide whether to answer the telephone. A professional such as a doctor, lawyer, or broker might use software to key the incoming telephone number to a client or patient database, from which information can be displayed before the phone is answered. Not only do they know who is calling, but potentially relevant information is also made available before the phone is picked up. The 911 emergency system greatly benefits people in trouble by displaying the number of an incoherent person or small child. Displaying the caller's number also helps reduce the number of obscene phone calls.

One drawback to this system is lack of privacy. Many people have unlisted phone numbers and should not have their numbers displayed whenever they make a call. Of course, caller ID can usually be disabled in such cases. The system will need to determine when a number should be displayed. All-digital systems do exist and standards are being developed for worldwide digital communication systems. Standards such as the Integrated Services Digital Network (ISDN) are discussed in Chapter 8. Another standard, ATM, the technology for a broadband ISDN system, is also discussed in Chapter 8.

- **Electronic media access:** Many people routinely make trips to their favorite video stores to rent a tape, or go to the library to borrow a book or look something up in an encyclopedia. Someday your television can be a two-way communications device.[*] You will be able to use it to access a library of movies, specials, or documentaries and view them at your convenience. Pay-per-view is already available in many locations, which allows you to select various movies showing at designated times (for a fee, of course). Similarly, you will be able to access books electronically from a library. Electronic access probably will not replace the practice of settling down at night with a good book, but it will be useful to those who want factual information such as that found in an encyclopedia or government document. Many well-known newspapers and magazines are already available in electronic form if you have an Internet connection.

- **Videoconferencing:** Every day millions of people spend part (often too much) of their day in meetings. Sometimes they must travel long distances at significant cost to attend meetings. Videoconferencing allows people in different locations to see and hear each other in a real-time setting. They are able to converse

---

[*]Many cable systems already provide two-way communications using a device available from the cable service provider.

and display charts as though they were all in the same room. Until recently, videoconferencing has not been economical because of the enormous amount of information that multiple video images require. However, advances in desktop video technology, high-resolution graphics, PC applications, and compression techniques have changed the field. Once considered a luxury for only the largest corporations, videoconferencing is now accessible to a wide variety of businesses. Some people predict that full-motion video will someday be available at the desktop of any network user, although such a development certainly would necessitate significant changes in network protocols.[*]

- **Three-dimensional imaging:** Video images are two dimensional. The old "3-D" movies were accomplished by showing two different images of the same thing and then giving viewers special glasses. Each lens filtered out one of the images so that each eye received a slightly different image. The brain interpreted these signals differently, giving the perspective of what we call distance. Someday your television may be replaced by a holographic box in which real three-dimensional images are displayed. This development probably will not occur in the near future. Consider how long it has taken for high-definition television (HDTV) to get off the ground. It will be a while before people embrace the technology to the point where they will scrap their old televisions and buy new ones. Of course, with the commitment to the new digital broadcast television standards, this will happen sooner than some expected.

    But why stop at images? People weren't content to stop at voice transmissions. They had to figure out a way to send two-dimensional video images, then three-dimensional images. What about transmitting actual objects or, in the extreme case, people? Sound like science fiction? Of course it is, as anyone who has ever watched *Star Trek* knows. But so were all these other technologies at one time. Transmitting physical objects would be the ultimate in data communication.

- **Electronic locators:** Another seemingly sci-fi device allows people to wear a badge that tells a central computer their exact location. Similar devices are used today. For example, some trucking firms have installed transmitters in all of their trucks. The transmitter sends signals to a satellite, which forwards them to a company's computer and allows dispatchers to determine the truck's location. The accuracy of these systems can place a truck within several hundred feet anywhere in the country.

    These devices are starting to show up in automobiles. The car could have a small video display showing a state road map. Using the satellite tracking system, it could also display a blinking "you are here" mark showing the current location of your car. Such a system would be useful for someone lost on a

---

[*]We note that downloading video clips from the Internet is already common, but that is not what we mean here. Such video clips are downloaded and viewed locally. We refer to the ability to view full-motion video in real-time, that is, as it is actually occurring. That requires some real-time constraints that many network protocols do not provide. Chapter 8 will discuss one that does, Asynchronous Transfer Mode (ATM).

lonely country road. Similar systems might be even more useful as part of a boat's navigation system on open waters (minus the road map, of course).

- **Voice communications:** Currently, most data communication originates with computer devices such as terminals, scanners, display screens, or disk drives. Sophisticated processors now can be taught to recognize speech patterns. This is of great service to physically impaired people, who could control a wheelchair or a robot arm by talking to it. A similar device already allows an individual to program a VCR using voice commands.

- **Mind communications:** Can a computer read a person's mind? Before you scoff at the question, remember that each person produces a brain-wave pattern that is unique and detectable by an electroencephalograph. This author once saw a documentary in which a test subject was connected to such a device while watching the projected image of a ball being moved up, down, left, and right; his brain-wave patterns were recorded and stored by a computer for later reference. Next, the person looked at the ball projected on the screen and attempted to move it himself by thinking one of the four directions. The computer compared the brain-wave patterns generated by this exercise with those stored and issued commands to move the projected ball image in the correct direction. It worked! Can a computer read a person's mind? You be the judge.

Communications technologies will present many challenges. Perhaps the most significant ones relate to privacy and security. The tremendous amounts of information traveling through the air will invite unscrupulous people to attempt illegal reception and transmissions. How do you prevent people from getting things they should not see or have not paid for? How can you prevent people from disrupting a television network transmission and sending their own messages? These are not hypothetical situations; they have happened.

What about different governmental policies on the transmission and exchange of information? We cannot set up checkpoints at national borders to restrict or filter information. Should we restrict and filter information? If so, who defines the policies on what information is appropriate? How do we distinguish that from censorship?

The challenges are many, and we must be prepared to meet them. First, we must understand them and the technology that creates them. It is time to begin.

Review Questions

1. What is the difference between contention and collision?

2. Name five standards-making agencies and at least one standard for which each is responsible.

3. What is a switchboard?

4. List five communications applications and how they might be used.

5. What is an open system?

6. List five ways of organizing a local area network.

7. What is a de facto standard? Give an example of one.

8. What is meant by a layered protocol? Why are protocols layered?

9. Match the functions in the table with the OSI layer that performs them.

OSI LAYER	FUNCTION
Physical	Activity definition
Data link	Bracketing
Network	Buffering
Transport	Contention
Session	Data compression
Presentation	Definition of a signal's electrical characteristics
Application	Dialog management
	Electronic mail
	Encryption and decryption
	Error detection
	Establishing and releasing a connection
	File transfers
	Format conversion
	Multiplexing
	Quarantining
	Remote job entry
	Routing
	Switching
	Synchronization
	Token passing

10. Distinguish between even and odd parity.

11. Distinguish between message and packet-switching.

12. What are the major differences between a two-way handshake and a three-way handshake protocol?

13. Are the following statements TRUE or FALSE? Why?

    a. The first computer was developed to aid in establishing communications systems.

    b. Telstar was a satellite designed to transmit television and telephone signals across the Atlantic Ocean.

c. An open system is one that allows free access to a variety of computing and information services.

d. A computer network can connect many types of storage devices even if they store information in different formats.

e. Two pairs of devices can communicate simultaneously along a common bus if each pair is at opposite ends of the bus.

f. A fully connected LAN topology is most common because it allows direct transfer of information between any two devices.

g. Standards eliminate the inconsistencies between computing devices.

h. The seven-layer OSI model would, if fully implemented, allow any two computing devices to communicate provided there is a way to physically transfer the information between them.

i. Layered protocols allow lower layers to be implemented independent of the higher layers and vice versa.

j. Datagrams are better than virtual circuits at dealing with congestion in networks.

k. Establishment of an OSI transport connection requires only that one side make the connection request and the other side acknowledge it.

14. Which network topologies allow token passing?

15. Which of the OSI model layers deal primarily with network operations?

16. Distinguish between upward and downward multiplexing.

17. Discuss the merits and drawbacks of having a caller's telephone number displayed on a viewing screen whenever the telephone rings.

18. What is the difference between the communication of data and the communication of information?

Exercises

1. Make a sketch outlining the LAN topology at your school or place of business.

2. Which of the applications listed in Section 1.1 have you used? Why have you used them?

3. What types of devices are connected to the LAN at your school or place of business? Are they likely to be found in other LANs? Why or why not?

4. Suppose a bidirectional token ring network connects eight devices numbered 1 through 8 in clockwise order. What device failures would prevent device 1 from sending messages to device 4?

5. Suppose the network in the previous exercise had n devices. Is it possible for two devices to fail and for all the remaining devices to still be able to communicate? If so, under what conditions can this situation occur?

6. In Figure 1.20, list four routes through which A can communicate with F. How many are there all together? (Assume a route does not pass through a node more than once.)

7. Consider the following frames:

$$011010001010001 \; x$$
$$100111000101101 \; x$$
$$100001100011000 \; x$$

Suppose x is the parity bit. What must x be to establish even parity? Odd parity?

8. Argue that if exactly two bits are altered during a transmission, simple parity checking will not detect the error.

9. In general, when will simple parity checking detect an error? When will errors go undetected?

10. What is the reason for using sequence numbers in the three-way handshake protocol?

11. Give examples of videoconferencing that your school or place of business has used.

12. What aspect of data communications will have the most significant impact on your personal or professional life?

13. Section 1.5 described an example in which a person gave a computer commands to move an image of a ball simply by thinking up, down, left, or right. One can argue correctly that this is a long way from reading a person's mind. How would you respond to that argument?

14. How many direct connections would there be in a fully connected topology containing n nodes?

REFERENCES

1. [Ch90] Champine, G., D. Geer, and W. Ruh. "Project Athena as a Distributed Computer System." *Computer,* vol. 23, no. 9 (September 1990), 40–51.

2. [Le90] Levy, E. and A. Silberschatz. "Distributed File Systems: Concepts and Examples." *Computing Surveys,* vol. 22, no. 4 (December 1990), 321–74.

3. [Qu90] Quarterman, J. S. *The Matrix: Computer Networks and Conferencing Systems Worldwide,* Bedford, MA: Digital Press, 1990.

4. [Sa90] Satyanarayanan, M. "Scalable, Secure, and Highly Available Distributed File Access." *Computer,* vol. 23, no. 5 (May 1990), 9–22.

5. [Sh90] Sherman, K. *Data Communications: A User's Guide,* 3rd ed. Englewood Cliffs, NJ: Prentice-Hall, 1990.

6. [Sp91] Spragins, J. D., J. L. Hammond, and K. Pawlikowski. *Telecommunications Protocols and Design.* Reading, MA: Addison Wesley, 1991.

7. [St97] Stallings, W. *Data and Computer Communications,* 4th ed. New York: Macmillan, 1994.

8. [Ta96] Tanenbaum, A. S. *Computer Networks,* 3rd ed. Englewood Cliffs, NJ: Prentice–Hall, 1996.

9. [Ta90] Tanenbaum, A. S. et al. "Experiences with the Amoeba Distributed Operating System." *Communications of the ACM,* vol. 33, no. 12. (December 1990), 46–63.

10. [To75] Tomlinson, R. S. "Selecting Sequence Numbers." *Proceedings of the ACM SIGCOMM/SIGOPS Interprocess Communications Workshop* (1975), 11–23.

CHAPTER 2

TRANSMISSION FUNDAMENTALS

Information networks straddle the world. Nothing remains concealed. But the sheer volume of information dissolves the information. We are unable to take it all in.
—**Günther Grass,** German author

This chapter covers the basics of communication. It begins with discussions of the various media used to transmit data and then addresses the issue of why there are different ways of transmitting data. In other words, what are their advantages and disadvantages?

Many factors help determine the best way to connect communication devices:

- Cost of a connection
- Amount of information that can be transmitted per unit of time
- Immunity to outside interference
- Susceptibility to unauthorized "listening"
- Logistics (how you connect a printer to a mainframe differs depending on whether the printer is on a different floor in the same building or in a different building across a 12-lane highway)

Once devices are connected, you might think the hardest part is done and the devices can easily communicate. Unfortunately, this is not correct. One major problem is in the way information is presented. For example, two people stand talking to each other face to face. If they speak the same language, communication usually (but not always!) occurs. If they speak different languages and neither understands the other's language, communication usually does not occur. Different computers may not represent data the same way. The resulting problems must be dealt with by communications protocols. Section 2.3 discusses some of the standard ways of representing data. Even if two devices represent data the same way, problems may still occur. We must consider the way in which data are transmitted. For example, computers transmit data using **digital signals,** that is, sequences of specified voltage levels. Graphically, they are often represented as a square wave (Figure 2.1a). In this figure the horizontal axis represents time and the vertical axis represents the voltage level. The alternating high and low voltage levels constitute the sequence over a period of time.

Computers sometimes communicate over telephone lines using **analog signals,**[*] which are formed by continuously varying voltage levels. They are most often represented by their characteristic sine wave (Figure 2.1b). Now we have another problem: Digital and analog signals transmit data in different ways. As a result, if a computer is going to communicate over an analog phone line, we need to find a way to convert signals of one type to signals of another and back again.

Section 2.4 discusses analog and digital signals. It presents their limitations and reports on two famous results that specify limits on the amount of data that can be transmitted per unit of time. Section 2.5 describes modulation and demodulation techniques. Finally, Section 2.6 covers modems, common devices used for modulation and demodulation. It also covers intelligent modems and standards.

2.1   COMMUNICATIONS MEDIA

There are three types of transmission media, each with many variations. The first is a conductive metal such as copper or iron. We will show how an electric current traveling along a wire can be used to transmit data. The second medium is a transparent glass or plastic strand that transmits data using light waves. The third requires no physical connection at all and relies on electromagnetic waves such as those found in noncable television and radio broadcasts.

Figure 2.1   Analog and Digital Signals

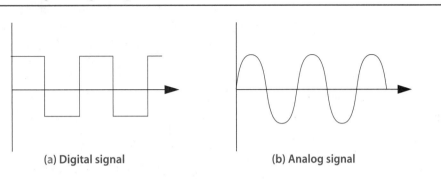

(a) Digital signal   (b) Analog signal

---

[*]Although much of the telephone system is digital, most telephones are devices designed to send and receive analog signals. A computer typically uses a modem to convert its digital signals to an analog format before transmitting. We will discuss modems later in this chapter.

One factor to consider in a discussion of communications media is cost. For example, wires, cables, and strands all have different manufacturing costs. In addition, the devices to which they attach have various costs.

Another factor to consider is the number of bits each communications medium can transmit per unit of time. Two measures are important: bit rate and bandwidth. The **bit rate** is a measure of the number of bits that can be transmitted per unit of time. The typical unit of measure is **bits per second (bps).** Depending on the medium and the application, bit rates commonly range from a few hundred bps to billions of bps.

Before defining bandwidth, let us take a closer look at what a signal is. Many analog signals, for example, exhibit the sine wave pattern of Figure 2.2. It is an example of a **periodic signal,** which means it repeats a pattern or cycle continuously. The **period** of a signal is the time required for it to complete one cycle. The signal in Figure 2.2 has a period of p. A signal's frequency, f, is the number of cycles through which the signal can oscillate in a second. The unit of measurement is cycles per second, or **hertz (Hz).** For example, suppose p from Figure 2.2 was 0.5 microsecond (μsec). Because 0.5 μsec is the same as 0.5×10^{-6} second, the signal's frequency is $1/(.5 \times 10^{-6})$, or 2,000,000 Hz. The frequency and period are related by

$$f = \frac{1}{p}$$

A given transmission medium can accommodate signals within a given frequency range. The **bandwidth** is equal to the difference between the highest and lowest frequencies that may be transmitted. For example, a telephone signal can handle frequencies between 300 Hz and 3300 Hz, giving it a bandwidth of 3000 Hz. In terms of audible sounds, this means that very high- or low-pitched sound cannot pass through the telephone system. Most human speech falls within this range and consequently is easily recognizable. The loss of high- and low-frequency sounds, however, will cause a problem for someone wanting to listen to and appreciate the New York Philharmonic over the telephone.

Sometimes the term *bandwidth* is used when referring to the number of bits that can be transmitted. Technically, bandwidth and bit rates are different, but there is an

Figure 2.2   Periodic Signal

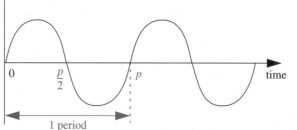

important relationship between them. This complex relationship will be explored in more detail in Section 2.4.

To transmit bits between two devices there must be a way for a signal to travel between them. Typically, this requires either a physical connection or the ability to use electromagnetic waves such as those used by radio and television. This section discusses several ways of making physical connections: twisted-pair wire, coaxial cable, and optical fiber. It also discusses wireless communications using microwave and satellite transmission.

CONDUCTIVE METAL

Twisted Pair   One of the oldest transmission media is conducting metal, which was used to transmit information as early as 1837, when Samuel Morse invented the telegraph. Basically, it is a circuit consisting of a power source, a switch, and a sensor (Figure 2.3). The switch, at location *A,* can be opened or closed manually, thus controlling whether current flows. A sensor, at location *B,* detects current and creates the clicking sound with which you are probably familiar from TV and movie Westerns. Figure 2.3 shows a telegraph system allowing transmission in just one direction. Other designs exist that allow transmissions in both directions (Ref. [Sh90]). Opening and closing the switch in different patterns controls the frequency and duration of signals sent to location *B.* The familiar Morse code, which we present in Section 2.3, associates data with different signal patterns.

Copper wire is probably the most common way of connecting devices. Copper is used because of its electrical conductive properties. That is, electricity flows through copper with less resistance than through many other materials. In addition, copper is more resistant to corrosion than other conducting metals such as iron, a property that makes it a good choice in places where it is exposed to moisture or humidity.

One of the most common uses of copper is in the **twisted pair** in which two insulated copper wires are twisted around each other. The insulation prevents the conductive metal in each wire from making contact and thus short-circuiting the circuit. A common use of twisted-pair wire is the transmission of a balanced signal.

Figure 2.3   One-Way Telegraph System

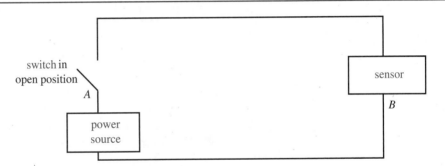

This means that each wire carries current but that the signals are 180° out of phase with each other.[*] The effects on each current from outside electromagnetic sources nearly cancel each other, resulting in a signal that degrades less rapidly. The twisting helps counteract any electrical capacitance that may build up as the current travels the length of the wire.

Twisted pairs often are bundled together and wrapped in a protective coating that allows the bundled cable to be buried. Such cables can be rated, in part, by the number of twists per unit length of wire. A larger frequency of twists provides a greater reduction in capacitance and also helps reduce crosstalk, the electromagnetic interference between adjacent pairs. For a long time, this medium was the primary mode of telephone communications and is still common in connecting a home telephone to a nearby telephone exchange. It is also common in connecting low-speed devices such as computer terminals to a high-speed network.

Even though copper is a good conductor, electrical resistance still occurs, and a signal transmitted over a copper wire will eventually distort and lose strength (**attenuate**). In practice, this means there is a limit on the twisted pair's length before the transmitted signal becomes distorted beyond recognition.

If the wire must connect two points separated by a long distance, a repeater must be inserted between the two points (Figure 2.4). A **repeater** is a device that intercepts a transmitted signal before it has distorted and attenuated too badly and then regenerates the signal and retransmits it. A logical question to ask is, How far apart must repeaters be spaced? The space between repeaters depends on characteristics such as the type of signal and the bandwidth and current carrying capacity of the wire. Many signals may be transmitted for miles before signal regeneration is necessary. With repeaters, there is no limit on how far a signal can be transmitted.

A twisted pair has a bandwidth of up to 250 kHz (1 kHz = 1000 Hz) for analog signals. Digital signal data rates vary with distance. For example, a local area net-

Figure 2.4   Two Points Connected Using a Repeater

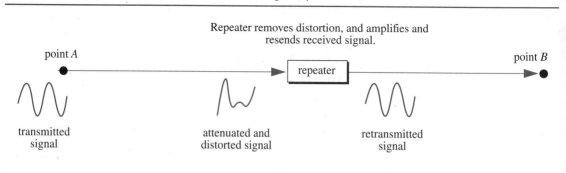

Repeater removes distortion, and amplifies and resends received signal.

point A

point B

repeater

transmitted
signal

attenuated and
distorted signal

retransmitted
signal

---

[*]By contrast, an unbalanced signal uses one wire to carry the current while the other is held at ground potential. Unbalanced signals are typically more susceptible to interference than balanced signals. We'll discuss this further in Section 3.2.

work protocol known as Fast Ethernet uses twisted pair and operates at 100 Mbps over a segment length of 100 meters. Twisted pair can also support a 2400 bps rate for up to 10 miles.

Coaxial Cable   Another common medium is **coaxial cable** (Figure 2.5), which consists of four components. First is the innermost conductor, a copper or aluminum wire core. As with the twisted pair, the core carries the signal. An insulation layer surrounds the core and prevents the conductor from making contact with the third layer, typically a tightly wound wire mesh.[*] The wire mesh acts as a shield, protecting the core from electromagnetic interference. It also protects the core from hungry rodents looking for a free meal. The last layer is what you see on the cables connecting your VCR to your television set, a plastic protective cover.

The wire mesh shield provides excellent protection from extraneous electrical signals. Consequently, coaxial cable has a bandwidth of about 500 MHz (1 MHz = 1,000,000 Hz) and can achieve data rates of up to 500 Mbps.[†] However, coaxial cable is more expensive than twisted pair.

Coaxial cable typically transmits information in either a baseband mode or a broadband mode. In **baseband mode,** the cable's bandwidth is devoted to a single stream of data. Thus, the high bandwidth capability allows high data rates over a cable. This is typical in local area networks, where only one data stream is present at any time. With **broadband,** the bandwidth is divided into ranges. Each range typically carries separate coded information, which allows the transmission of multiple data streams over the same cable simultaneously. Special equipment is used to combine the signals at the source and separate them at the end. Cable television is an example of multiple signals (one for each channel) traveling a single section of cable. We will further discuss combining signals in Section 3.3 under multiplexing.

Figure 2.5   Coaxial Cable

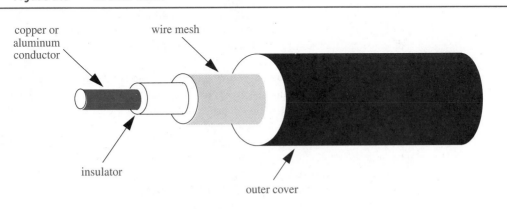

* Sometimes a solid metal conductor is used instead of a mesh on cables that do not need much flexibility.

† Actual data rates may vary with distances.

OPTICAL FIBER

There are several problems (or at least limitations) associated with using conducting metal to transmit signals. One problem is that electrical signals are susceptible to interference coming from sources such as electric motors, lightning strikes, and other wires. We will see in Section 2.4 that this interference limits the amount of data that can be transmitted. In addition, wires and cables are heavy and bulky, especially when bundling them together. It may not seem so at first, but think about carrying several thousand feet of cable during a morning stroll. In fact, AT&T reports that a 4.5-pound spool of optical fiber can carry the same amount of information as 200 reels of copper wire weighing more than 1600 pounds.

This weight places limitations on the installation of wire in high-traffic areas or in hard-to-reach areas such as closets or through long, narrow crawl spaces. Also, the characteristics of electrical signals and resistance properties of conducting metal place limits on the types of signals that can be sent and the distance that signals travel before they degrade. In turn, this limits the amount of information that can be sent per unit of time.

One alternative is **optical fiber.** It uses light, not electricity, to transmit information. Telephone companies make widespread use of optical fiber, especially for long-distance service. It is impervious to electrical noise and has the capacity to transmit enormous amounts of information. In addition, optical fibers are very thin (compared with cables), which allows many of them to be bundled together in much less space than old-fashioned cables require. For those faced with the task of routing them through conduits, above ceilings, or between walls, this is a big advantage.

Optical fibers are becoming more common in computer networks. High-capacity CDs and increased integration of computers and video imaging are generating a need for networks with high bandwidth capabilities. Section 6.3 discusses the Fiber Distributed Data Interface (FDDI), a standard for fiber networks. Reference [Po91] discusses the economics of installing optical fiber in a variety of cases.

The principles that make optical fiber viable are grounded in physics, specifically optics and electromagnetic wave theory. We do not intend to go into a detailed discussion of these topics, but we feel it is important to cover some of the basics so you will have an idea of how it works.

To begin, consider a light source directed toward some surface (Figure 2.6). The surface represents a boundary between two media such as air and water. Let α be the angle at which the light wave intersects the boundary. Some of the light will reflect back at an angle α with the plane and some will cross the boundary into the other medium. This is **refraction.** However, the angle the direction of light makes with the boundary changes. In other words, if β is the angle at which the light wave travels from the boundary, $\beta \neq \alpha$. Next you might ask whether β is larger or smaller than α. If you did, congratulations. That's a good question.

If $\beta > \alpha$ (as it is in Figure 2.6), we say the second medium has a higher optical density than the first (as water has a higher density than air). However, if the first medium has a higher optical density, then $\beta < \alpha$. Refraction explains why a lens in a pair of eyeglasses will distort the normal view, or why objects under water appear

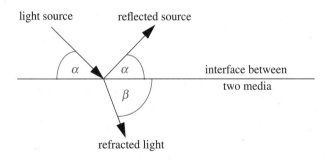

Figure 2.6   Light Refraction and Reflection

distorted if viewed from above the surface. The light reflected off the objects we see is distorted, making them look different.

The relation between β and α is of interest. Physicists use a measure known as the **index of refraction** to describe it. It is defined by

$$\frac{\cos(\alpha)}{\cos(\beta)}$$

Thus, an index of refraction less than 1 means light is traveling into a less optically dense medium whereas an index of refraction of greatrer than 1 means it is traveling in to a more optically dense medium. Remember, angles β and α are between 0° and 90°, so that cos(α) < cos(β) means α > β, and vice versa.

Another interesting phenomenon occurs when the index of refraction is less than 1 (α > β). When α is less than a certain critical angle, there is no refracted light. In other words, all the light is reflected. This is what makes fiber optics work.

The three main components to a fiber optic filament are the core, the cladding, and a protective cover. The core is made from very pure glass or plastic material. The cladding surrounds the core. It is also glass or plastic but is optically less dense than the core. How pure is the core? As we will see, an optical fiber works by allowing light to travel through the core. In some cases the fiber is up to 20 miles long. Because light travels from end to end we can think of the core as 20 miles thick. Thus, imagine a block of glass so pure that a chunk 20 miles thick is nearly transparent.

Next question: How does light enter the fiber? A light source such as a light-emitting diode (LED) or a laser is placed at one end of the fiber. Each is a device that responds to an electric charge to produce a pulse of light typically near the infrared frequency of 10^{14} Hz. The **laser** produces a very pure[*] and narrow beam. It also has a higher power output, allowing the light to propagate farther than that produced by an

---

[*]Light often consists of many wavelengths, or colors, as indicated by the fact that light passing through a prism is divided into its component rainbow colors. A laser can produce "pure" light, or light consisting of very few wavelengths.

LED. The LED produces less-concentrated light consisting of many wavelengths. LEDs are less expensive and generally last longer. Lasers normally are used where a high data rate is needed over a long distance, such as in long-distance telephone lines.

The light source emits short but rapid pulses of light that enter the core at different angles. Light that hits the core/cladding boundary at less than the critical angle is totally reflected back into the core, where it eventually hits the boundary on the opposite side of the core. Because the angle of reflection is the same, it is again totally reflected back into the core. The effect is that the light bounces from boundary to boundary as it propagates down the core. Eventually, the light exits the core and is detected by a sensor. Light that hits the boundary at an angle greater than the critical one is partly refracted into the cladding and absorbed by the protective cover. This prevents light from leaking out and being absorbed by other nearby fibers.

There is a potential problem with light propagating down a core. If the core is fairly thick (relative to a wavelength of light), then light enters it at many places and at many different angles. Some of the light essentially goes down the center of the core, but some hits the boundary at different angles (Figure 2.7). The study of electromagnetic waves (specifically Maxwell's equations) tells us that some of the reflecting rays interfere with one another. Consequently, there is a finite number of angles at which the rays reflect and propagate the length of the fiber. Each angle defines a path or a mode. Fiber that transmits light this way is called **step index multimode fiber.**

Light that reflects at larger angles (measured relative to horizontal) reflects more often and travels a greater distance than light that reflects at smaller angles. Consequently, it takes a bit longer to get to the other end of the fiber. This phenomenon is called **modal dispersion.** Imagine many people racing down a hallway. Some are running down the center, and others, who are blindfolded, are bouncing off the walls. We know who will win that race.

Modal dispersion is a problem if the fiber is too long. Light from one pulse (reflecting at small angles) could actually catch up with light emitted from a previous pulse (reflecting at larger angles), thus eliminating the gap in between. The sensors no longer see pulses of light; they see a steady stream of light rays, and any information that was coded in the pulses is destroyed.

One way of addressing the problem of modal dispersion is to use a **graded-index multimode fiber.** It makes use of another phenomenon related to the fact that

Figure 2.7 Step-Index Multimode Fiber

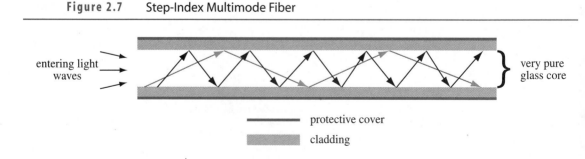

entering light waves

very pure glass core

protective cover

cladding

the speed of light depends on the medium through which it travels: Specifically, light travels faster through less optically dense media.

A graded-index multimode fiber (Figure 2.8) also has a core, cladding, and protective cover. The difference is that the boundary between core and cladding is not sharply defined. In other words, moving out radially from the core, the material becomes gradually less dense. Consequently, as light travels radially outward it begins to bend back toward the center, eventually reflecting back. Because the material also becomes less dense, the light travels faster. The net result is that although some light travels a greater distance, it travels faster, and modal dispersion is reduced.

Another way of dealing with modal dispersion is to eliminate it. How? you may ask. Earlier we stated that there is a finite number of modes at which light can propagate. The exact number depends on the core's diameter and the light's wavelength. Specifically, reducing the core's diameter decreases the number of angles at which light can strike the boundary. Consequently, it also reduces the number of modes. If we reduce the diameter enough, the fiber has only one mode. Cleverly, this is called **single-mode fiber** (Figure 2.9).

How far must we reduce the diameter? Another principle of physics relates the ability to reflect an electromagnetic wave (such as light) to the size of the reflector. Specifically, it tells us that to reflect a light ray in the manner we have described, the reflector must be larger than the wavelength of the reflected light. Because the reflector here is wrapped around the core, its size depends on the core's diameter. The relationship between frequency and wavelength states that

$$\text{wavelength} = \frac{\text{speed of light}}{\text{frequency}}$$

Light traveling through optical fibers has a frequency of approximately 10^{14} Hz, so its wavelength evaluates to approximately 2×10^{-6} meters, or 2 microns

Figure 2.8   Graded-Index Multimode Fiber

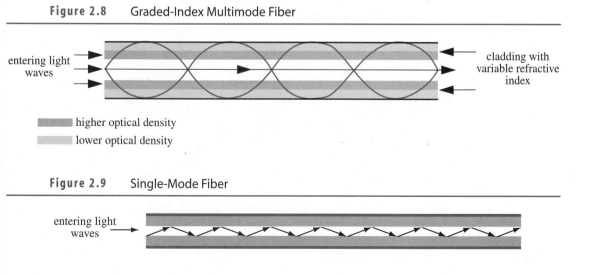

higher optical density
lower optical density

Figure 2.9   Single-Mode Fiber

(1 micron = 10^{-6} meters). Thus, single-mode fibers typically have a diameter measured in microns (typically 4–8, sometimes smaller), very thin indeed (many fibers are as thin as a human hair). Its small diameter makes the fiber more fragile and difficult to splice. Consequently, it is most often used in long-distance trunk lines, applications where handling and splicing are minimal.

Optical fiber technology has many advantages over conducting metal:

- It can transmit data more quickly.
- It has very low resistance. Thus, signals can travel farther without repeaters. For example, repeaters may be placed up to 30 miles apart; cable requires them every couple of miles.
- It is unaffected by electromagnetic interference, because the signals are transmitted by light.
- It has very high resistance to environmental elements such as humidity. This property makes it well suited for coastal areas.

On the other hand, current computers are electronic devices, so the use of optical fiber requires the conversion of electrical signals to light rays and vice versa. This process adds an extra level of complexity. In addition, optical fibers are more difficult than copper wire to tap into or splice together. Components can be added relatively easily to a copper bus by tapping into it, but much more care is necessary when tapping into a glass fiber.

WIRELESS COMMUNICATIONS

All modes of communication using conductive metal or optical fiber have one thing in common: Communicating devices must be connected physically. Physical connection is sufficient for many applications, such as connecting PCs in an office or connecting them to a mainframe within the same building. It is acceptable for short distances, but expensive and difficult to maintain for long distances. Imagine a coaxial cable connected to NASA flight control headquarters hanging out the back end of the space shuttle or a cable hanging between two towers in New York and London!

In many situations, a physical connection is not practical or even possible. Suppose participants in a proposed network are in two different buildings separated by an eight-lane highway. Stringing a cable over the highway or disrupting traffic to lay underground cable probably will not meet with approval by city planners. The network participants need a way of communicating without a physical connection, that is, wireless communications.

Wireless transmissions involve **electromagnetic waves.** As they are a significant part of a physics course, we will not attempt a thorough discussion of them. For our purpose, it is sufficient to say they are oscillating electromagnetic radiation caused by inducing a current in a transmitting antenna. The waves then travel through the air or free space, where they may be sensed by a receiving antenna. Free radio and TV transmit signals this way.

Figure 2.10 shows the electromagnetic wave spectrum. The radio waves are used for both radio and television transmissions. For example, television VHF (very high frequency) broadcasts range from 30 MHz to 300 MHz, and UHF (ultra high frequency) broadcasts range from 300 MHz to 3 GHz.[*] Radio waves are also used for AM and FM radio, ham radio, cellular telephones, and shortwave radio. Each of these communications is assigned a frequency band by the Federal Communications Commission (FCC). Some properties of electromagnetic radiation are important to communications. One is a previously stated relation between the wavelength and frequency:

$$\text{wavelength} = \frac{\text{speed of light}}{\text{frequency}}$$

Consequently, high-frequency waves have short wavelengths and vice versa. Table 2.1 shows some actual values.

Physics tells us that low-frequency waves, when broadcast from the ground, tend to reflect off the upper levels of the atmosphere with little loss. By bouncing back and forth between the atmosphere and the ground, such signals can travel far, following the curvature of the earth. Shortwave (between 3 and 30 MHz) radios, for

Figure 2.10 Electromagnetic Waves

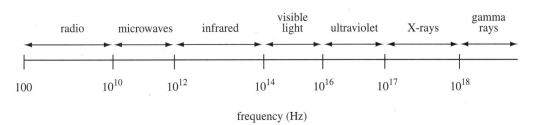

Table 2.1 Wavelength as a Function of Frequency

FREQUENCY (HZ)	APPROXIMATE WAVELENGTH (METERS)
10^2	3×10^6
10^4	3×10^4
10^6	300
10^8	3
10^{10}	0.03
10^{12}	0.0003

---

[*]MHz is megahertz, or 10^6 Hz. GHz is gigahertz, or 10^9 Hz.

example, have been known to receive signals from halfway around the world. Higher-frequency signals tend to reflect with more loss and typically do not travel as far (as measured across the earth's surface).

Low-frequency waves also require a very long antenna. Perhaps some of you remember a controversy in the 1970s and 1980s that involved an attempt by the Navy to install a large (more than 50 miles long) antenna in the upper peninsula of Michigan. Its purpose was submarine communication using extremely low frequency (ELF) signals in the less than 300 Hz range. The controversy over Project ELF centered around the potential health risks of people exposed to such electromagnetic radiation. Even today, there is much concern over potential health risks from radiation caused by devices such as power lines and computer terminals (Ref. [Br89]).

Two types of wireless communication are particularly important: microwave and satellite transmissions.

Microwave Transmissions   Microwave transmissions typically occur between two ground stations. Two properties of microwave transmission place restrictions on its use. First, microwaves travel in a straight line and will not follow the earth's curvature as some lower-frequency waves will. Second, atmospheric conditions and solid objects interfere with microwaves. For example, they cannot travel through buildings.

A typical mechanism for transmitting and receiving microwave transmissions uses the parabolic dish reflector (Figure 2.11). No doubt you have seen them in backyards (for receiving satellite signals for television), on top of buildings, or mounted on a tower in the middle of nowhere (Figure 2.12). The last are commonly used for telephone communications. More recently, the 18-inch satellite dish has become popular among many consumers as a way of receiving numerous television stations and for pay-per-view selections.

Figure 2.11   Parabolic Dish Receiving Signals

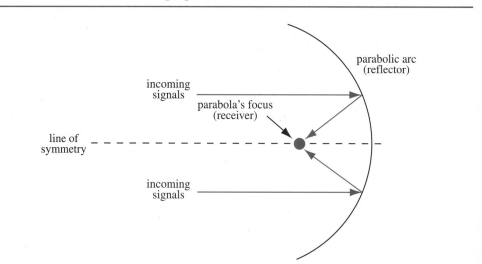

Figure 2.12   Microwave Transmission Tower (Courtesy of AT&T Archives)

Parabolic dishes use a well-known but probably forgotten fact from precalculus mathematics. Given a parabolic curve, draw a straight line perpendicular to a line tangent to the vertex. This is the line of symmetry. All lines parallel to the line of symmetry reflect off the curve and intersect in a common point called the **focus.** Figure 2.11 shows how this is applicable to receiving transmissions. The actual dish is not the receiver, just a reflector. Because it has a parabolic shape, incoming signals are reflected and will intersect at the focus. Placing the actual receiver there allows the signals to be received accurately. (As a side note, parabolic reflectors are used to illustrate the whispering phenomenon at museums. Two parabolic dishes are placed at opposite ends of the room facing each other. A person at the focal point of one speaks softly, and the voice is reflected directly to the other one. A second person listening at its focal point hears the first one's voice.)

Another type of antenna is the horn antenna (Figure 2.13). Transmitting antennas are often this type. (Figure 2.12 shows both horn and parabolic dish antennae.) The horn antenna consists of a cylindrical tube called a **waveguide.** It acts to guide the waves and transmit them directly into a concave reflector. The reflector's shape is designed to reflect the microwaves in a narrow beam. The beam travels across an unobstructed region and is eventually received by another antenna. The next time you take a leisurely drive in the countryside, look around and you may see both types of antenna mounted on towers. (But don't look too long; there are other cars on the road!)

Because there must be a direct line of sight between the transmitter and receiver, there is a limit on how far apart they can be. The limit depends on the tower's height, the earth's curvature, and the type of terrain in between. For example, antennae on tall towers separated by flat land can cover long distances, typically 20 to 30 miles, although higher towers or towers constructed on a hilltop can increase the distance. In some cases, antennae are separated by short distances within city limits. However, there will be a problem if someone constructs a building directly in the line of sight.

If transmissions must travel a long distance, several repeater towers may be placed in between (Figure 2.14). One antenna transmits to its neighbor, which in turn transmits to its neighbor. Proceeding this way allows transmissions between sites whose line of sight cuts through the earth.

Satellite Transmission   Primarily, satellite transmission is microwave transmission in which one of the stations is a satellite orbiting the earth (Figure 2.15). It is

Figure 2.13   Horn Antenna

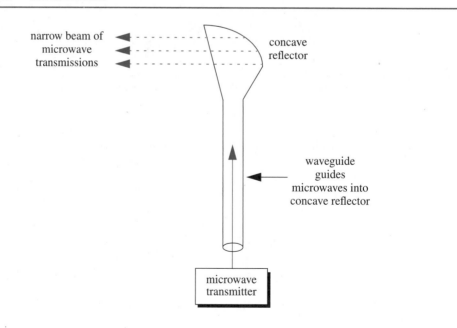

narrow beam of
microwave
transmissions

concave
reflector

waveguide
guides
microwaves into
concave reflector

microwave
transmitter

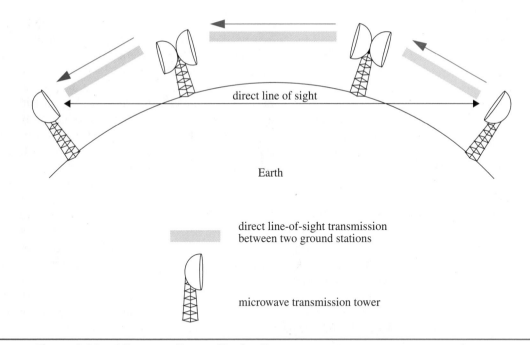

direct line-of-sight transmission between two ground stations

microwave transmission tower

Figure 2.14   Microwave Towers Used as Repeaters

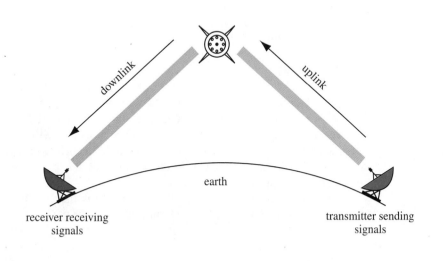

Figure 2.15   Satellite Communications

certainly one of the more common means of communication today. Applications include telephone, television, news services, weather reporting, and military use.

Many of you have probably heard of Arthur C. Clarke. He is best known as a science fiction author whose many novels include the *Space Odyssey* trilogy. Few people know that Clarke is a physicist who, in 1945, wrote about the possibility of using satellites in space for worldwide communication (Ref. [Cl45]). In 1945 this idea was science fiction; today, it is common science. At the time, Clarke did not believe that satellite communications would be economically or technically feasible until the 21st century (Ref. [Hu90]). Instead, it took just 20 years and the invention of the transistor for satellite communications to become a reality.

It began with a historic event on October 4, 1957, an event that shook American society and political leaders. On that day, the then–Soviet Union launched the Sputnik satellite. Sputnik entered a low earth orbit (560 miles high) and sent electronic "beeps" to the ground. As it moved across the sky, the ground station had to rotate its antenna to track it. By today's standards it was not sophisticated, but then it was truly remarkable because it showed that communication between the earth and an object in space was possible.

Because the satellite moved across the sky, communication was possible for only a short time. As it dropped below the horizon, communication ceased until it later appeared above the other horizon. Such a situation is inappropriate for many of today's applications (but not all). Imagine cable TV or a telephone conversation being interrupted every time the satellite dropped below the horizon! (Of course, if it could be synchronized to occur at the start of each commercial, perhaps the concept would have merit.) Realistically, a satellite remaining in a fixed position would allow a continuous transmission, certainly an important criterion for mass media applications. The question is, How can a satellite remain in a fixed position without falling down?

Geosynchronous Satellites   Satellite orbits are predictable using mathematical models based on Kepler's laws of planetary motion. The idea is fairly simple. Given a height, a certain velocity is needed to keep an object in orbit. Higher velocities will send the object out of orbit and into space. Lower velocities will be insufficient to counteract gravitational force and the object will fall. In other words, given a height, the orbital velocity is determined. Kepler's third law relates the time to revolve around a planet to the height of an orbit.

Specifically, suppose the period P of a satellite is the time it takes to rotate around another planetary body. Kepler's third law states that,

$$P^2 = KD^3$$

where D is the distance between the satellite and the planet's center and K is a constant depending on gravitational forces. In other words, higher orbits (larger D) mean a longer period.

A logical question is, At what orbital height will a satellite have a 24-hour period? According to Kepler's law, the answer is 22,300 miles above the equator, considerably higher than the Sputnik traveled. The answer has great significance. Because the earth takes 24 hours to rotate on its axis, an orbiting satellite at that height appears stationary to a ground observer. This is called a **geosynchronous orbit**. If the observer were a transmitter or receiver, the satellite would remain in a position that is fixed relative to the observer, and communications need not be interrupted.

Sputnik and many early satellites were in much lower orbits. Technology simply did not provide rocket engines powerful enough to boost them into higher orbits. Consequently, they rotated around the earth in less than 24 hours, which is why they appear to move across the sky when observed from the surface. Today, powerful rockets boost communications satellites much higher into geosynchronous orbits. Three equally spaced satellites at 22,300 miles above the equator can cover almost the entire earth's surface (Figure 2.16), except some polar regions.

Satellite communication is straightforward. Each satellite has several **transponders,** devices that accept a signal within a specified frequency range and rebroadcast it over a different frequency. A ground based transmitter sends a signal (**uplink**) to a satellite, where one of the transponders relays the signal back down to earth (**downlink**) to a different location (Figure 2.15). Satellite communications are now commonly used to transmit telephone and television signals. Many people have their own receivers for cable television reception. In some locations it is difficult to drive through the countryside and not see a satellite receiving dish in someone's backyard. Of course, this is now old technology, with increasing numbers of people using 18-inch dishes mounted on roofs, back porches, and on top of televisions.

Satellites commonly send and receive over a wide range of frequencies, with each transponder handling signals in a specified range. Typically, the uplink and

Figure 2.16   Satellites in Geosynchronous Orbit above the Equator

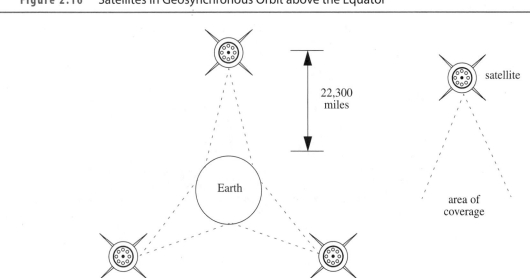

downlink frequencies differ so that they do not interfere with each other. Table 2.2 shows four common bands used in commercial satellite communications and the associated uplink and downlink frequencies. There are also other bands devoted solely to military and government use.

An important fact to remember about satellite transmission is that different signals in the same frequency range must not overlap. Consequently, this limits the number of satellites that can transmit within a particular band and places constraints on how close two satellites can be to each other (more about that later). The C band was the first to be used and is commonly used for broadcast television and VSAT applications (also discussed later). It is becoming saturated in part because of the explosion of worldwide media applications and in part because C band frequencies are also used in ground-based microwave transmissions.

With the world moving toward digital communications, the growth of digital satellite systems, and the migration of the broadcast television industry to high-definition television signals (HDTV), more information must be transmitted. As Section 2.4 will show, higher frequencies will allow more information to be sent per unit of time. Consequently, the Ku band is also used by commercial television carriers. A problem with higher frequencies (especially those approaching the Ka band) is that atmospheric conditions such as rain or moisture cause more interference. The problem becomes worse if the ground station is farther away (measured across the earth's surface) and the signal must travel through more atmosphere (Figure 2.17). This problem can be corrected by boosting the power of a signal or by designing more sophisticated receivers to filter out noise. In fact, the stronger signals sent in the Ku band allow the use of smaller antennae or dishes. Many of you are familiar with the 18-inch dishes you can buy in many electronic stores to pick up digital television signals. But many of us old dinosaurs remember when large satellite dishes mounted in the backyard were required. Ku signals also allow a smaller beam width, enabling transmissions to smaller geographic regions.

As signals move into the Ka range the interference problem becomes severe. As of this writing, the cost of manufacturing equipment to overcome these problems is still too high to see large-scale applications use signals in this range. Still, such applications are being planned for the future, as we will see shortly when we discuss low earth orbit satellites.

At the lower end of the frequency spectrum, the L band is used primarily for mobile satellite communications. This means that communications between cars,

Table 2.2	Satellite Frequency Bands	
BAND	**UPLINK FREQUENCY RANGE (GHZ)**	**DOWNLINK FREQUENCY RANGE (GHZ)**
L	1.6465–1.66	1.545–1.5585
C	5.925–6.425	3.7–4.2
Ku	14.0–14.5	11.7–12.2
Ka	27.5–30.5	17.7–21.7

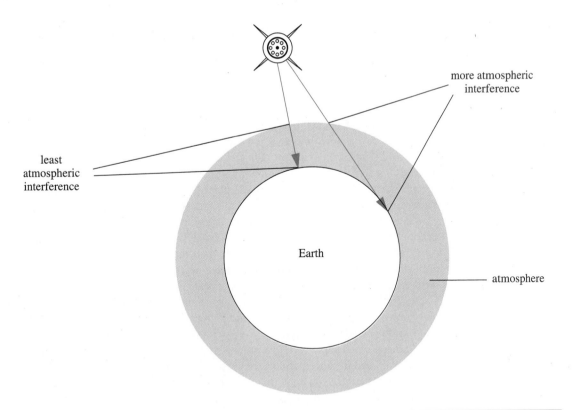

least atmospheric interference

more atmospheric interference

Earth

atmosphere

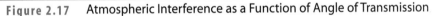

Figure 2.17   Atmospheric Interference as a Function of Angle of Transmission

trucks, boats, or anything mobile are relayed through satellites. The lower frequency allows the use of equipment that is smaller, lower in cost, and requires less power. Such applications can be found in the trucking industry, where dispatchers can locate trucks within a range of just a few hundred feet (on a continental scale). Applications also exist as navigation aids: Planes, boats, and automobiles can use the system to plot their own current locations.

Geosynchronous satellites transmit a signal that can be received anywhere on earth as long as there is a direct line-of-sight path. This type of broadcasting is useful for broadcast television transmission and pay-per-view movie services, in which the receivers are widely dispersed and do not have access to cable signals. Other applications, such as for military uses, must restrict the geographic areas that can receive signals. Special antennae that provide beam shaping allow a signal to be concentrated in a smaller area such as a city. The future will provide spot beam antennae, which will allow transmissions to a single site.

Currently, there are many hundreds of satellites orbiting the planet providing communications for different applications that send and receive signals in the C and Ku bands, so how can a satellite discriminate signals that were not meant for it? For example, suppose ground stations 1 and 2 send to satellites 1 and 2, respectively, using the same frequency (Figure 2.18). The area the signal covers depends on the angle of signal dispersion. If two satellites are too close or the angle of dispersion is too large, both satellites receive both signals. Consequently, neither can tell which signal to ignore.

If the dispersion angles are smaller and satellites are sufficiently far apart, however, no two satellites will receive signals from more than one station (Figure 2.19). The FCC defines U.S. satellite positions. For example, it has defined positions at 2° increments between 67° and 143° west longitude for U.S. communications using the C band. This is closer together than the previous 4° separation allowed. Satellites transmitting signals in the Ku band may be placed at 1° increments. Increased needs require more satellites, which must be placed closer together. As a result, ground stations must have smaller dispersion angles for transmitted signals.

Satellite communications have created problems. For example, how do you prevent unauthorized reception of signals? For that matter, how do you define unauthorized reception of a signal that travels through the public airwaves? Legalities are not often clear-cut. For example, there have been different views on whether it is legal to receive cable television's pay channels such as HBO using satellite dishes. Cable companies claim they lose revenue by such access. Dish owners claim the signals travel through public airspace, and anyone should be able to receive them as they would any television signal.

Perhaps worse, how do you prevent unauthorized transmission via satellite? There have been instances of intruders sending harmless messages via satellite. But what about an intrusion that disrupts communications? Considering how many applications rely on satellite communications, this could be disastrous. In many

Figure 2.18   Satellite Receiving More Than One Signal

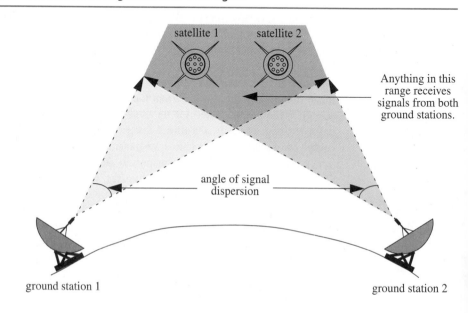

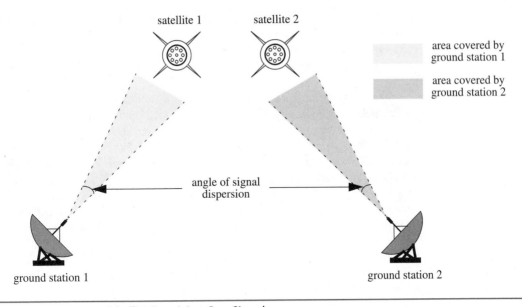

Figure 2.19   Satellite Receiving One Signal

cases, satellite signals are scrambled or encrypted to make the signal unintelligible to unauthorized receivers. One incident, on April 27, 1986, involved a video hacker who called himself "Captain Midnight" interrupting an HBO showing of the movie *Falcon and the Snowman*. He transmitted a signal over a satellite link that overpowered HBO's movie signal. He claimed it was done to protest the scrambling of signals. Chapter 4 deals with encryption and security in more detail.

Not all satellites are for telephones, weather forecasting, and military applications. Many private industries see satellites as an alternative to the telephone system, especially where a need exists for data transmission over a long distance. Using the phone system and going through many switches makes data transfer less reliable, and heavy usage may cause longer response times. The solution may be the **very small aperture terminal (VSAT)** system, developed in the 1980s. A VSAT system commonly connects a central location with many remote ones. For example, the central location may contain a large database to which many regional offices or users need access. Communication between two sites is via a satellite and requires the use of small antenna dishes that can be placed to allow easy access to the central location.

VSAT equipment may connect directly to user equipment such as workstations or controllers. Many applications rely on VSAT systems, especially those that require high data rates for short periods of time. Examples include the National Weather Service, news services, credit card verifications, automatic tellers, car rental agencies, and others (Ref. [Hu90], [Po91], and [Ro93]).

Low Earth Orbit Satellites   Geosynchronous satellites are particularly useful for broadcast-type transmissions. Dishes can be aimed at a fixed point in the sky and can send or receive signals as needed. **Low earth orbit (LEO) satellites** do offer some advantages that geosynchronous satellites do not. Applications such as military surveillance require that a satellite not remain in a fixed position. A lower orbit also allows the satellite to move relative to the earth's surface and scan different areas.

LEO satellites also require less powerful rockets and, with prior arrangement with NASA, can be transported to orbit in the space shuttle. Power requirements are also less because of the reduced distance that signals must travel. However, for global communications applications, LEO satellites have not been heavily used because the satellite is not always within range of earth-based transmitters and receivers. However, that is changing!

In theory, LEO satellites could be used for communications if there were a sufficient number of them in orbit. Figure 2.20 illustrates how. If a sufficient number of satellites were in a low earth orbit they would all move relative to the ground. For example, in Figure 2.20a, a ground station has established communications with satellite *A*. Because satellite *A* is in low earth orbit, it is moving with respect to the ground station. As such, it will eventually fall below the horizon, making direct communication with the ground station impossible until it has revolved around the earth and appears over the opposite horizon. However, rather than waiting for satellite *A*, there is another satellite (*B*) also in low earth orbit. The two satellites are positioned so that when *A* falls below the horizon (Figure 2.20b), *B* rises above the other horizon. It can pick up the communication with the ground station that *A* had to abandon.

Figure 2.20   Ground Station Communicating with LEO Satellites

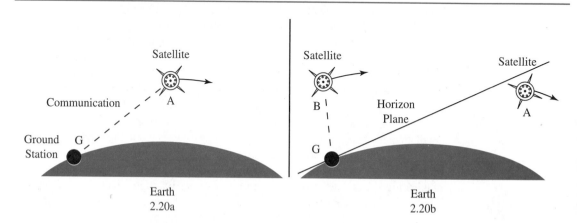

When *B* eventually falls below the horizon there will be yet another to take its place. If there are a sufficient number of LEO satellites, there will always be one capable of communicating with the ground station and all points on the planet, even the most desolate ones, will be within range of a LEO satellite. As a result, any two locations on the planet will be connected as Figure 2.21 shows. One station (site *X* in Figure 2.21) communicates with the nearest available LEO satellite. The orbiting LEO satellites execute a protocol allowing them to exchange information. The protocol will allow *A's* message to be relayed to the LEO satellite nearest to site *Y* and downlinked to the site.

Although as of this writing there is no fully operational global network using LEO satellites plans are underway to create one. In 1987 engineers at Motorola's

Figure 2.21   Two Arbitrary Stations Communicating Using LEO Satellites

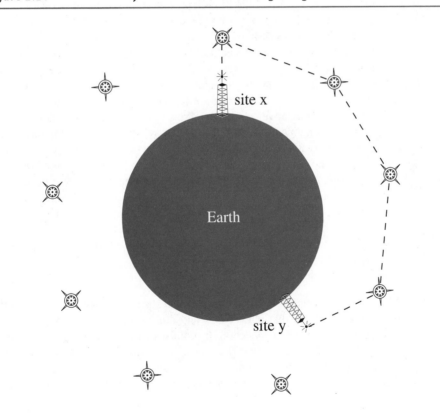

Satellite Division conceived of a global network consisting of 77 LEO satellites. Named **Iridium** after the 77th element in the periodic table, the project has grown into an international consortium of telecommunications and industrial companies. Current plans now call for 66 satellites in low earth orbits at a height of about 420 nautical miles. Communications with ground stations would use the L band, but intersatellite communications would be in the Ka band. Atmospheric conditions that pose an interference problem for satellite-to-ground communications become less of a problem above the atmosphere.

Another player is the Teledesic Corporation. Founded in 1990, its current principal shareholders are Craig McCaw, communications pioneer, and William Gates, Chairman and CEO of Microsoft. The Teledesic network plans to use 840 interlinked LEO satellites to provide global access to a broad range of voice, data and video communications. In fact, the February 27, 1998 issue of *USA Today* reported the launch of the first test satellite into orbit. The intent is to provide a network for the delivery of services by others as opposed to marketing services directly to the user. It is designed to provide broadband connections as opposed to the narrowband mobile voice service of the Iridium project. In this sense, there is a significant difference from the Iridium project. In fact, about the only thing the two have in common is the use of LEO satellites.

The large number of satellites will allow each one to service a relatively small cell about 53 kilometers across. This size allows a fairly refined division of the earth's surface and can be configured to account for countries' international boundaries. Although the satellites move relative to the earth, each one will remain in a fixed position relative to other satellites in its orbital plane. Plans call for the satellites to communicate using a fast packet-switching technology based on the Asynchronous Transfer Mode (ATM) protocol.[*]

Yet another system is the Celestri system which is designed to network both LEO and geosynchronous satellites and provide access to a broadband network infrastructure. Projected uses include the provision of video and data services to both communication carriers and international corporations. The system would also connect to land-based devices to provide an interface to the Internet and corporate and entertainment networks. Also projected are real-time Internet access and HDTV broadcast for residential use.

Wireless LANs   One of the more interesting recent developments is the **wireless LAN,** a system that allows PCs and other typical LAN devices to communicate without a physical connection. It promises many uses where cabling is impractical or for people who rarely stay in one spot. For example, medical personnel could use notebook computers connected to a wireless LAN as they visit patients in their rooms (Ref. [Sa93]). Executives might use a wireless LAN to access information

---

[*]We will discuss ATM in Chapter 8. Other references providing treatment of the ATM protocol are [Bl95] and [Bl97].

during important meetings. They can also be used in laboratories where excessive cables are a hindrance to those who need to move around frequently. PCs might access data stored on a server or print to a "connected" printer using the wireless connection. The wireless connection also allows equipment to be moved easily without worrying about disconnecting and reconnecting wires.

There are other applications for wireless LANs. Reference [Di92] describes a couple of them. One of interest is a wireless LAN installed at Edwards Air Force Base. This system uses a combination of optical fiber and microwave transmissions to connect test facilities and laboratories over 30 miles of desert. Their need to test-fire rockets required equipment that had to be isolated. Connecting devices using optical fiber over the rough desert terrain would have been an expensive venture, and the alternative use of microwave links has proved to be very reliable.

A drawback of wireless LANs is that they don't have the data rate capacities of their wired counterparts. Currently emerging standards are proposing 1 Mbit and 2 Mbit rates, depending on how the signals are sent. Consequently, although a wireless LAN might prove useful for a physician calling up a patient's record with a notebook computer, the available data rates won't provide timely access to X-rays and CAT scan results. The reason is that images require many more bits for accurate representation. Reference [Ne95a] examines some of the equipment used for wireless LANs and provides a summary.

A Working Group for wireless local area networks is developing the IEEE 802.11 standard. The current draft specifies a layer 2 protocol and three separate layer 1 specifications. The layer 2 protocol has some similarities with those found in an Ethernet, which we discuss in Chapter 6. It will also provide for authentication and privacy. There are actually three layer 1 specifications. Two involve communication using spread spectrum radio waves, and the other uses infrared light waves. Spread spectrum radio involves sending a radio signal over a broad frequency spectrum. It results in a secure transmission because only devices that know how the signal was constructed can receive and decode it. Infrared light transmission uses light waves in the infrared range. Its major disadvantage is that it requires a direct line-of-sight transmission because light cannot penetrate nontransparent solid objects. In other words, walls get in the way with infrared transmission but not with radio transmission. References [Da95] and [Ne95b] provide many more details about wireless LANs. The website http://stdsbbs.ieee.org/groups/802/11/ contains information on the current status of the emerging IEEE 802.11 standard.

SUMMARY

This section has described many different transmission media. You might ask, Which one is best? The answer is not easy. In data communications, newer technologies do not necessarily make older ones obsolete. Indeed, development of fiber optics and satellite communications has not obviated the need for twisted pair or coaxial cable. Each medium has a place in the communications world. Table 2.3 compares the media discussed here.

Table 2.3 Comparison of Transmission Media

	TWISTED PAIR	COAXIAL CABLE	OPTICAL FIBER	MICROWAVE	SATELLITE
Data rate	Varies depending on wire length and thickness. A Fast Ethernet local area network runs at 100 Mbps.	Up to 800 Mbps has been achieved for 1 to 2 kilometers.	Bit rates in the 2 Gbps to 3 Gbps range are becoming common. Rates as high as 28 Gbps have been reported.	Depends on the signal's frequency. Rates can vary between approximately 10 Mbps to 300 Mbps.	Like microwaves, it depends on the frequency (10–300 Mbps).[*] As the Ka band becomes more commonly used, expect the rates to increase.
Susceptibility to interference	Electrical interference from nearby wires or motors.	Shielding eliminates much of the electrical interference.	Immune to electrical interference.	Solid objects cause interference. Needs direct line of sight between both ends.	Interference caused by atmospheric conditions. Becomes worse at higher frequencies.
Distance	Depends on thickness and data rate. Can travel up to 5–6 miles without repeaters.	Also depends on data rates. Can travel up to 5–6 miles without repeaters.	Up to 60 miles.	20–30 miles, but depends on height of antenna and terrain between both ends.	Worldwide.
Typical uses	Useful where space is limited or where high data rates are not needed such as behind a wall leading to a terminal.	Often used as the primary communication medium in a computer network.	Commonly used in long-distance phone lines. Also popular as the primary communication medium in a computer network.	Typically used where laying a cable in not practical, e.g.; telephone service in sparsely populated areas or data communication between two sites in a metropolitan area. Some potential in LAN connection.	Worldwide communication. Applications include phone, military, weather and television.

Table 2.3   *(continued)*

	TWISTED PAIR	COAXIAL CABLE	OPTICAL FIBER	MICROWAVE	SATELLITE
Comments	Can be shielded to allow higher data rates at longer distances.	New devices can be attached easily. Also easy to splice.	Difficult to splice. Adding new devices is difficult.	New construction between the two sites will cause problems.	Difficult to prevent unauthorized reception. Also a delay caused by long distances traveled.

Note: 1 Kbps = 2^{10} bits per second $\approx$ 1000 bits per second

1 Mbps= 2^{20} bits per second $\approx$ 1 million bits per second

1 Gbps= 2^{30} bits per second $\approx$ 1 billion bits per second

*This is for each transponder. Since a satellite can contain up to two dozen transponders, the aggregate data rate for one satellite is the sum of data rates for each transponder.

2.2   COMMUNICATION SERVICES AND DEVICES

TELEPHONE SYSTEM

Of all the inventions in the past century, the telephone certainly has had one of the most profound effects on our lives. The ability to call almost anywhere in the world by specifying (dialing) a few numbers is absolutely incredible. But the telephone is more than just voice communications among friends and relatives; it is becoming indispensable to businesses using it for computer communications. The ability to transfer information across a computer network or by fax is now commonplace.

The telephone works by converting sound into electrical energy (Figure 2.22). What we perceive as sound is caused by small fluctuations in air pressure (sound waves). The waves travel through the air, causing some objects to vibrate. The same principle causes old windows or light fixtures to rattle during a thunderstorm. It also allows us to hear: The waves cause the eardrum to vibrate and send signals to the brain.

The telephone mouthpiece consists of a chamber filled with carbon granules (Figure 2.22). Two electrical contacts are connected to the chamber. As you speak into the mouthpiece, the sound waves cause a diaphragm covering the chamber to vibrate. As it vibrates it exerts varying pressure on the carbon granules. Higher pressure causes them to be compacted more closely, which in turn, causes them to be a better conductor of electricity. Less pressure has the opposite effect. The net result is that varying amounts of electricity caused by the sound are conducted. On the receiving end, the electricity activates a voice coil, causing an attached speaker to vibrate. The vibrating speaker causes changes in air pressure, which we interpret as sound.

To place a phone call, the caller enters a sequence of digits by dialing or touching buttons. Each digit sends a code to a local exchange office, which interprets

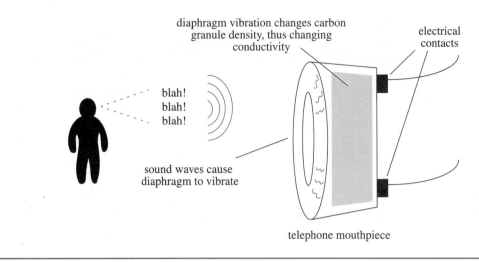

telephone mouthpiece

Figure 2.22   Converting Sound Waves to Electric Signals

the sequence and determines the destination. If there is an available route to the destination and the phone is not busy, two signals are sent. The first goes to the destination and causes the phone to ring. The second goes to the source and alerts the caller that the phone is now ringing.

Because the signals are separate, it is interesting to note that a caller does not actually hear the phone ringing. In fact, because of delays in the circuits you might not hear the ring until after it occurs. Perhaps you have had the experience of having someone answer your call before you heard a ring. Common perception is that it is caused by gremlins in the line or the mystical ability of the phone system. Now you know that it happens only because someone answered the phone before the second signal got back to you.

The code for each digit depends on whether you have tone or pulse dialing. With tone dialing, each digit sends a tone consisting of a unique pair of frequencies. With pulse dialing, each digit generates from 1 to 10 pulses. Each pulse actually corresponds to opening and closing a circuit, similar to depressing the hook. In fact, if your fingers are fast enough, you can actually dial a number by rapidly depressing the hook the proper number of times for each digit.

Call Routing   The way in which phone calls are routed is an amazing feat of engineering. Remember, we are discussing a network connecting many millions of users. The first part of this network is the local loop. It consists of phones connected by copper wires running along the familiar telephone pole or in underground cables to a local exchange.* The local exchange contains switching logic and determines where to route a call. If the call is to a phone with the same exchange (first three digits of

---

*Other terms used in place of *local exchange* include the end office, central office, or class 5 office.

the number), the connection can be made directly to the destination. Otherwise the routing strategy depends on the call's destination.

Figure 2.23 shows the major components (centers) of the telephone office. The class 1 regional centers are the fewest in number and cover the largest areas (typically multistate regions). Classes 2, 3, 4, and 5 are increasingly more numerous and cover smaller areas. Those covering the largest areas are owned by long-distance carriers, and others are owned by local companies. Table 2.4 summarizes this information. We will provide a brief discussion of the roles these centers play in the complex system

Figure 2.23 Telephone Network

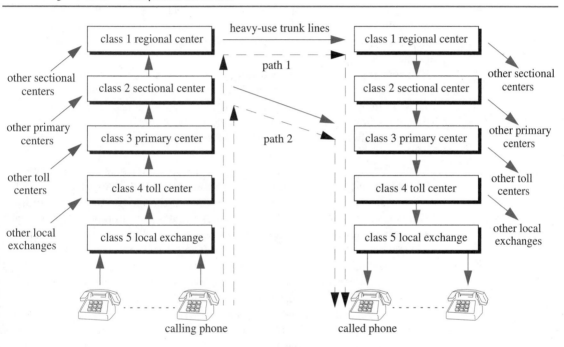

Table 2.4 Major Centers in Telephone Network

CENTER	OWNER	AREA COVERED
Class 1 regional center	Long-distance carrier	Multistate
Class 2 sectional center	Long-distance carrier	Statewide
Class 3 primary center	Local company or long-distance carrier	Metropolitan
Class 4 toll center	Local company	One or more cities
Class 5 local exchange	Local company	Neighborhood

of routing phone calls. For more detailed information, consult References [B189], [Ch84], [Pi81], [Wa85], and [Sh90].

Class 1 centers connect to many class 2 centers. Similarly, class 2 centers connect to many class 3 centers, and so on. At the top of the hierarchy, class 1 centers are connected by high-capacity trunk lines, which are capable of transmitting many phone conversations simultaneously. In general, any two phones can connect by going up the hierarchy from the local exchange to the regional center, across a trunk to another regional center, and back down to the proper local exchange (path 1 in Figure 2.23). This is not always the best route, however. Ideally, we would like a call to go through as few centers as possible. The extreme would be to have a direct connection between every pair of phones on this network but, of course, this is unrealistic. In some cases, there may be many phone calls between one sectional center and another primary center. In such cases, it is useful to place another high-capacity trunk line between them as a shortcut to bypass some of the centers and provide alternate routes (path 2 in Figure 2.23).

There are many trunk lines connecting different classes of centers. These connections, driven largely by the traffic between two areas, provide many alternate routes. In the unlikely event that all routes are operating at peak capacity, the call will not go through and the caller will receive a busy signal. However, current state-of-the-art hardware and software make this event highly unlikely.

Private Branch Exchange   In addition to the public telephone system there are also private telephone systems, called **private branch exchanges (PBX)**. Other common names are **private automatic branch exchange (PABX)** and **computer branch exchange (CBX)**. A PBX is a computer designed to route telephone calls within a company or organization. This system is especially useful for larger organizations whose many employees must be able to contact one another. A PBX gives the organization complete control over its voice and data communications facilities rather than relying on the telephone company for support. As you might expect, there are advantages and disadvantages. The organization must pay for the hardware, software, and personnel to maintain the system. On the other hand, if the company is large enough and its needs great enough, this may be a cost-effective way of establishing communications.

But a PBX is more than just a telephone system. When a PBX is installed, wires connect every office, conference room, or any location where a telephone may be used. Consequently, designers often elect to install additional wire pairs, cable, or optical fibers. The intent is to make them available for data traffic between computers or peripherals. In many cases, the additional wiring is installed even though there is no immediate need for data traffic. The extra cost of installing some redundant wiring is far below the cost for another installation in the future.

The PBX performs many of the same functions as a local area network, but there are important differences between them. For example, a local area network typically has a broadcast ability. This means one device can send a message to all or a group of devices connected to the network. A PBX typically is used for point-to-point communication. On the other hand, a PBX can define a circuit between communicating devices, something not typical of a LAN. This feature is an advantage if you need to exchange large amounts of data quickly between two devices. A detailed discussion of a PBX and its comparison with a LAN is beyond the purpose or scope of this book. If you are interested, References [Ro91], [Bl89], and [Sh90] contain such detailed discussions. Reference [Mu91] surveys some of the uses people are finding for PBXs.

INTEGRATED SERVICES DIGITAL NETWORK

The telephone system is still very much dependent on analog signals for communications, at least at the user's end. Digital technology has provided significant advances in the telephone system with fiber optics and digital switches, but one part of the telephone network is still very much analog: the last mile, or the pair of wires that runs from the local exchange to the user's premises. Because the telephone was (and still is) used mainly for voice communications, this setup made sense, but it is rapidly changing. Every year digital communications make up a larger portion of the telephone system traffic.

An alternative is to integrate both voice and data into a completely digital worldwide communications system. One such system is called the **Integrated Services Digital Network (ISDN)**. It is being used in many locations, but many others have been slow to adopt this particular standard. Instead of just a telephone, you would also have a video screen. If fully implemented, it would provide a whole new range of services. For example, because the signals are digital, incoming signals that cause the phone to ring could contain the name and phone number of the caller. This would be an advantage to doctors, brokers, or anyone who deals with clients. They could see the information displayed on a screen and even access the client's file from a database before answering the phone. It would also benefit the 911 emergency service by displaying the name of a caller who might be unable to speak.[*] Furthermore, it would certainly discourage obscene or nuisance phone calls. It is analogous to saying, "Hello my name is——and I am going to make an obscene call." On the negative side, additional measures would have to be taken to provide privacy for those with unlisted phone numbers.

With ISDN, the telephone book would become obsolete. Instead, the information in it would be stored in a database accessible through your telephone. Looking up telephone numbers becomes a database search similar to those done at a library or at a bank. Furthermore, any changes in a phone number would be available immediately.

The technology for such a system exists, so why don't we have it? One answer, in a single word, is cost. Many millions of private and business telephones would be affected. In addition, long-distance carriers and local services each have their own ISDN interface definitions. Getting everyone together will take time and effort (and money), and justifying the cost is difficult. For those with computers or terminals at

---

[*]911 emergency services already have the ability to trace an incoming call, but ISDN would probably make the system easier and cheaper to use.

home with data transfer needs, a strong case can be made. But what about Aunt Martha or Uncle Morris, who primarily use the telephone to reach out and call friends and family? What will a digital system mean to them, especially if they have never used a computer?

Another problem is that some see ISDN as a system that became obsolete before it was fully implemented, citing ISDN's relatively slow 64 Kbps bit rate. In addition, protocols such as broadband ISDN (B-ISDN) and Asynchronous Transfer Mode (ATM) have proved to be important new technologies and have provided competition to ISDN. The details of all these systems are important to the field of data communications, but we need to cover some ground before we can describe them. Thus, we defer these topics to Chapter 8.

CELLULAR PHONES

No doubt many of you have seen another technological development embraced by many, the **cellular telephone** (Figure 2.24). It is also known as a **car telephone** or **cellular radio.** Primarily, it allows its user to communicate over the telephone system when he or she is away from traditional phones, such as in a car. The term *cellular* pertains to the way a geographic area is divided to allow communications. It

Figure 2.24 Cellular Telephone (Courtesy of AT&T Archives)

is divided into multiple regions, or cells (Figure 2.25), each of which has a reception and transmission station. A network switching office (NSO) has a computer that controls all the cells and connects them to the telephone system.

The cellular phone is actually a two-way radio capable of communicating with a cell station. The boundaries between cells are not as well defined as Figure 2.25 indicates. Near the cell boundaries the cellular phone is potentially within range of several stations. Each of the stations continuously transmits, so a phone can determine which is closest by determining which signal is strongest. When a call is made from a cellular phone, the phone communicates with the closest station (Figure 2.26). The station in turn communicates with the NSO, which is capable of interfacing with the regular telephone system.

Receiving a call is a little more complex, as there is no way of knowing in which cell the cellular phone is located. However, each cellular phone, just like any phone, has a unique identification number. When it is called, the NSO transmits it to all the cell stations under its control. Each station then broadcasts the number. Because the cellular phone is continuously monitoring broadcasts, it hears its ID broadcast and responds. The station, hearing the response, relays the response to the NSO, which completes the connection.

A potential problem exists when a user moves into an adjacent cell. The station with which his or her phone is communicating eventually will be out of range. The NSO monitors signals received from cell stations, and if it detects that a

Figure 2.25   Cellular Grid

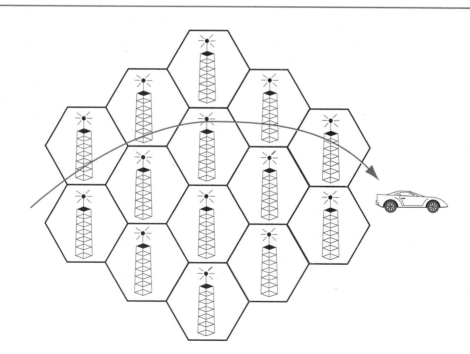

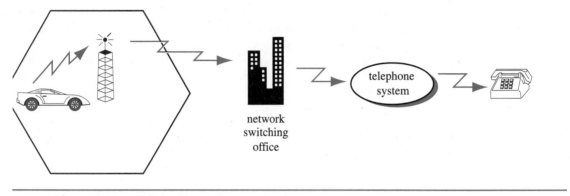

network
switching
office

Figure 2.26   Cellular Phone Communication

signal is becoming weak, it can reassign communication to another cell. The assignment occurs quickly so there is no noticeable interruption for voice communications. If the phone is being used for data transmission, however, there may be some loss.

Using the cell phone for data communications conjures up an image of someone racing down the highway in the driver's seat with a PC or fax machine in his or her lap. Certainly if you do this or know someone who does, please let me know so I can stay off the road. But some data transfer on the highway is not as bizarre as it sounds initially. For example, an ambulance has a legitimate need for data transfer when it sends an accident victim's vital signs to the hospital.

FAX MACHINES

Another device that became popular during the late 1980s is the **facsimile machine (fax)** (Figure 2.27). Capable of transmitting drawings, letters, or diagrams over the phone in a matter of seconds, it has become an indispensable device for many.

Fax machines are based on a principle similar to that used for displaying an image on a PC's video screen, on a television set, or in a photograph. The images that appear to be lines and colors are nothing more than dots, but they are too small to be seen individually unless you put your nose against the screen and look closely.

A fax machine works by taking a picture of the image to be sent and converting it to a binary format. You enter a sheet of paper into the fax much as you would a copier. The sheet is divided into many dots, each representing a portion of the paper. We call this a **bit map representation**, as each dot may be stored as one bit of data. Each dot is black or white (binary 0 or 1), depending on what is on that part of the paper. The dots then are transmitted as binary data and reassembled at the other end. For example, Figure 2.28 shows how the letters in the word "Hello" may be represented using a bit map. For simplicity, we have shown only a few large dots; a typical bit map may use 200 dots per inch. More dots provide better-quality transmissions. Fewer dots give a grainy look to the received image.

Figure 2.27   Fax Machine (Courtesy of AT&T Archives)

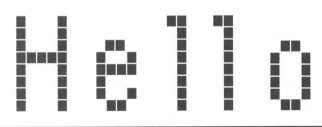

Figure 2.28   Bit Map Representation of "Hello"

Most fax machines do not simply take a picture and transmit the resulting dots. Proceeding that way would require long transmission times for simple documents. For example, suppose a fax recognizes 200 dots per inch. A little arithmetic shows that there are 200 × 200, or 40,000, dots for one square inch. But a typical sheet of paper measures 8 1/2 by 11 inches, or 93.5 square inches. At 40,000 dots per square inch, a typical sheet requires 40,000 × 93.5, or 3,740,000, dots. Using a typical transmission rate of 28.8 K bits per second, we need 3,740,000/28.8 K, or more than 2 minutes, to send the image on one sheet of paper.

Your first reaction might be, "I have used a fax machine and it didn't take nearly that long." Well, you are correct. Most fax machines will not take that long because they use data compression. Rather than sending each dot individually, the fax groups the dots and defines an equivalent binary representation for the group using fewer bits. For example, suppose a part of the image has 800 black dots in succession. Instead of sending 800 black dots, you might send 1 black dot preceded by the number 800. Because 800 has a binary representation of 1100100000 (10 bits), the transmission requires 11 bits (don't forget 1 bit for the dot). Clearly, this is a significant reduction. There are other ways compressing data; Chapter 3 discusses compression in more detail.

2.3   CODES

The previous section described common transmission media and some of their characteristics. Whether the medium uses light, electricity, or microwaves, we must answer perhaps the most basic of all communications questions: How is information coded in a format suitable for transmission? This and the next two sections answer this question.

Because most data communication is between computers and peripheral devices, we start with the basics of computer storage. Computers are digital devices; they operate by opening and closing tiny electrical switches programmed on a chip. This explanation is an oversimplification, but it is not our intent to discuss computer and CPU architecture. Rather, we take the view that regardless of implementation, all the switches are in one of two states: open or closed. Symbolically, we represent these bits, the smallest units of information a computer can store, by 0 or 1.

By themselves, bits are not particularly useful, as each can store only two distinct pieces of information. Grouping them, however, allows for many combinations of 0s and 1s. For example, grouping two bits allows $2^2 = 4$ unique combinations (00, 01, 10, and 11). A group of three allows $2^3 = 8$ combinations. They are formed by taking each of the four previous combinations and appending either a 0 or a 1. In general, a group of n bits allows 2^n combinations. (Can you prove this?) Grouping bits therefore allows you to associate certain combinations with specific items such as characters or numbers. We call this association a code. There is nothing difficult about a **code.** Anyone can define a code in any way. The trick is getting others to use the same code. If you get enough people to use it, you can ask IEEE or ITU to make it a standard.

Many codes exist. One of the more annoying problems in communications is to establish communications between devices that recognize different codes. It is as frustrating as trying to converse with someone who does not speak your language. To make life in communications a little easier, some standard codes have been devised. But just to make sure that life doesn't get too easy and manufacturers get too complacent, there are different, incompatible standards! (One of the more profound statements in the field of communications is, "The only problem with standards is that there are so many of them.")

The code you use depends on the type of data you are storing. Codes used for representing integers and real numbers vary widely and depend on the computer architecture. Typical codes can be found in almost any book on computer organization (such as Ref. [St96]). We will focus strictly on character codes.

ASCII CODE

The most widely accepted code is the **American Standard Code for Information Interchange (ASCII)**. It is a seven-bit code that assigns a unique combination to every keyboard character and to some special functions. It is used on most, if not all, PCs and many other computers. Each code corresponds to a printable or unprintable character. Printable characters include letters, digits, and special punctuation such as commas, brackets, and question marks. *Unprintable* does not mean those that are banned from newspapers, televisions, or personalized license plates. Rather, it corresponds to codes that indicate a special function such as a line feed, tab, or carriage return.

Table 2.5 shows characters and their ASCII codes written in both a binary and hexadecimal format. For example, the letter *M* has the ASCII code of 1001101. Using hexadecimal notation allows us to group the bits as 100-1101 and write the code as 4D. Please note that the use of D here has no relation to the character *D*. It is simply the hexadecimal notation for the four bits 1101.

Table 2.5   ASCII Codes

BINARY	HEX	CHAR	BINARY	HEX	CHAR	BINARY	HEX	CHAR	BINARY	HEX	CHAR
0000000	00	NUL	0010000	10	DLE	0100000	20	SP	0110000	30	0
0000001	01	SOH	0010001	11	DC1	0100001	21	!	0110001	31	1
0000010	02	STX	0010010	12	DC2	0100010	22	"	0110010	32	2
0000011	03	ETX	0010011	13	DC3	0100011	23	#	0110011	33	3
0000100	04	EOT	0010100	14	DC4	0100100	24	$	0110100	34	4
0000101	05	ENQ	0010101	15	NAK	0100101	25	%	0110101	35	5
0000110	06	ACK	0010110	16	SYN	0100110	26	&	0110110	36	6
0000111	07	BEL	0010111	17	ETB	0100111	27	'	0110111	37	7
0001000	08	BS	0011000	18	CAN	0101000	28	(	0111000	38	8
0001001	09	HT	0011001	19	EM	0101001	29	)	0111001	39	9
0001010	0A	LF	0011010	1A	SUB	0101010	2A	*	0111010	3A	:
0001011	0B	VT	0011011	1B	ESC	0101011	2B	+	0111011	3B	;
0001100	0C	FF	0011100	1C	FS	0101100	2C	,	0111100	3C	<
0001101	0D	CR	0011101	1D	GS	0101101	2D	-	0111101	3D	=
0001110	0E	SO	0011110	1E	RS	0101110	2E	.	0111110	3E	>
0001111	0F	SI	0011111	1F	US	0101111	2F	/	0111111	3F	?

Table 2.5 *(continued)*

BINARY	HEX	CHAR	BINARY	HEX	CHAR	BINARY	HEX	CHAR	BINARY	HEX	CHAR
1000000	40	@	1010000	50	P	1100000	60	'	1110000	70	p
1000001	41	A	1010001	51	Q	1100001	61	a	1110001	71	q
1000010	42	B	1010010	52	R	1100010	62	b	1110010	72	r
1000011	43	C	1010011	53	S	1100011	63	c	1110011	73	s
1000100	44	D	1010100	54	T	1100100	64	d	1110100	74	t
1000101	45	E	1010101	55	U	1100101	65	e	1110101	75	u
1000110	46	F	1010110	56	V	1100110	66	f	1110110	76	v
1000111	47	G	1010111	57	W	1100111	67	g	1110111	77	w
1001000	48	H	1011000	58	X	1101000	68	h	1111000	78	x
1001001	49	I	1011001	59	Y	1101001	69	i	1111001	79	y
1001010	4A	J	1011010	5A	Z	1101010	6A	j	1111010	7A	z
1001011	4B	K	1011011	5B	[	1101011	6B	k	1111011	7B	{
1001100	4C	L	1011100	5C	\	1101100	6C	l	1111100	7C	|
1001101	4D	M	1011101	5D	]	1101101	6D	m	1111101	7D	}
1001110	4E	N	1011110	5E	^	1101110	6E	n	1111110	7E	~
1001111	4F	O	1011111	5F	-	1101111	6F	o	1111111	7F	DEL

To illustrate how a transmission may work, suppose a computer sends the data in Figure 2.29 to a printer that recognizes ASCII codes. Assume the codes are sent leftmost one first. As the printer receives each code, it analyzes it and takes some action. Thus, receiving the codes 4F, 6C, and 64 causes it to print the characters O, l, and d. The next two codes, 0A and 0D, correspond to unprintable characters. Table 2.5 shows them as LF (line feed) and CR (carriage return), respectively. When the printer receives 0A it prints nothing but activates the mechanisms to advance to the next line. The code 0D causes the print mechanism to return to its leftmost position. At this point, subsequent printable characters appear on the new line beginning in the leftmost column (Figure 2.29).

Other control characters besides LF and CR are described in Table 2.6. We will discuss a few of them further in Section 5.2. We also note that some control characters vary depending on equipment and systems. We intend this information to be instructional; anyone wishing to write communications software should consult the appropriate manuals for an exact description of each control character.

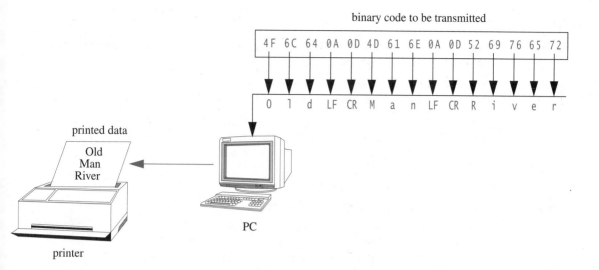

binary code to be transmitted

| 4F | 6C | 64 | 0A | 0D | 4D | 61 | 6E | 0A | 0D | 52 | 69 | 76 | 65 | 72 |

| O | l | d | LF | CR | M | a | n | LF | CR | R | i | v | e | r |

printed data

Old
Man
River

printer

PC

Figure 2.29   Transmitting an ASCII-Coded Message

Table 2.6   ASCII Control Characters

ACK
: Acknowledgment indicates an acknowledgment for a transmission sent previously. Chapter 5 discusses the concept of acknowledgments more thoroughly.

BEL
: Bell causes the receiving device (usually a CRT or terminal) to emit an audible sound usually heard as a "beep." This signal is commonly used to attract the user's attention when special messages are sent or when something significant is about to happen (Figure 2.30).

BS
: Back Space causes the print mechanism or cursor to move backward one position. This "control character" can be used to print two characters in one position (useful for underlining) or to print a character in boldface (print the same character twice in the same position). On a CRT it replaces the first character with the second one.

CAN
: Cancel causes previously submitted data to be canceled.

CR
: Carriage Return causes the print mechanism or cursor to return to the leftmost print position. Note: This character is independent of a line feed.

DC1,
DC2,
DC3,
DC4
: Device Controls correspond to special functions or features dependent on the device. For example, DC1 and DC3 sometimes correspond to X-ON and X-OFF characters generated by the control-Q and control-S keyboard sequences. If a device's buffers are filling up, it can send an X-OFF character to the sender, causing it to stop sending. Sending an X-ON causes transmission to continue.[*]

Table 2.6 (continued)

DLE	Data Link Escape acts as a toggle switch causing the device to interpret subsequently received characters differently.
EM	End of Medium indicates the physical end of a storage medium.
ENQ	Enquire is used to request that a remote station identify itself.
EOT	End of Transmission indicates the end of a transmission.
ESC	Escape causes one or more subsequent characters to be interpreted differently. For example, sending the escape code followed by the codes for the characters [, 2, and J to a VT100 terminal will clear the screen.
ETB	End of Transmission Block indicates the end of a block of data.
ETX	End of Text indicates the end of text transmission. Used in conjunction with STX.
FF	Form Feed is used with special forms or screens. It causes the print mechanism or cursor to advance to the beginning of the next form or screen.
FS, GS, RS, US	Used as separators. The first letter indicates what is being separated (File, Group, Record, or Unit).
HT	Horizontal Tab causes the cursor or print mechanism to advance to the next selected tab stop.
LF	Line Feed advances to the next line.
NAK	Negative Acknowledgment indicates that an expected transmission was not received or was received incorrectly.
NUL	Null is used as a filler (to occupy space where there are no data) in a partially filled record.
SI	Shift In indicates that subsequent character codes correspond to characters in the standard set (e.g., ASCII). Used in conjunction with SO.
SO	Shift Out indicates that subsequent character codes correspond to nonstandard characters. It can be used to go beyond the ASCII character set without defining additional codes. Used in conjunction with SI.
SOH	Start of Heading indicates the beginning of a header containing information about a transmission. It may contain an address, length of message, or data used for error checking.
SP	Space (blank) character. Blanks are not an absence of data but are legitimate characters in their own right.
STX	Start of Text indicates the beginning of text transmission. Used in conjunction with ETX.
SUB	Substitute character is used in place of a character that may have been damaged during transmission.
SYN	Synchronous character is used for synchronizing transmissions.
VT	Vertical Tab causes the cursor or print mechanism to advance to the next preassigned print line.

---

[*]A student's first exposure to X-ON and X-OFF often occurs by accident. For example, suppose you enter a command to a terminal to print a file (such as one containing machine language) containing unprintable characters. The file's contents are incorrectly interpreted as ASCII-coded characters. If one of the codes corresponds to an X-OFF character, the terminal interprets it as a command to stop sending characters. Consequently, anything the user types is not transmitted, which causes the terminal to freeze up.

Figure 2.30   Significant Event Requiring Use of BEL Character

EBCDIC CODE

The second most common code is the **Extended Binary Coded Decimal Interchange Code (EBCDIC),** used primarily on IBM mainframes and peripherals. It is an eight-bit code, thus allowing up to 256 different characters. Like the ASCII code, there are printable and unprintable characters. Table 2.7 shows the EBCDIC codes (both binary and hexadecimal format) and associated characters. In this case, the letter *M* has the EBCDIC code of 11010100. As before, hexadecimal notation allows us to group the bits as 1101-0100 and write the code as D4.

As many of the control characters are similar to the ASCII ones, we will not provide another complete description of them here. If you need to know their specific functions, consult a technical manual for the appropriate device.

BAUDOT, MORSE, AND BCD CODES

The ASCII and EBCDIC codes are the most common in computer communications. You will encounter them most of the time. To be complete, however, we should mention the Baudot, Morse, and binary-coded decimal (BCD) codes.

Table 2.7   EBCDIC Codes

BINARY	HEX	CHAR	BINARY	HEX	CHAR	BINARY	HEX	CHAR	BINARY	HEX	CHAR
00000000	00	NUL	00100000	20	DS	00100000	40	SP	01100000	60	–
00000001	01	SOH	00100001	21	SOS	00100001	41		01100001	61	/
00000010	02	STX	00100010	22	FS	00100010	42		01100010	62	
00000011	03	ETX	00100011	23		00100011	43		01100011	63	
00000100	04	PF	00100100	24	BYP	00100100	44		01100100	64	
00000101	05	HT	00100101	25	LF	00100101	45		01100101	65	
00000110	06	LC	00100110	26	EOB	00100110	46		01100110	66	
00000111	07	DEL	00100111	27	ESC	00100111	47		01100111	67	
00001000	08		00101000	28		00101000	48		01101000	68	
00001001	09		00101001	29		00101001	49		01101001	69	
00001010	0A	SMM	00101010	2A	SM	00101010	4A	¢	01101010	6A	
00001011	0B	VT	00101011	2B		00101011	4B	.	01101011	6B	,
00001100	0C	FF	00101100	2C		00101100	4C	<	01101100	6C	%
00001101	0D	CR	00101101	2D	ENQ	00101101	4D	(	01101101	6D	-
00001110	0E	SO	00101110	2E	ACK	00101110	4E	+	01101110	6E	>
00001111	0F	SI	00101111	2F	BEL	00101111	4F	|	01101111	6F	?
00010000	10	DLE	00110000	30		01010000	50	&	01110000	70	
00010001	11	DC1	00110001	31		01010001	51		01110001	71	
00010010	12	DC2	00110010	32	SYN	01010010	52		01110010	72	
00010011	13	DC3	00110011	33		01010011	53		01110011	73	
00010100	14	RES	00110100	34	PN	01010100	54		01110100	74	
00010101	15	NL	00110101	35	RS	01010101	55		01110101	75	
00010110	16	BS	00110110	36	UC	01010110	56		01110110	76	
00010111	17	IL	00110111	37	EOT	01010111	57		01110111	77	
00011000	18	CAN	00111000	38		01011000	58		01111000	78	
00011001	19	EM	00111001	39		01011001	59		01111001	79	
00011010	1A	CC	00111010	3A		01011010	5A	!	01111010	7A	:
00011011	1B		00111011	3B		01011011	5B	$	01111011	7B	#
00011100	1C	IFS	00111100	3C	DC4	01011100	5C	*	01111100	7C	@
00011101	1D	IGS	00111101	3D	NAK	01011101	5D	)	01111101	7D	'
00011110	1E	IRS	00111110	3E		01011110	5E	;	01111110	7E	=
00011111	1F	IUS	00111111	3F	SUB	01011111	5F	¬	01111111	7F	"
10000000	80		10100000	A0		11000000	C0	{	11100000	E0	
10000001	81	a	10100001	A1		11000001	C1	A	11100001	E1	
10000010	82	b	10100010	A2	s	11000010	C2	B	11100010	E2	S
10000011	83	c	10100011	A3	t	11000011	C3	C	11100011	E3	T

Table 2.7 *(continued)*

BINARY	HEX	CHAR	BINARY	HEX	CHAR	BINARY	HEX	CHAR	BINARY	HEX	CHAR
10000100	84	d	10100100	A4	u	11000100	C4	D	11100100	E4	U
10000101	85	e	10100101	A5	v	11000101	C5	E	11100101	E5	V
10000110	86	f	10100110	A6	w	11000110	C6	F	11100110	E6	W
10000111	87	g	10100111	A7	x	11000111	C7	G	11100111	E7	X
10001000	88	h	10101000	A8	y	11001000	C8	H	11101000	E8	Y
10001001	89	i	10101001	A9	z	11001001	C9	I	11101001	E9	Z
10001010	8A		10101010	AA		11001010	CA		11101010	EA	
10001011	8B		10101011	AB		11001011	CB		11101011	EB	
10001100	8C		10101100	AC		11001100	CC		11101100	EC	
10001101	8D		10101101	AD		11001101	CD		11101101	ED	
10001110	8E		10101110	AE		11001110	CE		11101110	EE	
10001111	8F		10101111	AF		11001111	CF		11101111	EF	
10010000	90		10110000	B0		11010000	D0	}	11110000	F0	0
10010001	91	j	10110001	B1		11010001	D1	J	11110001	F1	1
10010010	92	k	10110010	B2		11010010	D2	K	11110010	F2	2
10010011	93	l	10110011	B3		11010011	D3	L	11110011	F3	3
10010100	94	m	10110100	B4		11010100	D4	M	11110100	F4	4
10010101	95	n	10110101	B5		11010101	D5	N	11110101	F5	5
10010110	96	o	10110110	B6		11010110	D6	O	11110110	F6	6
10010111	97	p	10110111	B7		11010111	D7	P	11110111	F7	7
10011000	98	q	10111000	B8		11011000	8D	Q	11111000	F8	8
10011001	99	r	10111001	B9		11011001	D9	R	11111001	F9	9
10011010	9A		10111010	BA		11011010	DA		11111010	FA	|
10011011	9B		10111011	BB		11011011	DB		11111011	FB	
10011100	9C		10111100	BC		11011100	DC		11111100	FC	
10011101	9D		10111101	BD		11011101	DD		11111101	FD	
10011110	9E		10111110	BE		11011110	DE		11111110	FE	
10011111	9F		10111111	BF		11011111	DF		11111111	FF	

The oldest is the **Morse code**. Developed by Samuel Morse in 1838, it was used in telegraph communications. Table 2.8 shows the code as a sequence of dots and dashes. A unique aspect of this system is that the letter codes have varying lengths; for example, the letter *E* corresponds to a single dot, and the letter *H* has four dots. The varied code length allows messages to be sent quickly. In the original telegraph, an individual sent a message by tapping a switch to open and close the circuit. For example, suppose each letter's code length is 5 (a code length of 4 would allow only

Table 2.8 Baudot, Morse, and BCD Codes

CHARACTER	BAUDOT CODE	MORSE CODE	BCD CODE	CHARACTER	BAUDOT CODE	MORSE CODE	BCD CODE
A	00011	. -	110001	S	00101	. . .	010010
B	11001	- . . .	110010	T	10000	-	010011
C	01110	- . - .	110011	U	00111	. . -	010100
D	01001	- . .	110100	V	11110	. . . -	010101
E	00001	.	110101	W	10011	. - -	010110
F	01101	. . - .	110110	X	11101	- . . -	010111
G	11010	- - .	110111	Y	10101	- . - -	011000
H	10100	. . . .	111000	Z	10001	- - . .	011001
I	00110	. .	111001	0	10110	- - - - -	001010
J	01011	. - - -	100001	1	10111	. - - - -	000001
K	01111	- . -	100010	2	10011	. . - - -	000010
L	10010	. - . .	100011	3	00001	. . . - -	000011
M	11100	- -	100100	4	01010	. . . . -	000100
N	01100	- .	100101	5	10000	. . . . .	000101
O	11000	- - -	100110	6	10101	-	000110
P	10110	. - - .	100111	7	00111	- - . . .	000111
Q	10111	- - . -	101000	8	00110	- - - . .	001000
R	01010	. - .	101001	9	11000	- - - - .	001001

$2^4 = 16$ possible combinations). The time it takes to send a message is proportional to five times the number of letters in the message. If some of the letters required fewer taps, the telegrapher could send the message more quickly. To take the greatest advantage of a varying-length code, the most common letters were assigned short codes. This method helped reduce the average code length.[*] To illustrate, consider sending the alphabet. A code length of 5 for each of 26 characters requires 130 taps to send the message. Using the Morse code, the same transmission requires only 82 taps.

The code developed by Jean-Marie-Emile Baudot was dubbed, not surprisingly, the **Baudot code.** It uses five bits for each character and letter (see Table 2.8). Originally designed for the French telegraph, it is still used today in telegraph and telex communications.

The observant reader might notice that a five-bit code allows $2^5 = 32$ possible combinations, but that there are 36 letters and digits (not to mention other symbols not listed in Table 2.8). If you carefully scrutinize the table you can see some dupli-

---

[*]Some modern codes also have variable lengths, which significantly affects transmission costs. Chapter 3 discusses them in more detail.

cate codes. For example, the digit 1 and the letter Q have the same code. In fact, each digit's code duplicates that of some letter. (Can you find them?)

A logical question is, How can we tell a digit from a letter? The answer is by using the same principle that allows a keyboard key to represent two different characters. On a keyboard, the shift key allows the same key to generate the code for one of two characters. The Baudot code assigns the five-bit codes 11111 (shift down) and 11011 (shift up) to determine how to interpret subsequent five-bit codes. Upon receiving a shift down, the receiving device interprets all subsequent codes as letters. The interpretation continues until a shift up is received. Then all subsequent codes are interpreted as digits and other special symbols. Thus, sending the message "ABC123" requires the following Baudot code (read from left to right):

```
11111      00011   11001   01110   11011     10111   10011   00001
shift down   A       B       C    shift up     1       2       3
```

The last code we discuss is the **binary-coded decimal (BCD)** code, common in many early IBM mainframe computers. One of the reasons for it was to facilitate the entry and subsequent computation of numeric data. For example, if a programmer wanted to enter the number 4385, he or she had to punch the digits 4, 3, 8, and 5 on a punched card. (Remember, we are talking about the dinosaur age of computers.) Each digit then was read by a card reader.

Instead of combining the codes for each digit and creating one representation for the precise numeric equivalent, each digit was stored using the BCD code shown in Table 2.8. This method was considered easy and efficient, especially when there was a lot of data input. The processing unit was then able to do arithmetic between numbers stored in that format. For compatibility reasons, many architectures still support computations between numbers stored in a BCD format. As computer technology evolved and new applications were found, there was a greater need to store non-numeric data. Consequently, the BCD code was expanded to include other characters. Technically, the expanded code is called the **Binary-Coded Decimal Interchange Code (BCDIC)**.

2.4   ANALOG AND DIGITAL SIGNALS

At this point we have covered two primary areas of data transmission: the medium and the symbolic representation of data. Now it is time to combine them. In other words, now that we know how data may be stored symbolically, how does that relate to electrical signals, microwaves, or light waves? The next logical step is to relate physical signals to the symbolic representation of data. More simply put, what does a 0 or a 1 actually look like as it travels through a wire, optical fiber, or space?

The answer depends in part on whether we use analog or digital signals. Remember, an analog signal is a continuously varying signal oscillating between two values. A digital signal has a constant value for a short time and then changes to a different value. Figure 2.1 shows the difference. Concepts of frequency, bandwidth, and periodicity discussed in Section 2.1 apply to both signal types.

DIGITAL ENCODING SCHEMES

There is a natural connection between digital signals and digitally encoded data. Data stored digitally are represented by a sequence of 0s and 1s. Because digital signals can alternate between two constant values, we simply associate 0 with one value and 1 with the other. The actual values used are not important here. With electrical signals, they are sometimes equal but opposite in sign. To keep the discussion general, we will refer to them as "high voltage" and "low voltage."

NRZ Encoding   Perhaps the simplest encoding scheme is the **nonreturn to zero (NRZ).** A 0 is transmitted by raising the voltage level to high and a 1 is transmitted using a low voltage. Thus, any sequence of 0s and 1s is transmitted by alternating appropriately between high and low. The name NRZ refers to the fact that the voltage level stays constant (i.e., does not return to zero) during the time a bit is transmitted. Figure 2.31 shows the NRZ transmission of the binary string 10100110.

NRZ coding is simple, but it has a problem. Look at the transmission in Figure 2.32. What is being transmitted? Your answer should be "A sequence of 0s." Well, that's true, but how many zeros? To this question, you should respond that it depends on the duration of one bit. Now suppose we tell you that graphically, the duration corresponds to a line one millimeter long. All you have to do is measure the length of the line and convert to millimeters. This calculation will tell you the number of one-millimeter segments there are and, consequently, the number of 0 bits. In theory this method works, but in practice it may not. Suppose one person used a ruler and constructed 1000 one-millimeter line segments end to end. How long is the resulting line? The answer should be one meter, but imprecisions in taking measurements and actually drawing the lines will probably result in a line close to but not exactly one meter long. Thus, a second person measuring the line will conclude there are slightly more or less than 1000 segments. Even if the first person were lucky and

Figure 2.31   NRZ Encoding

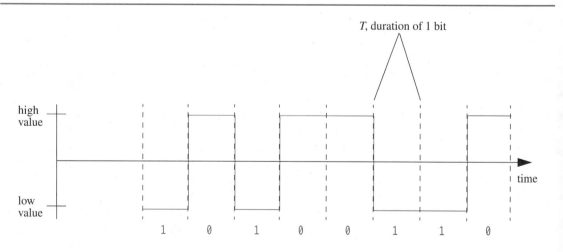

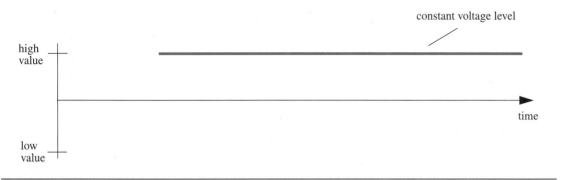

Figure 2.32   NRZ Encoding of a Sequence of 0s

measured accurately, imprecisions in the second person's measurements will cause a discrepancy.

What does this have to do with data transmissions? When a device transmits a digital signal for one bit, it generates a constant signal for a certain duration, say T. An internal clock defines the timing. The receiving device must know the duration of the signal so it can sample the signal every T units. It also has an internal clock defining the timing. So all that is needed is to make sure both clocks use the same T.

Next question: Do all the clocks in your house have the same time down to the last second? Mine don't. Unfortunately, any physical device is subject to design limitations and imperfections. There will almost certainly be very small differences between the clocks that cause one's signal sampling to drift from the other's transmission. It is similar to synchronizing two clocks on New Year's Day, only to find that by the year's end they differ slightly. Similarly, musicians in an orchestra may all start playing at the same time with the same tempo, but unless they watch the conductor and listen to one another, their tempos may begin to drift. It won't take much timing drift to destroy the piece, making it sound as though it were played by the author and his colleagues.

Communicating devices need some mechanism for making sure their timing does not vary, much like the conductor makes sure the musicians stay synchronized. With a constant signal, there is no synchronizing mechanism. However, if the signal changes, the changes can be used to keep the devices synchronized. Some schemes force signal changes for that reason.

Manchester Encoding   The **Manchester code** uses signal changes to keep the sending and receiving devices synchronized. Some call it a **self-synchronizing code**. To avoid the situation of Figure 2.32, it distinguishes between a 0 and 1 by changing the voltage. Specifically, it represents a 0 by a change from high to low and a 1 by a change from low to high. Figure 2.33 shows the Manchester-encoded transmission of the bit string 01011001. As the figure shows, the signal will never be held constant for a time longer than a single bit interval. Even for a sequence of 0s or 1s, the signal will change in the middle of each interval. This change allows the

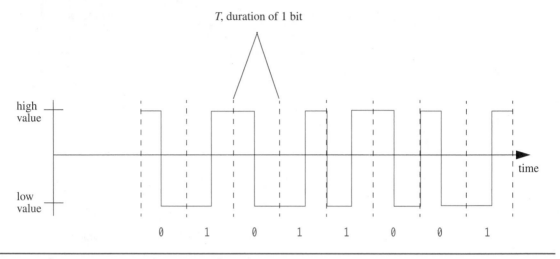

Figure 2.33   Manchester Encoding

receiving device's clock to remain consistent with the sending device's clock. A disadvantage of Manchester encoding is that twice the bandwidth is needed. That is, the signals must change twice as frequently as with NRZ encoding.

A variation of this method is called **differential Manchester encoding.** Like Manchester encoding, there is always a signal change in the middle of each bit interval. The difference is in what happens at the beginning of the interval. A 0 causes the signal to change at the start of the interval. A 1 causes the signal to remain where it was at the end of the previous interval. Thus, a 0 may go from low to high or high to low depending on the initial value of the signal. Figure 2.34 shows the dif-

Figure 2.34   Differential Manchester Encoding

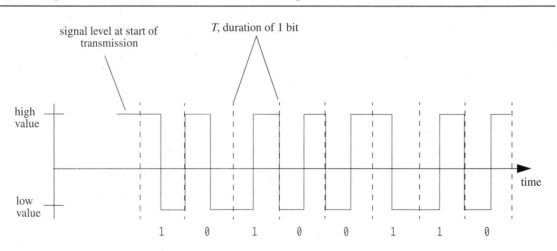

ferential Manchester encoding for the bit string 10100110. In this case, 0s and 1s are distinguished by whether there is a change in the signal at the beginning of the interval. Detecting changes is often more reliable, especially when there is noise in the channel. It is also useful when someone reverses connecting wires, which reverses high and low values. (Now, you might ask who in their right minds would switch the two connecting wires. There are several possible answers. First is someone in a hurry. Second is someone who just made an honest mistake. It happens!) With differential encoding you don't have to mark the wires to indicate which has the high voltage and this, in turn, makes the wire less expensive.

ANALOG SIGNALS

Dealing with analog signals adds complexity to data communications. One problem is that digital computers are incompatible with analog transmission media. Because much of the telephone system is analog, and analog is a major medium for computer communications, the problem must be dealt with. That is, we need a device that converts a digital signal to an analog one (**modulation**) and another that converts an analog signal to digital (**demodulation**). A modem (short for modulation/demodulation) does both. The next two sections discuss the functions and standards of modems. Here we provide an important theoretical foundation for analog signals.

To start, we will define an analog signal more carefully. Earlier we stated that an analog signal is a continuously varying signal between two values, and we used a diagram similar to those in Figure 2.35 to illustrate. This definition is certainly true, but it is far from a complete description. The signal in Figure 2.35a may be represented mathematically by a simple trigonometric function $y = \sin(t)$. In other words, Figure 2.35a is the graph of $y = \sin(t)$. But we can alter sine functions in many ways and thus affect the resulting signal. In general, an analog signal is characterized by its frequency, amplitude, and phase shift.

If the signal varies with time and repeats a pattern continuously, the **period** is the time it takes to complete the pattern once. Such a function is periodic. In Figure 2.35a, the period is 2π. However, by changing the function to $y = \sin(Nt)$, we change the period to $2\pi/N$ (Figure 2.35b). To see this, as t goes from 0 to $2\pi/N$, the sine function's argument (Nt) goes from 0 to 2π. In general, if $N > 1$, the period is smaller than 2π. If $N < 1$, the period is bigger than 2π.

The period is related to the **frequency,** the number of times the signal oscillates per unit of time. Its units of measurement are cycles per second or, equivalently, hertz (Hz). Specifically, if f is the frequency and p is the period, then

$$f = 1/p$$

Thus, the signal of Figure 2.35b has a frequency of $N/2\pi$.

The **amplitude** defines the values between which the signal oscillates. Because $y = \sin(t)$ oscillates between 1 and −1, then $y = A \times \sin(t)$ oscillates between A and $-A$ (Figure 2.35c).

The last way to change a signal is through a **phase shift.** Graphically, this is a horizontal shift in the graph of a sine function. In general, we can achieve a horizontal

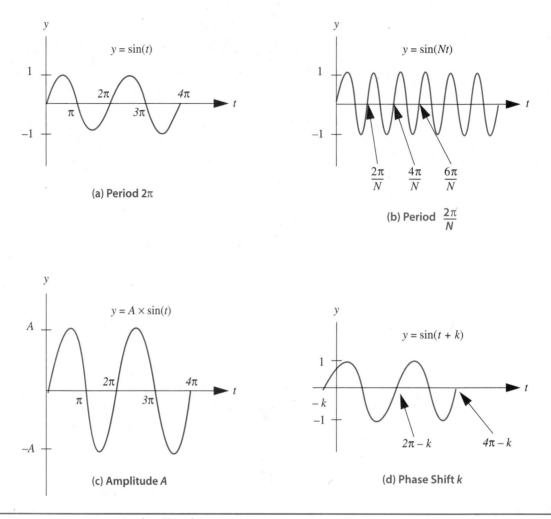

Figure 2.35   Analog Signals

shift by adding or subtracting from the argument. For example, if $k > 0$, the graph of $y = \sin(t + k)$ (Figure 2.35d) is that of Figure 2.35a shifted to the left k units. This change is easily verified by evaluating both functions at different values of t.

Fourier's Result   We now see that an analog signal is more complex than a simple sine wave (graph of a sine function). In general, its amplitude, frequency, and phase shift can all vary with time and thus create complex functions. Perhaps the most familiar example of an analog signal is the one produced by speaking into the telephone (Figure 2.36). As you speak, you vary the sounds you make in order to form words. Your voice also gets louder or softer depending on whether you are having an argument with your boss or speaking to your fiancé. Speaking louder or softer or in a higher or lower pitch creates sound that translates to electrical analog signals. The

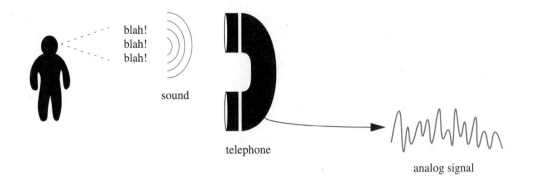

Figure 2.36   Sound Creating an Analog Signal

amplitude reflects the volume and the frequency reflects the pitch. (At this point, there is no simple sound equivalent corresponding to a phase shift.) The result is a complex combination of signals that represents your voice.

The problem now is how to transmit complex signals. There are infinitely many ways of varying the amplitude, frequency, and phase shift. Furthermore, electrical engineering tells us that different signals can experience different amounts of distortion. How do engineers design hardware to do the job? Do they design different hardware and transmission media for different signal types? Do the functions that represent different analog signals require separate analysis?

The answer to the last two questions is no. A famous mathematician, Jean Baptiste Fourier, developed a theory stating that any periodic function can be expressed as an infinite sum of sine functions of varying amplitude, frequency, and phase shift. The sum is called a **Fourier series**. Its importance is that no matter how complex periodic functions are, they all consist of the same components.

In more mathematical terms, suppose $s(t)$ is a periodic function with period P. One form for Fourier's results states that

$$s(t) = \frac{a_0}{2} + \sum_{i=1}^{\infty} \left[a_i \times \cos\left(\frac{2\pi it}{P}\right) + b_i \times \sin\left(\frac{2\pi it}{P}\right) \right]$$

(There are other forms, but this suits our needs here.)

The coefficients a_i, $i = 0, 1, 2, \ldots$ and b_i, $i = 1, 2, 3, \ldots$ are determined using

$$a_i = \frac{2}{P} \int_{-P/2}^{P/2} s(t) \times \cos\left(\frac{2\pi it}{P}\right) dt \quad \text{for } i = 0, 1, 2, 3, \ldots$$

and

$$b_i = \frac{2}{P} \int_{-P/2}^{P/2} s(t) \times \sin\left(\frac{2\pi it}{P}\right) dt \quad \text{for } i = 0, 1, 2, 3, \ldots$$

We won't derive or provide a rationale for these equations. We simply present them for the purposes of explaining the limitations of different communications media. If you are interested, you can find a more complete description of the Fourier series in References [Bl89], [Ta71], and [Wa91]. What is important to us is that Fourier analysis tells us that every periodic signal is a sum of analog signals with different frequencies and amplitudes. We conclude from this statement that the ability to send and analyze an analog signal depends on the range of frequencies (bandwidth) the medium is capable of handling.

Consider an example. Let $s(t)$ be defined by

$$s(t) = \begin{cases} 1 \text{ for } 0 \le t < \pi; \, 2\pi \le t < 3\pi; \, 4\pi \le t < 5\pi; \text{ etc.} \\ -1 \text{ for } \pi \le t < 2\pi; \, 3\pi \le t < 4\pi; \, 5\pi \le t < 6\pi; \text{ etc.} \end{cases}$$

Figure 2.37a shows its graph. Because it is periodic (with a period of 2π), we can write it as a Fourier series. In this case all constants a_i, for $i \ge 0$, are 0. Constants b_i are defined by

$$b_i = \begin{cases} 0 \ \text{ if } i \text{ is even} \\ \dfrac{4}{\pi i} \text{ if } i \text{ is odd} \end{cases}$$

We have used calculus to determine these values and will not duplicate the calculations here. If you are familiar with integration techniques, you should verify the results. If not, just focus on the bottom line, which is that we can write the periodic function as

$$s(t) = \sum_{i = 1 \text{ and } i \text{ odd}}^{\infty} \frac{4}{\pi i} \sin(it)$$

Calculating an infinite sum is likely to take some time (probably more than you are willing and able to give). The best we can hope to do is to approximate the function using a finite number of terms—but we must accept the tradeoffs. We can get an approximation quickly using few terms. Unfortunately, the approximation is not very accurate. Of course, we can easily improve the approximation by using more terms, which gives us better accuracy but takes more effort. Figures 2.37b through 2.37f show the graph of the approximation using 1, 3, 5, 11, and 21 terms. As the figures show, using just a few terms creates an approximation that barely resembles the original function. However, as we use more terms, the graph becomes flatter over each interval and the jumps between 1 and –1 occur more quickly.

Applications of Fourier's Results   Again you might ask, "So what?" Well, Fourier's results are essential to the study of communications. Transmitting a complex analog signal over a medium with a limited bandwidth is the same as approximating the function using some of the Fourier series terms. We can use this principle

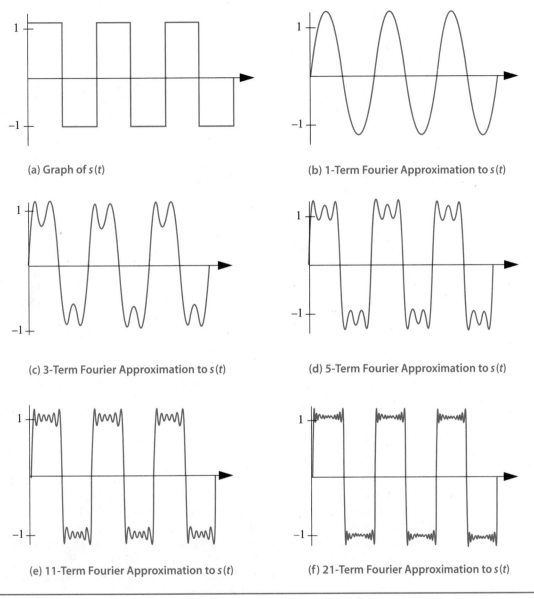

(a) Graph of $s(t)$

(b) 1-Term Fourier Approximation to $s(t)$

(c) 3-Term Fourier Approximation to $s(t)$

(d) 5-Term Fourier Approximation to $s(t)$

(e) 11-Term Fourier Approximation to $s(t)$

(f) 21-Term Fourier Approximation to $s(t)$

Figure 2.37 Fourier Approximations

to explain why, for example, listening to someone's CD player over a telephone is different from listening to it in person.

High-fidelity equipment is capable of producing sounds within a bandwidth of several tens of thousands of Hz. (Actual bandwidth, of course, depends on the equipment.) It can produce sounds ranging from about 30 Hz (cycles per second) to

20,000–30,000 Hz. The telephone, on the other hand, can transmit signals between approximately 300 Hz and 3300 Hz. Consequently, the original signal loses its very low and very high frequency components. The audible effect is that low bass and high treble sounds are lost, and the result is a less than clear sound. Fourier's results also explain why a person's voice never sounds exactly the same over the phone as in person. However, in this case, a normal voice does not have the range of sounds that an instrument has; that is, most of the voice frequencies are within the bandwidth of a telephone. Thus, although there is some loss of tonal quality, enough is saved to understand completely what is being said.

Fourier's results are also used in defining hardware. For example, a **filter** will block certain frequencies while allowing others to pass. Filters have a wide range of applications. For example, an equalizer attached to a stereo can be adjusted to bring out certain tones in music. If we want to highlight bass sounds or accentuate higher-pitched sounds such as soprano voices or a flute on the high end of the music scale, we can set the equalizer to vary the frequencies blocked by the filter.

Another example is in cable television. A bewildered consumer may wonder how a television can receive as many as 100 channels. The answer lies in the ability to view a complex signal as many simple ones. Each channel is assigned a certain range of frequencies, and a signal defining the sound and pictures is created using frequencies within that range. The physical cable transmits one signal consisting of the sum of signals from all channels. This process, **multiplexing,** is discussed in more detail in Chapter 3. Selecting a channel on a television simply allows frequencies within a certain range to pass. Television circuits analyze them and produce sounds and pictures.

BIT RATE

Nyquist Theorem and Noiseless Channels   The next step in the discussion of signals is to relate them to bit transfer. Computer networks now use all forms of transmission for this purpose. Furthermore, as the needs and capacities continue to grow, fundamental questions must be asked. For example: Given a particular medium, how many bits can be transferred? The **bit rate** is used to describe a medium's capacity and is measured in bits per second (bps). An important result in communications theory relates the bit rate to the bandwidth. Simply put, a higher-bandwidth medium is capable of a higher bit rate. The relation between them is so strong that many people often use the terms interchangeably.

Before describing the relation, let's make sure we understand the mechanism behind the transfer of bits. Figure 2.38 illustrates the main components. Basically, a transmitter sends a signal representing a bit string. The receiver "listens" to the medium and creates a bit string based on the signal it receives.

Let's take a close look at the signal. First we represent the bit string, by $b_1 b_2 \ldots b_n$. The transmitter alternately analyzes each string and transmits a signal component uniquely determined by the bit values. Once the component is sent, the transmitter gets another bit string and repeats the process. The dif-

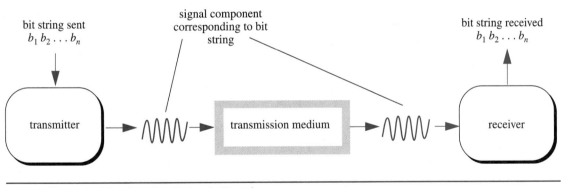

Figure 2.38 Sending Data via Signals

ferent signal components make up the actual transmitted signal. The frequency with which the components change is the **baud rate.**

Precisely how the transmitter determines each component is the topic of the next section and is not important here. If you would like something more concrete for now, just think of a unique signal amplitude for each bit combination. For example, the signal components may have up to 2^n different amplitudes, one for each unique combination of values for $b_1 b_2 \ldots b_n$.

At the receiving end, the process is reversed. The receiver alternately samples the incoming signal and generates a bit string. The bit string, of course, depends on the sample. For this process to work, the receiver must be able to sample with a frequency equal to the baud rate. (If it samples less frequently than components can change, some can go unsampled, and the result is lost data.)

Consequently, the bit rate depends on two things: the frequency with which a component can change (baud rate) and n, the number of bits in the string. Many people often use the terms *baud rate* and *bit rate* interchangeably. Based on our discussion, we now see that this idea is not correct. In fact,

$$\text{bit rate} = \text{baud rate} \times n$$

This would seem to imply that one can always increase the bit rate by increasing either the baud rate or n. This is true, but only up to a point. Some classic results put an upper bound on the data rate.

The first result is surprisingly old, dating back to the 1920s, when Harry Nyquist developed his classic theory. References [Wa91] and [Bl95] provide a more formal treatment. We will not prove it here, but we will state it and explain its importance to data communications. First, Nyquist showed that if F is the maximum frequency the medium can transmit, the receiver can completely reconstruct a signal by sampling it $2f$ times per second. (We interject here that he assumed absolutely no noise or distortion altered the signal. That is, he assumed a perfectly noiseless channel. We discuss noisy channels shortly.) Another way of saying this is that the receiver can reconstruct the signal by sampling it at intervals of $1/(2f)$ second or twice each period (remember, one period = $1/f$). For example, if the maximum frequency is 4000 Hz, the receiver need only sample the signal 8000 times per second. In other words, the signal can be recovered completely by sampling it every 1/8000th of a second.

Now, suppose the transmitter changed the signals at intervals of $1/(2f)$. In other words, the baud rate is $2f$. We then have the results of the **Nyquist theorem,** which states

$$\text{bit rate} = \text{baud rate} \times n = 2f \times n$$

Some books state the Nyquist theorem using the number of different signal components instead of n. In other words, if B is the number of different components, then

$$B = 2^n$$

or, equivalently,

$$n = \log_2 (B)$$

In such cases, we can write

$$\text{bit rate} = 2f \times \log_2 (B)$$

Table 2.9 summarizes some results assuming a maximum frequency of 3300 Hz, the approximate upper limit for the telephone system.

Noisy Channels   So far, this information seems to imply there is no upper bound for the data rate given the maximum frequency. Unfortunately, this is not true for two reasons. First, more signal components mean subtler changes among them. For example, suppose a signal's amplitude must be less than or equal to 5 volts and that each component is determined by amplitude only. If we used two components defined by $2^1/_2$ and 5 volts, the signals differ by $2^1/_2$ volts. However, using 16 signal components requires a difference of about $^1/_3$ volts between adjacent amplitudes. The receiver must be more sophisticated (and more expensive) to be able to detect smaller differences. If the differences become too small, we eventually exceed the ability of a device to detect them.

The second reason occurs because many channels are subject to **noise,** which means a transmitted signal can be distorted. If the distortion is too large the receiver

Table 2.9	Results of Nyquist's Theorem for a Maximum Frequency of 3300 Hz		
	N, NUMBER OF BITS PER SIGNAL COMPONENT	*B*, NUMBER OF SIGNAL COMPONENTS	MAXIMUM BIT RATE
	1	2	6600 bps
	2	4	13200 bps
	3	8	19800 bps
	4	16	26400 bps

cannot reconstruct the signal. For example, consider the digital signal in Figure 2.39a. (We use a digital signal simply because it is easier to illustrate. A similar discussion can certainly be made for analog signals.) The transmitter sends two signals, each of which oscillates between two voltage levels. However, the transmitted signal is subjected to some noise and the received signal differs from it. The distortion is not too great, so the received signal still pretty clearly defines two voltage levels. Thus, it would not be too difficult to reconstruct them.

Figure 2.39b shows a similar situation, except in this case the original two voltage levels differ by less. Now when noise occurs the two distorted signals overlap voltage levels and it is difficult, if not impossible, to reconstruct the original signal from the received one.

Shannon's Result   We have learned that noise can alter and possibly destroy information. Whether the information can be reconstructed depends on how powerful the noise is. For example, a little static electricity is not going to do much to transmissions from a 50,000-watt radio transmitting tower. However, a lightning strike can do amazing things to computer communications. The difference, of course, is the strength of the noise relative to that of the transmitted signal.

Electrical engineers use a parameter called the **signal-to-noise ratio** to quantify how much noise there is in the presence of a signal. We define it as *S/N,* where *S* is the signal power and *N* is the noise power. You may also recognize it as a specification on audio equipment to measure clarity of sound. A large ratio means a clear signal; a small one indicates more distortion. In high-fidelity equipment, high signal-to-noise ratios indicate a higher-quality sound (although in some cases the

Figure 2.39   Effect of Noise on Digital Signal

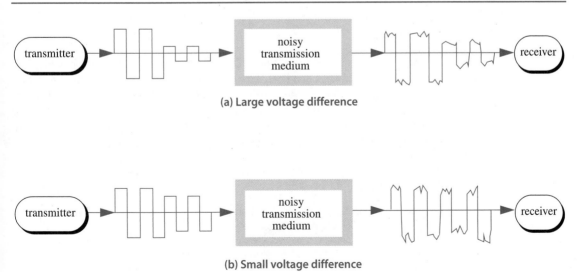

(a) Large voltage difference

(b) Small voltage difference

improved quality may be measurable but not audible). Because S is usually much larger than N, the ratio is often scaled down logarithmically and expressed as

$$B = \log_{10}(S/N) \text{ bels}$$

Here, bel is the unit of measurement. So, for example, if S is 10 times as large as N ($S = 10 \times N$), then $B = \log_{10}[(10 \times N)/N] = \log_{10}(10) = 1$ bel. Similarly, $S = 100N$ yields 2 bels, $S = 1000 \times N$ yields 3 bels, and so on.

Perhaps a more familiar term is the *decibel (dB)*. We define it as $1 \text{dB} = 0.1$ Bel. To better understand what this means in terms of S and N, let's look at another example. Consider a rating of 25 dB. It is equivalent to 2.5 bels and means $B = \log_{10}(S/N) = 2.5$. This equation, in turn, forces S/N to be $10^{2.5}$ or, equivalently, $S = 10^{2.5} \times N = 100\sqrt{10} \times N \approx 316N$.

In the 1940s, Claude Shannon went beyond Nyquist's results and considered noisy channels. He related the maximum data rate not only to the frequency but also to the signal-to-noise ratio. Specifically, he showed that

$$\text{bit rate} = \text{bandwidth} \times \log_2(1 + S/N) \text{bps}$$

The formula states that a higher bandwidth and signal-to-noise ratio allow a higher bit rate. If the noise power increases, however, the allowable bit rate decreases. The idea behind this relation is that if the signal-to-noise ratio is too small, noise can render two different signals indistinguishable.

Again, we illustrate with an example showing the practical upper limit for data transfer over telephone lines. The telephone system has a bandwidth of approximately 3000 Hz and a signal-to-noise ratio of about 35 dB or 3.5 bels. This rating implies that $3.5 = \log_{10}(S/N)$ or $S = 10^{3.5} \times N \approx 3{,}162N$. Using these values in Shannon's result yields

$$\text{bit rate} = \text{bandwidth} \times \log_2(1 + S/N) = 3000 \times \log_2(1 + 3162) \text{ bps}$$
$$\approx 3000 \times 11.63 \text{ bps}$$
$$\approx 34{,}880 \text{ bps}$$

As a final note, we stress that this is not just a theoretical result with little bearing on network users and consumers. In particular, it has a very real implication for modem users. During the 1980s, 2400 bps and 9600 bps modems became common. Higher rate modems were available but rather expensive. The 1990s saw modems accommodate up to 28.8 kbps and 33.6 kbps. However, according to Shannon's result, a bit rate of around 35,000 bps is an upper limit for conventional modems.[*]

---

[*]Yes, we are aware that, as of this writing, modems with 56 kbps rates have been advertised routinely. At first this may seem to violate Shannon's result. However, it does not because Shannon's result applies to two analog modems communicating over a telephone network. The 56 kbps modem can achieve the high rates when used to connect with an Internet service provider. As such, it takes advantage of the fact that there is no analog-to-digital conversion at that end. We discuss such modems further in Section 2.6.

2.5   MODULATION AND DEMODULATION

The previous section described transmission using analog and digital signals. If either analog or digital signals were used exclusively, communications would be simplified and this section would not be needed. In reality, there is a wide mix of analog devices communicating using digital signals and digital devices communicating using analog signals. Furthermore, there are good reasons for not converting everything to either digital or analog.

For example, by now you know that computers are digital devices. In fact, most computer communications such as terminal-to-computer or computer-to-disk transmissions use digital signals. In addition, most local area networks rely entirely on digital signals. So where do analog signals enter the picture? The answer is remote communications. Many people use PCs in their home to communicate with a computer at work. PCs also allow access to bulletin boards, stock quotations, and airline reservation systems. In most cases there is no direct connection such as a local area network. The physical connection uses existing hardware found in the telephone system. However, because the telephone is an analog device, the PC cannot communicate with it directly.

The solution to this problem is a device that converts a PC's digital signals to analog signals: a **modem** (short for modulation/demodulation). It fits between a PC and the telephone (Figure 2.40). The PC sends a digital signal out its modem port, where the modem intercepts it and converts (modulates) it to an analog signal. From there it goes through the telephone system and is treated as any voice signal. The process is reversed at the receiving end or for any signal destined for the PC. The analog signal comes through the phone line and into the modem, and the modem converts it to a digital signal and sends it to the PC via the modem port.

The most common example of analog devices communicating using digital signals is the telephone system. Section 2.2 described how voice sounds are converted to analog signals. In the old days of the telephone system, the analog signals were transmitted over wire or cable to the receiving telephone, where they were converted into sound. Today's fiber technology has changed completely the way a voice is transmitted. Perhaps you have seen television commercials describing how optical fibers carry thousands of telephone conversations. Because optical fibers transmit digital signals, a device called a **codec** (short for coder/decoder) translates the analog voice signal into a digital equivalent (Figure 2.41). The digital signal is then

Figure 2.40   Computer Data Transmitted over Telephone Lines

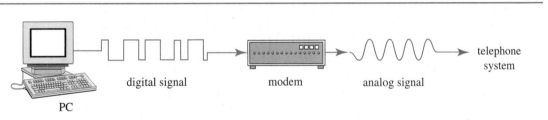

digital signal   modem   analog signal

PC

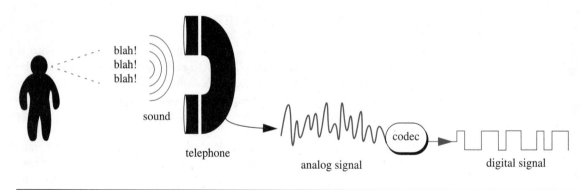

blah!
blah!
blah!

sound

telephone

analog signal

codec

digital signal

Figure 2.41 Voice Information Transmitted Digitally

transmitted. At some point it is converted back to an analog signal so it can be con-verted to sound by the telephone's receiver.

The purpose of this section is to explain how digital signals are converted to analog and vice versa. We will cover digital-to-analog and analog-to-digital conver-sion methods. Section 2.6 will discuss modem operations and modem standards.

DIGITAL-TO-ANALOG CONVERSION

Converting a digital signal to an analog one is not difficult. Basically, all you need to do is assign a group of one or more bit values to a particular analog signal. The pre-vious section described three ways of varying an analog signal: by frequency, ampli-tude, and phase shift.

Frequency Modulation   The first method, **frequency shift keying (FSK)**, also called **frequency modulation (FM)**, assigns a digital 0 to one analog frequency and a 1 to another. For example, if 0 corresponds to a higher frequency and 1 to a lower one, Figure 2.42 shows the analog signal resulting from the bit string 01001. For each bit, the modem transmits a signal of the appropriate frequency for a specified

Figure 2.42 Frequency Shift Keying (Two Frequencies), One Bit per Baud

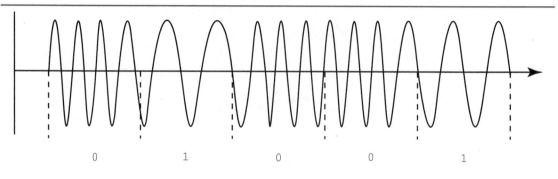

0   1   0   0   1

period of time. The period, and hence the number of cycles, varies. (Section 2.6 gives some specifics for particular modems.)

Using only two frequencies means that each signal change sends one bit of data. This is a case in which the baud rate (how often a signal can change) and bit rate are the same. Alternative forms of frequency modulation could use more frequencies. For example, because two bits can have one of four combinations, we could assign each pair to one of four frequencies. Thus, each frequency change conveys two bits of data; that is, the bit rate is twice the baud rate.

In general, n bits can have one of 2^n combinations, and each can be assigned to one of 2^n frequencies. In this case, the bit rate is n times the baud rate.

Amplitude Modulation   **Amplitude shift keying (ASK),** also called **amplitude modulation (AM),** is similar to frequency shift keying. The difference, as you might suspect, is that each bit group is assigned to an analog signal of a given magnitude. Also, as with FSK, a bit group may have one, two, or more bits, again defining a relation between the bit rate and baud rate.

To illustrate, suppose we designate four magnitudes as A_1, A_2, A_3, and A_4. Using these designations, Table 2.10 shows how two bits are associated with each magnitude. Figure 2.43 shows the analog signal for the bit string 00110110. In this case, the bit rate is twice the baud rate. Each of the two bits (starting from the leftmost ones) defines a signal with the appropriate magnitude. As with frequency shift keying, the signal is transmitted for a fixed period of time.

Phase Modulation   **Phase shift keying (PSK),** also called **phase modulation (PM),** is similar to the previous techniques. The signals differ by phase shift instead of frequency or amplitude. Typically, a signal's phase shift is measured relative to the previous signal. In such cases, the term **differential phase shift keying (DPSK)** is often used. As before, n bits can be assigned a signal having one of 2^n phase shifts, giving a technique in which the bit rate is n times the baud rate.

Quadrature Amplitude Modulation   Any of these simple techniques can be used with any number of different signals. More signals means a greater bit rate with a given baud rate. The problem is that a higher bit rate requires more signals and thus reduces the differences among them. As the previous section discussed, this creates difficulties because we need equipment that can differentiate between signals whose

Table 2.10   Signal Association for Amplitude Modulation

BIT VALUES	AMPLITUDE OF GENERATED SIGNAL
00	A_1
01	A_2
10	A_3
11	A_4

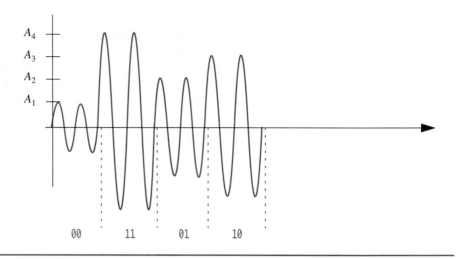

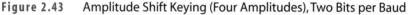

Figure 2.43   Amplitude Shift Keying (Four Amplitudes), Two Bits per Baud

frequencies, magnitudes, or phase shifts differ by just a little. In addition, noise may distort signals so that differences between two signals may be unmeasurable.

One common approach is to use a combination of frequencies, amplitudes, or phase shifts, which allows us to use a larger group of legitimate signals while maintaining larger differences among them. A common technique is **quadrature amplitude modulation (QAM)**, in which a group of bits is assigned a signal defined by its amplitude and phase shift.[*]

For example, suppose we use two different amplitudes and four different phase shifts. Combining them allows us to define eight different signals. Table 2.11 shows the relation between three-bit values and the signal. We define the amplitudes as A_1 and A_2 and the phase shifts as 0, $1/(4f)$, $2/(4f)$, and $3/(4f)$, where f is the frequency. The shifts correspond to 1/4, 2/4, and 3/4 of a period, respectively.

Figure 2.44 shows the changing signal resulting from the transmission of the bit string 001-010-100-011-101-000-011-110. (The hyphens are inserted for readability only and are not part of the transmission.) To understand why the signal looks this way, let's proceed carefully. The first three bits, 001, define a signal with amplitude

---

[*]An electrical engineer may disagree with this definition. Quadrature amplitude modulated signals are created by adding two analog signals with the same frequency. One signal corresponds to a sine function and the other to a cosine. (Sine and cosine functions differ by a 90° angle, hence the term *quadrature*.) This means the signal has the form $C \times \sin(x) + D \times \cos(x)$. Variable x varies with time depending on the signal's frequency, and C and D depend on the initial signal. However, trigonometry shows that $C \times \sin(x) + D \times \cos(x)$ may also be written as $A \times \sin(x + P)$, where $A = \sqrt{C^2 + D^2}$ and $P = \text{Arcsin}(C/\sqrt{C^2 + D^2})$. Thus, for our purposes, we can think of the signal as one with a varying amplitude and phase shift.

Table 2.11   Signal Association for Quadrature Amplitude Modulation

BIT VALUES	AMPLITUDE OF GENERATED SIGNAL	PHASE SHIFT OF GENERATED SIGNAL
000	A_1	0
001	A_2	0
010	A_1	$1/(4f)$
011	A_2	$1/(4f)$
100	A_1	$2/(4f)$
101	A_2	$2/(4f)$
110	A_1	$3/(4f)$
111	A_2	$3/(4f)$

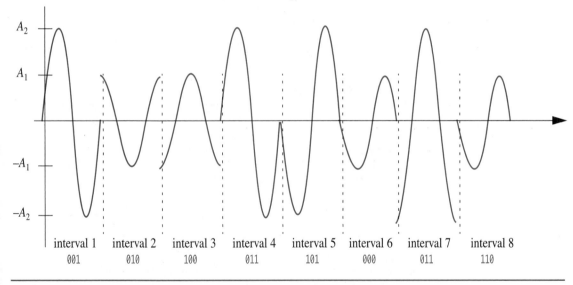

Figure 2.44   Quadrature Amplitude Modulation (Two Amplitudes and Four phases), Three bits per Baud

A_2 and phase shift 0. Consequently, as discussed in the previous section, the signal starts at 0 volts and oscillates between A_2 and $-A_2$. As before, the number of cycles depends on the frequency and the length of time the signal is transmitted. We have drawn one cycle for convenience.

The next three bits, 010, define a signal with amplitude A_1 and phase shift $1/(4f)$. Thus, as Figure 2.44 shows, the signal oscillates between A_1 and $-A_1$. Now, with no phase shift the signal would start at 0 and increase to A_1. However, as the previous section discussed, a positive phase shift corresponds to a left horizontal shift in the graph. To help illustrate, Figure 2.45 shows (a) a graph with no phase shift and (b) one with a phase shift of $1/(4f)$.

To understand the graph in Figure 2.45b, recall that $p = 1/f$ where p is the period. In other words, $1/(4f)$ corresponds to one fourth of a period, and the graph in Figure 2.45b is that of Figure 2.45a shifted left one fourth of a period. Therefore, it can be viewed as starting at its maximum, decreasing to its minimum, and rising again to its maximum. In effect, we can view the first one-fourth of a period, the part where it goes from 0 to its maximum, as being cut out. This phenomenon is exactly what the second interval in Figure 2.44 shows.

The third set of three bits, 100, defines a signal with amplitude A_1 and phase shift $2/(4f)$. Before we explain its effect, examine the signal at the end of the second interval. It is currently at its maximum of A_1. Now if there were no phase shift, the signal would just continue starting at A_1 and decrease to $-A_1$. But a phase shift of $2/(4f)$ means that half of a period is eliminated. Because the previous signal ended at its maximum, half of a period corresponds to that part of the signal that decreases from A_1 to $-A_1$. Consequently the signal begins at its minimum value at the start of the third interval.

Now let's provide a general description of how to generate a signal from a three-bit group. The signal generated by a three-bit group depends on where the previous signal ends. The phase shift is relative to that ending point. Table 2.12 defines

Figure 2.45   Effect of Phase Shift on a Signal

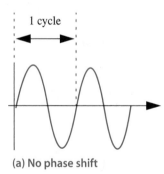
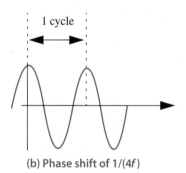

(a) No phase shift   (b) Phase shift of $1/(4f)$

Table 2.12   Rules for Signal Definition Using Quadrature Amplitude Modulation

POSITION OF PREVIOUS SIGNAL	NO PHASE SHIFT	1/4 PERIOD PHASE SHIFT	2/4 PERIOD PHASE SHIFT	3/4 PERIOD PHASE SHIFT
At 0, increasing	Start at 0, increase	Start at maximum	Start at 0, decrease	Start at minimum
At maximum	Start at maximum	Start at 0, decrease	Start at minimum	Start at 0, increase
At 0, decreasing	Start at 0, decrease	Start at minimum	Start at 0, increase	Start at maximum
At minimum	Start at minimum	Start at 0, increase	Start at maximum	Start at 0, decrease

the new signal as a function of the phase shift and the position of the previous signal. Keep in mind that the minimum or maximum in the first column refers to that of the previous signal, whereas the minimum or maximum in the second through fifth columns refers to the current signal.

Let's show how to apply this table in defining the signal over the fourth interval in Figure 2.44. The position of the previous signal (in interval 3) is at its minimum. Moreover, the bits 011 define a signal of amplitude A_2 and phase shift $1/(4f)$. Thus the signal is defined by the bottom row of the third column: It starts at 0 and increases to its maximum of A_2, just as the figure shows.

Note that a three-bit value will not always define the same signal. For example, intervals 4 and 7 both correspond to 011, but the signals are different. Of course, they both have the same amplitude. However, the phase shift is relative to where the previous signal ended. As a result, even though the phase shifts are both $1/(4f)$, the two signals start at different intervals. Another observation worth noting is that the same signal in two different intervals may correspond to different bit values. For example, intervals 6 and 8 have the same signal but the bits are different. (Why?)

Other ways of modulating using combinations of amplitude, frequency, and phase shift are presented in Section 2.6 during its discussion of modem standards.

As the previous section discussed, higher bit rates can be achieved by associating more bits per baud and using more signal definitions. However, recall that using more signals reduces the differences among them and increases the probability that a small amount of noise can make one signal look like another. If this happens, the receiving modem interprets the signal incorrectly and sends the wrong bits to its device.

One method of dealing with incorrect transmissions is, **Trellis-coded modulation (TCM)**, which uses correction mechanisms. It adds extra bits to a group in such a way that only certain bit combinations are valid. The expanded groups then define a signal using a modulation technique similar to QAM. The signals are defined in such a way that if noise makes one look like another, the distorted signal defines an invalid bit sequence. As a result, the receiver knows the received signal was incorrect.

We will not provide a detailed discussion of TCM at this point, but Chapter 4 will discuss error detection and correction methods in detail. We do note that TCM is a standard in some modems with high bit rates.

ANALOG-TO-DIGITAL CONVERSION

Some analog-to-digital conversions are nothing more than the reverse of what we have just discussed. The modem examines incoming signals for amplitudes, frequencies, and phase shifts and generates digital signals accordingly. These analog signals have constant characteristics, at least over short intervals. What about analog signals whose characteristics change continually? The most obvious example may be analog signals produced by a sound such as a voice. They are more complex than those generated by digital data and require alternative conversion techniques.

Pulse Amplitude Modulation   One approach to digitizing an analog signal is **pulse amplitude modulation (PAM)**. In this simple process an analog signal is sampled at regular intervals and then a pulse with amplitude equal to that of the sampled signal is generated. Figure 2.46 shows the result of sampling at regular intervals.

Pulse Code Modulation   PAM-generated signals look digital, but because a pulse may have any amplitude the signal has analog characteristics. One way of making the pulses truly digital is to assign amplitudes from a predefined set to the sampled signals. This process is called **pulse code modulation (PCM)**. For example, suppose we divide the amplitude range into a set of 2^n amplitudes and associate an n-bit binary number with each one. Figure 2.47 shows a division into eight values ($n = 3$).

As before, we sample the analog signal periodically. But this time we choose one of 2^n amplitudes that most closely matches the sample's amplitude. We then encode the pulse using the corresponding bit sequence. The bit sequence can then be transmitted using whatever digital transmission is in use. By sampling at regular intervals at a rate of s per second, we achieve a bit rate of $n \times s$ bits per second. Figure 2.47 shows the process. The first sample corresponds to 001, the second to 010, and so on.

Figure 2.46   Pulse Amplitude Modulation

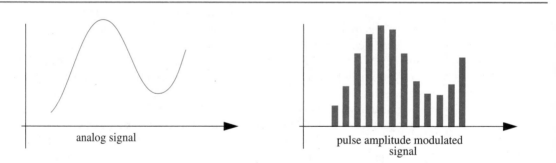

Figure 2.47   Pulse Code Modulation

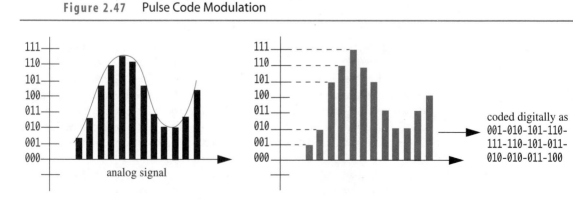

At the receiving end, the bit string is divided into groups of n bits and the analog signal is reconstructed. The accuracy of the reconstruction depends on two things. The first is the sampling frequency s. Sampling at a frequency less than that of the signal can cause some oscillations to be missed completely (Figure 2.48). Consequently, the reconstructed signal can be a poor approximation to the original one. Thus, we must sample frequently enough to preserve all the characteristics of the original signal. It would seem, therefore, that more samples are better. This conclusion is true, but only up to a point. Recall the Nyquist result from the previous section. It stated that sampling a signal at a rate twice its frequency is sufficient to preserve the signal's information. Now we have a nice application for the Nyquist result. If the original signal's maximum frequency is f, anything larger than $s = 2f$ will not provide a better approximation than with $s = 2f$.

The second factor that affects accuracy is the number of amplitudes from which to choose. Figure 2.47 showed just eight amplitudes for simplicity. With relatively large differences between the sampled signal and the pulse, the reconstructed signal becomes distorted. Reducing differences between adjacent pulse amplitudes helps reduce distortion.

One more note: Higher sampling frequencies and more pulse amplitudes create higher-quality transmissions, but at a price. Each produces more bits per second, requiring a higher bit rate, which costs more.

There are several common applications of PCM. One is the digitizing of voice signals over long-distance telephone lines. A worldwide standard makes 8000 samples per second and uses 8 bits per sample. In accordance with the Nyquist result, this frequency represents a little more than twice the maximum voice frequency your telephone can handle. It also requires a bit rate of 8×8000, or approximately 64K bps.[*]

Figure 2.48   Sampling at Too Low a Frequency

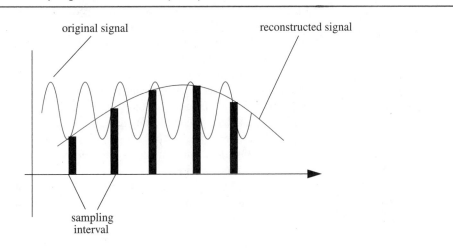

original signal

reconstructed signal

sampling
interval

---

[*] In practice, optical fibers used by long-distance carriers have much higher bit rates because they are capable of carrying many phone conversations simultaneously by multiplexing. Section 3.3 discusses this in more detail.

Another application is in compact disc (CD) technology. The music on a CD is coded optically in a digital format using PCM. To preserve the high quality of sound, however, PCM coding requires a higher frequency and more bits per pulse. Actual values depend on specific equipment. For example, we checked the owner's manual of a CD player and found the following technical specifications:

Sampling frequency: 44.1 kHz

D-A conversion: 16-bit linear

The D-A, as you might guess, refers to digital-to-analog. Sixteen bits allows approximately 64,000 sample amplitudes. The sampling frequency of approximately 44,000 samples per second is slightly more than twice the listed frequency response range of 2Hz to 20,000 Hz. The term *linear* means the pulse amplitudes are distributed evenly.[*]

There are other modulation techniques, but we will not elaborate here. For example, pulse duration modulation varies the duration of equal-amplitude pulses to code information. Differential pulse code modulation measures differences in consecutive samples. Delta modulation is a variation on differential pulse code modulation that uses just one bit per sample. For more information on these and other modulation techniques, consult Reference [Bl95].

2.6   MODEMS AND MODEM STANDARDS

Now that we have discussed how to communicate via telephone line, you may think that we are done, and that all you need is a modem to connect to the telephone system to communicate with anything else using a modem connection. Well, you might as well say, "I just bought a computer and now I can do wonderful things with it."

In the early 1980s, when PCs (often advertised as "home computers") first became available, a lot of people rushed to be among the first to have access to these new and powerful tools. However, many overlooked one, small detail. They had to learn how to use software, which was not an easy task for the novice (it wasn't always an easy task for the professional either).

In addition, many people who did manage to learn software found that their friends and colleagues bought different computers and learned different software. These differences made sharing and communicating next to impossible. The key words that apply to modems as well are *software* and *compatibility*. Figure 2.49 shows a modem connected to a PC. Of course, most modems today are installed internally and cannot be seen. The modulation techniques we have described explain how digital signals are changed to analog. But to get the signals to the modem in the first place, and to retrieve digital signals that the modem creates from telephone signals, we need software.

---

[*]In some cases, such as in telephone systems, the amplitudes are not distributed evenly. There are more pulse amplitudes in a range where values are more likely to occur. This uneven distribution, called *companding,* can improve voice quality without using more bits for each sample.

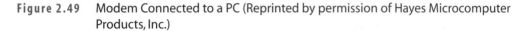

Figure 2.49   Modem Connected to a PC (Reprinted by permission of Hayes Microcomputer Products, Inc.)

Now suppose you have software and attach the PC to the modem. When it receives analog signals it must know how they were modulated. Likewise, when it modulates, it must use a scheme that the modem at the receiving end can understand. If the two modems do not understand the same modulation schemes they will not communicate. We need compatibility to do this.

Fortunately, the standards to which modem manufacturers adhere define bit rate, baud rate, and the modulation scheme. The best-known standards, defined by ITU-T, typically are identified by V.*xx*, where *xx* is an identifying number. There are also AT&T or Bell modems very similar to certain ITU-T standards.

We will start by describing a couple of the older, but simpler, standards and progress to more current ones. The ITU-T V.21 modem modulates using frequency shift keying. One bit defines the frequency; consequently its bit rate and baud rate are the same (300, very slow by today's standards).

The frequency assignment depends on whether the modem has originated (**originate mode**) or received (**answer mode**) a call. If the modem is in originate mode, it sends a 0 using 980 Hz and a 1 using 1180 Hz. In answer mode, a 0 corresponds to 1650 Hz and a 1 to 1850 Hz. Using two sets of frequency allows full-duplex communication (discussed in Section 3.1). For now, it means that data can be transmitted in both directions at the same time.

If the baud rate is 300, the signal's duration is $1/300 \approx .0033$ second. In the early days of communications, the relatively long duration made the signal less susceptible to noise. If some of it was distorted, there was enough left to be recognized by the unsophisticated (by today's standards) modems. Today's more sophisticated devices can use much shorter durations, thus increasing both baud and bit rate.

The AT&T 103 modem works similarly. It uses 1070 Hz for a 0 bit and 1270 for a 1 bit in originate mode, and 2025 Hz for a 0 bit and 2225 for a 1 bit in answer mode. Another standard is the V.22 modem. It uses phase shift keying associating two bits with each phase shift. It has a baud rate of 600 and a bit rate of 1200. Frequency and amplitude are constant.

SIGNAL CONSTELLATION

Current modems work by changing more than just one of an analog signal's components, typically the phase shift and amplitude (QAM). This change allows more differences to be introduced into signal components and, as a result, more bits per component. QAM methods can visually be described by a **signal constellation,** a diagram that uses points plotted on a coordinate system to define all legitimate signal changes. Figure 2.50 shows how to interpret one point. It is quantified by its length (distance from the origin) and the angle it makes with the horizontal axis. Recall from the previous section that length and angle (phase shift) are defined by variables C and D amplitudes of the sine and cosine functions that create the QAM signal. Each point defines a legitimate signal change. The signal's amplitude corresponds to the point's distance from the origin, and the phase shift corresponds to the angle with the horizontal.

In general, angles on a signal constellation measure between 0° and 360°. Previously, however, we defined phase shifts as a fraction of a period ranging between zero and one period. To interpret the signal constellation correctly, we define a linear relationship between the angles in the constellation and the fraction of a period. Specifically, an angle of $x°$ corresponds to $x/360$ of a period. So, for example, an angle of 90° corresponds to 90/360 = 1/4 of a period.

Using this interpretation, Figure 2.51 shows the signal constellation for a V.22 modem. It shows four points all the same distance from the origin, which means the

---

Figure 2.50 Quantifying a Point on a Signal Constellation

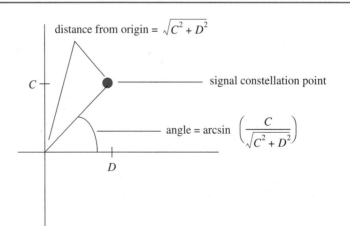

distance from origin = $\sqrt{C^2 + D^2}$

C

signal constellation point

angle = $\arcsin\left(\dfrac{C}{\sqrt{C^2 + D^2}}\right)$

D

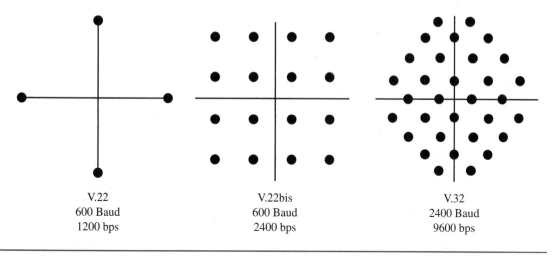

V.22	V.22bis	V.32
600 Baud	600 Baud	2400 Baud
1200 bps	2400 bps	9600 bps

Figure 2.51   Signal Constellations

amplitude does not change with the signal. These four points also make angles of 0°, 90°, 180°, and 270° with the horizontal axis. Therefore, legitimate phase shifts are none, one-fourth, one-half, and three-fourths of a period.

A more complex standard is the V.22bis standard. Figure 2.51 also shows its signal constellation of 16 points. The standard calls for 600 baud and 4 bits per baud, giving a data rate of 2400 bps. If you look carefully at the signal constellation you see there are 3 different amplitudes and 12 possible phase shifts. These figures should provide 36 combinations, but only 16 are used. The restriction is because of error-detection mechanisms.

The last signal constellation in Figure 2.51 corresponds to the V.32 standard. It is a 32-point constellation, using 2400 baud and 5 bits per baud. However, the data rate is $4 \times 2400 = 9600$ bps. The extra bit per baud occurs because the standard uses trellis coding. It is an error detection mechanism that creates a parity bit by defining additional signal components.

By looking at these signal constellations (and others), you might notice they have one thing in common. The points all seem to be spaced evenly. This feature is not just to create pretty constellation pictures. Modems, like grumpy people who have no appreciation for art, don't care what the picture looks like. The fact remains that most communications occur over noisy lines. To say that two signals differ by a 45° phase or that one's amplitude is twice the other is legitimate only in the absence of noise. The truth is, the phases may differ by $45° \pm x°$, where x corresponds to noise. Similarly, a signal's amplitude will actually be measured as $A \pm y$, where y corresponds to noise.

Figure 2.52 shows the effect of some noise on a signal constellation. A change in amplitude moves a constellation point farther from or closer to the origin. As a result, the point for the actual signal may be anywhere in the figure's shaded region. Similarly, a distorted phase shift can cause the point to move along a small circular

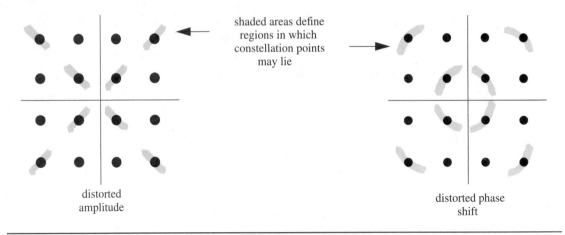

shaded areas define regions in which constellation points may lie

distorted amplitude

distorted phase shift

Figure 2.52 Distortion of Signal Constellation Points

arc. Worse yet, noise does not discriminate. Either type of distortion can occur independent of the other. The result is that the constellation point for a distorted signal may be anywhere within a circular region of where it should be.

If the initial points are separated enough and the noise is small enough, the noisy regions do not overlap. Consequently, a modem can recognize a distorted signal. However, if the noise is such that the regions overlap, then communication is impaired. If the point for a distorted signal lies in the intersection of two shaded regions, the modem cannot tell which one it should be in (Figure 2.53).

As you probably expect, there are many other modem standards. They vary in baud rate, bits per baud, and modulation technique. Newer standards also define error detection and correction methods and compression techniques. Table 2.13 summarizes some of the ITU-T standards. We must also note that many modems adhere to several standards, which is useful when communicating with a site that

Figure 2.53 Interpreting Constellation Points for a Distorted Signal

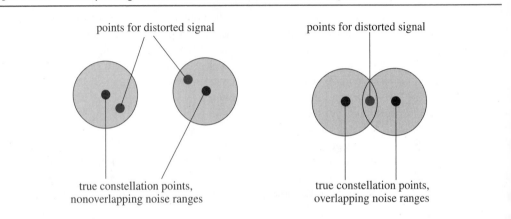

points for distorted signal

points for distorted signal

true constellation points, nonoverlapping noise ranges

true constellation points, overlapping noise ranges

Table 2.13   Some ITU-T V-Series Modem Standards

STANDARD	SUMMARY
V.21/Bell 103	300 bps bit rate using FSK.
V.22/Bell 212	1200 bps rate using PSK.
V.22bis	2400 bps rate using QAM.
V.27	4800 bps rate using PSK.
V.29	9600 bps rate using QAM (once a common standard for facsimile transmission).
V.32	9600 bps rate using QAM and trellis coding.
V.32bis	14400 bps rate using QAM and trellis coding.
V.34	33600 bps rate using QAM and trellis coding (commonly used in fax modems).
V.42	Standard for error correction techniques.
V.42bis	Standard using Lempel-Ziv methods (discussed in Chapter 3) for compression.

implements several of them. Typically, the modem can dial, exchange protocols, and then automatically choose the appropriate standard. These **autobaud modems** are convenient because users do not have to remember which phone number corresponds to which standard. They also allow users to communicate using any of several standards with the same modem and PC. Users can determine the standards by looking at the technical specifications in the owner's manual. There is usually a section specifying the data encoding mechanism at several data rates.

Still the modem evolution continues. As of this writing, vendors have been advertising 56 Kbps modems. We stated at the end of Section 2.4 that this seemed to exceed the theoretical data rate limits imposed by Shannon's result. However, these modems differ significantly from others in that they were designed with the assumption that communications will occur with an Internet service provider or corporate headquarters (Ref. [Ch97]). That is significant because communications equipment in those locations are typically based on digital technology. Consequently, there is no analog-to-digital conversion necessary and the noise typically introduced by conventional analog-to-digital converters is eliminated. As a result, Shannon's result does not apply.

Figure 2.54 helps explain. Conventional modem connections are similar to that described in Figure 2.54a. A PC sends a digital signal out of a port to a modem, which converts the signal to the required analog format. The analog signal goes through the telephone system's local loop to the nearest switching office, where it is converted back to a digital format. From there the digital signal is routed over a carrier system to another switching office that is closest to the remote site. The signal is converted back to analog and travels along another local loop to the remote site, where another modem converts the signal back to a digital format. There are four

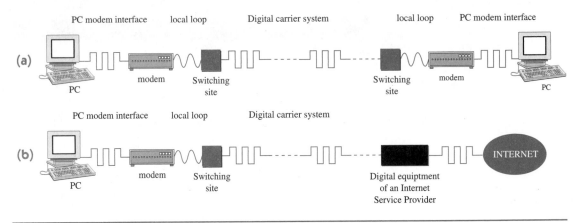

Figure 2.54   Connections Using a Modem

signal conversions in this process. In Figure 2.54b, these last two conversions do not occur. An Internet service provider has digital equipment that interfaces directly with digital carrier signals and is able to route them to the Internet without any analog-to-digital conversions. As a result, just two signal conversions occur at the user's end.

This reduction is significant because fewer analog-to-digital conversions mean less signal loss. The 56 Kbps modems are designed to exploit this fact. Another interesting feature about these modems is that they can often **download** (receive from a remote site) information more quickly than they can **upload** (send) it. The reason for this difference is that analog-to-digital conversions generally result in more signal loss than digital-to-analog conversions. Consequently, the analog signals the modem sends to the local switching office must have a lower frequency so that the loss does not corrupt the data. A lower frequency means a smaller data rate. When information is downloaded there is no analog-to-digital conversion prior to arriving at the modem. Thus, less noise is introduced and higher data rates are possible.

Of course, all this assumes that the local loop on the side of the modem is a line relatively free of noise, and there is often no guarantee that it is. Telephone equipment is designed to operate within certain constraints and often exceeds them. However, there is no guarantee that all phone lines will be able to support the 56 Kbps limit. In fact, estimates in Reference [Ch97] suggest that just 50% of U.S. connections are clean enough to support a 56 Kbps rate.

INTELLIGENT (HAYES COMPATIBLE) MODEMS

We continue our discussion of modems by discussing the **intelligent modem**, or **Hayes compatible modem**. As we have discussed, modems modulate and demodulate signals. However, almost every modem on the market does more. With appropriate software, a user can enter commands directing the modem to take certain actions such as dialing or answering the phone. Such intelligent modems have a processor to carry out these functions.

Hayes Microcomputer Products, Inc., developed a modem that has become commonplace. The Hayes modems are designed to respond to a set of instructions called **AT commands**. Using appropriate software, the user enters the letters *AT* followed by the command. Each command consists of one or more letters followed by parameters. Two common parameters are the D and T commands. The letter *D* represents *dial* and instructs the modem to dial the number that follows the command. The letter *T* indicates the modem should use *tone* dialing (as with push-button phones) as opposed to pulse dialing (as with rotary dials). To illustrate, a user wanting the modem to dial the number 555-1234 from a touch-tone phone would enter the command ATDT5551234.

In some cases, when dialing from within an organization you must first enter 9, wait for another dial tone, and then dial the number. How will a modem respond to this need? If it simply dials the numbers before the second dial tone, it may try to connect to an operator's recorded message saying, "Your phone call cannot be completed . . . ." You can instruct some modems to pause by including a comma (,) as part of the command. For example, if you must dial 9, wait, and then dial 555-1234, the appropriate command would be ATDT9,5551234.

Table 2.14 lists some common modem commands. Note that commands can be listed consecutively to form command strings such as the one described previously. We intend the following as a general overview and not as a complete command list. You should certainly consult your modem's manual for proper operation.

The commands of Table 2.14 can be entered from a PC using appropriate software. Some software also allows you to write several commands in a file. The files may be called **scripts** or **macros**; they allow the user to execute the commands on a file many times without having to type them each time. This feature is useful in cases where you frequently dial up the same line and go through the same logon procedures.

A last item worth mentioning is the use of modems in which a call waiting feature is available. Call waiting means that you hear an audible click if you are on the telephone and someone else is trying to call. The audible click is actually a brief, but temporary, disconnection. However, some modems will actually disconnect (go on hook) if this happens, thus terminating your connection. Others will not react to brief, temporary interruptions. Of course, if data were being transmitted during the interruption, there will be some loss. Certainly it is something you want to be aware of when you use a modem. Of course, call waiting can be disabled, usually by entering *70 on your phone before calling.

CABLE MODEMS

Our next topic is the cable modem, a device that has received considerable attention resulting, in part, from the upgrade of television cable delivery systems and the desire for faster bit rates for Internet connections. Whereas the conventional modem we have been discussing is designed to interface with analog components of the telephone system, the **cable modem** is designed to interface with the analog

Table 2.14   Example Modem Commands

COMMAND	FUNCTION
A	Put modem in answer mode. The modem will go off-hook (i.e., answer a call) when it detects an incoming signal.
AT	Stands for Attention code. Precedes most commands.
B	Use ITU-T V.22bis standard to communicate at 1200 baud.
D	Dial the following number.
E0, E1	Enables (E1) or disables (E0) echo printing of characters sent to the modem from the terminal.
H	Put modem on hook; that is, hang up.
H1	Put modem off hook.
Ln	Adjust speaker volume according to value of n.
P	Use pulse dialing. This is typical for rotary dial telephones. Typically appears following the D command.
Q0, Q1	Enables (Q0) or disables (Q1) returning result codes.
Sn	Display contents of register n on terminal.
Sn=x	Store value of x in register n.
T	Use tone dialing. Typically appears following the D command.
V0, V1	After receiving a command, a modem returns a result code. It may be displayed as digits (V0) or as words (V1).
W	Wait an amount of time specified by a register value. This can be used where you must wait for a dial tone.
Xn	Different values of n select a set of options for dialing and connect messages. For example, after the connection is made, you will see a message stating "CONNECT" or "CONNECT 2400," with the latter specifying the data rate at which the modem will operate. You can also specify whether to wait for a dial tone before dialing or to recognize a busy signal.

components of a cable TV (CATV) provider.[*] Many CATV subscribers are already familiar with the cable box that typically sits on top of a television. It is connected to a wall jack through which incoming CATV signals are transmitted. The box decodes incoming scrambled signals and sends them to the television for viewing. In many areas the box can also receive commands from a remote controller and send signals back to the cable company. This ability allows subscribers to order and watch pay-per-view movies.

---

[*] In the future all television signals will be entirely digital and current televisions will no longer be able to receive such signals without the aid of a converter. However, we're not there yet and must contend with analog signals for a while.

To some extent the cable modem is similar (Figure 2.55). Like a regular cable box, it can route TV signals to a television. However, it also has an extra output jack that can connect to a PC. In this capacity it functions much like the modems we have discussed, by converting between analog and digital signals. However, we'll soon see that there are important differences.

In effect, the cable modem is designed to give you access to the Internet via the CATV signals instead of calling an Internet service provider over the telephone. There are several advantages to this setup. One is that information can be transmitted using the high-frequency signals of CATV instead of the much lower frequencies of the telephone's local loop, resulting in much higher data rates (measured in Mbps instead of Kbps). Another advantage is that you will not need to dial in to make a connection; the connection is always there. A disadvantage is that although there are vendors making cable modems, there is not yet a standard governing the transportation of data over cable television networks. The lack of standards often means that different vendors' modems will not be compatible and consumers must take care when purchasing such devices.

Figure 2.56 shows the basic operation of a cable modem. Typically, a cable signal coming into a home has a frequency range of up to about 750 MHz. This signal is divided into many 6 MHz bands, each of which carries the signal from a particular station such as Discovery, ESPN, or CNN. Tuning in a channel effectively blocks out unwanted frequencies and allows only one 6 MHz signal to pass, enabling you to view the desired station. For Internet access, the cable company maintains a connection to the Internet through a provider. Information from the

Figure 2.55   Cable Modem Placement

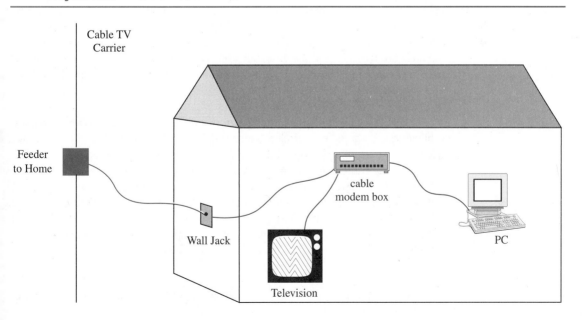

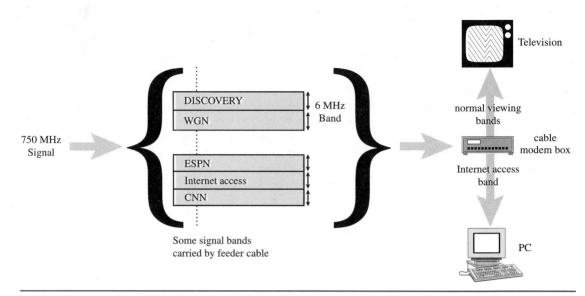

Figure 2.56 Cable Modem and Carrier Signals

Internet can then be downloaded onto a 6 MHz band somewhere between 42 MHz and 750 MHz.[*]

At the user's end the cable modem can access downloaded information by tuning into the appropriate 6 MHz band and converting those analog signals to a digital format. It then sends those signals through the appropriate port to a connected PC.

There are a number of techniques that can be used for modulating and demodulating, but two of the more popular are quaternary phase shift keying (QPSK) and Quadrature Amplitude Modulation (QAM64). Both are much more complex versions of similarly named techniques described in the previous section. QAM methods are typical for the high-bandwidth requirements of downloading information. Some estimates have placed download data rates at up to 36 Mbps. Many PCs are not capable of receiving data that quickly, however, so more realistic rates are between 3 Mbps and 10 Mbps.

The cable modem can also transmit information in the other direction (uploading). It can take information received from a PC and modulate it into a frequency range usually between 5MHz and 40 MHz. This is the range typically used by a two-way cable network for uploading. A problem is that signals in this range are more susceptible to electrical interference from home appliances. As a result, QPSK techniques are more common for uploading because they tend to be more robust. The drawback is that they have smaller bit rates. On the other hand uploading usually has smaller bandwidth demands. For example, sending email or commands usually requires much less data than downloading a graphic image.

---

[*]Downloaded signals are typically in bands above 42 MHz since lower-frequency signals are subject to more interference from home appliances.

There is another difference between modems and cable modems. Modems are often installed as cards in a PC. There is not yet a standard for connecting a cable modem to a PC, but using Ethernet (described in Chapter 6) connections is emerging as a common method. The cable modem converts analog signals to digital and sends them to the PC using the Ethernet protocols. Manufacturing cable modems as installable cards is an option but would require different cards for different makes of computers. Using an Ethernet connection allows a cable modem to use an already existing standard to connect to the computer. It also allows several PCs connected by an Ethernet LAN to share the cable modem.

As we have indicated, there is much work yet to be done on the creation of standards for the use of cable TV networks for data transport. The IEEE 802.14 Working Group has been chartered to develop such standards and quite a bit has been accomplished. Reference [He97] reviews some of the architectural options that are being considered for providing required services in an efficient but flexible manner.

NULL MODEMS

We close out this chapter with a brief reference to null modems. We know from previous discussion that PCs in two distinct sites could communicate if each had a modem connected to a telephone line. A logical question to ask is, If the PCs are in the same room can we just connect them directly? The answer is "sort of." Basically, a null modem is a device that allows such a connection. At this point in the text, however, we are not able to describe how a null modem works because we first need to discuss some additional protocols. Therefore, we mention null modems now because it seems logical to do so in a section about modems, but we must defer a more detailed discussion about them until after we have discussed some interface standards in Section 3.2.

2.7   SUMMARY

This chapter dealt mainly with communications media and equipment, applications, and communications theory. Primary communications media include twisted pair, coaxial cable, fiber optics, and microwave and satellite transmission. Electrically conducting media such as twisted pair and cable are cheaper than fiber and easier to tap into. However, they have smaller bandwidths and are subject to electrical interference.

Microwaves and satellites communicate through free space. That is, they require no physical connection. Satellites offer worldwide communications, and microwaves provide communication across distances where physical connections are impossible or impractical. Geosynchronous satellites remain in a fixed position relative to a position on the earth's surface and are useful in broadcast and communications applications. Low earth orbit (LEO) satellites continually move across the sky and a network of them is needed to provide a communications network. The data rates depend on the transmission frequencies. Higher frequencies provide higher data rates but are subject to more interference in the atmosphere.

Communication applications include VSAT (very small aperture terminal) systems, the telephone system, PBXs (private branch exchanges), ISDN (Integrated Services Digital Network), cellular phones, and fax machines. VSAT uses satellite technology and offers a viable alternative to the telephone system for many businesses and industries. The telephone system connects the largest number of people. For many years it was used primarily for voice communications, but each year finds more people using it for data communications. In fact, many organizations install a private system called a PBX for both voice and data. For many, it is a viable and economical alternative to the telephone system. For internal company communication, many PBXs bypass the central office but still have trunks to the interexchange telephone system.

Cellular telephones have provided telephone users freedom from a physical connection. An area is divided into regions, or cells, each of which has a transmitter capable of communicating with the telephone system. The cellular telephone then communicates with a transmitter within the cell.

Integrated Services Digital Network (ISDN) defines an all-digital communications network. It would transform the home telephone into a computer terminal that can be used for voice or data communications. It has been controversial over the years with many arguing that its 64 Kbps data rate is too slow for today's applications and that the much faster broadband ISDN and ATM are more viable technologies. On the other hand, vendors are still manufacturing ISDN-compatible devices and some argue there will be a place for ISDN.

The fax machine has combined the two technologies of copying and transmission. Like a copier, it reproduces images on paper. However, it reproduces them electronically and transmits them through the telephone system. The fax on the other end receives the signals and recreates the original image.

To transmit data, regardless of medium, we need to use a code, a mechanism that associates bit strings with certain information. The most common codes are ASCII (American Standard Code for Information Interchange) and EBCDIC (Extended Binary Coded Decimal Interchange Code). Each associates a bit string with each keyboard character and many special control functions. Other codes of importance are Baudot, Morse, and BCD (binary-coded decimal).

The next step is to determine what kind of digital or analog signal will define a 0 or 1 bit. Digital encoding schemes include NRZ (nonreturn to zero), Manchester, and Differential Manchester. NRZ assigns a fixed voltage level to a 0 and another to a 1. Both Manchester schemes (also called self-clocking codes) distinguish between a 0 and 1 by either a high-to-low or low-to-high voltage transition.

Analog signals convey information by changing amplitudes, frequencies, or phase shifts. In general, the number of bits per change depends on the number of allowable changes. Consequently, the bit rate depends on the baud rate. The Nyquist result and the sampling theorem together show that over a noiseless channel the bit rate $= 2f \times \log_2(B)$, where f is the maximum frequency and B is the number of different signals.

Claude Shannon extended the result to include noisy channels. His famous result states that the bit rate $=$ bandwidth $\times \log_2(1 + S/N)$, where S and N are the signal and noise power, respectively. This result puts a theoretical limit on the bit rate over any noisy channel.

A significant amount of communication involves connecting digital devices using analog signals and connecting analog devices using digital signals. Consequently, there is a need to study modulation and demodulation techniques. Digital-to-analog conversions often require changing an analog signal in response to a group of bits. Typical changes affect the amplitude (amplitude shift keying), frequency (frequency shift keying), or the phase shift (phase shift keying). Another technique known as quadrature amplitude modulation uses combinations of these changes.

One way of converting from analog back to digital is to simply reverse these processes. However, if the original signal is a complex analog signal such as voice, we need a different mechanism. One approach called PCM (pulse code modulation) samples an analog signal at regular intervals. It then associates a bit string with each sample and transmits it. On the receiving end the bits are received and the analog signal reconstructed.

Modems are perhaps the most familiar modulation/demodulation devices. They are used to connect digital devices such as computers via the telephone system. Modems use different modulation techniques, which are defined by standards. Two devices can communicate only if the modems on each end recognize the same standard. Most modems are also small special-purpose computers. They can respond to commands that a user, with the help of appropriate software, enters at a terminal. These intelligent, or Hayes compatible modems, are commonplace. Cable modems are designed to interface between a computer and the cable television signals that are widely available. The theory is that by having access to the much higher-frequency signals from CATV, data rates will be much higher than telephone modems will ever be able to achieve. Work is still in progress on the creation of standards for cable modem operations.

Data communications is a dynamic field of study. Researchers are continually increasing the data rates of different media and reducing their costs to make them technologically and economically feasible for more people than ever before.

Review Questions

1. List five transmission media and rank them in order of data rate capability.

2. Distinguish between a digital and an analog signal.

3. Distinguish between bit rate and bandwidth.

4. What three components completely describe an analog signal?

5. How are a signal's period and frequency related?

6. Distinguish between baseband and broadband modes.

7. Define the index of refraction.

8. What is the difference between a laser and LED in optical fiber communications?

9. List three modes for optical fiber communication and compare them.

10. Are the following statements TRUE or FALSE? Why?

    a. Direct microwave transmission can happen between any two surface points on earth.

    b. Satellite transmission requires a stationary communication satellite.

    c. Thicker optical fiber allows a higher data rate.

    d. Satellite transmission rates are limited only by the limitation of equipment to send and receive high frequency signals.

    e. Because LEO satellites move across the sky and fall below the horizon there are no practical uses for them in communications applications.

    f. Local area networks do not require a physical connection among their components.

    g. Satellite communications are practical only for the largest companies and agencies.

    h. A fax machine scans a page and transmits text information one character at a time.

    i. Light can travel through optical fiber at different speeds.

    j. Visible light and electromagnetic waves are the same.

    k. Optical fibers have a hollow center through which light passes and reflects off a reflective surface surrounding it.

11. Distinguish between a horn and a parabolic dish antenna.

12. List the five major components of the telephone system.

13. Describe how a cellular telephone works.

14. What is a very small aperture terminal system?

15. Which transmissions are susceptible to interference?

16. What is a periodic signal?

17. Why are the wires in a twisted pair twisted (as opposed to using parallel wires)?

18. What is the purpose of the cladding in optical fiber communications?

19. What was Sputnik?

20. List some advantages and disadvantages of LEO satellites versus geosynchronous satellites.

21. What is a private branch exchange?

22. What is the difference between a printable character and a control character?

23. What is the difference between the ASCII and the EBCDIC codes?

24. The Baudot code for the character 0 (zero) is the same as that for the character P. How can that be?

25. Distinguish among NRZ, Manchester, and differential Manchester digital encoding.

26. With all the precision equipment currently available, why does a long run of 0s or 1s present a problem when using an encoding scheme such as NRZ?

27. What baud rate is required to realize a 10 Mbps data rate using NRZ encoding? Using Manchester encoding?

28. Distinguish between the Nyquist and the Shannon results.

29. Define signal-to-noise ratio.

30. Suppose a transmission were free of noise. Does this imply that there is no limit on the maximum data rate that can be achieved with current equipment?

31. Given the proliferation of computing equipment using telephone lines, why is the telephone's bandwidth only approximately 3000 Hz?

32. Shannon's result relates data rates and bandwidth in the presence of noise. However, the amount of noise varies with the medium and source. How does Shannon's result account for it?

33. What does a modem allow you to do with a PC?

34. What is the difference between modulation and demodulation?

35. Distinguish among frequency modulation, amplitude modulation, and phase modulation.

36. What is quadrature amplitude modulation?

37. Distinguish between pulse code modulation and pulse amplitude modulation.

38. Why are there so many different modem standards?

39. What is a signal constellation?

40. What is an intelligent modem?

41. What is a cable modem?

42. If a modem supports several different standards, how does it know which one to use when you connect to another computer over a telephone line?

Exercises

1. If a satellite's orbital height is fixed, why is it not possible to change the time required to orbit the earth by changing the speed of the satellite?

2. Suppose a company is trying to establish communications among several sites in different parts of a large city. Would microwave links be a good idea? Why or why not?

3. Digital signals can be translated to analog signals by using relatively simple techniques such as varying the amplitude or frequency between two specified values. What is the advantage of using more complex schemes such as QAM?

4. Write a program that prompts its user with a message and a bell sound to input a number and echo print it.

5. Write a program that reads a character string and prints it on the screen moving the cursor from right to left rather than the usual left to right orientation.

6. Write a program that clears the screen.

7. What is the Baudot code for the character string SDG564FSDH65?

8. Table 2.5 shows ASCII codes for 0 through 9. Why is there not an ASCII code for 10?

9. Draw the digital signals for the bit string 0010100010 using each of the NRZ, Manchester, and differential Manchester digital encoding techniques. Assume the signal is "high" prior to receipt of the first bit.

10. What is the bit string associated with the following Manchester-encoded signal? What is the bit string if it is a differential Manchester-encoded signal?

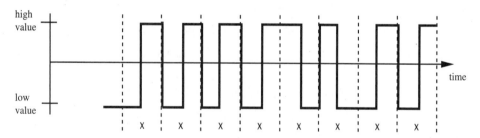

11. Draw analog signals corresponding to the following functions.

   a. $y = \sin(t)$

   b. $y = \sin(2t)$

   c. $y = 4\sin(2t)$

   d. $y = 2\sin(2t + \pi/2)$

   e. $y = 3\sin(t)$

   f. $y = \sin(t + \pi/4)$

   g. $y = \sin(2t - \pi/2)$

12. Assume the maximum analog frequency of a medium is 6000 Hz. According to the Nyquist result, what are the maximum bit rates for schemes that use one, two, three, and four bits per signal component?

13. According to Nyquist, what frequency is necessary to support a bit rate of 30,000 bps using only one bit per signal component? Three bits per signal component?

14. In your own words, what is the significance of Shannon's result?

15. What is the actual signal power (relative to the noise power) if the signal-to-noise ratio is given as 60 decibels?

16. What is the decibel rating if the signal power is twice the noise power?

17. Assume the maximum analog bandwidth of a medium is 6000 Hz. According to the Shannon result, what is the maximum bit rate if the signal-to-noise ratio is 40 decibels? 60 decibels?

18. According to Shannon, what bandwidth is necessary to support a bit rate of 30,000 bps assuming a signal-to-noise ratio of 40 decibels? What bandwidth is necessary if the number of decibels is doubled?

19. Suppose you want to achieve a bit rate of 64,000 bps using a maximum bandwidth of 10,000 Hz. What is the minimum allowable signal-to-noise ratio?

20. Can a phase shift of one period be used to distinguish signals?

21. Using QAM, is it possible for the exact same signal in two different intervals to correspond to different bit values?

22. Using QAM, do the same bits always correspond to the same analog signals?

23. Draw the QAM analog signal (carefully) that transmits the following bit string:

0010110101011010110

Assume the current analog signal is established as shown here. You need draw only one complete cycle for each modulation change.

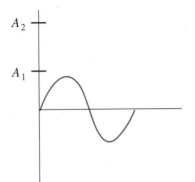

24.   Suppose a modem uses quadrature amplitude modulation as described by Table 2.11. What bit sequence corresponds to the following signal (starting with the second time interval)?

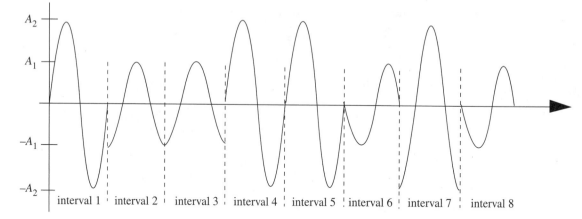

25.   Design a QAM technique that uses up to eight phase shifts and two amplitudes. How many bits per baud are there?

26.   Assume a QAM technique has up to m phase shifts and n amplitudes. How many bits per baud are there?

27.   Why don't modems use PCM techniques?

28.   If you have a CD player, examine its technical specifications and relate them to the discussions on PCM.

29.   Why can't professionals design modems with arbitrarily high baud rates and thus realize unlimited data rates?

30.   If you have a modem, write a short summary listing the standards it supports.

31.   Draw the signal constellation for a modem that uses the QAM defined by Table 2.11. Draw another one for the QAM techniques described by Exercise 25.

32.   Describe the signal changes (i.e., specify the amplitude and phase changes) associated with the signal constellations in Figure 2.51.

33.   How many bits correspond to one signal component using the V.21 standard? What is the duration for one signal component?

34.   Repeat Exercise 33 for the V.32 standard.

REFERENCES

1. [Bl89] Black, U. *Data Networks: Concept, Theory, and Practice.* Englewood Cliffs, NJ: Prentice-Hall, 1989.

2. [Bl95] Black, U. *ATM: Foundation for Broadband Networks.* Englewood Cliffs, NJ: Prentice-Hall, 1995.

3. [Bl97] Black, U. *Emerging Communication Technologies.* Englewood Cliffs, NJ: Prentice-Hall, 1997.

4. [Br89] Brodeur, P. *Currents of Death.* New York: Simon and Schuster, 1989.

5. [Ch84] Chorafas, D. N. *Telephony: Today and Tomorrow.* Englewood Cliffs, NJ: Prentice-Hall, 1984.

6. [Ch97] Cholewka, K. "56K Modems: The New Spin on Speed." *Data Communications,* vol. 26, no. 6 (May 1997), 93–103.

7. [Cl45] Clarke, A. C., "Extra-Terrestrial Relays: Can Rocket Stations Give World-Wide Radio Coverage?" *Wireless World* (October 1945).

8. [Da95] Davis, P. T. and C. R. McGuffin. *Wireless Local Area Networks.* New York: McGraw-Hill, 1995.

9. [Di92] Didio, L. *"Microwave LAN Links Rocket Test Site."* LAN Times, vol. 9, no. 20 (October 1992), 1, 102–104.

10. [He97] Hernandez-Valencia, E. J. "Architectures for Broadband Residential IP Services Over CATV Networks." *IEEE Network*, vol. 11, no. 1, (January 1997).

11. [Hu90] Hudson, H. *Communication Satellites.* New York: Free Press, 1990.

12. [Mu91] Mulqueen, J. "Users Rate PBXs." *Data Communications*, vol. 20, no. 7 (June 1991), 77–82.

13. [Ne95a] Newman, D. "Wireless LANs: How Far? How Fast?" *Data Communications*, vol. 24, no. 4, (March 1995), 77–86.

14. [Ne95b] Nemzow, M. *Implementing Wireless Networks.* New York: McGraw-Hill, 1995.

15. [Pi81] Pierce, J. R. *Signals: The Telephone and Beyond.* San Francisco: Freeman and Company, 1981.

16. [Po91] Politi, C. and J. Stein. "VSATs Give Corporate Networks a Lift." *Data Communications*, vol. 20, no. 2 (February 1991), 89–94.

17. [Ro93] Roussel, A. "VSAT Service Crosses the Border." *Data Communications,* vol. 22, no. 7 (May 1993), 73–78.

18. [Sa93] Saunders, S. "Wireless LAN Users: Take a Hike." *Data Communications,* vol. 22, no. 10 (July 1993), 49–50.

19. [Sh90] Sherman, K. *Data Communications: A User's Guide,* 3rd ed. Englewood Cliffs, NJ: Prentice-Hall, 1990.

20. [St96] Stallings, W., *Computer Organization and Architecture: Designing for Performance,* 4th ed. Englewood Cliffs, NJ: Prentice-Hall, 1996.

21. [Ta71] Taub, H. and D. Schilling. *Principles of Communications Systems.* New York: McGraw-Hill, 1971.

22. [Wa85] Wasserman, N. *From Invention to Innovation: Long Distance Telephone Transmissions at the Turn of the Century.* Baltimore: Johns Hopkins University Press, 1985.

23. [Wa91] Walrand, J. *Communications Networks: A First Course.* Boston: Richard D. Irwin, 1991.

CHAPTER 3

DATA COMMUNICATION

*The idea that information can be stored in a changing
world without an overwhelming depreciation of its value
is false. It is scarcely less false than the more plausible
claim that after a war we may take our existing
weapons, fill their barrels with cylinder oil, and coat
their outsides with sprayed rubber film, and let them
statically await the next emergency.*
— **Norbert Wiener** (1894–1964), U.S. mathematician

Chapter 2 discussed transmission fundamentals and the specific mechanisms required to transmit information. This chapter goes one step farther and discusses communication. You might ask, "What is the difference between transmission and communication?"

To answer, consider an analogy of human speech. We could discuss the mechanisms behind speech—how the vocal chords contract and expand to allow air to exit our lungs and form sound, and how the mouth manipulates these sounds to form what we call speech—but this is a long way from communicating. The words that come out must be organized to make sense. If they come out too quickly or too slowly, the speaker will not be understood. If many people speak simultaneously, no one is understood. If someone speaks a language you don't understand, communication is lost. If a sentence contains missing words or phrases (such as might occur when speaking in a second language), some meaning may be lost.

Electronic communication has similar problems. The receiver must know how message bits are organized to understand the message. The receiver must know how quickly they arrive to interpret the message. What happens if many people try to use a common medium simultaneously, as often occurs in a local area network (LAN)? Are there ways to transmit fewer bits and preserve the meaning of a message (presumably to save on transmission costs)?

This chapter discusses these topics. Section 3.1 discusses ways of communicating using serial, parallel, synchronous, and asynchronous transmission. It also contrasts one-way and two-way communications. The best way to ensure that devices send and receive in compatible ways is to adhere to standards. Section 3.2

discusses standards such as RS-232 and RS-449, which are commonly used to connect devices.

Sections 3.3 and 3.4 discuss ways that allow many messages to be transmitted on a single transmission medium. They discuss multiplexing and contention strategies common to LANs and the airwaves. Section 3.5 covers various data compression methods, which reduce transmission costs by transmitting fewer bits without losing any information.

3.1   TRANSMISSION MODES

A **transmission mode** defines the way in which a bit group goes from one device to another. It also defines whether bits may travel in both directions simultaneously or whether devices must take turns sending and receiving.

SERIAL AND PARALLEL TRANSMISSION

The first distinction we make is between serial and parallel transmission. **Parallel transmission** means that a group of bits is transmitted simultaneously by using a separate line (wire) for each bit (Figure 3.1a). Typically, the lines are bundled in a cable. Parallel transmissions are common especially where the distance between the two devices is short. For example, a PC-to-printer connection up to 25 feet is considered a safe distance. The most common examples are communication between a computer and peripheral devices. Other examples include communication among a CPU, memory modules, and device controllers.

Parallel transmission loses its advantage over longer distances. First, using multiple lines over long distances is more expensive than using a single one. Second, transmitting over longer distances requires thicker wires to reduce signal degradation. Bundling them into a single cable becomes unwieldy. A third problem involves the time required to transmit bits. Over a short distance, bits sent simultaneously

Figure 3.1   Parallel and Serial Transmission

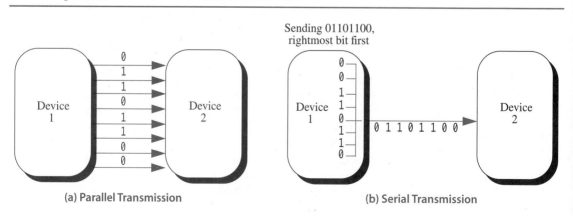

(a) Parallel Transmission   (b) Serial Transmission

will be received almost simultaneously. Over a long distance, however, wire resistance may cause the bits to drift a little and arrive at slightly different times, which can create problems at the receiving end.

Serial transmission provides an alternative to parallel transmission (Figure 3.1b). Using just one line, it transmits all the bits along it one after another. It is cheaper and more reliable than parallel transmission over long distances. It is also slower because the bits are sent one at a time.

The sending and receiving devices have an additional complexity. The sender must determine the order in which the bits are sent. For example, when sending eight bits from one byte the sender must determine whether the high-order or low-order bits are sent first. Similarly, the receiver must know where to place the first-received bit within the destination byte. It may seem like a trivial issue, but different architectures may number the bits in a byte differently and if the protocols do not agree on how to order the bits the information will be transmitted incorrectly.

ASYNCHRONOUS AND SYNCHRONOUS TRANSMISSION

There are two ways to provide serial communication: asynchronous and synchronous transmission. **Asynchronous transmission** means that bits are divided into small groups (usually bytes) and sent independently. The sender can send the groups at any time and the receiver never knows when they will arrive (somewhat like a visit from a long-lost relative!).

One common example is using a terminal to communicate with a computer. Pressing a key containing a letter, number, or special character sends an eight-bit ASCII code.[*] The terminal sends the codes at any time, depending on how well or fast you type. Internally, the hardware must be able to accept a typed character at any time. (We should note that not all keyboard entries are transmitted asynchronously. Some intelligent terminals can buffer entries and transmit an entire line or screen to the computer. This is synchronous transmission, which we discuss shortly.)

Terminal input is not the only example of asynchronous transmission. In some cases, data is sent to a line printer one byte at a time. Asynchronous transmission is typical of **byte-oriented input-output (I/O),** an operating systems term meaning that data is transferred a byte at a time.

There is a potential problem with asynchronous transmission. Remember that the receiver does not know when data will arrive until it gets there. By the time it detects it and can react, the first bit has come and gone. It is similar to someone coming up behind you unexpectedly and starting to talk. By the time you react and start listening, the first few words are missed. Consequently, each asynchronous transmission is preceded by a start bit (Figure 3.2). It alerts the receiver to the fact

---

[*]We haven't forgotten that we defined the ASCII code as a seven-bit code. However, in many cases the eight-bit is used for parity checking. We will discuss this in Chapter 4. Even without parity, you can think of a seven-bit code as an eight-bit code in which the leading bit is always 0. Since most memory consists of eight-bit bytes, this is the simplest way to store a seven-bit code.

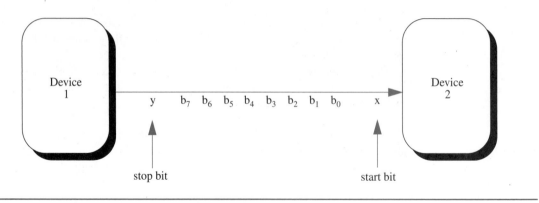

Figure 3.2 Asynchronous Transmission

that data is arriving. This gives the receiver time to respond and accept and buffer the data bits. At the end of the transmission, a stop bit indicates the transmission's end. By convention an idle line (one that is transmitting no data) actually carries a signal defining a binary 1. The start bit then causes the signal to change, corresponding to a 0. The remaining bits cause the signal to change depending on bit values. Finally the stop bit brings the signal back to the equivalent of a 1, where it stays until the next start bit arrives.

For example, suppose you enter the digits 321 at a terminal. Using an eight-bit extended ASCII code (with a leading 0) defines the following bits to be sent:

00110001 for the digit 1

00110010 for the digit 2

00110011 for the digit 3

Suppose we send each digit (leftmost bit first) separately using NRZ coding. Figure 3.3 shows the transmitted signal. In each case the start bit raises the signal, alerting the receiver that other bits will follow. When they have all arrived for that digit, the stop bit lowers the signal. It remains low until the next start bit raises it.

Figure 3.3 Asynchronous Transmission of the Digits 1, 2, and 3 Using NRZ Coding

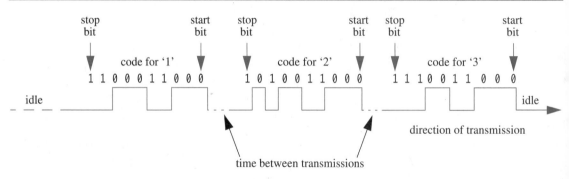

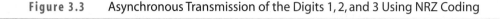

Asynchronous transmission is designed for use with slow devices such as keyboards and some printers. It also has a high overhead. In the example above, two extra bits are transmitted for every eight. This represents a 25% increase in the total transmission load. For slow devices that transmit little data, this is a small problem. However, for fast devices that transfer a lot of data, a 25% increase in load is significant.

With **synchronous transmission** much larger bit groups are sent. Instead of sending many characters separately, each with its own start and stop bit, they are grouped together and then transmitted as a whole. We call this group a **data frame** or **frame.**

The precise organization of a data frame varies with the protocol, discussed in Chapter 5. Data frames do have many common characteristics. Figure 3.4 shows the organization of a generic data frame. The orientation is rightmost bits first.

The first part of the frame contains **SYN characters,** unique bit patterns that alert the receiver that a frame is arriving. A SYN character is similar to the start bit discussed previously, except that here the pattern also ensures the receiver's sampling rate and the consistency of the rate at which the bits arrive.

Next are control bits, which may include the following elements:

- Source address specifying where the frame originated.
- Destination address specifying where the frame should go. This is important in networks in which a frame may go through several nodes to get to its destination. Each intermediate node uses the destination to determine where to route it. Chapter 7 discusses routing further.
- Actual number of data bytes.
- Sequence number. This is useful when many frames are sent and, for some reason, arrive out of order. The receiver uses the sequence numbers to reassemble them. Chapter 5 discusses this further.
- Frame type, distinguished by some protocols. Chapter 5 discusses some of these.

Figure 3.4   Synchronous Transmission

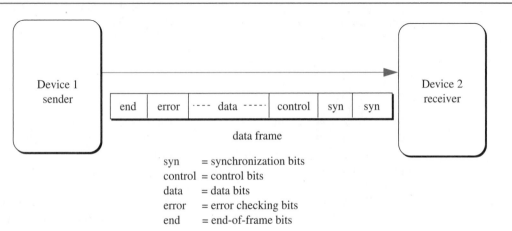

| end | error | ---- data ----- | control | syn | syn |

data frame

syn   = synchronization bits
control = control bits
data   = data bits
error   = error checking bits
end   = end-of-frame bits

The data bits define the information being sent. There are no start and stop bits between the characters. The error checking bits are used to detect or correct transmission errors. We know from Chapter 2 that electrical interference can distort signals. But how does the receiver know when this happens? Typically, the sender transmits extra bits that depend on the data. If the data is altered the extra bits are not consistent with the data. Chapter 4 discusses error detection and correction techniques.

The last part of the frame is an end-of-frame marker. Like the SYN characters, it is a unique bit string indicating that no more bits are arriving (at least until the start of the next frame).

Synchronous transmission generally is much faster than asynchronous. The receiver does not start and stop for each character. Once it detects the SYN characters, it receives all the others as quickly as they arrive. In addition, there is less overhead. For example, a typical frame may have 500 bytes (4000 bits) of data containing 100 bits of overhead (specifics will vary). In this case, the added bits mean a 2.5% increase in the total bits transferred. Compare that with the 25% increase with asynchronous transmission.

It should be noted that as the number of data bits increases, the percentage of overhead bits decreases. On the other hand, larger data fields require larger buffers in which to store them, putting a limit on the size of a frame. In addition, larger frames occupy a transmission medium for a longer uninterrupted amount of time. In an extreme case, this could cause excessive waiting by other users.

A third transmission mode we mention briefly is **isochronous transmission.** Like asynchronous, characters are not transmitted contiguously; that is, there may be gaps between them. The gaps are not arbitrary, however. The gap is equal to the amount of time needed to send an integral number of characters. That is, if T is the time required to send one character, the time between consecutive characters will be $n \times T$, where n is some integer.

In your readings you may encounter the term **bisync.** It is not a transmission mode in the same sense as asynchronous or synchronous. It is an acronym for **binary synchronous communications,** sometimes abbreviated as BSC, and is a protocol IBM introduced in the 1960s for synchronous communication between a computer and terminals. We will discuss it in Chapter 5.

Simplex, Half-Duplex, and Full-Duplex Communications

So far this chapter has dealt with ways to transmit information from one device to another, with a definite distinction between sender and receiver. This is an example of **simplex communications** (Figure 3.5). That is, communication goes only in one direction. The many examples include airport monitors, printers, television sets, or talking with an unsympathetic professor about a bad grade.

Other applications require a greater flexibility in which a device can both send and receive. The methods vary. Some use **half-duplex communications,** in which

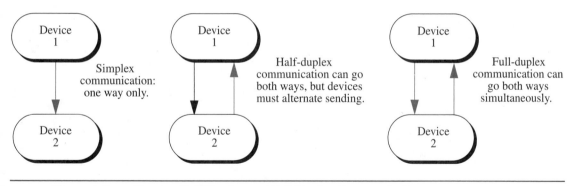

Figure 3.5   Simplex, Half-Duplex, and Full-Duplex Communication

both devices can send and receive, but they must alternate. It is used in two-way radios, some modems, and some peripheral devices. For example, the previously mentioned bisync protocol is half duplex.

The most flexible method is **full-duplex communications.** Here a device can send and receive simultaneously. When a device is sending over one line it may be receiving on another. Many computer terminals use full-duplex communications. This is evidenced by the ability to continue typing at the same time that information is being printed on the screen. Many modems are also full duplex.

Two-way communication becomes complex, especially over networks. Protocols must be used to make sure information is received correctly and in an orderly manner and to allow devices to communicate efficiently. Discussions of these issues will be covered in the next two chapters.

3.2   INTERFACE STANDARDS

Chapter 2 and the previous section described several ways to transmit information. One might conclude that as long as two devices use the same mechanisms to send and receive, they can communicate. Communication does not necessarily occur, however. If two people speak at the same time, neither listening to the other, they are not communicating. Common sense dictates that in order to communicate, they must take turns listening and speaking. Orderly discussions require that rules (protocols) be established that recognize an individual wanting to speak. Communications among devices must be guided similarly by protocols. Sending modulated signals to a device does no good if the device is not prepared to sense the signals and interpret them.

Figure 3.6 shows a typical arrangement of connected devices. The acronym DCE means **data circuit-terminating equipment,** and **DTE** means **data terminal equipment.** The DTE (a PC, for example) does not connect to a network directly. It communicates through a DCE (a modem, for example). We call the connection between the DTE and DCE the **DTE-DCE interface.** This section focuses on DTE-DCE interface standards.

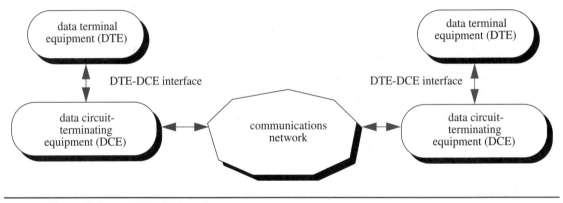

Figure 3.6   DTE-DCE Interface

RS-232 INTERFACE

One well-known standard is the **RS-232 standard.** It was developed by the Electronic Industries Association (EIA) in the early 1960s and has been revised several times. Probably the most common version, developed in the late 1960s, is known as RS-232-C. The technical level of detail differentiating the versions is beyond the scope of this text, but we will discuss the RS-232-C standard.[*]

The most obvious (visible) aspect of the standard is the number of lines (25) between the DTE and DCE. If the standard is fully implemented, the DTE and DCE are connected by a 25-line cable (sometimes called a DB-25 cable) connected to each device using a 25-pin connector (Figure 3.7). Each line has a specific function in establishing communication between the devices. Table 3.1 summarizes them and specifies the signal direction (i.e., whether the line is used to transmit from the DCE to the DTE or vice versa). The table also contains the EIA designation (circuit code) for each line.

We will not provide a thorough discussion of every connection, but we will describe the role some of the circuits play in a typical DTE-DCE connection. If you would like a more detailed description, consult a reference such as [Bl89] or [Sh90].

Figure 3.7   RS-232 Connector

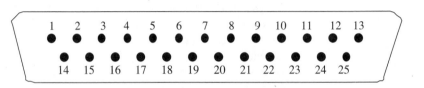

---

[*]Some years ago the EIA decided to replace the 'RS' designation with 'EIA'. Consequently, the standard is properly called the EIA-232 standard. However, because of its popularity and the fact that old habits die hard, the 'RS' designation is still commonly used.

Table 3.1   RS-232-C Circuit Definitions

CIRCUIT CODE	LINE NUMBER	SIGNAL DIRECTION	FUNCTION
AA	1		Protective ground. It is connected to the equipment frame and sometimes to external grounds.
AB	7		Electrical ground. All signal voltages are measured relative to this ground.
BA	2	DTE to DCE	Transmit data (TD). DTE transmits data to the DCE on this circuit.
BB	3	DCE to DTE	Receive data (RD). DTE receives data from the DCE on this circuit.
CA	4	DTE to DCE	Request to send (RTS). DTE uses this circuit to request permission from the DCE before it can transmit data.
CB	5	DCE to DTE	Clear to send (CTS). The DCE uses this circuit to give the DTE permission to transmit data.
CC	6	DCE to DTE	Data set ready (DSR). A signal on this line indicates the DCE has connected to a communications medium and is ready to operate. For example, if the DCE is a modem, this circuit indicates whether it is off-hook.
CD	20	DTE to DCE	Data terminal ready (DTR). A signal on this line indicates the DTE is ready to transmit or receive. It can be used to signal a modem when to connect to a communications channel.
CE	22	DCE to DTE	Ring indicator. Indicates the DCE is receiving a ringing signal (e.g., when a modem receives a call) from the communications channel.
CF	8	DCE to DTE	Data carrier detect (DCD). Indicates the DCE is receiving a carrier signal that meets suitability criteria from the communications network. Essentially, this means the DCE understands the incoming signal.
CG	21	DCE to DTE	Signal quality detector. Indicates whether there is a high probability the incoming signal is error free.
CH/CI	23	DTE to DCE or DCE to DTE	Data signal rate selector/indicator. Where two signal rates are possible from the DTE to the DCE, this line specifies which is used.
DA	24	DTE to DCE	Transmitter signal element timing. Provides clock signals to DCE used for timing in signal generation.
DB	15	DCE to DTE	Transmitter signal element timing. Similar to DA, except the DCE provides timing signals to the DTE for the signals the DTE sends.

(continues)

Table 3.1 *(continued)*

CIRCUIT CODE	LINE NUMBER	SIGNAL DIRECTION	FUNCTION
DD	17	DCE to DTE	Receiver signal element timing. Similar to DA, except the DCE provides timing signals to the DTE for the signals the DCE sends.
SBA	14	DTE to DCE	Secondary transmitted data. Same as BA except it uses a secondary channel.
SBB	16	DCE to DTE	Secondary received data. Same as BB except it uses a secondary channel.
SCA	19	DTE to DCE	Secondary request to send. Same as CA except it uses a secondary channel.
SCB	13	DCE to DTE	Secondary clear to send. Same as CB except it uses a secondary channel.
SCF	12	DCE to DTE	Secondary data carrier detect. Same as CF except it uses a secondary channel.
RL	21	DTE to DCE	Remote loopback. For testing, instructs DCE to return transmitted signals.
LL	18	DTE to DCE	Local loopback. Instructs local DCE to return transmitted signal.
TM	25	DCE to DTE	Test mode. Indicates DCE is in a test mode.

Suppose the DTE is a PC and the DCE is a modem. Chapter 2 discussed how a modem communicates with the analog world, so we now focus on the exchange between it and the PC. The first six circuits primarily are used to establish an exchange that ensures that neither device will send data when the other is not expecting it. Figure 3.8 shows the exchange that occurs over a period of time.

Since the DCE interfaces to a network on behalf of the DTE, it must know when the DTE is ready. The DTE indicates its readiness by asserting (sending a signal on) DTR circuit number 20 (time t_1 in Figure 3.8). The DCE senses the signal and responds by connecting (if it has not already done so) to the network. Once the DCE has connected and is also ready, it asserts DSR circuit number 6 (time t_2). Effectively, the DCE acknowledges the DTE's state of readiness and declares it also is ready.

Once they are both ready, the DTE requests permission to transmit data to the DCE by asserting RTS circuit 4 (time t_3). This circuit also controls the direction of flow in half-duplex communications. On sensing RTS, the DCE enters a transmit mode, meaning it is ready to transmit data over the network. It then responds by asserting the CTS circuit number 5 (time t_4). Finally, the DTE sends data over TD circuit number 2 (between times t_5 and t_6).

When the DCE detects an incoming signal from a network that it recognizes, it asserts DCD circuit number 8 (time t_7). As the signals come in, the DCE sends them

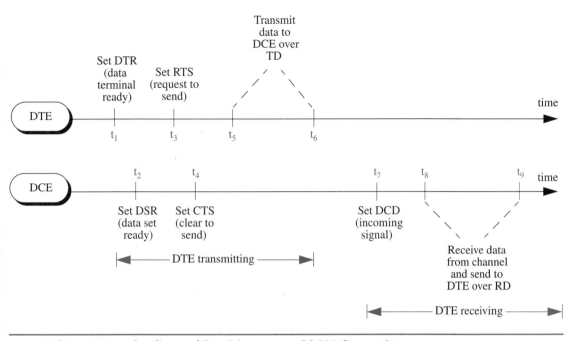

Figure 3.8   Sending and Receiving over an RS-232 Connection

to the DTE using RD circuit number 3. Some of the older modems had lights on the front that showed whenever certain lines were asserted. This signal provided the user with a chance to see what is actually occurring. In most cases, however, the lights flashed so rapidly that it was difficult to distinguish on from off.

RS-232 SUBSETS

If you look at the back of a PC or terminal you might notice that something seems inconsistent with our previous discussion. The connectors to the RS-232 ports do not have 25 pins. Remember that we have discussed the RS-232 standard. Whether a vendor chooses to implement the full standard is another matter. The fact is, many interfaces include only a subset of the RS-232 definitions.

To illustrate, many PC-to-modem connections use a cable with a 25-pin connector at one end and an 8- or 9-pin connector on the other. It sounds a bit like plugging a three-pronged plug into a two-hole socket, but there is a reason for the difference. For versatility, many modems comply with the complete standard. However, many users do not need to use the full range of RS-232 abilities. Primarily they need to communicate much as we have described in the most recent example. Consequently, modem ports generally require an 8- or 9-pin connector using the seven circuits described in the most recent example plus one or both grounds. This decision usually is driven by economics: Why implement (and pay for) the full range of abilities when there is little chance you will ever use them? Cables with different connectors on each end connect only the needed circuits. The extra lines on the modem side are not connected to the PC.

One drawback to the RS-232 standard is its limited bandwidth and distance. It is typically used for transmissions of 20,000 bits per second (bps) over a distance of up to 50 feet. In some cases, such as situations with little interference, longer distances are possible, but in those cases there are other standards, which we discuss shortly.

NULL MODEMS

Sometimes, you may want to allow two devices such as PCs to communicate directly, that is, with no network or DCEs between them. In such cases, your first reaction might be to connect their RS-232 ports with a cable and let the protocols do their job. After all, they both send and receive from the RS-232 ports. Using a simple cable, however, connects the same pins on each side. For example, the cable would connect pin 2 of each DTE. The problem is that both pins try to send over the same line. The first DTE sends data and the second receives it over line 2. Since the second DTE expects to receive data over line 3, the direct connection will not work. Similarly, since the cable connects pin 3 on each end, both expect to receive on the same circuit, but neither sends over it.

One solution to this problem is to connect the DTEs but cross some circuits. Figure 3.9 shows one way to do this using a null modem. A **null modem** may be either a cable connecting different pins on each connector or a device that simply crosses connections using existing cables. Either way, the result is the same. The null modem in Figure 3.9 connects pin 2 on one end to pin 3 on the other end. Consequently, when the DTE sends data using pin 2, it is routed to pin 3 on the other end, where it is received correctly.

Figure 3.9   Null Modem

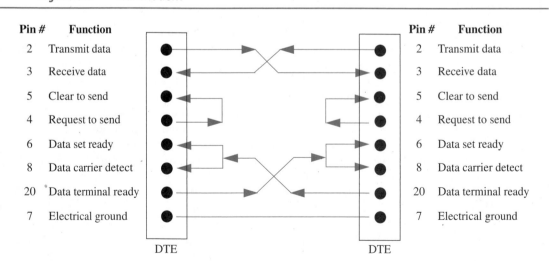

The null modem of Figure 3.9 also connects pins 4 and 5 of the same DTE. The reason for this is found in the example discussed previously. When a DTE wants to transmit, it must request permission and wait for a Clear to Send signal from the DCE. Since there is no DCE, the null modem routes a Request to Send signal (pin 4) back to pin 5. The DTE, sensing its own signal on pin 5, is fooled into thinking the DCE has responded with the Clear to Send message.

The other cross connections make sure each DTE is ready before any transmissions occur. As described previously, the DTE asserts the DTR line 20 when it is ready, expecting the DCE to respond by asserting DSR line 6. Here one DTE's line 20 is routed to the other's line 6, so that when each DTE signals it is ready the other receives that signal. Again, this fools the DTE into thinking its DCE has connected to a network and is also ready.

Figure 3.9 shows just one example of the many variations of null modems. They vary depending on device requirements and how much of the full RS-232 protocol they use. For other variations, see References [St94] and [Ru89].

RS-449 INTERFACE

As mentioned previously, the RS-232 standard was limited in bandwidth and distance. Another standard, **RS-449** (sometimes referred to as EIA-449), was designed to replace it and increase both distance and bandwidth. The RS-449 standard, unlike RS-232, differentiates between operational and electrical specifications. That is, RS-449 defines pin functions, but relies on one of two other standards, RS-422 or RS-423, for the electrical standards. We will discuss these standards shortly.

RS-449 defines a 37-pin connection and looks a lot like the one in Figure 3.7, except that it has more pins. Many of the circuit functions are similar to those of RS-232, and it also provides new ones for modem testing. Table 3.2 lists the circuits and their functions. The left set of columns in the table defines circuits that have similar counterparts in RS-232; the right columns define new functions. Describing each function in detail is beyond this book's goals; if you are interested in more detail consult References [Bl89] and [St94].

The two electrical standards, RS-422 and RS-423, correspond to balanced circuits and unbalanced circuits, respectively. An **unbalanced circuit** uses one line for signal transmission and a common ground. Thus, signal voltage levels are relative to that ground. A **balanced circuit** uses two lines for signal transmission. The transmitting device sends equal but opposite signals over each line. Balanced signals are less susceptible to noise and allow higher transmission rates over longer distances.

Figure 3.10 shows why balanced signals are more reliable. We have seen that a signal is partly determined by its voltage level. With an unbalanced signal the level is the difference between it and the ground. If noise occurs, the level can change and the signal may be interpreted incorrectly. With a balanced signal the lines have equal but opposite signals. In this case, the important measure is the difference between them, not an individual signal's level. The rationale is that if noise does occur it will affect both signals equally. The difference between them is still the same. Since the

Table 3.2   RS-449 Circuit Definitions

CIRCUIT CODE	PIN NUMBER	SIGNAL DIRECTION	FUNCTION
	1		Shield
SG	19		Signal ground
SD	4, 22	DTE to DCE	Send data
RD	6, 24	DCE to DTE	Receive data
RS	7, 25	DTE to DCE	Request to send
CS	9, 27	DCE to DTE	Clear to send
DM	11, 29	DCE to DTE	Data mode
TR	12, 30	DTE to DCE	Terminal ready
IC	15	DCE to DTE	Incoming call
RR	13, 31	DCE to DTE	Receiver ready
SQ	33	DCE to DTE	Signal quality
SR	16	DTE to DCE	Signal rate selector
SI	2	DCE to DTE	Signaling rate indicator
TT	17, 35	DTE to DCE	Terminal timing
ST	5, 23	DCE to DTE	Send timing
RT	8, 26	DCE to DTE	Receive timing
IS	28	DTE to DCE	Terminal in service
LL	10	DTE to DCE	Local loopback
NS	34	DTE to DCE	New signal
RC	20	DCE to DTE	Receive common
RL	14	DTE to DCE	Remote loopback
SB	36	DCE to DTE	Standby indicator
SC	37	DTE to DCE	Send common
F	16	DTE to DCE	Select frequency
SS	32	DTE to DCE	Select standby
TM	18	DCE to DTE	Test mode

receiving device measures only the difference between the signals, the noise hasn't destroyed the information that the difference represents.

This principle is similar to that used in providing homes with 220-volt circuits. Contrary to what some might believe, the current's voltage is not actually doubled. The 110-volt circuit uses two wires, one carrying 110 volts of electricity and the other a ground. With a 220-volt circuit, both lines carry an equal but opposite electric current (they differ in phase shift by 180°). The difference is 220 volts. (This principle also explains why birds can sit on high-voltage lines without being electro-

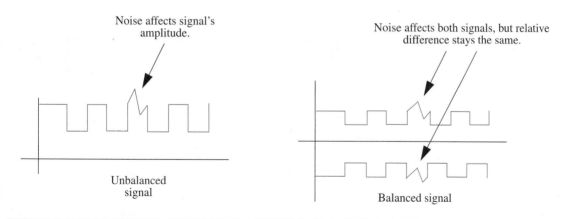

Figure 3.10   Effect of Noise on Balanced and Unbalanced Signals

cuted. As long as they don't touch anything connected to the ground the voltage difference between their toes is 0.)

RS-449 using a balanced signal can transmit up to 10 Mbps over short distances (about 40 feet). Lowering the data rate to 100 Kbps allows transmission up to about 4000 feet. Using an unbalanced circuit, the data rate is limited to 100 Kbps at 40 feet. It also allows for communications up to 4000 feet, but only at a data rate of 1200 bps.

RS-449 also allows for an optional nine-pin connector. The shield, signal ground, send, and receive are pins 1, 5, 9, and 6, respectively. It also defines a secondary data channel sending and receiving over circuits 3 and 4. The last three pins are for secondary channel control, defining a request to send, clear to send, and receiver ready as pins 7, 8, and 2.

X.21 INTERFACE

The **X.21 interface standard** is defined by ITU-T. It uses a 15-pin connector and, like RS-449, allows balanced (electrical standard X.27) and unbalanced (X.26 standard) circuits. There are a couple of significant differences between X.21 and the RS standards. The first is that X.21 was defined as a digital signaling interface. Experts agree that analog communications systems eventually will be replaced by entirely digital ones. Some see X.21 as an interim standard to ISDN (Integrated Services Digital Network). We will discuss ISDN, which some see as the future of worldwide communications, in Chapter 8.

The second difference involves how control information is exchanged. The RS standards define specific circuits for control functions. More control requires more circuits, thus making connections more inconvenient. The principle behind X.21 is to put more logic circuits (intelligence) in the DTE and DCE that can interpret control sequences and reduce the number of connecting circuits.

Table 3.3 shows the X.21 circuit definitions for a balanced circuit. The DTE uses just two circuits (T and C) to transmit to the DCE. Similarly, the DCE uses two

Table 3.3   X.21 Interface Standard for Balanced Circuit

CIRCUIT CODE	PIN NUMBER	SIGNAL DIRECTION	FUNCTION
	1		Shield
G	8		Signal ground
T	2, 9	DTE to DCE	Transmit data or control information
R	4, 11	DCE to DTE	Receive data or control information
C	3, 10	DTE to DCE	Contro
I	5, 12	DCE to DTE	Indication
S	6, 13	DCE to DTE	Signal element timing
B	7, 14	DCE to DTE	Byte timing

(R and I). The other circuits are used for timing signals in synchronous communications. With fewer circuits for transmission, more logic is needed to interpret the signals they carry. Typically, T and R are used to transmit bit strings, and C and I are in an ON (binary 0s) or OFF (binary 1s) state. Consequently, T and R are used for signaling and sending data and control information.

The signals on T, C, R, and I define the states (status) for the DTE and DCE. ITU-T defines many different states for X.21, but we will not elaborate on all of them here. (References [St94] and [Mo89] provide more detail.) We will, however, illustrate how the protocol works for a simple connection.

Figure 3.11 illustrates the signal exchange sequence as the DTE and DCE exchange information. To start, when both DTE and DCE are idle, the C and I circuits are both OFF and the T and R circuits transmit binary 1s. When the DTE wants to connect to a remote DTE, it begins sending 0s over T and sets C to ON (time t_1 in Figure 3.11). The DCE, sensing the change, responds by sending a sequence of + characters over R (time t_2). This is analogous to picking up the handset on a telephone and having the local switching office respond by transmitting the dial tone back to your phone.

If you were placing a phone call your next step would be to dial the number. The DTE responds similarly by transmitting control and data information over T (time t_3). This provides the DCE with necessary information, such as an address, to establish communications with a remote DTE via the network. As the DCE is trying to make the connection it sends a series of SYN characters over R. When the connection is established, the DCE informs the DTE by sending 1s over R and setting I to ON (time t_4).

At this point (time t_5), the DTE and DCE can exchange data, with the DTE using the T circuit and the DCE using R. Eventually, the DTE will decide to terminate its activities. It indicates its intention to the DCE by transmitting 0s over T and setting C to OFF (time t_6). The DCE confirms the intention by transmitting 0s over R and setting I to OFF (time t_7). Finally, the DCE disconnects by transmitting 1s over R

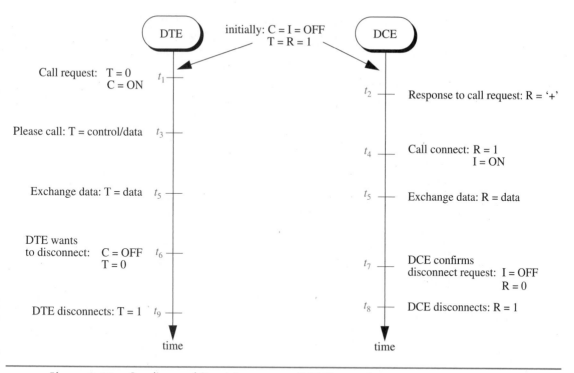

Figure 3.11   Sending and Receiving over an X.21 Connection

(time t_8), and the DTE disconnects by transmitting 1s over T (time t_9). This brings both devices to the idle state with which we began this example.

There are many other interface standards, but describing them all is far beyond the scope of this text. (Reference [Sh90] lists approximately 100 such standards.) We have described some of the most common or well-known standards here and will describe a couple of others later (that is, the X.25 network interface in Chapter 7 and ISDN in Chapter 8).

3.3   MULTIPLEXING

When it comes to data transmissions, it should not be hard to convince you that higher data rates are better. If you have ever upgraded to a faster PC, disk drive, or modem, you no doubt found that the faster response times helped you work more efficiently. Remember when the first $3^1/_2$-inch drives first became available? The ability to get a file in just a couple of seconds was a wonderful improvement over the $5^1/_4$-inch drives. And with the hard disk drives available today, we now have to find ways to amuse ourselves while waiting for anything on a $3^1/_2$-inch disk.

The same is true of networks and communications: Faster is generally better. Speed does have its drawbacks, however. First, it is more expensive; second, it has a point of diminishing returns. That is, after a certain point many users can't make use of the increased speed. For example, a common bit rate over networks is 10 Mbps. Some PC applications simply do not have the volume of data necessary to make use of that speed. Even if they did, many DTE-DCE interfaces don't provide data rates anywhere near 10 Mbps (remember the limits on the RS-232 interface from the previous section).

One response is to not worry about developing high-speed networks because most users cannot utilize their full potential. This solution has a serious flaw, however. Suppose the network shown in Figure 3.12 supports a bit rate of 64 Kbps (for simplicity, the DCEs are not shown). If the only activity involves two PCs communicating at that rate, the network serves its purpose. However, if several hundred PCs need to communicate with one another, the 64 Kbps limit will create quite a bottleneck. Increasing the bit data rate will reduce it. A good analogy is a major freeway system in a large city during rush hour. If traffic moves at 15 mph, the lines on entrance ramps will grow very long. If traffic moves at a normal speed of 55 mph, the cars will not wait as long to enter the freeway.

A second response to the problems of higher bit rates is to develop high-speed networks but somehow reduce the cost of connecting to them. In Figure 3.12, there is a

Figure 3.12   Many Users Communicating over a Network

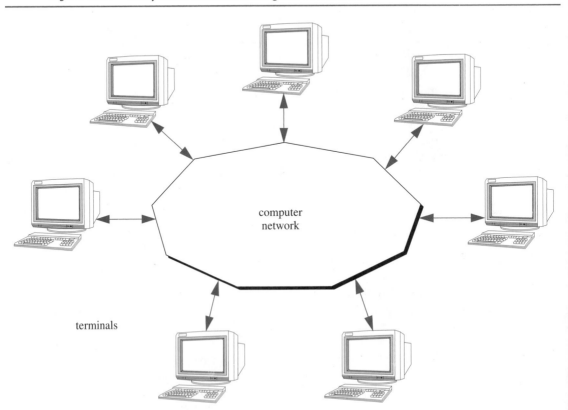

cost for each PC connection. Figure 3.13 shows a common alternative using a **multiplexer** (sometimes called **mux** to minimize transmission from the larynx and movement of muscles in and around the vocal cavity known as the mouth). It is a device that routes transmissions from multiple sources to a single destination. In Figure 3.13, the sources are PCs and the destination is the network. The multiplexer also routes transmissions in the reverse direction, from the network to any of the PCs.

In general, a multiplexer's output line to the network has a much higher bit rate than any of the input lines from the PCs. This way it can utilize the network's high bit rate and, by providing a single connection for multiple users, cut the cost per connection.

This description of multiplexing is just one of several depending on the signal types and the activity of the units connected to it. Next, we will describe specific multiplexing methods and provide an example used in long-distance telephone communications.

FREQUENCY-DIVISION MULTIPLEXING

Frequency-division multiplexing (FDM) is used with analog signals. Perhaps its most common use is in television and radio transmission. A multiplexer accepts analog signals from multiple sources, each of which has a specified bandwidth. The signals then are combined into another, more complex signal with a much larger

Figure 3.13   Multiplexing Low-Speed Devices

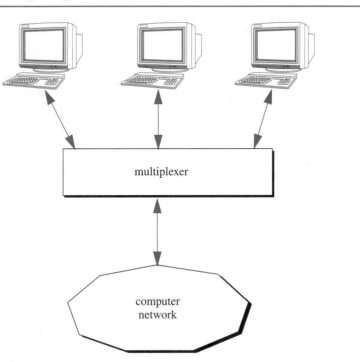

bandwidth. The resulting signal is transmitted over some medium to its destination, where another mux extracts and separates the individual components.

This method of multiplexing involves several steps. First, the available bandwidth of the transmission medium is divided into separate ranges or channels. For example, the bandwidth for broadcast television (54 Mhz to 806 MHz) is divided into 68 channels of 6 MHz each. VHF channels 2 to 13 correspond to 6 MHz bands between 54 MHz and 215 MHz. UHF channels 14 to 69 correspond to 6 MHz bands between 470 MHz and 806 MHz. Each channel corresponds to one of the multiplexer's input signals.

Next, a **carrier signal** is defined for each channel. It is changed (modulated) by the corresponding input signal to create another signal (modulated signal). There are several ways to do this. For example, Figure 3.14 illustrates amplitude modulation. The carrier signal has a specified frequency, typically centered in a channel's bandwidth. Its amplitude is changed to alternate between values depending on the other signal's maximum and minimum values.

A complete understanding of amplitude modulation requires some knowledge of the mathematical representation of wave forms and Fourier series. Consequently, a detailed explanation is beyond the scope of this text. If you want a more rigorous discussion, see References [St94], [Wa91a], and [St96]. We can, however, illustrate the process using a simple example.

Consider an analog signal corresponding to the formula $f(t) = [\sin(2\pi t)/4] + 0.5$. Figure 3.15 shows its graph between $t = 0$ and $t = 2$. Suppose the carrier signal corresponds to $g(t) = \sin(10 \times 2\pi t)$. Figure 3.15 does not show the graph of $g(t)$ but, if drawn, its graph would oscillate 20 times between 1 and −1 as t ranged from 0 to 2. Multiplying $f(t)$ and $g(t)$ generates the modulated signal shown in Figure 3.15.

In general, signals have much higher frequencies and correspond to complex sums of sine functions. Still, the process of amplitude modulation remains essentially the same as in the example. Other modulation techniques are frequency modulation and phase modulation. As you might expect, frequency modulation alters the frequency of the carrier depending on the input signal, and phase modulation alters

Figure 3.14   Amplitude Modulation

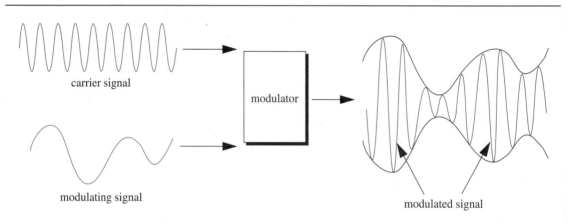

carrier signal

modulator

modulating signal

modulated signal

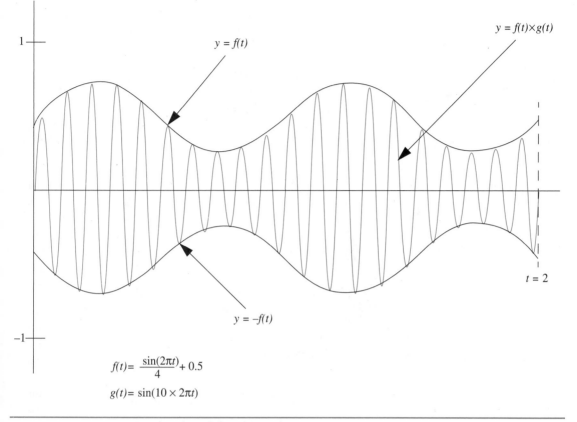

$$f(t)= \frac{\sin(2\pi t)}{4}+ 0.5$$

$$g(t)= \sin(10 \times 2\pi t)$$

Figure 3.15 Graphs of Modulated Signal

the signal's phase shift. Again, References [St94] and [Wa91a] contain more rigorous discussions.

In the last step of frequency-division multiplexing, the modulated signals from all the inputs are combined into a single, more complex analog signal (Figure 3.16). Its frequencies lie within the ranges of all the channels. The channels themselves are separated by **guard bands** (unused parts of the frequency range) in order to prevent interference between adjacent channels. The resulting signal is transmitted and another multiplexer receives it. It then uses bandpass filters to extract the individual modulated signals. Finally, the signals are demodulated and the original signals restored. In applications such as television and radio, the channel or frequency selectors specify which of the original signals is converted to sound and picture.

TIME-DIVISION MULTIPLEXING

In time-division multiplexing (TDM) many input signals are combined and transmitted together, as with FDM. TDM is used with digital signals, however. As a result,

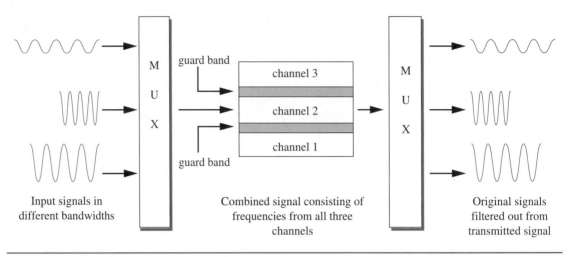

Figure 3.16 Frequency Division Multiplexing

TDM keeps the signals physically distinct but logically packages them together, in contrast to FDM, which combines them into a single, more complex signal.

Figure 3.17 illustrates TDM. Suppose A_i, B_i, C_i, and D_i (i = 1, 2, 3, . . .) represent bit streams from distinct sources. A few bits from each source are buffered temporarily in the multiplexer. The multiplexer scans each buffer, storing the bits from each in a frame, and then sends the frame. As it does so, it begins building a new frame by again scanning the input buffers for new data that has arrived. If the timing is right it will construct a new frame just in time to transmit it immediately

Figure 3.17 Time-Division Multiplexing

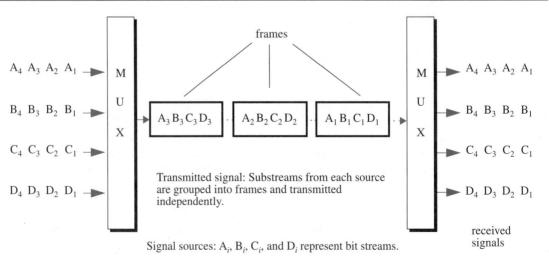

following the previous one. This process keeps the output line active and makes full use of its capacity.

In Figure 3.17 the bit streams A_1, B_1, C_1, and D_1 are buffered separately. The multiplexer packages them into a single frame and transmits it. It then follows by gathering A_2, B_2, C_2, and D_2 and sending another frame. The process continues as long as the sources are providing bit streams.

The multiplexer's design depends in part on the input and output transmission rates. For example, if source bits from the combined inputs arrive faster than the previous frame can be sent, frames are generated more quickly than they can be forwarded. If the multiplexer has no capacity to store the extra frames, they are lost. We must not supply the multiplexer with information faster than it can release it. On the other hand, if the source bits arrive too slowly, the previous frame will have been sent and the multiplexer has to wait for enough bits to arrive to form a new one. During this time the output line is idle and the multiplexer is not using it to its fullest capacity.

The optimal situation is when the global input rate (sum of rates from each source) equals the output rate. Suppose r_i is the input rate from the ith source and r_{output} is the multiplexer's transmission rate. Mathematically, we express this as

$$\sum_{i=1}^{n} r_i = r_{\text{output}}.$$ For example, if data from 10 sources arrived at a rate of 9.6 Kbps, the multiplexer should be able to send them at a rate of 96 Kbps. (We describe an alternative shortly.)

Another part of the multiplexer's design is the size of the frame components. One design defines A_i, B_i, C_i, and D_i as eight bits or one byte. In this case it is called a **byte multiplexer.** In other cases, A_i, B_i, C_i, and D_i are larger, containing many bytes (a block). In this case, strangely enough, it is called a **block multiplexer.**

STATISTICAL MULTIPLEXERS

Previously, we stated that an optimal design requires that the sum of input rates equals the output rate. However, sometimes this is not practical. In the previous example, we assumed that bits were arriving from each source continuously, but in many cases they arrive in bursts with periods of inactivity in between. This is especially true when the sources are terminals and the user alternates between thinking and typing. It is also true for an intelligent terminal where a user enters a screenful of data locally and sends the entire screen. There is a delay as the user enters another screenful of data.

In such cases there are two approaches for multiplexing the data. The first is to design the multiplexer to skip empty buffers and leave part of the frame vacant. For example, in Figure 3.17 suppose the third source was inactive. That is, C_1 C_2, C_3, and C_4 do not exist. Each frame would have space reserved for those bits, but would not contain any meaningful information. This has the advantage of keeping all the frames the same size and simplifying the protocols. The obvious disadvantage is that useless information occupies the transmission medium and thus wastes bandwidth.

Another approach is to have the multiplexer scan the buffers and create a variable-size frame depending on how many buffers contain data. We call this a **statistical multiplexer.** Some also use the term **concentrator.**[*]

Figure 3.18 shows how this works. Here all sources are active, but not at the same time. The symbol $\varnothing$ indicates that no information has arrived from a source. Initially bit streams A_1 and C_1 are buffered, but the others are empty due to inactivity at the sources. Therefore, the multiplexer puts A_1 and C_1 into a frame and sends it on its way. In the meantime A_2 and C_2, along with B_1, arrive. The multiplexer puts them together in another, larger frame and sends it. At this point there is inactivity from the C source, but the D source becomes active. Now A_3, B_2, and D_1 arrive. As before, the multiplexer puts them in a frame and sends it. This process continues as long as any of the inputs are active.

A complication with this approach is that sources are no longer assigned a fixed position in the frame. For example, in Figure 3.17 bits from each source always occupied the same positions in a frame. In Figure 3.18, this is not so. For example, bits from source B sometimes occupied the second or third positions (counting from the right). In such cases the frame format is more complex and requires additional information such as destination addresses. The receiving multi-

Figure 3.18 Statistical Time Division Multiplexing

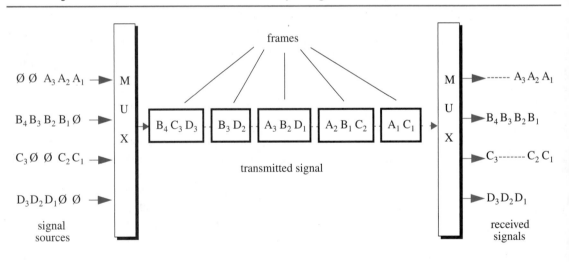

---

[*]Strictly speaking, the two terms are different. A *concentrator* is a more intelligent statistical multiplexer that allows us to do other things such as verify, acknowledge, and compress data. These are topics we discuss in Section 3.5 and in Chapters 4 and 5. The actual definitions often depend on to whom you talk. We will not make a distinction here. In fact, sometimes the term **asynchronous time-division multiplexer** is used.

plexer must have additional logic to seek out the addresses and route the information in the correct direction.

As defined, a statistical multiplexer may not fully use its output capacity. In the extreme case, if no sources are active there are no transmissions. The probability that none are active depends on how many sources there are. An astute observer may notice that we could connect additional sources to decrease this probability and keep the output line busier. If this happens, then $\sum_{i=1}^{n} r_i > r_{output}$. That is, the input capacity of the multiplexer is now larger than its output capacity.

Having a higher input rate is not necessarily a problem. Remember, r_i represents the capacity of the ith source, not its actual rate. If it is inactive, the actual bit rate is 0. The design assumes that although the sum of input rates is larger than r_{output} the sources are not all active at the same time. The ideal is where the combined input rate from active sources is equal to r_{output}. Since activity depends on the user, it is hard to predict and the ideal is difficult to achieve. There will be times when the combined input rate from active sources is smaller or even larger than r_{output}. In the latter case, additional logic and buffers must be designed in order to accommodate temporary surges in data. This is one reason they are sometimes called concentrators: They concentrate additional data for brief periods.

An analysis of statistical multiplexers can be difficult because of the random way in which the sources send data. Many questions must be asked. How frequently will the combined input rates exceed the output rate? How often will all sources be busy? How large must the internal buffers be to handle temporary surges? How long are the delays when surges occur? One approach to the analysis is the use of **queuing theory,** a field of mathematics that defines models for studying events such as waiting in lines (queues) for events to occur. It can be applied to many areas, including communications systems in which input streams may arrive in random patterns. In such cases the events are the transmissions over the output lines. References [St94], [Wa96], and [Ma72] contain introductory discussions of queuing theory.

T-1 CARRIER

We close this section with a discussion of a multiplexing standard used in long distance communications. Much of what we think of as the "telephone system" was designed to transmit digitized voice signals over high-speed media such as optical fiber or microwaves. In fact, AT&T developed a complex hierarchy of communications systems used to multiplex voice signals and transmit them all over the United States. The system is also used in other countries such as Canada and Japan. Still other countries use a similar but different system defined by ITU-T standards.

This system uses **time-division multiplexing** to combine many voice channels into one frame. Of the many ways to do this, one approach uses T-1 transmission and DS-1 signaling. The designations **T-1** and **DS-1** refer to the circuit and signal, respectively. For example, Figure 3.19 shows a DS-1 frame in which voice data is digitized using pulse code modulation (discussed in Chapter 2). It contains 193 bits divided into 24 slots (one for each channel) of 8 bits each. This leaves one extra bit called a **framing bit,** which is used for synchronizing.

Figure 3.20 shows how a T-1 carrier system works. Eight-bit voice samples are taken from each of 24 channels at a rate of 8000 per second. Each sample then occupies one slot in the DS-1 frame. According to the Nyquist theorem from Chapter 2, this is sufficient to maintain all the information in the original voice analog signal. Consecutive samples are stored in different DS-1 frames. The voice messages are thus transmitted using many DS-1 frames to another multiplexer. This one extracts the bits from each slot and routes them to their appropriate destination, where they eventually are converted back to analog signals. The result is converted into the original sound of the person's voice.

What is the bit rate of the T-1 carrier system? Each 8-bit slot is generated at a rate of 8000 per second for a rate of 64 Kbps. To support this speed, T-1 must transmit a DS-1 frame every 1/8000 of a second, or 8000 frames per second. In other words, it must transmit 8000×193 bits each second for a data rate of 1.544 Mbps. This rate is fast by some standards but pales when compared with the capabilities of optical fibers or microwaves. Consequently, there are other carrier and signal designations with more channels and faster bit rates. Table 3.4 summarizes some of them. A common approach is to multiplex signals from a low-speed carrier into a high-speed one. For example, the T-3 carrier could multiplex 7 DS-2 frames, 14 DS-1C frames, or 28 DS-1 frames, giving it the ability to carry 672 channels in each frame.

Voice data is not the only type that can be transmitted. Many companies lease phone lines to transfer digital information between computers. In fact, the principle behind the fax machine is to convert images on paper to digital signals and transmit them over telephone lines.

As a final note, we mention that the number of channels in each system can be increased by using different modulation techniques. Pulse code modulation digitizes voice information at a rate of 64 Kbps. Adaptive differential pulse code modulation digitizes voice information at 32 Kbps, which allows each of the carrier systems to support twice as many channels as listed in Table 3.4.

Figure 3.19   DS-1 Frame

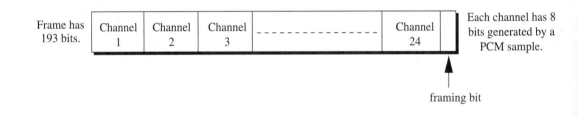

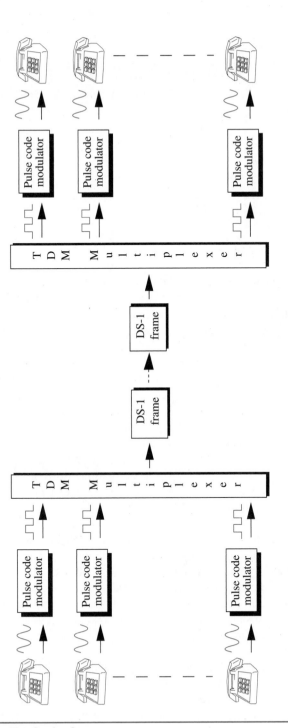

Figure 3.20   T-1 Carrier System

Table 3.4   North American Communication Carriers

CARRIER	FRAME FORMAT	NUMBER OF CHANNELS	DATA RATE IN MBPS
T-1	DS-1	24	1.544
T-1c	DS-1C	48	3.152
T-2	DS-2	96	6.312
T-3	DS-3	672	44.376
T-4	DS-4	4032	274.176

3.4   CONTENTION PROTOCOLS

Multiplexing (particularly TDM) goes a long way toward making a medium available to many users, but it is not enough. To route all users through a multiplexer onto a medium is unrealistic for two reasons. First, there may be too many users for a single multiplexer. Second, the logistics may prohibit a user from using a particular multiplexer.

A highway system provides a nice analogy. Interstate highway 94 connects Chicago and Seattle. In Chicago, many interchanges (the automobile's multiplexer) allow a driver access to the highway. But what if someone in Fargo, North Dakota, wants access to the highway in order to drive to Seattle? Would we expect her to first drive to Chicago, some 600 miles in the wrong direction? Of course not. She simply uses another access point to the interstate.

Communications media are similar. The multiplexer provides access for many users to one access point, but a large network requires many access points, just as the interstate highway system does. Access to the medium from many entry points is called **contention**. It is controlled with a **contention protocol**. Figure 3.21 shows what happens with no contention protocol in the highway system. Vehicles enter randomly and collisions occur periodically. At best they are unpleasant; at worst they are fatal. Fortunately, the highway system is not set up this way (although, with some drivers, you'd never know it). Figure 3.22 shows a common and simple contention strategy for traffic. This stop-and-go protocol uses traffic lights to control access. As long as motorists abide by the protocol they can avoid the situation shown in Figure 3.21. We assume that unless you are from a remote area in the Himalayas you are familiar with the details of this protocol and we won't discuss it further.

Communications require some protocol to ensure that transmitted data reaches its destination. This section explores some of the protocols used. Perhaps not surprisingly, there are many options depending on the actual medium, the amount of traffic, and the sophistication of the needs (which has a direct correlation to cost).

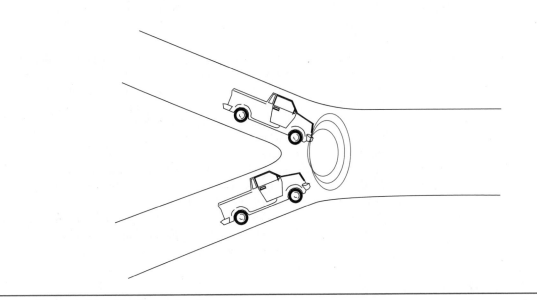

Figure 3.21   No Contention Protocol

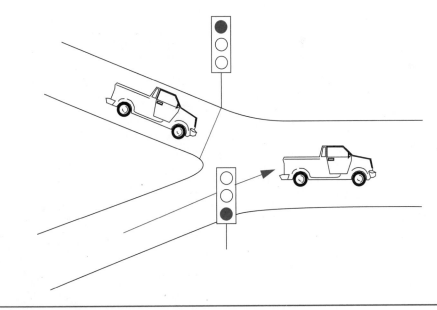

Figure 3.22   Stop-and-Go Access Protocol

ALOHA PROTOCOLS

One of the earliest contention protocols was developed in an area quite different from the remote area of the Himalayas. The **Aloha protocol** was developed at the University of Hawaii in the early 1970s. We also call it **pure Aloha** in contrast to another protocol we discuss shortly. The Aloha system was designed to establish communication among the islands using a packet radio system. The word *packet* or *frame*[*] refers to the information broadcast during a single transmission. Terminals (Figure 3.23) were connected to a radio channel, which in turn broadcast information from the terminal to a central facility called the Menehune. Stations broadcast frames at the same frequency. Consequently, the medium (the airspace) was truly shared. Any attempt to broadcast two different frames simultaneously using the same frequency disrupted both signals. The end result, of course, was that neither transmission was successful.

The Aloha protocol worked on a very simple principle. Essentially, it allowed for any station to broadcast at any time. If two signals collided, so be it. Each station

Figure 3.23   Aloha System

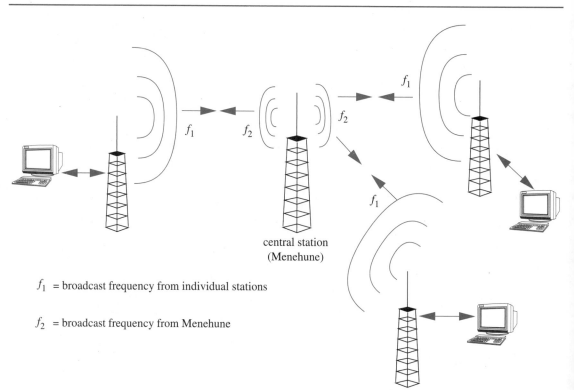

central station
(Menehune)

f_1 = broadcast frequency from individual stations

f_2 = broadcast frequency from Menehune

---

[*]Depending on the protocol, the term *packet* or *frame* may be used to indicate the contents of a single transmission. For now we continue to use the term *frame*.

would simply wait a random time and try again. The highway analogy would be to enter the freeway with your eyes closed. If you have a collision, get a new car and try again. Although it would be an expensive protocol for traffic control, it worked well for the Aloha system.

Collisions were detected quite easily. When the Menehune received a frame it sent an acknowledgment. It used a different frequency so as not to interfere with incoming signals. If a station received an acknowledgment, it concluded that its frame was transmitted successfully. If not, it assumed a collision occurred and waited to send again. Because each station waited a random time, the chance that two or more stations waited the same time was reduced. In turn this reduced the chances of a second collision. If they did collide a second time (perhaps even with another station) the same rules applied: Wait a random amount of time and try again.

In this type of situation, collisions occur not only when two stations send simultaneously, but also when two transmissions overlap even by the smallest amount. It does not matter if all or part of the frame is destroyed. It's like receiving a telephone call and hearing "I've got good news for you. You have just $%^#$%." If the "$%^#$%" represents static you don't know if you won the lottery, received an inheritance, or were elected to political office (good news?). What's lost is gone, and conventional wisdom dictates the entire frame be sent again.

The advantage of the Aloha protocol is its simplicity. It works very well if there are not many transmissions, but if a station broadcasts more frequently or there are more stations, the protocol is less effective. In either case, more collisions occur—just as they do on heavily traveled roads.

When we are faced with increased transmissions, what can we do to decrease the collisions? First, let us analyze a little more closely how collisions occur. As stated, a collision occurs if any part of two transmissions overlaps. Suppose that T is time required for one transmission and that two stations must transmit. The total time required for both stations to do so successfully is $2T$.

Next, consider an arbitrary interval of time $2T$. Unless one station begins its transmission at the start of the interval, completing both transmissions before the end of the interval is impossible. (Why?) Consequently, allowing a station to transmit at arbitrary times can waste time up to $2T$.

As an alternative, suppose we divide time into intervals (slots) of T units each and require each station to begin each transmission at the beginning of a slot. In other words, even if a station is ready to send in the middle of a slot, it must wait until the start of the next one (Figure 3.24b). This way, the only time a collision occurs is when both stations become ready in the same slot. Contrast this to the previous scenario (3.24a), where a collision occurs if the second station transmits when the frame is ready.

Requiring a station to transmit at the beginning of a time slot is the **slotted Aloha protocol**. According to the previous discussion, it would seem to perform better than the pure Aloha protocol. In fact, a rigorous analysis of both protocols shows that the slotted Aloha protocol does perform better. We'll not provide a detailed description of the analysis here, but we will summarize the findings and interpret them. More rigorous discussions are found in references [Wa91a], [St94], [Ro75], [Ru89], and [Mi87].

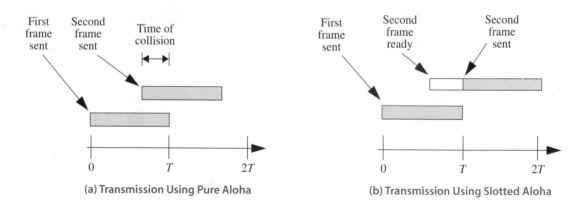

| (a) Transmission Using Pure Aloha | (b) Transmission Using Slotted Aloha |

Figure 3.24 Transmission Using Pure Aloha and Slotted Aloha

Intuitively, we know there is a relationship between the number of frames sent and the number sent successfully. A mathematical model can be created that, under certain assumptions, defines the relationship as follows.

Let G represent the traffic measured as the average number of frames generated per slot. Let S be the success rate measured as the average number of frames sent successfully per slot. (e is the mathematical constant 2.718 . . . .) The relationship between G and S for both pure and slotted Aloha is

$$S = Ge^{-2G} \text{ (pure Aloha)}$$

$$S = Ge^{-G} \text{ (slotted Aloha)}$$

Your next logical question is probably "So what? What does it mean?" For an answer, look at the graphs in Figure 3.25. The vertical axis represents S and the horizontal one represents G. Values for S range from 0 to 1. Since we have chosen the slot time to equal that required to send one frame, S can be no larger.

First note that both graphs have the same basic shape. If G is small, so is S. This makes sense since few frames will be sent successfully if there are only a few frames generated. As G increases so does S, up to a point. More transmissions mean more successfully sent frames, until they start colliding. At that point, which corresponds to the high point on each graph, the success rate decreases. As G continues to increase, S approaches 0. This corresponds to the situation in which there are so many frames that they are almost always colliding. It becomes a rare event when a frame gets through without colliding.

The model shows how the pure and slotted Aloha protocols compare. Differential calculus shows how to calculate the maximum value in each case. If you are familiar with the details, just take the derivative of each function with respect to G and equate with 0. In any case, the maximum for slotted Aloha occurs at $G = 1$, for which $S = 1/e \approx 0.368$. In other words, the best rate of successful transmissions is approximately .368 frames per slot time. Another way to say it is that about 37% of

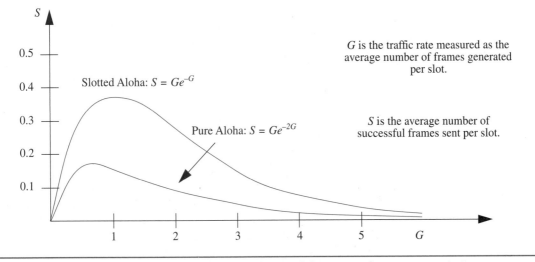

Figure 3.25   Success Rate for Slotted and Pure Aloha Protocols

the time will be spent on successful transmissions. The rest will be on collisions or idle time.

For pure Aloha, the maximum occurs at $G = 0.5$, for which $S = 1/2e \approx 0.184$. Again, this means that approximately 18% of the time is spent on successful transmissions.

At first it may seem strange that slotted Aloha generally won't provide a better success rate. Providing not much more than a frame every three lots seems like underachieving. But a critical assumption the models make is that frames become ready randomly. There is no intent to coordinate transmissions beyond waiting until the beginning of the next slot. As the model shows, this important assumption degrades performance.

Another question might be, Should we try to coordinate transmissions in order to achieve better efficiency? In general, the answer is no. If you were at a PC connected to a network, you would probably find it inconvenient to coordinate your network access with others. Most users want access on demand and expect the protocols and hardware to provide good response.

CARRIER SENSE MULTIPLE ACCESS

An observant person might ask, "Couldn't we improve on the success rate if the stations listened to the medium[*] for existing transmissions before sending its own?" They certainly have the capability to determine when frames are in transit. Why not

---

[*]Although the Aloha system was developed for packet radio, we use the term *medium* in a very general sense. Unless otherwise specified, it may be air space, fiber, cable, or twisted pair.

hold a frame until another has finished? This way a station would not destroy a frame currently being sent, and the success rate should improve.

The idea of listening makes sense and is used in many networks today such as Ethernet (actually Ethernet uses a variation of it that we describe later). We call this approach **Carrier Sense Multiple Access (CSMA).** In general, the protocol is described simply. If a station has a frame to send it does the following:

1. Listen to the medium for any activity.

2. If there is no activity, transmit; otherwise wait.

Does this system eliminate collisions? It will eliminate some but not all. A collision still can occur if two (or more) stations want to transmit at nearly the same time. If there is currently no activity, both conclude that it is safe to send and do so. The result, of course, is a collision. However, such collisions generally are less common because there is a very small time delay between when a station detects no activity and when its transmitted frame reaches other stations. In order for a collision to occur, another station must decide to transmit within this period of time. Since the interval is small, so is the probability that the second station will send a frame in that interval.

But collisions still can occur, and variations on CSMA try to improve efficiency by reducing the number of them. With one type, **p-persistent CSMA,** the station continues to monitor an active medium. When it becomes quiet, the station transmits with probability p ($0 \le p \le 1$). Otherwise it waits for one time slot (probability of $1 - p$). Note that if $p = 1$ the station always transmits when the medium is quiet. If $p = 0$ it always waits. With **nonpersistent CSMA,** the station does not continue to monitor the medium. It simply waits one time slot and again checks for activity. At this point it transmits, if the medium is idle; otherwise, it waits another time slot.

Collisions still can be a problem, especially with p-persistent CSMA. If two stations want to transmit at nearly the same time and the medium is idle, a collision occurs. Although collisions for this reason may not be common, they occur in other ways. For example, consider the case where $p = 1$. If two (or more) stations become ready while another is transmitting, both wait. But since $p = 1$, both stations send when the first is done and their frames collide. As more stations transmit, this scenario occurs more frequently and collisions become more of a problem.

One way to reduce the frequency of collisions is to lower the probability that a station will send when a previous one is done. For example, suppose two stations using a 0.5-persistent protocol are waiting. When the medium is idle, each sends with a probability of 0.5. Thus, four events occur with equal probability:

- They both transmit immediately.
- They both wait.
- The first sends and the second waits.
- The second sends and the first waits.

Rather than a certain collision, there is a 0.5 probability that one will be able to send the beginning of the next slot. (Note, however, that there is also a 0.25 probability that neither sends. This is another type of inefficiency that we will discuss shortly.)

Figure 3.26 shows the success rates of various p-persistent protocols. We will not discuss the equations that generate these curves because they are somewhat complex. However, we do consider the results and what they mean. If you are interested in the actual equations or their derivations, see Reference [Kl75].

In general, smaller values of p result in fewer collisions. However, the number of waiting stations increases and causes a proportionate increase in the chances no one will send at all. Still, as the number of stations increases, the traffic goes up. The probability that at least two will send simultaneously increases, and eventually collisions become a problem again.

With nonpersistent CSMA no station waits for the medium to be idle. Instead, each checks periodically and waits one time slot if it is busy. Thus, the only times collisions occur are when two stations detect a quiet medium at nearly the same time. As Figure 3.26 shows, the success rate increases with G and for large values of G is much better than that of persistent or Aloha protocols.

The success rate is only one statistic and can be misleading, however. As we defined it, the success rate is impressive, but it isn't achieved until there is a glut of frames that stations want to send. For example, the model's equations show that a

Figure 3.26   Success Rate of CSMA and Aloha Protocols

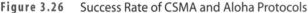

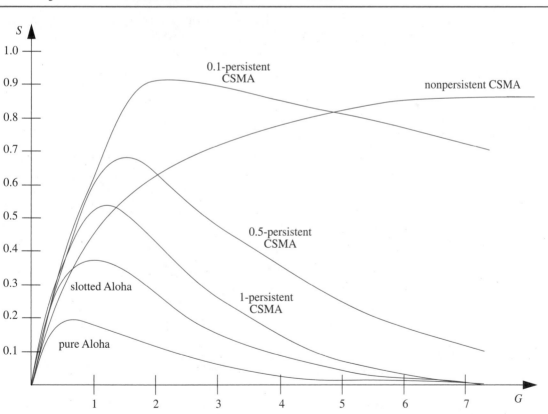

success rate of 0.9 is achieved when $G = 9$. In other words, 90% of the time is spent sending frames only when they are generated at a rate of 9 per slot. This is a rate that exceeds the medium's capacity by a factor of 9. In this case we have other problems far exceeding those caused by the protocol. The stations are saturating the medium, thus causing delays.

A good analogy here is a bank that hires only one teller on its busiest days. Customers wait about 45 minutes to make a deposit and complain to the manager. The manager responds by stating that the teller is busy most of the time and therefore there is no problem. It's now time to take your money and hide it in your mattress.

For smaller values of G, the persistent protocols have higher success rates because idle time is more of a problem for the nonpersistent protocols. If a station detects another transmitting, it waits a full slot. If the transmission ends well before that time, the medium is unnecessarily idle. For lighter traffic, the nonpersistent protocol is not aggressive enough.

COLLISION DETECTION

Another way to improve the success rates is to reduce the time during which collisions occur. Previously, when a station had a frame, it sent the whole thing and concluded that a collision occurred when it did not get responses. The problem is that the medium is unusable for others during the time the frame is colliding. Is there some way to have a station monitor the medium to listen for collisions? If so, it could stop transmissions immediately and decrease the time that signals are colliding.

Figure 3.27 illustrates. In Figure 3.27a, the time of collision spans from the transmission of the first frame to the end of the second one. The wasted time could

Figure 3.27   Collision with and without Detection

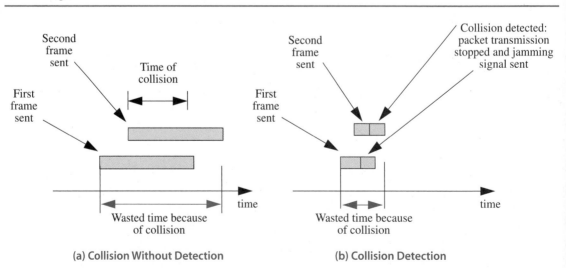

(a) Collision Without Detection

(b) Collision Detection

extend up to two time slots. In Figure 3.27b, both stations stop transmitting when the collision occurs. Typically each will send a jamming signal (a type of electronic scream) to ensure that all stations know a collision has occurred. In this case, the wasted time spans only part of a slot and the time to send a short jamming signal.

Such a protocol exists and is commonly used with CSMA. We call it **Carrier Sense Multiple Access with Collision Detection (CSMA/CD)**. CSMA/CD typically is used with one of the persistence algorithms. We summarize it as follows:

- If a medium is busy, the station waits per the persistence algorithm.
- If the medium is quiet, the station transmits the frame and continues to listen.
- If it detects a collision, it immediately stops transmitting and sends a short jamming signal.
- After a collision it waits a random amount of time before trying to send again.

The last step is important to reduce the chances that two frames will collide a second time. There is certainly no point in two stations waiting the same amount of time just to have their frames collide again.

Two issues that surface in a discussion of collision detection are frame size and transmission distance. If frames are too large, one station can monopolize the medium. On the other hand, collision detection requires that frames be at least a minimum size so that a station can detect a collision before it finishes sending the frame. If it detects a collision after the frame is sent, it does not know if its frame was involved. The frame may have reached its destination and two others collided. You might respond by suggesting that we could use the method described previously that looks for an acknowledgment. We could, but we would defeat the reason for collision detection in the first place: to avoid sending the entire frame before a collision occurs.

Next question: How small should a frame be? The answer depends on the maximum time it takes to detect a collision. Sometimes a collision is detected almost immediately. In other cases, the signal may travel a very long distance only to meet another signal. Even then the noise from the collision must travel back to the sending station. Consequently, in the worst case, the time to detect a collision is twice the time it takes a signal to span the longest distance covered by the medium.

As an example, suppose the following:

- A station sends frames over a coaxial cable at a rate of 10 Mbps.
- The largest distance between two stations on the cable is 2 km.
- A signal propagates along a cable at a rate of 200 m/μsec (meters per microsecond).

In the worst case, the frame travels 2 km (taking 10 μsec) before it collides with another. The corrupted signal then travels 2 km back to the sending station. The round trip takes a total of 20 μsec. Thus, a frame should require at least 20 μsec to send. A data rate of 10 Mbps is the same as putting out 10 bits per μsec; therefore, it could put out 200 bits in 20 μsec. This would mean that the frame should be at least 200 bits, or 200/8 = 25 bytes long. Chapter 6 discusses specific networks and protocols, and we will see that they do indeed specify minimum frame sizes.

The other problem in collision detection is distance. For example, listening and collision detection do not work well for satellite networks, in which the time required for a frame to travel from ground to satellite and back is approximately one quarter of a second. That may not sound like much, but in a world measured in microseconds it is a very long time. If a ground station listened for satellite transmissions it could detect only what was sent one quarter of a second ago. Consequently, it may hear nothing when in reality someone else's frame is speeding up to the satellite on a collision course with anything that might be sent.

A strong advantage of the protocols discussed so far is that the protocol need not be changed when new stations are added. A station need not have knowledge of any other particular station. The ability to add new stations without changing the protocol makes growth easier. A significant disadvantage, however, is the fact that collisions do occur. We have argued that the protocols can work well, yet there is no theoretical limit on the number of collisions that can occur. There is always a small chance that unusual delays will occur. For most applications a periodic delay is not serious, but they can be disastrous in real-time applications such as chemical and nuclear plants, air traffic control systems, or factory automation.

In some cases, the wait times after collisions occur are not completely random. One common technique defines the wait time as an integral multiple of a slot time. The number of slot times must be limited so a station does not wait excessively long.

Defining the limits is not easy, however. For example, if the limit were large, random waits may also be large and cause excessive idle time. On the other hand, the larger number of slot times from which to choose lessens the chance that two or more stations will choose the same and collide again. If the limit were fairly small, colliding stations would not wait long, but with fewer slot times to choose from the chances for a second collision increase.

A technique called **binary exponential backoff** varies the limit. It works in the following way:

- If a station's frame collides for the first time, wait 0 or 1 time slot (chosen randomly) before trying again.
- If it collides a second time, wait 0, 1, 2, or 3 slots (again, chosen randomly).
- After a third collision, wait anywhere from 0 to 7 slots.
- In general, after n collisions, wait anywhere from 0 to $2^n - 1$ slots if $n \leq 10$. If $n > 10$ wait between 0 and 1024 (2^{10}) slots.
- After 16 collisions, give up. There is probably an error somewhere and the inability to transmit the frame is reported to the controlling computer. In this case, other software or a network manager must investigate in order to determine the problem.

This approach clearly tries to minimize excessive waits by keeping the number of possible time slots small. After all, if two stations collide there is a 50% chance they will succeed on the next try (assuming that no other stations are sending).

If many stations collide, however, the chances are very small that even one will be successful on the next try. The successful one would have to choose either 0 or 1 slot with all the others making the other choice. By increasing the number of possible slots after each collision, the chances of colliding again decrease exponentially. The only time a large number of slots is possible is when all previous attempts have failed. In this case, long waits by some may be the only solution.

TOKEN PASSING

The previous protocols took a somewhat anarchistic approach to sending signals by allowing stations to send whenever they wanted. A logical question at this point is whether there is some way stations can agree in advance about who sends when. In other words, is there some way they can take turns?

Token Ring   The difficulty with many networks is that no central control or authority makes such decisions. Still, there is a way for all participating stations to agree on a protocol for taking turns: **token passing,** a common protocol used in office environments in token ring networks. In a token ring network (Figure 3.28), the stations are commonly PCs connected circularly to a wire or fiber medium. A **network interface card (NIC)** connects each to the network and contains the hardware and logic allowing a PC to communicate with the network.

The contention protocol here is an orderly one compared to the "send when you can" protocols discussed previously. The devices in a token ring execute a protocol

Figure 3.28   Token Ring Network

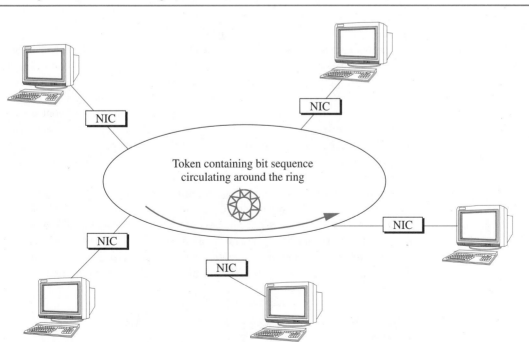

Token containing bit sequence
circulating around the ring

allowing them to take turns sending. The process involves a specially formatted frame called a **token.** It contains bit codes that the NIC recognizes and circles the ring visiting each NIC. According to the protocol, a PC can send when its NIC has the token.[*]

Chapter 6 describes exactly how stations exchange frames. In general, the concept is as follows. When a station receives the token, one of two things occurs. If it has nothing to send it simply sends the token on to its neighbor. If it does have something to send it inserts the data and the destination address into the token. It also changes some control bits to identify the token as a data frame (one containing information). Proceeding this way allows the token to visit each station and pick up data when it is available. (It's a lot like an electronic Federal Express traveling around picking up and dropping off frames.)

When a station receives a frame it examines the control bits. If they indicate that the frame contains no data, the station proceeds as before according to whether it has data to send. If the frame contains data, the station examines the destination address. If it is destined for some other station it just routes it to its neighbor. Otherwise the station copies the information and sends it to the PC. It then puts the frame back onto the ring. Eventually the frame returns to the sending station, which removes it and puts the token or another frame back onto the ring. Proceeding this way, the data eventually reaches its destination.

Token ring operations can be expanded to include prioritization and a reservation system that allows a station to reserve a token that already has data for future use. We will discuss these operations in Section 6.3.

Slotted Ring   Our description so far allows only one data frame per token. Thus a station will not send data until it receives an empty token. This fairly simple approach can have drawbacks, as Figure 3.29 shows.

Suppose station *A* wants to send many frames to station *C*. When it gets the token it inserts the first frame in it and routes it to its neighbor, station *B*. Station *B*, following the prescribed protocol, sends the frame to its neighbor. Eventually the frame gets back to station *A*. At this point, station *A* could send another frame.

Proceeding in this manner allows *A* to send all its frames without giving *B* a chance. With its transmissions delayed, station *B* sees the ring as slow and unresponsive. What can be done? One approach allows *B* to reserve a token as it passes by. We will explain this method in Chapter 6 when we discuss the IEEE token ring standard in detail.

Another approach is to use a **slotted ring.** It is also called the **Cambridge ring** because much of its development was done at the University of Cambridge. A slotted ring is much like a token ring except that it contains several rotating tokens, or slots. As before, slots may be empty or contain data. The protocol for sending is similar to that of the token ring: A station must wait for a free slot. In contrast, however, a station may not send any other frames until the slot that carried its previous

---

[*]In some situations this is not true. Chapter 6 provides a more detailed discussion of the token ring protocol.

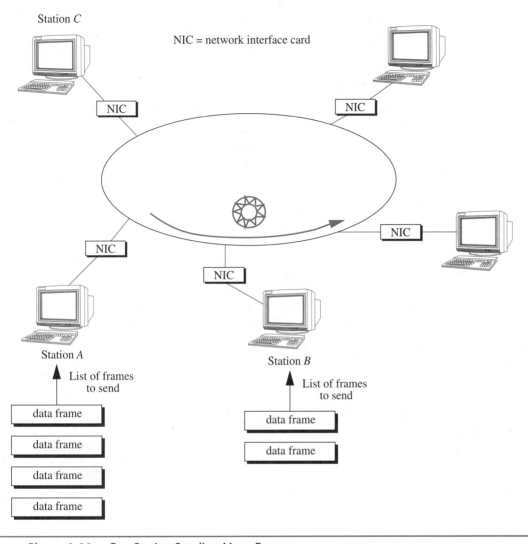

Station C

NIC = network interface card

NIC

NIC

NIC

NIC

NIC

Station A

List of frames
to send

| data frame |
| data frame |
| data frame |
| data frame |

Station B

List of frames
to send

| data frame |
| data frame |

Figure 3.29   One Station Sending Many Frames

data frame returns. This allows other free slots to pass it by and visit other stations, picking up their data frames.

The slotted ring is more suited to rings with a long distance around the ring's perimeter to accommodate the many slots. For example, we stated previously that a signal propagates along a cable at about 200 m/μsec. Suppose the ring supports a data rate of 10 Mbps, or 10 bits every μsec. This means that 1 bit travels 20 meters before the next one is put on the ring; in other words, 1 bit occupies 20 meters of the ring. Since more frames mean more bits occupying the ring, large rings are needed unless there are delays at each station caused by temporary storage of bits.

Rings have another advantage similar to that of the protocols discussed earlier. New stations can be added easily. When a station sends a frame to its neighbor it does not know if it has been added recently or has been there a long time. Consequently, stations need not be notified of changing neighbors.

One disadvantage is that one station can hog the token. In addition, a break in the link between two consecutive stations can bring the entire network down since the token cannot circulate. Another problem occurs if an NIC fails while it is sending a token onto the ring. The result is an incomplete and invalid token circulating the ring. Stations looking for the proper token format are waiting for something that is not on the ring. Yet another problem occurs if, for some reason, the station responsible for removing a frame fails. Every station passes the frame to its neighbor and the frame circulates forever. The abundance of token ring networks suggests that these problems all have solutions. We will present some solutions when we cover higher-layer protocols in Chapter 6.

Token Bus   The token bus network has applications in assembly line and factory automation environments. Physically, it looks like a common bus (Figure 3.30), but it communicates using a principle similar to that in the token ring. All of the stations are numbered and a token is passed among them in order of number. The highest-numbered station passes the token to the lowest-numbered one. The numbering scheme organizes the stations into a logical ring independent of their physical locations on the bus. That is, two stations numbered consecutively need not be physically adjacent.

Figure 3.30 Token Bus Network

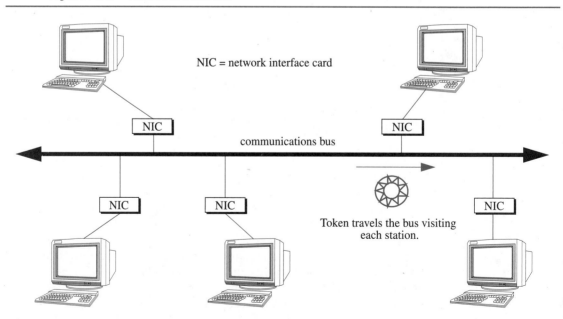

As with a token ring, the station with the token transmits. Because the stations are not connected physically in a ring, a station can transmit to any other directly. As with the previous protocols, the bus interface examines the addresses of transmitted frames and reads the frames destined for it.

The strongest proponents of the token bus were people interested in factory automation. The common bus structure allowed computer-controlled devices to be positioned along an assembly line. However, these proponents were uncomfortable with CSMA/CD approaches because there was no theoretical limit on the number of collisions that could occur and, consequently, no theoretical limit on frame delays. For obvious reasons they wanted to ensure that when a large piece of machinery came rolling down the assembly line, the computer-controlled devices would be ready to receive it.

Token bus protocols have one difficulty we have not yet encountered. A new station cannot be added as simply as with the previous protocols. Here, a station sends a token to its neighbor via the common bus, and since all stations sense the bus the station must know who or where its neighbor is. (No isolationism here.) Consequently, adding or deleting stations does require some additional work to be done to inform appropriate stations of the change. A discussion of this process requires some knowledge of higher-level protocols. We will revisit this topic more fully in Chapter 6.

SUMMARY OF PROTOCOLS

The contention protocols we have discussed in this section represent some of the most popular and important ones. We have summarized them in Table 3.5. Other protocols do exist. If you are interested in them, see References [St94] and [Ta96].

Table 3.5 Summary of Contention Protocols

PROTOCOL	SIGNIFICANCE	ADVANTAGES	DISADVANTAGES
Aloha	Variations are useful in satellite communications, where listening is not practical because of the time delay.	Simple approach.	Potential delays because a station may not know its frame has collided until well after it is sent.
p-persistent	Combined with CSMA/CD, a popular choice for the Ethernet and for a network.	Tends to decrease the chances of an idle medium.	May have excessive collisions under heavy traffic, wasting bandwidth of the medium.
Nonpersistent	According to the model the success rate does not decrease under heavy loads.	Reduces the number of collisions, especially under heavy loads.	Transmission medium may be idle even when there are stations wanting to send something.

(continues)

Table 3.5   *(continued)*

PROTOCOL	SIGNIFICANCE	ADVANTAGES	DISADVANTAGES
CSMA/CD	Combined with 1-persistence, it is commonly used with Ethernet.	Reduces the time of a collision.	No theoretical upper bound on the time it takes to transmit a frame successfully.
Token ring	Especially popular protocol used in office and business environments.	Simple interface because a station can only send to and receive from a neighbor. Upper bound on the time a station must wait before getting the token.	Unless recovery methods are built into the protocol, a malfunction at one station can destroy a token or break the ring, thus affecting the entire network.
Token bus	Originally favored by many interested in factory automation.	Upper bound on the time a station must wait before getting the token.	More difficult to add or delete a new station since its logical neighbors must be told of a change.

3.5   DATA COMPRESSION

With so many new applications requiring electronic communications there is an obvious trend to build faster and less costly ways of sending data. Chapter 2 mentioned some of the current areas of research, such as optical fiber, higher frequency microwaves, and faster modems. All have their place and will certainly contribute to the field.

Some applications, however, cannot wait for these new developments. Their demand has forced people to look for other ways to communicate quickly and cheaply. For example, consider one of the more significant developments of the 1980s, the fax machine. Chapter 2 described how the fax machine divides a sheet of paper into dots depending on the image on it. A typical fax uses 40,000 dots per square inch, resulting in nearly 4 million dots per page. Using a 9.6 Kbps modem[*] would require over six minutes to transmit. If you have ever used a fax machine you know it does not take that long.

Another example is color television signals. What we see as motion on a TV screen is actually a display of 30 pictures (frames) per second (the same principle behind motion pictures). Furthermore, each picture actually consists of approximately 200,000 dots or **pixels** (picture elements), each with different intensities of the primary colors of blue, green, and red. Various combinations allow the generation of different colors in the spectrum. This means a TV signal for one frame has to have information on the intensity of each primary color for each pixel. Since a signal

---

[*]This is slow by comparison to today's modems but was common when fax machines were becoming commonplace.

carries 30 frames per second, it would need a digital transmission capability of over 100 Mbps and, according to the Shannon's Result, require a signal bandwidth well above the 6 MHz currently allocated to each channel.

Both examples show that there are ways to get around the physical limits of different media. But how? The answer is **data compression,** a way to reduce the number of bits during transmission while retaining the meaning of the transmitted frame. It decreases both cost and time to send. Data compression has found uses in a variety of areas such as fax machines and the V.42 modem standards. It is also used in disk storage, and many software vendors compress programs on disks and CDs in order to conserve space.

The next logical question is, How do you eliminate bits and still maintain necessary information? For example, suppose the data in a large file consists entirely of strings of capital letters. How many data bits must be transferred? If the characters are stored as eight-bit ASCII codes, the number is $8n$, where n is the number of characters. However, if the information to be sent consists of uppercase letters only, we do not need the full eight-bit ASCII code. Can we devise a code that represents just capital letters? Yes! Table 3.6 shows a five-bit code using the numbers 0 through 25. Using this table, the sending station can substitute each five-bit code for the original eight-bit one. The receiving station can convert back. The result is that the information is sent and the number of data bits transferred is $5n$—a 37.5% reduction.

Again, many questions pop up (won't they ever stop?). What if there are control characters? What about lowercase letters? What if the data is not letters? These are valid questions and must be addressed. Table 3.6 is a very simple method of compression not suitable for many applications. Its main purpose is to show what compression is and what it can do. There are many other ways to compress data.

HUFFMAN CODE

The ASCII code and the code in Table 3.6 have one thing in common. All characters use the same number of bits. The **Huffman code** (Ref. [Hu52]) varies the number

Table 3.6   Alternative Code for Capital Letters

LETTER	CODE
A	00000
B	00001
C	00010
D	00011
⋮	⋮
X	10111
Y	11000
Z	11001

according to the frequency with which a character appears. Such a code is also called a **frequency-dependent code.** It assigns shorter codes to characters that appear more often, such as vowels and L, R, S, N, and T. (The frequency factor is why they are worth less in a Scrabble game and, except for the vowels, which are not worth any money, why they are often chosen on the game show *Wheel of Fortune.*) Thus, fewer bits are needed to transmit them.

For example, suppose Table 3.7 shows the frequencies (percentage of time they appear) of characters in a data file. To keep the example manageable we assume just five characters. If you want, you can do a similar example with all 26 letters.

Table 3.8 shows a Huffman code for these characters. Note that we say *a* Huffman code since, as we will show, it is not unique. We will show how to develop this code shortly.

Next, suppose the bit stream 01110001110110110111 was Huffman coded. If the leftmost bits were transmitted first, how do you interpret it? Fixed-length codes have an advantage. Within a transmission, we always know where one character ends and the next one begins. For example, in the transmission of ASCII-coded characters, every set of eight data bits defines a new character. This is not true of Huffman codes, so how do we interpret the Huffman-coded bit stream? How do we know where one letter ends and the next one begins?

The answer lies in a property of Huffman codes called the **no-prefix property.** That is, the code for any character never appears as the prefix of another code. For example, the Huffman code for *A* is 01, so no other code starts with a 01.

Table 3.7   Frequencies for the Letters *A* through *E*

LETTER	FREQUENCY
A	25%
B	15%
C	10%
D	20%
E	30%

Table 3.8   Huffman Code for the Letters *A* through *E*

LETTER	CODE
A	01
B	110
C	111
D	10
E	00

Figure 3.31 shows how to interpret a Huffman-coded string. As bits are received, a station builds a substring by concatenating them. It stops when the substring corresponds to a coded character. In the example of Figure 3.31, it stops after forming the substring 01, meaning that *A* is the first character sent. To find the second character, it discards the current substring and starts building a new one with the next bit received. Again, it stops when the substring corresponds to a coded character. In this case, the next three bits (110) correspond to the character *B*. Note that the substring does not match any Huffman code until all three bits are received. This is a consequence of the no-prefix property. The station continues this approach until all bits have been received. The data in Figure 3.31 consists of the character string ABECADBC.

Huffman Algorithm   The following steps show how to create a Huffman code.

1. To each character, associate a binary tree consisting of just one node. To each tree, assign the character's frequency, which we call the tree's **weight.**

2. Look for the two lightest-weight trees. If there are more than two, choose among them randomly. Merge the two into a single tree with a new root node whose left and right subtrees are the two we chose. Assign the sum of weights of the merged trees as the weight of the new tree.

3. Repeat the previous step until just one tree is left.

When completed, each of the original nodes is a leaf in the final binary tree. As with any binary tree, there is a unique path from the root to a leaf. For each leaf, the path to it defines the Huffman code. It is determined by assigning a 0 each time a left child pointer is followed and a 1 for each right child pointer.

Figure 3.32 (parts a through e) shows the construction of the Huffman code in Table 3.8. Figure 3.32a shows the five single-node trees with their weights. The trees for letter *B* and *C* have the smallest weights, so we merge them to give the results of Figure 3.32b. For the second merge there are two possibilities: merge the new tree with *D* or merge *A* with *D*. In this case we arbitrarily chose the first, and Figure 3.32c shows the result. Proceeding this way eventually gives the tree in Figure 3.32e. In it we see each left or right child pointer assigned a 0 or a 1. Following the pointers to a leaf node gives the Huffman code for the associated character. For example, following a left child (0) pointer and then a right child (1) pointer gets us to the leaf node for *A*. This is consistent with the Huffman code of 01 for the letter *A*.

Figure 3.31   Receiving and Interpreting a Huffman-Coded Message

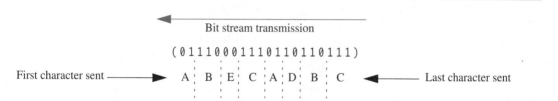

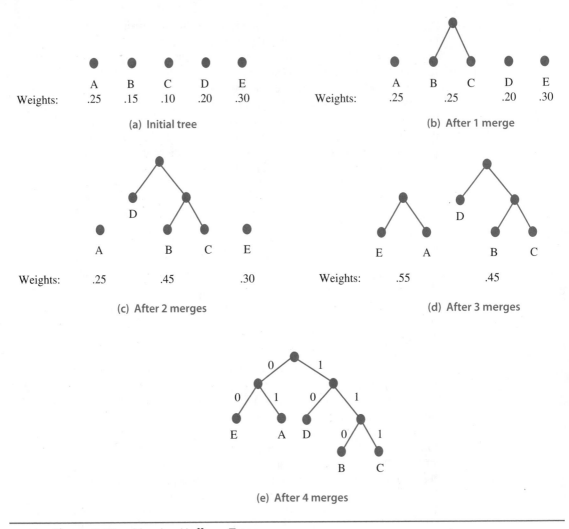

(a) Initial tree

(b) After 1 merge

(c) After 2 merges

(d) After 3 merges

(e) After 4 merges

Figure 3.32 Merging Huffman Trees

RUN-LENGTH ENCODING

Huffman codes do reduce the number of bits to send, but they also require that frequency values be known. As described, they also assume that bits are grouped into characters or some other repeatable units. Many items that travel the communications media, including binary (machine code) files, fax data, and video signals do not fall into that category.

The fax, for example, transfers bits corresponding to light and dark space on a sheet of paper. It does not transfer the characters directly. Consequently, there is a need for a more general technique that can compress arbitrary bit strings. One approach, called **run-length encoding,** uses a simple and perhaps obvious approach: It analyzes bit strings looking for long runs of a 0 or 1. Instead of sending all the bits, it sends only how many are in the run.

This technique is especially useful for fax transmission. If you were to examine closely the space in which a character is typed, potentially up to 70% to 80% is white space. The exact amount, of course, depends on the font and character. The actual dark spots from typed characters make up very little of a fax transmission. For example, note the amount of white space in a magnified representation of a lower-case *f* within one print position.

$$f$$

Runs of the Same Bit   There are a couple of ways to implement run-length encoding. The first is especially useful in binary streams where the same bit appears in most of the runs. In a fax example consisting primarily of characters, there will be many long runs of 0s (assuming a light spot corresponds to a 0). This approach just transmits the length of each run as a fixed-length binary integer. The receiving station receives each length and generates the proper number of bits in the run, inserting the other bit in between.

For example, suppose four bits are used to represent the run length. Consider the bit stream of Figure 3.33a. Figure 3.33b shows the compressed stream that is sent. The original stream starts with 14 zeros, so the first four bits in the compressed stream are 1110 (binary 14). The next four bits in the compressed stream are 1001 (binary 9 for the second run of nine 0s). After the second run there are two consecutive 1s.

Figure 3.33   Stream Prior to Compression and Run-Length-Encoded Stream

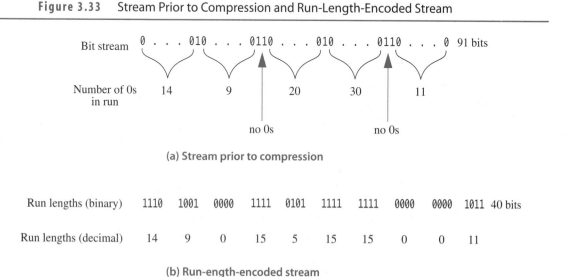

(a) Stream prior to compression

(b) Run-ength-encoded stream

However, this approach sees them as two distinct 1s separated by a run of no 0s. Consequently, the third group of four bits is 0000.

The fourth run has 20 zeros. Unfortunately, 20 cannot be expressed using four bits. In this case, the run length is expressed using a second four-bit group. The two four-bit numbers are then added to determine the run length. In Figure 3.33b, the 1111 (binary 15) and 0101 (binary 5) groups determine a run length of 20.

If the run length is too large to be expressed as a sum of two four-bit numbers, the method uses as many four-bit groups as necessary. The receiving station must know that a group of all 1s means the next group corresponds to the same run. Thus, it continues summing the group values and stops after it receives something other than all 1s. Consequently, the run of length 30 is represented by 1111, 1111, and 0000. In this case the 0s are needed to tell the station that the run stops at 30 zeros.

How would the compressed stream differ if the stream in Figure 3.33a started with a 1? Similar to the case for two consecutive 1s, the method considers the stream to actually start with a run of no 0s. Thus, the first four bits sent would be 0000.

This technique is best suited where there are many long 0 runs. As the 1 bits increase in frequency, the technique becomes less efficient. In fact, you might try to construct a stream where this approach actually generates a longer bit stream.

We had mentioned previously that Huffman codes are not suited for fax transmission. That is not entirely true. Certain runs often occur with greater frequency (blank lines and spaces between adjacent characters and examples). In such cases Huffman codes can be assigned to these runs.

Runs with Different Characters   Knowing that the same bit is involved simplifies matters since we only need to send the run length. But what about cases with runs of different bits or even characters? In such cases, your first response is probably correct: Send the actual character along with the run length. For example, the character string

HHHHHHHUFFFFFFFFFFFFFFFYYYYYYYYYYYYYYYYYYYYYYYDGGGGGGGGGGGG

might actually be sent as the alternating set of numbers and characters 7, H, 1, U, 14, F, 20, Y, 1, D, and 11, G.

RELATIVE ENCODING

The two compression techniques already discussed have their applications, but in certain cases neither provides much help. A common example is in video transmissions, where images may be very complex in contrast to the black and white transmission of a fax or a text file. Except perhaps for test patterns that appear before a station goes on the air, little in a video picture is repetitive. Consequently, neither of the previous methods offers much hope of compressing the signals for a picture.

Although a single video image may contain little repetition, there is a lot of repetition over several images. Remember, a typical television signal sends 30 pictures per second. Furthermore, each picture generally varies only slightly from the previous one. Over the course of a fraction of a second not much action occurs. Therefore, rather than trying to treat each frame as a separate entity and compress it, we might think about how much a frame differs from the previous one. Encoding that information and sending it has potential when the differences are small. This method is called **relative encoding** or **differential encoding.**

The principle is fairly straightforward. The first frame is sent and stored in a receiver's buffer. The sender then compares the second frame with the first, encodes the differences, and sends them in a frame format. The receiver gets the frame and applies the differences to the frame it has, thus creating the second frame the sender had. It stores the second frame in a buffer and continues the process for each new frame.

Figure 3.34 shows how it works. Here we represent a frame using a two-dimensional array of integers. We put no interpretation on their meaning; they're just easier to draw than video signals. The first frame contains a set of integers, and the second differs very little from the first. (The colored numbers are the ones that differ.)

The figure shows another two-dimensional array below the second frame containing 0s, 1s, and –1s. A 0 in any position means the element in that position of the frame is the same as that in the same position in the previous frame. A nonzero value indicates what the change is. So a 1 means the element in that frame position is one larger than the one in the same position in the previous frame. A –1 means it is one smaller. Certainly values other than 1 and -1 can be used. The point is that the frames to be sent contain long runs of 0s, making them candidates for run-length encoding.

LEMPEL-ZIV ENCODING

With run-length encoding we compressed by looking for runs of a character or a bit. The idea is to reduce repetitious or redundant transmissions. But not all redundancy

---

Figure 3.34   Relative Encoding

First frame	Second frame	Third frame
5 7 6 2 8 6 6 3 5 6	5 7 6 2 8 6 6 3 5 6	5 7 6 2 8 6 6 3 5 6
6 5 7 5 5 6 3 2 4 7	6 5 7 6 5 6 3 2 3 7	6 5 8 6 5 6 3 3 3 7
8 4 6 8 5 6 4 8 8 5	8 4 6 8 5 6 4 8 8 5	8 4 6 8 5 6 4 8 8 5
5 1 2 9 8 6 5 5 6 6	5 1 3 9 8 6 5 5 7 6	5 1 3 9 7 6 5 5 8 6
5 5 2 9 9 6 8 9 5 1	5 5 2 9 9 6 8 9 5 1	5 5 2 9 9 6 8 9 5 1

0 0 0 0 0 0 0 0 0 0	0 0 0 0 0 0 0 0 0 0
0 0 0 1 0 0 0 0 –1 0	0 0 1 0 0 0 0 1 0 0
0 0 0 0 0 0 0 0 0 0	0 0 0 0 0 0 0 0 0 0
0 0 1 0 0 0 0 0 1 0	0 0 0 0 –1 0 0 0 1 0
0 0 0 0 0 0 0 0 0 0	0 0 0 0 0 0 0 0 0 0
Transmitted frame is the encoded differences between the first and second frames.	Transmitted frame is the encoded differences between the second and third frames.

occurs in the form of single bit or character repetitions. In some cases, entire words or phrases may be repeated. This is especially true with large text files such as manuscripts. An author's writing style is often characterized by a choice of words or phrases that may be repeated frequently.

The **Lempel-Ziv**[*] **encoding** method looks for often-repeated strings and stores them just once. It then replaces multiple occurrences with a code corresponding to the original. This is one of the basic principles behind database management strategies: Store one piece of information in just one place and reference it through special codes. This technique is used by the UNIX compress command and in the V.42bis compression standard for modems.

For example, consider the following writing sample (Ref. [Cr90]):

> The tropical rain fell in drenching sheets, hammering the corrugated roof of the clinic building, roaring down the metal gutters, splashing on the ground in a torrent.

Several letter sequences are repeated. Ignoring case sensitivity, some of them are *the* , *ro*, *ing* Suppose we replace each of these strings with the special characters $\otimes$, $\oplus$, and $\varnothing$, respectively. The compressed string then becomes

> $\otimes$t$\oplus$pical rain fell in drench$\varnothing$ sheets, hammer$\varnothing$ $\otimes$corrugated $\oplus$of $\otimes$clinic build$\varnothing$, $\oplus$ar$\varnothing$ down $\otimes$metal gutters, splash$\varnothing$ on $\otimes$g$\oplus$und in a torrent.

This text did not compress the original by much, but you can't expect much repetition in a single sentence and compression is generally not very effective (or useful, for that matter) with short samples. With longer text and longer and more frequent repetitions the compression improves. The reason is that typical English text is filled with repetitions as evidenced, for example, by words such as *the, then, them, their, there, these,* and so forth. However, it's not only text data that can be subject to Lempel-Ziv compression. Any file can be considered as a sequence of ASCII-defined characters. If the file contains numerous character sequences that appear frequently, then it is a candidate for Lempel-Ziv compression.

An important characteristic of this method is that we make no assumptions about what the repeated strings look like, making it a more robust and dynamic algorithm. As a consequence, however, it may at first appear there is no efficient way to implement this algorithm. One reason is that it may appear that looking for repeated sequences adds considerable overhead to the algorithm. Then there is also the issue of decompression. Remember, compression algorithms do not have much value if we cannot reverse the process. How can we decompress? If we received the compressed string above, how could we possibly know what letter sequences correspond to the special symbols? One option would be to send a table of symbols showing the strings that they represent along with the compressed text. Of course, doing that partially counteracts the value of compressing in the first place.

---

[*]There are actually several different versions of Lempel-Ziv compression schemes. These variations may be called Lempel-Ziv, Lempel-Ziv-Welch, LZW, LZ77, LZ78, or even Ziv-Lempel. We will not make distinctions among the variations, but if you would like some further details you can consult Reference [Ho97].

It turns out that there is an efficient way to identify commonly repeated strings. Also, strange as it may seem, it is possible to determine the strings associated with the special symbols without having them transmitted with the compressed text. We will show how this works by outlining both a compression and a decompression algorithm. We will, however, shorten the example by compressing text consisting of only the three characters A, B, and C. To work with a full alphabet would require a lengthy example with potentially hundreds of steps to fully realize the value of compression. This limited example will preserve the fundamental logic behind the algorithms and accomplish our task in relatively few steps.

Figure 3.35 shows both the compression and decompression algorithms ([We84] and [Dr95]). These algorithms preserve the fundamental logic but are not intended to provide all the C language–specific details and declarations. We leave that as an exercise. The compression algorithm is based on the following central ideas:

1. Assign a code to each letter or character that is part of the initial text file (line 3 of the compression algorithm) and store in a code table.

2. Set up a loop and get characters one at a time from the file. We will use a buffered string (initially the first character, line 4) built by concatenating characters from the file.

3. In each pass of a loop, read one character and append it to a buffered string to form a new temporary string (line 7). If that temporary string has been encountered before (i.e., is in the code table), then move the temporary string to the buffer (line 10).

4. If the temporary string was not found in the code table, assign a code to the temporary string and store both code and string in the code table (line 14) and send the code associated with the buffered string (line 13). This code represents the compressed equivalent of the string. Last, reinitialize the buffered string to the single character that was just read (line 15).

Let's see how this algorithm works for a specific example. Suppose the characters to be read from the file are ABABABCBABABABCBABABABCBA. Table 3.9 shows the values of relevant variables and what action is taken at each step. Table 3.10 shows the results of the code table after the compression algorithm has finished. Initially, the code table contains just three entries: A, B, and C with associated codes 0, 1, and 2, respectively. As the algorithm adds new strings to the code table, we assume it creates successive codes, starting with 3, for each new string added. As you follow through each step remember that the tempstring is the buffered string with c appended to it.

At step 1 the algorithm looks for AB in the code table and fails to find it. It sends the code for the buffered string A (0), stores AB (code=3) in the code table, and defines the new buffered string to B. At step 2 the algorithm looks for BA in the code table and fails to find it. It sends the code for B (1), stores BA (code=4) in the code table, and defines the new buffered string to A. At step 3 it looks for AB in the code table and this time finds it. Nothing is sent and the new buffered string is AB. At step 4 the algorithm looks for ABA in the code table and fails to find it. It sends

COMPRESSION		DECOMPRESSION	
1	void compress (FILE * fieid)	1	void decompress
2	{	2	{
3	initialize(code table);	3	initialize(code table);
4	buffer=string consisting of first character from the file.	4	receive first code, call it prior;
5	while ((c=getc(fileid)) != EOF)	5	print the string associated with prior;
6	{	6	while (true)
7	tempstring=concat(buffer, c);	7	{
8	search for tempstring in the code table;	8	receive code, call it current; if no code then break;
9	if found	9	search for current in the code table;
10	buffer = tempstring;	10	if not found
11	else	11	{
12	{	12	c=1st character of string associated with prior;
13	send the code associated with buffer;	13	tempstring=concat(string associated with prior, c);
14	assign a code to tempstring; store both in the code table;	14	assign a code to tempstring; store both in the code table;
15	buffer=string consisting of one character c;	15	print tempstring;
16	}	16	}
17	}	17	else
18	send the code associated with buffer;	18	{
19		19	c=1st character of string associated with prior, c);
20		20	tempstring=concat(string associated with prior, c);
21		21	assign a code to tempstring; store both in the code table
22		22	print string associated with current
23		23	}
24		24	prior=current
25		25	}

Figure 3.35   Lempel-Ziv Compression And Decompression Algorithms

the code for the buffered string AB (3), stores ABA (code=5) in the code table, and defines the new buffered string to A.

This process continues and longer strings get stored in the code table. Also, the temporary strings are found in the code table more frequently and fewer transmissions occur. This causes the buffered string to become longer and when a code table lookup does fail, the transmitted code corresponds to a longer string. The result is better compression. Table 3.9 does not show the last few steps of the algorithm; we leave it as an exercise to complete it.

The next step is to describe the decompression algorithm. Remember, all the decompression algorithm has to work with is the initial code table of characters (in

Table 3.9   Run Time Results of Compression Algorithm

LOOP PASS	BUFFER	C	WHAT IS SENT	WHAT IS STORED IN TABLE	NEW BUFFER VALUE
1	A	B	0 (code for A)	AB (code=3)	B
2	B	A	1 (code for B)	BA (code=4)	A
3	A	B			AB
4	AB	A	3 (code for AB)	ABA (code=5)	A
5	A	B			AB
6	AB	C	3 (code for AB)	ABC (code=6)	C
7	C	B	2 (code for C)	CB (code=7)	B
8	B	A			BA
9	BA	B	4 (code for BA)	BAB (code=8)	B
10	B	A			BA
11	BA	B			BAB
12	BAB	A	8 (code for BAB)	BABA (code=9)	A
13	A	B			AB
14	AB	C			ABC
15	ABC	B	6 (code for ABC)	ABCB (code=10)	B
16	B	A			BA
17	BA	B			BAB
18	BAB	A			BABA
19	BABA	B	9 (code for BABA)	BABAB (code=11)	B

Table 3.10   Table Produced by Compression Algorithm[*]

String	A	B	C	AB	BA	ABA	ABC	CB	BAB	BABA	ABCB	BABAB	BABC	CBA
Code	0	1	2	3	4	5	6	7	8	9	10	11	12	13

[*]Input string: ABABABCBABABABCBABABABCBA
Transmitted code: 0 1 3 3 2 4 8 6 9 8 7 0

our case, the code table consisting of A, B, and C with codes of 0, 1, and 2) and the incoming code values. In our example the decompression algorithm's input is the sequence 0 1 3 3 2 4 8 6 9 8 7 0. We will show its output to be the same as the original string that was input to the compression algorithm. The beauty of the decompression algorithm is its ability to reconstruct the same code table based on this limited information. Let's see how it works for the first few steps. You might want to read the next paragraph very slowly, checking and double-checking references to the algorithms and specified tables.

Initially, the algorithm receives a code and calls it prior (line 4). It prints the string associated with prior that it finds in the code table (line 5). In this case, prior=0 and it prints the letter A. The algorithm then enters a loop. Table 3.11 shows relevant values with each pass of the loop and what is printed. In loop pass 1, the algorithm receives a current code of 1 (line 8). The current code is in the code table, so the algorithm executes lines 19 through 22 storing the tempstring/code pair (AB/3) in the code table and printing the string associated with the current code (B). Note that, as with compression, code values are assigned successively beginning with 3. In pass 2 the prior code is 1 and the new current code is 3. The current code is in the code table (by virtue of pass 1), so the algorithm again executes lines 19 through 22. It stores the tempstring/code pair (BA/4) in the code table and prints the string associated with the current code (AB). In pass 3 the prior code is 3 and the new current code is again 3. The current code is in the code table, so the algorithm once again executes lines 19 through 22. It stores the tempstring/code pair (ABA/5) in the code table and prints the string associated with the current code (AB).

The remaining steps follow along similar lines. The important thing to note is the way the code table is being constructed. Comparing what is being stored in the code table with what the compression algorithm stored there (Table 3.9) shows the code table being built the same way. Consequently, code table lookups produce the same strings and the code is decompressed. As you can see, the first printed letter (A) followed by the printed letters from the last column of Table 3.11 correspond to the initial string.

As a final note, we have shown the code table as a two-dimensional table, suggesting the use of linear searches to look for codes and strings. This will generally decrease the effectiveness of both algorithms a great deal. Instead of a table, a better

Table 3.11   Run-Time Results of Decompression Algorithm

Loop Pass	Prior (string)	Current (string)	Is Current Code in Table?	c	Tempstring/ Code Pair	What Is Printed (current or tempstring)
1	0 (A)	1 (B)	yes	B	AB/3	B (current)
2	1 (B)	3 (AB)	yes	A	BA/4	AB (current)
3	3 (AB)	3 (AB)	yes	A	ABA/5	AB (current)
4	3 (AB)	2 (C)	yes	C	ABC/6	C (current)
5	2 (C)	4 (BA)	yes	B	CB/7	BA (current)
6	4 (BA)	8	no	B	BAB/8	BAB (tempstring)
7	8(BAB)	6 (ABC)	yes	A	BABA/9	ABC (current)
8	6 (ABC)	9 (BABA)	yes	B	ABCB/10	BABA (current)
9	9 (BABA)	8 (BAB)	yes	B	BABAB/11	BAB (current)
10	8 (BAB)	7 (CB)	yes	C	BABC/12	CB (current)
11	7 (CB)	0 (A)	yes	A	CBA/13	A (current)

approach would be to use a dictionary-based data structure in which lookups can be performed much more efficiently. In fact, Lempel-Ziv algorithms are examples of a general class of algorithms called **dictionary-based compression algorithms.** We did not use a dictionary-based data structure here because such discussions belong in a data structures course and the details would have clouded our discussion of the Lempel-Ziv algorithm. If you would like further details on dictionary-based data structures, consult Reference [Dr95].

IMAGE COMPRESSION

One of the most significant advances in recent years is the integration of multimedia applications with computer programs and networks. With a click of a mouse we can access photographs, pictures of classic works of art on display in the Louvre, and even movie clips from the Internet or a CD-ROM. While it may at first seem a small step beyond the typical transmission of words and sentences, multimedia applications would simply not be feasible without some very sophisticated compression algorithms.

We will end this section on compression by investigating two widely used compression methods used in the transmission and storage of visual images. We examine how a single visual image such as a photograph can be compressed and follow up by looking at video, which is essentially a sequence of still images displayed at a fast rate to give the appearance of motion. However, before we get into compression methods we must first provide a little background on how visual images may be stored and why compression is necessary.

Pictures, whether they be photographs or images on a computer screen, are made up of a lot of very small dots. These dots are also called **picture elements** or **pixels.** If the picture is of high quality you probably cannot even see them unless perhaps you squint and place the picture very close to your eyes or use a magnifying glass. They are so densely packed that the sensory nerves in your eyes cannot distinguish them. In lesser-quality pictures the dots become more evident. For example, look very closely at a newspaper photograph and you may be able to see individual dots. Pull the picture further away and the dots blend together and the picture comes into view. One might try the same with a television picture, but parental warnings from long ago of "Don't sit so close or you'll go blind" are so deeply ingrained that they prevent me from making this recommendation.

We begin by discussing how pixels may be represented in computer memory. When we discussed fax transmissions we referred to images that are made up of black and white pixels. This allowed us to use either a 0 or a 1 for each pixel. However, a movie or picture truly made up of just black and white images would not be very satisfying to look at. In fact, the phrase *black and white* as applied to images of old movies or of photographs is really a misnomer. The fact is that these images consist of various shades of gray and each pixel must be able to represent a different shade. A common scheme is to use eight bits to represent 256 shades of gray (ranging from white to black).

Representing images becomes more complex when we add color. High-quality images allow a wide range of colors and we are able to distinguish among subtle changes in color or hue. Lesser-quality images may not distinguish among various shades of red and orange. For example, personal computers allow you to adjust the resolution of the screen to provide true color or to determine the color of the desktop, screen, icons, and title bars. In some cases you can customize your colors.

Video technology is based on the fact that any color can be represented by using a suitable combination of the primary colors red, green, and blue or RGB. Monitor screens contains three phosphors,[*] one for each primary color. The electronics inside a monitor uses three electron beams, one for each phosphor. By varying the intensity of each beam the amount of primary color emitted by each phosphor can be adjusted, and the result is virtually any color in the visual spectrum. The heart of the problem is in creating a data structure that represents the proper color mix for each pixel.

Just as we can use 8 bits to represent 256 shades of gray, we can use an 8-bit group to represent each of the three primary colors. The intensity of each electron beam can be adjusted according to the 8-bit value to produce the desired color. In fact, using 8 bits for each primary color means each pixel can be represented using 24 bits, which allows up to 2^{24} possible colors. Since the human eye cannot distinguish among so many colors, we think of it as true color.

We should note that there is an alternative representation for video images that also consists of three 8-bit groups. The difference is that one group represents **luminance** (brightness) and each of the other two represents **chrominance** (color). The luminance and both chrominance values are calculated from RGB values. For example, Reference [Ta96] states one possible relationship as

$$Y = 0.30R + 0.59G + 0.11B$$
$$I = 0.60R - 0.28G - 0.32B$$
$$Q = 0.21R - 0.52G + 0.31B$$

The letters R, G, and B represent values for each of the primary colors. The letters Y, I, and Q are used by the National Television Standards Committee[†] (NTSC) to represent the luminance and two chrominance values. There are other standards and different formulas relating the above quantities, but these are not relevant to our discussion. The important thing is that for each RGB value there is a YIQ value and vice versa. If you would like additional information on chrominance and luminance values, please consult Reference [Pe93].

The advantage of using luminance and chrominance is based on the sensory capabilities of the human eye, which is not uniformly sensitive to all colors. Our sensory system is more sensitive to luminance than to chrominance. This means that a small loss in chrominance values during a transmission may not be visually detectable. This is useful information when it comes to compressing images.

---

[*] A phosphor is a substance which emits energy in the form of light when its atoms are excited by an electron beam.

[†] The group that defines standards for broadcast television signals in the United States.

In the ensuing discussions we will not worry about whether pixels are represented using RGB or YIQ values. We only care that each pixel can be represented by three 8-bit groups, and our main concern is to reduce the number of bits for transmission or storage.

The next step is to consider the number of pixels in a typical picture. Certainly, this will vary with picture size. However, in order to have some number to work with let us assume a picture that fills up a VGA computer screen measuring 640 pixels by 480 pixels.[*] A little arithmetic tells us that this one image requires 24 × 640 × 480 = 7,372,800 bits. How does this affect Internet traffic? Considering the facts that video often consists of 30 images per second and that there are many images being transferred simultaneously to different users, the number of bits being pushed through approaches gigabit levels and higher. Without some way to compress and reduce the number of bits significantly, current technology just could not handle the traffic.

JPEG

JPEG is an acronym for the Joint Photographic Experts Group. It is a group formed as a cooperative effort by the ISO, ITU, and IEC. The compression standard, commonly known as **JPEG compression,** is used to compress both gray scale and photographic-quality color images. JPEG differs from previous compression techniques in an important way. Previous methods were examples of **lossless compression.** That is, the decompression algorithm was able to recover all of the information embedded in the compressed code. JPEG is **lossy:** The image obtained after decompression may not be the same as the original.

Whereas information loss is unacceptable in cases such as the transfer of executable files, some loss may be tolerable if the file contains an image. The reason is due to inherent limitations in the human optical system. The simple fact is that we cannot always see subtle differences in color. Thus, if a few color pixels have been changed slightly, we may never notice the difference. An analogy may be made to looking at paint samples in a store. One person may agonize for hours over several paint samples, all of which look the same to a spouse.

JPEG compression consists of three phases (Figure 3.36): the **discrete cosine transform (DCT), quantization,** and **encoding phases.** The second and third phases are fairly straightforward, but the DCT phase is rather complex. Much of the theory is based in mathematics, requiring a knowledge of topics such as calculus, Fourier transforms, and discrete cosine transforms. We will not go into the theory behind these topics, but if you have a sufficient mathematics background you might consult References [Fe92] and [Ra90]. We will, however, present some equations, go through a couple of examples, and explain how and why they work on images.

---

[*]Today's screens can display higher-quality images than 640 × 480. Also common are 800 × 600, 1024 × 768, 1152 × 864, and 1280 × 1024.

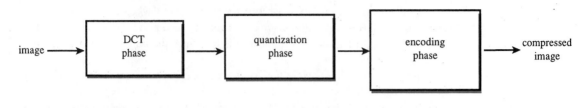

Figure 3.36 JPEG's Three Phases

DCT Phase JPEG begins by dividing an image into a series of blocks consisting of 8 × 8 pixels each. If the original image measured 640 × 480 pixels, the picture would consist of a series of blocks 80 across and 60 down (Figure 3.37). If the image consisted of gray scales only, then each pixel would be represented by an 8-bit number. We can therefore represent each block as a two-dimensional array containing eight rows and eight columns. The array's elements are 8-bit integers between 0 and 255, inclusive. The discrete cosine transform phase is applied to this array.

If the image is color, then each pixel can be represented by 24 bits or, equivalently, three 8-bit groups (representing either RGB or YIQ values; it doesn't matter here). Consequently, we can represent this 8 × 8 pixel block using three two-dimensional arrays, each with eight rows and eight columns. Each array represents pixel values from one of the three 8-bit groups. The discrete cosine transform is applied to each array.

Now we get to what the discrete cosine transform actually does. Basically, it is a function that takes a two-dimensional array with eight rows and columns and produces another two-dimensional array also with eight rows and columns. For example, if P represents the array of pixel values (with $P[x][y]$ representing the value in row x and column y), then the discrete cosine transform defines a new array, T (with $T[i][j]$ representing the value in row i and column j), as follows:[*]

$$T[i][j] = 0.25 C(i) C(j) \sum_{x=0}^{7} \sum_{y=0}^{7} P[x][y] \cos\left(\frac{(2x+1)i\pi}{16}\right) \cos\left(\frac{(2y+1)j\pi}{16}\right) \quad (3.1)$$

for $i = 0, 1, 2, \ldots, 7$ and $j = 0, 1, 2, \ldots, 7$ and where

$$C(i) = \begin{cases} 1/\sqrt{2} & \text{if } i = 0 \\ 1 & \text{otherwise} \end{cases}$$

We'll not derive this formula. Instead let's try to understand just what this formula does to the matrix P and under what circumstances it can lead to good com-

---

[*]Discrete cosine transforms have a more general definition depending on the size of the array on which they are operating. Since we are assuming an 8 × 8 array, this formula suits our purposes here.

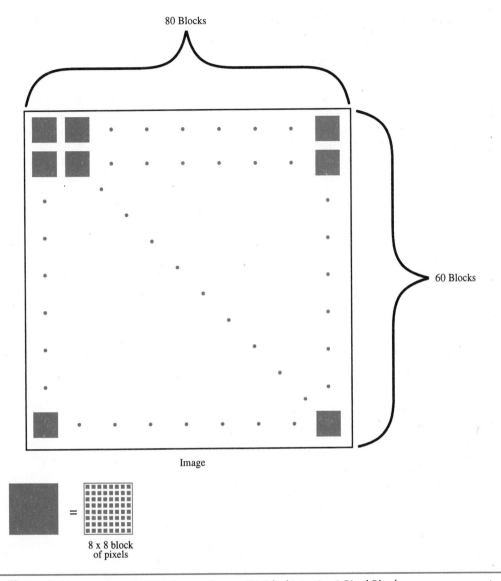

80 Blocks

60 Blocks

Image

8 x 8 block
of pixels

Figure 3.37   640 × 480 VGA Screen Image Divided into 8 × 8 Pixel Blocks

pression. The resulting matrix, T, contains a collection of values called **spatial frequencies.** Essentially, these spatial frequencies relate directly to how much the pixel values change as a function of their positions in the block. The value in $T[0][0]$ is called the **DC coefficient** and is related to the average of the values in the array P. (With i and j both equal to 0, the cosine functions are all 1.) The other values in T are called the **AC coefficients.** For larger values of i and j, pixel values get multiplied by cosine functions with a higher frequency.

Why is this important? Suppose that all of the P values were the same. This would correspond to an image consisting of a single color with no variation at all. In this case all of the AC coefficients correspond to sums of cosine functions that cancel each other out (since the P values could be factored out of the summations). The result is that the AC coefficients are all 0. If there is a little variation among the P values, then many, but not all, of the AC coefficients will be 0. If there is a lot of variation in the P values, there will be few AC coefficients that are 0.

Figure 3.38 shows the results of applying the discrete cosine transform on two different arrays. The first array (Figure 3.38a) contains P values that change uniformly. This would correspond to an image with uniform color changes and little fine detail. In this case, the T array contains many AC coefficients that are 0. Note how the AC coefficients become generally smaller as they get further away from the upper left position in the array. Values that are further away from that position correspond to high spatial frequencies, or fine detail in the image. Since this particular image has little fine detail, these values are small and mostly 0.

Figure 3.38   Discrete Cosine Transform Results on Two Different Arrays

P array

T array (values rounded to the nearest integer)

20	30	40	50	60	70	80	90
30	40	50	60	70	80	90	100
40	50	60	70	80	90	100	110
50	60	70	80	90	100	110	120
60	70	80	90	100	110	120	130
70	80	90	100	110	120	130	140
80	90	100	110	120	130	140	150
90	100	110	120	130	140	150	160

720	−182	0	−19	0	−6	0	−1
−182	0	0	0	0	0	0	0
0	0	0	0	0	0	0	0
−19	0	0	0	0	0	0	0
0	0	0	0	0	0	0	0
−6	0	0	0	0	0	0	0
0	0	0	0	0	0	0	0
−1	0	0	0	0	0	0	0

(a) *P* array representing small changes in the image

P array

T array (values rounded to the nearest integer)

100	150	50	100	100	150	200	120
200	10	110	20	200	120	30	120
10	200	130	30	200	20	150	50
100	10	90	190	120	200	10	100
10	200	200	120	90	190	20	200
150	120	20	200	150	70	10	100
200	30	150	10	10	120	190	10
120	120	50	100	10	190	10	120

835	15	−17	59	5	−56	69	−38
46	−60	−36	11	14	−60	−71	110
−32	−9	130	105	−37	81	−17	24
59	−3	27	−12	30	28	−27	−48
50	−71	−24	−56	−40	−36	67	−189
−23	−18	4	54	−66	152	−61	35
2	13	−37	−53	15	−80	−185	−62
32	−14	52	−93	−210	−48	−76	80

(b) *P* array representing large changes in the image

In the second case (Figure 3.38b), the *P* values change a lot throughout the array. This would correspond to an image with large color changes over a small area. In effect, it represents an image with a lot of fine detail. In this case, the AC coefficients are all nonzero.

In general, if the pixel values change more rapidly and less uniformly as a function of their position, the AC coefficients correspond to values with larger magnitudes. In addition, more of the higher spatial frequency values become nonzero. In summary, the AC coefficients are essentially a measure of pixel variation. Consequently, images with a lot of fine detail will be harder to compress than images with little color variation.

The spatial frequencies are not of much use to us unless there is a way to use them to restore the original pixel values. In fact, there is an inverse formula that will convert spatial frequencies back to pixel values:

$$P[x][y] = 0.25 \sum_{i=0}^{7} \sum_{j=0}^{7} C(i)C(j)T[i][j]\cos\left(\frac{(2x+1)i\pi}{16}\right)\cos\left(\frac{(2y+1)j\pi}{16}\right) \quad (3.2)$$

We will not prove or verify this claim. However, we leave it as an exercise to write a program that applies the above formula to the spatial frequencies of Figure 3.38. If you do it correctly, you will calculate the original pixel values.

Quantization Phase   The second, or quantization, phase provides a way of ignoring small differences in an image that may not be perceptible. It defines yet another two-dimensional array (call it *Q*) by dividing each *T* value by some number and rounding to the nearest integer. For example, suppose that

$$T = \begin{vmatrix} 152 & 0 & -48 & 0 & -8 & 0 & -7 & 0 \\ 0 & 0 & -0 & 0 & 0 & 0 & 0 & 0 \\ -48 & 0 & 38 & 0 & -3 & 0 & 2 & 0 \\ 0 & 0 & 0 & 0 & 0 & 0 & 0 & 0 \\ -8 & 0 & -3 & 0 & 13 & 0 & -1 & 0 \\ 0 & 0 & 0 & 0 & 0 & 0 & 0 & 0 \\ -7 & 0 & 2 & 0 & -1 & 0 & 7 & 0 \\ 0 & 0 & 0 & 0 & 0 & 0 & 0 & 0 \end{vmatrix} \quad (3.3)$$

If we divided each value by 10 and rounded to the nearest integer, we would have

$$Q = \begin{vmatrix} 15 & 0 & -5 & 0 & -1 & 0 & -1 & 0 \\ 0 & 0 & 0 & 0 & 0 & 0 & 0 & 0 \\ -5 & 0 & 4 & 0 & 0 & 0 & 0 & 0 \\ 0 & 0 & 0 & 0 & 0 & 0 & 0 & 0 \\ -1 & 0 & 0 & 0 & 1 & 0 & 0 & 0 \\ 0 & 0 & 0 & 0 & 0 & 0 & 0 & 0 \\ -1 & 0 & 0 & 0 & 0 & 0 & 1 & 0 \\ 0 & 0 & 0 & 0 & 0 & 0 & 0 & 0 \end{vmatrix} \quad (3.4)$$

The reason we might do this is to create another array with fewer distinct numbers and more consistent patterns. For example, array Q has more zeros in it and would likely compress better than T. Of course, doing this prompts a logical question: How can we go from Q back to T for decompression? The answer is simple: We can't. By dividing T values and rounding we have lost information. If we tried to reverse the operation and multiply each element in Q by 10, we would end up with

$$
T =
\begin{vmatrix}
150 & 0 & -50 & 0 & -10 & 0 & -10 & 0 \\
0 & 0 & 0 & 0 & 0 & 0 & 0 & 0 \\
-50 & 0 & 40 & 0 & 0 & 0 & 0 & 0 \\
0 & 0 & 0 & 0 & 0 & 0 & 0 & 0 \\
-10 & 0 & 0 & 0 & 10 & 0 & 0 & 0 \\
0 & 0 & 0 & 0 & 0 & 0 & 0 & 0 \\
-10 & 0 & 0 & 0 & 0 & 0 & 10 & 0 \\
0 & 0 & 0 & 0 & 0 & 0 & 0 & 0
\end{vmatrix}
\tag{3.5}
$$

There's no way to know, for example, that the two -10s in column 1 should have been -8 and -7 as in the T array from Equation 3.3. Consequently, if we applied Equation 3.2 to the above array we would end up with pixel values that are approximations to the originals. In other words, we have lost some of the color. If the loss is small, however, it may not be noticed.

In practice, dividing the T values by the same constant is not practical and often results in too much loss. What we really want to do is preserve as much information in the upper left portions of the array as possible because they represent low spatial frequencies. That is, they correspond to less subtle features of the image that would be noticed if changed. Values in the lower right portion correspond to fine detail and changes there might not be noticed as much. Consequently, the usual approach is to define a quantization array, call it U, with smaller values in the upper left portion and larger values in the lower right. Then we define Q using the formula

$$Q[i][j] = \text{Round}(T[i][j]/U[i][j]), \quad \text{for } i = 0, 1, 2, \ldots, 7 \text{ and } j = 0, 1, 2, \ldots, 7$$

where Round is a function that rounds to the nearest integer.

For example, if we use the T array from Equation 3.3 and

$$
U =
\begin{vmatrix}
1 & 3 & 5 & 7 & 9 & 11 & 13 & 15 \\
3 & 5 & 7 & 9 & 11 & 13 & 15 & 17 \\
5 & 7 & 9 & 11 & 13 & 15 & 17 & 19 \\
7 & 9 & 11 & 13 & 15 & 17 & 19 & 21 \\
9 & 11 & 13 & 15 & 17 & 19 & 21 & 23 \\
11 & 13 & 15 & 17 & 19 & 21 & 23 & 25 \\
13 & 15 & 17 & 19 & 21 & 23 & 25 & 27 \\
15 & 17 & 19 & 21 & 23 & 25 & 27 & 29
\end{vmatrix}
\tag{3.6}
$$

then the quantization would yield

$$
Q = \begin{vmatrix}
152 & 0 & -10 & 0 & -1 & 0 & -1 & 0 \\
0 & 0 & 0 & 0 & 0 & 0 & 0 & 0 \\
-10 & 0 & 4 & 0 & 0 & 0 & 0 & 0 \\
0 & 0 & 0 & 0 & 0 & 0 & 0 & 0 \\
-1 & 0 & 0 & 0 & 1 & 0 & 0 & 0 \\
0 & 0 & 0 & 0 & 0 & 0 & 0 & 0 \\
-1 & 0 & 0 & 0 & 0 & 0 & 0 & 0 \\
0 & 0 & 0 & 0 & 0 & 0 & 0 & 0
\end{vmatrix} \tag{3.7}
$$

Reversing the process and multiplying each element in Q by the corresponding element in U would generate

$$
T = \begin{vmatrix}
152 & 0 & -50 & 0 & -9 & 0 & -13 & 0 \\
0 & 0 & 0 & 0 & 0 & 0 & 0 & 0 \\
-50 & 0 & 36 & 0 & 0 & 0 & 0 & 0 \\
0 & 0 & 0 & 0 & 0 & 0 & 0 & 0 \\
-9 & 0 & 0 & 0 & 17 & 0 & 0 & 0 \\
0 & 0 & 0 & 0 & 0 & 0 & 0 & 0 \\
-13 & 0 & 0 & 0 & 0 & 0 & 0 & 0 \\
0 & 0 & 0 & 0 & 0 & 0 & 0 & 0
\end{vmatrix} \tag{3.8}
$$

It is still only an approximation to the original T of Equation 3.3, but there will generally be less loss in the lower spatial frequency areas of the array, which will preserve more of the less-subtle aspects of the original image. It may come at the expense of more loss in higher spatial frequency areas but, again, the losses would be less noticeable. Furthermore, the quantized array Q still has considerable redundancy, which should lead to some good compression.

We should note that JPEG does not prescribe the contents of U. It typically depends a great deal on the applications, and great efforts often go into finding a U that helps compress well with minimal loss.

Encoding Phase   Much of the discussion on JPEG so far has involved complex transformations and quantizing results. We have yet to compress anything. These steps exist primarily to transform the data into a form suitable for compression. The encoding phase finally does the compression. The main function of the encoding phase is to linearize the two-dimensional data from the Q array and compress it for transmission. A logical approach might be to linearize by transmitting Q one row at a time. With all the 0s that appear, we could use run-length coding. While this will certainly work, there is a better way.

Figure 3.39 illustrates how we can order the elements from the array Q from Equation 3.7. If we were to order the array elements by transmitting a row at a

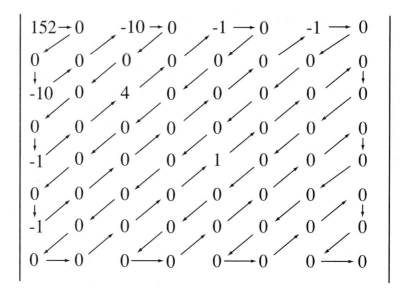

Figure 3.39   Order in which Array Elements Are Transmitted

time, starting with row 1, we would have the following runs of 0s (of length greater than 8):

- Run of length 9 from rows 1 and 2
- Run of length 13 from rows 3 and 4
- Run of length 11 from rows 5 and 6
- Run of length 15 from rows 7 and 8

If, however, we ordered the elements as indicated by the arrows in the figure, we have the following runs (of length greater than 8):

- Run of length 11
- Run of length 24

As we can see, there is a much longer run with this second order. We don't intend this to be a formal proof that this method of linearizing the elements is optimal. On the other hand, we make the argument that by following the arrows of Figure 3.39, elements representing higher spatial frequencies tend to be gathered together. That is not the case if we transmit a row or column at a time. Since the quantization array, U, often has larger values in the higher spatial frequency areas, the quantized values have a higher probability of being 0. By keeping the higher spatial frequency values together we have a higher probability of producing long runs of 0s, which, in turn, leads to better compression.

JPEG can also use some type of Huffman code for the nonzero values in cases where the DCT and quantization phases produce certain nonzero values with a higher frequency. Finally, since the 8×8 arrays represent only a small portion of an image, many arrays must be transmitted. In many images, consecutive arrays represent adjacent blocks that may differ little from each other. There is even the potential for transmitting differences among nonzero elements as opposed to the elements themselves, thus adding yet another dimension to the compression.

In summary, JPEG is complex and the amount of compression depends a great deal on the image and the quantization array. The quantization array is not prescribed by JPEG but rather depends on the application. Under the right conditions JPEG is known to produce compression ratios of 20:1 and better (meaning the transmitted file is 5% the size of the original). It is a complex method of compression that is of interest because of its widespread applications. Certainly, a more detailed discussion of JPEG is possible; if you are interested in such details, you can consult References [Wa91b], [Ho97], [Pe93], and [Ha97].

MPEG

Having described how to compress still images, the next logical step is to discuss video or motion pictures. However, before we deal with compressing those we must understand just how motion in a video clip is achieved. Motion, whether it be on the big screen, a television, or a video clip from a CD-ROM or the Internet on a monitor, is really not much more than just a rapid display of still pictures. Standards for video differ worldwide, but a common standard defined by the NTSC produces motion by displaying still pictures at a rate of 30 frames per second. This is fast enough to fool your eyes, giving the perception of true motion. Images produced at rates much slower than that produce motion that appears jerkier, which is reminiscent of some very old movies.

The group that defines standards for video compression is the Moving Pictures Expert Group (MPEG). Like JPEG, it is the result of a cooperative arrangement between ISO, IEC, and ITU, and people often use the phrase *MPEG compression* when referring to video compression. MPEG, however, is not a single standard. In fact, there are several standards, known as MPEG-1, MPEG-2, and MPEG-4. Yes, there was an MPEG-3, which was originally intended for high definition television (HDTV), but HDTV was added to the MPEG-2 standard instead. MPEG-1 was designed for video on CD-ROM and early direct broadcast satellite systems. MPEG-2 is used for more demanding applications, such as multimedia entertainment and HDTV. MPEG-4 is still in progress and is intended for videoconferencing over low-bandwidth channels.

At this level we will not worry about the different MPEG variations and are content to spend some time discussing MPEG-1 (which we will, from this point on, refer to as MPEG). As before, if you would like information beyond what we will present you can consult References [Di91], [Ho97], and [Ta96]. Also, MPEG actually compresses audio and video separately, and we will deal only with video compression. You can find a description of MPEG audio encoding in Reference [Ho97].

Since video is actually a series of still pictures, it seems logical to assume that MPEG uses JPEG compression or a variation of it to compress each image. While that is essentially true, using only JPEG compression for each still picture does not provide sufficient compression for most applications. In the last section, we stated that a still picture could contain 7,372,800 bits. At a 20:1 compression ratio we could reduce the image to 368,640 bits. However, remember that NTSC video standards specify 30 images per second, so that we would still need to transmit $30 \times 368,640 = 11,059,200$ bits per second. That's a lot, especially if it is being sent over shared channels being used by others who also want access to video.

What makes MPEG feasible is additional redundancy (**temporal redundancy**) found in successive frames. Basically, this means that no matter how much action you see in a video, the difference between two consecutive frames is usually quite small. Even popular action heroes require a couple of seconds to get blown across a room. That's a good 60 frames, and the hero may only travel a few feet from one frame to another. If you consider scenes with little action, consecutive frames may be almost identical. Since JPEG compresses information found on a single image, MPEG must deal with the temporal redundancy. Actually, we addressed this issue earlier in the section when we discussed relative encoding. Essentially, that technique sends a base frame and then encodes successive frames by computing the difference (which will contain little information), compressing, and transmitting it. The receiving end can reconstruct the frame based on the first base frame and the differences it receives.

To some extent this is what MPEG does, but, as you probably suspect, it is more complex than that. Calculating differences with prior frames works well to place figures that are moving across your view, since those figures are in a prior frame. But it does not work well for images that were not in a prior frame. For example, a completely new scene cannot be compressed this way. The difference between a new scene and an old one is large and you might as well just send the new scene. Another example involves objects hidden behind someone who is moving. As a person moves across a scene, objects that were hidden behind the person in a previous frame come into view in successive frames.

MPEG identifies three different types of frames:[*]

- **I-frame (intrapicture frame).** This is a self-contained frame that is, for all intents and purposes, just a JPEG-encoded image.

- **P-frame (predicted frame).** This frame is similar to what we have just discussed in that it is encoded by computing differences between a current and a previous frame.

- **B-frame (bidirectional frame).** This is similar to a P-frame except that it is interpolated between a previous and a future frame. (Yes, this sounds a bit peculiar, but we'll get to that).

There are two issues that need to be discussed. First is how and why the different frames types appear in a frame sequence. Second is how P- and B-frames are

---

[*]There is actually a fourth type of frame called a **DC-frame** which can be used for fast searches on devices such as tape recorders. It doesn't play a role in our goals here, so we won't discuss it.

reconstructed from other frames. We start by indicating that I-frames must appear periodically in any frame sequence. There are a couple of reasons for this. As we have stated, calculating differences works well when there is little difference between frames. But small differences from a fixed frame are usually localized over a relatively short period of time. Eventually, a scene changes or new objects come into view. If we try to measure everything relative to the very first frame, we will have little success. If we use a relative differencing and measure differences in consecutive frames, then any error introduced in one frame is propagated throughout subsequent frames. A second reason is appropriate in broadcast applications, where an individual can tune in at any time. If everything was encoded relative to the very first frame and you tuned in a bit late, you have nothing to which you can compare successive frames. Getting I-frames periodically ensures that differences are measured to relatively current scenes. It can also eliminate the propagation of errors.

Figure 3.40 shows a typical MPEG frame sequence. Sandwiched between two I-frames are four B-frames and a single P-frame. In general, the number of B-frames can vary, but typically there will be one P-frame between two groups of B-frames. The P-frame is essentially a difference from the prior I-frame, and the B-frames are interpolated from the nearest I- and P-frames. So, for example, the first two B-frames are interpolated from the first I-frame and the P-frame. The last two B-frames are interpolated from the last I-frame and the P-frame.

A logical question to ask is, How can we interpolate B-frames from frames we haven't received yet? The answer is that Figure 3.40 shows the frames in the order they are to be viewed, but that is not the order in which they are transmitted. The P-frame will be sent prior to the first two B-frames, and the second I-frame will be sent prior to the last two B-frames. The P-frame and two I-frames can then be buffered, and subsequently received B-frames can be decoded at the viewing end.

P-frames are coded using a method called **motion-compensated prediction,** which is based on concepts specified in ITU recommendation H.261. It works by dividing the image into a collection of macroblocks, each containing 256 pixels (16 horizontal and 16 vertical). Assuming each pixel has one luminescence and two chrominance values, the macroblock can be represented by three 16×16 arrays. To help speed things up, the two chrominance arrays are actually reduced to two 8×8 arrays. Figure 3.41 shows how that is done. The 16×16 array is viewed as a collection of 2×2 arrays of chrominance values. The average of each set of four chrominance values replaces the four values, and the result is an 8×8 array. Again, there is some loss in doing this, but the loss is often not perceptible.

Prior to sending a P-frame, an algorithm examines each macroblock and locates the best matching macroblock in the prior I-frame. It won't necessarily be in the

Figure 3.40   Typical MPEG Frame Sequence

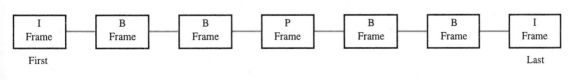

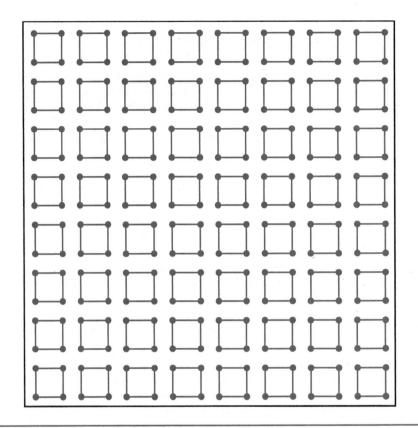

Figure 3.41 Reduction of a 16 × 16 Chrominance Array to an 8 × 8 Chrominance Array

same relative position[*] since we are assuming that images move from one frame to another. MPEG does not specify what constitutes a best-match—this is dependent on specific applications. Once the best-match macroblock is found, the algorithm calculates differences between the matching macroblocks and also calculates a **motion vector** (essentially a vertical and horizontal pixel displacement), which it stores along with the differences. This is done for all macroblocks in a frame, and the results are encoded and transmitted in a manner similar to that specified by JPEG. At the decoding end, the differences are used to reconstruct the macroblocks and the motion vectors are used to determine their position in the frame.

B-frame decoding is similar except macroblocks are interpolated from matching macroblocks in a prior and future frame. **Interpolation** is a way of predicting a value based on two existing values and is a common topic in numerical

---

[*]This does not mean the algorithm searches the entire frame looking for a best match. Typically, it looks at the macroblock in the same relative position and at others in nearby positions. This helps speed the encoding algorithm.

analysis. Figure 3.42 illustrates what we mean. If the horizontal line represents time and we know the values of some quantities (Y_P and Y_F, respectively) at some past and future times, we can estimate the value (Y_C) at the current time. One way is to draw a line connecting points corresponding to Y_P and Y_P and calculate the y-coordinate of that line at the current time. This is an example of linear interpolation. There are many other ways to interpolate, but that's another topic.

The important thing here is that both past and future frames can be searched to find matches for a macroblock, with differences and motion vectors calculated for each. The value of the macroblock and its correct placement in the current frame can then be interpolated from the matching macroblocks and the motion vectors. As previously stated, this is particularly useful when there is no good match for a macroblock in a previous frame, as can happen when new objects come into view. However, that object would likely be in a future frame and that information can be used to calculate and place a macroblock in the current frame.

Before we finish it is noteworthy to mention that despite the standards, MPEG encoding and decoding requires a lot of computing power. Finding matches and

Figure 3.42   Using Interpolation to Estimate a Value

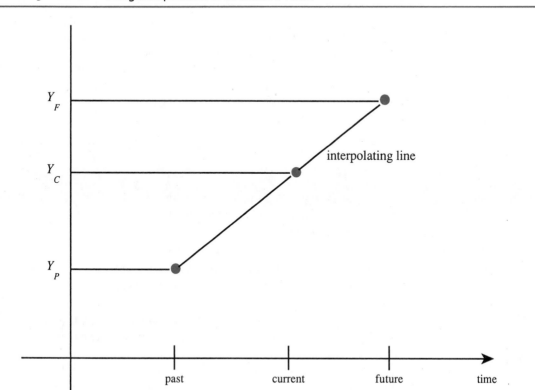

calculating motion vectors for a large number of bits is nontrivial. However, in many multimedia applications, video is recorded just once and stored in some medium. Since this is done well in advance of viewing, the time required for encoding is not that much of a concern. Viewing the video, however, is done frequently and in real time. Decoding must be done quickly or the motion appears jerky. Try looking at some multimedia applications using a PC that is a couple of years old and you will likely notice that the images do not flow with the smoothness of real video.

Faster CPUs certainly help, but the CPU does so many other things that this is not a long-term solution to the development of fast multimedia applications. One of the more significant developments in recent years is the MMX technology built into Pentium chips for multimedia applications. It enables applications such as MPEG (actually MPEG-2) decoding, thus resulting in significant overall performance increase. Describing MMX technology belongs in a computer architecture course, but because of its impact on MPEG-2 applications it is appropriate to mention it here. Further details regarding MMX technology and its impact on multimedia performance are found in Reference [Pe97].

SUMMARY OF COMPRESSION TECHNIQUES

The compression techniques discussed here are representative of schemes in actual use, but they by no means represent the entire spectrum of techniques. References [Ru89], [Ta96], and [Wa91a] mention other techniques, and References [Ne91] and [Ho97] are devoted completely to compression techniques (and are good reading for anyone seriously interested in the topic). Remember that compression techniques are designed for different types of transmissions. Table 3.12 gives a brief summary of the compression techniques discussed in this chapter.

Table 3.12   Summary of Compression Techniques

COMPRESSION TECHNIQUE	HOW IT COMPRESSES
Huffman code	Uses short bit patterns for more frequently used letters and longer ones for less frequently used letters.
Run-length encoding	Looks for long runs of a particular bit or character.
Relative encoding	Looks for small differences between consecutive frames.
Lempel-Ziv encoding	Looks for repeated occurrences of strings without assuming what those strings are.
JPEG	Compresses still images by applying discrete cosine transforms to 8×8 blocks of pixels, quantizing the results, and encoding the quantized frequency coefficients.
MPEG	Uses methods similar to JPEG compression but also takes advantage of redundancy between successive frames to use interframe compression by calculating differences between successive frames and using motion prediction techniques.

3.6   SUMMARY

This chapter dealt with data communication, which we see is a step above data transmission. It is one thing to send signals over some medium, but it is quite another to communicate effectively. We must be aware of the information inherent in the data and the measures necessary to make sure it reaches its destination. The chapter covered the following important topics:

- **Parallel and serial transmission.** Parallel transmission sends bits simultaneously using several lines; serial transmission sends them in sequence using a single line.

- **Synchronous and asynchronous transmission.** Asynchronous transmission sends each byte separately with a start and stop bit before and after the byte. Synchronous transmission groups bytes into a frame format and sends the entire frame.

- **Simplex, half-duplex, and full-duplex communication.** Simplex communication is one-way only. Half-duplex communication allows two-way communication, but the sending and receiving stations must alternate. Full-duplex communication allows both stations to send simultaneously.

- **Interface protocols.** The RS-232 protocol connecting a DCE and DTE is probably the most well known. It defines circuit definitions and rules that both devices must follow to communicate with each other. The RS-449 protocol was designed to improve on the RS-232 protocol by allowing faster data rates over longer distances. Because of its popularity, however, the RS-232 is still used frequently. The X.21 interface was designed for digital interfaces. Compared with the RS standards, it uses fewer lines between the DTE and DCE but requires more logic to interpret the exchanged signals.

- **Multiplexing.** Many applications do not need the full power of a high-speed network, or the cost may make separate connections prohibitive. A multiplexer can interface between several devices and a single network connection. Frequency-division multiplexers combine analog signals from different channels into a single analog signal. Time-division multiplexers put bit streams from different sources into a single frame of fixed length. Statistical multiplexers also combine bit streams into a single frame, but vary the frame size depending on which sources are sending data.

- **Contention protocols.** Since a network is meant to service many users, it must allow them all to communicate. This means making decisions when two or more users want to send simultaneously. One approach, the Aloha protocol, was designed for packet radio communication in the Hawaiian Islands. If two frames overlap, they collide. When the sending station hears no acknowledgment, it sends again. Slotted Aloha is similar, but requires that each station send only at the start of predefined time slots.

  CSMA took Aloha one step farther by listening to the medium before sending. It would send only if there was no traffic. If there was traffic its next step depended on which variation was used. With p-persistent CSMA, the station continued to monitor the medium. When the medium became quiet, there was a probability of p that the station would send. With nonpersistent CSMA, the station did not monitor the medium. It just waited a random number of slot times and tried again. The last variation, CSMA/CD, used a collision detection technique to stop sending if a station detected a collision. The intent was to decrease the amount of time during which frames collide.

Another protocol, token passing, is used in two types of networks: token ring and token bus networks. In both types, a special frame called a token circulates among the stations. A station can send only when it has the token. A token ring station is organized physically in a ring, and token bus stations communicate via a common bus.

- **Data compression.** One goal of data communications is to send information faster and more cheaply. One solution is to reduce the number of bits sent. The Huffman algorithm does this by assigning shorter codes to more frequently occurring symbols. Run-length encoding replaces long runs of a character or bit by the length of the run. Relative encoding measures the difference between successive frames and sends it. The Lempel-Ziv algorithm replaces redundant character sequences by a code. Decompression replaces the code by the string it represents. Finally, MPEG and JPEG are used for image compression. JPEG reduces the spatial redundancy found in many still pictures. MPEG must deal with not only spatial redundancy but also the temporal redundancy across consecutive frames.

Review Questions

1. Distinguish between serial and parallel communication.

2. Distinguish between synchronous and asynchronous communication.

3. List typical fields in a data frame and what they contain.

4. Distinguish among simplex, half-duplex, and full-duplex communication.

5. How does full-duplex communication prevent signals traveling in opposite directions from colliding?

6. Are the following statements TRUE or FALSE? Why?

    a. Parallel and serial communications require different types of cables.

    b. A PC normally connects directly to a network.

    c. An RS-232 interface requires a 25-pin connector.

    d. Two compatible PCs can communicate by installing a cable between each one's RS-232 port.

    e. Devices using an RS-232 interface can automatically communicate.

    f. Frequency-division multiplexing is a form of parallel communication.

g. Time-division multiplexing applies only to digital communications.

h. A time-division multiplexer allows its combined input capability to exceed its output capability.

i. The nonpersistent protocols outperform the persistent protocols in all cases.

j. 1-persistent is optimal among the *p*-persistent protocols because a station never waits voluntarily, thus wasting time.

7. Distinguish between a DTE and DCE.

8. What is a null modem?

9. In Figure 3.9, why is each DTE pin 20 connected to the other's pin 8?

10. In Figure 3.9, why are each DTE's pins 4 and 5 connected?

11. Distinguish between a balanced and an unbalanced circuit.

12. Distinguish between frequency-division multiplexing and time-division multiplexing.

13. What is a multiplexer?

14. What is a channel?

15. Distinguish among a carrier signal, a modulating signal, and a modulated signal.

16. What is a primary motivation for using a multiplexer?

17. Why does a DS-1 frame field have eight bits for each channel?

18. What are guard bands?

19. What is a contention protocol?

20. Describe the Aloha protocol, listing its advantages and disadvantages.

21. Distinguish between slotted and pure Aloha.

22. What is the difference between 0-persistent CSMA and nonpersistent CSMA?

23. Why does collision detection improve the performance of CSMA?

24. Why does the performance of persistent protocols degrade as *G* increases, whereas the reverse is true of a nonpersistent protocol?

25. What is the binary exponential backoff algorithm?

26. What is a token?

27. What is a slotted ring?

28. Distinguish between token ring and token bus networks.

29. Distinguish between data and information.

30. What is a Huffman code?

31. What is the Huffman code's no-prefix property?

32. What is a frequency-dependent code?

33. What does run-length encoding mean?

34. What is relative encoding?

35. What is Lempel-Ziv encoding?

36. Both the Lempel-Ziv and Huffman algorithms are similar in that they take advantage of repetitions. How do they differ?

37. What are the main differences between JPEG and MPEG compression methods?

38. Distinguish among I-, P-, and B-frames in the context of MPEG encoding.

Exercises

1. Why do asynchronous communications require additional start and stop bits? What is wrong with letting the first bit in a transmission act as a start bit and the last one act as a stop bit?

2. Since parallel communications transmit bits simultaneously, why not design parallel communications with an arbitrarily large number of parallel lines to decrease transmission time?

3. What is a minimal set of circuits required to establish a full-duplex communication over an RS-232 Interface?

4. Why must the DTE assert an RTS (Request to Send) circuit before sending to the DCE, but the DCE is not required to assert any Request to Send line prior to sending to the DTE?

5. Some null modems connect a DTE's pin 20 to its own pins 5 and 6. What purpose does this serve?

6. Some null modems connect a DTE's pin 4 to its own pin 5 and to the other DTE's pin 8. What purpose does this serve?

7. RS-449 was designed to replace RS-232 and, in fact, can do anything RS-232 can. Yet RS-232 remains a dominant standard. Why do you suppose this is true?

8. If you have a PC or access to a terminal that has an RS-232 interface, check the manual to determine what circuits are used.

9. Write a program to produce a graph of a modulating signal and a modulated signal similar to those of Figure 3.15.

10. Suppose five devices are connected to a statistical time division multiplexer (similar to the situation in Figure 3.18) and that each produces output as shown here. Construct the frame that the multiplexer sends.

```
Device 1: . . . . Ø  A₃  Ø  A₂  A₁
Device 2: . . . . B₄ B₃  Ø  B₂  B₁
Device 3: . . . . Ø  C₂  Ø  Ø   C₁
Device 4: . . . . D₅ D₄ D₃  D₂  D₁
Device 5: . . . . Ø  Ø  E₂  Ø   E₁
```

11. What is the purpose of adding 0.5 to the sine function to form $f(t)$ in Figure 3.15? That is, what happens if that term is eliminated?

12. Discuss the significance of the graphs in Figure 3.25.

13. Comment on the following statement:

> With 1-persistent CSMA a waiting station always transmits when the medium is clear. Why not change the protocol so that when a medium is clear the station waits the amount of time it would take for another station's transmission to reach it? If it is still clear, then transmit. This should decrease the chances of two waiting stations colliding.

14. Comment on the usefulness of a 0-persistent CSMA.

15. Suppose three stations using a 0.5-persistent protocol are waiting for an idle medium.

a. What is the probability of a collision when the medium clears?

b. What is the probability of a successful transmission when the medium clears?

c. What is the probability that no station will send anything when the medium clears?

16. Repeat Exercise 15, but assume the stations use a 0.25-persistent protocol.

17. Suppose two stations using CSMA/CD and the binary exponential backoff algorithm have just sent transmissions that have collided.

a. What is the probability that they will collide again during the next time slot?

b. What is the probability that both stations will transmit successfully during the next two time slots?

c. What is the probability that they will collide two more times? Three more times?

18. Suppose three stations using CSMA/CD and the binary exponential backoff algorithm have just sent transmissions that have all collided.

a. What is the probability that they will all collide again during the next time slot?

b. What is the probability that all three stations will transmit successfully during the next three time slots?

c. What is the probability that any two will collide during the next time slot?

19. Suppose the binary exponential backoff algorithm is altered so that a station will always wait 0 or 1 time slots regardless of how many collisions have occurred. How is the effectiveness changed?

20. Assume n is some positive integer. Suppose the binary exponential backoff algorithm is altered so that a station will always wait anywhere between 0 and 2^n-1 time slots regardless of how many collisions have occurred. How is the effectiveness changed?

21. Can you devise a four-bit code similar to that in Table 3.6?

22. Devise a Huffman code for letters whose frequency of occurrence is in the following table.

LETTER	FREQUENCY
A	15%
B	25%
C	20%
D	10%
E	10%
F	20%

Without constructing them, how many different Huffman codes could you create?

23. Compress the following bit stream using run-length encoding. Use five bits to code each run length. Parenthesized expressions indicate runs.

1 (33 zeros) 1 (25 zeros) 1 1 1 (44 zeros) 1 (2 zeros) 1 (45 zeros)

Express the length of the compressed stream as a percentage of the original.

24. With run-length encoding, how many 0s must appear in a run before the code actually compresses?

25. Give an example of a situation in which run-length encoding would perform better (worse) than a Huffman code.

26. Comment on the following statement:

In an era of megabit and gigabit transmissions, compression schemes will save only the smallest fractions of a second. Therefore, the time saved is not worth the additional overhead of compressing bits.

27. Use the Huffman code from Table 3.8 and interpret the following bit stream (starting from the leftmost bit).

1100111001000100011110110

28. Which of the following are Huffman codes? Why?

CHARACTER	CODE	CHARACTER	CODE	CHARACTER	CODE
A	01	A	10	A	1
B	001	B	001	B	01
C	10	C	11	C	000
D	110	D	101	D	001
E	010	E	000	E	0001

29. Fill in language-specific details and implement the Lempel-Ziv algorithms of Figure 3.35.

30. How do the algorithms of Figure 3.35 change if we use a full alphabet?

31. Complete Table 3.9.

32. Run the Lempel-Ziv compression and decompression algorithms starting with the string below. Create tables similar to Tables 3.9, 3.10, and 3.11.

BBABAABBAABACBACBACBABAAABAA

33. Write a program that applies Equation 3.2 to the spatial frequencies in each of Figures 3.38a and 3.38b.

34. Perform a discrete cosine transform (Equation 3.1) on the following pixel array. You should write a program to do the calculations.

```
10 10 10 10 10 10 10 10
10 20 20 20 20 20 20 10
10 20 30 30 30 30 20 10
10 20 30 40 40 30 20 10
10 20 30 40 40 30 20 10
10 20 30 30 30 30 20 10
10 20 20 20 20 20 20 10
10 10 10 10 10 10 10 10
```

REFERENCES

1. [Bl89] Black, U. *Data Networks: Concept, Theory, and Practice.* Englewood Cliffs, NJ: Prentice-Hall, 1989.

2. [Cr90] Crichton, M. *Jurassic Park.* New York: Ballantine Books, 1990.

3. [Di91] Didier, L. "MPEG: A Video Compression Standard for Multimedia Applications." *Communications of the ACM,* vol. 34, no. 4 (April 1991), 46–58.

4. [Dr95] Drozdeck, A. and D. Simon, *Data Structures in C.* Boston: PWS, 1995.

5. [Fe92] Feig, E. and S. Winograd, "Fast Algorithms for Discrete Cosine Transformations." *IEEE Transactions on Signal Processing,* vol. 40. (September 1992) 2174–2193.

6. [Ha97] Hankerson, D., G. A. Harris, and P. D. Johnson. *Introduction to Information Theory and Data Compression.* Boca Raton, FL: CRC Press, 1997.

7. [Ho97] Hoffman, R. *Data Compression in Digital Systems.* New York: Chapman and Hall, 1997.

8. [Hu52] Huffman, D. "A Method for the Construction of Minimum Redundancy Codes." *IRE Proceedings,* vol. 40 (September 1952), 1098–1101.

9. [Kl75] Kleinrock, L. and F. Tobagi. "Random Access Techniques for Data Transmission over Packet-switched Radio Channels." *AFIPS Conference Proceedings,* vol. 44 (1975), 187.

10. [Ma72] Martin, J. *Systems Analysis for Data Transmission.* Englewood Cliffs, NJ: Prentice-Hall, 1972.

11. [Mi87] Mitrani, I. *Modeling of Computer and Communication Systems.* London: Cambridge University Press, 1987.

12. [Mo89] Moshos, G. *Data Communications: Principles and Problems.* St. Paul, MN: West, 1989.

13. [Ne91] Nelson, M. *The Data Compression Book.* Redwood City, CA: M & T Books, 1991.

14. [Pe93] Pennebaker, W. B. and J. L. Mitchell. *JPEG Still Image Data Compression Standard.* New York: Van Nostrand Reinhold, 1993.

15. [Pe97] Peleg, A., S. Wilkie, and U. Weiser. "Intel MMX for Multimedia PCs." *Communications of the ACM,* vol. 40, No. 1 (January 1997), 25–38.

16. [Ra90] Rao, K. R. and P. Yip. *Discrete Cosine Transform-Algorithms, Advantages, Applications.* London, Academic Press, 1990.

17. [Ro75] Roberts, L. "ALOHA Packet System with and without Slots and Capture." *Computer Communications Review,* vol. 5 (April 1975), 28–42.

18. [Ru89] Russel, D. *The Principles of Computer Networking.* Cambridge University Press, 1989.

19. [Sh90] Sherman, K. *Data Communications: A User's Guide,* 3rd ed. Englewood Cliffs, NJ: Prentice-Hall, 1990.

20. [St94] Stallings, W. *Data and Computer Communications,* 4th ed. New York: Macmillan, 1994.

21. [St96] Stanley, W. *Network Analysis with Applications,* 2nd ed. Englewood Cliffs, NJ: Prentice-Hall, 1996.

22. [Ta96] Tanenbaum, A. S. *Computer Networks,* 3rd ed. Englewood Cliffs, NJ: Prentice-Hall, 1996.

23. [Wa91a] Walrand, J. *Communications Networks: A First Course.* Boston: Richard D. Irwin, 1991.

24. [Wa91b] Wallace, G. "The JPEG Still Picture Compression Standard." *Communications of the ACM,* Vol. 34, no. 4 (April 1991), 30–44.

25. [Wa96] Walrand, J. and P. Varaiya. *High-Performance Communication Networks.* San Francisco: Morgan Kaufmann, 1996.

26. [We84] Welch, T. "A Technique for High-Performance Data Compression." *Computer,* vol. 17, no. 6 (May 1984), 8–19.

CHAPTER 4

DATA SECURITY AND INTEGRITY

Who could deny that privacy is a jewel? It has always been the mark of privilege, the distinguishing feature of a truly urbane culture. Out of the cave, the tribal teepee, the pueblo, the community fortress, man emerged to build himself a house of his own with a shelter in it for himself and his diversions. Every age has seen it so. The poor might have to huddle together in cities for need's sake, and the frontiersman cling to his neighbors for the sake of protection. But in each civilization, as it advanced, those who could afford it chose the luxury of a withdrawing-place.
—**Phyllis McGinley** (1905–1978), U.S. poet, author

4.1 INTRODUCTION

Chapters 2 and 3 dealt with many of the mechanisms necessary to transmit information. All of these methods, no matter how sophisticated, are not sufficient to guarantee effective and safe communications. Consider an example in which you receive the following message via electronic mail:

I heard from your brothel in New Orleans. Plan to meet there tomorrow.

Your reactions could be anything from confusion to shock to terror. What if your spouse got the message first? There is no way for your spouse to know that the message should have read:

I heard from your brother in New Orleans. Plan to meet there tomorrow.

What happened? The person sending the message is not a practical joker. He or she actually sent the innocuous message. The problem was in the message transmission. The letter *r* from the word *brother* was ASCII coded as 1110010. Unfortunately, some electrical interference changed the middle four bits 1001 to 0110, and the bit string received was 1101100, the code for the letter *l*.

I think we would all agree that a system that allows altered messages to be delivered is less than desirable. But the fact is that errors do occur. Any message transmitted electronically is susceptible to interference. Sunspots, electrical storms, power fluctuations or a digger hitting a cable with a shovel can do amazing and unpredictable things to transmissions. We simply cannot allow shuttle astronauts to receive incorrect navigational instructions or Swiss banks to deposit a million dollars more than they should (unless it's into my account!). Any communications system must deliver accurate messages.

The ability to detect when a transmission has been changed is called **error detection.** In most cases, when errors are detected the message is discarded, the sender is notified, and the message is sent again. We will discuss protocols that do this in Chapter 5. In other cases when an error is detected it may actually be fixed without a second transmission. This is called **error correction.** The sender never knows the message was damaged and subsequently fixed. The bottom line is that the message eventually is delivered correctly.

Integrity is not enough, however. Another issue is security. When you go to the bank, you don't normally show your deposit slips and balances to the person standing in line with you. For the same reasons, electronic funds transfers between banks must be secure so that unauthorized people cannot get access to your financial arrangements. Not just banks, but many other communications systems as well must be secure. Ideally, they should provide easy access to authorized people and no access to unauthorized people. But how can you have security when information is sent over microwaves and satellites? The information travels freely through the air, and unauthorized reception is virtually impossible to enforce. Even with cable it may be difficult to prevent someone from finding an isolated spot in a closet or basement and tapping into the cable.

One common approach to secure transmissions, strangely enough, does not worry about unauthorized reception. Why worry about what you cannot prevent? Instead, this approach alters (encrypts) messages so that even if they are intercepted by unauthorized people they are not intelligible. Encryption is common in cable television (CATV) transmission. Anyone with CATV can receive the premium movie stations, but the signals are scrambled so that viewing is impossible. If you pay your local cable company the appropriate fees they will unscramble the signals for you or give you a device that does so. Only then may you watch all the available movies.

In this chapter, we deal with the issues of integrity and security. Sections 4.2 through 4.4 discuss different ways to detect and correct transmission errors. They show that some techniques are implemented easily but are not very effective, whereas other, more complex techniques are very effective. Effectiveness at the expense of simplicity is an almost universal trade-off.

Sections 4.5 and 4.6 present different ways of encrypting information and some of the issues surrounding encryption standards. True to the universal trade-off just mentioned, some simple encryption schemes are not very secure and some theoretically difficult ones are very secure. We finish the chapter by discussing some of the most serious threats to computer and communications security: worms, viruses, and hackers. We will describe them and discuss some common approaches to battling them.

4.2   PARITY CHECKING

Most error detection techniques require sending additional bits whose values depend on the data that is sent. Thus, if the data is changed the additional bit values no longer correspond to the new data (at least in theory). Probably the most common approach is **parity checking,** which involves counting all the 1 bits in the data and adding one more bit to make the total number of 1 bits even (even parity) or odd (odd parity). The extra bit is called the **parity bit.** We will base our discussions on an even parity and leave it to the reader to construct similar discussions for odd parity.

To illustrate, suppose the number of 1 bits in the data is odd. By defining the parity bit as 1, the total number of 1 bits is now even. Similarly, if the number of 1 bits in the data is already even, the parity bit is 0. Consider the bit streams in Figure 4.1. The first one has four 1 bits. Therefore, its parity bit is 0. The second one has five 1 bits, so its parity bit is 1.

PARITY CHECKING ANALYSIS

Parity checking will detect any single-bit error. The parity bit is transmitted with the data bits and the receiver checks the parity. If the receiver finds an odd number of 1 bits, an error has occurred. Single-bit errors are very rare in electronic transmissions, however. For example, suppose an error occurred because of a brief power surge or static electricity whose duration is a hundredth of a second. In human terms, a hundredth of a second is barely noticeable. But if the data rate is 64 Kbps (kilobits per second), approximately 640 bits may be affected in that hundredth of a second. When many bits are damaged we call this a **burst error.**

How does parity checking work for arbitrary burst errors? Suppose two bits change during transmission. If they were both 0, they change to 1. Two extra 1s still make the total number of 1 bits even. Similarly, if they were both 1 they both change to 0 and there are two fewer 1 bits, but still an even number. If they were opposite values and both change, they are still opposite. This time the number of 1 bits remains the same. The bottom line is that parity checks do not detect double-bit errors.

In general, if an odd number of bits change, parity checking will detect the error. If an even number of bits change, parity checking will not detect the error. The conclusion is that parity checks will catch about 50% of burst errors, and a 50% accuracy rate is not good for a communications network.

Figure 4.1   Detecting Single-Bit Errors Using Parity Checking

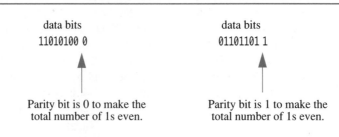

Does this make parity checks useless? The answer is no, for two reasons. First, some computer memory organizations store the bits from a byte or word on different chips. Thus, when the word is accessed the bits travel different paths. In such cases the malfunction of one path can cause a single-bit error. Such architectures often use additional memory chips for parity bits. (The details are beyond the scope of this text.) The second reason is that parity checking is the basis for other, more sophisticated detection techniques, discussed in this and the next sections.

DOUBLE-BIT ERROR DETECTION

Since a single parity check will detect any single-bit error, you might guess that extra parity checks can detect multiple errors. They can, up to a point. For example, suppose we wanted to detect double-bit errors. One approach is to use two parity checks, one for the odd-numbered bits and one for the even-numbered bits. Figure 4.2 shows how to do this. In the figure, one parity bit is used for positions 1, 3, 5, and 7 and the other for positions 2, 4, 6, and 8. Consequently, if any single bit or any two consecutive bits are changed, one or both parity checks fail.

You might respond by asking what happens if two even- (or odd-) numbered bits change. The answer is simple: It doesn't work. Even though this method provides a little more error checking than single parity checks, it still won't detect all errors. It is possible to define additional parity checks to account for different combinations of errors, but the choice of which positions to check becomes more difficult. In addition, the number of parity bits increases, resulting in more transmission overhead. Nevertheless, one error correction method does use this approach; we will discuss it in Section 4.4.

BURST ERROR DETECTION

Trying to detect errors in arbitrary positions (burst errors) certainly can be difficult. But perhaps we are approaching this problem the wrong way. Earlier we stated that some

Figure 4.2   Detecting Consecutive Double-Bit Errors Using Parity Checking

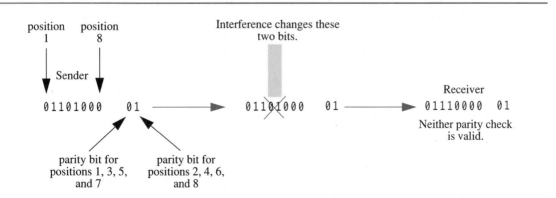

computer memory organizations store bits from a byte in separate chips. The bits travel different paths and the byte is assembled afterward. We can use this idea in communications as well. Frequently, messages (especially long ones) are divided into smaller, more manageable units called **frames.** Rather than sending all bits from one frame together, we can send them separately. Transmitting just one bit of information is not very efficient, however. It is analogous to writing a letter, cutting out the words and stuffing them into separate envelopes, and mailing them. On the other hand, if there are many frames to send perhaps we can transmit many bits together but just one from each frame. The sender has to disassemble them and the receiver reassemble them.

Figure 4.3 illustrates this principle. Create a two-dimensional bit array in which each row corresponds to one frame. The first column contains the first bits from each frame, the second column contains the second bits from each frame, and so on. The figure shows 10 frames of 5 bits each. Next we construct a single parity bit for each frame, which gives us an extra column. Now instead of sending each frame with its parity bit, we send each column separately. In Figure 4.3 we would send six columns consisting of 10 bits each.

Now suppose a burst error occurs and interferes with one transmission. At the most, one bit from each original data frame is actually changed, and the parity checks will detect them. In Figure 4.3, column 4 was damaged, making all the bits 0.[*] The receiver performed the parity checks and found that five of them failed. It does not know which column is the culprit, so it will request a retransmission of all the columns.

Figure 4.3   Detecting Burst Errors Using Parity Bits

	Sender				Receiver	
Row (frame) number	Parity bit for one row			Row number		Parity bit for one row
1	01101	1		1	01101	1
2	10001	0		2	10001	0
3	01110	1		3	01100	1*
4	11001	1		4	11001	1
5	01010	0	Burst error occurs and	5	01000	0*
6	10111	0	destroys column four,	6	10101	0*
7	01100	0	making it all zeroes.	7	01100	0
8	00111	1		8	00101	1*
9	10011	1		9	10001	1*
10	11000	0		10	11000	0
Column number	12345	6		Column number	12345	6

* Parity bit is not correct

---

[*] Note that a burst error does not necessarily change every bit. The bits in a transmission may or may not be damaged. In this example some of the 0s were present in the original frame; some were not. The point is that the receiver has no way of knowing which ones are correct.

This method will guarantee error detection for any single burst error whose duration is less than the time to send one column. But what about burst errors affecting two or more columns? Let's consider the case for two columns. Earlier we said that parity checks will not detect a case in which two bits actually change. Therefore, the only way a burst error affecting two columns can go undetected is when either two bits or no bits are actually changed in each row. In other words, the error must actually change the same bits in each of the two columns.

What are the odds of this happening? Suppose columns i and j were affected by burst errors. Suppose the bits from column i are affected randomly (i.e., there is no predictable pattern of which ones actually change). Now consider any bit from column j. It either changed or it didn't (pretty conclusive, right?). Therefore there is a 1/2 probability that the same thing happened to it that happened to the corresponding bit in column i. If there are n bits in a column, there is a probability of $(1/2)^n$ that either two or no bits are changed in each row and the error goes undetected.

For large n, most burst errors that affect two different columns will be detected. For example, if $n = 20$ the probability the errors will not be detected is $(1/2)^{20} = 1/1,048,576$. This corresponds to a success rate of about 99.9999%. As the number of affected columns increases, the chances that all parity checks are successful become even more remote.

A major disadvantage of this approach is the assembling and reassembling of the frames, which causes quite a bit of overhead. Fortunately, there is another method that is theoretically more difficult to understand, but has an efficient implementation and is very accurate.

4.3   CYCLIC REDUNDANCY CHECKS

In the previous section we saw that parity checking by itself is not very reliable. However, if we combine frames into two-dimensional bit arrays and send them one column at a time, parity checking can be very reliable. A problem with this approach is that an error is not detected until after all the columns are sent. Consequently, the receiver does not know which columns are incorrect. Thus there is no choice but to retransmit all the columns—a lot of extra work for a single error. The problem is compounded if another error occurs as the columns are being sent the second time.

Is there a way to send a frame and determine immediately whether there was an error? In this section we discuss a method called **cyclic redundancy check (CRC)** that does exactly that. We also show that it is a very reliable method that can be implemented efficiently.

CRC is a rather unusual but clever method that does error checking via polynomial division. Your first reaction is probably, "What does polynomial division have to do with transmitting bit strings?" The answer is that the method interprets each bit string as a polynomial. In general, it interprets the bit string

$$b_{n-1}b_{n-2}b_{n-3} \ldots b_2 b_1 b_0$$

as the polynomial

$$b_{n-1}x^{n-1} + b_{n-2}x^{n-2} + b_{n-3}x^{n-3} + \ldots + b_2x^2 + b_1x + b_0$$

For example, the bit string 10010101110 is interpreted as

$$x^{10} + x^7 + x^5 + x^3 + x^2 + x^1$$

Since each b_i is either 0 or 1, we just write x^i when b_i is 1 and do not write any term when b_i is 0.

We outline the CRC method below. We also assume all computations are done modulo 2.

1. Given a bit string, append several 0s to the end of it (we will specify how many and why later) and call it B. Let $B(x)$ be the polynomial corresponding to B.

2. Divide $B(x)$ by some agreed-on polynomial $G(x)$ (**generator polynomial**) and determine the remainder $R(x)$.

3. Define $T(x) = B(x) - R(x)$. Later we will show that $T(x)/G(x)$ generates a 0 remainder and that the subtraction can be done by replacing the previously appended 0 bits with the bit string corresponding to $R(x)$.

4. Transmit T, the bit string corresponding to $T(x)$.

5. Let T' represent the bit stream the receiver gets and $T'(x)$ the associated polynomial. The receiver divides $T'(x)$ by $G(x)$. If there is a 0 remainder the receiver concludes $T = T'$ and no error occurred. Otherwise, the receiver concludes an error occurred and requests a retransmission.

Before you throw your hands up in despair, we agree that questions need answering. Why do we perform each of these steps? Is there any validity to the receiver's conclusion after dividing $T'(x)$ by $G(x)$? How accurate is this method? Must a sender and receiver go through all this work each time a frame is sent? However, we cannot answer these questions until we have covered a few preliminaries. We assume you have some knowledge of polynomials and polynomial operations using real numbers, but we will provide a brief summary of modulo 2 division of polynomials.

POLYNOMIAL DIVISION

Figure 4.4 shows an example of polynomial division $T(x)/G(x)$ where

$$T(x) = x^{10} + x^9 + x^7 + x^5 + x^4$$

and

$$G(x) = x^4 + x^3 + 1$$

This is just like polynomial division from an algebra course except that the calculations use modulo 2 arithmetic. Modulo 2 addition and subtraction are defined by

$$
x^4 + x^3 + 1 \overline{\smash{\big)}\begin{array}{l} x^6 \qquad\qquad + x^3 \quad + x \\ x^{10} + x^9 \quad\quad + x^7 \qquad + x^5 + x^4 \end{array}}
$$

$$\underline{x^{10} + x^9 \qquad\qquad + x^6}$$
$$x^7 + x^6 + x^5 + x^4$$
$$\underline{x^7 + x^6 \qquad\qquad + x^3}$$
$$x^5 + x^4 + x^3$$
$$\underline{x^5 + x^4 \qquad\qquad + x}$$
$$x^3 \qquad + x \qquad \text{remainder}$$

Figure 4.4 Calculation of $(x^{10} + x^9 + x^7 + x^5 + x^4)\,/\,(x^4 + x^3 + 1)$

$$0 + 0 = 0$$
$$1 + 0 = 1$$
$$0 + 1 = 1$$
$$1 + 1 = 0$$

and

$$0 - 0 = 0$$
$$1 - 0 = 1$$
$$0 - 1 = 1$$
$$1 - 1 = 0$$

Note that modulo 2 addition and subtraction are the same as and, in fact, correspond to the exclusive OR operation. This is an important fact we use later when we discuss CRC implementation.

Figure 4.5 shows the same division using synthetic division. You might recall from the same algebra class that it is a shortcut that uses only the coefficients of the polynomials (in this case, bit strings). Remembering to use zeros where there are no polynomial terms, the coefficient list for $x^{10} + x^9 + x^7 + x^5 + x^4$ is 11010110000 and for $x^4 + x^3 + 1$ is 11001.

HOW CRC WORKS

Let's now describe how CRC works. Suppose we want to send the bit string 1101011, and the generator polynomial is $G(x) = x^4 + x^3 + 1$. (We will discuss some criteria for choosing $G(x)$ later.)

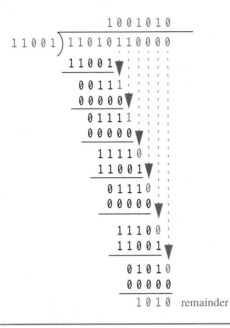

Figure 4.5 Synthetic Division of $(x^{10} + x^9 + x^7 + x^5 + x^4) / (x^4 + x^3 + 1)$

Step 1: Append 0s to the end of the string. The number of 0s is the same as the degree of the generator polynomial (in this case, 4). Thus the string becomes 11010110000.

Step 2: Divide $B(x)$ by $G(x)$. Figures 4.4 and 4.5 show the result for this example, giving a remainder of $R(x) = x^3 + x$, or its bit string equivalent of 1010. Note that we can write this algebraically as

$$\frac{B(x)}{G(x)} = Q(x) + \frac{R(x)}{G(x)}$$

where $Q(x)$ represents the quotient.

Equivalently, we can write

$$B(x) = G(x) \times Q(x) + R(x)$$

Step 3: Define $T(x) = B(x) - R(x)$. Since the subtraction takes the difference of coefficients of like terms, we calculate the difference by subtracting the bit strings associated with each polynomial. In this case, we have

11010110000	bit string B
− 1010	bit string R
11010111010	bit string T

Note that the string T is actually the same as string B with the appended 0s replaced by R. Another important fact, as shown by Figure 4.6, is that if we divide $T(x)$ by $G(x)$ the remainder is 0.* The sender then transmits the string T.

Step 4: If the string T arrives without damage, dividing by $G(x)$ will yield a 0 remainder. But suppose that during transmission string T is damaged. For example, suppose that four bits in the middle changed to 0 and the string arrives as 11000001010. The receiver synthetically divides it by $G(x)$ and the remainder is not 0 (Figure 4.7). Since the remainder is not 0, the receiver concludes that an error has occurred. (*Note:* This is not the same as saying that dividing a damaged string by $G(x)$ will always yield a nonzero remainder. It can happen, but if $G(x)$ is chosen wisely it occurs only rarely. We will discuss this topic next.)

ANALYSIS OF CRC

The mechanisms of CRC are fairly straightforward. The question we have yet to answer is whether the method is any good. Will the receiver always be able to detect a damaged frame? We relied on the proposition that a damaged frame means that dividing by $G(x)$ yields a nonzero remainder. But is this always true? Is it possible to

Figure 4.6 Dividing $T(x)$ by $G(x)$

```
             1001010
      11001 )11010111010
             11001
              00111
              00000
               01111
               00000
                11111
                11001
                 01100
                 00000
                  11001
                  11001
                   00000
                   00000
                    0000 remainder
```

*There is an analogy using integers that says if p and q are integers and r is the integer remainder obtained by dividing p by q, then $p - r$ is evenly divisible by q. For example, 8/3 generates a remainder of 2 and 8 – 2 is evenly divisible by 3.

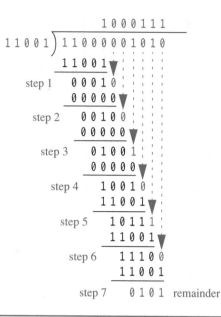

Figure 4.7 Division of Received Polynomial by $G(x)$

change the bit string T in such a way that dividing by $G(x)$ does give a zero remainder?

A complete and detailed proof requires knowledge of factorization properties of polynomial rings (a field in abstract mathematics), and we will not provide one here. Instead, we will provide a brief discussion to give some sense of why it works. To begin, let's specify more accurately what we are looking for. Changing the bits in T is analogous to adding some unknown polynomial to $T(x)$. Thus, if T' represents the received string and $T'(x)$ the associated polynomial, then $T'(x) = T(x) + E(x)$, where $E(x)$ is unknown to the receiver of T'. In the previous example,

string $T = 11010111010$ corresponds to $T(x) = x^{10} + x^9 + x^7 + x^5 + x^4 + x^3 + x$

string $E = 00010110000$ corresponds to $E(x) = x^7 + x^5 + x^4$

string $T' = 11000001010$ corresponds to $T'(x) = x^{10} + x^9 + x^3 + x$

Don't forget that the addition is done using the exclusive OR operation. So, for example, adding the x^7 terms from $E(x)$ and $T(x)$ yields $x^7 + x^7 = (1+1) \times x^7 = 0$.

The question we must answer, therefore, is, When will $(T(x) + E(x))/G(x)$ generate a zero remainder? Since $(T(x) + E(x))/G(x) = T(x)/G(x) + E(x)/G(x)$ and the first term has a zero remainder, the latter term determines the remainder. Therefore, the question can be reformulated: For what polynomials $E(x)$ will $E(x)/G(x)$ have a zero remainder?

We can now make the following statement:

Undetected transmission errors correspond to errors for which $G(x)$ is a factor of $E(x)$.

The next question is, Under what conditions is $G(x)$ a factor of $E(x)$? Let's examine the simplest case first, where just one bit in T changes. In this case $E(x)$ is just one term, x^k for some integer k. The only way $G(x)$ can be a factor of x^k is if $G(x)$ is x raised to some power. So as long as we choose $G(x)$ with at least two terms it won't happen. Thus CRC will detect all single-bit errors.

Next, consider a burst error of length $k \leq r = $ degree $G(x)$.[*] Suppose $T(x)$ is represented by

$$t_n t_{n-1} \cdots \underbrace{t_{i+k-1} t_{i+k-2} \cdots t_i}_{k \text{ affected bits}} t_{i-1} \cdots t_1 t_0$$

and $t_{i+k-1} \cdots$ and t_i are the first and last bits to be damaged. The bits in between have been damaged arbitrarily. This means that

$$E(x) = x^{i+k-1} + \ldots + x^i = x^i \times (x^{k-1} + \ldots + 1)$$

Therefore,

$$\frac{E(x)}{G(x)} = \frac{x^i \times (x^{k-1} + \ldots + 1)}{G(x)}$$

Now, suppose we chose $G(x)$ so that x is not a factor of $G(x)$. Consequently, $G(x)$ and the x^i from the previous fraction have no common factors. Thus, if $G(x)$ is a factor of the numerator then it must in fact be a factor of $(x^{k-1} \ldots +1)$. Remember, however, that since we chose $k \leq r$ then $k - 1 < r$, and $G(x)$ cannot be a factor of a polynomial having a smaller degree.

We therefore draw the following conclusion:

If x is not a factor of $G(x)$, then all burst errors having length smaller than or equal to the degree of $G(x)$ are detected.

Consider next a burst error of any length in which an odd number of bits is affected. Since $E(x)$ has a term for each damaged bit, it contains an odd number of terms. Therefore, $E(1)$ (exclusive OR of an odd number of 1s) evaluates to 1. On the other hand, suppose that $x + 1$ is a factor of $G(x)$. We can therefore write $G(x) = (x + 1) \times H(x)$, where $H(x)$ is some expression.

Now look at what happens if we assume that an undetected error occurs. Recall that an undetected error means that $G(x)$ is a factor of $E(x)$. This means that $E(x) = G(x) \times K(x)$, where $K(x)$ is the other factor of $E(x)$. Replacing $G(x)$ with $(x + 1) \times H(x)$ yields $E(x) = (x + 1) \times H(x) \times K(x)$. Now, if this equation is evaluated at $x = 1$,

---

[*]The degree of a polynomial is its highest power of x.

the $x + 1$ factor makes $E(1)$ evaluate to 0. This is in direct contrast to the previous claim that $E(1)$ evaluates to 1.

Clearly both cannot occur. If we maintain our assumption that $x + 1$ is a factor of $G(x)$, then the other assumption of an undetected error damaging an odd number of bits cannot happen. In other words:

> If $x + 1$ is a factor of $G(x)$, then all burst errors damaging an odd number of bits are detected.

The last case we consider is a burst error with length > degree $G(x)$. From our previous discussion we have

$$\frac{E(x)}{G(x)} = \frac{x^i \times (x^{k-1} + \ldots + 1)}{G(x)}$$

But this time since we assume that $k - 1 \geq r = $ degree $G(x)$, it is possible that $G(x)$ is a factor of $(x^{k-1} + \ldots + 1)$. The question is, What are the chances this will happen? Let's first consider $k - 1 = r$. Since the degree of $G(x)$ is also r, then $G(x)$ is a factor of $(x^r + \ldots + 1)$ means that $G(x) = (x^r + \ldots + 1)$. Now, the terms between x^r and 1 define which bits are actually damaged. Since there are $r - 1$ such terms, there are 2^{r-1} possible combinations of damaged bits. If we assume all combinations can occur with equal probability, there is a probability of $1/2^{r-1}$ that the combination matches the terms of $G(x)$ exactly. In other words, the probability of an error going undetected is $1/2^{r-1}$.

The case for $k - 1 > r$ is more complex and we do not discuss it here. However, it can be shown that the probability of an undetected error is $1/2^r$. References [Pe72] and [Mo89] provide a more rigorous analysis of error detection codes.

CRC is widely used in local area networks (LANs), where there are standard polynomials for $G(x)$, such as the following:

CRC-12: $x^{12} + x^{11} + x^3 + x^2 + x + 1$

CRC-16: $x^{16} + x^{15} + x^2 + 1$

CRC-ITU: $x^{16} + x^{12} + x^5 + 1$

CRC-32: $x^{32} + x^{26} + x^{23} + x^{22} + x^{16} + x^{12} + x^{11} + x^{10} + x^8 + x^7 + x^5 + x^4 + x^2 + x + 1$

In general, CRC is very effective if $G(x)$ is chosen properly. Specifically, $G(x)$ should be chosen so that x is not a factor but $x + 1$ is a factor. In this case, CRC detects the following errors:

- All burst errors of length $r < $ degree $G(x)$
- All burst errors affecting an odd number of bits
- All burst errors of length $= r + 1$ with probability $(2^{r-1} - 1)/2^{r-1}$
- All burst errors of length $> r + 1$ with probability $(2^r - 1)/2^r$ (The CRC-32 polynomial will detect all burst errors of length > 33 with probability $(2^{32} - 1)/2^{32}$. This is equivalent to 99.99999998% accuracy rate. Not bad!)

CRC IMPLEMENTATION USING CIRCULAR SHIFTS

Finding an accurate error detection method is half the battle. The other half is finding a way to implement it efficiently. Considering the nearly countless number of frames that travel across networks, an efficient implementation is essential.

Having learned about CRC, your first reaction might be to write a program to do polynomial division. However, during the time it takes to run such a program, several other frames will probably arrive. As we take the time to verify each of those, even more will arrive and a real bottleneck will occur. It's like having the cashier at a grocery store call for a price check on every item in your cart. Meanwhile, the customers behind you start making nasty remarks, and the Eskimo pies in your cart are melting!

Can we divide two polynomials and get the remainder quickly? Do we even need to go through a complete division when all we really need is the remainder? The quotient was never used. Let's take a close look at Figure 4.7, which showed the synthetic division. The entire process can be visualized as nothing more than a sequence of shifts and exclusive OR operations between the divisor and parts of the dividend.

One widely used CRC implementation uses a circuit constructed depending on the generator polynomial $G(x)$. Since there are standard polynomials, these circuits can be mass produced. The circuit contains a shift register and does exclusive OR operations according to the following rules:

- Interpret $G(x) = b_r x^r + b_{r-1} x^{r-1} + \ldots + b_2 x^2 + b_1 x + b_0$ where b_i is either 0 or 1, $i = 0, \ldots r$. The number of bit positions in the register is r. The rightmost position corresponds to b_0 and the leftmost to $b_{r-1} x^{r-1}$.

- An exclusive OR circuit lies to the right of any position for which the associated value of b_i is 1.

- A bit string enters the register one bit at a time starting with the rightmost position.

- As new bits enter, each bit in the register is shifted left one position. Each bit goes through exclusive OR circuits where they exist, forming one operand in the exclusive OR operation.

- The bit in the leftmost position is routed to each of the exclusive OR circuits, forming the second operand in each exclusive OR operation.

Figure 4.8 shows the register and exclusive OR circuits for the polynomial $G(x) = x^4 + x^3 + 1$. Note the exclusive OR symbol to the right of the positions corresponding to x^3 and 1, and none to the right of the positions corresponding to the missing terms x^2 and x. Initially, the register contains all 0s.

This figure shows the same computations as in Figure 4.7. At step 0, the first bit of the incoming string (dividend from Figure 4.7) has been shifted to the leftmost register position. At step 1, the leftmost bit is routed to each exclusive OR and everything else shifted left. Note that the register's contents are exactly the same as the result of the first exclusive OR operation from step 1 in Figure 4.7.

Each step defines the same process of shifting left and doing exclusive OR operations. The register's contents at each step are always the same as the results of

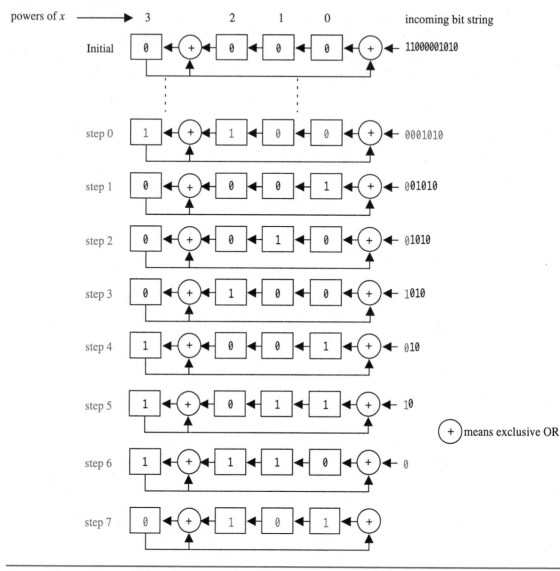

Figure 4.8   Division Using Circular Shifts

similarly labeled steps from Figure 4.7. By the time the bits from the incoming string have all been moved into the register, the register's contents are the remainder (step 7 in Figures 4.7 and 4.8).

Error detection using CRC is an accurate and widely used method. It can also be implemented efficiently, requiring time proportional to the string's length. The standard generator polynomials allow the entire method to be designed into hardware (chips), thus further enhancing its efficiency.

4.4   HAMMING CODES

As stated previously, when errors are detected there are typically two choices: resend the original frame or fix the damaged frame. The latter choice requires a method to not only detect an error but also to determine precisely which bits were affected. The simple parity checks could not do this.

SINGLE-BIT ERROR CORRECTION

A method developed by R. W. Hamming involves creating special code words from data to be sent. The **Hamming code** requires the insertion of multiple parity bits in the bit string before sending. The parity bits check the parity in strategic locations. The idea is that if bits are altered, their positions determine a unique combination of parity check errors. When a frame is sent, the receiver recalculates the parity checks. If any fail, the combination of failures tells the receiver which bits were affected. The receiver then can set the bits to their correct values. This technique is quite common for memory addressing and transferring bits from registers to RAM and back.

Let's illustrate how a Hamming code works for the simplest case, the detection and correction of any single-bit error. Suppose that frames consist of eight bits. Label them as $m_1 m_2 m_3 m_4 m_5 m_6 m_7 m_8$. The next step is to define parity bits for parity checks in select positions. The logical questions are How many parity checks do we use? and Which positions does each one check?

If we use one parity check, it will either fail or succeed. From this we can conclude that an error either occurs or does not occur. It says nothing about where an error might be. If we use two parity checks, one of four things can happen: They both fail; they both succeed; the first fails and the second succeeds; the second fails and the first succeeds. These four cases might be used to convey four events: no error or a bit error in one of three positions. Since there are more than three bit positions, two checks are not enough.

In general, if n parity checks are used, there are 2^n possible combinations of failures and successes. We must associate each bit position with a unique combination to allow the receiver to analyze the parity checks and conclude where an error occurred (if one occurred). However, in order to account for every bit position, we need n so that 2^n is larger than the number of bits sent. We also must remember that each additional parity check requires another bit to be sent.

Table 4.1 shows the relationship between n and the number of bits sent, assuming we start with an 8-bit frame. As it shows, if we use four parity checks there are 16 possible combinations of parity successes and failures. The four additional parity bits with the eight original bits means 12 bits are actually sent. Thus, 13 events are possible: There is no error or there is a single-bit error in one of 12 positions.

The next step is to associate a combination with a unique event. To do this, construct four parity bits p_1, p_2, p_3, and p_4 and insert them into the frame as shown in Figure 4.9. Each parity bit establishes even parity for selected positions listed in the

Table 4.1   Number of Combinations of Parity Successes and Failures as a Function of n

n (NUMBER OF PARITY CHECKS)	NUMBER OF BITS SENT	2^n (NUMBER OF COMBINATIONS OF POSSIBLE PARITY SUCCESSES AND FAILURES)
1	9	2
2	10	4
3	11	8
4	12	16

figure. The next questions are Why put the parity bits in those positions? and How did we determine the positions for each parity check?

To answer these questions, let's make an observation about the positions in each parity check. The first parity check involves all the odd-numbered positions. These positions, if written in binary, all have 1 as the least significant digit. If you write the positions covered by the second parity check in binary, they all have 1 as the second least significant digit. Similarly, the positions covered by the third and fourth parity checks have 1 as the third and fourth least significant digit, respectively.

How does this help us? Create a four-bit binary number b_4, b_3, b_2, and b_1 where $b_i = 0$ if the parity check for p_i succeeds and $b_i = 1$ otherwise ($i = 1, 2, 3,$ or 4). Table 4.2 shows the relationship among erroneous bit positions, invalid parity checks, and the four-bit number. As the table shows, the four-bit binary number and the erroneous bit position coincide.

When a receiver gets a transmitted frame, it performs each of the parity checks. The combination of failures and successes then determines whether there

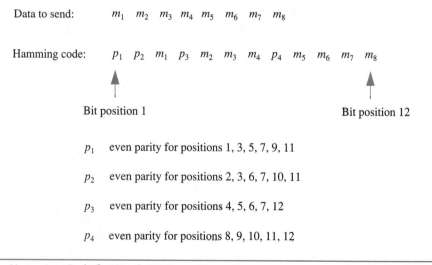

Data to send: m_1 m_2 m_3 m_4 m_5 m_6 m_7 m_8

Hamming code: p_1 p_2 m_1 p_3 m_2 m_3 m_4 p_4 m_5 m_6 m_7 m_8

Bit position 1   Bit position 12

p_1 even parity for positions 1, 3, 5, 7, 9, 11

p_2 even parity for positions 2, 3, 6, 7, 10, 11

p_3 even parity for positions 4, 5, 6, 7, 12

p_4 even parity for positions 8, 9, 10, 11, 12

Figure 4.9   Hamming Code for Single-Bit Error Correction

Table 4.2   Bit Position Errors and Associated Parity Errors

ERRONEOUS BIT POSITION	INVALID PARITY CHECKS	$b_4, b_3, b_2,$ AND b_1
No error	None	0000
1	p_1	0001
2	p_2	0010
3	p_1 and p_2	0011
4	p_3	0100
5	p_1 and p_3	0101
6	p_2 and p_3	0110
7	$p_1, p_2,$ and p_3	0111
8	p_4	1000
9	p_1 and p_4	1001
10	p_2 and p_4	1010
11	$p_1, p_2,$ and p_4	1011
12	p_3 and p_4	1100

was no error or in which position an error occurred. Once the receiver knows where the error occurred, it changes the bit value in that position and the error is corrected.

To illustrate, consider the example in Figure 4.10. Here we see the initial frame 0 1 1 0 0 1 1 1 and the Hamming code 0 1 0 1 1 1 0 1 0 1 1 1 to be transmitted. You should go through the computations to convince yourself that the parity bits establish even parity in the correct positions.

Figure 4.11 shows the received frame 0 1 0 1 0 1 0 1 0 1 1 1. Now, if we perform each parity check, we see that the checks for p_1 and p_3 are invalid. That is, there is an odd number of 1 bits in positions 1, 3, 5, 7, 9, and 11, and in positions 4, 5, 6, 7, and 12. Thus, according to Table 4.2, the error is in bit 5. Since bit 5 is 0, the receiver changes it to 1 and the frame is corrected.

Figure 4.10   Bit Stream Before Transmission

$$
\begin{array}{llllllll}
\text{Data:} & 0 & 1 & 1 & 0 & 0 & 1 & 1 & 1 \\
 & m_1 & m_2 & m_3 & m_4 & m_5 & m_6 & m_7 & m_8
\end{array}
$$

$$
\begin{array}{lllllllllllll}
\text{Hamming code:} & 0 & 1 & 0 & 1 & 1 & 1 & 0 & 1 & 0 & 1 & 1 & 1 \\
 & p_1 & p_2 & m_1 & p_3 & m_2 & m_3 & m_4 & p_4 & m_5 & m_6 & m_7 & m_8
\end{array}
$$

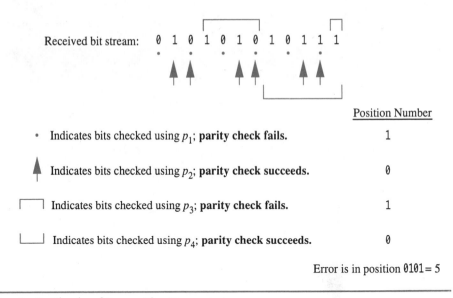

		Position Number
•	Indicates bits checked using p_1; **parity check fails.**	1
▲	Indicates bits checked using p_2; **parity check succeeds.**	0
⌐⌐	Indicates bits checked using p_3; **parity check fails.**	1
⌊⌋	Indicates bits checked using p_4; **parity check succeeds.**	0

Error is in position 0101 = 5

Figure 4.11   Parity Checks of Frame After Transmission

MULTIPLE-BIT ERROR CORRECTION

We can make similar comments about single-bit error correcting codes that we made about single-bit error detection codes. That is, single-bit errors are not common in data communications. One response to this information applies when there are many data frames to send. We can create a Hamming code for each, visualize all the Hamming codes as a two-dimensional bit array, and transmit the array one column at a time. If a single burst error affects no more than one column, no more than one bit in each row is destroyed. The receiver can determine the original data. The second response is to generalize Hamming codes for double- or multiple-bit error correction. Such codes do exist, but we will not discuss them here. The number of extra bits becomes quite large and is used in very specialized cases. If you are interested, References [Ko78] and [Ha80] discuss them.

COMPARISON OF ERROR DETECTION AND ERROR CORRECTION

Which is better, error detection or error correction? The answer, as you might expect, is that neither is better, at least in a general sense. Correction techniques generally require more overhead and cannot always be justified in applications where errors occur rarely. It is usually much cheaper just to ask for a retransmission. Typically, most computer networks fall into this category.

As errors occur with more frequency, the extra overhead due to increased transmissions becomes a problem. In such cases, it may be cheaper to include additional correction bits rather than clutter the media with excessive redundant transmissions.

Error rate is not the only consideration. Time may be a critical factor. Sending a frame again will take time; how much depends on many factors such as the traffic, data rate, and distance. In most cases, a short delay in receiving an email message or a file from a LAN server is not so bad. A real-time environment in which messages must be delivered on time to avoid disaster cannot afford even small delays, however, deep-space probes, in which signals require many hours to reach their destination, are severely handicapped if a message must be retransmitted, especially when there is a high probability that interference will occur again. Imagine an astronaut saying, "Hello, NASA . . . can't read you. What's that about an impending collision with an alien spacecraft?"

4.5   ENCRYPTION AND DECRYPTION

Error detection and correction methods help prevent people from getting incorrect information. Another potentially dangerous problem is the illegal or unauthorized reception of information. Such cases involve the usual sender and receiver, plus a third party who intercepts a transmission not intended for him or her (Figure 4.12). The worst part is that neither sender nor receiver may be aware of the unauthorized reception until the guilty party has used the intercepted information for some purpose such as blackmail, criminal fraud, or a breach of national security. By then the damage is done. Clearly, if we are going to send sensitive information over some medium we would like some assurance of privacy.

With so much information being broadcast using microwaves and satellites it is virtually impossible to prevent unauthorized reception. Portable antenna dishes can be placed almost anywhere to receive information from a satellite. Even cable systems are susceptible. They frequently run through basements, isolated closets, and under streets. Finding a secluded spot and tapping the cable is not difficult.

As a result, much effort has gone into ways to make information unintelligible to unauthorized receivers. The idea is that even if they do receive the transmission

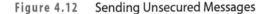

Figure 4.12   Sending Unsecured Messages

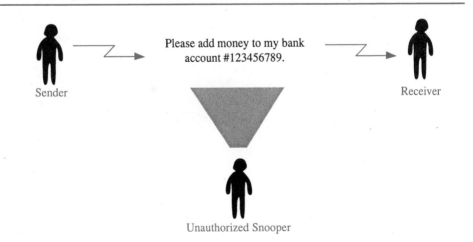

they won't be able to understand its contents. The rendering of information into a different, unintelligible form is called **encryption.** The authorized receiver must be able to understand the information, so he must be able to change the encrypted data to its original form. We call this **decryption.** We also use the terms **plaintext** for the original message and **ciphertext** for the encrypted one.

Figure 4.13 illustrates the process. The sender uses an encryption key (usually some character or numeric constant) to change the plaintext (P) into a ciphertext (C). We write this symbolically as $C = E_k(P)$, where E and k represent the encryption algorithm and key, respectively. If some unauthorized person gets C, its unintelligible form makes it useless. Eventually the receiver gets C and decrypts it to get the original message. We write this symbolically as $P = D_{k'}(C)$, where D and k' represent the decryption algorithm and key. In general, $P = D_{k'}(E_k(P))$. Also, in many cases (but not always) $k = k'$.

As usual, questions arise. How do the encryption and decryption algorithms work? Is an encrypted message really unintelligible to an unauthorized receiver? If

Figure 4.13   Sending Encrypted Messages

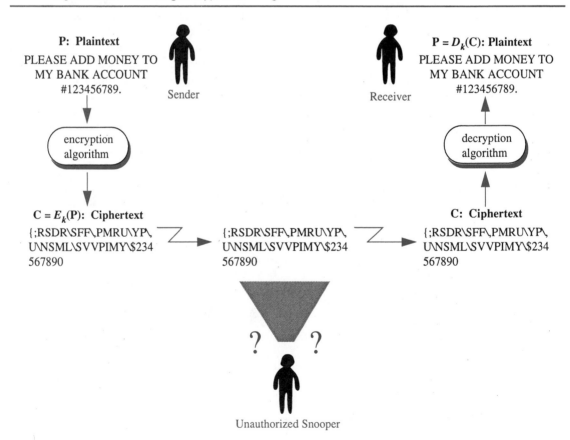

an unauthorized receiver knows how the message was encrypted can she decrypt it? Ideally an encrypted message should be impossible to decrypt without knowing the decryption algorithm and key. Unfortunately, most completely secure codes are analogous to unsinkable ships such as the *Titanic:* As soon as you are sure it is secure someone will prove you wrong.

CAESAR CIPHER

One of the earliest and simplest codes replaces each plaintext character with another character. The choice of a replacement depends only on the plaintext character. This method is called a **monoalphabetic cipher** or **Caesar cipher,** reputedly dating back to the days of Julius Caesar. For example, you might add 1 (the encryption key) to the ASCII code of each character. Thus, A becomes B; B becomes C; and so on. This approach is widely used, occurring in places such as children's television shows, decoder rings, and the backs of cereal boxes. Figure 4.13 used a Caesar cipher. Can you determine the rationale behind the letter substitutions?

The decryption algorithm normally reverses the encryption steps. In the previous example, subtracting 1 from the ASCII codes of each ciphertext character yields the original plaintext character. This is a case in which the encryption and decryption keys are equal. We should point out that the example could have changed the ASCII codes by any constant.

Although they are simple to describe and certainly seem to yield unintelligible messages, Caesar ciphers are rarely used in serious applications. They are relatively easy to decode without knowledge of the original encryption method because the code does nothing to disguise frequently used letters or combinations. For example, the most commonly used letters in English are E, T, O, A, and N. Thus, if a certain letter appears frequently in a ciphertext, there is a high probability it is one of these common letters rather than a Q or Z. This gives a potential codebreaker a place to start.

To illustrate, consider the following ciphertext (from Figure 4.13). Pretend you never saw the plaintext.

```
{;RSDR\SFF\,PMRU\YP\,U\NSML\SVVPIMY\$234567890
```

The most common ciphertext characters are \ (seven times), S (four times), and R, P, and M (three times each). Consequently, there is a high probability they are substitutions for E, T, O, A, and N, or even a blank space.

The next step would be to try various combinations of the common plaintext characters in place of the ciphertext ones. For example, after several attempts you might come up with the following partially decrypted character string (decrypted characters are in bold type):

```
{;EADE\AFF\,ONEU\YO\,U\NANL\AVVOINY\$234567890
```

To continue, you might further observe that most messages have blanks between the words and that the most common character (\) might represent a blank. You try it and generate

```
{;EADE AFF ,ONEU YO ,U NANL AVVOINY $234567890
```

Next you might look at the YO and the AFF and ask how many two-letter words end in the letter O or how many three-letter words begin with A followed by a repeated letter. There are not many, so you might try replacing the Y with a T and the F with a D. Now you have

{;EADE ADD ,ONEU TO ,U NANL AVVOINT $234567890

By making some educated guesses, we have the message half decrypted. It would not be difficult to continue making educated guesses and finish decrypting. (It's really a lot like playing the game Hangman or the equivalent television show, *Wheel of Fortune*.) The important point to emphasize here is that a secure code should not preserve particular letter sequences or the frequency with which letters occur.

POLYALPHABETIC CIPHER

One way to change the frequencies and destroy common sequences is to use a **polyalphabetic cipher.** Like the monoalphabetic cipher, it replaces each character with another. The difference is that a given plaintext character is not always replaced with the same ciphertext one. We can choose a replacement depending not only on the actual plaintext character but on its position in the message as well.

An example of a polyalphabetic cipher is a **Vigenère cipher.** It uses a two-dimensional array of characters (its encryption key) in which each row contains the letters of the alphabet. Figure 4.14 shows an example. The first row (row zero) contains the letters written from A to Z. The second row has the letters written from B to Z followed by A at the end. Each subsequent row is formed by moving each letter from the previous row left one position, with the leftmost character being moved to the rightmost position.

To replace a letter, let i be its relative position (first position is relative position zero) in the message and j its relative position in the alphabet. Let V be the array. Replace the letter with the one in $V[(i \bmod 26), j]$. Figure 4.15 shows a procedure written in partial C code that does this, assuming the plaintext letters are all upper-

---

Figure 4.14   Key for Vigenère Cipher

row 0:   A B C D E F G H I J K L M N O P Q R S T U V W X Y Z

row 1:   B C D E F G H I J K L M N O P Q R S T U V W X Y Z A

row 2:   C D E F G H I J K L M N O P Q R S T U V W X Y Z A B

row 3:   D E F G H I J K L M N O P Q R S T U V W X Y Z A B C

row 24:   Y Z A B C D E F G H I J K L M N O P Q R S T U V W X

row 25:   Z A B C D E F G H I J K L M N O P Q R S T U V W X Y

```
int encrypt(char P[], char C[], char V[26] [26]);
                        /* is the plain text*/
                        /* is the cipher text*/
                        /* is the Vigenere cipher key*/

{
  int i, j;

  for i = 0 to end of plaintext
  {
    j = P[i] - 'A' ;              /* relative position of P[i] in the alphabet */
    C[i] = V[i % 26] [j];         /* % is the mod operator in C */
  }
}
```

Figure 4.15   Encryption Algorithm for Vigenère Cipher

case.[*] For example, suppose the word THE appears three times in a message, beginning in positions 25, 54, and 104. Table 4.3 shows the required calculations and the substituted ciphertext letters. As the table shows, the three occurrences of the word THE encrypt to SHF, VKI, and TIG.

The Vigenère cipher seems to solve the repetition problems, but in fact it has only reduced them. Repetitions and patterns still occur. For example, the two encrypted words SHF and TIG may seem dissimilar, but they are not. Can you see a relation between them? The letters in TIG are the alphabetic successors to the letters

Table 4.3   Letter Substitutions Using the Vigenère Cipher

PLAINTEXT LETTER	i = (RELATIVE POSITION IN MESSAGE)	i MOD 26	j RELATIVE POSITION IN ALPHABET	CIPHERTEXT LETTER
T	25	25	19	S
H	26	0	7	H
E	27	1	4	F
T	54	2	19	V
H	55	3	7	K
E	56	4	4	I
T	104	0	19	T
H	105	1	7	I
E	106	2	4	G

---

[*]It also assumes that the letters correspond to consecutive binary codes such as in the ASCII code.

in SHF. To a professional trying to break a code, this is a very big clue to the encryption method.

In fact, all of the encrypted forms of THE share a similarity. Consider two consecutive letters occupying the same relative positions in each of two encrypted versions of THE. The difference (modulo 26) of their ASCII codes is the same. For example, the differences between the ASCII codes of S and H, T and I, and V and K are all 11. The common differences occur because each row of the matrix in Figure 4.14 is essentially in alphabetic order. The only exception is the transition point from Z to A.

This problem can be fixed by making each row a random permutation of the alphabet, but even that will not be enough, at least for long text. Since there are 26 rows, there are essentially 26 ways to encrypt a letter or a word. In a long message common words may appear several hundred times. With only 26 different ways to encrypt the word, repetitions will still occur. They will just be a little harder to find.

Again, you might respond by using even more rows in the matrix, each with a unique permutation of the alphabet, to provide more ways to encrypt words, thus reducing the repetitions. Indeed, 26! (approximately 4×10^{26}) unique permutations of the alphabet provide many alternatives. In the extreme case we could use a number of rows equal to the length of the message. Here each row is used just once during encryption, thus avoiding any repetition (except for statistically random ones). The problem now, however, is that the encryption key is longer than the message. Communicating it to authorized receivers and storing it securely become problems.

TRANSPOSITION CIPHER

A **transposition cipher** rearranges the plaintext letters of a message (rather than substituting ciphertext letters). One way to do this is to store the plaintext characters in a two-dimensional array with m columns. The first m plaintext characters are stored in the array's first row, the second m characters in the second row, and so on. Next we determine a permutation of the numbers 1 through m, and write it as $p_1, p_2, \ldots, p_m$. The permutation may be random or determined by some secret method. Either way, the final step is to transmit all the characters in column p_1, followed by those in column p_2, and so forth. The last set of characters transmitted are those in column p_m.

To illustrate, suppose the following message's characters are stored in a two-dimensional array with five columns (Table 4.4).

MISS PIGGY KERMIT ANIMAL AND FOZZIE BEAR

Suppose the column numbers are rearranged as 2, 4, 3, 1, 5. That is, the characters in column 2 are transmitted first, followed by the characters in columns 4, 3, 1, and 5, respectively. Therefore, the transmitted message looks like

IIKTMNZBSGRAL IASGE ADZEMP IIAO YMN FER

The transmitted message looks nothing like the original, but if the receiver knows the number of columns and the column number permutation, he can easily reconstruct the message. This is done by storing incoming characters in columns in the

Table 4.4   Two-Dimensional Array Used for the Transposition Cipher

COLUMN NUMBERS				
1	2	3	4	5
M	I	S	S	
P	I	G	G	Y
	K	E	R	M
I	T		A	N
I	M	A	L	
A	N	D		F
O	Z	Z	I	E
	B	E	A	R

order of the permutation. In the previous example, the incoming characters would be stored in column 2 followed by columns 4, 3, 1, and 5. This is another example in which the decryption algorithm is defined by essentially reversing the steps of the encryption algorithm.

The problem with the transposition cipher is that it is not very secure. For one thing, letter frequencies are preserved. On reception, an unauthorized receiver could analyze the ciphertext and notice the high frequency of common letters. By itself this is an indication that letter substitutions were probably not used and that this may be a transposition cipher. The next step in breaking the code would be to group the characters and store them in different columns. The receiver would not try column arrangements randomly but would instead try arrangements that yielded commonly used sequences such as THE, ING, or IS in a row. This process would reduce the number of guesses greatly and provide a lot of help and information to the unauthorized but highly motivated receiver.

BIT-LEVEL CIPHERING

Not all transmissions are character sequences. Consequently, not all encryption methods work by manipulating or substituting characters. Some work at the bit level. One method defines the encryption key as a bit string. The choice is determined randomly and secretly. The bit string to be transmitted is divided into substrings. The length of each is the same as the length of the encryption key. Each substring is then encrypted by computing the exclusive OR between it and the encryption key.

In this case the decryption does not reverse the encryption steps, as in previous methods, but instead repeats them. In other words, to decrypt we compute the exclusive OR between the encryption key and each of the encrypted substrings. Here, the encryption and decryption keys are the same.

Figure 4.16 demonstrates that doing the exclusive OR operation twice produces the original string. But does it always work this way? Yes! To see how, let p_i be any plaintext bit and $\oplus$ represent the exclusive OR operation. During the encryption/ decryption process p_i is exclusively OR'd with either 0 or 1 twice. If it is 0 we have

$$(p_i \oplus 0) \oplus 0 = (p_i) \oplus 0 = p_i$$

If it is 1 we have

$$(p_i \oplus 1) \oplus 1 = p_i \oplus (1 \oplus 1) = p_i \oplus (0) = p_i$$

Either way, performing the exclusive OR twice generates the original bit p_1.

The security of this code depends largely on the length of the encryption key. A short key means the original string is divided into many substrings with each encrypted separately. With many substrings, there is a greater chance that repetitions will occur. Since they are encrypted using the same key, the encrypted substrings are also repeated. As before, the repetitions can help an unauthorized receiver trying to break the code.

Using longer encryption keys means longer but fewer substrings. In the extreme case, the length of the encryption key is the same as that of the message to be sent. In this case, each bit is encrypted using a unique bit in the key. If the key's bits are truly random, no patterns will exist in the encrypted string and the code is truly unbreakable without trying every possible decryption key. Such unbreakable ciphers are also called **one-time pads.**

This method (where the key length is equal to the original string length) is similar to the polyalphabetic cipher, in which each character was substituted using a unique key. The difference is essentially that between bit or character substitutions. Like the polyalphabetic cipher, the drawback is the large key that must be communicated to the receiver, thus making the method somewhat unwieldy.

DATA ENCRYPTION STANDARD

The encryption methods discussed so far are not terribly complex. In fact, when used with short keys they're not even very good because the ciphertext contains many clues that help an unauthorized person break the code. With longer keys, however, the ciphertext becomes more cryptic. In the extreme case, the code is virtually unbreakable. The difficulty is that long keys make implementation more difficult.

There is another approach that keeps the keys short and uses complex procedures to encrypt the data. One such method, the **Data Encryption Standard (DES),**

Figure 4.16 Encryption Using Exclusive OR Bit Operation

```
1101100101001    Plaintext
1001011001010    Encryption key
0100111100011    Ciphertext = plaintext exclusive-or'd with the encryption key
1001011001010    Decryption key (same as the encryption key)
1101100101001    Plaintext = ciphertext exclusive-or'd with the decryption key
```

was developed by IBM in the early 1970s. It was adopted as a standard in 1977 by the U.S. government for all commercial and unclassified information. The logic of this widely used method is built into hardware (VLSI chips) to make it even faster.

The DES divides a message into 64-bit blocks and uses a 56-bit key. It uses a complex combination of transpositions (rearrangement of bits), substitutions (replacing one bit group with another), exclusive OR operations, and a few other processes on each block to eventually produce 64 bits of encrypted data. In all, the 64-bit block goes through 19 successive steps, with the output of each step being input to the next step.

Figure 4.17 shows the primary steps. The first step does a transposition on the 64 data bits and the 56-bit key. The next 16 steps (labeled *encryption* in the figure) involve many operations, which we will describe shortly. Each step is the same except that it uses a different key derived from the original. The important thing now is that the output from one step is the input to the next. The second-to-last step (*swap* in the figure) swaps the first 32 bits and the last 32 bits. The last step is another transposition. In fact, it is the reverse of the transposition done in the first step. The result is 64 bits of encrypted data.

Figure 4.18 outlines the primary operations of each of the middle 16 steps. In the figure we represent a bit string with a letter and a numeric subscript. The subscript indicates the number of bits in the string. For example, K_{56} refers to the 56-bit

Figure 4.17 Outline of the DES

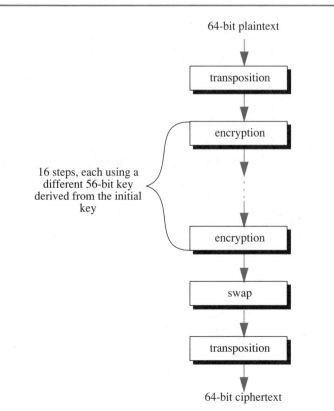

64-bit plaintext

transposition

encryption

16 steps, each using a different 56-bit key derived from the initial key

encryption

swap

transposition

64-bit ciphertext

Figure 4.18   One of Sixteen Encryption Steps of the DES

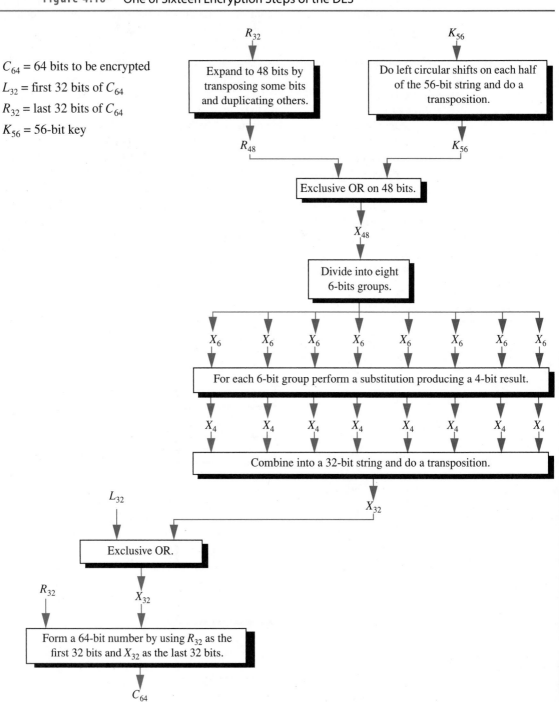

C_{64} = 64 bits to be encrypted

L_{32} = first 32 bits of C_{64}

R_{32} = last 32 bits of C_{64}

K_{56} = 56-bit key

R_{32}

Expand to 48 bits by transposing some bits and duplicating others.

K_{56}

Do left circular shifts on each half of the 56-bit string and do a transposition.

R_{48}

K_{56}

Exclusive OR on 48 bits.

X_{48}

Divide into eight 6-bits groups.

X_6 X_6 X_6 X_6 X_6 X_6 X_6 X_6

For each 6-bit group perform a substitution producing a 4-bit result.

X_4 X_4 X_4 X_4 X_4 X_4 X_4 X_4

Combine into a 32-bit string and do a transposition.

L_{32}

X_{32}

Exclusive OR.

R_{32}

X_{32}

Form a 64-bit number by using R_{32} as the first 32 bits and X_{32} as the last 32 bits.

C_{64}

string used as a key, and X_{48} is a 48-bit string resulting from some intermediate operation. When reading through the ensuing discussion, remember that even though we use the symbol X throughout the figure, it represents different strings at each stage. This method seems more sensible than using different names for each operation.

First, DES divides C_{64} (the 64 bits being encrypted) in half. The first 32 bits are L_{32} and the remaining 32 bits are R_{32}. Next, it expands R_{32} to a 48-bit string by transposing some of the bits and duplicating others. We label the result as R_{48} to reinforce the fact that it is determined completely from R_{32}. The algorithm also changes the 56-bit key by dividing it in half and doing a circular bit-shift on each half. The number of bits shifted depends on which of the 16 steps the algorithm is in. The point is that each step uses a different key. After the shifts the key is transposed. The result is labeled K_{56}.

Next, the algorithm does an exclusive OR operation between R_{48} and the first 48 bits of K_{56}. The result is labeled X_{56}. Next, X_{48} is divided into eight 6-bit groups (X_6.) Each 6-bit group goes through a substitution algorithm and is replaced by a 4-bit group X_4. The resulting eight 4-bit groups are then combined and subjected to another transposition, giving another 32-bit group X_{32}. The algorithm then does an exclusive OR operation between this string and L_{32}. Again, we call the result X_{32}. Finally, the algorithm creates a 64-bit string by using R_{32} as the first 32 bits and X_{32} as the last 32 bits.

Confusing? Well, it is supposed to be. IBM's intent was not to design a method everyone understands easily. The idea was to design a method that consists of many convoluted steps and is virtually impossible to reproduce without prior knowledge of the encryption key.

This entire process is done 16 times. Each time, the input is the result of the previous step and a different key is used. We have left out many details, such as how the transpositions are done or how the 6-bit groups are substituted with 4-bit groups. Some of these details are not difficult. For example, the following C procedure does a transposition of the elements of array b.

```
void transposition
(sometype b[N], int t[N])      /* b is an array of elements to be transposed */
                               /* t contains the numbers from 0 to N-1 in random
                                     order */

{
  sometype temp [N];           /* temporary storage for elements in b */
  int i;                       /* used for subscripting */
  for (i=0; i<N; i++)          /* copy elements into temporary storage */
    temp[i] = b[i];
  for (i=0; i<N; i++)          /* as i increases, t[i] is used to get elements
                                     randomly from */

    b[i] = temp[t[i]];         /* positions in array temp */
}
```

The details of making substitutions depend largely on the substitution rules, which we won't discuss here. If you are interested, References [St95a] and [St95b] provide detailed descriptions of the DES algorithm.

Without doubt, the algorithm is complex, as it consists of many convoluted steps. On the other hand, when the DES algorithm is complete, a 64-bit string has been replaced with another 64-bit string, making it essentially a substitution cipher—although we admit that the rules for the substitution are obscure.

The standardization of the DES has been controversial (see Ref. [Ko77]). One argument is that despite the complexity the DES isn't secure enough. Indeed, when IBM researchers began working on the problem they used a 128-bit key. But, at the request of the National Security Agency (NSA), it was reduced to 56 bits. Furthermore, the reasons behind the reduction to 56 bits haven't been made public. You might ask, "So what? What's the difference between using a 56-bit key and a 128-bit key?"

The difference is in how an unauthorized receiver might try to break the code. The DES was designed so that the decryption algorithm uses the same key as the encryption algorithm and uses the same steps, but in reverse. An unauthorized receiver can break the code simply by trying the decryption algorithm with every possible key. Of course, with $2^{56} \approx 7 \times 10^{16}$ possible key values, that will take a while. On the other hand, the development of faster processors and massively parallel processor systems allows computers to make computations a lot faster than they once could. Consequently, this number is not as big as it used to be, and to some it is uncomfortably small.

Another factor contributing to the controversy is that some people feel the rationale behind substitutions in the DES algorithm was never fully explained. The fear is that there may be something in the substitution that could compromise the cipher's integrity. These factors have led to speculation that the NSA was uncomfortable with a code that even it would have trouble breaking. Remember, with the widespread use of electronic mail, the availability of DES chips, and the emergence of digital voice transmission, there is a lot of DES-encrypted information. The inability to decrypt when necessary must make NSA officials just a bit jittery. To make matters worse, there have been reports that the government has tried to suppress research or publication dealing with more secure ciphers (Ref. [Sh77]).

CLIPPER CHIP

In April of 1993 the controversy surrounding encryption and alleged government intervention heated up again when the Clinton administration announced plans for a new security initiative. The initiative outlined the plans for a new technology called the **Clipper Chip,**[*] a government-designed and -built encryption computer chip that could be used in security devices. These devices, in turn, could be used in ordinary communications equipment such as telephones or fax machines.

The way it works is rather straightforward (Figure 4.19). The Clipper Chip contains an encryption algorithm designed into its microcircuits. Suppose you make a telephone call and want to begin a secure conversation, that is, a conversation that

---

[*]Although the term *Clipper* is commonly used, the official name for the technology was *capstone*.

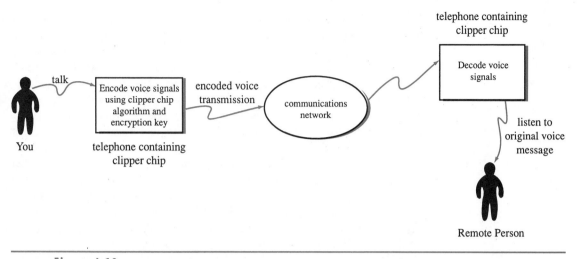

Figure 4.19   Clipper Chip Encryption

cannot be intercepted and understood by a third party. All you would need to do is press a button and your security device and the remote one would exchange encryption keys.[*] The security device would then route anything you say, along with the encryption key, to the Clipper Chip, which encodes your voice signals. The telephone system then transmits your encoded message. At the other end the remote device decodes the voice transmission using its Clipper Chip (which it could do because of the encryption key exchange) and restores your original voice message. The net result is that the remote person hears your voice as in any telephone conversation. However, any third party that might tap into your conversation gets only the encoded voice signals.

The initiative was motivated by two major concerns. The first was the need for privacy of telephone conversations and for protection of any sensitive information transmitted by telephone, fax, or computer. The second was to be responsive to the needs of law enforcement individuals when sensitive information corresponds to illegal activities. These both sound like laudable goals, so why the controversy?

First, the Clipper Chip was designed by engineers in the NSA with no input from private industry [Si96]. Given the ongoing tension that exists between civil libertarians and government officials, this fact alone was sufficient fodder for controversy, but there was more. The method used for encryption is called the **SkipJack algorithm,** which was developed by the NSA and whose details remain classified. This caused suspicion among some, who argued that the algorithm cannot be subjected to the same testing processes as other algorithms, whose details are freely available. Some also saw this as a violation of the Computer Security Act, a law

---

[*]There are various protocols to observe when exchanging encryption keys to ensure that the keys are not intercepted. We will discuss one option called the Diffie-Hellman key exchange in the next section.

passed by Congress in 1987 that was intended to limit the NSA's role in the development of standards. Proponents for classifying the algorithm argued that keeping details secret had nothing to do with making the algorithm more secure. Instead, the intent was to prevent unauthorized construction of devices that were compatible with authorized ones but that did not implement certain law enforcement features.

This brings us to another controversial aspect, which involves the encryption keys themselves. Suppose someone using a telephone or other communications device were suspected of illegal activities. A common tool used by law enforcement officials is wiretapping, or the monitoring of communications. If the suspect is encrypting all communications, the wiretap provides no useful information. Further, if the encryption method is a good one it cannot be broken in a reasonable amount of time. At the heart of the issue is whether private citizens have the right to "unbreakable" encryption techniques and whether and when law enforcement officials have the right to listen to private conversations. This is something that prompts long debates. The FBI and other law enforcement agencies urged the inclusion of a feature in the Clipper Chip that would allow them to determine the encryption key and, subsequently, decode encrypted information.

To do this, each Clipper Chip has the following information:

- K. An 80-bit session key used to encrypt transmitted messages. This is what law enforcement officials need to know to make the wiretap effective.
- F. An 80-bit family key. All chips in a group have the same one.
- N. A 30-bit serial number unique to each chip.
- S. An 80-bit secret key, also unique to each chip and used by law enforcement officials.

The last key, S, is the one at the center of the controversy. As stated, each Clipper Chip generates an encrypted voice message, E_k (message). It also generates a law enforcement field $E_F(E_S(K) + N)$.[*] This last expression is important, so let's examine it closely. Essentially, the Clipper Chip produces its own session key as output, albeit in encrypted form. All you need is the method for getting it. Figure 4.20 outlines the necessary steps.

Once a wiretap has been court approved, officials apply D_F to the law enforcement field to get $E_S(K) + N$. The family key F is not secret, so that is not a problem; in theory, anyone could do it. At this point, officials can extract the serial number of the chip and the encrypted session key $E_S(K)$. All that remains is to apply D_S to get the session key. Since S is secret, this is not easy, but there is a way. However, let's first examine how S is created.

The secret key S is actually defined using two other keys according to the formula $S = S_1 \oplus S_2$ ($\oplus$ is the bitwise exclusive OR). The keys S_1 and S_2 are also secret

---

[*] As we did earlier in this section, we use E to represent an encryption method. A subscript following E corresponds to the encryption key. The + in the expression $E_s(K) + N$ refers to concatenating N's bits to those of $E_s(K)$.

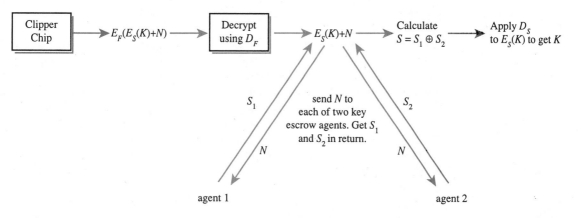

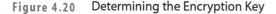

Figure 4.20   Determining the Encryption Key

and are maintained by two different **key escrow agencies.** These are agencies designed to keep and protect valuable information. When a particular Clipper Chip is constructed, one representative from each agency is present. Each representative selects a random 80-bit number, which is subjected to a series of calculations. One agent produces S_1 and the other produces S_2 for a particular chip. Neither agent knows what the other chose or ended up with. The secret key is then calculated as $S = S_1 \oplus S_2$ and was programmed into the chip. One agent records S_1 and N (chip serial number) and the other records S_2 and N. Each returns that valuable information to his agency, where it is kept in a secure location. The important thing here is that the secret key S is not stored in any one place. This provides an extra level of security since neither S_1 nor S_2 alone provide any useful information. In fact, the computers that calculate S and program the chip may even be destroyed as an added security measure.

Once the law enforcement officials obtain the chip's serial number they can send a copy to each key escrow agency, along with proof that a wiretap was authorized. Each agency responds by sending its portion of the key associated with the specified serial number. The officials eventually obtain both S_1 and S_2, calculate S, and apply D_S to $E_S(K)$ to get the session key, K. At this point they are able to decrypt any messages encrypted using E_K and the wiretap is successful.

Part of the concern centered on the key escrow agents, who were in charge of key components, and the mechanisms in place to store and protect keys. Many argue that the escrow agencies should be separate from law enforcement agencies. A major concern again is a person's right to privacy. The argument is that having one law enforcement agency getting key components from itself or another law enforcement agency has the potential for misuse. By using independent agencies with no official ties to law enforcement, a citizen's right to privacy is better protected. If you are interested in knowing more about the mechanisms for key escrow systems, you can consult Reference [De96].

KEY DISTRIBUTION AND PROTECTION

All of the methods discussed so far assume that the decryption key is derivable from (or equal to) the encryption key. Consequently, the best encryption method in the world is no good if the key cannot be kept secret. Therefore, we face another problem: How does the sender communicate the key to the receiver (**key distribution** or **exchange**)? For example, Clipper Chips exchange keys prior to beginning a secure conversation. Your first suggestion might be for the sender simply to send the key. But, as before, what if an unauthorized receiver gets it? Encrypt it, you might say—but what method should the sender use? How does the sender communicate that method's key to the receiver? This does not solve the problem; it merely redefines it.

Maintaining a key's secrecy is not an easy task, but there are options. For example, the two persons communicating could meet in some clandestine location (such as a local McDonald's restaurant) and agree on a key. But sometimes logistics do not allow such meetings (or maybe the principal parties are vegetarians). Another option would be to transport a key under armed guard. This conjures up images of people with attaché cases handcuffed to their wrists surrounded by people with bent noses and their hands hidden inside their suit coats.

Merkle's Puzzles   Such options exist, no doubt, but there are other, more academic solutions. One technique, described in Reference [Me78], involves the use of puzzles. A **puzzle** is an encrypted message containing a potential encryption key, an identifying number, and a predefined pattern. In order for a sender and a receiver to agree on an encryption key, the following steps occur:

1. The sender sends n puzzles, each encrypted with a separate key. The receiver does not know the encryption key and must break the code as any unauthorized receiver would. Typically the encryption key is not too large, allowing the receiver to attack the code by brute force if necessary.

2. The receiver chooses a puzzle randomly and breaks the code. The receiver knows when the code is broken because of the pattern inserted into the puzzle.

3. The receiver extracts the encryption key from that puzzle and sends a message back specifying the ID of the puzzle he has broken.

4. The sender receives the puzzle ID and assumes the receiver solved the puzzle and obtained the key in it. Both sender and receiver can now communicate using the agreed-on encryption key.

You might wonder, if the intended receiver can get a key this way, why can't an unauthorized one? The answer is that the intended receiver randomly chooses which puzzle to solve. The unauthorized receiver does not know which puzzle is chosen and is left with few choices other than to try to solve all n puzzles. If n is large, however, solving all the puzzles will take a lot of time (more time than this person has, we hope). Meanwhile, the sender and receiver communicate while the eavesdropper is trying to solve the right puzzle.

Shamir's Method   Another method of key distribution, Shamir's method, is used in a different scenario. Suppose the information to be encrypted is so sensitive that no one person can be trusted to send or receive it. We want to store the key in such a way that at least k people must be present to determine it. We further assume that any k people with appropriate clearance will suffice. That is, we impose no requirement that any particular person or persons be present.

Storing the key in any one spot will not work, as this violates the condition that k people must be present. We could divide the key into k distinct pieces and distribute the pieces. If each person gets one piece we have a constraint on who may be present (only those with mutually distinct pieces). If we give several pieces to any person, fewer than $k - 1$ persons have the remaining pieces, which violates the condition that at least k persons must be present.

Shamir's method (Ref. [Sh79]) is a clever one based on polynomial interpolation. Specifically, suppose that $p(x) = a_0 + a_1x + a_2x^2 + . . .+ a_{k-1}x^{k-1}$ is a polynomial of degree $k - 1$. Suppose also that (x_1,y_1), (x_2,y_2), . . ., (x_k, y_k) are known points on the graph of $p(x)$ and that $x_i \neq x_j$ whenever $i \neq j$. Then these k points determine the polynomial $p(x)$ uniquely and from them we can determine the values of $a_0, a_1, . . . ,$ and a_{k-1}.

In Shamir's method the polynomial $p(x)$ is constructed so that one of the coefficients (say a_0) is the encryption key. Each person who is cleared to send or receive information is given precisely one data point on the graph of $p(x)$, making sure that no two data points have the same x-coordinate. Any group of k persons can provide k unique data points. All of the data points allow them to determine the polynomial and consequently the key.

If there are fewer than k people, there are not enough data points to determine the polynomial uniquely. Even so, a small group of subversives could pool their data points and determine relationships among the a_i, which could yield hints to the key's value. Shamir's method avoids this possibility by doing all the computations using modular arithmetic.

Diffie-Hellman Key Exchange   Diffie-Hellman key exchange works by having a sender and receiver exchange calculated values from which an encryption key can be computed. The calculations use other numbers, which do not need to be kept secret. For example, suppose two people agree to use two integers, g and n, in the calculation of the encryption key. Figure 4.21 shows an exchange between two people, A and B (their parents must have liked simple names), and illustrates who knows what.

First, A picks an integer x and calculates and sends the value of g^x modulo n to B. Similarly, B independently selects a value of y and sends g^y modulo n to A. If

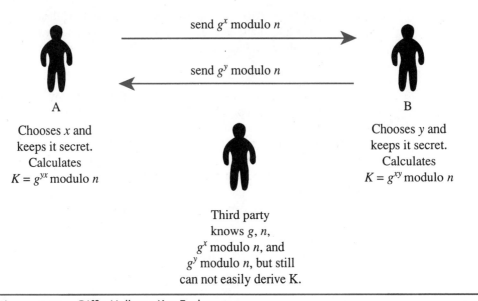

send g^x modulo n

send g^y modulo n

A

Chooses x and
keeps it secret.
Calculates
$K = g^{yx}$ modulo n

B

Chooses y and
keeps it secret.
Calculates
$K = g^{xy}$ modulo n

Third party
knows g, n,
g^x modulo n, and
g^y modulo n, but still
can not easily derive K.

Figure 4.21   Diffie-Hellman Key Exchange

there is a third party listening to this conversation, we assume he knows g and n along with whatever else is being transmitted. Meanwhile, A gets g^y modulo n and raises it to the power of x, getting g^{yx} modulo n. B gets g^x modulo n and raises it to the power of y, getting g^{xy} modulo n. Using properties of modular arithmetic, g^{yx} modulo n and g^{xy} modulo n are equal. Both A and B use this as the encryption key.

What about the snooping third party? As stated, he knows both g and n and can determine the values of g^x modulo n and g^y modulo n from snooping on the communications line. But since both A and B keep the values of x and y secret, the third party cannot complete the calculations to get the encryption key. This, by itself, does not make the line secure. A logical question to ask is, If the third party knows g, n, g^x modulo n, and g^y modulo n, can he derive the values of x and y from them? In effect, the third party needs to calculate a logarithm of g^x modulo n or g^y modulo n. There are conditions that n and g can satisfy which make such derivations very difficult. At the very least, both g and n must be very large (perhaps a thousand bits). We won't provide a discussion of the conditions that must apply and why they are sufficient, as that gets us into mathematical number theory. If you are interested in this topic, References [Sc94] and [St95a] have more detail.

4.6   PUBLIC KEY ENCRYPTION

All of the previous encryption methods share one feature. If an unauthorized receiver intercepts the ciphertext and, for some reason, knows the encryption algorithm and key (E_k), then the decryption method ($D_{k'}$) is easy to determine. For example, if the ciphertext for a Caesar cipher was determined by adding k to the ASCII codes of the plaintext, we simply decrypt by subtracting k from the ASCII codes of the ciphertext. Similarly, if we know the key for the Vigenère cipher, it is a simple matter to decrypt the ciphertext. You should convince yourself that we can make similar comments about the other methods discussed so far.

It certainly seems reasonable that knowing E_k makes decryption trivial. Like many other reasonable things, however, it is not true. In 1976, Diffie and Hellman (Ref. [Di67]) proposed the use of encryption methods for which the decryption algorithm and key are not determined easily even when both the encryption method and key are known. The rationale is that even if an unauthorized person knows the encryption algorithm and key, that knowledge is of no use in helping him or her decrypt the ciphertext.

There is another advantage to such methods. Suppose someone needs to get secret messages from many sources (Figure 4.22). Rather than having each source use a different encryption method, they can all use the same one, E_k. Only the receiver knows the decryption method $D_{k'}$. In fact, E_k could be made public. Since $D_{k'}$ cannot be derived from that knowledge, there is no danger. Even different senders cannot decrypt others' messages despite the fact they use the same encryption method.

Such systems are called **public key cryptosystems.** Typical uses include a bank receiving sensitive financial requests from many customers or a military command center receiving reports from various locations. It also is being used in networking software such as Novell's NetWare 4.0.

Figure 4.22   Multiple Senders Using the Same Encryption Method

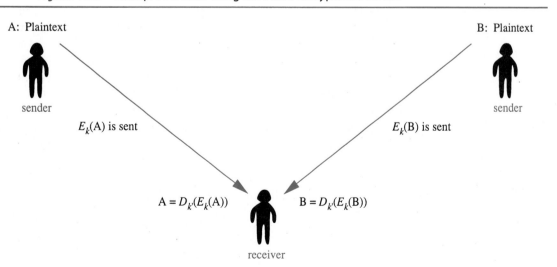

A: Plaintext

sender

$E_k(A)$ is sent

$A = D_{k'}(E_k(A))$

B: Plaintext

sender

$E_k(B)$ is sent

$B = D_{k'}(E_k(B))$

receiver

RSA ALGORITHM

The RSA algorithm (named after its developers, Rivest, Shamir, and Adleman), described in Reference [Ri78], uses modular arithmetic and the factorization of very large numbers. The ciphertext is surprisingly easy to calculate and very difficult to break, even when E_k is known. Some of the theory behind this algorithm is based in mathematical number theory, specifically in notable results known as Fermat's Theorem and Euler's Theorem. We won't diverge into a discussion of number theory, but if you have the inclination, Reference [St95a] summarizes some of the important number theoretic results.

To describe how this method works, we consider messages consisting of capital letters only. However, the method can be generalized to include a larger character set. The following steps describe the RSA encryption algorithm and include an example to illustrate the steps.

1. Assign a simple code to the letters, such as 1 through 26 for A through Z, respectively.

2. Choose n to be the product of two large prime numbers p and q. (A prime number has no factors except itself and 1.) In practice, a large prime number consists of 200 or more digits. However, we will conserve space and energy by using $n = p \times q = 11 \times 7 = 77$.

3. Find a number k that is relatively prime to $(p - 1) \times (q - 1)$. Two numbers are relatively prime if they have no common factors except 1. In our example, we choose $k = 7$, which is relatively prime to $(p - 1) \times (q - 1) = 10 \times 6 = 60$. The number k is the encryption key. You might ask, Can we always find a number k with this property? The answer is yes. A well-known result in number theory proves it.

4. Divide the message into components. In general, each component will contain many letters to avoid repeated components. However, for our example, we will have just one letter per component. If the message is "HELLO," the components are H, E, L, L, and O.

5. For each component, concatenate all the binary codes of each letter in the component and interpret the resulting bit string as an integer. Here, each component has just one letter. So, the integers are 8, 5, 12, 12, and 15 (the numbers assigned to the letters originally).

6. Encrypt the message by raising each number to the power of k. However, do all arithmetic modulo n. In our example, this requires the following computations:

8^7 modulo 77; 5^7 modulo 77; 12^7 modulo 77; 12^7 modulo 77; 15^7 modulo 77

The results are the encrypted message. Here the calculations evaluate to 57, 47, 12, 12, and 71, respectively. (We will show how to make this calculation shortly.) Note that here the two 12s indicate a repeated letter. This is a consequence of having one letter per component. If a component contains several letters, repetitions like this are avoided.

The receiver gets the encrypted message 57, 47, 12, 12, and 71. How does she decrypt it? The following steps show the decryption method and continues the example to illustrate each step.

1. Find a value k' for which $k \times k' - 1 = 0$ modulo $(p-1) \times (q-1)$. This means that $(k \times k') - 1$ is evenly divisible by $(p-1) \times (q-1)$. The value for k' is the decryption key. In this example, $(p-1) \times (q-1) = 60$, and $k' = 43$ works nicely. That is, $7 \times 43 - 1 = 300$ is divisible by 60. Again, you might ask, Can a value k' always be found? Yes! Again, famous results in number theory by Euler and Fermat prove this.

2. Raise each encrypted number from step 6 to the power k', and do the arithmetic modulo n. The results are the original component numbers from step 5. In our example, this requires the following calculations:

$$57^{43} \text{ modulo } 77;\ 47^{43} \text{ modulo } 77;\ 12^{43} \text{ modulo } 77;\ 12^{43} \text{ modulo } 77;$$
$$71^{43} \text{ modulo } 77$$

The results are the original numbers: 8, 5, 12, 12, and 15.

Using previous notation, $E_k(x) = x^k$ modulo n and $D_{k'}(y) = y^{k'}$ modulo n, so we have $D_{k'}(E_k(x)) = (x^k)^{k'}$ modulo n. As long as k and k' are chosen as described, $(x^k)^{k'}$ modulo n evaluates to x. Once again, verification of this lies in the work of number theorists.

The encryption and decryption algorithms are surprisingly simple. Both involve exponentiation and modular arithmetic. But there is a potential problem: How do you calculate the exact modular value of a number like 71^{43}? This particular number evaluates to approximately 10^{79} and is actually very small compared with numbers that occur in practice. It certainly seems to be an intimidating calculation. We are interested only in modular arithmetic, however, so we can take some shortcuts that allow you to do this on any calculator. Let's illustrate by calculating 71^{43} modulo 77.

The first step is to write the exponent as a sum of powers of 2. Doing this, we get

$$71^{43} = 71^{32+8+2+1} = 71^{32} \times 71^8 \times 71^2 \times 71^1 \tag{4.1}$$

Now $71^2 = 5041 = 36$ modulo 77. Again, this means 5041 and 36 have the same integer remainder on dividing by 77. Since Equation 4.1 requires only the modular value, we can replace 71^2 by 36. Furthermore, we can write 71^8 as $(71^2)^4$. Again, since we need only the modular value this is the same as 36^4. Similarly, the modular equivalent of 71^{32} is $(71^2)^{16}$, or 36^{16}. Therefore, Equation 4.1 reduces to

$$71^{43} = 36^{16} \times 36^4 \times 36 \times 71 \text{ modulo } 77 \tag{4.2}$$

As you can see, we have reduced the necessary calculations significantly. But we can go farther. Proceeding in a similar fashion we have $36^2 = 1296 = 64$ modulo 77. Consequently, we can write $36^4 = (36^2)^2 = 64^2$ modulo 77 and $36^{16} = (36^2)^8 = 64^8$ modulo 77. Now Equation 4.2 reduces to

$$71^{43} = 64^8 \times 64^2 \times 36 \times 71 \text{ modulo } 77 \tag{4.3}$$

Of course, we can continue the process to get

$$71^{43} = 64^8 \times 64^2 \times 36 \times 71 \text{ modulo } 77$$
$$= 15^4 \times 15 \times 36 \times 71 \text{ modulo } 77$$
$$= 71^2 \times 15 \times 36 \times 71 \text{ modulo } 77$$
$$= 36 \times 15 \times 36 \times 71 \text{ modulo } 77$$
$$= 15 \text{ modulo } 77$$

There's no calculation here that cannot be verified by any calculator.

The RSA algorithm is relatively easy to implement, but is it secure? The encryption algorithm requires n and k, and the decryption algorithm requires n and k'. Now, suppose you intercept an encrypted message and that you know n and k. It doesn't seem like it should be difficult to determine k'. But remember, k' is chosen so that $(k \times k') - 1 = 0$ modulo $(p - 1) \times (q - 1)$. Therefore, all you need to do is find p and q, the factors of n. But if n is very large, say on the order of 200 digits, this is very difficult (or at least very time consuming) to do.[*]

DIGITAL SIGNATURES

Another interesting use for public key cryptosystems is in verification. For example, when you make a withdrawal from a bank you must fill out a form and sign it. Your signature verifies your identity. If you later claim you never made the withdrawal, the bank can produce the form with your signature. Of course, you can always claim the signature was forged and sue the bank. If the case goes to court the bank can produce a handwriting expert who can verify the signature is yours. Consequently, you will lose the suit and the bank's loan officers will probably not approve your request for a mortgage on your new house.

But consider a slightly different scenario. You send a request electronically to your Swiss bank account to transfer a large sum of money to your ex-spouse's account. What can the bank do if you later claim you never made the request, especially since your ex-spouse took the money and moved to Bolivia? There is no signature on file for a handwriting expert to analyze. The bank might respond by stating a password had to be entered to authorize the request and only you knew the password. Of course, the bank's computers also have the password somewhere to verify it when you enter it. You might claim that someone got the password from the bank's records and that therefore, the bank is at fault for not providing proper protection.

Is there a way for the bank to prove it was not at fault and to verify it was you who made the request? Figure 4.23 illustrates the general problem. Someone sends a message, receives a response, and then claims he never sent it. Can the receiver verify the claim is false? Verifying the identity of a sender is called **authentication**.

---

[*]According to wire service reports at the time of this writing, Purdue University researchers were using large computers in attempts to factor a 167-digit number.

Figure 4.23   Sender Denying Sending a Message

One method of authentication is to use a **digital signature.** Essentially, it involves encrypting a message in a way that only the sender would know. More specifically, it uses an encryption key only the sender knows. It is similar to a password except that passwords are also stored in the receiver's files for verification. The encryption key is nowhere except in the sender's possession. The sender might claim someone stole it, but since the receiver has no record of the key, the receiver is not at fault. It's like losing the key to your home. Ultimately, you are responsible.

Figure 4.24 shows how to send encrypted messages containing a digital signature. It uses two pairs of public key encryption/decryption methods. We label them $(E_k, D_{k'})$ and $(E_j, D_{j'})$, where the public keys are j and k and the private keys are k' (known only to the sender) and j' (known only to the receiver). Furthermore, the pairs should have the following properties:

$$E_k(D_{k'}(P)) = D_{k'}(E_k(P)) = P \text{ and } E_j(D_{j'}(P)) = D_{j'}(E_j(P)) = P$$

We have already stated that an encryption followed by a decryption yields the original message, but we also require the reverse to be true. That is, decrypting first and then encrypting also yields the original.

Suppose the sender wants to send an encrypted message and identify himself. If P is the plaintext message, the sender calculates $E_j(D_{j'}(P))$ and sends it.[*] The receiver applies $D_{j'}$ to the message. Since $D_{j'}$ and E_j are inverse operations, the result

---

[*] Sometimes the sender may apply $D_{k'}$ only to his signature or ID and then encrypt everything. This is faster than altering the entire message twice, especially if the message is long.

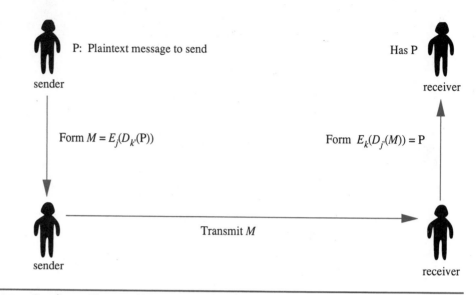

P: Plaintext message to send

Has P

sender

receiver

Form $M = E_j(D_{k'}(P))$

Form $E_k(D_j(M)) = P$

sender

receiver

Transmit M

sender

receiver

Figure 4.24 Sending a Message Using a Digital Signature

$D_{k'}(P).$[*] The receiver stores $D_{k'}(P)$ in the event the sender eventually denies sending the message. Next the receiver applies E_k, giving $E_k(D_{k'}(P)) = P$, and the message is received.

Now suppose the sender denies sending the message. To authenticate the sender's identity, the receiver supplies both $D_{k'}(P)$ and P to an arbiter (someone who must decide who is lying). The arbiter applies E_k (the public key encryption method) to $D_{k'}(P)$ and gets P. This shows that the message P is derived from $D_{k'}(P)$. Furthermore, since $D_{k'}(P)$ was determined using a private key not derivable from E_k, the arbiter concludes that $D_{k'}(P)$ could have been constructed only by someone with knowledge of the private key k'. Since the sender is the only person with that knowledge, the sender is guilty as charged.

AUTHENTICATION USING HASH-BASED SCHEMES

The ability to authenticate the sender of a message is certainly important in an age of electronic transfers. However, the method we have just described authenticates by encrypting the entire message. Consequently, this blurs the distinction between providing security and authentication. In some cases, we are not concerned about hiding the contents of a message as much as ensuring that it is authentic. This is useful in cases where the message might be a contract, a letter of recommendation, or anything with legal implications. Is there a way to ensure that once a document has reached electronic form it cannot be altered without detection?

---

[*]If just the sender's ID was altered the first time, the receiver now has the plaintext and the ID altered by $D_{k'}$.

One approach uses a **hash function** H (also called a **message digest**) to associate a unique fixed-length value with a document. If M is the document then $H(M)$ represents the **hash value** or **message digest value.** Next, apply a private key decryption algorithm represented by $D_{k'}$ to $H(M)$ and store the result, $D_{k'}(H(M))$ along with the document (Figure 4.25). If the authenticity of the document is in question, then do the following:

1. Calculate the message digest value of the document in question.

2. Apply a public key encryption algorithm to the decrypted message digest value $D_{k'}(H(M))$ stored with the document (use a public key encryption algorithm that complements the private key decryption algorithm applied to $H(M)$). The result is $E_k(D_{k'}(H(M))) = H(M)$.

3. Compare these two values. If they disagree, someone has tampered with the document.

This simple explanation raises a logical question: How hard is it to tamper with a document and not change the message digest value? For example, a simple hash function will sum the byte values (interpreted as integers) in the document. An exchange of two bytes will alter the document but leave the message digest value the same. This is an important question and is critical to the development of an authentication method.

Figure 4.25   Authenticating a Document

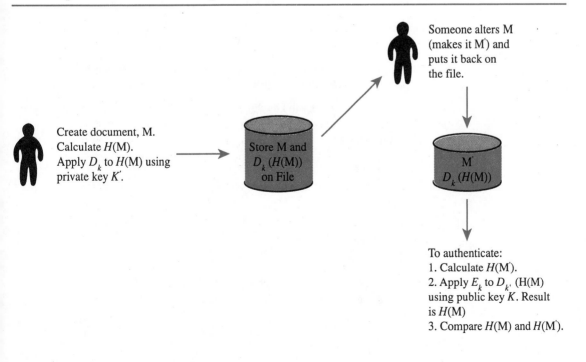

Create document, M.
Calculate $H(M)$.
Apply D_k to $H(M)$ using
private key K'.

Store M and
$D_k(H(M))$
on File

Someone alters M
(makes it M') and
puts it back on
the file.

M'
$D_k(H(M))$

To authenticate:
1. Calculate $H(M')$.
2. Apply E_k to $D_{k'}(H(M)$
using public key K. Result
is $H(M)$
3. Compare $H(M)$ and $H(M')$.

The answer lies in the creation of one-way hash functions. A **one-way hash function** H is one that satisfies the following conditions:

- Let M be a message or document of arbitrary length. Then H is a function that associates a unique fixed-length value with M. Mathematically, we write $H(M) = V$.
- $H(M)$ is easy to calculate. This is important to develop an efficient algorithm.
- Given a value for V, it is difficult to find an M for which $H(M) = V$. This criterion is the reason for the *one-way* qualifier. A direct implication of this is that if M is a message and $V = H(M)$ then it is difficult to find another message M' for which $H(M') = V$.
- It is difficult to find two messages M_1 and M_2 for which $H(M_1) = H(M_2)$. This may seem the same as the previous criterion but, as we will soon show, there is a subtle but important difference.

One might question the need for such tight conditions on the hash function. After all, even if a message or document could be altered without changing the message digest value, wouldn't the change be noticeable? The answer is a resounding No! In 1979 a now well-known article by Yuval [Yu79] described the **birthday attack,** a technique that can be used to generate two documents with the same message digest value if the message digest is not strong enough.

The technique is so named because of its similarity to a common problem described in a probability course. The problem is stated as follows:

> Given an arbitrary collection of people in a room, how many must there be so that the probability that one of them shares your birthday is greater than 0.5?

The answer is one-half the number of days in a year, or 183.

A related problem is

> Given an arbitrary collection of people in a room, how many must there be so that the probability that any two of them share a birthday is greater than 0.5?

It is often a surprise to many to know that the answer is 23. The reason the number is lower than expected is because we don't care which birthdays match.

This is a special case of a more general problem, stated as follows:

- Let $X = \{x_1, x_2, x_3, \ldots, x_k\}$ and $Y = \{y_1, y_2, y_3, \ldots, y_k\}$ be two sets of numbers.
- Each number is random and lies between 1 and 2^m, respectively (m is some positive integer).
- Let $P(m, k)$ be the probability that X and Y have at least one number in common. In other words, $x_i = y_j$ for some i and j.
- What must k be so that $P(m, k) \geq 0.5$?

It turns out that the answer to the above question is $k \approx 2^{m/2}$. We won't provide the mathematical proof of this, but if you have the background, Reference [St95a] has the details.

So what does this have to do with authenticating documents? Suppose an unscrupulous person, Mr. X, works for a city building inspector and is helping to publish a list of inspection reports. Mr. X prepares each report, based on input from the building inspector, and then gives it to the building inspector for approval. Upon approval the inspector runs a program that calculates a message digest value and gives the document to Mr. X for eventual publication. Suppose there is a project that does not pass inspection but for which Mr. X has been paid by the contractors to see that a positive report is published anyway. How can Mr. X achieve this?

Suppose the message digest produces a value between 1 and 2^{64}. The birthday attack has Mr. X preparing two reports. One is a valid but unfavorable report; the other is not valid but is favorable to the contractor. Mr. X can create several variations of each report, each of which has essentially the same content. For example, Mr. X might find several words for which synonyms can be substituted or places where a pronoun can be substituted for a proper noun. Even replacing two consecutive spaces with one constitutes a change. If Mr. X can identify 32 places in each report where a substitution can be made, then there are 2^{32} variations of each report. That is how many combinations of substitutions are possible.

If the message digest applied to each report generates a 64-bit number, then there is a 50-50 chance that Mr. X can find a valid and invalid report generating the same message digest value. Computationally it would not be that difficult. Granted, 2^{32} is a large number of variations for which to calculate message digest values by hand, but a computer program would not have that much trouble with it. Consequently, Mr. X can provide the proper valid report to the inspector, who, in turn, generates the message digest number for it. When Mr. X gets the validated report he can substitute the invalid report with the same message digest number and publish the false report.

The flaw in this process is not in the scheme itself but in the size of the message digest number. For example, if the message digest value were a 128-bit number instead, then the probability of finding two matches from the 2^{32} variations of each report is extremely small. In fact, Mr. X would need 2^{64} versions of each document to have a 50-50 chance of finding a match. The sheer amount of time needed to do this makes the attempt at fraud computationally infeasible. Of course, this last statement is subject to change as computers become faster and more powerful.

The next logical question to ask is, What kinds of hashing schemes are available? One such algorithm is the **MD5 algorithm** developed by Ron Rivest at MIT [Ri92]. The algorithm produces a 128-bit message digest value. It divides the message into 512-bit blocks (some padding may be necessary to get a full 512-bit block) and operates on each block. Each block is subjected to four rounds of operations that use various bit operations and factor in values from a sine function. Eventually, a result is generated, which is used as input to encrypt the next block. It is a complex process; if you'd like to see some details, References [St95a] and [Sc94] provide them. Another algorithm is the **Secure Hash Algorithm (SHA)** which was developed by the NSA and NIST. It is more secure in that it produces a 160-bit message digest value. Like MD5, it operates on 512-bit blocks, subjecting each to a convoluted sequence of bit operations. Again, details can be found in References [St95a] and [Sc94].

Summary of Encryption Methods

Table 4.5 provides a brief summary of the encryption methods discussed in Sections 4.5 and 4.6.

Encryption Potpourri

We have just scratched the surface regarding privacy issues, encryption methods, and key distribution. As with other topics in this text, whole books have been

Table 4.5   Summary of Encryption Methods

Method	Relationship between Encryption and Decryption Keys	Comments
Caesar cipher	They are same. If we add k to the plaintext, we subtract k from the ciphertext.	Each plaintext character is replaced with a ciphertext character. All occurrences of a character combination translate to the same ciphertext.
Polyalphabetic cipher	They are the same.	Replaces a plaintext character with a ciphertext character. Replacement character depends on plaintext character's position in the message. Larger keys reduce the frequency of letter combinations in the ciphertext, but it becomes more unwieldy.
Transposition cipher	They are the same.	Makes no attempt to disguise the plaintext letters. This method can provide clues to someone trying to break the code.
Bit-level cipher	They are the same.	Performs exclusive OR operations between a key and message segments. Short keys allow some letter combinations to be encrypted the same way. Longer keys do not, but they become unwieldy.
DES	They are the same.	Uses a complex collection of transpositions, substitutions, and exclusive OR operations to disguise the translation process. Still, it defaults to a substitution cipher for 64-bit segments.
RSA algorithm	They are related by some well-known results in number theory.	Encrypts by raising numbers to powers that depend on large prime numbers. Determining the decryption key, even when the encryption key is known, requires the factoring of very large numbers, which can take a very long time.
Clipper Chip and SkipJack algorithm	They are the same.	Details of the algorithm are classified.

written on the subject of encryption. The past few years have seen an incredible growth of Internet applications, especially the World Wide Web, and this growth will likely continue. As the number of people becoming electronically active grows, so does the need for privacy and security. We could continue on this topic for quite some time, but there are other topics to cover. Table 4.6 provides a short description of some other topics and some references useful for further reading. In particular, if you are looking for detailed coverage of a wide variety of encryption methods and the source code for some, then Reference [Sc94] is a good source.

Table 4.6 Further Topics in Encryption

TOPIC	OUTLINE	REFERENCES
Digital Signature Standard (DSS)	The DSS has been adopted by the NIST as a standard and is based on a signature method called ElGamal. Instead of using prime factors of very large numbers, ElGamal is based on the calculation of discrete logarithms. That is, it is based on a relationship $y = x^k$ (modulo p) where $y, x,$ and p are the public keys and k is the private key. Under proper conditions the algorithm is considered quite secure.	[St95a], [St95b], [Sc94]
Firewalls	The tremendous growth of the Internet has raised serious concerns about the security of connected networks and the information in PCs connected to those networks. Web browsers allow access to numerous resources, and network managers must keep their systems secure. A firewall allows a wide variety of network configurations within an organization but protects it from outside attack. Essentially, all communications to and from any location outside the organization must go through a specific system that runs security software. The idea is to place security measures where they are needed most—at access points to the network. On the other hand, if the firewall's security measures are compromised the intruder may have free access to internal systems. Firewalls also do not protect information from attack from within an organization.	[Op97], [Si96], [Ch95]
Key distribution and escrow	In order to decrypt codes, private keys must be distributed to appropriate recipients. In addition, law enforcement officials argue that under certain conditions there must be a way to get access to those keys. Consequently, how private keys are stored, protected, and accessed is an issue. In the section on the Clipper Chip we discussed one approach, but there are others. The cited reference discusses key distribution, and the March 1996 issue of the *Communications of the ACM* has several articles devoted to key escrow.	[St95b]

(continues)

Table 4.6   *(continued)*

TOPIC	OUTLINE	REFERENCES
Legal, social, ethical, and political issues	Developing secure codes is serious business. We have outlined some of the controversy surrounding the NSA and the development of encryption techniques. In fact, commercial encryption products were once treated as munitions, making them subject to the same rules as an F-16 fighter jet. If you were caught selling them overseas without a proper license you were an international arms trafficker. In 1996, President Clinton issued an executive order that would transfer jurisdiction over commercial encryption exports from the State Department to the Commerce Department when the Commerce Department developed regulations to implement the order. Still, not all encryption algorithms are considered exportable and information regarding some cryptographic algorithms still remains classified information. In addition, the Department of Commerce may still refer export license applications to the State Department and other agencies for review. This is a complex and very controversial issue. The debate between those arguing for the right to privacy and those opposed to privacy when it hinders law enforcement will be ongoing. In addition to the cited references, most of the December 1995 issue of the *Communications of the ACM* deals with ethics and computer use. It's excellent reading.	[Sc94], [Ta96], [Fo94], [La96]
Pretty Good Privacy (PGP)	PGP is a freeware email security program developed by Philip Zimmerman. It includes public key encryption, authentication, digital signatures, and compression. It runs on many platforms and uses algorithms that have been thoroughly reviewed, such as RSA for public key encryption, MD5 for message digests, and the IDEA algorithm (Ref. [Sc94]) for regular encryption. It had received some notoriety because of its free accessibility via the Internet, which allows it to be "exported" to foreign countries. The U.S. government argued that because cryptographic software is considered munitions, this situation was in violation of export laws. More recent versions were developed outside of the United States to circumvent this problem.	[GA94], [St95a], [Zi95]
Privacy Enhanced Mail (PEM)	PEM is a standard designed to provide for secure email over the Internet. It is a protocol package that provides encryption, authentication, and key management capabilities. PEM is described in four documents: RFC 1421, RFC 1422, RFC 1423, and RFC 1424.* Algorithms used by PEM include DES for encryption and RSA and MD5 for authentication and digital signatures.	[Ke93], [St95a], [Sc94]

---

*RFC is an acronym for Request for Comments, a series of research notes covering a wide array of topics such as Internet protocols, network management, email, network standards, and a lot more. RFCs are numbered and have the form RFC xxxx. Many RFCs are available via the Internet.

4.7   VIRUSES, WORMS, AND HACKERS

Up to now we have considered the integrity and security of data as it travels along some medium. We answered questions about detecting data that has been damaged and disguising data so unauthorized persons cannot understand it. Other serious threats to the security and integrity of information are computer viruses and worms.

Strictly speaking, viruses and worms may be less of a computer network problem and more of an operating system or human behavior problem. Although networks certainly facilitate the spread of some viruses, just being connected to one does not mean viruses are going to jump into your computer and eat your disks. In fact, two main reasons that viruses and worms exist are security holes in operating systems and careless behavior by PC users.

On the other hand, network connections are not without danger, as victims of the Internet worm incident (discussed shortly) can testify. Access to electronic bulletin boards and connectivity among computers all over the world make the existence of worms and viruses a serious problem. Consequently, a chapter on security must at least discuss them and their capabilities.

INFECTING FILES

A **virus** is a collection of instructions attached to an executable file that does something the original executable file was not designed to do. On PCs, a virus commonly attaches to a file with the .EXE or .COM extension. On a Macintosh, a file's resource fork typically is infected. When a virus attaches to a file, we say the file is **infected. Worms** are a lot like viruses, but they usually appear as a separate program. Like a virus, they are an intrusion to the system and are potentially damaging to the system's security.

Figure 4.26 shows one way to differentiate between an infected and an uninfected file. There are other ways and, if interested, you should consult References [Sp90] and [Ka94]. The uninfected file contains executable code that runs when it is referenced. In an infected file, however, the virus has placed a branch command to the virus's code. When the user calls on the infected file to do some task, the branch command transfers control to the virus code first. The virus does its deed and executes another branch to begin the requested task. As far as the user is concerned, the requested task is done. Unless the virus performed an obvious task such as erasing the hard disk, the user may not know the virus exists.

What is a virus capable of doing? Unfortunately, just about anything. A virus may do "harmless" tasks such as displaying Christmas trees on your PC during the holiday season.[*] It may be very destructive and erase your hard disk or destroy your file system. In these cases the effects usually can be minimized, but only if you have backups! If not, you're in serious trouble.

---

[*] Some "harmless" viruses may actually do a great deal of harm, even if they do not explicitly destroy or damage existing information. We will see a few examples shortly.

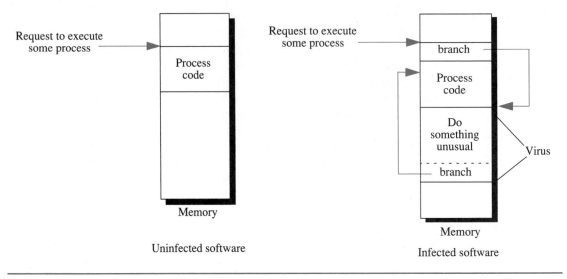

Request to execute some process → Process code

Memory

Uninfected software

Request to execute some process → branch / Process code / Do something unusual / branch — Virus

Memory

Infected software

Figure 4.26   Virus on an Executable File

The worst viruses do not cause massive destruction immediately. Instead, they are very subtle, making small (and usually unnoticeable) changes in files as they run. Over a period of time the small changes compound and eventually are noticed. By that time, the information has been corrupted. Worse yet, if you made backups diligently they also may be infected. Restoring the uninfected versions of the files may be difficult.

How does the virus attach itself to an executable file? The first step is to bring an infected file into your computer and run it. Once it runs, the attached virus can infect files in different ways. For example, it might probe your file system looking for other executable files (Figure 4.27). With a little knowledge of a file system this is not difficult. Whenever it finds an executable file the virus can execute instructions to duplicate itself and store the copy on the file, as in Figure 4.27.

Such viruses can be detected more easily than others. The process of seeking executable files and changing them requires extra disk activity. Consequently, if you notice a lot of disk activity when you do a simple task, be suspicious. On the other hand, it's very easy to be preoccupied with what you are doing and not even notice the hardware. If the virus is subtle and infects only a few files, you may not notice the extra activity, especially with a fast hard drive.

MEMORY-RESIDENT VIRUSES

Rather than scanning the disk's file system, the virus may copy itself into memory and wait for an executable file to be stored in memory. When a file enters, the virus attacks it. Picking the files off one by one as they enter memory is a much more subtle type of attack—not unlike a sly predator hiding and waiting for its prey to arrive unsuspecting, only to become the predator's next meal.

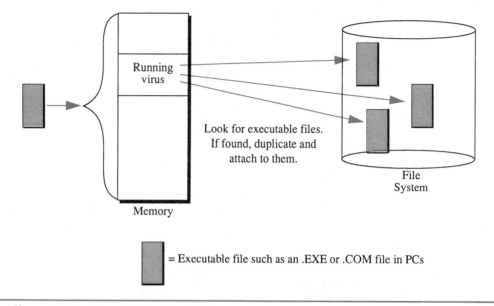

= Executable file such as an .EXE or .COM file in PCs

Figure 4.27   Virus Duplicating Itself

But how does a memory-resident virus become activated? It is still a program and cannot be activated until it is called. On PCs some viruses take advantage of internal interrupt mechanisms. Typically BIOS and operating system service routines are located via an interrupt table or interrupt vector. The **interrupt table** is a collection of addresses to service routines. When a user requires a service or when some asynchronous event occurs that needs action, the operating system locates the required service by finding its address in the table and begins executing the program at that location. A memory-resident virus will change the interrupt table to create addresses that locate the virus instead (Figure 4.28). Consequently, when an interrupt occurs, the routine located via the table's address is called. In this case, it is the virus, which does its deed. As before, it may try to disguise what it did by calling the intended service routine, making the user think everything is progressing normally.

VIRUS EVOLUTION

The history of the computer virus goes back to 1949, a time when most people did not even know computers existed. John Von Neumann wrote a paper entitled "Theory and Organization of Complicated Automata" describing a theory that computer programs could in fact multiply. It outlined, in effect, the model for a computer virus. Since the only computers then were just a few huge mainframes and the only programmers were engineers, there was not much interest in Von Neumann's theories. However, that has changed.

Before the mid-1980s computer viruses were virtually nonexistent. Since then viruses have increased both in number and in complexity, as have the methods for

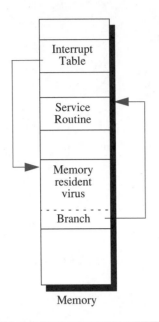

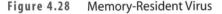

Figure 4.28 Memory-Resident Virus

detecting and eliminating them. Software vendors offer a range of antivirus software packages designed to locate known viruses on a PC. The problem is that as antivirus packages become more sophisticated so do the viruses they seek. A logical question to ask is: How do viruses become harder to detect? References [Na97] and [Ka94] explore some of the history and evolution of viruses and antivirus programs. We summarize the topic here.

We begin by examining how simple viruses are detected. Early viruses in the mid-1980s were quite simple and small in number. Antivirus programs worked by looking for a virus **signature,** a sequence of bytes (corresponding to machine language instructions) contained in the virus. Since there were not very many viruses, the number of signatures was small and looking for them was not a serious problem.

As time passed two things happened to make virus detection more difficult. First, more viruses were written. Second, the proliferation of software and growth in disk capacities provided more places for viruses to hide. Simply looking for a wider variety of virus signatures throughout a disk's files became a time-consuming process. To compensate, antivirus researchers noted a couple of things: Most viruses are not lengthy programs, and viruses typically placed themselves at the beginning or end of an executable file (recall Figure 4.26). Consequently, antivirus programs concentrated their searches at the beginning and end of such files, thus significantly increasing the efficiency of their search.

Virus programmers began to realize that in order to be successful they had to hide the virus' signature, or at least disguise it so it would not be recognizable. Encryption is the tool they began to use. By subjecting virus code to an encryption algorithm (even a simple Caesar cipher) the signature was altered and antivirus software would not find it. The only problem was that a program whose machine instructions are encrypted won't run.

The way around this was to insert a decryption algorithm with the virus in a file (Figure 4.29). When making a call to a process, a branch at the process' entry point transfers control to a decryption algorithm. The algorithm runs and decrypts the contents of memory containing the encrypted virus. Once decrypted the virus can execute, do its nasty deeds, and transfer control to the process. Since this happens in memory, the virus remains in encrypted form in the file and its signature remains disguised.

To make things more difficult for antivirus researchers, the virus could even be written to use a different encryption key each time it infected a new file. Consequently the same virus would look different with each file it infected.

Antivirus programmers responded by designing software to look for byte patterns common to decryption algorithms. The problem here was that code for decryption algorithms is short and often similar to code for legitimate programs. For example, does the following code represent a Caesar cipher decryption algorithm or simply a task to update information in an array?

```
for (i=0; i<s; i++)
    m[i]+=k;
```

Actually, it can be either and it's difficult to distinguish without knowing the context in which it is used.

Figure 4.29   Encrypted Virus on an Executable File

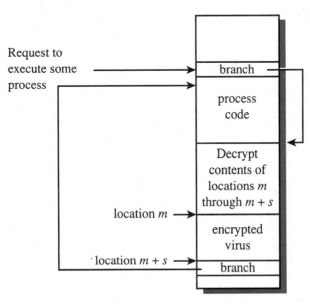

Memory

In order to eliminate an inordinate number of false alarms, antivirus programs use a technique called **X-raying.** Essentially the programs take a suspected encrypted virus and subject it to a collection of decryption algorithms known to be used with viruses. They then examine the decrypted result and look for virus signatures. This method has proved to be successful.

Not to be foiled, the virus programmers responded by creating the **polymorphic virus.** Essentially, it is a virus that mutates when it infects a new file. This is similar to biological viruses (such as the AIDS virus) that often mutate, making them resistant to treatment. A polymorphic virus uses a mutation engine to change the code for the decryption algorithm each time the virus infects a file. Any experienced programmer knows that there are many ways to generate code to accomplish a specific task. The polymorphic virus just takes advantage of that fact. Consequently each copy of a polymorphic virus is not only encrypted with a different key but uses a different decryption routine to decrypt it. For antivirus programs looking for a specific byte sequence characteristic of a virus or decryption algorithm, this is a serious problem.

How can you locate a virus when you don't know what it looks like? There has been some success at analyzing byte strings produced by mutation engines and detecting patterns. The problem is that some of the more complex engines are capable of producing well over a billion forms of decryption algorithms. The huge number of signatures that are possible make any signature-seeking detection methods impractical.

However, any computer virus must eventually decrypt and reveal itself in order to execute. This is the key that has allowed a successful response to the polymorphic virus. The difficulty is that if the antivirus programs wait until then, it is too late. Some current virus detection techniques use **generic decryption (GD)** technology. In a sense, it is a technique that fools the virus into revealing itself early, before it has a chance to do damage.

More accurately, GD antivirus software contains a CPU emulator. When it examines a file, it executes software that simulates the execution of the file. If the file contains a polymorphic virus, it will decrypt itself and its signature pattern will be revealed. By periodically invoking signature-seeking routines, the virus can be detected. Even if the virus decloaked and executed before being detected, it is only a simulation and no real harm is done.

However, what if the file does not contain a virus? At some point the simulation must terminate or no real work would ever get done. The simulation might execute a specific number of instructions and then, if no virus is found, terminate. Still that is not foolproof. A virus can contain all kinds of do-nothing instructions at the start. Examples include NOP instructions (literally instructions that do nothing) or an instruction that adds 0 to a register. The purpose of such instructions is to delay the real activity of the virus and to create the illusion of an innocuous program, at least for a while. Thus, if the simulation is too short, it might miss some viruses. On the other hand, if it is too long then the user gets impatient while waiting for the detection program to complete and writes to the vendor to complain about lousy responses.

The war between virus authors and everyone else continues. Current antivirus software is effective and efficient but new viruses continue to show up, forcing many to invest significant time and money in protecting their resources.

VIRUS SOURCES

Where do viruses come from? Initially they are created by individuals who for whatever reason try to invade a system. Whether it is done as a prank or as an unprincipled and malicious act of destruction is usually of no consequence. What is destroyed is destroyed and reasons are of no value to the victim.

Like any biological virus, computer viruses are spread by sharing. We saw how a file can become infected. Consider what happens if an infected file is copied to a disk and the disk is inserted in another computer. When the infected file is run, the other computer's files can become infected. If any of those are copied to a disk and transported to yet another computer, the virus spreads further. Obviously you want to be very careful about where you get software.

The growing use of networks and communications has compounded the problem. What happens if an infected file gets into an electronic bulletin board, commercial software, or a network file server? The virus now has the potential to spread to thousands of users in a short period of time. The growth rate of the virus can stagger the imagination.

Don't infer from this discussion that bulletin boards, networks, and commercially distributed software are a haven for viral infections. Reputable bulletin board operators and vendors go through great effort to make sure their software is not infected. Still, in this business there are no guarantees. In 1988 there was an incident in which a commercial software package contained a virus that displayed a peace message and then erased itself. This is an example of a "harmless" virus doing damage. It may be harmless in the sense that it neither destroys files nor steals valuable information. The vendor, however, will have to rebuild its damaged reputation and restore consumer confidence in its products. The company could lose business, which in turn can force layoffs. To a vendor and its employees, such incidents are far from harmless.

Given that viruses are unavoidable, how can you deal with them? As with most illnesses, prevention is your best bet. Many virus detection packages are available. Sometimes a virus detection package scans any disk inserted into a drive looking for viruses. If it detects one it sounds a warning and, in some cases where the disk is a floppy, ejects it. The user then can request the package to remove the virus or can replace all the infected files with uninfected backups (making sure first that they are uninfected).

THE INTERNET WORM

One of the more famous instances of intrusion was the Internet worm. Several interesting and accessible articles describe the worm, its effects, and how it worked. For detailed accounts see References [Sp89], [Ro89], [Se89], and [De90].

In November 1988 a Cornell graduate student released a worm into the Internet, a worldwide collection of wide area networks running the TCP/IP protocol.[*] It invaded thousands of Sun 3 and VAX computers running variants of the 4 BSD UNIX operating system. This worm was of the so-called harmless variety; it did not damage any information or give away any of the secret passwords it uncovered.

On the other hand, it was a serious breach of security. It replicated quickly throughout the Internet, clogging communications and forcing many systems to be shut down. It also forced many experts to spend days tracking the source of the problem and cleaning up after it. It caused an FBI investigation to determine whether there was a violation of the 1986 Computer Fraud and Abuse Act and resulted in an indictment of the perpetrator. The case went to court, and a federal jury found the defendant guilty. The defendant was sentenced to three year's probation, fined $10,000, and ordered to do 400 hours of community service [Mo90]. So much for harmless worms! (Computer worms and viruses are federal crimes and in most cases will be investigated by the FBI. Federal laws are stricter than most state laws.)

The worm itself was written in C and attacked UNIX systems through flaws in the software. It used several techniques, each of which is described in Reference [Sp89]. In one approach, it used a utility called **fingerd** that allows one user to obtain information about other users. The *fingerd* program is designed to accept a single line of input from a remote site (a request) and send back output corresponding to the request (Figure 4.30). The flaw that was exploited was that the fingerd program's input command (the C language gets command) did not check for buffer overflow. Consequently, a worm running on a remote machine could connect to the fingerd program and send a specially constructed message that overflowed the fingerd program input buffer.

Figure 4.30   The fingerd Utility

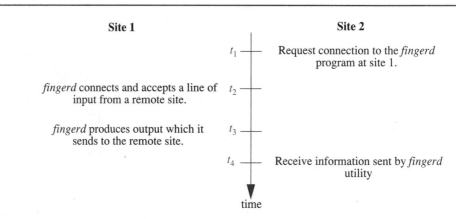

[*]We will discuss the Internet, wide area networks, and the TCP/IP protocol in Chapter 7. Specific knowledge of what they are and how they work is not needed for this discussion. The important fact here is that hundreds of thousands of computers worldwide are interconnected.

Figure 4.31 shows what happened. The transmitted message overflowed the input buffer and overwrote parts of the system stack. However, the stack contains a return address (of the calling procedure) to be referenced when *fingerd* is done. Because of the overflow, this address was changed to point to some instructions stored in the buffer. Consequently, when *fingerd* finished, control returned to the "program" located by the new return address. This "program" effectively replaced *fingerd* with the UNIX shell (interface or command interpreter). The result was that the worm was now connected to the shell. From that point the worm communicated with the shell and eventually sent a copy of itself, thus infecting the new machine. The worm then proceeded to inspect system files looking for connections to other machines it could infect.

It also attacked a password file trying to decipher user passwords. Deciphering a password allowed the worm to attack other computers where that user had accounts. An interesting note here is that the passwords were all stored in encrypted form using the DES. In theory, deciphering the passwords without the key is next to impossible. The worm took a rather straightforward approach, however. It simply guessed passwords, encrypted them, and looked for matches. In theory, the number of possible passwords is huge, making this an impractical method of seeking passwords. However, the worm used words from an online dictionary and in many cases found matches. In some cases, over 50% of the passwords were uncovered (Ref. [Sp89]). The moral of this story is don't use passwords commonly found in a dictionary.

COMPUTER HACKERS

Widespread connectivity has opened many doors for another security threat, the computer hacker. Basically, a **hacker** is someone who writes programs just for the sheer enjoyment of writing them. Some people see hackers as unprincipled people who try to gain unauthorized access to a computer system, often by exploiting security holes in operating systems and determining user passwords.

Figure 4.31   Intruding into the System

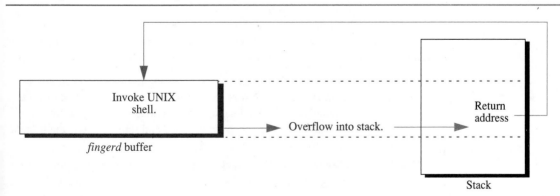

Why do unprincipled hackers do what they do? That's tough to answer. Some people believe that most hackers see breaking into a system as a challenge or a game. They either do not realize or do not care about the consequences of their actions to others. To some, looking at private information does not carry the same stigma as intruding on the privacy of a person's home. This does not necessarily make such people less dangerous, however. Some people believe the perpetrator of the Internet worm did not have malicious intent since the worm did not try to destroy information. Nevertheless, its effect was far-reaching and very disruptive. People who hack with the sole purpose of stealing or altering information do exist. They often accept the risk of getting caught or perhaps do not even care. Reference [La87] discusses the motives of some hackers and suggests that there are some very dangerous people doing the hacking.

The existence of widespread networks has created the potential for more severe and potentially dangerous problems (Ref. [Na91]). For example, one hacking incident described in References [St88] and [St89] received widespread publicity. It started with a 75-cent accounting error at Lawrence Berkeley Laboratory (LBL) in August 1986 and led to the arrest of a West German hacker. The hacker attacked many computers on MILNET (a military production network) and passed information to the KGB, the secret police of the former Soviet Union. In 1990 a West German court convicted him of espionage for the KGB.

References [St88] and [St89] provide fascinating reading. They detail the activities of many people as they monitored the intruder's efforts and eventually tracked him to his West German location. They characterized the intruder as not particularly resourceful but very persistent, using primitive attack methods such as guessing passwords. As with the Internet worm, many of his attacks were successful simply because of the widespread use of common words as passwords.

4.8 SUMMARY

This chapter dealt primarily with two topics: the security and integrity of transmitted information. Integrity means making sure that information that is received is the same as that which is sent. Security means making sure only authorized people get access to transmitted information.

Sections 4.2 through 4.4 dealt with two approaches to integrity. The first approach is to develop methods to detect damaged transmissions and simply ask for a retransmission when they occur. Two methods of error detection were discussed.

- **Parity bits.** This method is geared primarily for single-bit error detection, as it is only 50% accurate for burst errors. However, it can be useful when bits are transmitted separately, such as is done in some computer memory architectures, or if single bits from many messages are grouped and sent. It also is the foundation of an error correction technique.

- **Cyclic redundancy checks.** This method is based on the theory of polynomial division. Bit strings are interpreted as polynomials. CRC bits are created so that a message divided by a generator polynomial yields a zero remainder. Dividing a received message by the generator polynomial and checking the remainder yields a very high probability that errors are detected. This method is commonly used and is implemented easily using circular shift circuits and a register. Certain polynomials have been declared as standards.

The second approach to integrity involves detecting and correcting errors. This is most useful when a retransmission is too costly or violates time constraints. The Hamming code establishes a collection of parity bits for strategic positions. If any single-bit error occurs, the position will affect a unique combination of parity checks. This not only allows the error's detection but also provides its position. Knowing its position subsequently allows the bit to be corrected.

Sections 4.5 and 4.6 discussed encryption as a security method. The idea is to disguise information so that even if it does fall into the wrong hands it cannot be understood. The tricky part of encryption is to determine a method so that an unauthorized receiver cannot analyze the ciphertext and reverse the encryption process (decrypt). Several methods were discussed:

- **Caesar cipher.** This method substitutes one character for another. It preserves common letter sequences and is relatively easy to break.

- **Polyalphabetic cipher.** Like the Caesar cipher, one character is substituted for another. The difference is that the substitution choice for a common character varies depending on the letter's position in the message.

- **Transposition cipher.** This method makes no attempt to disguise the characters but instead rearranges them.

- **Exclusive OR bit operations.** The key is a bit string. An exclusive OR operation between it and parts of the message encrypts the message.

- **Data Encryption Standard (DES).** This method is essentially a substitution cipher, but the rules for the substitution follow many convoluted steps, thus making the process difficult to reverse without knowing the encryption steps. The method is controversial, as some feel that the National Security Agency weakened the standard from the original proposal. The speculation was that the NSA did not want an encryption method it would have trouble breaking.

- **RSA algorithm.** This method is an example of a public key cryptosystem that encrypts by treating a bit string as a number and raising it to a very large power using modular arithmetic. It is also unique among the methods discussed in that the decryption key (private key) is very difficult to determine even when the encryption key (public key) is known.

Other issues involving encryption, such as key distribution and digital signatures, were discussed. Key distribution means communicating keys in a secure way. One method, Merkle's puzzles, involves sending many encrypted messages (each with a different key) and having the receiver choose one randomly, break the code, and determine the key. Another, Shamir's method, involves using a key as part of a polynomial expression. Then, points that the polynomial's graph pass through are distributed. To determine the key, a minimal number of people are needed to provide enough points to determine the original polynomial. A third technique, Diffie-Hellman key exhange, called for a sender and receiver to exchange calculated values from which an encryption key can be derived. Part of the calculation is kept secret and the lack of that information makes deducing the key by a third party very difficult.

Digital signatures are a way of authenticating the author of an encrypted message. The idea is to encrypt using a private key and decrypt using a public one. If the author later disputes ownership of the message, the receiver can provide both the received ciphertext and the plaintext. Since the private key is known only to the author, then only the author could have sent the message. A message digest is a way of providing authenticity of a document without encrypting the document. Essentially, it associates a fixed-length number with a document, which is encrypted and stored with the document. It is difficult to tamper with the document without changing the message digest value.

The Clipper Chip was a controversial development in part because it uses algorithms designed by the NSA. It also includes a protocol allowing access to a user's private key under certain circumstances (typically when illegal activities are suspected). Since there is a distrust of government by many, especially where privacy is concerned, it has enflamed the ongoing discussion between right-to-privacy groups and law enforcement officials who argue that privacy is not a right in cases where illegal activities are happening.

The last topics on security were viruses, worms, and hackers. Viruses are programs that attach themselves to other programs. What they do varies and can be very destructive. Like viruses, worms represent invasions into a system, but they are not actually part of another program, as viruses are. Computer hackers are individuals who attempt to break through a system's security. They may try to steal private information or plant viruses or worms in order to do damage. Two rather famous cases of intrusion were the Internet worm, which invaded thousands of computers on the Internet, and the West German programmer who attacked computers on MILNET and sold information to the former KGB.

Review Questions

1. What is a parity bit?

2. Distinguish between even and odd parity.

3. Distinguish between error correction and error detection.

4. What is a burst error?

5. Are the following statements TRUE or FALSE? Why?

   a. It is not unusual to lose a bit or two during a transmission.

   b. Although an accurate technique, CRC is time-consuming because it requires a lot of overhead.

   c.   A generator polynomial can be chosen arbitrarily as long as both sender and receiver know it.

   d.   CRC will detect a burst error of arbitrary length as long as the number of bits affected is odd.

   e.   Error correction codes are more efficient than error detection codes since they obviate the need for retransmissions.

   f.   The Caesar cipher has no real value where serious security is needed.

   g.   Public key encryption allows different people to use the same encryption key even when they are not supposed to know what another person is sending.

   h.   The most serious viruses destroy a lot of data very quickly.

   i.   Viruses that do not destroy information or otherwise compromise a computer system are harmless.

6.   What is a cyclic redundancy check?

7.   Under what conditions will CRC detect the following errors?

   a.   Single-bit errors

   b.   Double-bit errors

   c.   Burst errors of length less than or equal to the degree of the generator polynomial

   d.   Burst errors of length greater than the degree of the generator polynomial

8.   What conditions should a generator polynomial satisfy? Why?

9.   Classify the errors that a CRC method will always detect.

10.   Classify errors that a CRC method will not detect.

11.   What is a shift register?

12.   What is a Hamming code?

13.   Distinguish between encryption and decryption.

14.   Distinguish between ciphertext and plaintext.

15.   What is a Caesar cipher?

16.   Distinguish between a monoalphabetic and a polyalphabetic cipher.

17.   What is a Vigenère cipher?

18.   What is a transposition cipher?

19.   If the encryption key is long enough, encryption techniques such as bit-level ciphering are truly unbreakable. Why aren't they used more?

20.   What is the Data Encryption Standard (DES)?

21. What was the controversy surrounding DES?

22. Why has the Clipper Chip proved controversial?

23. What is the purpose of using key escrow agents to hold the keys used in the SkipJack algorithm?

24. What are Merkle's puzzles?

25. What is Shamir's method for key distribution?

26. How does public key encryption differ from regular encryption?

27. What is a digital signature?

28. What are the main features of the RSA algorithm?

29. What makes the RSA algorithm so difficult to break?

30. How do authentication and digital signatures differ?

31. What is the significance of the birthday attack?

32. Distinguish between a virus and a worm.

33. What is an infected file?

34. List some ways you can help prevent the spread of computer viruses.

35. What is the UNIX fingerd utility?

36. What is a memory-resident virus?

37. What was the Internet worm?

Exercises

1. Construct an argument showing that simple parity checking detects errors only when an odd number of bits change.

2. Consider the double parity check approach discussed in Section 4.2. What can you say about its effectiveness with a burst error of length n?

3. Suppose some static of duration 0.01 second affects the communication line for a 14,400 bps modem. How many bits could be affected?

4. Consider the error detection technique described by Figure 4.3. What is the probability that two distinct burst errors will go undetected? Assume each burst error has duration less than the time to send one column.

5. Why does $0 - 1 = 1$ using modulo 2 subtraction?

6. What polynomial corresponds to the following bit string?

0110010011010110

7. Calculate the remainder of the following division using the methods described by Figures 4.4 and 4.5:

$$\frac{x^{12} + x^{10} + x^7 + x^6 + x^5 + x^3 + x^2}{x^7 + x^4 + x^2 + 1}$$

8. Suppose you want to transmit the data 100111001 and the generator polynomial is $x^6 + x^3 + 1$. What bit string is actually sent?

9. Draw the circular shift register and exclusive OR circuits for the CRC-12 and CRC-16 standard polynomial.

10. Calculate the remainder of the following division using circular shifts:

$$\frac{x^{12} + x^{10} + x^7 + x^6 + x^5 + x^3 + x^2}{x^7 + x^4 + x^2 + 1}$$

11. Investigate the documentation for the LAN at your university or company and determine what method of error detection (if any) is used.

12. Suppose the generator polynomial had the term x as a factor. Give an example of an undetected error.

13. Suppose we want to devise a single-bit error-correcting Hamming code for a 16-bit data string. How many parity bits are needed? How about for a 32-bit data string?

14. The following 12-bit Hamming-coded (single-bit correction) string was received. What ASCII-coded letter does it represent?

110111110010

15. Construct Hamming codes for each of the following characters: A, 0, and {.

16. Assume a sender has the following data frames:

Frame Number	Data
1	0 1 1 0 1 0 0 1
2	1 0 1 0 1 0 1 1
3	1 0 0 1 1 1 0 0
4	0 1 0 1 1 1 0 0

Suppose the sender constructs a Hamming code for each frame, forms a two-dimensional bit array, and sends it one column at a time. What does the receiver get if an error makes the fifth column all 0s? Apply error correction methods to the received data and correct it.

17.   Develop a Hamming code capable of correcting any single-bit errors and detecting double-bit errors for an eight-bit data string.

18.   Suppose the four-bit number $b_4 b_3 b_2 b_1$ described by Table 4.2 forms a number exceeding 12. What does that mean?

19.   Write a computer program to take 8 bits of data and create the 12-bit Hamming code.

20.   How were the letter substitutions in Figure 4.13 determined?

21.   Write a program to encrypt and decrypt using a Caesar cipher. The program should request the encryption key as input.

22.   The following message was encrypted using a Caesar cipher. What is the original message?

fcvceqoowpkecvkqpucpfeqorwvgtpgvyqtmu

23.   Write a decryption algorithm to decrypt ciphertext created by the encryption algorithm in Figure 4.15.

24.   Consider the transposition cipher applied to Table 4.4. What is the transmitted message if the columns are rearranged as 5, 1, 4, 2, and 3?

25.   Write a program to accept a binary string and a binary key. It should then use the key to encrypt the string using bit-level ciphering.

26.   Consider the bit string 0010110101010000111111101001101 and the key 10110. Use the key to encrypt and then decrypt the string using bit-level ciphering.

27.   Suppose that the rows (except row 0) in the key of Figure 4.14 are rearranged so that the ASCII codes of the first letters in two consecutive rows differ by 3 (instead of the current 1) modulo 26. Use the resulting key to encrypt the following message:

TIME FLIES LIKE AN ARROW FRUIT FLIES LIKE A BANANA[*]

28.   Repeat the encryption process of the message "HELLO" discussed in Section 4.6 using a different encryption key but with the same value for n.

29.   Suppose you intercepted the following encrypted message:

20 5 21 3 49 4 49 3 4 15

You also know that the encryption key is $k = 7$ and that it was determined using $n = 55$. Decrypt this message. Assume A through Z were initially coded using 1 through 26, and a blank was initially coded using 27.

---

[*] Apologies to Groucho Marx.

30. Using $n = 47$, $g = 5$, $x = 10$, and $y = 12$, verify that the Diffie-Hellman key exchange works. What is the encryption key?

31. Calculate 95^{91} modulo 121.

References

1. [Ch95] Chapman, D. and E. Zwicky. *Building Internet Firewalls.* Sebastopol, CA: O'Reilly & Associates, 1995.

2. [De90] Denning, P., ed. *Computers Under Attack: Intruders, Worms, and Viruses.* Reading, MA: Addison-Wesley, 1990.

3. [De96] Denning, D. E. and D. K. Branstad. "A Taxonomy for Key Escrow Encryption Systems." *Communications of the ACM,* vol. 39, no 3 (March 1996), 34–40.

4. [Di67] Diffie, W. and M. E. Hellman. "New Directions in Cryptography." *IEEE Transactions on Information Theory,* vol. 13 (November 1967), 644–654.

5. [Fo94] Forcht, K. *Computer Security Management.* Danvers, MA: Boyd & Fraser, 1994.

6. [Ga94] Garfinkel, S. *PGP: Pretty Good Privacy.* Sebastopol, CA: O'Reilly & Associates, 1994.

7. [Ha80] Hamming, R. W. *Coding and Information Theory.* Englewood Cliffs, NJ: Prentice-Hall, 1980.

8. [Ka94] Kane, P. *PC Security and Virus Protection Handbook.* New York: M&T Books, 1994.

9. [Ke93] Kent, S. T. "Internet Privacy Enhanced Mail." *Communications of the ACM,* vol. 36, no. 8 (August 1993), 42–47.

10. [Ko77] Kolata, G. B. "Computer Encryption and the National Security Agency Connection." *Science,* vol. 197 (July 1977), 438–440.

11. [Ko78] Kohavi, Z. *Switching and Finite Automata Theory,* 2nd ed. New York: McGraw-Hill, 1978.

12. [La87] Landreth, B. and H. Rheingold. *Out of the Inner Circle: A Hacker's Guide to Computer Security.* Bellevue, WA: Microsoft Press, 1987.

13. [La96] Laudon, K. "Markets and Privacy." *Communications of the ACM,* vol. 39, no. 9 (September 1996), 92–104.

14. [Me78] Merkle, R. C. "Secure Communications Over an Insecure Channel." *Communications of the ACM,* vol. 21, no 4 (April 1978), 294–299.

15. [Mo89] Moshos, G. *Data Communications: Principles and Problems.* St. Paul, MN: West, 1989.

16. [Mo90] Montz, L. "The Worm Case: From Indictment to Verdict." In *Computers Under Attack: Intruders, Worms, and Viruses,* ed. Peter Denning. Reading, MA: Addison-Wesley, 1990.

17. [Na91] National Research Council. *Computers at Risk.* Washington, DC: National Academy Press, 1991.

18. [Na97] Nachenberg, C. "Computer Virus-Antivirus Coevolution." *Communications of the ACM,* vol. 40, no. 1 (January 1997), 46–51.

19. [Op97] Oppliger, R. "Internet Security: Firewalls and Beyond." *Communications of the ACM,* vol. 40, no. 5 (May 1997), 92–102.

20. [Pe72] Peterson, W. W. and E. J. Weldon. *Error Correcting Codes,* 2nd ed. Cambridge, MA: MIT Press, 1972.

21. [Ri78] Rivest, R. L., A. Shamir, and L. Adleman. "On a Method for Obtaining Digital Signatures and Public Key Cryptosystems." *Communications of the ACM,* vol. 21 no. 2 (February 1978), 120–126.

22. [Ri92] Rivest, R. L. "The MD5 Message Digest Algorithm." RFC 1321, April 1992.

23. [Ro89] Rochlis, J. and M. Eichin. "With Microscope and Tweezers: The Worm from MIT's Perspective." *Communications of the ACM,* vol. 32, no. 6 (June 1989), 689–698.

24. [Sc94] Schneier, B. *Applied Cryptography.* New York: Wiley, 1994.

25. [Se89] Seeley, D. "Password Cracking: A Game of Wits." *Communications of the ACM,* vol. 32, no. 6 (June 1989),700–703.

26. [Sh77] Shapely, D. and G. B. Kolata. "Cryptology: Scientists Puzzle over Threat to Open Research, Publication." *Science,* vol. 197 (September 1977), 1345–1349.

27. [Sh79] Shamir, A. "How to Share a Secret." *Communications of the ACM,* vol. 22, no 11 (November 1979), 612–613.

28. [Si96] Simonds, F. *Network Security: Data and Voice Communications,* New York: McGraw-Hill, 1996.

29. [Sp89] Spafford, E. "The Internet Worm: Crisis and Aftermath." *Communications of the ACM,* vol. 32, no. 6 (June 1989), 678–687.

30. [Sp90] Spafford, E., K. Heaphy, and D. Ferbrache. "A Computer Virus Primer." In *Computers Under Attack: Intruders, Worms, and Viruses,* ed. Peter Denning. Reading, MA: Addison-Wesley, 1990.

31. [St88] Stoll, C. "Stalking the Wily Hacker." *Communications of the ACM,* vol. 31, no. 5 (May 1988), 484–497.

32. [St89] Stoll, C. *The Cuckoo's Egg: Tracking a Spy Through the Maze of Computer Espionage.* New York: Doubleday, 1989.

33. [St95a] Stallings. W. *Network and Internetwork Security.* Englewood Cliffs, NJ: Prentice-Hall, 1995.

34. [St95b] Stinson, D. *Cryptography: Theory and Practice.* Boca Raton, FL: CRC Press, 1995.

35. [St96] Stallings, W. *Computer Organization and Architecture,* 4th ed. Englewood Cliffs, NJ: Prentice-Hall, 1996.

36. [Ta96] Tanebaum, A.S., *Computer Networks,* 3rd ed. Englewood Cliffs, NJ: Prentice-Hall, 1996.

37. [Yu79] Yuval, G. "How to Swindle Rabin." *Cryptologia.* vol. 3, no. 3 (July 1979), 187–190.

38. [Zi95] Zimmerman, P. *The Official PGP User's Guide.* Cambridge, MA: MIT Press, 1995. 237

CHAPTER 5

PROTOCOL CONCEPTS

*Knowledge in the form of an informational commodity
indispensable to productive power is already, and will
continue to be, a major—perhaps the major—stake in
the worldwide competition for power. It is conceivable
that the nation-states will one day fight for control of
information, just as they battled in the past for control
over territory, and afterwards for control over access to
and exploitation of raw materials and cheap labor.*
—**Jean François Lyotard,** French philosopher

5.1 INTRODUCTION

Almost everything we have discussed so far has dealt with a single transmission
from a sender to a receiver. Whether we discussed digital or analog signals, compression, contention, security, or integrity, the discussion was generally aimed at a
single transmission or frame. Most communications are more complex than that.
The following issues also should be considered:

- What if the transmitted message is very long? Examples include large data files
  or a copy of a speech given at a political rally. Treating the entire message as a
  single transmission entity monopolizes the medium. This is fine for the sender
  but not so good for anyone else waiting to transmit.

- How do we react to damaged transmissions? In the previous chapter we stated
  that the receiver simply requests a retransmission. But how does the receiver do
  this? Does the sender's protocol depend entirely on the receiver's ability to
  notify him of damaged frames? Should the sender conclude that a frame arrived
  correctly if the receiver sends no such request? What happens if the receiver's
  request for a second transmission is itself damaged or lost?

- What if the sending and receiving computers work at different speeds? For
  example, you might download a data file from a supercomputer to a ten-year-
  old PC. Or perhaps the receiver is busier than the sender. In general, how do

you prevent a sender from overwhelming a receiver with more data than the receiver can handle?

- What happens if a sender's frame gets lost? For example, the damaged part of a frame may include the receiver's address. If so, the frame will never be delivered. We know the receiver can detect damaged frames. But what happens if a receiver gets nothing? Does it mean a frame was lost or that nothing was sent? How does the receiver distinguish between the two?

- In our previous examples, the distinction between sender and receiver was sharp. What if both want to send and receive simultaneously? It's a lot like talking and listening at the same time. We all do it on occasion but some of what we hear is lost. We do not want our receivers to lose information.

This chapter discusses two important functions necessary to establish and maintain effective communications: error control and flow control. **Error control** defines how a station checks frames for errors and what it does if it finds them. Sections 4.2 and 4.3 discussed ways of detecting errors but did not address what happened afterward. A common approach is for the receiving station to send a message to the sending station indicating that an error occurred. What the sending station does next varies, and we discuss several protocols. The message is effectively a request to resend the frame, so this type of error control is often called **automatic repeat request (ARQ).**

Flow control defines the way in which many frames are sent and tracked and how the stations do error control. It determines when frames can be sent, when they cannot be sent, and when they should be sent a second time. In general, flow control protocols ensure that all of the related frames arrive at their destination accurately and in order.

As with any topic, protocols range from simple to complex. Section 5.2 discusses relatively simple flow control protocols. The protocols range from sending one frame at a time (stop and wait) to sending all of them at once (unrestricted flow). This section also discusses the use of special signals or specific byte values to indicate when to send data. The latter is analogous to a traffic signal regulating traffic flow onto a highway. As long as the light is green, traffic can enter the highway. But when the highway traffic reaches a certain saturation point the light turns red, halting any additional flow onto the highway.

Section 5.3 defines a more complex approach that numbers the frames and sends only a few at a time. The sender then waits for acknowledgment before sending more. The go-back-n protocol discussed in Section 5.3 assumes that frames arrive in the same order in which they were sent. The selective repeat protocol also discussed in Section 5.3 allows for cases in which frames might be delayed and delivered out of order.

Discussing protocols and how they work is one thing. Verifying that they are correct is quite another. For simple algorithms, verification is often easy, but the complex ones require some special tools. Section 5.4 discusses some verification tools such as Petri nets and finite state models. Its orientation is more theoretical, and it may be skipped without loss of continuity.

The final two sections take a practical approach and discuss actual protocols in use today. Section 5.5 discusses data link protocols such as High-level Data Link Control (HDLC) and binary synchronous communications (BSC). Section 5.6 discusses Kermit, a common file transfer protocol.

5.2   BASIC FLOW CONTROL

SIGNALING

This section introduces relatively elementary approaches to flow control useful in simple communications systems. The first approach, **signaling,** is straightforward (Figure 5.1). The sender transmits data as long as the receiver is able to receive it. The receiver may not be able to receive data all the time, however. For example, the buffers that hold received data may be filling up, or the receiver may not be ready if it is doing other things. In such cases, the receiver sends a signal to the sender. On receipt of the signal, the sender stops transmitting. The protocol also allows for another signal to be sent when the receiver is again ready to receive more data. This approach is analogous to a nonproductive argument in which one person says, "Stop! I don't want to hear any more."

Figure 5.1   Flow Control Using Signaling

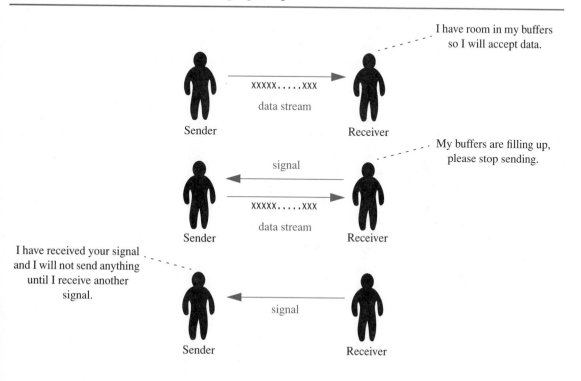

DTE-DCE Flow Control   Section 3.2 discussed one way to signal readiness to send and receive data over an RS-232 interface. It involved sending signals over specified lines (DTR and DSR) to indicate a state of readiness. When the DTE wanted to send to the DCE, it sent another signal (RTS) requesting to send. It then waited for a Clear to Send signal (CTS) before transmitting. The details are in Section 3.2 so we won't rehash old material here.

X-ON/X-OFF   The RS-232 interface was complex in that it required separate lines for separate signals. Another approach is to send the signal as part of the transmitted data. This is called **inband signaling.** In this case, the receiver has to analyze the incoming data looking for any special signals to which it must respond.

The ASCII character set defines two control characters for flow control (see Table 2.4 in Section 2.3). Symbolically, they are DC3 (ASCII code 19) and DC1 (ASCII code 17), also called X-OFF and X-ON, respectively.[*] They are commonly used for flow control between a terminal and mainframe. Figure 5.2 shows how this works.

The figure assumes full-duplex communications, so there is no distinction between a sender and receiver. Stations A and B both send to and receive from each other. If A's buffers are starting to fill up it can respond by inserting the X-OFF character into the data it is sending to B. When the X-OFF character arrives, B sees it and stops transmitting its data to A. (Note, however, that A is still sending to B.) If A has more room in the buffers later, A can send the X-ON character to B, which signals B that it is permissible to resume transmitting.

When one station sends the X-OFF character, it continues to receive data for a short time because of the small delay between the time the X-OFF character is sent and the time the other station can respond to it. Consequently, a station usually will send when data in its buffers exceeds some threshold value.

Your first exposure to this protocol may have been by accident. For example, a common activity in a programming class is to list text files on the screen. Occasion-

Figure 5.2   Flow Control Using Inband Signaling

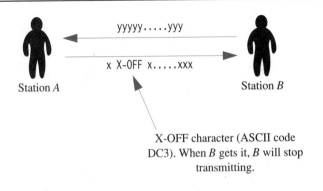

Station A

Station B

yyyyy.....yyy

x X-OFF x.....xxx

X-OFF character (ASCII code DC3). When B gets it, B will stop transmitting.

---

[*]They also correspond to the control-S and control-Q keyboard sequences.

ally, through a mistake or inattention, you might try to list a binary file such as an executable file. The result usually is the appearance of strange characters on the screen, some beeping noises, and random cursor movement. In some cases, the terminal becomes unresponsive to further keyboard entries. That is, the keyboard freezes on you. Since most bytes in a binary file do not correspond to printable characters, the terminal often responds to their contents in unexpected ways. Line feed, vertical tab, or horizontal tab codes cause the cursor to move randomly. The characters may also contain the BEL code (hexadecimal code 07), causing the beeping sound. (This should destroy popular belief that the beeps are a warning that the terminal is about to self-destruct.)

The freezing problem occurs if one of the file's bytes contains an X-OFF character. Because the terminal received the X-OFF character, it responded by stopping transmission back to the computer. Thus, if you make subsequent keyboard entries they are not sent, and the terminal freezes. Solutions range from turning off the terminal or entering a local mode at the terminal and clearing communications.

Another common use of this protocol occurs when printing a large file on the screen. To prevent information from scrolling off the screen you can enter a control-S (hold the control key and enter S) from the keyboard to freeze the screen. Control-S sends an X-OFF character, which stops the transmission of the file. Later, having read what you wanted, you can enter control-Q, which sends the X-ON character and allows the file's transmission to resume.

FRAME-ORIENTED CONTROL

Protocols such as X-ON/X-OFF are byte oriented and are typical of asynchronous communications (Section 3.1). That is, transmission can start and pause at any given byte. Synchronous communications (Section 3.1) are frame oriented and require more organization. Information is sent and retrieved in larger pieces, not as a byte stream. Because a station must be able to buffer all the bytes in a frame it receives, different protocols are used to restrict the number of frames that can be sent. How the restrictions are applied, of course, varies.

Another consideration is that those who send and receive information usually do not care about the frames and their structure. Indeed, if you send a file from a PC to a mainframe over a modem you do not want to be bothered with these details. You simply want to enter a command to send a file and have the software worry about the details. Consequently, most protocols divide the information to be sent into frames of the appropriate format and send them. Figure 5.3 illustrates how this is done in a typical case.

Someone or something that we call a **patron** has information it must send to another. The patron typically is a user or a higher layer in a multilayer protocol. The sender gets enough information (a **packet**) from the patron to put into one frame and transmits the frame. The receiver gets the frame, extracts the packet, and gives it to the patron that it serves. This process is repeated using as many frames as needed to transmit all the information.

Typically, the sender, receiver, and patrons of Figure 5.3 define consecutive layers in some communications software. This is typical of the interaction between the data link (sender and receiver) and network layer (patron) in the OSI model. Flow control also exists in higher-layer protocols such as TCP/IP and is part of IBM's SNA architecture. (We describe each of these later in this book.) At this point, where the sender, receiver, and patron exist is not important. Flow control exists in different models and in different layers. However, it is important to realize that flow control typically is part of the interaction between two consecutive layers in some protocol.

Unrestricted Protocol   The easiest protocol, **unrestricted protocol,** assumes the receiver either has an unlimited capacity to receive frames or processes them fast enough so that buffer space is always available. Figure 5.4 shows the sender and receiver logic written in partial C code.[*] The sender and receiver use the primitive calls send and receive. Typically, they are calls to a layer below the sender and receiver that take care of details required to transmit the frame or retrieve it.

The sender executes a loop repeatedly as long as there is information to send. With each pass of the loop it gets a packet from its patron, puts it into a frame, and sends the frame. It sends frames repeatedly and makes no effort to limit the number

Figure 5.3   Sending and Receiving between Patrons

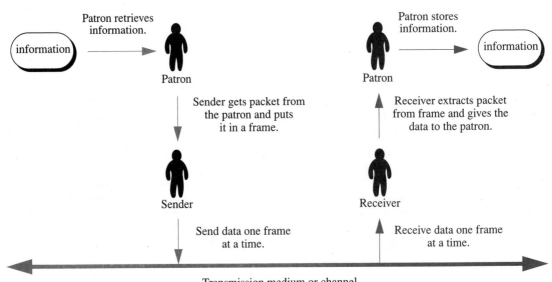

Transmission medium or channel

---

[*]We make no attempt to write syntactically correct code. We will combine C syntax with informal statements to convey the program's meaning without a lot of language detail. A good exercise is to modify all the protocols we discuss into syntactically and logically correct programs.

```
void send_data;                        void receive_data;
{                                      {
  while there are packets to send        while there are frames to receive
  {                                      {
    get packet from the patron;            wait for frame to arrive;
    put packet into a frame;               receive(frame);
    send(frame);                           Extract packet from the frame;
  }                                        Give packet to the patron;
}                                        }
                                       }
```

Sender code	**Receiver code**

Figure 5.4   Unrestricted Flow Control

it sends. The receiver also executes a loop repeatedly. We assume the receiver is always capable of receiving a frame. With each pass through the loop, the receiver waits (i.e., exists in a suspended or wait state) until a frame arrives. The arrival causes the receiver to wake up and receive the frame. It extracts the packet and passes it to its patron and then goes back into a wait state until another frame arrives.

This approach does not consider any of the problems we have discussed previously. There is no attempt to check for damaged, lost, or delayed frames or to control the number of frames sent. It assumes that every frame will arrive without damage and in the order sent. It is much like our dependence on the Post Office when we mail letters.

Stop and Wait Protocol   This protocol differs from the previous one in two ways. First, every time the receiver gets a frame it sends an acknowledgment back to the sender. The acknowledgment is another frame specifying whether the received frame was damaged. Second, after sending a frame the sender waits for an acknowledgment before sending another frame. Thus rather than sending all the frames in rapid sequence, this protocol sends one, waits for an acknowledgment, sends another, waits for an acknowledgment, and so on. We call this the **stop and wait protocol.** In some ways it represents the opposite extreme of the previous method. Whereas the unrestricted protocol sent the maximum number of frames per unit of time, this one sends the minimum number.

Figure 5.5 outlines the sender's and receiver's protocol. The receiver protocol is similar to the unrestricted one. It consists of an infinite loop in which it waits for a frame to arrive. When a frame arrives, the receiver checks it for damage. Whether it uses CRC or some form of parity checking discussed in Chapter 4 is not relevant at this level of the discussion. The important thing is that it can detect a damaged frame.

If the frame was not damaged, the receiver defines an error field in a record structure called ack as 0. It proceeds to extract the packet from the frame and give it to the patron. If the frame was damaged the error field of ack is set to 1. It does not

```
void send_data;                              void receive_data;
{                                            {
  damaged=0;                                   while there are packets to receive
  while there are packets to send              {
  {                                              Wait for frame to arrive;
    if (!damaged)                                receive(frame);
        /* !0 is the same as true in C */        Examine frame for transmission error;
    {                                            if no transmission error
      Get packet from the patron;                {
      Put packet into a frame;                     ack.error=0;
    }                                              Extract packet from the frame;
    send(frame);                                   Give packet to the patron;
    Wait for acknowledgment to arrive;           }
    receive(ack);                                else
    if ack.error                                   ack.error=1;
      damaged=1;                                 send(ack);
    else                                       }
      damaged=0;                             }
  }
}
```

Sender code   **Receiver code**

Figure 5.5   Stop and Wait Flow Control

extract a packet from the frame and the patron gets nothing. In any case, the receiver sends the acknowledgment back to the sender. Since the error field specifies the status of the received frame, the sender can respond accordingly.

The sender executes a loop repeatedly, sending frames and waiting for acknowledgments. Prior to sending a frame, the sender must decide whether it should send a new one or resend the old one. It does this through a local variable called damaged whose value indicates the status of the most recently sent frame (1 means the frame was damaged; 0 means it was not). Initially, it is 0. At the beginning of the loop, the sender checks damaged. If it is 0, the sender gets a new packet from the patron, puts it into a frame, and sends it. If damaged is 1, the sender sends the current frame (the one it sent earlier). Either way, it waits for an acknowledgment after sending the frame. When the acknowledgment arrives, the sender checks the error field, which the receiver defined. If the error field indicates the previous frame was damaged, the sender defines damaged = 1. Thus, the next time through the loop, the sender does not get new data from the patron but resends the frame. If damaged = 0, the sender gets a new packet in the next pass and sends it.

As we have described it, stop and wait seems preferable to the unrestricted protocol. Still, it has some shortcomings:

- If the sender's frame is lost, the receiver never sends an acknowledgment, and the sender will wait forever.
- If the receiver's acknowledgment is lost, the same thing happens.
- If the acknowledgment is damaged, the sender may draw the wrong conclusion and make the protocol fail.
- The sender certainly does not overwhelm the receiver with too many frames, but perhaps it has gone to the other extreme. Both sender and receiver do a lot of waiting. It's analogous to a teacher giving an assignment one question at a time. The student takes the question home, works on it, brings it back to school, gives it to the teacher, waits for the teacher to grade it, gets another question, and does the same thing all over again. In some cases it would be far more efficient to take all the questions home, finish them, and return them the next day.

These observations need responses, and the next two sections provide them. Before discussing more complex protocols, however, let's introduce the notion of protocol efficiency.

PROTOCOL EFFICIENCY

We can measure efficiency in several ways. For example, how much buffer space does the protocol require? With the stop and wait protocol there is never more than one frame being sent at a time, so a buffer capacity of one frame is sufficient. With the unrestricted protocol they may arrive faster than the receiver can formally receive them. Therefore, they must be stored in the interim. The number stored depends on how fast they arrive and how quickly the receiver can dispense them. In any case, the stop and wait protocol requires less space and can be considered more efficient from that perspective.

Another measure of efficiency is **channel utilization.** What percentage of the time is the channel transferring data frames? Channel utilization is complex because it depends on several factors such as the distance between the sender and receiver, signal speed over the channel, the bit rate, frame size, and the amount of time needed to construct and send a frame.

Let's illustrate with an example. Assume the following definitions, with the numbers in parentheses to be used in the example:

R = transmission rate (10 Mbps or 10 bits per μsec)

S = signal speed (200 meters per μsec)

D = distance between the sender and receiver (200 meters)

T = time to create one frame (1 μsec)

F = number of bits in a frame (200)

N = number of data bits in a frame (160)

A = number of bits in an acknowledgment (40)

We begin by determining the amount of time needed to construct and send a frame (Figure 5.6). Assume the sender begins at time zero. The sender will have gotten information and put it into a frame at time T. The next step is to transmit the frame (put its bits on the channel). Since R is the data rate, then $1/R$ is the time needed to transmit one bit. Therefore, F/R is the time needed to transmit one frame. The total time used so far is $T + F/R$.

Once the sender has transmitted the frame, the bits require time to travel through the channel to the receiver. The travel time is D/S. Thus, after the last bit is transmitted, it requires another D/S time units to reach the receiver. Therefore, the receiver receives the last bit at time $= T + F/R + D/S$. Note that the amount of time a frame is in transit is $F/R + D/S$.

For the stop and wait protocol the receiver must send an acknowledgment. A similar argument shows that the time required for the sender to receive the acknowledgment is $T + A/R + D/S$.[*]

Next question: How much time elapses between sending two data frames? With the unrestricted protocol, the sender starts building the next frame as soon as it has transmitted the last bit from the previous one. With stop and wait, the sender must wait for each acknowledgment. Therefore, the elapsed time between sending two consecutive frames is

$$\text{time} \; = \; T + \frac{F}{R} \quad \text{for the unrestricted protocol} \tag{5.1}$$

and

$$\text{time} \; = \; \left(T + \frac{F}{R} + \frac{D}{S} \right) + \left(T + \frac{A}{R} + \frac{D}{S} \right)$$

$$= \; 2\left(T + \frac{D}{S} \right) + \frac{F + A}{R} \quad \text{for the stop and wait protocol} \tag{5.2}$$

Figure 5.6   Time Required to Send a Frame to a Receiver

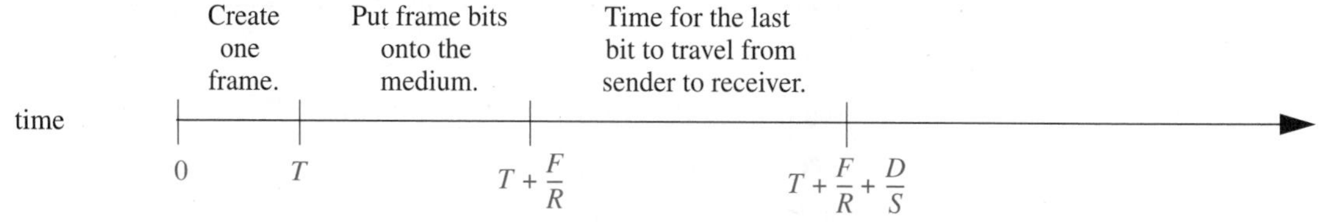

| | Create one frame. | Put frame bits onto the medium. | Time for the last bit to travel from sender to receiver. |

time

$0 \qquad T \qquad\qquad T + \dfrac{F}{R} \qquad\qquad T + \dfrac{F}{R} + \dfrac{D}{S}$

---

[*] Strictly speaking, the amount of time needed for the receiver to construct the acknowledgment frame is different from T. However, specifics depend on CPU speed, efficiency of compiled code, and software scheduling. To simplify matters, we just assume both the sender and receiver can construct a frame in the same amount of time.

Previously, we stated that the amount of time a data frame is actually in transit is $F/R + D/S$. Thus, if we define P as the percentage of time during which frame bits occupy the channel, we have

$$P \text{ (unrestricted protocol)} = 100 \times \frac{\dfrac{F}{R}}{T + \dfrac{F}{R}}$$

$$= 100 \times \frac{\dfrac{200 \text{ bits}}{100 \text{ bits/}\mu\text{sec}}}{1 \mu\text{sec} + \dfrac{200 \text{ bits}}{10 \text{ bits/}\mu\text{sec}}} \qquad (5.3)$$

$$\approx 95\%$$

and

$$P \text{ (stop and wait protocol)} = 100 \times \frac{\dfrac{F}{R} + \dfrac{D}{S}}{2\left(T + \dfrac{D}{S}\right) + \dfrac{F + A}{R}}$$

$$= 100 \times \frac{\dfrac{200 \text{ bits}}{10 \text{ bits/}\mu\text{sec}} + \dfrac{200 \text{ meters}}{200 \text{ meters/}\mu\text{sec}}}{2\left(1 \mu\text{sec} + \dfrac{200 \text{ meters}}{200 \text{ meters/}\mu\text{sec}}\right) + \dfrac{200 \text{ bits} + 40 \text{ bits}}{10 \text{ bits/}\mu\text{sec}}} \qquad (5.4)$$

$$\approx 75\%$$

Thus, if we measure efficiency solely by channel utilization, the unrestricted protocol is more efficient.

Another useful measure is the **effective data rate.** It is the actual number of data bits (as opposed to the maximum number of bits or capacity) sent per unit of time. To calculate the effective data rate, we divide the number of data bits (N) sent by the elapsed time between sending two frames. Continuing with our example, we have the following:

$$\text{effective data rate (unrestricted protocol)} = \frac{N}{T + \dfrac{F}{R}}$$

$$= \frac{160 \text{ bits}}{1 \mu\text{sec} + \dfrac{200 \text{ bits}}{10 \text{ bits/}\mu\text{sec}}} \qquad (5.5)$$

$$\approx 7.6 \text{ bits/}\mu\text{sec} = 7.6 \text{ Mbps}$$

and

$$\text{effective data rate (stop and wait protocol)} = \frac{N}{2\left(T + \dfrac{D}{S}\right) + \dfrac{F + A}{R}}$$

(5.6)

$$= \frac{160 \text{ bits}}{2\left(1 \ \mu\text{sec} + \dfrac{200 \text{ meters}}{200 \text{ meters}/\mu\text{sec}}\right) + \dfrac{200 \text{ bits} + 40 \text{ bits}}{10 \text{ bits}/\mu\text{sec}}}$$

$$\approx 5.7 \text{ bits}/\mu\text{sec} = 5.7 \text{ Mbps}$$

It is important to note that raw bit rate capacity does not guarantee that much data will be moved. In this example, the stop and wait protocol realizes only about 57% of the channel's actual capacity. The effective data rate depends very much on the protocols, frame sizes, distance traveled, and so on. For example, increasing the frame size will increase the effective data rates (assuming there is a proportionate increase in the frame's data bits). This may not be obvious from the previous equations, but try it and see what happens. Can you determine what effect increases in the other variables will have on the effective data rate?

These measures provide only part of the total picture, and we make no claim that the unrestricted protocol is better just because its effective data rates and channel utilization are higher. Other factors to consider are the users the protocols serve, the amount of data to transfer, and the fact that the channel will be used by others. The fact is that these two protocols represent two extremes (send everything at once and send one frame at a time), and some commonly used protocols fall somewhere in between. The next two sections discuss two of them.

5.3   SLIDING WINDOW PROTOCOLS

The previous protocols work reasonably well if the number of frames and the distance between stations are not large. If the number of frames becomes large, the unrestricted protocol can flood the channel and overwhelm the receiver. Equation 5.6 shows what happens with the stop and wait protocol if the distance increases. The D in the denominator forces the effective data rate to decrease. In theory, choosing D large enough makes the rate arbitrarily small.

Since communications often occur over large distances and involve large amounts of data, alternative protocols are needed. One approach is a compromise between the unrestricted and stop and wait protocols called a **sliding window protocol.** It numbers the frames to be sent and defines a **window** as a subset of consecutive frames. If the window contains i frames numbered starting with w (w and i are integers), then the following statements are true (Figure 5.7):

- Every frame numbered less than w has been sent and acknowledged.
- No frame numbered greater than or equal to $w + i$ has been sent.
- Any frame in the window has been sent but may not yet have been acknowledged. Those not yet acknowledged are **outstanding frames.**

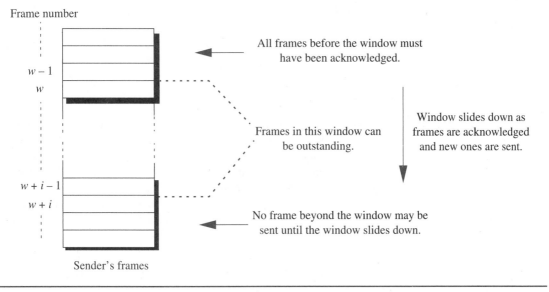

Frame number

w − 1

w

w + i − 1

w + i

All frames before the window must
have been acknowledged.

Frames in this window can
be outstanding.

Window slides down as
frames are acknowledged
and new ones are sent.

No frame beyond the window may be
sent until the window slides down.

Sender's frames

Figure 5.7   A Sliding Window Protocol

Initially, the window contains frames starting with frame 0. As the patron provides packets, the window expands to include new frames, which then are sent. A limit on the window's size, however, limits the number of outstanding frames. When the limit is reached, the sender takes no more packets from the patron. As outstanding frames are acknowledged, the window shrinks to exclude acknowledged frames. Subsequent to this the window can expand again to include more new frames to send.

As the window changes, the previous conditions must always be met and the window must always contain frames numbered consecutively. For example, if frame $w + 1$ is acknowledged but frame w is not, the window will not change until frame w is acknowledged. Even if every frame was acknowledged except frame w, the window will not change. Frames are excluded from the window in the same order in which they were included.

This approach is a compromise because it allows multiple (but not necessarily all) frames to be sent before receiving acknowledgments for each. The maximum window size defines the number of frames that may be outstanding. If the window size is 1, we have essentially the stop and wait protocol. If the window size is greater than the total number of frames, we have essentially the unrestricted protocol. Adjusting the window size can help control the traffic on a network and change the buffering requirements.

There are two common implementations of a sliding window protocol. The **go-back-*n* protocol** requires frames to be received in the same order they are sent.[*] The **selective repeat protocol** does not. Go-back-n is simpler as the receiver rejects every frame except the one it is supposed to receive. Selective repeat requires the receiver to be able to hold onto frames received out of order before passing them on to a higher layer in the correct order.

FRAME FORMAT

With these protocols we drop a previous assumption and eliminate the sharp distinction between sender and receiver. That is, we assume a more realistic model in which two stations (A and B) are sending to (and receiving from) each other (Figure 5.8). This is a conversational or full-duplex mode of communication. Thus the protocol must be able to not only send frames but receive them as well.

Let's review briefly what a frame actually contains. Figure 5.9 shows typical fields. We will see some specific formats in Sections 5.5 and 5.6. The frame fields are as follows:

- **Source address.** This is the address of the station sending the frame. It is often needed so that a station receiving a frame knows where to send an acknowledgment.

- **Destination address.** This is the address where the frame should be sent. It is needed so that a station can determine which frames are destined for it.

- **Frame number.** Each frame has a sequence number starting with 0. If this field has K bits, the largest number is $2^K - 1$. More than 2^K frames causes complications, which we discuss shortly.

Figure 5.8   Two-Way Communication between Stations A and B

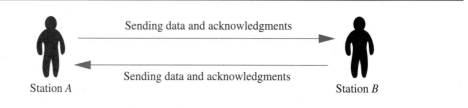

Sending data and acknowledgments

Sending data and acknowledgments

Station A Station B

Figure 5.9   Typical Frame Format

Source	Destination	Number	ACK	Type	...Data...	CRC

[*]The reason frames can arrive out of order varies. It is a lot like the Post Office. The letter you mailed on Monday will probably arrive before the one you mail on Tuesday, but don't bet your retirement pension on it. Heavy traffic, hardware or software failures, and damaged frames can all contribute to delaying or even losing a frame.

- **ACK.** The integer value of this frame is the number of a frame being acknowledged. Note that because a station both sends and receives, it can avoid sending a separate acknowledgment by including the acknowledgment in a data frame. This is called **piggybacking.**

- **Type of frame.** This field specifies the type of frame. For example, a data frame has type "data." However, there may be occasion to acknowledge a frame separately. Piggybacking can be used only when there is data to send; without data, the protocol uses separate acknowledgments using a frame of type "ACK." We also use a type "NAK" for negative acknowledgment for problem situations. For example, the protocol sends a NAK frame when a received frame is damaged or if the wrong one has arrived. In either case, the protocol is letting the other station know something went wrong.

- **Data.** This represents the information in a data frame.

- **CRC.** This corresponds to the bits used for error checking (Section 4.3).

GO-BACK-n PROTOCOL

The go-back-n protocol has several identifying features:

- Frame numbers must lie between 0 and $2^K - 1$ (K = number of bits in the number field), inclusive. If there are more than 2^K frames, frame numbers are duplicated. For example, suppose $K = 6$ and there are more than 64 frames to send. Frames 0 through 63 are numbered 0 through 63. However, frames 64 through 127 are also numbered 0 through 63. In general, frames are all numbered consecutively modulo 2^K. We will see that this feature puts restrictions on the window size in order to allow the stations to correctly interpret the frame numbers.

    This also requires a slight adjustment in how we define a window. We still require that the window contain frames numbered[*] consecutively. However, we now consider 0 as the next frame number after $2^K - 1$. For example, if $K = 6$ then frames numbered 62, 63, 0, 1, 2, etc., are consecutive modulo $2^6 = 64$.

- The receiving station always expects to receive frames in order (modulo 2^K) of frame number. If it receives one out of order, it ignores the frame and sends a NAK for the frame it expected. It then waits until the correct one arrives.

- If a frame arrives and is damaged, the receiving station ignores it and sends a NAK for it.

- A receiving station does not acknowledge each received frame explicitly. If a sending station receives an acknowledgment for frame j and later receives one for frame k ($k > j$), it assumes all frames between j and k have been received correctly. This reduces the number of acknowledgments and lessens network

---

[*]From this point when we refer to a *frame number*, we mean the value that appears in the number field of the frame.

traffic. Of course, the station sending the acknowledgments must make sure the assumption is valid.

- A station uses the piggyback approach whenever possible to acknowledge the most recently received frame. However, if no data frames are sent during a period of time, the station sends a separate acknowledgment frame. An **ACK timer** is set whenever a data frame arrives. The ACK timer counts down and stops only when the station sends something. The rationale is that when a data frame arrives it should be acknowledged within a period of time defined by the ACK timer. If there are no outgoing frames the timer continues to count down to 0. If the timer reaches 0 (expires), the station sends a separate acknowledgment frame in lieu of the piggyback acknowledgment. If the station sends a frame as the timer counts down, the timer stops because an acknowledgment goes with the frame.

- The sending station buffers the packets from all frames in the window in the event it has to resend them. Packets are removed from the buffer as they are acknowledged.

- If a station does not receive an acknowledgment for a period of time, it assumes something went wrong and that one or more outstanding frames did not reach their destination. It then uses a **frame timer,** one for each frame, which is set whenever a data frame is sent. The frame timer counts down and stops only when the associated frame is acknowledged. If the frame timer expires, the protocol resends every frame in the window.

  The rationale for sending all outstanding frames is that the receiving station rejects any frame with the wrong number. If the receiving station got the first frame in the window, the sending station should have received an acknowledgment. Not getting one, the sending station assumes something happened to it. It also reasons that since the receiving station did not get the first frame, it would have rejected all subsequent frames. Thus, all frames must be present. If there are n frames, it goes back to the beginning of the window to resend them. Hence the term go-back-n.

How many frames can the sending protocol have outstanding at one time? In other words, what is the maximum window size? If frames are numbered between 0 and $2^K - 1$, the window size can be no larger than 2^K. If it were, there would be more than 2^K frames outstanding. Consequently, there will be two different outstanding frames with the same number. When the sending station receives an acknowledgment for that number, it has no way of telling which of the two frames is actually being acknowledged. For example, suppose $K = 3$ and the first nine frames are outstanding. The first eight frames are numbered 0 through 7. The last one is numbered 0. If the sending station receives an acknowledgment for frame 0, it does not know if it corresponds to the first or the last frame.

From this, we conclude that the window size must be less than or equal to 2^K. However, if the window size is equal to 2^K, an unfortunate sequence of events still can make the protocol fail. Suppose $K = 3$, and consider the events shown in Figure 5.10.

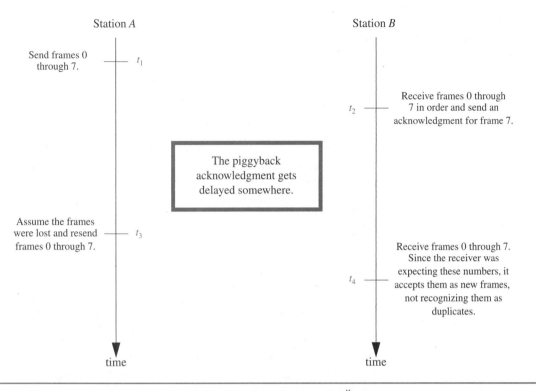

Figure 5.10   Protocol Failure When Window Size Equals 2^K

Assume both stations have been exchanging frames prior to time t_1. At time t_1 station A sends frames 0 through 7 to station B. Station B receives each of them in the correct order and at time t_2 sends an acknowledgment for the most recent one received, number 7. Unfortunately, this acknowledgment gets lost because of a hardware or software error somewhere or a hungry gremlin with a voracious appetite for frames.

Station B has no way of knowing the acknowledgment was lost and is waiting for the frame after frame 7 (frame 0). Station A, on the other hand, does not receive the acknowledgment and does not know whether the frames arrived or not. Following the protocol, it resends frames 0 through 7 at time t_3. At time t_4 station B receives frame 0. The problem is that this frame 0 is a duplicate of the previous frame 0. But station B is expecting a new frame 0 and has no way of knowing it has received a duplicate. It therefore accepts the duplicate as a new frame, and the protocol fails.

The problem occurs because two consecutive windows contain the same frame numbers. Station B had no way of knowing which window frame 0 was in. Reducing the window size by 1 corrects this problem. Figure 5.11 shows what happens if similar events happen with the reduced window size. Here, station A sends frames 0 through 6 at time t_1 and station B receives them all. At time t_2 station B acknowledges

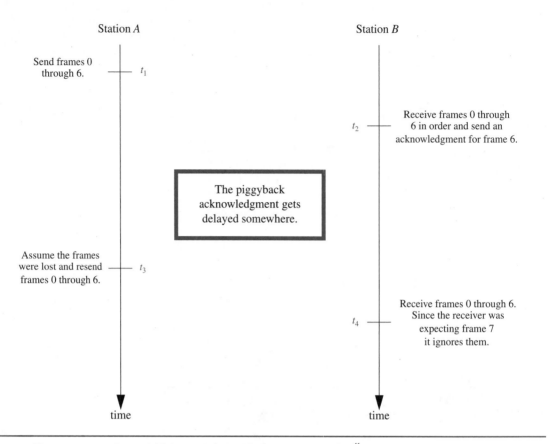

Station A   Station B

Send frames 0
through 6. — t_1

t_2 — Receive frames 0 through
6 in order and send an
acknowledgment for frame 6.

The piggyback
acknowledgment gets
delayed somewhere.

Assume the frames
were lost and resend — t_3
frames 0 through 6.

Receive frames 0 through 6.
Since the receiver was
t_4 — expecting frame 7
it ignores them.

time   time

Figure 5.11   Protocol Success When Window Size Equals $2^K - 1$

frame 6 and the acknowledgment gets lost. The difference now is that station B is expecting to receive frame 7. When station A resends frames 0 through 6 (at time t_3), they arrive at B at time t_4. Since they are not what B is expecting, B ignores them. Eventually B sends another acknowledgment, which A receives (we hope).[*] Station A advances its window to include frame 7 and the protocol continues. From this, we conclude that the window size must be strictly less than 2^K or the go-back-n protocol can fail.

We are finally ready to present a more detailed description of the go-back-n protocol. Figure 5.12 shows a partially coded C program containing the logic and variable names. Figure 5.7 should also help you understand the use of protocol variables w and i. As before, we make no attempt to be syntactically correct or worry about whether the code compiles correctly. The intent is to describe how the protocol

---

[*]We have not yet explained how we know B sends another acknowledgment. When we discuss specifics of the algorithm we will describe how the protocol guarantees the acknowledgment.

```
#define MAX=2^K;                        /* K = number of bits in the
                                           frame.number field */

#define N=MAX-1;                        /* N is the maximum window size and largest frame
                                           number */

#define increment(x) x=(x+1) % MAX;     /* Increment x modulo MAX */
void go_back_N;
{
  int w=0;                              /* First position in the window */
  int i=0;                              /* Current size of window */
  int last=N;                           /* Frame number of last data frame received */
  packettype buffer[MAX];               /* Packet buffers */
  while (the earth rotates on its axis)
  {
    wait for an event;
    if (event is "packet from patron") && (i<N)
    {                                   /* If frame fits in the window, send it */
      get packet from the patron and store in buffer[(w+i) % MAX] ;
      construct frame with frame.ack=last, frame.type=data, and frame.number=(w+i) % MAX;
      send frame;
      reset frametimer(frame.number);   /* Define timer for expected ACK of this frame*/
      stop acktimer;                    /* Stop ACK timer since an ACK is piggybacked */
      i++;                              /* Increase window size by 1 */
      continue;                         /* Skip to the end of the while loop */
    }
    if (event is "expired acktimer")
    {                                   /* No frames have been sent in a while. Send a
                                           special ACK frame */
      Construct and send a frame with frame.type=ack and frame.ack=last;
      continue;
    }
    if (event is "expired frametimer")
    {                                   /* Have not received an ACK in a while; resend all
                                           frames in the window */
      for (j=w; j is "between" w and (w+i-1) % MAX; increment(j) )
      {
        construct and send a data frame as before with packet from buffer[j];
        reset frametimer(j);            /* Start timer for expected ACK of this frame*
      }
        stop acktimer;                  /* Stop ACK timer; an ACK is piggybacked */
        continue;
    }
    if (event is "damaged frame arrives")
    {
```

Figure 5.12   Go-back-*n* Protocol *(continues on next page)*

```
          Construct a frame with frame.type=nak and frame.ack=last and send it;
          stop acktimer;                  /* Stop ACK timer; an ACK is being sent */
          continue;
      }
      if (event is "undamaged frame arrives")
      {                                   /* Remove all frames "between" w and frame.ack
                                             from window */
          receive(frame);
          for (j=w; j is "between" w and frame.ack; increment(j) )
          {
            i--;
            stop frametimer(j);           /* Stop frame timer; the ACK has been received */
          }
          w=(frame.ack+1) % MAX;
          if (frame.type==data) && (frame.number==((last+1) % MAX))
          {                               /* If data frame is received in sequence, pass it to
                                             the patron */
                                          /* Ignore any frame received out of sequence */
            increment(last);
            extract packet from the frame and give it to the patron;
            if acktimer not active then
              reset acktimer;             /* Start ACK timer for the frame being accepted */
            continue;
          }
          if (frame.type == nak)
          {                                 /* resend all buffered packets */
            for (j=w; j is "between" w and (w+i-1) % MAX; increment(j) )
            {
              construct and send a data frame as before with packet from buffer[j];
              reset frametimer(j);        /* Start timer for expected ACK of this frame*/
            }
            stop acktimer;                /* Stop ACK timer; an ACK is piggybacked */
            continue;
          }
          if (frame.type==data) && (frame.number!=(last+1) % MAX)
          {                               /* Send a NAK for the frame that was expected */
            construct and send a frame with the frame.type=nak and frame.ack=last;
            stop acktimer;                /* Stop ACK timer; an ACK is piggybacked */
          }
      }                                   /* end of "undamaged frame arrives" event */
    }                                     /* end of while loop */
  }                                       /* end of go_back_N */
```

Figure 5.12   *(continued)*

works without becoming mired in language-specific details. The important thing to remember is that both stations are running a copy of the algorithm as they exchange frames. That is, each station responds to events that correspond to it sending and receiving frames. Read the following discussion and algorithm carefully and slowly; the algorithm is complex.

The algorithm consists of a loop controlled by a condition that should remain for a very long time. If this condition becomes false, protocol failure is of little consequence by comparison. As the algorithm loops, it responds to events as they occur. If multiple events have occurred during one pass of a loop, the algorithm chooses one randomly and responds to it. We do not care how it chooses. That is system dependent. Presumably it will respond to the other events with subsequent passes of the loop.

With each pass through the loop, the station waits for an event to occur. The five events and the protocol's responses are as follows:

1. The patron has delivered a packet. If the window size (i) is its maximum value (N), nothing happens and the event remains pending until the window size decreases. If the window size is less than N, the protocol builds a data frame containing the packet. It also defines a piggyback acknowledgment of the last frame sent (frame.ack = last) and specifies the frame number (frame.number = (w + i) % MAX where MAX = 2^K). The expression (w + i) % MAX also defines which buffer the packet is stored in. After buffering the packet and sending the frame, it increments the window size by one (i++) and resets the corresponding frame timer. It also stops the ACK timer.

   The ACK timer, as explained previously, detects long periods of time during which no frames are sent. Since one is sent, the ACK timer is stopped. The frame timer is to detect a long period of time during which the specified frame is not acknowledged. By resetting a timer, we begin the countdown.[*]

2. An ACK timer has expired. When no data frames are sent, the other station does not receive any piggybacked acknowledgments. In order to keep the other station aware of what the current station is receiving, the protocol sends a special acknowledgment frame when the ACK timer expires. Its sole purpose is to acknowledge the most recently received frame (frame.ack = last).

3. A frame timer has expired. If the protocol has not received an acknowledgment in a while, something may have gone wrong. Perhaps the acknowledgments were lost or the frames in the current window were lost. Since the protocol does not know which, it assumes the worst and resends all the frames in the window

---

[*]How timers are implemented is not pertinent to our discussion. There could be an internal interrupting clock or the protocol could just build a list of records for each timer, timestamp each record, and check the list periodically. We leave the details to someone who is willing to implement the protocol as a programming exercise.

("between"[*] buffer slots w and $(w + i - 1)$ % MAX). It also resets each of the frame timers in order to provide enough time for the newly sent frames to get to their destinations and an acknowledgment to return before assuming another error occurred. Last, it stops the ACK timer since a piggybacked acknowledgment is also being sent.

4. A damaged frame arrives. A damaged frame is ignored. If the damaged frame was the expected one, the protocol eventually will ignore all subsequently numbered frames. The protocol therefore must notify the other station that a problem occurred so it can resend all of its buffered frames. The protocol does this by sending a frame of type NAK. The station also ACKs the last frame it did receive correctly and stops the ACK timer.

5. An undamaged frame arrives. This is the most complex part of the protocol. The first thing the protocol does is receive the frame. Then it checks the piggyback acknowledgment and removes all frames that have been acknowledged from the window. It does this by decreasing the window size by one for each frame "between" w and frame.ack. It also stops the frame timers for the acknowledged frames. It then redefines the beginning of the window (w) to locate the first frame not acknowledged: (frame.ack + 1) % MAX.

   If the frame contains data, the protocol determines whether it has the expected number, ((last + 1) % MAX). Remember, the variable last represents the most recently received frame. Thus, the number after it is the one expected. If the received frame is the expected one, the protocol extracts the packet and gives it to the patron. It also increments the value of last, thus remembering the new frame most recently received. Then it sets the ACK timer, defining the time during which it should send an acknowledgment.

   If the frame is a NAK frame, the protocol resends all frames in the window as it did with the expired frame timer event. If the frame is a data frame, but not the one expected, the protocol ignores it but sends a NAK frame.

SELECTIVE REPEAT PROTOCOL

The go-back-n protocol works well, especially over reliable channels. When frames are rarely lost, damaged, or delayed, the assumption that they arrive in the order they were sent is usually valid. In the few cases where there is a problem, little time is lost by resending all outstanding frames. As the reliability decreases, however, the overhead of resending all frames in a window when just one is damaged or arrives out of order becomes excessive. A logical question to ask is this: Why not allow the receiving station to receive frames out of order and sort them when they

---

[*]We define "between" w and $(w + i - 1)$ % MAX in a modulo MAX sense. If $w \leq (w + i - 1)$ % MAX, "between" has its conventional meaning. If $w \geq (w + i - 1)$ % MAX, "between" includes those numbers from w through MAX − 1 and 0 through $(w + i - 1)$ % MAX. For example, suppose MAX = 16. If $w = 3$ and $(w + i - 1)$ % 16 = 12, "between" means values from 3 through 12, inclusive. If $w = 12$ and $(w + i - 1)$ % 16 = 3, "between" means values 12, 13, 14, 15, 0, 1, 2, and 3.

all arrive? This question is answered by another sliding window protocol called **selective repeat.**

The selective repeat protocol is similar to go-back-*n* in the following ways:

- Frame formats are similar and frames are numbered using a *K*-bit field (Figure 5.9).
- The sender has a window defining the maximum number of outstanding frames.
- It uses piggybacked acknowledgments where possible and does not acknowledge every frame explicitly. If a frame is acknowledged, the sending station assumes that all prior ones have also been received.
- The protocol uses NAKs for damaged frames and frames received out of order.
- It uses timers to send special acknowledgment frames during periods of low traffic and to resend frames that have not been acknowledged for a while.

The similarities end here. Probably the most apparent difference is that the selective repeat protocol defines two windows, one each for the sending and receiving parts of the protocol (Figure 5.13). Thus, each station using a selective repeat protocol has both a sending and a receiving window. The sending window is the same as for the go-back-*n* protocol. It defines which frames may be outstanding.

The receiving window defines which frames can be received. As with the sending window, frames in the receiving window are numbered consecutively (modulo 2^K, where K = number of bits used for the frame number). Thus, the receiving station is not required to receive frames in order. A frame arriving out of order can be received as long as it is in the window. However, you will recall that

Figure 5.13   Sending and Receiving Windows for Selective Repeat Protocol

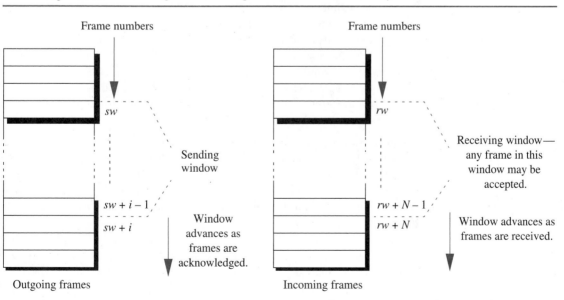

part of the protocol's responsibility is to deliver packets to its patron in the proper order. Thus the protocol needs a buffer for each frame in the window. Out-of-order frames are buffered until their predecessors arrive. Then the protocol can deliver them in the correct order.

Other differences between selective repeat and go-back-*n* are listed here, along with the former protocol's responses:

- If an arriving frame is in the receiving window, it is buffered. However, it is not given to the patron until all of its predecessors (within the window limits) have also arrived. Thus, whenever a frame is buffered, the protocol checks the window slots prior to the new arrival. If they all contain packets the protocol delivers them to the patron and advances the window.

- Whenever an out-of-order frame is received, the protocol sends a NAK for the frame it was expecting. The rationale is that an out-of-order frame signals that something may have happened to the one expected frame. The NAK notifies the sender of a possible loss. Remember, though, that as long as the received frame is in the window, it is still accepted.

- If a frame timer expires, only the timed-out frame is resent. With go-back-*n*, all outstanding frames are resent. With selective repeat, the receiving station may have received the other frames, and unless they also time out, there is no need to resend them.

- If the protocol receives a NAK, it resends just the frame specified by the NAK. Go-back-*n* resends all outstanding frames. The rationale for sending just one frame is the same as that for a frame timer expiration.

- A piggyback acknowledgment doesn't necessarily acknowledge the frame most recently received. Instead, it acknowledges the frame immediately prior to the one at the beginning of the receiver's window (i.e., the last one delivered to the patron). The rationale is that acknowledging the most recently received frame does not allow the sending station to conclude that prior frames have also been received. Remember, the most recent frame may have arrived out of order. Effectively that would force an acknowledgment for each frame. Acknowledging the last frame delivered to the patron allows the sending station to conclude that prior frames have also been delivered and thus received. Again, the result is fewer overall acknowledgments.

With the go-back-*n* algorithm we saw that there were constraints on the window size. Specifically, the window size had to be strictly less than 2^K or the protocol could fail with certain events. Constraints also exist with the selective repeat protocol. Suppose the maximum sending window size and receiving window size are equal. In that case, the constraint is that both must be less than or equal to one-half of 2^K (i.e., 2^{K-1}).

To see what can happen otherwise, let's consider a couple of examples. In both examples we will use $K = 3$, so that $2^K = 8$. In the first example, suppose the sending window meets the constraint and has a maximum size of 4. But consider what happens if the receiving window is larger, say 5 (Figure 5.14).

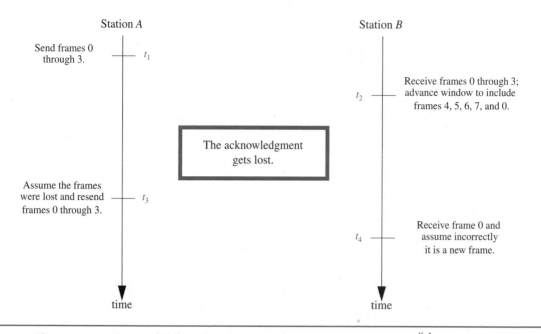

Figure 5.14   Protocol Failure: Receiving Window Size Is Greater Than 2^{K-1}

At time t_1 station A sends the maximum number of frames, frames 0 through 3. Since station B has a window size of 5, it can accept any frame numbered between 0 and 4, inclusive. At time t_2, B receives frames 0 through 3. Since they are in the window, they are accepted and passed to the patron. B then advances its window to include frames 4, 5, 6, 7, and 0.

Meanwhile, the acknowledgment that B sends is lost. Eventually A gets tired of waiting and assumes something went wrong. Consequently, as dictated by the protocol, A resends frames 0 through 3 (time t_3). Since frame 0 is in the receiving window, B accepts it (time t_4), not realizing it is a duplicate of the previous frame 0. The protocol fails.

Similar problems can occur if the receiving window size meets the constraint but the sending window does not. For example, suppose this time that A's window size is 5 and B's window size is 4 (Figure 5.15). At time t_1, A sends frames 0 through 4. Since B's window size is 4 it can accept only frames 0 through 3. But suppose frame 4 was delayed because it met an attractive frame going the other way and "did lunch" before arriving. Meanwhile frames 0 through 3 arrive and are accepted (time t_2). B advances its window to include frames 4 through 7.

When frame 4 eventually arrives, it is within the new window and is accepted. The window advances again and now includes frames 5, 7, and 0. At this point B sends something to A with the acknowledgments piggybacked. The same mysterious gremlin that ate the previous acknowledgments is insatiable and gets another one. Again, A gets tired of waiting and resends frames 0 through 4 (time t_3). The frames

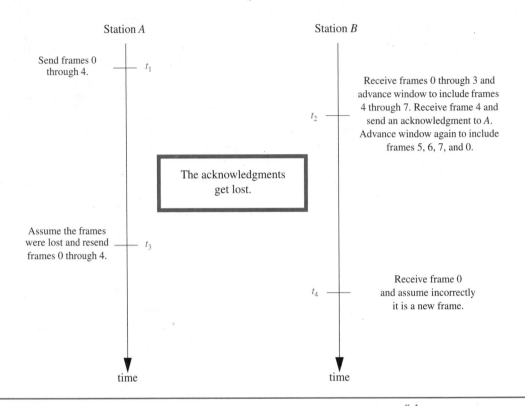

Station A   Station B

Send frames 0
through 4. t_1

                                         Receive frames 0 through 3 and
                                         advance window to include frames
                                         4 through 7. Receive frame 4 and
                                    t_2 send an acknowledgment to A.
                                         Advance window again to include
                                         frames 5, 6, 7, and 0.

The acknowledgments
get lost.

Assume the frames
were lost and resend t_3
frames 0 through 4.

                                         Receive frame 0
                                    t_4 and assume incorrectly
                                         it is a new frame.

time   time

Figure 5.15   Protocol Failure: Sending Window Size Is Greater Than 2^{K-1}

finally get through (the gremlin is resting from its lunch) and since frame 0 is within the receiving window, it is accepted (time t_4). Again, B does not recognize that it is a duplicate of the previous frame 0, and the protocol fails.

Each of these problems can be corrected by making both window sizes equal to 4. In fact, these problems could have been eliminated by using window sizes of 5 and 3 instead of 5 and 4 (or 3 and 5 instead of 4 and 5). The problem occurs when the receiving window advances to the point of including new frame numbers still in the sending window. This can happen when the two sizes sum to a value larger than 2^K (the number of distinct frame numbers). By reducing the window sizes so that this won't happen we eliminate that type of problem. Typically, the window sizes are the same (2^{K-1}).

Figure 5.16 contains a partially C-coded algorithm for the selective repeat protocol. It is designed similarly to the go-back-n protocol in that it loops continuously, responding to events as they occur. Both sending and receiving windows have size $N = 2^{K-1}$.

The algorithm has a few additional variables that the go-back-n algorithm does not have. In addition to the sending buffer (sbuffer) there is a receiving buffer (rbuffer). Since each window size is N, both buffers are defined as packet arrays with N elements. This generates another difference from the go-back-n algorithm. With

```
#define MAX=2^K;                      /* K = number of bits in the frame.number field */
#define N=MAX/2;                      /* N = maximum sending window size, actual receiving window
                                         size, and number of buffers */
#define increment(x) x=(x+1) % MAX;   /* Increment x modulo N */
#define prior(x) (x==0 ? MAX-1 : x-1) /* Return integer prior to x modulo N */
void selective_repeat;
{
  int frame_no=0;                     /* Maintain frame numbers of outgoing frames */
  int sw=0;                           /* First position in sender's window */
  int rw=0;                           /* First position in receiver's window */
  int i=0;                            /* Current size of sender's window */
  packettype sbuffer[N];              /* Sender's packet buffers */
  packettype rbuffer[N];              /* Receiver's packet buffers */
  int status[N];                      /* Status of frame in receiving window. 1 means it arrived;
                                         0 means it has not */

  while (Hades does not freeze over)
    {
    wait for an event;
    if (event is "packet from patron") && (i<N)
      {                               /* If frame fits in window, send it */
      Get packet from the patron and store it in sbuffer[(sw+i) % N];
      construct frame with frame.ack=prior(rw), frame.type=data, and frame.number=frame_no;
      send frame;
      increment(frame_no);            /* Define number of next outgoing frame */
      reset frametimer(frame.number); /* Start timer for expected ACK of this frame */
      stop acktimer;                  /* Stop ACK timer; an ACK is piggybacked */
      i++;                            /* Increase sending window size by 1 */
      continue;                       /* Skip to the end of the while loop */
      }
    if (event is "expired acktimer")
      {                               /* No frames have been sent in a while. Send a special
                                         ACK frame */
      Construct and send a frame with frame.type=ack and frame.ack=prior(rw);
      continue;
      }
    if (event is "expired frametimer")
      {                               /* Have not received an ACK in a while; resend frame */
      fn = frame number corresponding to the timer;
      construct and send as before a data frame with packet from sbuffer[fn % N];
      reset frametimer(fn);           /* Start timer for expected ACK of this frame */
      stop acktimer;                  /* Stop ACK timer; an ACK is being sent */
      continue;
      }
    if (event is "damaged frame arrives")
```

Figure 5.16   Selective Repeat Protocol *(continues on next page)*

```
  {
    Construct a frame with frame.type=nak and with frame.ack=prior(rw); send it;
    stop acktimer;                    /* Stop ACK timer; an ACK is being sent */
    continue;
  }
  if (event is "undamaged frame arrives")
  {                                   /* Remove all frames "between" sw and frame.ack from
                                         sender's window */
    receive(frame);
    for (j=sw; j is "between" sw and frame.ack; increment(j) )
    {
      i--;
      stop frametimer(j);             /* Stop frame timer; the ACK has been received */
    }
    sw=(frame.ack+1) % MAX;
    if (frame.type==data) && (frame.number != rw)
  {
    construct a frame with frame.type=nak and frame.ack=prior(rw) and send it;
    stop acktimer;                    /* Stop ACK timer; an ACK is being sent */
  }
  if (frame.type==data) && (frame.number is in the receiving window) && (status[frame.number % N]==0)
  {                                   /* If data frame is in the window and has not yet arrived,
                                         buffer it */
    extract packet from the frame and put in rbuffer[frame.number % N];
    status[frame.number % N]=1;
    for(;status[rw % N]==1; increment(rw) )
    {                                 /* Give received packets stored in consecutive window
                                         slots to the patron */
      extract packet from rbuffer[rw % N] and give to patron;
      status[rw % N]=0;
    }
    reset acktimer;                   /* Start ACK timer for frames being accepted */
  }
  if (frame.type == nak) && ( framenum = (frame.ack+1) % MAX is in the sending window)
  {                                   /* Resend the frame the receiving station expected to
                                         receive */
    construct and send a frame with packet from sbuffer[framenum % N];
    reset frametimer(framenum % N);   /* Start timer for expected ACK of this frame */
    stop acktimer;                    /* Stop ACK timer; an ACK is being piggybacked */
    continue;
  }
    }
  }
  }
}
```

Figure 5.16   *(continued)*

go-back-*n* the packets are stored in buffer slots subscripted by the frame number. Here there are twice as many frame numbers as buffer slots. To avoid using an excessive number of buffers, the buffer subscript is equal to the frame number modulo *N*.

Another variable not present in the previous algorithm is the status array. Since arriving frames can be buffered in random order, we use the status array to determine whether a buffer slot is empty. A value of status[i] = 1 means buffer number *i* contains a packet. A value of 0 means it does not.

As the algorithm loops continuously, it responds to events. We list the events and the protocol's response here. Because of the similarities to the go-back-*n* protocol, we will not discuss each step in detail. We will concentrate only on those parts that differ from go-back-*n*.

1. The patron has delivered a packet. The protocol responds much as the go-back-*n* protocol does. If the sending window size is its maximum value, nothing happens. Otherwise it buffers the packet, builds a frame, and sends it. It also piggybacks an acknowledgment for the frame prior to the one in the beginning of the receiving window (frame.ack=prior(rw)). The macro named prior subtracts 1 modulo 2^K. Unlike the increment macro, it does not change the variable passed to it.

2. An ACK timer has expired. The protocol sends an ACK frame acknowledging the frame prior to the one in the beginning of the receiving window.

3. A frame timer has expired. Instead of resending every outstanding frame, the protocol sends only the frame corresponding to the expired timer. How the frame is determined depends on how the timers are implemented. As before, there could be an interrupt mechanism identifying the frame number or some list containing time values and frame numbers.

4. A damaged frame arrives. The protocol sends a NAK frame containing an acknowledgment for the frame prior to the one in the beginning of the receiving window.

5. An undamaged frame arrives. After receiving the frame the protocol removes all frames that have been acknowledged from the window. If the frame contains data, the protocol checks to see if it arrived in order. In other words, is the frame number equal to the number corresponding to the beginning of the receiving window? If not, a NAK frame is sent back.

   Next, the protocol checks two more conditions: Is the received frame in the window, and has its packet not yet been buffered? The packet may have been buffered already if the frame arrived previously but an ACK was late in getting back to the sending station. In that case the frame would have timed out and the protocol would have sent it again. By checking the value of status[frame.number % N] we avoid the extra work of extracting a packet that is already buffered.

   If both conditions are met, the packet is extracted and stored in the buffer. Next, the protocol determines whether it can advance the receiving window and deliver packets to the patron. It does this by checking consecutive positions in the status array. It stops when it finds the first empty window slot.

Finally, if the frame is a NAK frame, the protocol examines the value in frame.ack. When a NAK is sent, the frame.ack field contains the number of the frame prior to the one in the beginning of the receiving window. This means something happened and the receiving protocol did not get the frame it expected ((frame.ack+1) % MAX). If this frame is still in the sending window, the protocol must send it. (Can you construct a scenario in which this frame is not in the sending window?)

SLIDING WINDOW PROTOCOL EFFICIENCY

Section 5.2 analyzed the unrestricted and stop and wait protocols and showed that the protocol can affect the amount of actual data transmitted per unit of time (effective data rate). We saw that the effective data rate also depended on raw bit rate, distance between stations, frame size, and other factors. A full-fledged analysis for sliding window protocols is much more difficult because other factors contribute to the effective data rate. Such factors include the rate at which frames are lost or damaged, the timer values used to determine when special ACK frames are sent, and the number of data frames in the reverse direction carrying piggybacked acknowledgments.

We will provide an analysis for sliding window protocols under certain assumptions. Specifically, we will assume that lost or damaged frames do not happen. We also assume consistent traffic in both directions to make the most use of piggybacked acknowledgments. The latter assumption allows us to ignore ACK timers because they won't be used. If you are interested in a more complete analysis of sliding window protocols, see References [Ta96] and [Wa91].

All things being equal, a sliding window's effective data rate should lie between that of the unrestricted and stop and wait protocols. But what effective rate can we expect from the sliding window protocols? How does the window size affect it?

Recall from Section 5.2 the following definitions and values used in the examples:

R = transmission rate (10 Mbps or 10 bits per μsec)

S = signal speed (200 meters per μsec)

D = distance between the sender and receiver (200 meters)

T = time to create one frame (1 μsec)

F = number of bits in a frame (200)

N = number of data bits in a frame (160)

A = number of bits in an acknowledgment (40)

Let's add one definition to that list:

W = window size (4 frames)

To begin, we observe that two cases can occur with a sliding window protocol. The first is that the sender's window never reaches its maximum size. This will happen when the first acknowledgment arrives before all the frames in the window are sent. Once this happens, and assuming there are no delays at the other end, the sender never has to wait for an acknowledgment. In other words, old frames are removed from the window as fast as new ones are added to it. In effect, the sending protocol behaves just like the unrestricted protocol.

In the second case, when all W frames have been sent and the first acknowledgment has not yet arrived (Figure 5.17), the protocol must wait for it. When it does arrive the protocol then can send the next frame. If the acknowledgments arrive at the same rate that data frames are sent, W more frames are sent before the protocol must wait again. In other words, the protocol sends W frames, waits for the first acknowledgment, sends W more frames, waits for an acknowledgment, and so on. This protocol now resembles stop and wait. However, instead of sending and waiting for individual frames, it sends and waits for a window full of frames.

Mathematically, these two cases can be distinguished by comparing the time to send W frames with the time to send one frame and receive an acknowledgment. From Equation 5.1, the time to build and send one frame is $T + F/R$. Thus, the time to build and send W frames is $W \times (T + F/R)$. From Equation 5.2, the time to send a

Figure 5.17   Sending All Windowed Frames and Waiting

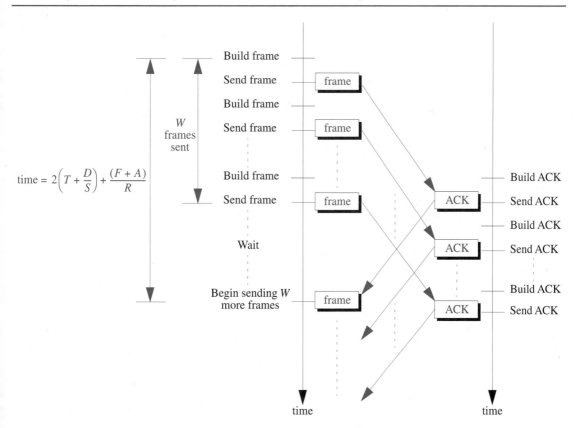

frame and receive an acknowledgment (assuming the acknowledgment comes back right away) is $2(T + D/S) + (F + A)/R = 2(T + D/S) + 2F/R = 2(T + D/S + F/R)$. In this equation we substituted F for A because acknowledgments arrive piggybacked on data frames (of size F) instead of via separate ACK frames (of size A).

Consequently, we have

$$\text{Case 1 (unrestricted protocol): } W\left(T + \frac{F}{R}\right) > 2\left(T + \frac{D}{S} + \frac{F}{R}\right)$$

$$\text{Case 2 (window-oriented stop and wait): } W\left(T + \frac{F}{R}\right) < 2\left(T + \frac{D}{S} + \frac{F}{R}\right)$$

In the first case we have, from Equation 5.5,

$$\text{effective data rate } = \frac{N}{T + \dfrac{F}{R}} \text{ (unrestricted version)}$$

Because our sample values satisfy the condition of Case 1, the effective data rate evaluates to

$$\frac{160 \text{ bits}}{1 \text{ }\mu\sec + \dfrac{200 \text{ bits}}{10 \text{ bits/}\mu\sec}} \approx 7.6 \text{ bits/}\mu\sec = 7.6 \text{ Mbps}$$

The effective data rate for Case 2 is derived from Equation 5.6. This equation was derived under the assumption that just one frame was sent. As we now send W frames in the same amount of time, we replace N with $W \times N$. Remembering to replace A with F, we have

$$\text{effective data rate } = \frac{W \times N}{2\left(T + \dfrac{D}{S}\right) + \dfrac{2F}{R}} \text{ (window-oriented stop and wait version)}$$

Since our sample values do not satisfy the condition of Case 2, using them in this equation would yield a nonsensical value. If we increase the distance (D) from 200 meters to 5,000 meters, however, the values will satisfy the condition of Case 2. Using these values, we have

$$\text{effective data rate } = \frac{4 \times 160 \text{ bits}}{2\left(1 \text{ }\mu\sec + \dfrac{5000 \text{ meters}}{200 \text{ meters/}\mu\sec}\right) + \dfrac{2 \times 200 \text{ bits}}{10 \text{ bits/}\mu\sec}}$$

SUMMARY OF PROTOCOLS

We have discussed four flow control protocols: stop and wait, unrestricted, go-back-n, and selective repeat. In some ways (excluding timers, ACKs, and NAKs) they can all be viewed as variations of a sliding window protocol (Table 5.1). For example,

Table 5.1   Comparison of Flow Control Protocols

	STOP AND WAIT PROTOCOL	UNRESTRICTED PROTOCOL	GO-BACK-N PROTOCOL	SELECTIVE REPEAT PROTOCOL
Sending window size	One frame	Unlimited number of frames	Less than 2^K	Less than or equal to 2^K minus receiving window size
Receiving window size	One frame	Unlimited number of frames	One frame	Less than or equal to 2^K minus sending window size

go-back-n is essentially selective repeat in which the receiving window has just one frame. In stop and wait, both windows have just one frame. The unrestricted protocol has unlimited frame sizes.

5.4   PROTOCOL CORRECTNESS

In the previous sections we have presented some protocols and the conditions under which they seem to work correctly. Note that we say "seem to work." This uncertainty is necessary because we have not proved that they do work. Providing formal proof or verification that a protocol works is very difficult, and we leave such formal methods to courses in software engineering or advanced courses in protocol design. In this section we introduce two basic tools of verification.

FINITE STATE MACHINES

Much of what we perceive to be continuous or analog is, in fact, a collection of separate or discrete events. Perhaps the most common example is a motion picture. As we munch popcorn, sip sodas, or stretch our arms and yawn we view the action on the screen as a flowing or continuous movement. In reality, it is a rapid display of still pictures shown through a projector. This view allows us to see a movie in a new way as a collection of individual pictures. It is not the most desirable way to watch some of the classics, but it is precisely the way movie personnel such as special effects technicians must see a movie. They see a sequence of pictures to be spliced, cut, and altered to create the proper effect.

Computer algorithms also can be viewed as a sequence of "pictures." The computers that run them are digital devices. Their actions are controlled and synchronized by internal clocks and driven by the programs they run. Each clock pulse defines a new set of internal values and, for a brief period (length of a clock pulse), nothing changes. In a sense, the entire architecture is frozen in time and the collection of internal values defines a picture of the **machine state.** With the next clock pulse they change, defining a new machine state. This process continues repeatedly, defining a sequence of machine states.

Similarly, we can view an algorithm as a sequence of states. Each state is defined in part by the values of program variables at an instant in time. In theory, we can categorize (list) all possible states and the events that cause a change from one state to another. The term **finite state machine** (sometimes **finite state model**) corresponds to this categorization. An event that causes a change of state is called a **state transition.**

Viewing an algorithm in this discrete way allows us to represent it through a directed graph called a **state transition diagram (STD).** Recall that a directed graph consists of a set of vertices and edges. Each vertex represents a state and usually is represented visually by a dot or circle. Each edge is an ordered pair of vertices and usually is represented visually by an arrow from the first vertex to the second. Through graph theory we can analyze the state transition diagram and draw conclusions with regard to the reachability of certain states or possible sequences of events (transitions).

Figure 5.18 shows a state transition diagram. It has six different states, and the arrows show the possible transitions. For example, if the system is currently in state S_1, three different events could occur, one causing the system to move to state S_2, the others causing it to move to state S_4 or S_5.

By analyzing the graph we can draw conclusions about the system it represents. For example, note that there are no edges pointing to S_1. This means there are no transitions to state S_1. If this graph represented an algorithm designed to respond to events, this observation could mean a flaw in the algorithm's logic. That is, the algorithm does not respond to any event that puts the system into state S_1. If this is in contrast to what we know about the system, we have detected a flaw.

This graph shows another potential problem. Suppose an event occurs that causes a transition to state S_5. It can respond only to events that cause it to move to state S_6. Once there, it can only go back to state S_5. In other words, once this model progresses to state S_5 or S_6, it will remain in one of those two states forever. This might correspond to an infinite loop or a **deadlock** (waiting for an event that will never happen). As before, this most likely represents a flaw in our algorithm.

STD for a Simplified Go-back-*n* Protocol   How can we apply this diagram to an actual protocol? First consider the go-back-*n* protocol with a sender window size of

Figure 5.18   General State Transition Diagram

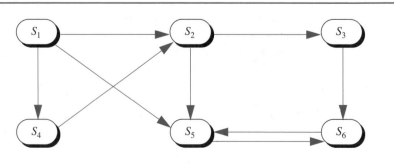

1 and a one-bit frame number field. Assume that no timeouts or transmission errors occur, all data goes in one direction only (sender to receiver), and the receiver acknowledges each frame received. Essentially, it is the stop and wait protocol with frame numbers. The following events occur:

- Send frame 0.
- Receive frame 0; send ACK 0.
- Receive ACK 0; send frame 1.
- Receive frame 1; send ACK 1.
- Receive ACK 1; send frame 0.

We can associate four distinct states with this protocol. They are labeled by ordered pairs (x, y) in Figure 5.19. The value of x is either 0 or 1 depending on the ACK number for which the sender is waiting. Similarly, y is either 0 or 1 depending on the frame number for which the receiver is waiting. Thus, state (0,0) means the sender has sent frame 0 and is expecting its acknowledgment. It also means the receiver is waiting for frame 0.

The arrival of frame 0 is an event that causes a transition from state (0,0) to (0,1). The receiver has received frame 0, sent its acknowledgment, and is now waiting for frame 1. However, the sender is still waiting for an acknowledgment to frame 0. When that acknowledgment arrives the sender accepts it, sends frame 1 next, and begins waiting for its acknowledgment. This is state (1,1) because the receiver is still waiting for frame 1. The sending and receiving of frames and acknowledgments continues and the states in Figure 5.19 occur in clockwise order.

An observant reader might ask: Aren't there really more states associated with this protocol? For example, there is a period of time after the sender receives the acknowledgment but before it sends its next frame. Shouldn't there be a state for which the sender is waiting for the patron to provide a packet? Yes! In fact, we could go to the extreme and define a state corresponding to the execution of each step in the algorithm. But does it pay to do so?

Defining states is an important design issue. Ideally, we would like to define states that represent significant steps in a system's evolution and not worry about insignificant or trivial differences. But determining what is significant is often difficult

Figure 5.19   STD for a Stop and Wait Protocol with Frame Numbers

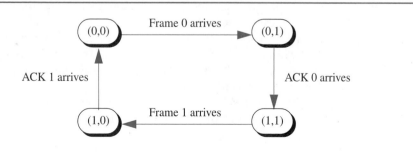

and depends a great deal on what is being modeled. There are often many levels of refinements to which we can subject an STD. We will give an example showing how to do a refinement and how an STD can locate flaws in a system. Our purpose here, however, is only to introduce the concepts, and we will not provide elaborate STDs. If you are interested in more detail or a higher level of discussion, References [Ta96], [Wa91], [Li87], and [Ru89] can provide it.

STD for a Faulty Go-back-*n* Protocol

Consider the previous version of the go-back-*n* protocol. This time we assume a window size of 2, which, according to Section 5.3, can fail. To help, Figure 5.20 shows the algorithm with the restrictions (e.g., the sender receives only ACKs or NAKs, the receiver receives only data, and frame numbers alternate between 0 and 1).

Figure 5.21 represents a first approximation to an STD showing some states and state transitions. In this case, we categorize each state by what the sender or receiver is waiting for. Specifically, we represent each state by an ordered triple (a, b, c) defined as follows:

- If the sender is waiting for an ACK to frame 0 then $a = Y$. Otherwise, $a = N$.
- If the sender is waiting for an ACK to frame 1 then $b = Y$. Otherwise, $b = N$.
- If the receiver is waiting for frame 0 then $c = 0$. Otherwise $c = 1$.

For example, suppose the model is in state $(N, N, 0)$. The sender is expecting no ACKs and the receiver is waiting for frame 0. If the sender sends frame 0 the model moves to state $(Y, N, 0)$. The sender now expects an ACK for frame 0. While in this state, two other events can happen. The first is that the sender sends frame 1, in which case the model moves to state $(Y, Y, 0)$. The other event is that frame 0 arrives and is accepted and the receiver sends an ACK. In this case the receiver now waits for the next frame and the state is $(Y, N, 1)$.

You should take the time to follow some arrows and understand why the states change as shown. As you do so, you might find some anomalous events. For example, consider the following two ways to move from state $(N, N, 0)$ to state $(Y, Y, 0)$:

1. Send frames F0 and F1.
2. Send F0; F0 accepted and A0 sent; send F1; F1 accepted and A1 sent.

In the first case just one event can happen next: F0 arrives and is accepted. The other events shown (A0 and A1 accepted) cannot happen because neither acknowledgment has been sent yet. Similar reasoning shows that in the second case the only event that can occur next is that A0 or A1 is accepted. F0 cannot arrive because it has already done so. (We will assume that frames do not clone themselves as they travel, resulting in an invasion of an army of frames.) The point is that Figure 5.21 does not distinguish between cases 1 and 2 and shows events that may be impossible depending on how a state was reached.

The problem is that we have not refined our state definitions to accurately portray the system. One solution is to refine the state definitions to include the frames actually

```
void send_data;
{
#define increment(x) x=(x==0 ? 1 : 0);
int w=0;
int i=0;
packettype buffer[2];
while there are packets to send
{
  wait for an event;
  if (event is "packet from patron") && (i<2)
  {
    get packet from the patron and store in
      buffer[(w+i) % 2];
    construct and send frame with
      frame.number=(w+i) % 2;
    reset frametimer(frame.number);
    i++;
    continue;
  }
  if (event is "expired frametimer")
  {
    resend one or both frames in window;
    reset one or both frametimers;
    continue;
  }
  if (event is "undamaged frame arrives")
  {
    receive(frame);
    remove any acknowledged frames from window;
    decrement i by number of frames removed;
    stop frametimers for acknowledged frames;
    w=(frame.ack+1) % 2;
    if (frame.type == nak)
    {
      resend frames in the window;
      reset frametimers;
    }
  }
}
}
```

Sender code

```
void receive_data;
{
#define increment(x) x=(x==0 ? 1 : 0);
int last=-1;
while there are packets to receive
{
  wait for an event;
  if (event is "damaged frame arrives")
  {
    Construct a frame with frame.type=nak and
      frame.ack=last and send it;
    stop acktimer;
    continue;
  }
  if (event is "undamaged frame arrives")
  {
    receive(frame);
    if (frame.number != last)
    {
      increment(last);
      extract packet from the frame and give it to
        the patron;
      if acktimer not active then reset acktimer;
      continue;
    }
    if (frame.number == last)
    {
      construct and send a frame with the
        frame.type=nak and frame.ack=last;
      stop acktimer;
    }
  }
  if (event is "expired acktimer")
  {
    Construct and send a frame with frame.type=ack
      and frame.ack=last;
    continue;
  }
}
}
```

Receiver code

Figure 5.20   Go-back-*n* Protocol for One-Way Data Transfer (Window Size = 2)

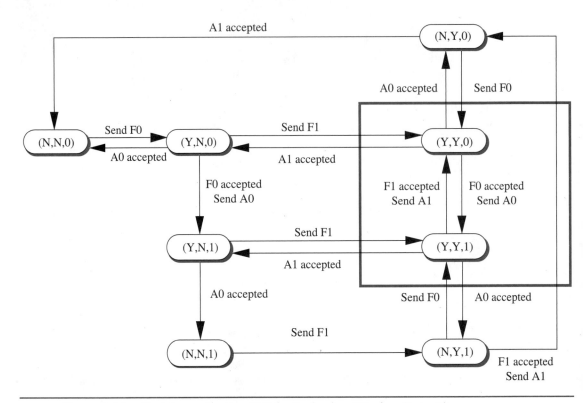

Figure 5.21   First Approximation STD for Go-back-*n* (Window Size = 2)

in transit, which will allow us to distinguish between the two cases (and others). It will also create additional states and state transitions and make the diagram more complex.

Figure 5.22 shows a partial refinement of the STD's boxed-in region from Figure 5.21. This refinement also shows how the STD can locate flaws in our design. We have further defined each state by specifying not only what the stations are waiting for but what is actually in transit. We represent this by adding an ordered pair (x, y) to each state. Variable x defines which frames are actually in transit (0 for frame 0, 1 for frame 1, B for both, and N for neither). Similarly, y specifies which acknowledgment is in transit. For example, state $(Y, Y, 0) : (B, N)$ means the sender is waiting for an acknowledgment to frames 0 and 1 and that these frames are still in transit. The receiver is waiting for frame 0 and there are no acknowledgments in transit. We have also included additional events that cause state changes. (There are other events we have not shown, but these are sufficient for our needs.)

We next show how this refined model can expose a problem. Recall from your data structures course that a path through a graph is a list of nodes where every two adjacent nodes in the list are connected by an edge. In an STD, a path defines a sequence of events. The graph of Figure 5.22 shows a path (actually a cycle) in which both $(Y, Y, 0)$ and $(Y, Y, 1)$ appear. Consider what happens if we follow the

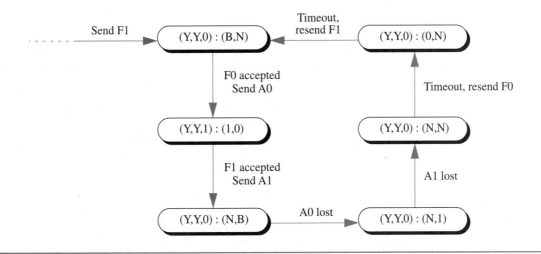

Figure 5.22   Partial Refinement of STD from Figure 5.21

cycle repeatedly. This defines a sequence of events that causes the receiver to alternately expect and receive frames 0 and 1. However, none of the events corresponds to sending new frames (just resending old ones). This means the receiver repeatedly accepts new frames even though no new ones are being sent. That is, the receiver is accepting old frames as if they were new, just as we discussed in Section 5.3.

In general, STDs can be used to trace sequences of events and intermediate states. If a path exhibits state changes that should not occur given the events, there is a flaw in the model.

PETRI NETS

Like a finite state model, a **Petri net** uses a graph to represent states and transitions, but the way it does so is different. A Petri net consists of four parts:

1. **Places.** Represented visually by circles, places correspond to part of a state. This is one difference from the finite state model. Each vertex of an STD represents a complete state; with a Petri net we may need several places to represent the complete state. We'll see an example shortly.

2. **Transitions.** Represented visually by a short horizontal or vertical line, transitions show movement between places.

3. **Arrows.** Arrows connect a place to a transition or vice versa. A place at the source of the arrow is called the **input place** of the transition to which the arrow points. Any place pointed to by the arrow is the **output place** of the transition at the arrow's source.

4. **Tokens.** Tokens, represented by heavy dots inside places, collectively define the current state of the system.

A Petri net can be represented by a graph. A graph vertex may be either a place or a transition, and an edge is an arrow. With STDs, state transitions are defined by moving from one vertex to another along an edge. With Petri nets, they are defined by the way tokens move from one place to another. Thus, the next step is to define the rules by which tokens can move:

- A transition is **enabled** if each of its input places contains a token.
- Any enabled transition can **fire.** That is, tokens are removed from each of the input places and tokens are stored in each of the output places. After firing, there may be more or fewer tokens, depending on the number of input places and output places.
- One transition fires at a time. If several transitions are enabled, however, the choice of transition is indeterminate. For our purposes, this means the choice is made arbitrarily. Because firing transitions will correspond to real events, we do not want rules to dictate the order in which they occur.

Part (a) of Figure 5.23 shows a Petri net just before firing. There are two transitions, T1 and T2, but only T1 is enabled (all of its input places have tokens). Part (b) shows the Petri net after firing. The tokens are removed from each input place of T1. Next a token is put into each of the output places of T1. Other tokens in places associated with a different transition remain where they are.

Next, let's see how we can use a Petri net to model a protocol. The one we will use is the go-back-n protocol of Figure 5.20, changed to use a window of size 1.

Figure 5.23   Petri Net Before and After Firing

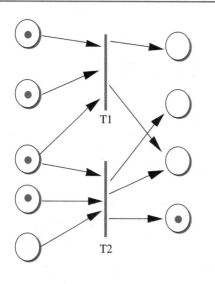

(a) Before firing

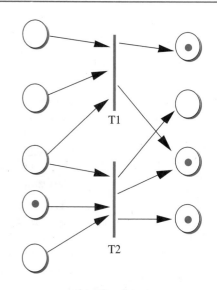

(b) After firing

Figure 5.24 shows part of the Petri net for it. As before, we have left out some parts of the Petri net to simplify the diagram and our discussion.

Instead of trying to describe the state of the system in one vertex, we divide the system into its parts and represent the state of each. In this case, the system consists of a sender, receiver, and channel between them. Thus, the system state depends on what the sender and receiver are waiting for and what is on the channel, just as with our previously refined STD. Specifically, the sender has two states, each represented by a place. The sender is waiting for an acknowledgment for frame 0 (Wait for A0) or for frame 1 (Wait for A1). The receiver also has two states: waiting for frame 0 (F0) or frame 1 (F1). The four places in the middle correspond to what is on the channel. F0 and F1 are places corresponding to frame 0 or 1 being transmitted. A0 and A1 correspond to the acknowledgments for frame 0 or 1 being transmitted.

The tokens in Figure 5.24 show the current state of the system. The sender has sent frame 0, which is currently on the channel. The receiver is waiting for it and the sender is waiting for an acknowledgment of it.

Next let's consider the transitions. Transitions correspond to events that can occur, and their input places correspond to states that must exist before the event can occur. For example, look at the first transition for the sender labeled "Receive A1,

Figure 5.24   Partial Petri Net for Go-back-*n* with Sender Window Size = 1

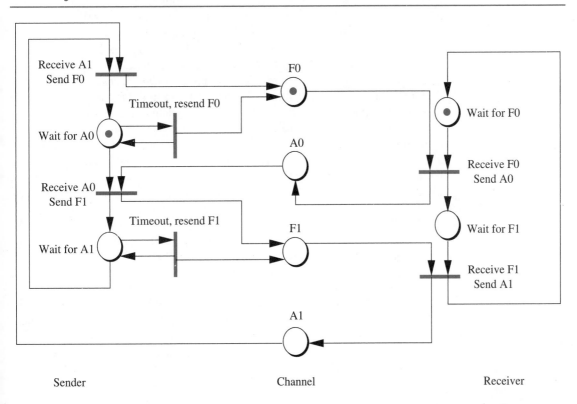

Send F0." It has two input places, "Wait for A1" for the sender and "A1" for the channel. A firing of this transition means the sender has received an ACK for frame 1 and has sent the next frame, F0. However, for this to occur the sender must be waiting for A1, and A1 must be on the way. Thus, for the transition to fire, tokens must be in these two input places. We can make similar arguments about the other transitions for the sender and the receiver.

This Petri net also has two timeout transitions. Each has one input place corresponding to the sender waiting for an ACK. For example, suppose the sender is waiting for A0 (token in that place). The corresponding timeout transition is enabled. This does not mean it will fire, however. It means it *could* fire. If a frame timer expires, the timeout transition fires. If that happens, the token is removed from the input place and others are placed in the two output places. One of them is the F0 place for the channel, indicating that frame 0 is being sent. The other output place is the same as the input place, meaning the sender is again waiting for A0.

Confused? Let's trace token movement for a sequence of typical events. Parts (a) through (d) of Figure 5.25 show Petri nets corresponding to successive transition firings. Places, transition, and arrows are as in Figure 5.24, but we have eliminated the labels to simplify the diagram. The token placement in Figure 5.25a is the same as in Figure 5.24. The sender is waiting for A0, the receiver is waiting for F0, and F0 is on the channel. Together they define the system state. At this point two transitions are enabled (marked with *): the first timeout transition for the sender and the transition for the receiver labeled (from Figure 5.24) "Receive F0, Send A0."

Suppose the latter transition fires. The tokens are removed from the two input places and new ones put into places as shown in Figure 5.25b. The system is in a new state. The sender is still waiting for A0, which is now on the channel. The receiver is now waiting for F1. Again, two transitions in Figure 5.25b are enabled. They are the timeout and the reception of A0. Again, the latter transition fires, and the tokens are moved to their positions in Figure 5.25c. Again the system is in a new state. The sender has sent F1, which is on the channel, and is waiting for A1. Meanwhile the receiver is still waiting for F1. If the receiver gets the frame, the tokens move to their positions in Figure 5.25d. The sender is still waiting for A0, which is on its way, and the receiver is waiting for F0. If the acknowledgment arrives, the Petri net changes again and token placement is as in Figure 5.25a. Thus, if frames and acknowledgments are communicated without error these four Petri nets describe the changing system states.

Earlier we stated that the Petri net of Figure 5.24 does not include transitions for every possible event. For example, there is always a token in one of the channel's places, implying there is always something on the channel. This, of course, is not true. A token on the channel could get lost or destroyed, resulting in a state in which the sender and receiver both are waiting but nothing is on the channel (something our Petri net doesn't show). This state is fixed easily by making each of the channel's places an input place for a new transition labeled "lost." None of these transitions would have an output place. Thus, whenever something is on the channel one of these transitions is enabled. If it fires, the token is removed from the input place. With no output place, that token disappears. Eventually a timeout transition would fire and place a token into one of the places again.

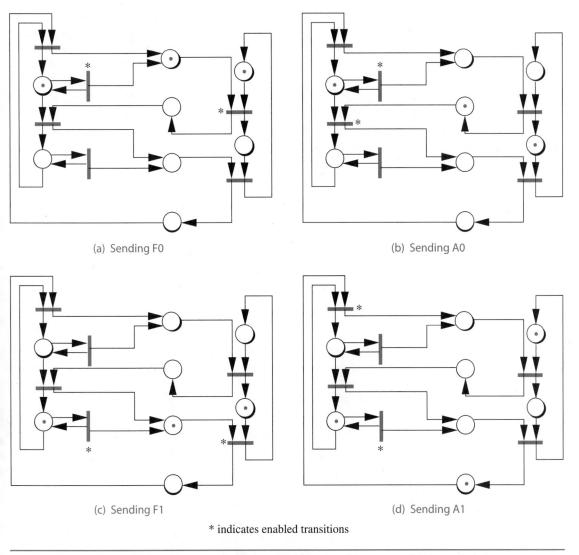

(a) Sending F0

(b) Sending A0

(c) Sending F1

(d) Sending A1

* indicates enabled transitions

Figure 5.25 Firing Sequence for Normal Exchange of Frames and Acknowledgments

Another way we could refine the Petri net is to divide the sender's transitions into two separate ones. In our model, when the sender gets an ACK it immediately sends out the next frame. We assume there are always frames to send but that may not be the case. We could define new sender places corresponding to situations in which the sender has to wait for a packet from its patron. We encourage you to consider some of the cases and redraw the Petri nets (see questions at the end of the chapter).

As with STDs, Petri nets can be analyzed to look for protocol errors. For example, if tokens could never reach certain places, certain states could not be represented by the Petri net. If they are known to be possible, our model would be in error. Another error would be indicated if tokens moved through certain places without landing in places in between. For example, suppose a sequence of firings resulted in Petri nets in which a token moves alternately between the receiver's places in Figure 5.24. If, in these same Petri nets, one of the sender's places never gets a token, an error exists because the Petri nets indicate the receiver is getting frames but the sender is not sending them.

If you are interested in further study or other examples of Petri nets, see References [Ta96], [Wa91], and [Pe81].

5.5   DATA LINK CONTROL PROTOCOLS

We have discussed general concepts of flow control and the maintenance of data frame exchange. Now it is time to present some specific protocols. Those we present here are called **data link control protocols** because they are found in or are similar to protocols in the OSI data link layer. Their primary responsibility is to manage and control the flow of frames between two stations.

HIGH-LEVEL DATA LINK CONTROL (HDLC)

HDLC is a bit-oriented protocol that supports both half-duplex and full-duplex communications. (We discussed half duplex and full duplex in Section 3.1.) By *bit oriented* we mean that the protocol treats frames as bit streams. In other words, it does not recognize or interpret byte values as some protocols discussed previously (such as X-ON/X-OFF) do. Defined by ISO, HDLC is used worldwide.

Three types of stations run the HDLC protocol:

- **Primary station** (sometimes called the **host station** or **control station**). It manages data flow by issuing commands to other stations and acting on their responses. We will see some examples later in this section. It also may establish and manage connections with multiple stations.

- **Secondary station** (sometimes called the **target station** or **guest station**). It responds to commands issued by a primary station. Furthermore, it can respond to just one primary station at a time. It does not issue commands to other stations (although it can send data).

- **Combined station.** As the name implies, it can act as both primary and secondary station. It can issue commands to and respond to commands from another combined station.

Stations running HDLC can communicate in one of three modes:

- **Normal response mode (NRM).** In NRM, the primary station controls the communication. That is, the secondary station can send only when the primary station instructs or allows it to do so. This operational mode is common in two configurations. In a **point-to-point link** (Figure 5.26a), the primary station communicates with a single secondary station. In a **multipoint link** (sometimes called a **multidrop link**), the primary station can communicate with several secondary stations (see Figure 5.26b). Of course, it must manage and keep separate the different sessions it maintains with each of them.

- **Asynchronous response mode (ARM).** Like NRM, ARM involves communication between a primary station and one or more secondary stations. Here, however, the secondary station is more independent. Specifically, it can send data or control information to the primary station without explicit instructions or permission to do so. However, it cannot send commands. The responsibility for establishing, maintaining, and eventually ending the connection still resides with the primary station. This mode is most common in the point-to-point links of Figure 5.26a.

- **Asynchronous balanced mode (ABM).** ABM is used in configurations connecting combined stations (Figure 5.26c). Either station can send data, control information, or commands. This is typical in connections between two computers and in the X.25 interface standard (discussed in Chapter 7).

Figure 5.26   HDLC Configurations

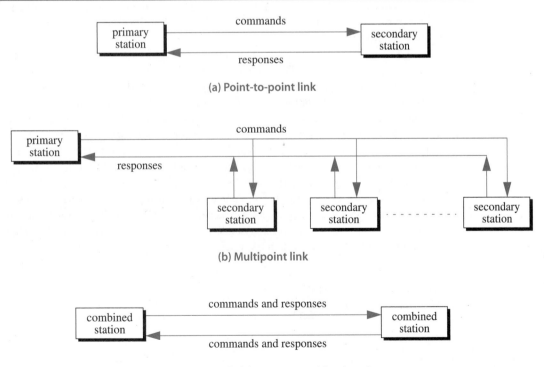

(a) Point-to-point link

(b) Multipoint link

(c) Point-to-point link between combined stations

Frame Format   HDLC frames are similar to the general formats discussed previously. Figure 5.27 shows the frame format. Some of the fields can occur in one of two sizes. The smaller size defines a standard format and the larger an extended format. Which format is used must be decided when the link is established.

There are three different types of frames. They differ in the contents of the control field and whether the frame actually contains data. We will first discuss the fields common to all types and then differentiate among them.

The **flag field** marks the beginning and end of each frame and contains the special bit pattern 01111110. A station receiving this pattern knows an HDLC frame is on its way. Since the frame size may vary, the station examines arriving bits and looks for this pattern to detect the frame's end. This pattern presents a problem: Since the protocol is bit oriented, the data fields (and others, as well) can consist of arbitrary bit patterns. If the flag pattern exists in another field, won't the station interpret it incorrectly as the end of the frame? We certainly do not want to constrain the data to disallow certain bit patterns from appearing.

Fortunately, this problem has a relatively easy solution called **bit stuffing.** The sending station monitors the bits between the flags before they are sent. If it detects five consecutive 1s (Figure 5.28), it inserts (stuffs) an extra 0 after the fifth 1. This breaks any potential flag pattern and prevents it from being sent. Now the data is no longer correct, so the receiving station must correct it. Whenever five consecutive 1s are followed by a 0, it assumes the 0 was stuffed and removes it. Since the flag field is not subjected to bit stuffing by the sending station, it is the only place where the flag pattern can appear.

The **address field** is self-explanatory. It has 8 bits for the standard format and 16 bits for the extended. The extended format allows a greater number of stations to be identified. If a primary station sends the frame, the address field defines the identity of the secondary station where the frame is being sent. This is necessary in multipoint configurations where there are several secondary stations. If a secondary station is sending the frame, the address field contains the sender's identity. As there is only one primary station and secondary stations do not send to each other, the destination address is not needed. The source address is needed to let the primary station know where a frame originates.

In some cases the field may contain a **group address** or **broadcast address** (all 1s). A frame with a group address is accepted by all secondary stations in a predefined group. One with a broadcast address is accepted by every secondary station with which the primary station has established a link.

Figure 5.27   HDLC Frame Format

number of bits:	8	8 or 16	8 or 16	variable	16 or 32	8
	Flag	Address	Control	- - - - - Data - - - - -	FCS	Flag

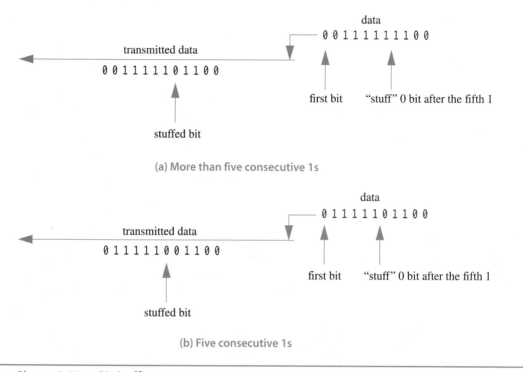

Figure 5.28   Bit Stuffing

The **data field** contains the data, and its length is variable. We will see that in some cases there is no data and this field does not exist. The **frame check sequence (FCS)** is used for CRC error detection. The field may be 16 (standard format) or 32 (extended format) bits long. Most common is a 16-bit field defined as described in Section 4.3 using the CRC polynomial $x^{16} + x^{12} + x^5 + 1$.

The **control field** is 8 (standard format) or 16 (extended format) bits long and is used to send status information or issue commands. Its contents depend on the frame's type. The three types are information frame, supervisory frame, and unnumbered frame. Figure 5.29 shows the format for each using the standard format. With the extended format, the fields are larger or the frame contains unused bits; the differences are not important here.

The first one or two bits define the frame type. As Figure 5.29 shows, an information frame always starts with 0, a supervisory frame always starts with 10, and an unnumbered frame always starts with 11. These definitions allow the receiving stations to determine the type of an arriving frame.

Information frames are used primarily to transfer information (data field of Figure 5.27) using either the go-back-*n* or the selective repeat sliding window protocols. The fields N(R) and N(S) are similar to what we previously called frame.ack and frame.number, respectively. Specifically, N(R) (number of received frame) is a piggyback acknowledgment indicating that all frames up to N(R) − 1 have been received.

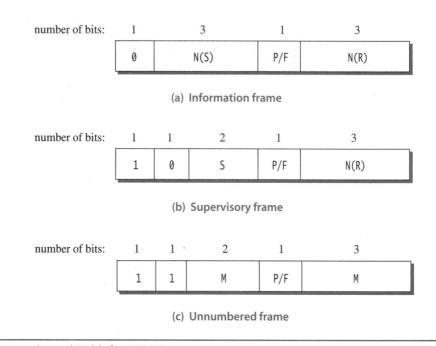

number of bits: 1   3   1   3

| 0 | N(S) | P/F | N(R) |

(a) Information frame

number of bits: 1   1   2   1   3

| 1 | 0 | S | P/F | N(R) |

(b) Supervisory frame

number of bits: 1   1   2   1   3

| 1 | 1 | M | P/F | M |

(c) Unnumbered frame

Figure 5.29   Control Fields for HDLC Frames

Equivalently, the station is currently expecting a frame numbered N(R). Similarly, N(S) is the number of the frame being sent. The fields N(R) and N(S) are either three bits (standard frame) or seven bits (extended frame) long. Consequently, frame numbers and arithmetic such as N(R) − 1 are modulo 8 (2^3) or modulo 128 (2^7).

The P/F bit stands for poll/final bit. Its meaning depends on whether the frame is being sent by a primary (poll bit) or secondary station (final bit). The primary station can request a response from a secondary station by sending it a frame with the P bit set to 1. For example, the primary station may want to know if the secondary station has any data to send or may request its status with regard to some ongoing process. In any case, the secondary station is expected to respond (we'll see some examples shortly). When sent by a secondary station, the F bit indicates that the current frame is the last in a sequence of frames.

Supervisory frames are used by either station to indicate its status or to NAK frames received incorrectly. The N(R) and P/F bits do the same thing as in information frames. The differences are in the two-bit S field, which is defined as follows:

- **RR: Receive ready** (00). When a station wants to indicate it is ready and able to receive information, it sends an RR frame. The RR frame is also used to acknowledge received frames periodically when there is no outgoing data (recall the discussion of ACK timers in Section 5.3).

- **REJ: Reject** (01). This is similar to the NAKs discussed using the go-back-*n* protocol. It requests that the other station resend all outstanding frames starting with the one whose number is specified by N(R). This can occur if a frame arrives out of order or damaged.

- **RNR: Receive not ready** (10). If a station's buffers are filling or it detects an error on its side of the link, it can stop the flow of incoming frames by sending an RNR frame.

- **SREJ: Selective reject** (11). This is similar to the NAKs discussed using the selective repeat protocol. It requests that the other station resend the frame whose number is specified by N(R).

Whereas the information and supervisory frames control and manage the transfer of frames, the **unnumbered frames** establish how the protocol will proceed. For example, we stated previously that HDLC can use go-back-n or selective repeat, it can use different frame sizes, and it can communicate in one of three modes. How do the stations decide when to do what?

Part (c) of Figure 5.29 shows the unnumbered frame format. The two fields marked M together define five flags whose values define the communication protocol. A primary station sends commands and a secondary station responds to commands by setting these flags appropriately. Table 5.2 lists some of the possible commands and responses that can be coded in an unnumbered frame.

HDLC Example   The following example describes the process of establishing a link, exchanging frames, and terminating the link. Figure 5.30 shows a possible sequence of exchanges between two stations, A (primary station) and B (secondary station). We will assume a go-back-n protocol. Vertical arrows represent passing time. Slanted arrows between them indicate the sending of frames and their direction. Text at the arrow's source specifies the frame's contents. Text at the arrow's end specifies what happened when the frame arrived. To simplify the figure, no text appears in cases where the frame was accepted without error.

To begin, Figure 5.30a shows how a connection might be established. Station B starts by sending an unnumbered frame with the function RIM. This is a request that the primary station (A) send an unnumbered frame with function code SIM. When B receives the SIM it begins its initialization procedure as mentioned previously and acknowledges receipt of the SIM by sending another unnumbered frame with function UA. When A receives UA it knows that B is initializing. In this case, A decides the response mode will be ARM and sends another unnumbered frame with that function. When B receives the frame, it again acknowledges by sending another UA frame. When A receives the acknowledgment the stations are ready to communicate.

Figure 5.30b shows an example exchange of frames. Since the response mode is ARM, A and B both begin sending information frames (i frames). B sends its first two frames with frame numbers N(S) = 0 and 1. In both cases, N(R) is 0. Since B has not received anything yet, it is expecting the first frame (number 0). Meanwhile, A sends its first three frames with numbers N(S) = 0, 1, and 2. In the first two frames, N(R) = 0 because A has not received anything yet. However, A receives a frame from B after it sends its second frame. Consequently, with the third frame, A sets N(R) = 1, thus acknowledging its receipt of frame 0.

Table 5.2 HDLC Unnumbered Frame Functions

Function (C = Command; R = Response)	Meaning
SNRM: Set normal response mode (C)	Communicate using normal response mode and standard frame format.
SNRME: Set normal response mode extended (C)	Communicate using normal response mode and extended frame format.
SARM: Set asynchronous response mode (C)	Communicate using asynchronous response mode and standard frame format.
SARME: Set asynchronous response mode extended (C)	Communicate using asynchronous response mode and extended frame format.
SABM: Set asynchronous balanced mode (C)	Communicate using asynchronous balanced mode and standard frame format.
SABME: Set asynchronous balanced mode extended (C)	Communicate using asynchronous balanced mode and extended frame format.
DISC: Disconnect (C)	Initiates a disconnect between the two stations. The disconnect is completed when the other station responds with a UA function (see below).
RSET: Reset (C)	Each station tracks the values of N(R) and N(S) as frames come and go. If an error occurs (say at a higher level than HDLC), the data link control may have to reinitialize the frame exchange. RSET resets the tracked values of N(R) and N(S) to a previously established value.
SIM: Set initialization mode (C)	Instructs the other station to initialize its data link control functions.
UP: Unnumbered poll (C)	A poll (request) to get status information from a specified station.
UI: Unnumbered information (C or R)	Used to send status information. Typically sent following a UP or SIM.
XID: Exchange identification (C or R)	Allows two stations to exchange their identification and status.
RIM: Request initialization mode (R)	Request from a secondary station that the primary station send SIM.
RD: Request disconnect (R)	Request from a secondary station that the primary station initiate a disconnect by sending a DISC frame.
DM: Disconnect mode (R)	Tells the primary station that the secondary station is not operational (i.e., in a disconnect mode).
UA: Unnumbered acknowledgment (R)	Used to acknowledge previously sent commands such as a set mode or disconnect.

(continues)

Table 5.2 *(continued)*

FUNCTION (C = COMMAND; R = RESPONSE)	MEANING
TEST: Test (C or R)	Request to the other station to send a test response. The sending station may put something in the data field for the receiving station to return to test the link.
FRMR: Frame reject (R)	Used to indicate an arriving frame was rejected. The REJ function rejects frames that are damaged or received out of order. FRMR is used if, for example, a control field is defined incorrectly or a frame that was never sent is acknowledged.

Figure 5.30 Communicating Using HDLC

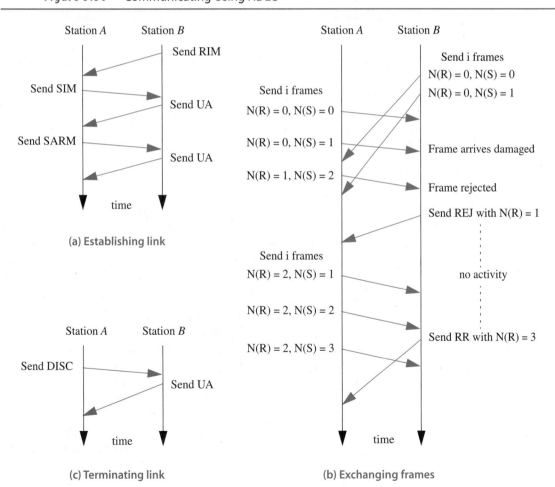

(a) Establishing link

(c) Terminating link

(b) Exchanging frames

Next, suppose the second frame that *A* sends arrives damaged. *B* sends a supervisory frame containing the function code REJ and N(R) = 1. This frame does two things: It acknowledges that *B* received frame 0 from *A* and states that an error occurred and that *A* should resend everything beginning with frame 1. Meanwhile, *B* is still expecting frame 1 so when the next frame arrives, *B* rejects it as being out of order.

Eventually, *A* receives the REJ frame and resends frames beginning with the specified number. If it has three frames to send they contain N(S) = 1, 2, and 3. Note that N(R) is now 2 in each of these frames. This is because while we were discussing what *B* did with the damaged frame, *A* received another (its second) i frame. These three frames eventually reach *B*. However, *B* has entered a period of inactivity and cannot piggyback any acknowledgments. Consequently, between the arrival of frames 1 and 2, its timer expires. It sends a supervisory frame with function code RR, which reaffirms that *B* is still ready to accept frames and acknowledges the receipt of frame number 2 (sets N(R) = 3). Using RR here is a lot like listening on the telephone to your eccentric aunt complain about her neighbors. You hold the phone by your ear while you make a batch of cookies and respond every five minutes or so with a "Yes, Aunt Mabel."

Frame exchanges like this occur until both stations have finished sending. Station *A* decides it is time to disconnect by sending an unnumbered frame with function code DISC (Figure 5.30c). When *B* receives the frame, it acknowledges it by sending a UA frame. When *A* receives the acknowledgment, it knows both sides have agreed to disconnect and it terminates the link. (Don't hang up on Aunt Mabel without her consent; you might be in her will!)

OTHER BIT-ORIENTED PROTOCOLS

HDLC is not the only bit-oriented protocol. Several others are very similar to HDLC. Some are actually modified subsets of HDLC, and others provide some additional functions. In general, their frame formats and function codes differ little from the previous discussions. Therefore, we will not discuss each in detail, but will mention them and where they are used. If you are interested, Reference [Ha96] provides some additional detail. The other protocols are as follows:

- **Synchronous Data Link Control (SDLC).** HDLC was derived from SDLC, which was developed by IBM in the early 1970s. IBM had submitted SDLC to the ISO for acceptance. ISO modified it and renamed it HDLC. Effectively, SDLC is IBM's equivalent to HDLC. (If you sit on the other side of the fence, HDLC is ISO's equivalent to SDLC). SDLC uses go-back-*n* and is part of IBM's Systems Network Architecture (SNA), discussed in Chapter 8. It is typically used in IBM terminal-to-computer communications.

- **Advanced Data Communications Control Procedure (ADCCP).** IBM also submitted SDLC to ANSI for acceptance. As all good standards organizations do, they modified it and renamed it ADCCP.

- **Link access protocols (LAP).** There are several link access protocols. The ITU adopted and modified HDLC for use in its X.25 network interface standard (discussed in Chapter 7). Originally it was labeled LAP, but subsequently was changed to LAPB (B for balanced). It allows devices to be connected to packet-switched networks. A variation on LAPB is LAPD, the link control for the Integrated Services Digital Network (ISDN). ISDN is an entirely digital communications system being defined by ITU. It is designed to eventually replace the telephone system. LAPD allows devices to communicate over the ISDN D channel (discussed in Chapter 8).

- **Logical link control (LLC).** LLC (an IEEE standard) is also similar to HDLC but is used in local area networks (LAN). It allows LANs to connect to other LANs and to wide area networks.

BINARY SYNCHRONOUS COMMUNICATIONS PROTOCOL

The binary synchronous communications protocol, often referred to as the **BSC** or **bisync protocol,** was made popular by IBM. It is used with synchronous, half-duplex communications and uses a stop and wait flow control. As with the previous protocols, it can be used in point-to-point or multipoint connections. It is perhaps most typical in multipoint connections where the primary station is a CPU and the secondary ones are terminals. It is older than the bit-oriented protocols we have discussed, but it is still used in enough applications to warrant its discussion.

Unlike the previously discussed protocols, BSC is **byte oriented.** That is, the stations interpret frames as a sequence of control and data bytes. Byte values can be interpreted using either the ASCII or EBCDIC character sets.[*] BSC uses several different frame formats. Figure 5.31 shows three typical ones: a control frame format and two data frame formats. We discuss the control frame first and then discuss the difference between the transparent and nontransparent data frames shortly. In each case, the frame starts with two **SYN characters.** Primarily, they allow the receiver of the frame to divide the bit stream into bytes (i.e., where one byte ends and the other begins). Two SYN characters are used to reduce the probability of receiving a false frame. Random transmission noise can simulate any byte; however, there is a much lower probability of producing two false SYN characters than just one SYN character, which would cause the receiver to mistakenly react to the false frame. (Reference [Sh90] provides a bit-level discussion of how the receiver checks for SYN characters.)

The SYN bytes are followed by one or more control bytes. In a **control frame** (Figure 5.31c), the control bytes constitute the bulk of the information transmitted. Control information is similar to what we have discussed previously. It can acknowledge frames received correctly, NAK those received incorrectly, or request a response

---

[*]It may be interesting to note that BSC can also be used with a lesser-known six-bit code called Transcode. (Then again, maybe not.)

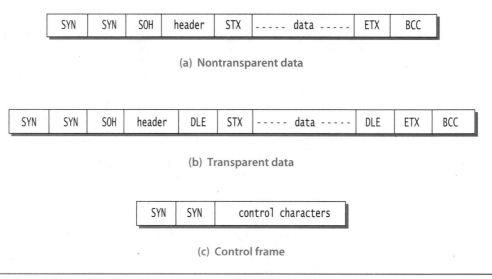

Figure 5.31   BSC Frame Formats

from another station. We will discuss a few of them in detail. Table 5.3 provides a short summary of typical control characters and their functions.

In a data frame, the first control byte is SOH (start of header). It tells the receiving station that successive bytes in the arriving frame contain header information. **Header information** will vary, but typically contains the identity or address of the sending or receiving stations. For example, a destination identifier is needed when a primary station is sending something over a multipoint line, and a receiving identifier is needed when a primary station is receiving something from it.

The header information is followed by an STX character (Figure 5.31a) or a DLE-STX combination (Figure 5.31b). In the first case, STX indicates the start of text. This means that successive bytes represent data. However, since the number of data bytes can vary, the protocol needs a way to specify the end of them. It does this by using the ETX (end of text) character. Thus, a receiving station receives and accepts the bytes as data until it encounters ETX.

In some cases an ETB character (Table 5.3) is used in place of ETX. For example, suppose a sending station needs to send a message that will not fit into one data frame. The obvious solution is to send multiple frames. But now, the receiving station needs to know not only the end of the data in a frame, but also which frame contains the last of the data. In the first and successive blocks the sender inserts an ETB (end of transmission block) character in place of ETX. In the last block it uses ETX.

For applications in which the data consists of printable character codes this is a simple way to indicate its end. But what about binary files whose data consists of bytes with random bit patterns? What happens if a frame's data contains an ETB or ETX character (Figure 5.32)? What is to prevent the receiving station from

Table 5.3   BSC Control Characters

BSC CHARACTER	MEANING
ACK: Acknowledge	Verifies that a block of data was received correctly. Since BSC is a half-duplex, stop and wait protocol, ACK also tells the sender that it may send the next frame.
DLE: Data link escape	Typically used with STX. The DLE/STX sequence specifies that all successive bytes, including control bytes up to a DLE/ETX or DLE/ETB sequence, are to be treated as data. Afterward, any control character is interpreted accordingly.
ENQ: Enquiry	Requests a response from another station. Responding stations might send a data frame or an ACK or NAK, depending on their status.
EOT: End of transmission	Indicates end of transmission and tells the stations they may disconnect.
ETB: End of transmission block	If a message requires many frames, ETB indicates the end of an intermediate frame.
ETX: End of text	Indicates the end of the last frame in a multi-frame message or the end of a frame in a single-frame message
NAK: Negative acknowledgment	Indicates the previous frame was received incorrectly.
NUL: Null	Used as a filler character where frames must be a minimal length.
SOH: Start of header	Indicates the start of header information in the frame.
STX: Start of text	Indicates the start of data within the frame.
SYN: Synchronous idle	Two SYN characters are at the start of each frame, alerting the station of an arriving frame.

Figure 5.32   Encountering Control Bytes in Data

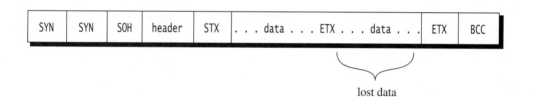

lost data

interpreting it as a control byte and missing the remaining data? A station using the BSC protocol handles this by preceding the STX character with a **DLE character.** The DLE, which stands for **data link escape,** acts like a toggle switch. When the receiving station sees the DLE-STX pair, it disables any checking for control bytes such as ETX or ETB. Moreover, the checking remains disabled until the receiving station encounters another DLE character. Once this DLE is encountered, the receiving station enables its checking for ETX or STX characters.

At first glance it may seem we have not solved any problems. What if the data contains a DLE character? The protocol gets around this problem by disguising DLE characters in its data. Figure 5.33 shows how. A sending station examines the characters it sends as data. Whenever there is a DLE character, it inserts an extra DLE character. This process is called **byte stuffing** and is similar to bit stuffing, discussed previously; it just operates on a different level. Thus, when a receiving station encounters a DLE it looks for a second one following immediately. If it finds one, it knows the second one is bogus and accepts the first as data. If not, it knows the DLE is not data and enables control character checking. Data delimited this way is called **transparent data.** That is, the data field's contents are transparent to the receiving station. Data delimited with STX and ETX (or ETB) only is **nontransparent data.**

The last character from the formats shown in Figure 5.31 is **BCC, block check character.** It is used in BSC's error checking method. The BCC field's contents depend on which error checking method is used. If the protocol uses the CRC check, BCC will correspond to the CRC-16 polynomial (see Section 4.3). In other cases, BSC uses a **longitudinal redundancy check.** This method visualizes the frame as a two-dimensional bit array where each row represents one byte. For each column a parity bit is determined from the bits in that column and is stored in the BCC field.

Frame Exchange   Because BSC is a half-duplex protocol using stop and wait flow control, the process of sending and acknowledging frames is simplified. Figure 5.34 shows a typical sequence of events. Station *A* (primary station) sends an ENQ control frame to *B*. Since ENQ frames request a response, station *B* sends an acknowledgment. After *A* receives the acknowledgment, *A* and *B* exchange a sequence of data frames and acknowledgments. If *B* receives a frame correctly it

Figure 5.33   Byte Stuffing

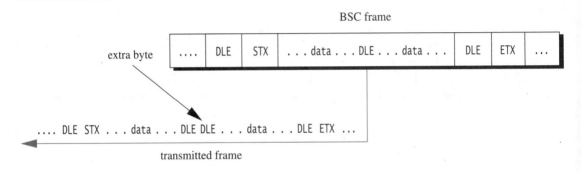

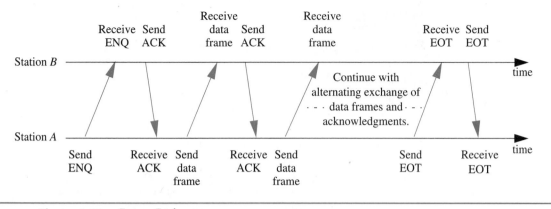

Figure 5.34   Frame Exchange

sends a control frame containing the ACK control character. When *A* receives it, the ACK character indicates the previous frame has been received. Consequently, *A* sends the next one. This exchange continues as long as *A* has frames to send. When *A* has no more data to send it sends an EOT frame. *B* responds by sending its own EOT frame. When *A* receives it the connection between the two is terminated.

Naturally there are provisions for responding to damaged frames or for using timers to check for lost frames. But since these methods do not differ significantly from what we have discussed previously, we will not duplicate the discussions.

SUMMARY: DATA LINK PROTOCOLS

HDLC (and its many variations) and BSC represent two of the most common data link protocols. Table 5.4 summarizes the main differences between them.

Table 5.4   Comparison of BSC and HDLC Protocols

HDLC	BSC
Full duplex	Half duplex
ARQ with go-back-*n* or selective repeat flow control	ARQ with stop and wait flow control
Bit-oriented protocol	Byte-oriented protocol
Code independent	Requires ASCII, EBCDIC, or Transcode
One frame format specifying three frame types	Multiple frame formats
Achieves data transparency through bit stuffing	Achieves data transparency through byte (DLE) stuffing
Bit flags delimit frames	SYN , ETX, and ETB characters delimit frames
Uses control field for control information	Uses control frames for control information

5.6 CASE STUDY: KERMIT

We finish this chapter by describing **Kermit,** a popular file transfer protocol. By now, we have covered enough material to describe adequately how a specific protocol runs. We choose Kermit because it is available on most, if not all, the major platforms. We describe only the aspects of Kermit that relate to what we have discussed thus far. If you are interested in an in-depth study, Reference [Da87] does a thorough and understandable job.

Kermit was written at Columbia University in the early 1980s in response to a growing demand to transfer mainframe files to a new and emerging technological wonder, the floppy disk. Kermit is unique in that it is not proprietary software. In other words, it doesn't cost anything. It is exchanged freely and is widely available. Its availability has allowed many people to study it and make suggestions for improving it. Consequently, Kermit has grown and appears in many versions.

Because there are so many versions the features we discuss here may or may not be true for your version. We intend this discussion to be general and to relate to the topics we have discussed previously. For complete details you should consult the documentation at your site.

The name Kermit probably seems familiar. Indeed, Kermit is named after one of the late Jim Henson's Muppet characters. According to daCruz (Ref. [Da87]), the name Kermit was chosen because the Muppet frog is "a pleasant, unassuming sort of character" and the protocol designers liked the association. To justify its use they tried to think of a phrase for which Kermit was an acronym. After failing in their attempt, they decided to use the name anyway and requested (and got) permission from Henson Associates, Inc. to do so.

To transfer a file between two computers, each must run a copy of Kermit. Figure 5.35 shows the general approach involving a PC and a remote computer con-

Figure 5.35   Kermit File Transfer

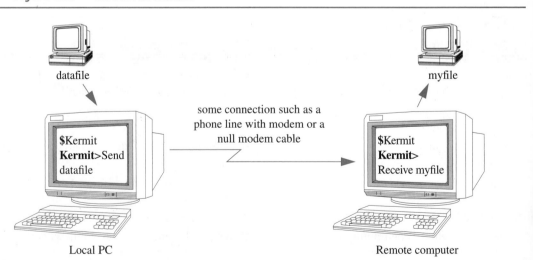

datafile

myfile

some connection such as a
phone line with modem or a
null modem cable

$Kermit
Kermit>Send
datafile

$Kermit
Kermit>
Receive myfile

Local PC

Remote computer

nected by a phone line and modem. The PC's user runs some communication software to log on to the remote machine. Once logged on, he or she calls Kermit by entering its name. The user then enters the command Receive myfile. At this point, the Kermit running on the remote computer is waiting for a file to arrive. The boldface characters in the figure indicate system prompts (which will vary with the system).

Next, the user calls Kermit from the local PC and enters the command Send datafile. This activates the PC's Kermit. At this point, the user's interaction is done and Kermit does the rest. It looks for a file named "datafile" on the local PC and divides it into packets, the number depending on the size of the file and a packet. The PC Kermit constructs and sends frames through the modem and phone lines using the techniques, standards, and protocols described in Chapters 2 through 5. When the frames arrive at the remote computer, its Kermit receives them. If there are no errors, it extracts the packets and creates a file named "myfile." Once all the packets have been reassembled, the PC's Kermit informs the user the file transfer was successful.

From the user's perspective, the transfer was almost trivial. Two commands on each end were enough to do the job. But each of the topics discussed in the previous four chapters must be addressed somewhere, making the transfer far from trivial.

FRAME FORMAT

Kermit is a byte-oriented protocol. As with BSC, the Kermit frame consists of a sequence of bytes. Each byte's placement in the frame determines its meaning. Figure 5.36 shows the frame format and, as you might expect, it differs little from what we have discussed previously. It contains the ASCII SOH character, a frame number, and data. It also contains the number of bytes or length of a frame. This differs from previous protocols in which variable-length frames were terminated by a special character. With Kermit, the receiving station finds the frame's end by counting the number of bytes and comparing with the length field.

Each frame also contains an error checking field. Error checking may be done using the CRC method or checksums. The **checksum** method computes a modular sum of frame bytes treated as integers. The sum is stored and sent with the frame. The receiving station recalculates the sum and compares it with the stored sum. Any discrepancy indicates an error.

Finally, each frame has a type field represented by a character. Kermit's frame types are similar to previously discussed types. Table 5.5 summarizes some of them. A complete list is found in Reference [Da87].

Figure 5.36   Kermit Frame Format

SOH	Length	Number	Type	... data ...	ErrorCheck

Table 5.5 Kermit Frame Types

FRAME TYPE	MEANING
B	Break transmission. Indicates the two communicating stations should disconnect.
D	Data frame.
E	Error. Indicates a fatal error has occurred and the data field specifies the error.
F	File header. Contains the name of the file that will be sent.
G	Generic command. The data field contains one of a number of commands and optional parameters that can be sent to the other station.
N	Negative acknowledgment.
S	Send initiation. Sent to the receiving Kermit. It indicates a file will be coming soon and contains parameters (discussed shortly) used in the protocol.
Y	Acknowledgment frame. Used to acknowledge both data and control frames.
Z	End of file frame. Indicates that all frames for the file have been sent.

PROTOCOL

Kermit was written as a half-duplex (but will support full-duplex), stop and wait[*] protocol for a point-to-point connection. The station (*A*) that sends the first file starts by sending an initiation frame (type S) to the other station (*B*). As specified in Table 5.4, this frame informs the receiving station that it will be receiving frames. The S frame and its eventual acknowledgment contain parameters on which the stations must agree in order for the protocol to work correctly if *A* and *B* exchange several files. The S frame contains parameters such as the following:

- **The longest frame that *A* expects to get.** This prevents *B* from sending *A* more than it can handle.

- **Timeout period.** This specifies how long *B* should wait for a frame before a timeout occurs.

- **Control prefix character.** If a file's data includes certain control characters, sending them can have unexpected effects if a device such as a modem intercepts and interprets them. To avoid misinterpretation of data, Kermit replaces a control character with two printable characters. The first is an agreed-on prefix

---

[*]Newer versions of Kermit do support a sliding window protocol.

such as the character #. A must tell B which prefix character to use so that A can recognize it.

The second character is obtained by adding 64 to the control character's code, thus making it a printable character (see Table 2.4 in Section 2.3). For example, if the control characters X-ON and X-OFF appeared as data they would be sent as the two-letter sequences #Q and #S, respectively. When B receives a two-character sequence starting with #, it discards the # and subtracts 64 from the second character. (What do you think happens if # was actually part of the original data?)

- **Eighth-bit prefix character.** Many versions of Kermit are written to transfer seven-bit ASCII text files. However, the seven-bit codes are often stored in eight-bit bytes with the eighth bit being 0. In such cases, an eighth bit is replaced by a parity bit determined from the other seven. When the file arrives, a 0 bit replaces the parity bit. A problem can occur when binary files are sent because all eight bits in a byte are meaningful. If the eighth bit is replaced with a parity bit then it is lost for good and the protocol fails.

  One option for dealing with binary files is to use an eighth-bit prefix character. If the eighth bit in a byte is 1, the seven remaining bits are sent with parity. However, the sending Kermit will insert the agreed-on prefix character (such as an &) prior to it. If the eighth bit is 0 then no eighth-bit prefix is sent. When the receiving Kermit sees the & character, it removes it and concludes that the eighth bit of the next byte is a 1. Otherwise it concludes that the eighth bit is 0.

- **Run-length encoding prefix.** In Section 3.5, we discussed run-length encoding, a data compression method that replaces long strings of a character with a single occurrence of it preceded by the number of times it occurs. Kermit also can provide run-length encoding. However, the receiving Kermit must be able to determine when it receives a run-length-encoded string. For example, suppose it receives two consecutive bytes 0000 0111 (binary 7) and 0100 0001 (ASCII code for A). Are these data, or do they represent a run-length-encoded string? To differentiate the two cases, the sending Kermit inserts a special prefix (such as ~) prior to a run-length-encoded string. Thus, when the receiving Kermit sees the character ~, it concludes the following characters define a run-length-encoded string.

Figure 5.37 shows a typical exchange of Kermit frames. Station A starts by sending an S frame containing the previous information. B responds by sending a Y frame (acknowledgment). The Y frame may also contain the previous information. This exchange allows each station to inform the other what it expects. Next, A sends an F frame specifying the name of the file it will send. Again, B responds by acknowledging the F frame by sending another Y frame. Sending data frames proceeds as described in previous sections, with B acknowledging the ones it receives correctly and sending NAKs (N frames) when it receives a damaged frame or times out. When the last frame has been sent, A sends a Z frame indicating the entire file has been sent. Again, B responds with an acknowledgment. Finally, if there is no more work to be done, A sends a B frame indicating its intention to disconnect. B acknowledges it and the disconnection occurs.

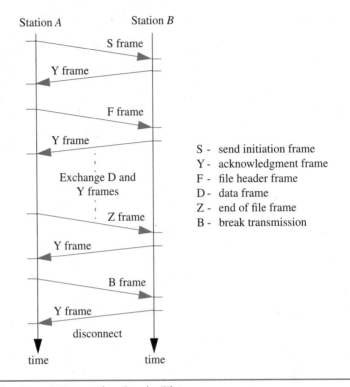

Figure 5.37   Kermit Protocol to Send a File

Commands

Many people who use Kermit do not know how it works. In many cases they do not want or need to know. However, they do need to know how to interact with it to perform necessary tasks. We finish this section by discussing some of the more common commands to which Kermit responds. Remember, this description is general, and all commands may not be available on every Kermit. Reference [Da87] lists approximately 100 commands; to completely cover each one in detail, spelling out where they are used, is far beyond our scope here. However, Table 5.6 lists some of the commands that relate to previous discussions.

Kermit is included here primarily because of its widespread use, but the reader should not conclude that it is the only file transfer protocol. There are others, such as XMODEM, XMODEM-CRC, XMODEM-1K, WXMODEM, YMODEM, and ZMODEM. The differences among them, including frame sizes and formats, error checking methods, and control characters used, are not huge. On the other hand, as anyone who has ever written a program knows, even the smallest differences can make protocols incompatible. If you are interested in further distinctions, Reference [Ra96] has a short discussion of each protocol.

Table 5.6   Some Kermit Commands

COMMAND	FUNCTION
clear	Clears buffers and removes deadlocks caused if each station sends the other an X-OFF character.
get	Request (usually to a file server) for a specified file. It differs from receive, which assumes the other station has issued a send command independent of the receive. The get command requests that the server send it.
receive	Tells Kermit to wait for a file that will be arriving. If the command specifies a file name, the incoming file will be stored under that name. If not, the file will be stored under the name specified in the file header (F frame). It is expected that a file has been (or will be) sent; otherwise, the wait is very long.
send	Tells Kermit to send one or more files to the other station. It is expected the other station can receive it.
set baud	Defines the baud rate.
set block-check	Specifies how error checking will be performed. As stated previously, the choices are a checksum or cyclic redundancy check.
set delay	Defines how much time Kermit waits before sending the first frame in response to a send command. This is needed when a user is running two Kermits and enters a send command. He or she needs time to get to the other Kermit to enter the receive command before frames start arriving.
set duplex	Specifies whether the connection is half or full duplex.
set parity	Establishes how and if parity is used. Choices are ODD (for odd parity), EVEN (for even parity), MARK (parity bit always 1), SPACE (parity bit always 0), or NONE (no parity, all eight bits are data). It is essential that both Kermits use the same method.
set receive	Used to establish previously discussed parameters such as the maximum frame length and prefix characters for incoming frames.
set send	Used to establish previously discussed parameters such as the maximum frame length and prefix characters for outgoing frames. The parameters can be changed by a send receive command entered at the other Kermit.
set timer	Used to enable or disable the timeout mechanism.
set window	Allows Kermit to use a sliding window protocol (go-back-n) instead of the typical stop and wait protocol to improve overall efficiency. A parameter for this command specifies the window size (between 0 and 31).
set {send or receive} packet-length	Changes the default frame size[*] to send or receive. The default maximum is 94, but an extended version of Kermit allows frame sizes up to 9000.
set {send or receive} timeout	Specifies how long a station should wait for a frame before responding with a negative acknowledgment.

[*]Typical Kermit terminology uses the term *packet* where we have used *frame*. Some books interchange the two terms freely and others make a very careful distinction between them. The reader should be careful with this terminology.

5.7 SUMMARY

In previous chapters we discussed details necessary for the transmission of a single frame, but Chapter 5 considered multiple frames. Specifically, it discussed protocols that deal with the following issues:

* Tracking multiple frames and their acknowledgments.
* Responding to frames that arrive damaged.
* Responding when a frame or acknowledgment never arrives or arrives late.

Several protocols were discussed. The unrestricted protocol simply sends all frames and assumes the receiver has enough buffer space to handle them. It also assumes that all frames arrive correctly. The stop and wait protocol sends one frame at a time, waiting for an acknowledgment to each. These two represent extremes in protocol design.

A sliding window protocol represents a compromise between the two extremes. It defines a window for the sending station containing frames that can be sent but not yet acknowledged. Adjusting the window size can make it behave more like an unrestricted or a stop and wait protocol. We discussed two different sliding window protocols. The go-back-n protocol requires that the receiving station accept all frames in the order they are sent. If one arrives out of order, the receiving station does not accept it and the sending station must resend it. The selective repeat protocol defines a window for the receiving station. The receiving station then can accept any frame in its window. It buffers them and eventually delivers them in order to its patron.

Both sliding window protocols respond to frames that arrive damaged or out of order by sending negative acknowledgments (NAKs). A station receiving a NAK must resend frames. Under the go-back-n protocol it resends all outstanding frames, but under the selective repeat protocol it resends only the NAK'd frame. Each protocol also relies on timers so that if an acknowledgment is not received within a period of time, the station assumes one or more frames are lost and resends them.

With both sliding window protocols there are restrictions on the window size. Generally, with the go-back-n protocol, if there are 2^K distinct frame numbers, the sender's window must have fewer than 2^K frames. With selective repeat, the sum of the sender's and receiver's windows must not exceed 2^K. Violating these restrictions does not mean the protocol will fail, but it does mean the protocol is subject to failure if a certain sequence of events occurs.

The algorithms are complex, and providing a formal mathematical proof is outside the scope of this text. However, Section 5.4 introduced two tools that can be used for verification: state transition diagrams and Petri nets. Both use directed graphs to represent the states and state transitions of a system, but they differ in the way they do so. State transition diagrams use nodes for states and edges for state transitions. The execution of an algorithm thus can be equated to defining paths through the state transition diagram. Petri nets are more complex. They use places, transitions, arrows, and tokens. The collection of tokens corresponding to places defines the state of the system. Tokens move from place to place subject to rules that allow transitions to fire. In both cases, the models can be analyzed to detect anomalies that can occur.

Sections 5.5 and 5.6 discussed specific examples of flow control protocols used in practice. The three main protocols discussed were HDLC, BSC, and Kermit.

HDLC is an example of a bit-oriented protocol. That is, its frames are treated as bit streams. It is defined by the ISO for point-to-point or multipoint connections, is used for half- and full-duplex communications, and can use either the go-back-n or selective repeat protocol. It defines different frame types and uses them to exchange data, commands, or control information.

BSC is a byte-oriented protocol; the frames are treated as byte streams. It also is used in point-to-point or multipoint connections, but is typically used with half-duplex communications and uses a stop and wait protocol. Like HDLC, it defines different frame types to exchange data, commands, and control information.

Kermit is a popular file transfer protocol written at Columbia University and is a public domain program (i.e., distributed without charge). Kermit is a byte-oriented protocol used primarily in point-to-point connections. Depending on the version, it can run in half- or full-duplex mode and can use either a stop and wait or sliding window protocol.

All three of these protocols (and many others) represent different ways to do the same thing. In all cases, the stations exchange frames according to specified rules. They differ in those rules and the types of frames they recognize. Because of these differences, two or more stations must run the same protocols in order to communicate. If either station is unaware of what the other is sending it, communication is impossible.

Review Questions

1. What is automatic repeat request error control?

2. What is flow control?

3. What are X-ON and X-OFF characters?

4. What is an unrestricted flow control?

5. What is stop and wait flow control?

6. Are the following statements TRUE or FALSE? Why?

   a. Unrestricted flow control generally has a better channel utilization than the stop and wait flow control.

   b. Unrestricted flow control really amounts to no flow control.

   c. Unrestricted and stop and wait flow control are special cases of a sliding window protocol.

   d. Sliding window protocols can work with any size window.

e. The go-back-n algorithm will resend several frames even if just one fails to arrive at its destination.

f. For the selective repeat protocol, the receiving window size is independent of the sending window size.

g. Petri nets and finite state machines represent two different ways to accomplish the same thing.

h. HDLC is a byte-oriented protocol.

i. HDLC can use either a selective repeat or go-back-n protocol.

j. Kermit is a half-duplex byte-oriented protocol.

7. Distinguish between bit rate and effective data rate.

8. Define two measures of transmission efficiency.

9. What important role does an acknowledgment play in a flow control protocol?

10. What is a sliding window flow control protocol?

11. What is a piggybacked acknowledgment?

12. Why are frames numbered modularly rather than being allowed to increase as large as needed?

13. List typical fields in a data frame.

14. Distinguish between a frame timer and an ACK timer.

15. What purpose does the window size play in a sliding window flow control protocol?

16. Distinguish among an ACK, a NAK, and a data frame.

17. What are the major differences between the go-back-n and selective repeat protocols?

18. What is the constraint on the sending window size for the selective repeat protocol?

19. For the selective repeat protocol, what is the relationship between the sending and receiving window size?

20. What is a finite state machine (or model)?

21. What is a state transition diagram?

22. What is a Petri net?

23. Define the terms place, transition, arrow, and token as applied to Petri nets.

24. What does it mean when a transition "fires"?

25. Distinguish between a byte-oriented and a bit-oriented protocol.

26. What are the three communication modes of HDLC? Describe each one.

27. What is bit stuffing and why is it necessary?

28. Distinguish among a primary station, secondary station, and combined station.

29. Distinguish among the main HDLC frame types.

30. Define the four status types a supervisory frame can indicate.

31. What is a broadcast address?

32. List other protocols similar to HDLC and each one's sponsoring organization.

33. List the main differences between the HDLC and BSC protocols.

34. What is a SYN character?

35. What is a data link escape?

36. Distinguish between transparent and nontransparent data.

37. What is byte stuffing?

38. Distinguish among end of transmission, end of transmission block, and end of text characters.

39. What is Kermit?

40. List some of the Kermit frame types.

41. What is a control prefix character?

42. What is an eighth-bit prefix character?

43. What is a run-length encoding prefix?

Exercises

1. What happens if *A* and *B* from Figure 5.2 both insert X-OFF characters into their data streams?

2. With the X-ON/X-OFF protocol, why does one station send X-OFF before the buffers are full instead of waiting until they are full?

3. Modify the unrestricted protocol in Figure 5.4 to reflect the following changes:

   a. The sender has a fixed number of frames to send.

   b. A frame could be damaged.

4. What are effective data rates for the unrestricted protocol and stop and wait protocol given the following values:

   R = capacity (16 Mbps)
   S = signal speed (200) meters per μsec

D = distance between the sender and receiver (200 meters)

T = time to create one frame (2 μsec)

F = number of bits in a frame (500)

N = number of data bits in a frame (450)

A = number of bits in an acknowledgment (80)

5. For each variable (except signal speed and the number of data bits) in Exercise 4, how will an increase in its value affect the effective data rate for both the unrestricted and stop and wait protocols? For each case, give credence to your answer by doubling the value from that in Exercise 4 and calculating the effective data rate.

6. The scenario in Figure 5.10 shows one way the go-back-n protocol can fail if the window size equals the maximum number of sequence numbers. Describe another way the protocol can fail under the same assumption.

7. Consider the go-back-n algorithm of Figure 5.12 with a window size of 7. Describe the actions of both sending and receiving protocols, specifying variable values and buffer contents, in the following cases. What is the current state of each protocol after responding to the events specified?

   a. Station A sends frames 0 through 6. Station B receives them in order, but frame 4 was damaged.

   b. Station A sends frames 0 through 6 and station B receives them in order. Station B sends one data frame to A (which A receives correctly) after receiving frame 4 but before receiving frame 5.

   c. Same scenario as in (b) but the data frame sent to A is damaged.

   d. Station A has 12 frames to send to B, but B has nothing to send to A.

8. How could the go-back-n algorithm of Figure 5.12 fail under each of the following conditions?

   a. Remove the check for expired acktimer.

   b. Remove the check for expired frametimer.

   c. Remove the check for condition (i < N) in the first if statement in the main loop.

   d. Remove the statement w = (frame.ack+1) % MAX from the code under the last event check.

9. Reproduce the scenarios of Figures 5.14 and 5.15 with both window sizes equal to 4 and show that the protocol does not fail.

10. Consider the selective repeat algorithm of Figure 5.16 with window sizes of 4. Describe the actions of both sending and receiving protocols, specifying variable

values and buffer contents, in the following cases. What is the current state of each protocol after responding to the events specified?

a.   Station *A* sends frames 0 through 3. All except frame 2 arrive. Frame 2 is lost.

b.   Station *A* sends frames 0 through 3. They arrive at *B* in the order 0, 1, 3, 2.

c.   Station *A* sends frames 0 through 3. Station *B* receives frames 0 and 1 and sends a piggyback acknowledgment, which *A* receives.

d.   Same scenario as in (c), but the acknowledgment gets lost.

11.   Consider the selective repeat protocol of Figure 5.16. Construct a scenario in which the condition `frame.type==nak`, but the second condition following it does not hold.

12.   How could the selective repeat algorithm of Figure 5.16 fail under each of the following conditions?

a.   Remove the check for expired `acktimer`.

b.   Remove the check for expired `frametimer`.

c.   Remove the check for condition (`i < N`) in the first `if` statement in the main loop.

d.   Remove the statement `sw = (frame.ack+1) % MAX` from the code under the last event check.

13.   Consider the analysis of the sliding window protocol in Section 5.3 and assume the following values:

> R = transmission rate (10 Mbps or 10 bits per μsec)
> S = signal speed (200 meters per μsec)
> D = distance between the sender and receiver (unknown)
> T = time to create one frame (1 μsec)
> F = number of bits in a frame (200)
> N = number of data bits in a frame (160)
> W = window size (4 frames)

At what distance will the first acknowledgment arrive precisely when the last frame in the window is sent? What is the effective data rate?

14.   Consider your answer to Exercise 13. What happens to the effective data rate if the window size increases? Decreases?

15.   Repeat Exercise 14 for each of the other parameters.

16.   Consider the state transition diagram of Figure 5.21. Why is there no state transition from (Y, N, 1) to (Y, N, 0)?

17. Expand the boxed-in area of Figure 5.21 to include the states (Y, N, 0) and (Y, N, 1) and refine, resulting in an expansion of Figure 5.22.

18. Consider the Petri net of Figure 5.24. Consider the case that a sender receives an ACK but may not have the next frame to send. That is, it must wait for the patron to give it a packet. What does the new Petri net look like?

19. Draw the sequence of Petri nets (similar to those in Figure 5.25) for the following sequence of events:

    a. Send F0.

    b. Timeout, resend F0.

    c. Receiver gets F0 and sends A0.

    d. Sender gets A0 and sends F1.

    e. Timeout, resend F1.

20. A timeout could occur after the receiver gets a frame and sends the ACK but before the sender gets the ACK. Thus the sender would resend a frame that the receiver is not expecting. Modify the Petri net of Figure 5.24 to account for this possibility.

21. What is the transmitted binary string after bit stuffing the following (leftmost bit first)?

    01011111101111101111111101111

22. Redraw Figure 5.30b, but assume that *B* sends SREJ (instead of REJ) when it detects the error.

23. Redraw Figure 5.30b, but assume that *B* has sent four information frames, which arrived at *A* before *A* sent the second batch of frames. Also assume *B*'s third frame is damaged in transit.

24. Section 5.5 described byte stuffing by inserting an extra DLE character whenever DLE occurs in data. The intent was to avoid misinterpreting a "data DLE" as a "control DLE." Why can't we achieve the same effect simply by using STX prior to data bytes, and if ETX or ETB occurs in the data, just insert an extra one?

25. Write a program that does byte stuffing on a character string. Write a complementary one that accepts a byte-stuffed character string and removes the stuffed bytes.

26. Section 5.6 discusses sending an S frame containing the specification of various prefixes such as a #, &, or ~. This was done to identify certain encoding schemes. But what happens if any of these characters is part of a file's data? What prevents the receiving station from interpreting it as a particular prefix? (*Hint*: We have faced similar problems previously.)

27. Refer to the discussion of prefix characters in Section 5.6 and code the following strings.

    a. Text string AJKKKKKKKKKKKDK

    b. Binary string 01011010 01011010 10010110 01011001 10011010

REFERENCES

1. [Da87] da Cruz, F. *Kermit: A File Transfer Protocol.* Bedford, MA: Digital Press, 1987.

2. [Ha96] Halsall, F. *Data Communication, Computer Networks, and Open Systems,* 4th ed. Reading, MA: Addison-Wesley, 1996.

3. [Li87] Lin, F., P. Chu, and M. Liu. "Protocol Verification Using Reachability Analysis: The State Space Explosion Problem and Relief Strategies." *Proceedings of the ACM SIGCOMM 1987 Workshop,* 1987, 126–135.

4. [Pe81] Peterson, J. *Petri Net Theory and the Modeling of Systems.* Englewood Cliffs, NJ: Prentice-Hall, 1981.

5. [Ra96] Ramos, E., A. Schroeder, and A. Beheler. *Computer Networking Concepts.* Englewood Cliffs, NJ: Prentice-Hall, 1996.

6. [Ru89] Russel, D. *The Principles of Computer Networking.* Cambridge University Press, 1989.

7. [Sh90] Sherman, K. *Data Communications: A User's Guide,* 3rd ed. Englewood Cliffs, NJ: Prentice-Hall, 1990.

8. [Ta96] Tanenbaum, A. S. *Computer Networks,* 3rd ed. Englewood Cliffs, NJ: Prentice-Hall, 1996.

9. [Wa91] Walrand, J. *Communications Networks: A First Course.* Boston: Richard D. Irwin, 1991.

CHAPTER 6

LOCAL AREA NETWORKING

*The more the data banks record about each one of us,
the less we exist.*
—**Marshall McLuhan** (1911–1980), Canadian
communications theorist.

6.1 NETWORK TOPOLOGIES

Up to this point we have focused on communication between two stations and, with the exception of multiplexing and contention in Sections 3.3 and 3.4, have not considered the larger picture of connecting many stations. This chapter and the next discuss different connection strategies and the protocols needed to maintain communication among many stations. This chapter deals with local area networks (LANs), and Chapter 7 deals with wide area networks (WANs). The differences between *local* and *wide* are partly in the geographic area covered as well as the protocols. LANs typically connect PCs, printers, and file servers located in a building or cluster of buildings. By contrast, WANs connect devices located throughout a city, state, country, and even the world. In fact, with the development of LEO satellites on the horizon, even the world will no longer be a limitation.

We begin with a discussion of the different LAN topologies (configurations) shown in Figure 6.1. Perhaps the two most common topologies are the bus and ring. In a **bus topology** (Figure 6.1a) a single communication line, typically a twisted pair, coaxial cable, or optical fiber, represents the primary medium, which we call a **segment.** Any station wanting to send to another does so over the segment. Only one station may send at a time, however. In a **ring topology** (Figure 6.1b), all the stations are arranged in a ring, with each station connected directly only to its two neighbors. If a station wants to send to another, the message must pass through all of the stations in between (either clockwise or counterclockwise). It's a little like neighborhood gossip that spreads from neighbor to neighbor.

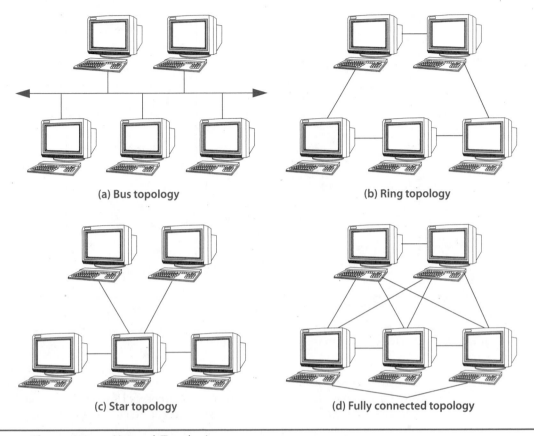

(a) Bus topology

(b) Ring topology

(c) Star topology

(d) Fully connected topology

Figure 6.1   Network Topologies

Other topologies are the star topology and a fully connected topology. In a **star topology** (Figure 6.1c) one station (often a mainframe or file server) is a logical communication center for all others. Any two communicating stations must go through it. Finally, a **fully connected topology** (Figure 6.1d) connects every pair of stations directly. Fully connected topologies represent an extreme case and are rarely used in practice (except perhaps in small isolated cases). Therefore we will not discuss them further.

An advantage of the bus topology is its simplicity. The segment may run through one or more buildings, with feeder lines going to specific offices or classrooms (Figure 6.2) and connecting to PCs. It may run the length of an assembly line, connecting devices necessary for the assembly of a product such as an automobile. Because of the linear organization, adding new stations or removing old ones is relatively easy.[*]

[*]Be cautious of this statement. Insertion and deletion of stations depends on more than topology. Two very different protocols, Ethernet and token bus, both use the linear organization. We will see that the way in which stations are added and deleted is more different.

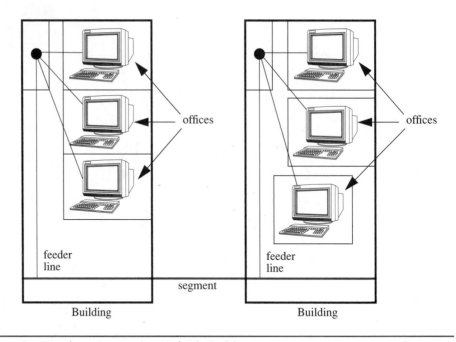

offices

offices

feeder
line

feeder
line

segment

Building

Building

Figure 6.2 Bus Topology Connecting Multiple Buildings

A disadvantage of the linear organization is that only one station can send at a time. With many applications this limitation poses no problem. However, as the number of transmissions increases, serious bottlenecks can occur. You might want to refresh your memory by reviewing the discussion of contention protocols in Section 3.4.

Ring topologies allow multiple stations to send using one or more tokens that circulate the ring. Recall from Section 3.4 that a token is a special frame and a station in possession of it may send. The most common ring networks use just one token but some protocols have provisions for more. Ring topologies are common in office environments where multiple PCs must communicate among themselves or with a file server or shared printer.

Sections 6.2 through 6.4 discuss three standards for bus and ring networks: the Ethernet, token ring network, and token bus network. The discussions cover the protocols used to control and maintain the integrity of the network. We will see that the differences among these standards go far beyond the diagrams we have drawn so far.

As the need to communicate increases, the bus and ring topologies become less effective. Greater needs usually require more flexibility than these topologies can provide. As the number of frames increases, the LANs become saturated and performance degrades. Recall again from Section 3.4 how too many frames affect efficiency.

One way to avoid serious bottlenecks is to use more LANs, thus reducing the number of stations per LAN. This solution helps maintain performance at an acceptable level. However, dividing all the stations into multiple LANs raises the question

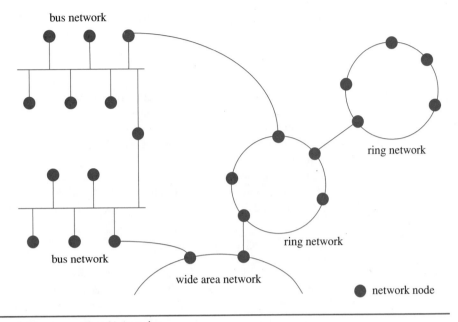

Figure 6.3   Interconnecting Networks

of which stations are assigned to which LANs. A corollary to Murphy's law states that no matter how you group them, two stations on two different LANs will need to communicate. Consequently, we must provide some way for communication across LANs. This invariably leads to connecting networks in a manner similar to that in Figure 6.3. The figure shows two bus and two ring networks. Any two stations on a LAN communicate using the LAN's protocols. In addition, connections between LANs allow cross communications. Locating the proper stations across LANs can be tricky. Section 6.5 discusses methods of connecting LANs and the protocols that allow inter-LAN communication.

After studying various LAN protocols you realize that a lot of software is necessary to make them function. There are two ways to get such software: Write it or buy it. Since most people buy it, we present a case study of one of the more popular network software products, Novell NetWare. We chose this package because it is popular and because books are available for anyone wanting more information.

6.2   ETHERNET: IEEE STANDARD 802.3

Ethernet has a bus topology. Stations contend for the segment using a form of the CSMA/CD contention protocol (Section 3.4). It is commonly used to connect PCs, workstations, printers, file servers, and even mainframes. Part of the Ethernet's history dates back to 1973. In his Ph.D. thesis, Robert Metcalfe described much of his research on LAN technology. After graduation, he joined the Xerox Corporation and worked with a group that eventually implemented what became known as the **Ethernet.** The Ethernet is named after **ether,** the imaginary substance that many once believed occupied all of space and was the medium through which light waves propagated.

Later, the concepts of the Ethernet were written up and proposed to the IEEE as a standard for LANs. The proposal had the backing of Xerox, Intel, and DEC. The IEEE eventually adopted it as a standard, and it is now referred to as **IEEE standard 802.3.** It is worth noting that two other proposals were made to IEEE at about the same time. One was backed by General Motors and the other by IBM. With such influential organizations promoting particular standards, IEEE officials no doubt had difficulties deciding which of the three was most appropriate for a LAN standard. They compromised and made all three LAN standards. The other two standards, 802.5 and 802.4, are the subjects of the next two sections.

RELATION TO OSI

To fully understand the IEEE 802.3 standard (and other LAN standards as well), it is important to understand where it fits in a layered design and how it relates to other topics we have discussed thus far. Recall from Section 1.4 the seven-layer OSI reference model. Network operations typically are defined by the lowest three layers: the physical, data link, and network layers. The data link layer performs services for the network layer and assumes the existence of the physical layer. Specifically, the data link layer is responsible for accurate communication between two nodes in a network. This involves frame formats, error checking, and flow control, all of which we have discussed so far. In general, however, these topics are independent of the network topology. For example, error-checking algorithms do not care whether a frame was sent via bus or ring.

As a result, the data link layer is further divided into two sublayers, the **logical link control (LLC)** and the **medium access control (MAC)** (Figure 6.4). LLC handles logical links between the stations, whereas MAC controls access to the transmission medium. The LLC is also a standard (IEEE 802.2) and is based on the HDLC protocol discussed in Section 5.5. Primarily, the LLC provides service to the network layer and calls on the MAC for specific tasks.

The IEEE 802.3 standard is a MAC protocol. You will see that the token ring and token bus standards discussed in the next two sections are also MAC protocols. Again, we see how the layering of software allows different lower-level protocols with the same higher-level ones. Many of the topics we have discussed are independent of the network topology, which gives them a great deal of flexibility and marketability.

ETHERNET COMPONENTS

Although Ethernet is classified as a bus topology, there are actually several ways to connect devices. Figure 6.5 shows a possible connection between a PC and an

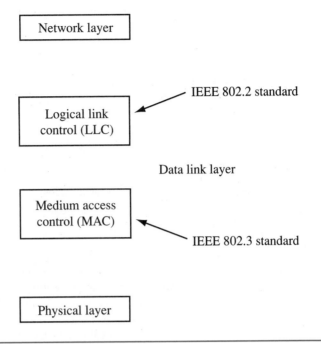

Figure 6.4   Data Link Layer Refinement

Ethernet segment (cable).[*] Although we use the example of a PC you should remember that other devices also can be connected to the cable. Electronic terminators are placed at both ends of the cable. They prevent electronic echoing of signals back and forth through the cable, which creates false signals and causes confusion. It's a little like calling a radio talk show and listening to yourself as you talk. Your voice is usually delayed in order to avoid broadcasting nasty words. Thus, speaking and hearing your delayed words can be disorienting.

A PC can connect to the cable, but it requires some hardware. First, a **transceiver** clamps onto the cable using a vampire clamp, a device with a pin that pierces the outer covering of the cable and makes contact with the cable's core. The transceiver's primary function is to create an interface between the PC and the cable. One of its functions is to transmit bits onto the cable using CSMA/CD contention, which allows it to determine when there is information moving along the cable and to detect collisions when they occur. The transceiver communicates with the PC using a **transceiver cable.** Some call it an **Attachment Unit Interface (AUI) cable.** The cable consists of five twisted pairs. Two are used to send data and control information to the PC. Two more are used for receiving data and control information. The

---

[*]This is representative of a *thick Ethernet*, more formally known as a 10Base5 cable. We'll discuss this and other cable specifications shortly.

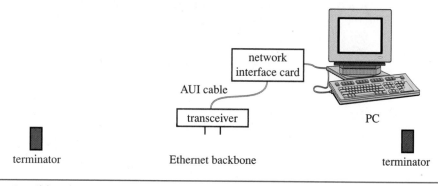

Figure 6.5   Possible Ethernet Connection

fifth pair can be used to connect to a power source and ground. A transceiver can communicate with several devices using a multiplexer.

The transceiver cable connects to the PC through a **network interface card (NIC)** installed in the PC. The NIC contains the logic necessary to buffer data and move it between the transceiver cable and the PC's memory. It also does error checking, creates frames, determines when to retransmit after collisions occur, and recognizes frames destined for its PC. In short, it performs those functions appropriate for the MAC layer protocol. It also relieves the PC's processor from these tasks and allows it to attend to typical PC activities.

To put things in perspective, let's describe and sequence the activities required for a PC to send data to another PC. The steps are as follows:

1. The sending PC executes network software that puts a packet of information in the PC's memory. It then signals the NIC via its internal bus that a packet is waiting to be sent.

2. The NIC gets the packet and creates the correct frame format, storing the packet in the frame's data field. It then waits for a signal from the transceiver, which is monitoring the segment waiting for a chance to send.

3. When the transceiver detects a quiet cable it signals the NIC, which then sends the frame to the transceiver. The transceiver transmits the bits onto the cable, listening for any collisions. If none occur, it assumes the transmission was successful. If a collision does occur, the transceiver notifies the NIC. The NIC executes the binary exponential backoff algorithm of Section 3.4 to determine when it should try again. If collisions continue to occur it will signal the network software, which will provide the user with an error message or execute some algorithm in response to the error.

4. The transceiver at the receiving end monitors cable traffic. It copies frames from the cable and routes them to the NIC at that end.

5. The NIC then does a CRC error check. If there is no error, the NIC checks the destination address in the frame. If it is destined for its PC, the NIC buffers the frame's data (packet) in memory and generates an interrupt, thus informing the PC that a packet has arrived.

6. The PC executes network software and determines whether the packet can be accepted according to the flow control algorithms discussed in Chapter 5. If it can, the PC gets the packet from memory for further processing. If not, the network software responds according to the protocols at the next higher layer.

CABLE SPECIFICATIONS

There are actually several different variations of the Ethernet standard as defined by IEEE 802.3. They differ, for example, by the medium used in a segment, the maximum segment length, the number of stations that can connect to it, and the data rates. Table 6.1 lists some of the specifications. All use Manchester encoding except 10Broad36, which uses differential phase shift keying (recall Section 2.5), and 100BaseF, which uses optical fiber communication.

The original proposal defined the 10Base5 cable, a 50-ohm, 10-millimeter diameter coaxial cable. Some also called it **Thick Wire Ethernet** or just **ThickNet,** a clear reference to the thick unwieldy cable. The thicker 10-mm cable typically ran through basements or under floors, and devices connected to it as described in Figure 6.5. There are some drawbacks to the 10Base5 cable. First, it is relatively expensive. Also, its large diameter does not allow the cable to bend very much.

In order to allow cheaper LANs more suited to PC environments, the 10Base2 cable was added to the standard. The smaller diameter allows the cable to bend more easily, an important feature when trying to route cable around corners and into cabinets. It is also cheaper and has been dubbed **Cheapernet.** It is also called **Thin Wire**

Table 6.1   Cable Types for IEEE 802.3

CABLE TYPE	SEGMENT	MAXIMUM SEGMENT LENGTH (METERS)	DATA RATE (MBPS)
10Base5	50-ohm coaxial cable, 10-mm diameter	500	10
10Base2 (Cheapernet)	50-ohm coaxial cable, 5-mm diameter	200	10
10Broad36	75-ohm coaxial cable	3600	10
1Base5	Unshielded twisted pair	500	1
10BaseT	Unshielded twisted pair	100	10
100BaseF	Multimode optical fiber	2000	100
100BaseT (Fast Ethernet)	Unshielded twisted pair	100	100

Ethernet or **ThinNet.** The additional flexibility allows a different connection than that shown in Figure 6.5. The thinner, more flexible 10Base2 cable can be connected directly to a PC using a T-connector (Figure 6.6). Done this way, all the interfacing electronics and logic can be combined into a NIC installed in the PC. This method also helps reduce the cost of the LAN. A drawback of 10Base2 is that the thinner cable has more electronic resistance and cannot span as long a distance.

Another addition to IEEE 802.3 is the 10Broad36 cable, which uses broadband transmissions rather than the baseband transmissions of 10Base5 and 10Base2. It uses a 75 ohm coaxial cable such as that used with cable television. The 1Base5 and 10BaseT types both use unshielded twisted pair instead of cable. With 1Base5, the data rate is decreased to 1 Mbps between stations up to 500 meters apart. The 10BaseT maintains the 10 Mbps data rate but reduces the maximum distance between stations to 100 meters.

Physically, both 1Base5 and 10BaseT are star topologies (1Base5 is commonly referred to as **StarLAN**), but both behave like a bus topology logically. That is, all the stations are connected to a central hub. A sending station transmits to the hub, which regenerates the signal and broadcasts it to all the stations. Thus, every station sees each transmission, just as in the bus topology. Collisions occur when the hub receives two transmissions simultaneously. Then it broadcasts a special signal alerting the stations that a collision has occurred. The logic in a device behaves no differently than if a shared cable were used.

These configurations have several advantages. First, they are useful in buildings where the physical configuration is not conducive to linear connections. In addition, they allow networks to be implemented using existing wiring, which is often installed when office buildings are built. Finally, the centralized communications control simplifies diagnostics and testing.

The 10BaseT standard has become quite common, but the 10 Mbps data rate is an issue. With so many graphic-oriented user interfaces, CAD systems, and the large data needs of many organizations, there is a need for faster rates. In 1995, IEEE

Figure 6.6   T-Connector

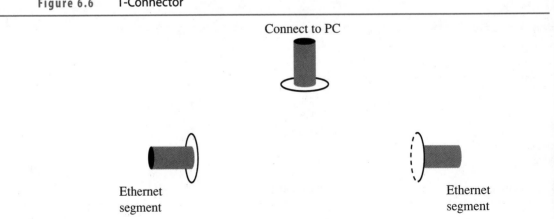

Connect to PC

Ethernet
segment

Ethernet
segment

added 100BaseT to the 802.3 group of protocols.* It is similar to 10BaseT in its use of a central hub and the use of twisted pair wire. However, it supports a 100 Mbps data rate. Consequently, many refer to it as **Fast Ethernet.**

Despite the attraction of 100 Mbps speeds, a Fast Ethernet is not for everyone. First of all, many PCs cannot make use of that speed. That is, they don't have the capacity of producing or receiving bits at that rate. Even if a new NIC were installed, the PC's internal CPU and bus may be too slow to accommodate 100 Mbps. It would be like connecting a garden hose to a fire hydrant. Furthermore, many organizations (probably the majority) use networks mostly for email and relatively simple PC applications such as word processing and spread sheets. On the other hand, file servers connected to heavily used networks can benefit from this speed. CAD (computer-aided design) systems also have a need for large data rates, and their performance can suffer under a relatively slow 10 Mbps rate.

Finally, the 100BaseF "cable" from Table 6.1 is really an optical fiber. It boasts the same 100 Mbps data rate as the Fast Ethernet but offers the noise immunity typical of optical fiber. It also has much longer segments, making it useful in places where network devices are spread out, perhaps in different buildings dispersed over a large plot of land.

When the first edition of this text was written, 10 Mbps Ethernets were the norm and we reported that work toward 100 Mbps Ethernets was in progress. Now that 100 Mbps Ethernets are gaining popularity, what's next? The next step seems to be development of gigabit-rate Ethernets. Gigabit LANs are getting industry support, and IEEE working groups have produced spec documents describing Gigabit LANs. However, whereas Fast Ethernet was to some extent a faster version of 10BaseT, Gigabit Ethernets require different technology. Some question whether twisted pair will support such a high rate and indicate that optical fiber is the likely choice. Some have also raised questions about the quality of service that it provides. Others point out that any new technology will go through growing pains and that time is needed to sort through some of the difficulties. For a discussion on Gigabit Ethernets and some of the concerns, you can consult References [Ro97] and [Lo97].

The previous discussion articulates some of the fundamental differences among the versions of IEEE 802.3. There are more, but the level of detail is beyond this book's goals. If you would like to see some more detail on some of the variations we have discussed, References [St90] and [Jo96] provide it.

CONNECTING SEGMENTS

Each 802.3 variation has a maximum segment length, which is necessary because signals degrade as they propagate along the segment. But what can you do if, for example, the total distance spanned by a 10Base5 cable exceeds 500 meters?

---

*Perhaps more accurately, the result of the 100 Mbps network proposal was called 802.3u and is an addendum to the 802.3 standard.

The 802.3 committee considered this problem and solved it by allowing multiple segments to be connected. Figure 6.7 shows one way to do this. The 500-meter limit is seen as the maximum distance over which an unamplified signal can still be recognized. However, many sites use multiple segments connected by a **repeater,** a device that receives a signal, regenerates it, and retransmits it. The regeneration allows the signals to travel longer distances. In general, the 802.3 standard allows two computers to be separated by no more than four repeaters.[*]

Increasing distance is not the only reason to connect multiple segments. In a system of many stations with varied needs, a good design may be to isolate the stations with similar needs and allow them to communicate over a single segment. This design reduces traffic on each segment and increases efficiency. In another scenario, security may demand that some stations be isolated from others on a separate segment. Such designs, however, introduce problems not solved by connecting the segments with a repeater. Section 6.5 discusses some of these problems in more detail and some solutions to those problems.

FRAME FORMAT

Figure 6.8 shows the Ethernet frame format. As with previous frame formats, there are no surprises. It contains the usual information:

- **Preamble.** A seven-octet[†] pattern consisting of alternating 0s and 1s is used for synchronization. Recall that synchronization establishes the rate at which bits are sampled. It's similar to the late Lawrence Welk's preamble of "uh-one-an-uh-two" to establish the timing and synchronize his orchestra.

Figure 6.7   Connecting Two Segments

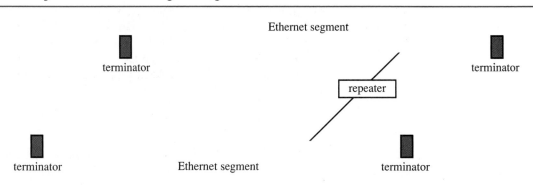

---

[*]In general, there may be many segments in a network. The four-repeater constraint applies only to the path between two computers.

[†]An *octet* is really a byte, but since the LLC is a bit-oriented protocol, we can't call eight bits a byte. Instead we call them an octet.

number of octets

7	1	2 or 6	2 or 6	2	46–1500	4
Preamble	Start of frame delimiter	Destination address	Source address	Data field length	Data ¦ Pad	Frame check sequence

Figure 6.8 Ethernet Frame Format

- **Start of frame delimiter.** The special pattern 10101011 indicates the start of a frame.
- **Destination address.** If the first bit is 0, this field specifies a specific station. If it is 1, the destination address is a group address and the frame is sent to all stations in some predefined group specified by the address. Each station's interface knows its group address and responds when it sees it. If all bits are 1, the frame is broadcast to all stations.
- **Source address.** Specifies where the frame comes from.
- **Data length field.** Specifies the number of octets in the combined data and pad fields.
- **Data field.** Self-explanatory.
- **Pad field.** The data field must be at least 46 octets (more about this shortly). If there is not enough data, extra octets are added (padded) to the data to make up the difference.
- **Frame check sequence.** Error checking using 32-bit CRC.

From Figure 6.8, we see an upper and lower limit (from 46 to 1500) on the number of data and pad octets. The upper limit is used to prevent one transmission from monopolizing the medium for too long. The lower limit is to make sure the collision techniques work properly. In Section 3.4 we stated that frame sizes must be a minimum length so a sending station can detect a collision before sending the frame's last bit. The length is determined by the distance a frame travels, a bit's propagation speed, the data rate, and the delays caused by any repeaters. Considering all these factors, the 802.3 standard defines a minimum frame length as 512 bits (64 octets). If all the fields (except the pad) in Figure 6.8 have the smallest number of octets possible, the total comes to 18 octets. The 46 pad octets then make up the difference.

EFFICIENCY

We now address one measure of the efficiency of the 802.3 standard. As we have stated previously in this text, there are many ways to define efficiency, and we leave more extensive treatments of the topic to References [Ll96], [Wa91], [Be92], and [Wa96]. The measure we address here defines the average amount of time to make a successful transmission. It should depend on several factors such as the data rate, cable length (including repeaters), frame size, and the number of stations. We will see that this is indeed true.

We begin by dividing time into slots of T units each (there was a similar division in Section 3.4). Typically, T is the maximum amount of time needed to detect a collision and is also the maximum round-trip propagation time between the two farthest points on the network. Figure 6.9 helps show why they are the same. Suppose that station A sends a frame. The frame takes $0.5T$ to reach the farthest point (station B). Suppose that just prior to the frame's arrival, B sends. Remember, the frame has not yet reached B, so B still detects an idle medium. Thus, a collision occurs at approximately $0.5T$ after the frame was sent. The collision's noise must propagate back to A before A can detect it, which requires another $0.5T$, for a total time equal to T.

What are the chances a station will send a frame successfully during a time slot? It depends on two things: the total number of stations and the probability of a given station sending during the slot. Suppose N is the total number of stations, each of which sends with probability p_s ($0 \leq p_s \leq 1$) during slot time T. Equivalently, the probability that a station does not send during T is $1 - p_s$.

The probability (P) of a frame being sent without collision during a slot time is the probability that one station sends (p_s) times the probability that all others do not [$(1 - p_s)^{N-1}$] multiplied by N (because any of the N stations could be the one that sends). We therefore write

$$P = N \times p_s \times (1 - p_s)^{N-1}$$

Equivalently, $1 - P$ is the probability that a frame is not sent successfully, due either to a collision or to the fact that no one sent anything.

We would like to know under what conditions the largest number of frames are sent successfully. They can be found by finding the largest value for P. Calculus

Figure 6.9   Maximum Time to Detect a Collision

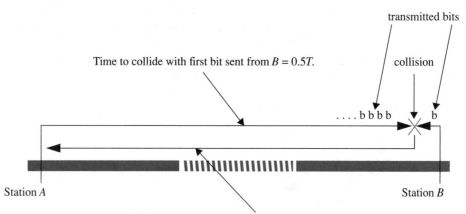

transmitted bits

Time to collide with first bit sent from $B = 0.5T$.

collision

.... b b b b   b

Station A

Time for collision noise to propagate back to $A = 0.5T$.

Station B

techniques allow us to maximize P by taking its derivative, equating to 0, and solving for p_s. We leave the details to those who know calculus, but doing so yields

$$p_s = \frac{1}{N} \quad \text{and} \quad P = \left(1 - \frac{1}{N}\right)^{N-1}$$

This result is of more theoretical than practical[*] interest because a station generally does not know how many others there are and therefore cannot adjust its probability of sending to achieve the maximum. We will, however, use this definition of P in later calculations.

The next question we pose is, How many time slots pass before a frame is sent successfully? We call this the **contention period** (C) and express it as a weighted average or a sum of terms, each of which is the product of the number of slots a station waits (say, i) times the probability of waiting that many slots. Mathematically, we write this as

$$C = \sum_{i=0}^{\infty} (i \times \text{probability of waiting } i \text{ slots})$$

Because the probability that a frame is not sent successfully during one time slot is $(1 - P)$, the probability of no successful transmissions for i slots is $(1 - P)^i$. In addition, the probability of waiting i slots followed by a successful transmission is $(1 - P)^i \times P$. Therefore, we write

$$C = \sum_{i=0}^{\infty} i \times ((1 - P)^i \times P)$$

Evaluating infinite sums is not something we care to do often but, as before, calculus comes to the rescue and allows this equation to be simplified as

$$C = \frac{1 - P}{P} = \frac{1}{P} - 1$$

Before we go on, let's stop and reflect: What does this all mean? (No, we haven't changed this into a philosophy text, but a little reflection can benefit computer scientists, too.) First of all, remember that because P is a probability, it lies between 0 and 1. Second, according to this equation, small values (near 0) for P cause a large average contention time, whereas larger values (near 1) make C nearly 0. The ideal would be zero contention, which would mean that each frame is sent successfully during the first time slot. But that is not realistic. We already have stated that the maximum value for P is $P = (1 - 1/N)^{N-1}$. Plugging this into the definition of C yields $C = (1 - 1/N)^{1-N} - 1$.

---

[*]One must be careful not to infer, however, that anything theoretical is not practical or useful. Theoretical limits or values often are used as benchmarks against which measures are made to estimate efficiency.

Next, as N gets large, P approaches the number $1/e \approx 1/2.718$ (another calculus tidbit). Consequently, C approaches $e - 1 \approx 1.718$. Thus, the best average contention period as the number of stations gets large is about 1.7 time slots. Furthermore, this occurs only if the probability of a station sending decreases in proportion to the number of existing stations.

In practice, however, p_s will not depend on the number of stations. A station will try to send what it needs regardless of how many other stations there are. If we repeated the previous analysis with p_s defined as a constant, say k, then we would have $P = N \times k \times (1 - k)^{N-1}$. In this case P approaches 0 as N gets large. Consequently, C approaches infinity as N gets large. The result is very long or unending contention with nothing getting through.

As our last step, we define the **percent utilization** (U) as the amount of time spent on transmitting a frame as a percentage of the total time spent on contending and transmitting. Assume the following definitions:

R = transmission rate

F = number of bits in a frame

T = slot time

Since C is the number of contention intervals, then $T \times C$ is the contention time. Also, the time required to transmit a frame is F/R. Therefore, we can define the percent utilization as

$$U = 100 \frac{\dfrac{F}{R}}{\dfrac{F}{R} + T \times C} \tag{6.1}$$

Let's consider an example. Consider an 802.3 LAN (10Base5) with 500 stations connected to five 500-meter segments. The data rate is 10 Mbps, and the slot time (defined by the standard) is 51.2 µsec.[*] If all stations transmit with equal probability, what is the channel utilization using a frame size of 512 bytes?

Pertinent variables have the following values:

$$F = 512 \times 8 = 4096 \text{ bits}$$

$$\frac{F}{R} = \frac{4096 \text{ bits}}{10 \text{ Mbps}} \approx 0.000410 \text{ seconds or } 410 \text{ µsec}$$

$$C = \left(1 - \frac{1}{N}\right)^{1-N} - 1 = \left(1 - \frac{1}{500}\right)^{1-500} - 1 \approx 1.716$$

$$U = 100 \frac{410}{410 + 51.2 \times 1.716} \approx 82\%$$

---

[*] In this case the slot time is larger than it would be for a single 2500-meter segment because the standard includes delays at the repeaters.

What happens if someone tries to exceed the 802.3 limits by adding more stations or increasing the maximum distance between stations? This model provides us with some theoretical limits. Let's consider the case for very large N. The best possible scenario causes C to approach $e - 1 \approx 1.718$. Thus the best possible channel utilization is

$$U = 100 \frac{\dfrac{F}{R}}{\dfrac{F}{R} + T \times 1.718}$$

Simplifying and substituting 51.2 for T and 410 for F/R yields

$$U = 100 \frac{410}{410 + 51.2 \times 1.718} \approx 82\%$$

6.3   TOKEN RING: IEEE STANDARD 802.5

Token ring LAN is defined by the IEEE standard 802.5. Like Ethernet, the token ring is a MAC protocol sitting between the logical link control (LLC) and the physical layer in the OSI model. Data rates for token ring networks are listed as 4 Mbps and 1 Mbps, although IBM token rings can run at 4, 16, or 100 Mbps. Transmission occurs using the differential Manchester coding techniques described in Section 2.4.

Stations on a token ring LAN are connected in a ring using a NIC (Figure 6.10). A station can send directly only to its neighbors, and in most cases only to one neighbor (counterclockwise in Figure 6.10). If a station wants to send to another station on the ring, the frame must go through all the intermediate interfaces. Ring contention is handled through a token (a special frame) that circulates past all the stations. The specifics of claiming tokens and sending frames are involved, and we will discuss them later in this section. For now, we provide a very general and simple description of the process.

When a token arrives at a station one of two things occurs. If a station does not have data to send it routes the token to its neighbor. If a station does have something to send it claims the token, removes it from the ring, and sends a frame in the token's place. The frame then travels along the ring and each station examines its destination address. If the destination address does not match the current station's address, the station routes the frame to its neighbor. If it does match, the destination station copies the frame, sets some status bits in it, and routes the frame to its neighbor. The frame continues along the ring until it eventually arrives at the station that created it. This station removes the frame from the ring, generates a new token, and sends the token back onto the ring.

Two observations can be made almost immediately. The first is that ring contention is more orderly than with an Ethernet. Each station knows when it can send and sends only to its neighbor. An immediate consequence is that there is no wasted bandwidth due to collisions. The second observation is that the failure of one station can cause network failure. Unlike an Ethernet, every station participates in the

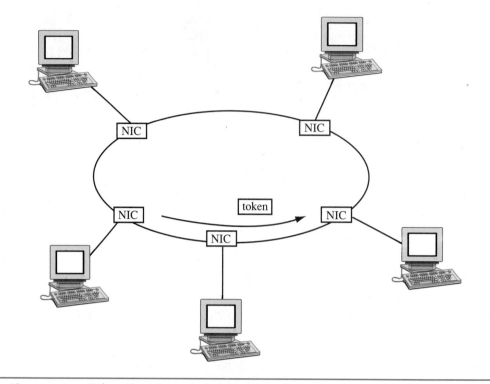

Figure 6.10   Token Ring Network and Circulating Token

routing of tokens or data frames. If a station fails it may not route a received token or data frame, thus causing it to disappear from the ring.

The latter problem can be solved by using the configuration in Figure 6.11. Instead of connecting neighboring stations directly, they all communicate through a wire center. The configuration resembles a star topology physically, but it is still a ring logically. That is, a station still sends only to its neighbor, but the bits travel through the wire center.

The wire center contains a bypass relay for each station that can respond to current or commands from that station. If a station fails or loses power, the relay bypasses that station. For example, if *A* sends to *C,* the frame goes from *A* to the wire center. It then goes to *B,* which routes it back to the center, where it is routed to *C.* If *B* fails, the relay causes the frame received from *A* to bypass *B* and go directly to *C.* The wire center is used mainly to improve reliability while preserving the token ring protocol.

On a token ring network, the notion that the token moves from station to station is generally correct, but it does not occur the way you might think. For example, a station does not receive the entire token before passing it on. To illustrate, suppose a token ring network had the following characteristics:

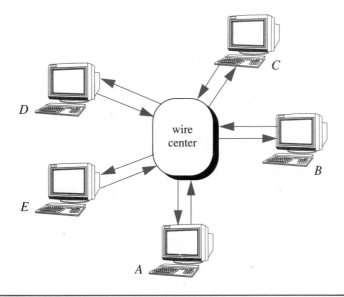

Figure 6.11   Token Ring Network Using Wire Center

- 20 stations, each separated by 10 meters, for a total ring length of 200 meters
- Transmission at 4 Mbps, or one bit every 0.25 μsec
- Propagation speed of 200 m/μsec

According to these characteristics, each bit would travel the ring in 1 μsec. But if the bits are sent at a rate of one every 0.25 μsec, no more than four bits are ever on the ring at any time. This is a problem because if no stations have anything to send, the token won't even fit on the ring, much less circulate around it. In order to get more bits on the ring, there is a delay at each station allowing it to examine each bit before deciding whether to copy it or repeat it. The delay is typically one **bit-time,** the time required for one bit to be transmitted. For a 4 Mbps data rate, the bit-time is 0.25 μsec.

In our example, if each station had a one bit-time delay, 24 bits would fit on the ring. As we will see, a token is 24 bits and the ring would accommodate the token. If the number of stations were reduced, however, fewer bits would fit and the token would be too big. Typically, to make the circulating token independent of the number of stations on the ring, one monitor station will have an extra delay to allow all 24 bits to fit on the ring. This monitor station is discussed further under ring maintenance in this section.

TOKEN AND FRAME FORMATS

We already stated that a token is simply a special frame. Figure 6.12 shows both the token and frame formats. The four fields labeled "destination address," "source

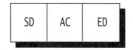

(a) 3-octet token

number of octets

1	1	1	2 or 6	2 or 6	0–5000	4	1	1
SD	AC	FC	Destination address	Source address	....data....	Frame check sequence	ED	FS

(b) Variable-octet frame

```
     SD (starting delimiter):  J K 0 J K 0 0 0
        AC (access control):  p p p t m r r r
                              p p p: priority bits
                                  t: token bit
                                  m: monitor bit
                              r r r: reservation bits
      ED (ending delimiter):  J K 1 J K 1 I E
        FC (frame control):  f f z z z z z z
                              f: frame type bits
                              z: control bits
         FS (frame status):  a c x x a c x x
                              a: address recognized bit
                              c: frame copied bit
                              x: undefined bit
```

Figure 6.12   Token and Frame Formats

address," "data," and "frame check sequence" have the same meanings as those we have discussed in previous sections, so we will not elaborate again. The destination address may be an individual, group, or broadcast address. The data field has no theoretical maximum length, but there is a limit on how long a station can transmit uninterrupted, which puts a practical limit of about 5000 data octets.

Each frame has a **starting delimiter (SD)** and **ending delimiter (ED)** that designate a token's boundaries. SD has the special signal pattern JK0JK000. The 0s are binary 0s as defined by the differential Manchester code. The symbols J and K correspond to special signals. To understand what they are, recall that the differential Manchester code defines a signal transition (high to low or low to high) in the middle of each signal interval. The J and K signals violate that rule. The J signal starts out like a 0 but there is no transition in the middle. Similarly, the K signal starts out like a 1 and has no transition. Sometimes these signals are referred to as **non-data-J** and **non-data-K.** Because these signals do not conform to the

Manchester code for defining bits, they can never appear as part of any information. This makes them useful for indicating special conditions such as the start or end of a frame.

The ending delimiter has the signal pattern JK1JK1IE. The symbols J and K are the same as in the SD. The 1s are binary 1s. The two remaining bits correspond to an intermediate frame bit (I) and an error bit (E). As before, a communication between two stations may consist of many frames. Bit I is 0 in the last frame and 1 otherwise. Bit e is set to 1 whenever an error (such as a frame check sequence) is detected.

The second octet in each frame is the **access control (AC).** Its bits convey different meanings. The bit labeled t stands for **token bit** and determines the frame type. A token has $t = 0$ and a data frame has $t = 1$, thus allowing a station to determine what it is receiving. The remaining bits deal with ring maintenance and token reservation, discussed later. The third frame octet is the **frame control (FC),** which also deals with ring maintenance.

The last octet is the **frame status (FS)** and has two copies (in case of errors) each of an **address recognized bit** (bit a) and a **frame copied bit** (bit c). The sending station initially sets bits a and c to 0. If the destination station is on the ring it sets a to 1, indicating that the address has been recognized. If the destination station copies the frame it also sets bit c to 1. Note that the presence of the destination does not automatically mean the frame is copied. Status set at a higher layer (such as LLC) may temporarily prohibit receiving any frames. We have discussed such possibilities in the sections on sliding window protocols.

The frame status field tells the sending station whether the destination station is on the ring and, if it is, whether it copied the frame. If the destination station is there but did not copy the frame, the sending station presumably can try to resend the frame later.

RESERVING AND CLAIMING TOKENS

The process of capturing tokens and sending data frames at first glance seems relatively simple. Once a station sends a frame and subsequently drains it from the ring, it creates and sends the token to its neighbor, who has the first opportunity to claim the token. Proceeding in this way allows the stations to transmit in the order in which they are connected. This process also puts an upper limit on the length of time a station must wait for a token.* But can we override this order? Are there ways to give a station a higher priority and thus allow it to send ahead of others? This certainly would be useful in cases where the token ring services high-priority or real-time devices.

To prioritize and allow stations to capture tokens in a different order, we assume that every station as well as the circulating token has a priority. The station's priority is defined locally, and the token's priority is defined by the three **priority bits** in the

---

*This statement assumes there is a limit on the length of time that a station may possess the token. In fact, a token-holding timer, with a default of 10 msec, specifies how long a station can control a token.

AC field. A station can claim a token only if its priority is greater than or equal to the token's priority. This forces lower-priority stations to pass available tokens, even if the station has something to send. Only stations with priority higher than or equal to the token's priority can claim the token.

This system raises important questions: Who defines the token's priority? How is it done? Initially, one of the stations sends a token with priority 0. Afterward, the answer lies in the system's **reservation system,** the protocol used to reserve tokens and define priorities.

Suppose a station receives a token with a higher priority than its own priority (we'll see how this can happen shortly) or receives a data frame. Either way, the station cannot send. However, the station may be able to put in a request (reservation) for the token for the next time it arrives. To do this, a station examines the incoming **reservation bits.** If the value stored there is smaller than the station's priority, it stores its own priority there, thus making the reservation. If the value is larger, the station can make no reservation at this time. Presumably some other station with a higher priority, but still lower than the token's priority, already made a reservation and it cannot be preempted by a lower-priority station. (Indeed, try booking your favorite suite at a five-star hotel when the English Prime Minister has already reserved that floor of the hotel.)

When a station drains a frame and creates a new token, it examines the reservation bits of the incoming frame. If it sees that some station has made a reservation, it defines the new token's priority as the reservation value. It then stores both the old priority and the new one (which is now the current priority) locally on a stack. Afterward, it is designated as a **stacking station**—only it can restore the token to its original priority. Thus, when this token begins to travel the ring, it is claimed by the first station with a higher or equal priority. Lower-priority stations are ignored in favor of the higher-priority ones.

Figure 6.13 shows a pseudocoded algorithm that describes the priority and reservation system. Each station executes it as frames and tokens arrive. The algorithm is simplified somewhat, as it does not show the receipt of frames destined for a station or deal with a station sending multiple frames. We intend the figure to focus only on making reservations and determining priorities, but it may be expanded as an exercise.

The algorithm refers to a frame's reservation bits and priority bits as frame.res and frame.priority, respectively. Similar notation is used for a token's bits. Like previous algorithms it is event driven, where the event is the arrival of a frame or token. If a frame arrives, the station determines whether the frame originated there (condition 1) or elsewhere (condition 4). If it originated elsewhere and the current station has a frame to send, it tries to make a reservation. If the station's priority is larger than the contents of frame.res (condition 5), it makes the reservation. If not, it makes no reservation. Either way, it passes the frame to its neighbor.

If the frame originated at the current station it must drain the frame and create a new token. The question that the station must now answer is, What priority should the new token have? There are two possible answers.

```
     while (Peter Pan lives in the Never Land)
     {
        wait for an event;
        if (event is "frame arrives")
        {
1          if (frame originated at current station)
           {
              drain frame;
2             if (frame.res > frame.priority)
              {
                 create and send token with token.priority = frame.res and token.res = 0;
                 put old and new priorities on stack and designate this station as a stacking station;
                 continue;
              } /* end - frame.res > frame.priority */
3             if (current station is stacking station for this frame)
              {
                 create and send token with token.priority = max(token.res, old priority on stack);
                 if token.res is used replace the current priority at the top of the stack with it;
                 if the old priority from the stack is used, pop the old and current priorities from the stack
                    and discontinue the stacking station designation if that stack is empty;
                 continue;
              } /* end - current station is stacking station for this frame */
              create and send token with token.res = frame.res and token.priority = frame.priority;
           } /* end - frame originated at current station */
4          if (frame originated elsewhere)
           {
5             if (there is a frame to send) && (station priority > frame.res) store sending priority
                 in frame.res ;
              send frame;
           }
        } /* end - event is "frame arrives" */
        if (event is "token arrives")
        {
6          if (current station is stacking station for this token)
           {
              create token with token.priority = max(token.res, old priority on stack);
              if token.res is used replace the current priority at the top of the stack with it;
              if the old priority from the stack is used, pop the old and current priorities from the stack
                 and discontinue the stacking station designation if that stack is empty;
           }
7          if (there is a frame to send)
           {
```

Figure 6.13   Token Ring Protocol to Reserve and Claim a Token *(continues on next page)*

```
8               if (station priority >= token.priority)
                    claim token, create, and send frame;
                else
9                   if (station priority > token.res)
                        store sending priority in token.res;
            } /* end - frame to send */
            send frame or token;
        } /* end - event is "token arrives" */
    } /* end of while loop */
```

Figure 6.13   *(continued)*

First, suppose some station with a higher priority than the frame's priority has made a reservation (condition 2). The station gives the token a priority equal to that of the station making the reservation (contents of `frame.res`). It also defines `token.res = 0` to give any station a chance to make another reservation. But raising the token's priority is an awesome responsibility. Any station that does this also has the responsibility of lowering it later when the only stations with something to send have a priority lower than the token's priority. At that point the station must recognize a token whose priority it raised and lower it. To achieve this, the station (designated as a stacking station) stores the old and new (now current) priorities on a stack whenever it raises the priority.

The second answer occurs when the reservation on the incoming frame was made by a station with a lower priority than the frame's priority. This means that as the frame travels the ring, no station that wants to send has a high enough priority to do so. Consequently, the new token's priority must be lowered, but which station has the authority to do so? If the current station did not raise the priority it cannot lower it. Thus, it simply creates a token with the same priority and reservation value as the incoming frame's (last statement under condition 1). Presumably the token will reach the stacking station, which will lower the priority.

However, if the current station is the stacking station[*] (condition 3), it creates a new token with a lower priority. Next question: What is the new priority? The stacking station compares the incoming reservation value with its old stacked priority and chooses the larger value. If the reservation value is larger, it replaces the current priority on the stack. The station is still the stacking station because it has not restored the priority that existed prior to its becoming the stacking station. If the reservation value is not larger, the token gets the old stacked priority. The old and current priorities are popped from the stack and, if the stack is empty, the station is

---

[*]There may actually be several stacking stations because a token's priority can be raised by more than one station. What we really need here is the station that became a stacking station most recently. The station can determine this by comparing the frame's priority field with the current priority on the station's local stack. If they are the same, the current station can lower the token's priority. If not, then another station raised the priority and must subsequently lower it.

no longer a stacking station. Note that the stacking station designation is removed only when the stack is empty, as the station could be a stacking station from a previous priority increase.

Now consider what happens when a token arrives. If the station is a stacking station (condition 6) it proceeds as we have just discussed. Afterward, it determines whether there is a frame to send (condition 7). If so, it compares the token's priority with the station's priority (condition 8). If the station has a high enough priority it claims the token. If not, it compares its priority with the value specified by the reservation bits (condition 9). Again, if it has a high enough priority it makes the reservation. Finally, it sends either the token or the frame (if it created one) to its neighbor.

This discussion is general and describes the major aspects of the priority and reservation system. Now it is time to see an example. Suppose four stations are ready to transmit (Figure 6.14) and that each has just one frame to send. Suppose also that station C has just captured the token and is sending its frame. We now apply the algorithm to the situation of Figure 6.14.

To help follow the algorithm, Table 6.2 summarizes what happens at each station as a frame or token travels the ring. The first column lists the steps. The second column indicates the station receiving the frame or token. The third column lists the conditions from Figure 6.13 that are true when the frame or token arrives. The fourth column specifies whether it sends a frame or token. The last two columns specify the priority and reservation values (values 0 through 7) of the outgoing frame or token. We begin the discussion at the point where station C has just captured a token and sent its frame.

We pick up the algorithm after C sends the frame, so the first line in Table 6.2 corresponds to the arrival of a frame at D (step 1). In this case, conditions 4 and 5 are true. That is, the frame did not originate at D, D has a frame to send, and its priority is higher than that of the incoming frame. As a result, D stores its priority (2) in

Figure 6.14   Reserving Tokens on a Token Ring

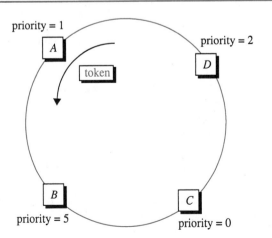

Table 6.2 Activities as Token and Frame Travel the Ring

STEP	ARRIVING AT	CONDITION	STATION SENDS	PRIORITY	RESERVATION
1	D (frame)	4 and 5	Frame	0	2
2	A (frame)	4	Frame	0	2
3	B (frame)	4 and 5	Frame	0	5
4	C (frame)	1 and 2	Token	5	0
5	D (token)	7 and 9	Token	5	2
6	A (token)	7	Token	5	2
7	B (token)	7 and 8	Frame	5	0
8	C (frame)	4	Frame	5	0
9	D (frame)	4 and 5	Frame	5	2
10	A (frame)	4	Frame	5	2
11	B (frame)	1	Token	5	2
12	C (token)	6	Token	2	2
13	D (token)	7 and 8	Frame	2	0
14	A (frame)	4 and 5	Frame	2	1
15	B (frame)	4	Frame	2	1
16	C (frame)	4	Frame	2	1
17	D (frame)	1	Token	2	1

frame.res and passes the frame to its neighbor. When A receives the frame (step 2), only condition 4 is true (A's priority is too low). When B receives the frame (step 3), it reacts as D did previously, increasing frame.res to 5. The frame finally arrives back at C (step 4), the originating station, where it is drained from the ring. Because conditions 1 and 2 are true, C creates and sends a token with priority = 5 and becomes the stacking station. D receives the token (step 5) but cannot capture it because the token's priority is too high. However, it does set the reservation value to 2 and sends the token to A (step 6). A's priority is too low, so it sends the token to B (step 7). Station B claims the token (conditions 7 and 8) and sends a frame.

The frame circulates as before and eventually comes back to B (step 11). B drains the frame and creates a token. Notice now that the token's reservation field contains 2 and the priority is 5. Since B was not the stacking station (C was at step 4), it sends a token with the same priority and reservation values as that in the received frame. When C receives the frame (step 12), it sees condition 6 as true and lowers the token's priority to 2. The old priority is still on the stack and C still remains the stacking station. Although the remaining steps are similar to those that already have occurred, you should go through them. Note that Table 6.2 can be expanded to the point at which all stations have sent their frames and the token's priority is reduced to 0 again. We leave this as an exercise.

RING MAINTENANCE

The discussions so far suffice to describe token ring operations as long as nothing goes wrong. This is a dangerous assumption to make, however. Things can and do go wrong; for example:

- A station sends a short frame over a long ring (where the last bit is sent before the first one has come back) and subsequently crashes. It is not able to drain the frame. A frame that is not drained is an **orphan frame.**

- A station receives a frame or token and crashes before it can send it. Now there is no token circulating and the stations waiting to send wait forever.

- Line noise damages a frame. Which station has the responsibility of fixing it?

Some problems can be handled by giving one of the stations a few additional responsibilities and designating it a **monitor station.** For example, to detect an orphan frame a station initially creates a frame with the monitor bit in the access control octet (Figure 6.12) set to 0. When the monitor receives a frame, it sets the bit to 1. An orphaned frame is not drained from the ring, causing it to arrive at the monitor a second time with the bit already equal to 1. The monitor drains the frame and generates a new token.

The monitor also can detect a lost token using a built-in timer. The timer is defined depending on the ring's length, number of stations, and maximum frame size. Whenever the monitor sends a frame or token it starts the timer. If the monitor receives no other frame or token before the timer expires it assumes it was lost and generates a new token.

Some problems even the monitor station cannot solve. For example, what if the malfunctioning station is the monitor station? What if a break in the ring causes a lack of tokens? Sending new ones does nothing to correct the problem.

These problems are handled using **control frames,** as shown in Table 6.3. The control bits in the FC octet (Figure 6.12b) define the frame's function. When a new station enters the ring it sends a **duplicate address test frame** that stores its own address in the destination field. This frame ensures that the station's address is

Table 6.3 Token Ring Control Frames

FRAME TYPE	CONTROL BITS IN FC	MEANING
Active monitor present	000101	Informs stations a monitor is operational and initiates the neighbor identification procedure.
Beacon	000010	Locates ring faults.
Claim token	000011	Elects a new monitor.
Duplicate address test	000000	Checks for duplicate addresses.
Purge	000100	Clears the ring.
Standby monitor present	000110	Carries out the neighbor identification procedure.

unique among those in the ring. When the frame returns, the station checks the address-recognized bit in the frame's status field. If it is 0 there is no other station with that address; if it is 1 the station's address is a duplicate. The station removes itself from the ring and reports the error.

If a new monitor station must be chosen, one or more stations submit bids to become the monitor station. The one with the highest address gets the job. The problem is that none of the stations knows which one that is. To determine this, each one sends a succession of **claim token (CT) frames.** When a station receives a claim token frame it compares the token's source address with its own. If the token's source address is larger the station stops sending its own frames and repeats the ones it receives. If the token's source address is smaller the station drains it from the ring and continues to send its own frames. Consequently, a CT frame never makes it past another competing station with a higher address and the only CT frames to circumnavigate the ring come from the station with the highest address. When this station receives its own CT frame it considers itself duly elected as monitor station—after a very short campaign and without the help of PAC contributions.

When a station is elected monitor and periodically thereafter, it sends an **active monitor present (AMP) frame** to notify the other stations that there is an active monitor station. If for some reason the monitor malfunctions, no AMP frames are sent. The other stations have timers that expire when they do not detect an AMP frame over a period of time. When this happens they make bids to become the new monitor by sending a CT frame, as discussed previously.

Before a monitor station creates and sends a new token it first sends a **purge frame.** Meanwhile it drains everything it receives, including the returning purge frame, to make sure the ring is clear before sending a new token or AMP frame.

The **standby monitor present (SMP) frame** is part of the neighbor identification procedure. When the monitor sends the AMP frame it sets the *a* bits in the status field equal to 0. The first station receiving it (downstream neighbor) records the source address and sets the *a* bits in the status field to 1 before repeating the frame. That station now knows its immediate upstream neighbor. The *a* bits are set to 1 to inform the other stations in the ring that the arriving frame is not from their immediate neighbor. After receiving the AMP frame from its upstream neighbor, the station sends an SMP frame (also with the *a* bits equal to 0). Its downstream neighbor receives the frame, records the source address, sets the *a* bits to 1, and repeats it. After a while it sends its own SMP frame and its downstream neighbor reacts similarly. This cascading effect causes each station to send its own SMP frame to inform its downstream neighbor of its identity. Because the *a* bits are set by the first station receiving each SMP frame, each station can distinguish a frame that its upstream neighbor originated and a frame that the upstream neighbor repeated.

A **beacon frame** is used to inform stations that a problem has occurred and the token-passing protocol has stopped. Previously we stated that each station has a timer to detect an absence of AMP frames. When this happens, the station does not know whether the monitor malfunctioned or whether there was a break in the ring. In the latter case, sending a CT frame serves no purpose. Consequently, a station detecting a problem sends a continuous stream of beacon frames containing the address of its upstream neighbor. If they return, the station assumes there is no break (or it has been corrected) and begins sending CT frames as before. If the beacons do not return in a specified amount of time, the station concludes there is a break somewhere and reports the error to a higher layer in the protocol. If the station receives beacons from another station, it suspends sending its own and repeats the ones it receives. Eventually, if there is a break, the only station sending beacon frames (Figure 6.15) is the one downstream from the break.

One last function of the monitor is to make sure the token fits on the ring. Previously we discussed the fact that the number of bits that fit on the ring depends on the ring's length and the delays at each station. If both parameters are small, the number of bits that will fit is small. This is not a problem when a frame is being sent because a station can be sending a frame's bits at the same time it is receiving previously sent ones. A circulating token, however, is not drained until it is claimed and it must fit on the ring. The monitor inserts extra delays to allow a full token to occupy the ring and circulate.

EFFICIENCY

The discussion on token ring efficiency is mercifully short compared with similar discussions of other protocols. This is because there are no collisions to waste bandwidth and complicate the efficiency. The CSMA/CD contention suffers badly under heavy loads, but token rings achieve very high rates of efficiency. For example, suppose we consider the percent utilization, defined in Section 6.2. Recall that it is the amount of time spent on an actual successful transmission as a percentage of the

Figure 6.15   Locating a Ring Break

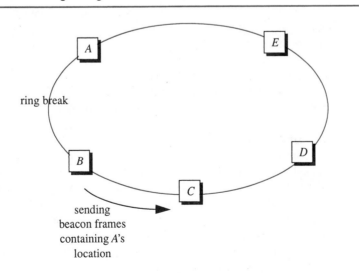

total time spent on contending and sending. Here *contending* means waiting for a free token. To illustrate, assume the worst case of maximum traffic. That is, each station has something to send each time a token arrives. The percent utilization is

$$U = 100 \times \frac{\text{time to send a frame}}{\text{time to send a frame} + \text{time to send a token}}$$

Tokens, however, typically are much smaller than frames and travel much smaller distances (the distance between two stations as opposed to the ring's circumference). This means the time to send a token is very small compared with the time to send a frame. Thus the percent utilization is close to 100%.

This short discussion does not mean there is no basis for further analysis. Indeed there is, but it is not within the scope of this text. If you are interested, References [Wa91] and [St94] provide more analysis of the token ring.

OTHER RING NETWORKS

Fiber Distributed Data Interface   The 802.5 token ring networks are not the only ring networks that solve contention using token passing. Another standard is the **Fiber Distributed Data Interface (FDDI)** developed by ANSI and also classified as an ISO standard (ISO 9314). FDDI is not really a local area network since it was designed to span distances of up to 200 kilometers with a 100 Mbps data rate. FDDI was developed at a time when most local area networks produced data rates of 10 Mbps or less. With its 100 Mbps data rate, some predicted that FDDI would obviate the need for then current LAN designs. However, as mentioned in previous sections, LAN standards have evolved to the 100 Mbps data rate range and provided competition for FDDI. Furthermore, FDDI hardware tended to be more expensive, making Fast Ethernets and 100 Mbps token rings more attractive to many. FDDI, however, did find a niche in the market as a backbone used to connect multiple LANs using devices called **bridges.** Connecting LANs with bridges is something we discuss later in this chapter.

Someone not familiar with the differences among protocols might call it a token ring over fiber. That classification is not entirely correct, although there are many similarities between FDDI and the token ring we have described. For example, both connect stations in a logical ring and both rely on a circulating token to determine which one can send. Both also use token-holding timers to specify how long a station can control a token

Unlike 802.5 token ring networks, FDDI uses a multimode or single-mode optical fiber. Multimode is more common because the standard calls for a data rate of 100 Mbps and multimode fiber can achieve that rate more economically. FDDI standards allow a 200-kilometer ring connecting up to 1000 stations. FDDI also connects stations using two rings instead of one. The second ring can be used to send tokens and frames in parallel with the first one (Figure 6.16a). Another advantage of two rings is that in case of a ring break the rings can be joined to create a single logical ring (Figure 6.16b).

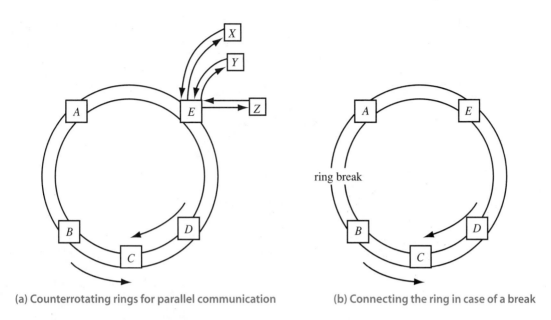

(a) Counterrotating rings for parallel communication   (b) Connecting the ring in case of a break

Figure 6.16   Counterrotating Rings

Two types of stations are the **single-attachment station (SAS)** and **double-attachment station (DAS).** An SAS connects only to one ring and a DAS connects to both. Single-attachment stations are typically workstations, whereas double-attachment stations may correspond to interconnecting units. For example, in Figure 6.16a, station E is a DAS, connected to both the outer and inner rings. However, there are several other stations, X, Y, and Z, each connected to E using only the outer ring. A token going through the inner ring would pass through E and skip X, Y, and Z. A token going through the outer ring would pass through the stations in the order E-Z-E-Y-E-X. The inner ring connects fewer stations and should provide better efficiency. The outer ring can service more devices. It's a little like express lanes along a major urban highway. They are designed to let traffic flow more efficiently because there are fewer access points. Another advantage of this is, for example, if Y should fail, station E can bypass it, thus allowing a token to travel from X through E to Z.

Another difference between token ring and FDDI is how a signal is transmitted. Recall that the token ring uses differential Manchester transmission signals. Its advantage is that it is self-synchronizing. The transition in the middle of each interval, however, means the baud rate must be twice the bit rate. For FDDI this would mean that a 200 million baud rate is needed for a 100 Mbps bit rate. Instead of requiring such a high baud rate, the approach is to transmit the bit stream as a sequence of on/off light pulses. The problem is that long strings of 0s or 1s mean long constant signals. As we discussed in Section 2.4, this can cause a loss of synchronization.

To lower the baud rate requirement and to maintain a synchronization ability, FDDI uses a **4 of 5 code** in conjunction with an **NRZI (nonreturn to zero invert)** technique. NRZI is similar to NRZ except that the signal remains constant as long as

0s are being sent but changes each time a 1 is sent. Thus a string of 0s still means a constant signal, but a string of 1s causes the signal to change with each 1.

For every four bits of data, a 4B/5B encoder creates a five-bit code, as shown in Table 6.4. Each set of five bits is then transmitted using NRZI. Using this scheme, a signal will change at most five times for each four data bits. This means that a 100 Mbps bit rate can be achieved using a 125 million baud rate. At the same time, the 4B/5B encoder never codes more than two consecutive binary 0s for data, ensuring that the signal is never constant for long periods. The bottom line is that this method preserves the self-synchronizing ability using a baud rate just 25% higher than the bit rate.

Frame and token formats in FDDI are similar to those of the token ring. In fact, comparing Figures 6.17 and 6.12 shows only two differences. First is that each FDDI frame or token begins with a preamble. It contains 16 or more Idle control signals (80 or more binary 1s). The preamble causes a signal change, with each 1 bit resulting in the signal oscillating at its maximum baud rate. It is used to establish synchronization. The other difference is that the access control (AC) field is eliminated in the frame and is replaced by the frame control (FC) field in the token. Some of the bits in these and other fields are different from their counterparts in the token ring, but those differences are not important to our discussion. If you are interested, Reference [St90] describes the functions of each bit.

One interesting note is that the elimination of the AC field along with its reservation and priority bits suggests a significant change in claiming tokens. When a sta-

Table 6.4   4 of 5 Code Definition

DATA BITS	ENCODED BITS	CONTROL SYMBOLS	ENCODED BITS
0000	11110	Halt	00100
0001	01001	Idle	11111
0010	10100	Non-data-J	11000
0011	10101	Non-data-K	10001
0100	01010	Quiet	00000
0101	01011	Reset	00111
0110	01110	Set	11001
0111	01111	Terminate	01101
1000	10010		
1001	10011		
1010	10110		
1011	10111		
1100	11010		
1101	11011		
1110	11100		
1111	11101		

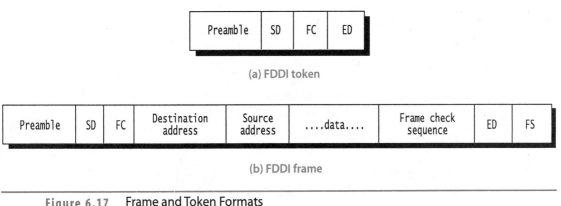

(a) FDDI token

(b) FDDI frame

Figure 6.17   Frame and Token Formats

tion claims a token it inserts a frame onto the ring, as in the token ring. This time, however, instead of draining the token the sending station reinserts it immediately after the frame. This way the token is always on the ring and any station has the opportunity to insert a frame when the token passes by.

Figure 6.18 illustrates in more detail. Suppose stations A, B, and C have frames frA, frB, and frC to send. When the token reaches A (Figure 6.18a), only the token (T) is on the ring. When A gets the token it sends the frame followed by the token (Figure 6.18b). When the frame and token reach B, B repeats the frame, sends its own, and puts the token back onto the ring (Figure 6.18c). After passing station C (Figure 6.18d), the ring contains all three frames followed by the token.

After comparing the token ring with FDDI you might ask, Why doesn't the IEEE standard allow multiple frames in its token ring? There are a couple of ways to answer this. First, for a long time the 4 Mbps data rate with a single token met the

Figure 6.18   FDDI Ring Contents

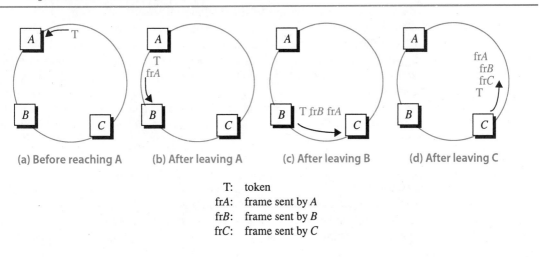

(a) Before reaching A   (b) After leaving A   (c) After leaving B   (d) After leaving C

T: token
frA: frame sent by A
frB: frame sent by B
frC: frame sent by C

users' needs. (It still meets many users' needs; not everyone needs a Cadillac of LANs.) With fiber, however, a single small frame does not make the best use of the increased capacity. For example, sending relatively short frames past 1000 stations over 200 km of fiber means that much of the fiber is idle. It's like building a six-lane highway between two rural communities to be used by occasional tourists and a haywagon. It can be done, but most will agree the cost is not justified—and the haywagon will not reach its destination any faster.

The same is true of fiber. Its increased capacity is best used with a lot of traffic, and single small frames do not constitute heavy traffic. Having larger frames or more of them, however, will increase the traffic. In this case using multiple frames is the choice. Still we return to the question: Can't IEEE change the standard? Technically, yes, but that defeats the purpose of standards. Standards exist to maintain consistency, and changing them regularly creates inconsistency, which is little different from having no standards at all. But that does not mean new standards cannot be defined to meet growing needs.

FDDI-II Despite the speed of FDDI, one feature is that it still delivers information in the form of packets. Since packets vary in size, information tends to arrive at a station at an uneven rate. While this is just fine for many applications, it does not work well for multimedia applications. In order to provide for continuous video and sound, information must arrive at a constant rate. The alternative is gaps in both sound and picture. In response to the growing need for multimedia applications, FDDI-II was developed as an upgrade to FDDI. It is designed to provide a circuit-switching service capability while still maintaining compatibility with FDDI's packet-oriented service.

To accomplish this FDDI-II has two modes of operation. Its basic mode is similar to FDDI, providing information transfer using circulating frames and tokens. Its hybrid mode provides for circuit-switching services. It operates by having a specially designated station issue a framing structure called a **cycle** at regular intervals (once every 125 µsec). This is equivalent to 8000 cycles generated each second. Each cycle contains 16 subdivisions (**channels**), each with 96 bytes. Generating 8000 cycles per second, each with a 96-byte capacity, produces an overall bit rate of 6.144 Mbps for each channel, delivered at a fixed rate and suitable for multimedia applications. While multimedia applications have emerged as an important topic in networks, we will not discuss FDDI-II further and will leave details such as the cycle's format and mode of operation to other references, such as [St93] and [Bo94]. To give multimedia applications their proper due, Chapter 8 discusses Asynchronous Transfer Mode (ATM), a protocol developed largely with multimedia applications in mind.

Slotted Rings A **slotted ring** (also called a **Cambridge ring** because it was developed at the University of Cambridge) consists of several rotating slots. **Slots,** similar to tokens, are specially formatted frames that circulate the ring (Figure 6.19). Unlike a token, however, each slot is similar to an empty frame, having 8 bits of space for a destination and source address, 16 bits for data, and some status bits. If

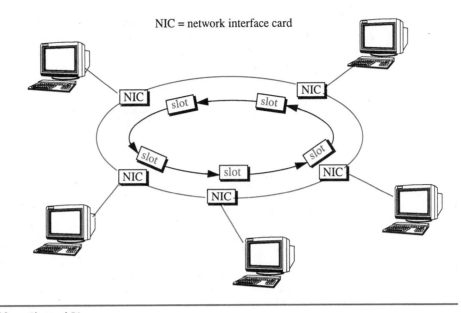

NIC = network interface card

Figure 6.19   Slotted Ring

an empty slot passes a station that has something to send, the station stores the necessary address and as much data as will fit. If a slot is full the station waits for the first empty slot. When the slot returns, the sending station marks the slot as empty by changing one of its status bits. If the station has more data to send it will not use the same slot but will wait for the next empty slot. This forces empty slots onto the ring and prevents one station from monopolizing the slots.

We should note that slotted rings allow many bits to be on the ring simultaneously. Previous discussions showed the number of bits on a ring to be typically small. However, by using longer rings or longer propagation delays at each station, the number of bits on the ring simultaneously can be increased to meet the requirements of multiple slots.

6.4   TOKEN BUS: IEEE STANDARD 802.4

The third and last MAC protocol we discuss is the token bus protocol. It combines features of the Ethernet and the token ring protocols. For example, the token bus operates on the same principle as the token ring. The stations are logically organized into a ring and a token passes among them. A station wanting to send something must wait for the token to arrive. Here, however, the stations communicate via a common bus as in an Ethernet. For example, Figure 6.20 shows five stations, *A* through *E*, connected to a bus. If the logical order is *A-B-C-D-E*, then *A* starts by sending a token to *B* along the bus. As with Ethernet, each station is capable of receiving it, but the token's destination address specifies which station gets it. When

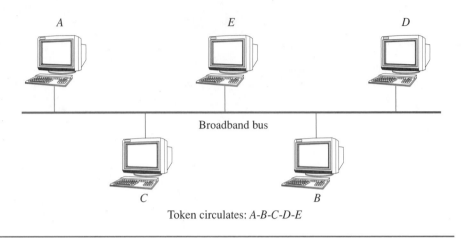

Token circulates: *A-B-C-D-E*

Figure 6.20   Token Bus

B receives the token, it has permission to send a frame. If it has no frame it sends a token to *C*. Similarly, *C* sends either a token to *D* or a data frame, and so on.

Generally, a station receives a token from its predecessor and sends a token to its successor. Another immediate difference between the token bus and token ring is that token bus stations must know their predecessor and successor. They must know their successor so they know which destination address to put in the token. The reasons for knowing their predecessor will be discussed later.

Token bus networks have the most support from those involved in factory automation and process control, applications that require real-time processing. The real-time environments made many people nervous about embracing the 802.3 standard because there was no theoretical limit on the number of collisions that could occur. This meant that there was no theoretical limit on the delays one of the network components could experience. With large objects moving down the assembly line, the possibility of unexpected delays was unacceptable (reminiscent of the old television gag where pies or pieces of candy are rolling down the assembly line faster than the worker can pack them). In addition, the token ring did not satisfy their needs. First, the physical ring is not the best fit for the linear organization of an assembly line. Second, the point-to-point connections made the system susceptible to disaster if one of the links failed. Thus, their solution was to use the linear organization to fit the physical environment but a logical ring order to put an upper limit on the time a station must wait for a token.

There also are some differences between the bus of the IEEE 802.5 and 802.3 physical layers. The token bus specifies signals to be sent over a baseband cable or a broadband cable like that used for cable television. It allows for three different modulation schemes: continuous FSK (baseband), phase coherent FSK (baseband), and multilevel duobinary AM/PSK (broadband). As these are variations on the modulation schemes discussed in Section 2.5, we will not discuss them further. If you are interested in specifics, you can consult References [St90] and [Mo89]. Data rates may be as high as 10 Mbps, depending on the modulation technique.

Figure 6.21 shows the token bus frame format. All the fields in the frame are similar to similarly named fields discussed previously. The only difference is that there is no special token format. The FC field specifies whether the frame contains data, is a token, or is any of several other control frames we will discuss shortly. Remember, since the tokens are sent along a bus the destination and source addresses must be specified.

TOKEN BUS OPERATIONS

The linear physical topology coupled with the logical ring organization adds some complexity to the token bus operations. For example, how is a new station added to the network? With token ring it is added between two others and automatically gets the token from its upstream neighbor. In a token bus a predecessor must be determined and notified of its new successor. Similarly, if a station is removed, its predecessor must be informed so it does not send the deleted station any tokens.

How is the logical order determined? Typically, the stations' addresses determine the order, but how do the stations notify each other where they are? How does each one determine who its predecessor and successor are? What makes these questions difficult is that no one station has a global view of anything. Each knows only what it has and what arrives on incoming frames. With no central control the stations must somehow exchange information and come to some consensus about order. It's a bit like an anarchistic society establishing some order without agreeing to any centralized government.

The answers to these questions lie in the different control frames and the rules for using them. Table 6.5 shows the different token bus control frames, their FC fields, and a brief summary of their use.

Removing Stations   What happens when a station leaves the ring? Suppose the token passes through three stations in the order *A, B,* and *C.* Suppose station *A* has the token and has nothing to send. It creates a new token addressed to *B* and sends it.

Figure 6.21   Token Bus Frame Format

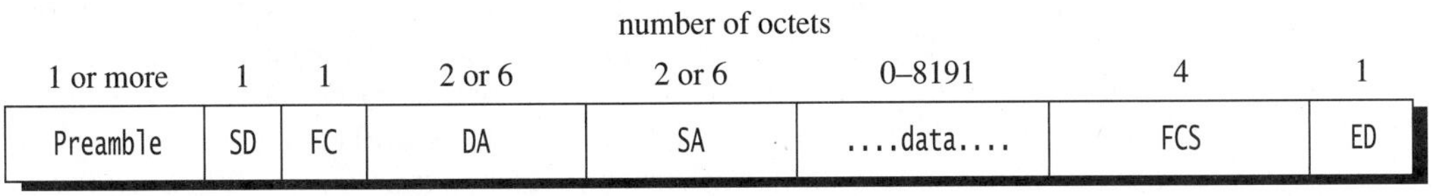

				number of octets			
1 or more	1	1	2 or 6	2 or 6	0–8191	4	1
Preamble	SD	FC	DA	SA	....data....	FCS	ED

SD: Start delimiter
FC: Frame control
DA: Destination address
SA: Source address
FCS: Frame check sequence
ED: End delimiter

Table 6.5   Token Bus Control Frame Types

FRAME TYPE	FC FIELD	FUNCTION
Claim token	00000000	Used in a protocol to establish who gets the token initially or following a recovery.
Resolve contention	00000100	Used in an arbitration protocol when two or more stations attempt to enter the logical ring simultaneously.
Set successor	00001100	Used to define a new successor to a specified station.
Solicit successor 1	00000001	Used in a protocol that invites certain stations to enter the logical ring.
Solicit successor 2	00000010	Same as solicit successor 1 but pertains to different stations.
Token	00001000	The holder of this frame has permission to transmit data.
Who follows	00000011	Used in a protocol to determine a station's successor.

Similarly, if B has nothing to send it sends a token to C. Now suppose B leaves or malfunctions and is no longer in the ring. Either way, the result is the same: A sends a token to B, but since B no longer exists the token effectively disappears. Meanwhile, C and all subsequent stations wait for a token that will not arrive.

To deal with this problem, whenever A sends a token to its successor B, it listens for a response. After B receives the token, it sends a token to its successor or a frame (depending on whether it has data to send) containing B's address. Since the frame or token travels along the bus, A can detect it. Thus, A knows its successor received the token. On the other hand, if A detects no response in a reasonable time it suspects a problem. In the event the problem may be transmission interference, it sends the token again and listens. If it hears the expected response, it concludes the token has been sent successfully.

If it still does not hear a response, it proceeds on the assumption that B is no longer there. The logical thing to do is to send all subsequent tokens to B's successor, but A does not know who it is. To find out, A broadcasts a **who follows frame** specifying B (in the data field) as its current successor. The frame is a request for B's successor to identify itself. Each station is able to examine this frame and determine whether it is B's successor. One station, in this case C, recognizes that it is B's successor and responds by sending a set successor frame to A (whose address was also in the who follows frame). When A receives this frame it redefines its successor as C and sends the token.

This scenario applies when B leaves the ring unexpectedly. If it voluntarily leaves, a different protocol is followed. In this case B waits for the token and then sends a **set successor frame** to *A* specifying *C* as *A*'s new successor. *A* records the information and *B*'s final activity is to send the token to *C*. When the token eventually returns to *A*, *A* sends it to its new successor, *C*.

Adding Stations   Adding new stations is a bit more complex. The insertion protocol does not allow a new station to insert itself into the ring. Rather, a new station must wait for an existing station to invite it into the ring. It's like attending a party at a fashionable country club: Don't try to get in without an invitation. Periodically (i.e., according to timers) each station sends a **solicit successor 1 frame** specifying its own and its successor's addresses and waits a sufficient time for a station to respond. If none respond, the station assumes no one wants to enter and passes the token to its successor. If there is a station with an address between the two specified ones it may now submit a bid to enter the ring. It does so by sending a set successor frame to the station extending the invitation. That station records its new successor and sends its next token there.

For example, Figure 6.22 shows a token bus containing three stations, *A*, *B*, and *C*. Two new stations, *X* and *Y*, want to enter but have not yet done so. That is, they are physically connected but do not participate in the token passing. Assume the addresses are ordered $A > X > B > C > Y$ and that the token must follow that order. At some point *A* sends a solicit successor 1 frame specifying *A*'s and *B*'s addresses. Only *X*'s address is between them, so *X* sends a set successor frame to *A*. *A* recognizes *X* as its new successor and sends all subsequent tokens to *X*.

Since the solicit successor 1 frame is an invitation to stations with an address between two given ones, a new station with an address less than or greater than all others will never respond. The **solicit successor 2 frame** is used for those stations. The station with the smallest address sends it periodically, specifying the current and successor's addresses (the smallest and largest addresses). Any station with an even smaller or larger address responds as before by sending a set successor frame. In the example of Figure 6.22, station *Y* cannot enter the ring until station *C* broadcasts a

Figure 6.22   Adding New Stations to a Token Bus

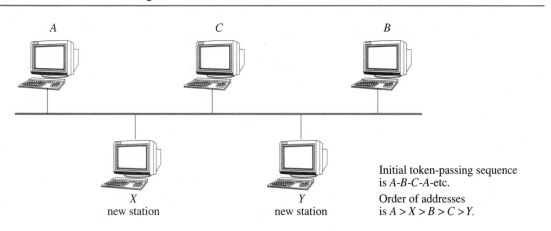

Initial token-passing sequence
is *A-B-C-A*-etc.

Order of addresses
is $A > X > B > C > Y$.

X
new station

Y
new station

solicit successor 2 frame. Then Y sends C its set successor frame and enters the ring as C's successor and A's predecessor.

This approach works well when stations enter one at a time. But what happens if two or more stations respond to a solicit successor frame?[*] For example, if the stations of Figure 6.22 were ordered $A > X > Y > B > C$, then both X and Y would respond to a solicit successor frame from A. When multiple stations respond, their frames collide and the station sending the solicit successor frame hears the noise. It responds by sending a **resolve contention frame.** Each of the colliding stations receives this frame and places itself into one of four groups, depending on the first two bits of its address.

If a station's address begins with 00 it sends another set successor frame immediately. Otherwise it waits one, two, or three time slots, depending on whether its address begins with 01, 10, or 11, before sending another set successor frame. However, if a waiting station detects a set successor frame on the ring, it stops trying to enter the ring until it receives another invitation. This prioritizes the contending stations and forces some of them to back off from trying to enter.

After sending a resolve contention frame the station again listens. If it receives a set successor frame it proceeds as described previously and allows the station into the ring. However, it could detect another collision (if two or more addresses have the same first two bits), in which case it sends another resolve contention frame and waits. This time the colliding stations place themselves into one of four groups depending on the second pair of bits in their address. As before, a station sends a set successor frame immediately or waits one, two, or three time slots to do so.

Every time the soliciting station hears a collision it sends another resolve contention frame. Each successive frame causes the colliding stations to use the next pair of address bits to determine their group, thus reducing the number of stations trying to enter. Eventually, only one station's set successor frame will get through, and it will join the ring. The only way collisions will occur with every pair of address bits is if two stations have the same address, which, of course, we don't allow.

LOST TOKENS

We have discussed how to bring stations into the ring one at a time assuming a previous ring order already has been established. We have discussed what to do if a station due to receive a token malfunctions. But what about a more difficult question: What happens if the station holding the token malfunctions? For example, suppose station A receives the token and sends a frame. Its predecessor detects the frame and concludes the token has been passed successfully. Now suppose station A malfunctions after it sends the frame but before it can pass the token to its successor. Station A goes down and takes the token with it. All the others are now waiting for a nonexistent token.

---

[*]From this point we no longer distinguish between the solicit successor 1 and solicit successor 2 frames.

The logical solution is for some station to take the initiative and reintroduce a token into the ring. But which one does it? How is that decision reached? Again, the difficulty is caused by the fact that there are many stations waiting and any number of them may take the initiative. There must be a way to resolve the conflicts.

When a station does not receive a token in a reasonable amount of time, a timer expires, alerting the station that a token has not arrived. The station responds by sending a **claim token frame.** This is an attempt to notify all other stations that it is trying to claim the token. After sending the frame it listens to the bus for any other such transmissions. If it detects none it concludes it is the only station trying to claim the token. It creates a new token and sends it to its successor. The ring is operational again.

The solution is more complex if several stations' timers expire and they all send claim token frames. In this case they all begin executing a contention-resolving algorithm. Each station sending the frame pads the data field (adds bits) to make the total frame length equivalent to zero, two, four, or six slot times. The first two bits of the station's address determine the frame's length. After sending the frame, the station continues to listen to the bus for another time slot. If another station sends a longer frame, the listening station detects it and drops its claim for the token. The effect is that stations sending shorter claim token frames than other stations give up their claim.

When several stations send equal length frames, if the listening station does not detect another frame it sends another claim token frame whose length depends on the second pair of address bits. Again it listens for at least one slot time and proceeds as just described. If a station sends a third claim token frame it uses the third pair of address bits to determine its length. If necessary, it continues to send claim token frames using subsequent pairs of address bits. The only way two stations could repeatedly send the same length claim token frames is if every pair of address bits is identical. Since this cannot happen (all stations have unique addresses), eventually one station prevails with the longest frame and gets the token.

Ring Initialization

All of the previous discussion has assumed that some logical order already existed prior to a particular situation. But what about the initial startup? Remember, each station knows its own address but has no knowledge about other stations. Which one gets the token initially? When a station gets it, to whom does it send the token? In other words, how is the logical ring order determined?

This situation is much like the lost-token situation. Initially, many stations are connected to the ring, but there is no token. Therefore, the logical approach is to proceed as before. Each station goes through the process of sending and resending claim token frames until one station gets it. The difference here is that the station with the token does not know who its successor is and does not know where to send the token. As a result it sends the token to itself. This is not as ludicrous as it seems. Effectively we have just defined a logical ring containing one station whose successor and predecessor are itself. However, the token-passing protocol is now in effect, and all the other stations are viewed as new stations waiting to enter the ring. Consequently, the station in the ring eventually sends a solicit successor frame and another station enters the ring. Over a period of time solicit successor frames are sent, thus allowing all of the waiting stations to enter the ring.

PRIORITIZING FRAMES

The token bus does not prioritize stations and tokens as did the token ring, but it does define priorities for data to be sent. Each station maintains four priorities, or **service classes,** numbered 0, 2, 4, and 6. The classes are ordered with class 0 having the lowest priority and class 6 having the highest. As information comes down to the MAC layer from a higher layer, the protocol determines the information's priority. The protocol then creates data frames and stores them in one of four queues (one for each class) that the station maintains (Figure 6.23).

When a station gets a token, it sends class 6 frames first. If there are none it looks for class 4 frames, then class 2 frames, and finally class 0 frames. A station sends frames in a class until either a timer expires or there are no more frames in that class. Afterward, the station passes the token to its successor or sends frames from the next lowest class.

To control frame transmissions each station maintains two timers: a **token-holding timer (THT)** and a **token-rotation timer (TRT).**[*] The THT is the max-

Figure 6.23   Prioritizing Frames

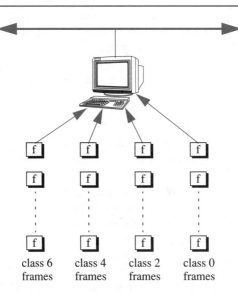

class 6   class 4   class 2   class 0
frames   frames   frames   frames

---

[*]Actually, there are three token-rotation timers, one for each of classes 0, 2, and 4. To simplify our discussion we assume all three timers are equal and are represented by TRT. If you are interested, Reference [St90] discusses the more specific case and provides a more detailed analysis.

imum time a station may spend sending class 6 frames. The TRT determines the maximum time for a token to rotate around the ring. It also determines the maximum time allowed for the station to send frames in the lower classes. On receipt of the token a station starts its THT and sends class 6 frames until there are no more or until the THT expires. The station starts its TRT prior to sending the token to its successor. The timer then continues counting while the token travels the logical ring. When the token returns and the station has sent its class 6 frames, the remaining time on the TRT determines how long it has to send any remaining frames. If other stations had little to send the current station has more time sending frames. If other stations send more frames the current one sends fewer. The intent is to minimize delays as the token travels the logical ring.

Figure 6.24 shows pseudocode of the logic behind sending frames. When a token arrives, the station starts the THT timer and sends class 6 frames until the THT expires or there are no more class 6 frames. It then sends class 4 frames until the TRT expires or there are no more class 4 frames. It performs similarly for class 2 and class 0 frames. Finally, when the station has finished sending frames, it starts the TRT and sends the token to its successor. The TRT continues counting the entire time the token is traveling the ring.

For example, suppose a token circulates among four stations in the order *A-B-C-D*. As the token arrives at *A*, Table 6.6 shows how many frames of each class each station has to send and the time left on each station's TRT. We simplify the example by assuming that all frames are the same size and require the same amount of time to send. Suppose timer units are slot times, the time required to send one frame. That is, THT = 6 means a station can send up to six class 6 frames at a time.

When *A* gets the token, it sends six class 6 frames and two class 4 frames. It then sets its TRT to 32 before sending the token to *B*. Meanwhile, the time left on

---

Figure 6.24   Protocol for Sending Frames

```
while (Horton hears a Who)
{
  wait for arriving token;
  start THT timer;
  while (THT not expired) && (class 6 queue not empty)
    send class 6 frames;
  while (TRT not expired) && (class 4 queue not empty)
    send class 4 frames;
  while (TRT not expired) && (class 2 queue not empty)
    end class 2 frames;
  while (TRT not expired) && (class 0 queue not empty)
    send class 0 frames;
  set TRT timer;
  send token to successor;
} /* end of while loop */
```

Table 6.6   Stations with Frames to Send

STATION	NUMBER OF CLASS 6 FRAMES	NUMBER OF CLASS 4 FRAMES	NUMBER OF CLASS 2 FRAMES	NUMBER OF CLASS 0 FRAMES	TIME LEFT ON TRT
A	8	4	2	1	8
B	9	4	2	2	14
C	6	7	0	0	26
D	7	8	3	6	32

THT = 6
Maximum value in TRT = 32

B's, *C*'s, and *D*'s TRTs decreases by 8 (row 1 in Table 6.7). When *B* gets the token it can send only six class 6 frames. At that point both its THT and TRT expire and it sends the token. During this time the others' timers decrease by 6. When *C* gets the token it has 12 units left on its TRT and sends six class 6 tokens and six class 4 frames. Meanwhile, *D*'s TRT decreases to 6, and when it gets the token it can send only six class 6 frames. The token returns to *A* and the timers are as shown in row 4 of Table 6.7. The token continues to circulate; if there are no new frames, the remaining rows of Table 6.7 describe the number of frames sent and left, along with each station's TRT value.

Table 6.7   Station Information After Receiving Each Token

STATION GETTING TOKEN	NUMBER OF FRAMES SENT (NUMBER LEFT), BY CLASS				AMOUNT OF TIME LEFT ON TRT TIMERS PRIOR TO SENDING TOKEN, BY STATION			
	6	4	2	0	A	B	C	D
A	6 (2)	2 (2)	0 (2)	0 (1)	32	6	18	24
B	6 (3)	0 (4)	0 (2)	0 (2)	26	32	12	18
C	6 (0)	6 (1)	0 (0)	0 (0)	14	20	32	6
D	6 (1)	0 (8)	0 (3)	0 (6)	8	14	26	32
A	2 (0)	2 (0)	2 (0)	1 (0)	32	7	19	25
B	3 (0)	4 (0)	0 (2)	0 (2)	25	32	12	18
C	0 (0)	1 (0)	0 (0)	0 (0)	24	31	32	17
D	1 (0)	8 (0)	3 (0)	5 (1)	7	14	15	32
A	no frames to send				32	14	15	32
B	0 (0)	0 (0)	2 (0)	2 (0)	28	32	11	28
C	no frames to send				28	32	32	28
D	0 (0)	0 (0)	0 (0)	1 (0)	27	31	31	32

An important relation between the two timers guarantees a certain amount of high-priority traffic along the bus. Suppose there are n stations. If each station spends the full time allowed by the THT sending class 6 frames, the token will take at least $n \times$ THT time to circulate the ring once. (For this analysis, ignore the negligible time it takes to send a token to a successor.) In this case, if TRT $= n \times$ THT then each station's TRT expires after it sends its class 6 frames. Consequently, it sends nothing below class 6. In other words, class 6 frames get 100% of the bus's bandwidth.

Two conditions allow a station to send lower-priority frames. First is if one or more stations do not send the maximum number of class 6 frames. Second is if TRT $> n \times$ THT. The first depends on events beyond a designer's control. Therefore, to guarantee that class 6 frames do not monopolize the bus, we need TRT $> n \times$ THT. Even if each station spends the full time that THT allows sending class 6 frames, there will be time left for lower-class frames. Just how much depends on how much larger TRT is.

In general, if all stations have the maximum number of class 6 frames to send, we can guarantee a percentage of bandwidth equal to $100 \times n \times$ THT/TRT for them. For example, if we wanted to guarantee that 75% of the bus's bandwidth is available for class 6 frames, we define TRT $= 4n \times$ THT/3. Doing so yields $100 \times n \times$ THT/TRT $= 100 \times n \times$ THT/$[(4/3)n \times$ THT$] = 100 \times 3/4 = 75\%$. This type of control over the timer adds flexibility to the token bus in order to adapt to real-time situations.

6.5 INTERCONNECTING LANS

After reading about three very different standards for local area networks, you may be wondering, Doesn't this create confusion and inconsistencies among vendors and users? Let's put it this way: Some things in life are inescapable. Among them are death, taxes, and confusion among network users.

Different networks were designed for different people with very different goals. To assume they are isolated from one another is unrealistic, however. For example, within a large corporation different departments may have specific goals and approaches to their work. Departments of manufacturing, research and development, and marketing are very different. Different factors affect their decisions as they install computer systems or connect to networks. Consequently, they may adopt different and incompatible systems. The departments still must communicate, and if they use incompatible networks they have a problem. This leaves them with two possible solutions. The first is to force them all to adopt a specific network standard. Unfortunately, if the chosen network does not meet the goals and needs of a department then the choice is counterproductive. The second solution is to determine some way for different networks to communicate. Since most people expect computers and networks to be servants rather than masters, the second choice is preferable.

For example, consider the scenario of Figure 6.25, which represents networks used by a large corporation with departments in New York and Texas. Two New York departments and one Texas department each have installed their own LANs. New York stations A and B access file servers on their respective LANs using protocols

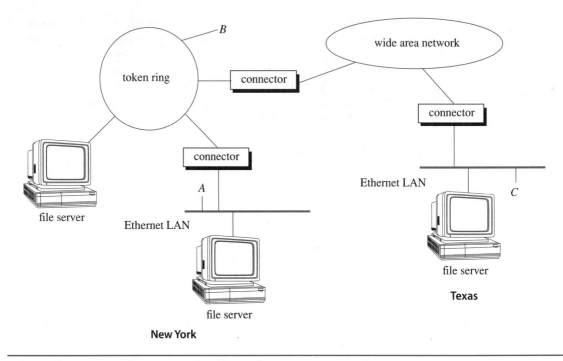

Figure 6.25   Interconnecting Networks

we have discussed in previous sections. Texas station *C* does similarly. However, all three stations need access to the other LANs periodically. The two New York networks can be connected directly, but distance prohibits a direct connection with the Texas LAN. Consequently, a larger wide area network[*] is used to connect Texas and New York.

The ability to connect networks is certainly not new. There are standards for software and connecting devices, and any computer vendor has many such products to sell. The question is where in the hierarchy of hardware and software these products fit. That is, what do they actually do? Models such as OSI provide several layers of protocols for computer networks. For example, suppose the two New York LANs of Figure 6.25 differ only in the MAC sublayer of the data link layer (Figure 6.4), but the wide area network is different at higher layers. A connection to the wide area network deals with more incompatibilities and is more complex than one connecting the two LANs.

In general, we can connect two identical networks at layer 1, which amounts to little more than an electronic connection to regenerate and repeat signals. We also

---

[*]The next chapter discusses wide area networks. For now, just think of it as a network spanning a larger geographical area than a LAN and having different protocols.

can connect two totally incompatible networks at the highest layer. Such a connection requires complete knowledge of both protocols and the ability to translate one to another. We also can connect anywhere between the highest and lowest layers, depending on the degree of compatibility between the two networks. This section discusses OSI layer 1 and layer 2 connections.

LAYER 1 CONNECTIONS

Figure 6.26 shows several networks connected using **repeaters,** devices connecting networks at the physical layer. A repeater accepts a frame's bits from a LAN to which it is connected and retransmits them onto another LAN. It assumes the LANs to which it is connected use the same protocols and same frame formats. A repeater's primary function is to regenerate signals, thereby extending the distance covered by the LAN.

In Figure 6.26 stations *A, B, C,* and *D* are each connected to a different LAN. Each station, however, will see any frame that any other sends. For example, *D* sees everything *A* sends. Whether they accept the frame depends on to whom the frame is addressed. The stations have no knowledge of the repeater's existence; as far as they are concerned, they are all connected by a single, but larger, LAN.

Repeaters do present problems, however. One is that more stations can access the medium, which leads to more traffic and can degrade LAN performance. For example, if *A* sends a frame to *E* (both on LAN L1), the repeaters still send the frame to LANs L2, L3, and L4. They have no built-in logic to know that *A* and *E* are on the same LAN and that repeating the frame is pointless. The result, of course, is that none of the other stations can send until station *A* has finished. A second problem is security. Generally, as more people have access to information, security is more difficult to implement. If *A* and *E* are exchanging sensitive information, the frames pass by all the other stations and the potential for a security breach increases.

Figure 6.26   LANs Connected with a Repeater

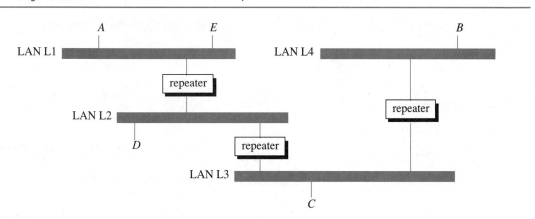

LAYER 2 CONNECTIONS

Another way to connect LANs is to use a **bridge,** a connector with the ability to execute a subset of a protocol. Typically a bridge is a connector at the OSI layer 2. As such it performs data link functions such as error detection, frame formatting, and frame routing. For example, suppose station *B* sends a frame on LAN L2 in the network configuration of Figure 6.27. Bridge B1 examines the destination address and, if it is destined for any station on LAN L1 (say *A*), accepts the frame and buffers it. (How B1 knows what is on L1 is a major issue that we discuss shortly.) If the frame is destined for a station on one of the other LANs, B1 ignores the frame. Thus, B1 acts like any other station selectively rejecting or accepting frames based on their destination.

If B1 accepts the frame, it executes error detection routines to determine whether the frame is correct. If there are no errors it sends the frame over LAN L1. If L1's frame format is the same as L2's, the bridge sends the frame as is. If it is different, the bridge must reformat the frame it received into a format consistent with L1's standard. In some cases, reformatting is a simple matter of reorganizing the fields, adding required ones, and dropping unnecessary ones. Unfortunately, as we soon will see, in some cases the reformatting causes other problems, some of which layer 2 protocols cannot handle.

Before discussing bridge design let's pose one last question: What are the reasons for using bridges in the first place? One reason is to enhance efficiency. With repeaters we saw that every frame propagates throughout each LAN, causing a lot of unnecessary traffic. To avoid this possibility a network designer can create a topology in which frequently communicating stations are on the same LAN. For example, each LAN of Figure 6.27 could correspond to a different department in a large company. Thus, stations within a department can communicate with each

Figure 6.27 LANs Connected with a Bridge

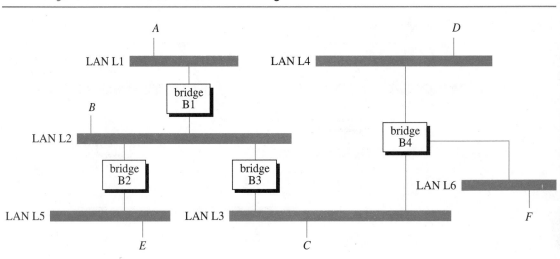

other, and the bridges do not forward any of the frames onto another LAN. For example, two stations can communicate over L1 at the same time two others communicate over L2. In general, communication within different LANs occurs in parallel, and efficiency is increased.

The bridges also allow interdepartmental communications when necessary. Furthermore, the interconnection strategy can be designed depending on the frequency of interdepartmental communication. For example, Figure 6.27 shows that LANs L1 and L2 communicate over one bridge, whereas communication between LANs L1 and L4 requires three bridges. This makes sense if communication between LANs L1 and L2 is more frequent. The figure also suggests that LANs L3, L4, and L6 communicate among each other equally often, as any two of them can communicate over one bridge.

Security is another reason for using bridges. Because bridges selectively resend frames they can prevent certain frames from propagating throughout the network. This procedure enhances security because some stations never see the transmissions of others. The bridge organization also can reflect different security levels. For example, LAN L1 might connect stations to a file server with the highest priority (one that contains the most sensitive information). LAN L2 might be the second-highest priority LAN, with just one bridge between it and L1. LANs L3 and L5 might have the next-lowest priority, with two bridges between them and L1. In general, each bridge provides an opportunity to block a frame from going to another LAN. Thus, the design can place more bridges between LANs to represent priority differences.

BRIDGING DIFFERENT TYPES OF LANs

Bridging becomes more difficult when connecting different types of LANs. One problem is that different LANs may have different bit rates. For example, suppose a bridge accepts frames from a fast LAN and forwards them to a slower LAN or to one where collisions have occurred. The frames may arrive faster than they can be forwarded. Consequently, there must be sufficient buffer space in the bridge to allow a backlog of frames. Bridge delays can cause other problems, such as timeouts in the flow control protocols. Timers are set to provide a reasonable time for a frame to reach its destination and an acknowledgment to be sent. Delays at bridges can cause excessive timeouts unless the station's network software adjusts them. Now, however, timers depend on interconnection strategies and we lose some of the transparency of the topology.

Frame formatting presents another problem. Recall from the three previous sections (also Figures 6.8, 6.12, and 6.21) that each LAN standard has a different frame format. Therefore, if a bridge connects two different LANs it must also reformat a received frame before resending it. On the surface, reformatting does not seem difficult, as it is primarily a rearrangement of information. Suppose a bridge connects an Ethernet and a token ring LAN, however. Frames on a token ring have a priority; those on an Ethernet do not. Therefore, a frame going from a token ring to an Ethernet loses its priority. Conversely, a frame going from an Ethernet to a token ring must be given a priority—but what? Usually a default is assigned. But what happens if a frame goes from a token ring to an Ethernet and then to another token ring? The frame has an initial priority, loses it when it goes on the Ethernet, and then gets another priority when it reaches the second token ring. There is no guarantee, however, that the initial and ending priorities are the same.

Yet another problem occurs due to the different maximum frame sizes with each LAN protocol. For example, both token ring and token bus may use frames larger than the maximum allowed on an Ethernet. Therefore, a large frame sent to an Ethernet station is not consistent with the Ethernet protocol. There are two possible solutions to this problem. The first is to make each station aware of the different LAN standards that may be encountered when it sends a frame. Then the station's network software can construct frames small enough so they meet the maximum size requirements of any LAN the frame may encounter. Many network packages allow this option. The problem is that each station's protocol now depends on the interconnection topology. Adding new bridges and LANs may require giving each LAN station new parameters. Since a major goal of communication is to create protocols that work regardless of the connection scheme, this is a significant constraint.

The second solution is for the bridge to break large frames into smaller ones. For example, Figure 6.28 shows a 5000 byte frame being sent to an Ethernet. Since the Ethernet does not allow frames above 1518 bytes, the bridge divides the frame into three pieces. The problem with this is that flow control protocols at the data link layer depend on the sending and acknowledging of frames. When a sending station sends a frame it anticipates that the receiving station will or will not receive it. There is no provision for the receiving station to receive what amounts to part of a frame.

The situation is not hopeless, however. Additional logic can be added to the bridge that divides frames and provides for proper acknowledgment of each piece. The logic to do so resides above the data link layer protocol, so the connection between the networks must occur at a higher OSI layer. Devices that achieve this maintain some bridge functions and assume some functions of a router.[*] They are called **Brouters.**

Figure 6.28   Dividing a Large Frame into Smaller Ones

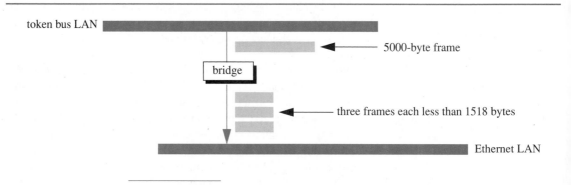

[*] A **router** connects two networks at the OSI layer 3.

BRIDGE ROUTING

For the rest of this section we assume that a bridge connects two similar LANs so we can focus on another bridge function: forwarding frames. By itself, forwarding frames is not difficult. The hard question is, How does a bridge know when to accept and forward a frame? For example, suppose bridge B3 in Figure 6.27 detects a frame on LAN L2. If the frame's destination is station A or E, B3 should ignore it. However, suppose the destination is D, C, or F. Station C is on LAN L3, and the only way to get to stations D or F is through L3. Therefore, the bridge must accept the frame and forward it on LAN L3. But how does B3 know that D, C, and F are accessible via L3? Worse yet, what if someone moves F from L6 to L5? How does the bridge know the station is no longer accessible via L3?

These questions may seem trivial at first because you, as the reader, can see the entire network drawn in a diagram. Having a global view of a situation always makes a problem easier. But the bridges do not have this view. They connect two or more LANs and see only what arrives on them. Furthermore, a bridge certainly cannot see what happens on a LAN several bridges away. The process of deciding which frames to forward and to where is called **bridge routing.** We will devote the rest of this section to discussing three approaches to it.

Fixed-Routing Bridges   One way to route frames is to program each bridge with each station's address and the LAN to which frames destined for that station should be forwarded. That information is then stored in a **routing table** (sometimes called a **forwarding database** or **routing directory**). Where a bridge routes a frame depends on the LAN on which the frame arrives. Each bridge has a routing table for each LAN to which it is connected. When a frame arrives on that LAN the bridge finds the destination address in the appropriate routing table. The table's entry specifies to which LAN the bridge should forward the frame.

To illustrate, Figure 6.29 contains routing tables for the bridges in Figure 6.27. Bridge B1 has two routing tables (Figure 6.29a), one each for LANs L1 and L2. When the bridge detects a frame on L1 it determines the destination address and looks for it in the routing table for L1. If the destination address is one of B through F, the bridge forwards the frame to L2, the only way to get to those stations. If the destination is A the bridge does not forward the frame and the frame stays on L1. Similarly, if the bridge detects a frame from L2 destined for A it forwards the frame to L1.

The tables in bridge B3 are similar. The bridge will forward any frame from L2 to L3 that is destined for C, D, or F. However, if a frame arrives on L2 and is destined for A, B, or E, the bridge will not forward it. Figure 6.27 shows that those stations cannot be reached by going from L2 to L3. You should read through the other tables and convince yourself that their entries accurately reflect the topology of Figure 6.27.

We call this approach **fixed routing** because we assume the tables' information does not change. In many dynamic network environments, however, this assumption is too restrictive. New stations may be added, old ones removed, and others moved

Source LAN L1		Source LAN L2	
Destination	Next LAN	Destination	Next LAN
A	—	A	L1
B	L2	B	—
C	L2	C	—
D	L2	D	—
E	L2	E	—
F	L2	F	—

(a) Bridge B1

Source LAN L2		Source LAN L5	
Destination	Next LAN	Destination	Next LAN
A	—	A	L2
B	—	B	L2
C	—	C	L2
D	—	D	L2
E	L5	E	—
F	—	F	L2

(a) Bridge B2

Source LAN L2		Source LAN L3	
Destination	Next LAN	Destination	Next LAN
A	—	A	L2
B	—	B	L2
C	L3	C	—
D	L3	D	—
E	—	E	L2
F	L3	F	—

(a) Bridge B3

Source LAN L3		Source LAN L4		Source LAN L6	
Destination	Next LAN	Destination	Next LAN	Destination	Next LAN
A	—	A	L3	A	L3
B	—	B	L3	B	L3
C	—	C	L3	C	L3
D	L4	D	—	D	L4
E	—	E	L3	E	L3
F	L6	F	L6	F	—

(a) Bridge B4

Figure 6.29   Routing Tables for Bridges in Figure 6.27

to different locations. Entire LANs may be added or removed. We need correct routing regardless of a station's location and network topology. This will provide the transparency that makes a network easier to use.

If we want to use routing tables in a more dynamic environment, we have two choices. One is to reprogram the bridges every time someone adds, deletes, or moves a station. In a dynamic environment this approach is not viable, so we are left with the second choice: determine some way for the bridges to update their routing tables automatically.

Transparent Bridges   We call bridges that create and update their own routing tables **transparent bridges.** They have their own standard (IEEE 802.1d). They are designed so that you can plug them in and have them work immediately regardless of topology and the stations' locations. There is no need to tell them where the stations are. They will determine that automatically and initialize their routing tables. They require no special programming. If a station moves from one LAN to another, each bridge learns this and updates its routing table accordingly. This ability to update its routing table is called **route learning** or **address learning.**

Route Learning   A bridge learns what to put in its routing table by observing traffic. Whenever it receives a frame it examines the source address. It then knows that the station sending the frame is accessible via the LAN on which the frame just arrived. The bridge examines each of its routing tables looking for the station's address. If a table entry indicates that the station is accessible over a different LAN, the bridge changes the entry to specify the LAN on which the frame arrived. Presumably the station moved to a different LAN.

To illustrate, consider again the routing tables of Figure 6.29 and the LANs of Figure 6.27. Now suppose station *D* moves from LAN L4 to LAN L1. The routing tables are now incorrect and the only stations able to send to *D* are those on the same LAN as *D*. Next, suppose *D* sends a frame to *E* on LAN L5. Bridge B1 routes the frame to L2. However, it also examines its routing tables (Figure 6.29a). Since the bridge received a frame from *D* on L1 it knows that *D* is in the direction of L1.[*] It therefore changes the fourth entry in each routing table and redefines them as follows:

SOURCE LAN L1		SOURCE LAN L2	
DESTI-NATION	NEXT LAN	DESTI-NATION	NEXT LAN
A	—	*A*	L1
B	L2	*B*	—
C	L2	*C*	—
D	—	*D*	L1
E	L2	*E*	—
F	L2	*F*	—

Bridge B1 now knows not to forward any frame from L1 that is destined for *D* and to forward any frame from L2 that is destined for *D* to L1. When bridge B2 detects *D*'s frame from L2 it updates its tables similarly. In this case B2 realizes *D* is accessible via L2. However, from B2's perspective this is no different from when *D* was on L4. As a result, the "updated" values are the same as the original ones.

Some questions still remain. Bridges B1 and B2 learned of *D*'s move only because *D* sent a frame that B1 and B2 had to forward. Bridges B3 and B4 still do not know of *D*'s move. Must they remain ignorant until *D* sends something their way? What if *D* never does? Do they remain in the dark forever? If so, frames sent to

---

[*]Note that B1 doesn't necessarily know *D* is on L1. For all it knows the frame may have gone through several bridges before getting to L1. The important thing is that the bridge knows in what direction to forward a frame.

D from LANs L3, L4, or L6 will never reach D. For that matter, what if D never sent the frame to E? Then not even bridges B1 and B2 are aware of D's move and nothing will reach D.

So far the discussion has dealt only with changing information. Another issue is how the tables are initialized. What do the bridges do at startup? Fortunately, the 802.1d specifications provide answers. Whenever a bridge updates a routing table entry it includes the time of update. Each bridge also maintains a timer. Whenever the timer expires the bridge examines each routing table entry. If the entry has not been updated since the timer was last set, the bridge removes the entries from the table. The bridge "reasons" that since it has not heard from those stations in a while their locations may not be accurate. Consequently, it maintains no routing information for those stations.

This action appears to make stations inaccessible if they did not move. However, when a bridge receives a frame destined for a station that has no entry in the routing table, the bridge uses a **flooding algorithm.** That is, it sends the frame over every LAN to which it is connected except the one on which the frame arrived. This serves two purposes: It guarantees the frame will reach its destination (assuming it exists), and it allows more bridges to see the frame and learn the direction of the sending station. This information keeps their routing tables current.

Consider the previous example in which D moves from L4 to L1 in Figure 6.27 and then sends a frame to E. If E has not sent anything for a while, its entries in each bridge are deleted. Therefore, when B1 receives D's frame it notes that there is no entry for E and automatically forwards the frame to L2. Similarly, B2 and B3 also forward the frame to L5 and L3, respectively. Finally, B4 forwards the frame to L4 and L6. The end result is that E gets the frame and each bridge forwards a frame from D and updates its routing table. Consequently, anything sent to D will be forwarded correctly (at least until the next timer expires).

The flooding algorithm also allows bridges to initialize their routing tables. Suppose a LAN is installed and all of the bridges' routing tables are empty. No bridge knows the location of any station. When a bridge receives its first frame from a LAN it sends it along every other LAN to which it is connected. Similarly, bridges on those LANs receive the frame and also forward it using the flooding algorithm. Before long the frame has reached every bridge and every LAN. In particular, the frame has reached its destination and every bridge knows the direction of the sending station.

As more stations send frames the bridges forward them using routing table entries or by flooding. As the frames propagate through the network, the bridges eventually learn the direction of the sending station and can forward frames without using the flooding algorithm.

Frame Propagation   The previous approach to designing transparent bridges and route learning worked well with the examples given. However, certain topologies can cause an endless propagation of frames and glut the network. To illustrate, suppose network designers decide to add a second bridge connecting two LANs. Adding a redundant bridge between two LANs is sometimes used to protect the system in the event of failures. If the first bridge fails, the second one is already in place and there is no (or very little) delay caused by the failure. This is particularly useful in real-time systems where delays caused by equipment failure can lead to a disaster.

For example, the simple LAN connection of Figure 6.30 shows two bridges between the same two LANs. Suppose the routing tables are empty and *A* sends a frame to *B*. Since neither bridge is aware of the other, each accepts the frame and forwards it onto LAN L2. Next, bridge B1 sees B2's frame and B2 sees B1's frame on L2. Since neither knows where *B* is, both bridges accept the frame and forward it onto LAN L1. Again each will see the other's frame and forward it back to L2. Until *B* identifies its location the frames will be transferred back and forth repeatedly between both LANs.

The situation is made worse if there is a third bridge (B3) connecting the LANs. If *A* sends one frame along L1, each bridge forwards it to L2, putting three frames on L2. Each bridge sees two of them (one from each of the other two bridges) and forwards them onto L1, putting six frames on L1. Each bridge now sees four frames (two from each of the other two bridges) and forwards them, putting twelve frames back on L2. This process continues, causing an explosion of frames that eventually clogs the system and brings communication to a standstill.

We illustrated the problem with a simple topology showing two bridges between two LANs. The potential for endlessly circulating frames exists in other topologies as well. In particular, two distinct routes between two stations will cause a loop in the topology. This means that a frame may leave a LAN via one route only to return via another. Figure 6.31 shows a topology with multiple routes between *A* and *B*. (We'll see what the costs mean shortly.) In fact, there are at least seven routes if we ignore routes going through the same bridge twice (can you find them?). To see the magnitude of this problem, suppose *A* sends *B* a frame and the bridges use the flooding algorithm. Suppose a frame takes the route from L1 to L4 through bridges B1 and B2. Bridge B6 will forward the frame back to L1. Bridge B4 will forward the frame to L3. From here B5 forwards it to L1, and B3 forwards it to L2. Next B1 forwards it to L1, B2 forwards it back to L4, and the process continues. As

Figure 6.30   Two Bridges Connecting Two LANs

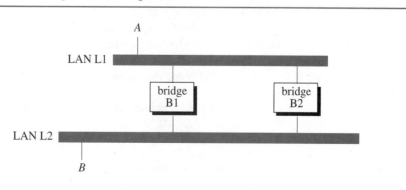

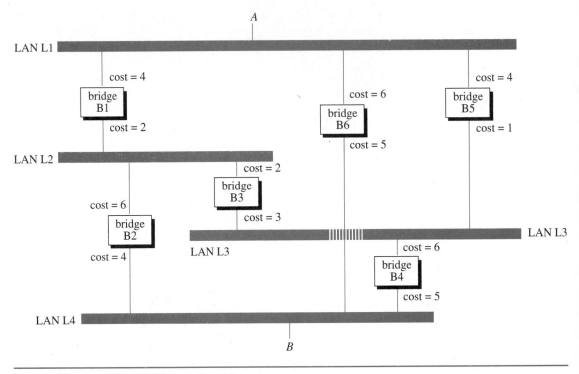

Figure 6.31   Multiple LANs with Loops

before, the single frame causes an unending increase in the number of frames moving through the network. If we consider the other routes from L1 to L4, the increase is even more rapid. The number of frames becomes excessive very quickly and the network shuts down.

Spanning Tree Algorithm   One approach to this problem is to eliminate the loops by not using certain bridges. We don't disconnect the bridges physically, but we prevent them from forwarding frames. Instead they are used as backups in case another bridge fails. The tricky part is determining which bridges are used and when they should automatically reconfigure if a bridge fails. As usual, we want to let the bridges do the work themselves and make the configuration transparent to the user. One solution calls for the bridges to execute a **spanning tree algorithm.** A **spanning tree,** a term from data structures, corresponds to a minimal subset of edges taken from a connected graph that connects the graph's vertices. The subset is minimal in that the spanning tree has no loops.[*] For more information on spanning trees, consult a reference on data structures, such as Reference [Dr95] or [Pa95].

---

[*]In data structures, the term *cycle* is often used in place of *loop*.

To make the algorithm work, we first associate a cost with each bridge-to-LAN connection, or **bridge port.** It may correspond to a bit rate at which a bridge port can transmit onto a LAN. Typically, lower bit rates mean a higher cost. The cost of sending a frame from one LAN to another is the sum of costs of ports in the route. In some cases, all costs are set to 1 so that the cost of a route is simply the number of bridges in it. Figure 6.31 shows the cost of each bridge port. The cost of sending a frame from L1 to L4 via bridges B1 and B2 is 6, the sum of the costs of going from B1 to L2 (2) plus B2 to L4 (4). Note that the costs associated with the B1 to L1 and B2 to L2 ports are not included here. They are used for frames going in the other direction.

Next, we visualize the LAN topology as a graph. The LANs and bridges are vertices and the connections between a LAN and a bridge are the edges. Figure 6.32 shows a graphical representation of the topology in Figure 6.31. The figure lists costs for each edge. Remember that as frames move through the graph, only costs from a bridge node to a LAN node accrue.

The spanning tree algorithm determines a set of edges that connect all the LAN nodes of Figure 6.32. Remember as we discuss the algorithm that we have the advantage of seeing the entire network topology; the bridges that execute the algorithm have no such view. They know only the LANs to which they are connected. This makes the algorithm more complex than it would be if executed by a processor that knows the entire topology.

To begin the spanning tree algorithm, the bridges elect one of their own (true partisan politics) to be a **root bridge.** It is usually the one with the lowest ID,

Figure 6.32   Graph Representation of the LAN Topology in Figure 6.31

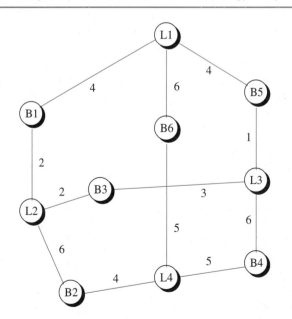

although priorities can be used. Using data structures terminology, the root bridge will be the root of the spanning tree. The bridges elect the root bridge by first sending a series of special frames called **bridge protocol data units (BPDUs)** at regular intervals. Each BPDU contains the bridge's ID, the port ID over which the frame was first sent, and the accumulated costs of ports over which it has been received. The latter is the cost of a path from the BPDU's current location back to its source.

When a bridge receives a BPDU it compares the source bridge's ID with its own. If its own ID is larger it knows it will not be the root bridge. It records the sending bridge's ID and the path cost to it, increments the path cost by the cost of the receiving port, and forwards the BPDU through all its other ports. It also stops sending its own BPDUs. If the bridge's ID is smaller than the one that sent the BPDU it will not forward the frame. It reasons that the sending bridge will never be elected so there is no point in forwarding its frames.

Eventually each bridge except the one with the lowest ID will stop sending frames because it knows it will not be the root bridge. The remaining bridge stops forwarding any frames it receives and eventually receives no more. After a time during which it receives no frames, it considers itself duly elected as root bridge. It and the other bridges then proceed to the algorithm's next step.

In the second step, each bridge determines its **root port,** the port corresponding to the cheapest path to the root bridge. Since each bridge previously recorded path costs for each BPDU received on each port, it simply looks for the cheapest. Each bridge subsequently will communicate with the root bridge using its root port.

The last step determines a **designated bridge** for each LAN. This is the bridge that eventually forwards frames from that LAN. The bridges elect a designated bridge by sending BPDUs over each LAN to which they are connected. A bridge will not send a BPDU to a LAN using a previously determined root port. Essentially, the root port determines the LAN in the direction of the root bridge. The algorithm now must determine if there are any LANs in any other direction.

Let's examine the activities from the perspective of a specific LAN. The LAN is carrying BPDUs from its bridges requesting to be the designated bridge. Each BPDU contains the cost to the root bridge from the bridge sending the BPDU. When a bridge receives a BPDU it compares the cost in it with its own cost to the root bridge. If its own cost is larger, it knows it will not be the designated bridge and gives up its claim. Eventually the only bridge not seeing a smaller cost becomes the designated bridge for the LAN. In the event there are two or more bridges with the same smaller cost, they use their IDs to break ties. The smallest ID wins.

After selecting designated bridges for each LAN, the spanning tree algorithm is complete. Every LAN is connected to its designated bridge and every bridge can communicate with the root bridge via its root port. This defines a unique path between any two LANs and avoids frame propagation resulting from flooding algorithms.

We now illustrate the spanning tree algorithm with an example. Consider the LAN topology of Figure 6.31 and the associated graph of Figure 6.32. The first step determines the root bridge. If we assume the bridges are numbered in increasing order from B1 through B6, then B1 is elected root bridge.

During the election process each bridge records the cost to the root bridge through each of its ports, and then selects the cheapest one. Figure 6.33 shows the root ports (designated by an arrow) and paths to the root bridge (designated by red lines). The path costs are also listed next to the arrows. For example, bridge B2's root port is the one connected to L2. The cheapest path is B2-L2-B1, for a cost of 6. Remember, we only accrue costs from bridges to LANs. B4's root port is the one connected to L3. The path to the root bridge is B4-L3-B3-L2-B1, for a cost of 8. As the figure shows, there are other paths but their costs are higher. You should take some time to understand why the other root ports were chosen as they were.

The last step determines the designated bridge for each LAN. The root ports connect bridges to some LANs, but there may be other LANs that are not part of the developing connection scheme. For example, in Figure 6.33 there is no root port connected to L4, and we need to determine a bridge to forward information from L4. To do this, bridges B2, B4, and B6 send BPDUs along L4 requesting to be the designated bridge. B4 states that its cost to the root bridge is 8; B2 and B6 indicate their cost to be 6. Consequently, B4 gives up its request because of its higher cost and B6 gives up its request because of its higher ID. Thus, B2 becomes the designated bridge for L4. Proceeding similarly, B3 is the designated bridge for L3, and B1 is the designated bridge for L1 and L2 (Figure 6.34).

Figure 6.34 shows the resulting spanning tree and Figure 6.35 relates it to the original network topology. The dotted lines indicate physical but not active connections. The bridges use these connections to send and receive BPDUs but not to forward frames in general. The tree connects all the LANs even though some of the

Figure 6.33   Graph After Determining Root Ports

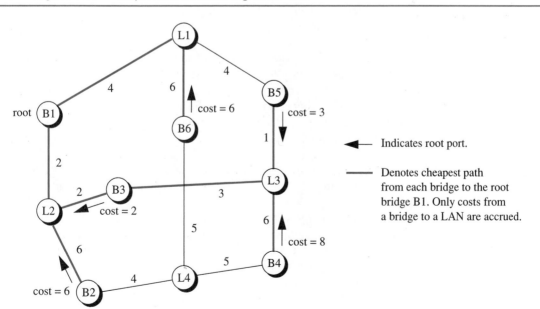

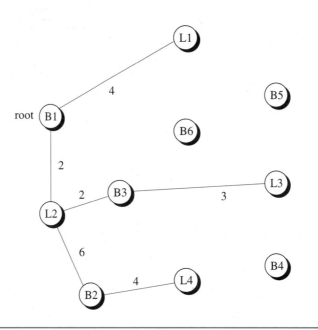

Figure 6.34　Graph After Determining Designated Bridges

bridges are not used. That is to be expected, however, as the bridges are redundant devices to be used in the event of a failure of another one. As long as no failure occurs, the LANs communicate using the topology of Figure 6.35.

In order to detect a bridge failure and reconfigure the connection scheme, each bridge maintains a timer called a **message age timer.** During the specified time, each bridge (even the ones not part of the spanning tree) expects to hear from the root bridge confirming its status as root bridge. When a bridge receives this confirmation, it resets its timer. The root bridge, of course, cooperates by sending a configuration BPDU periodically to confirm its status. If a bridge malfunctions, one or more bridges do not receive a configuration BPDU and their timers expire. If a bridge other than the root bridge fails, the affected bridges exchange BPDUs to elect a new designated bridge for their LANs. If the root bridge fails they must elect a new root bridge. Either way, they reconfigure the active topology dynamically.

Source Routing Bridges　The last approach to forwarding frames on a LAN interconnection puts the burden of routing on the individual stations instead of the bridges. Specifically, network software at the sending station determines a route to the destination and stores it in the frame (Figure 6.36). The route consists of a sequence of **route designators,** each consisting of a LAN and a bridge ID. When a bridge sees a frame, it determines whether there is a designator containing its ID and the ID of the LAN carrying the frame. If so, the bridge accepts the frame and forwards it to the LAN specified in the next designator.

For example, suppose *A* sends *B* (from Figure 6.31) a frame and specifies the route as L1-B5-L3-B4-L4. Both bridges connected to L1 see the frame, but since B5

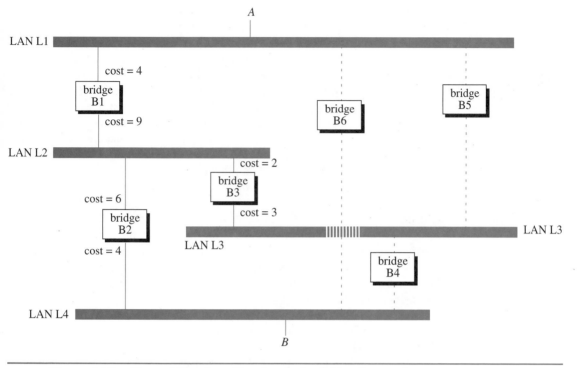

LAN L1

A

cost = 4

bridge
B1

cost = 9

LAN L2

cost = 2

bridge
B3

bridge
B6

bridge
B5

cost = 6

bridge
B2

cost = 3

LAN L3

LAN L3

cost = 4

bridge
B4

LAN L4

B

Figure 6.35   Network Topology Showing Active Bridge Connections

follows L1 in the sequence only B5 accepts it. B5 then forwards the frame to L3, where bridges B3 and B4 see it. Similarly, since B4 follows L3 in the sequence only B4 accepts the frame. Finally, B4 forwards the frame to L4, where station *B* eventually receives the frame.

At first this may seem like a variation of the fixed-routing strategy discussed at the beginning of this section. Each station must be aware of the interconnection strategy and be able to specify a path to any other station. It may seem the only way to do this is to program the topology's structure into each station, which would

Figure 6.36   Partial Frame Format for Source-Routing Bridges

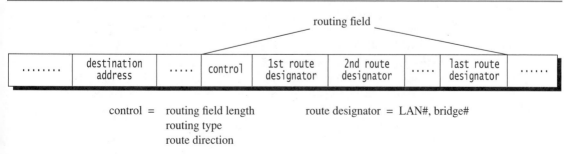

routing field

| .... | destination address | ..... | control | 1st route designator | 2nd route designator | ..... | last route designator | ...... |

control = routing field length   route designator = LAN#, bridge#
routing type
route direction

destroy its ability to reconfigure dynamically. However, this approach does allow a way for each station to learn the location of any other station and to determine the best path.

To determine the path, a station sends a frame to another station, effectively asking, "Where are you?" The receiving station gets the request and responds. When the sending station gets the response, it determines the best path. But how does the sending station know where to send the initial request when it does not know the destination? It doesn't. The bridges must help by executing a variation of the flooding algorithm to make sure the request and response are received. The determination of a route to the destination is called **route discovery.**

One way to do this is to send an **all-routes broadcast frame** to the intended destination station. The frame's control field specifies the frame type and notifies the bridges that they should forward the frame onto all available LANs. An exception, of course, is made for the LAN on which the frame arrived. The problem the bridges must solve is the uncontrolled growth of these frames that flooding can produce. To avoid propagation, a station sends an all-routes broadcast frame with the route designator fields empty and the control field's routing field length equal to 0. When a bridge receives the frame, it inserts its own and the incoming LAN's IDs to the routing field and increments the routing field length. To avoid forwarding a frame it received previously, the bridge examines the existing route designators. It will not forward a frame to a LAN whose ID was part of a route designator of the incoming frame.

When a frame finally arrives at its destination, the routing field contains the route used in getting there. The destination puts this route in the routing field of a **nonbroadcast frame** and sends it back to the source station. It also sets a directional bit in the control field to notify the bridges they should interpret the route designators in reverse order. When a bridge receives a nonbroadcast frame, it forwards or drops the frame according to the information in the routing field. When the source station receives all the responses, it chooses which route to use in subsequent transmissions to B. Presumably, it would examine the costs (calculated during the broadcast) and choose the cheapest. Alternatively, it could choose the one using the fewest bridges or choose based on bridge IDs.

Figure 6.37 shows an example of an all-routes broadcast from A to B. A sends a frame with no routing information in it. Bridge B1 gets the frame, puts the route designator L1-B1 in it, and forwards it to L2 and to L3. B2 gets it from L2, adds the route designator L2-B2, and forwards it to L4, where B eventually receives it. Meanwhile, B4 gets the other forwarded frame, adds the designator L3-B4, and forwards it to L4. Station B receives that frame as well. Note that B3 also sees the frame on L3 but does not forward it to L1 because L1 is in a route designator.

While all this is happening, B3 also receives the initial frame, adds the designator L1-B3, and forwards it to L3. Both B4 and B1 pick up that frame. B4 forwards it to L4, adding the designator L3-B4, and B1 forwards it to L2, adding the designator L3-B1. Finally, B2 forwards the frame from L2 to L4 and adds the designator L2-B2. Station B receives four frames via four different routes. With this approach the destination sends as many frames as it receives. As the number of

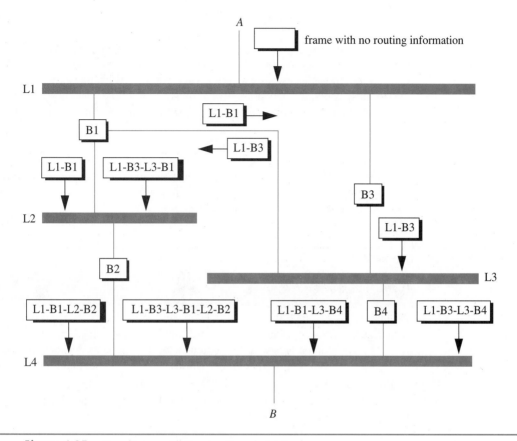

Figure 6.37 Sending an All-Routes Broadcast Frame

redundant bridges increases, so does the number of routes and the number of frames on the network.

Another approach to route discovery has the sending station transmit a **single-route broadcast frame.** Like the all-routes broadcast frame, it contains no routing information. This time, instead of broadcasting to all LANs each bridge forwards a frame only through a port that is part of a spanning tree. In this case the destination receives just one request. However, instead of relying on the spanning tree's route the destination station sends an all-routes broadcast frame as its response. The bridges forward the all-routes broadcast frame as before, determining the route as they do so. Eventually the source station receives many responses, one for each route and, as before, can choose the one it wants for subsequent frames. The advantage of this approach is that there are fewer frames traveling from source to destination (although there are just as many going the other way). The disadvantage is that the bridges must determine the spanning tree first.

SUMMARY

This section has discussed ways to connect LANs. Layer 1 connections simply repeat what they receive. Layer 2 connections do some error checking and frame reformatting. In some cases, frame reformatting is impossible due to limits on frame size. In those cases, the network software must create frames that meet the limits of any protocol they might encounter, or they pass the frames to higher layers that can divide them.

Most of the section dealt with routing frames across a LAN interconnection. It discussed three types of bridges: fixed routing, transparent, and source routing. Fixed routing is limited because it cannot respond to changing conditions dynamically. The other approaches can change, but they differ in where the changes occur. Table 6.8 summarizes the three approaches.

Table 6.8	Comparison of LAN Bridges		
	FIXED-ROUTING BRIDGES	**TRANSPARENT BRIDGES**	**SOURCE-ROUTING BRIDGES**
Ability to reconfigure	Limited. It is done by reprogramming the bridges with routing information.	High. Bridges maintain information on location of stations.	High. Each station must learn the route to its destination before sending.
Stations' responsibilities	None. They just send the frames and let the bridges do the work.	None. They just send the frames and let the bridges do the work.	They determine and maintain addresses.
Bridges' requirements	Routing tables.	Routing tables and the ability to both update them and execute a spanning tree algorithm.	Ability to broadcast or forward, depending on routing designators and ability to execute a spanning tree algorithm.
Routes used	Determined by designer.	Always along the spanning tree, but not necessarily the cheapest.	Stations can choose the cheapest routes to one another.
Dependence on topology	Some. Bridges must be programmed, but stations have no need to know.	None. Bridges learn where stations are relative to their ports dynamically and stations have no need to know.	Some. Bridges respond to routing information and spanning tree algorithms, but stations must determine a route to a destination.

6.6   CASE STUDY: NOVELL NETWARE

Much of this chapter has dealt with local area network standards and internet-working techniques. A logical way to conclude it is to discuss a commonly used commercial network operating systems: Novell NetWare. Novell NetWare contains the protocols necessary to allow communication among many types of PCs and devices. Most typical are printers; Macintosh computers; and PCs running DOS, Windows 3.1, Windows 95, Windows NT, OS/2, or UNIX. It will also run with Ethernet, token ring, and Arcnet protocols.* Typical uses allow PC users to access shared printers, data, applications software, and of course email. For example, if all the members of a department use the same word processor for their reports, there is probably no need for each person to have a separate licensed copy. Another option is to purchase a copy licensed for network use (often cheaper than many individual licenses) and make it available over the network.

Like any commercial product, there are several versions of NetWare. Examples include early versions written to run on 286 machines (NetWare 286 version 2.x), those written to make use of 386 and 486 architecture (NetWare 386 version 3.x), and the most recent version, NetWare 4.x, which can probably run on most anything you have. With perhaps a few exceptions we will not distinguish among versions. Our goal is to provide an overview of NetWare; we will concentrate on topics that are compatible with versions 3.x and 4.x because those are the most common ones. Those interested in a serious, detailed coverage can consult References [Ra94a], [Ra94b], [Ra94c], or [Si97].

NetWare Configuration

Figure 6.38 shows a typical network configuration running Novell NetWare. Most devices typically are PCs, often referred to as **client PCs, client workstations,** or **clients.** At least one PC is designated as a **file server** running all of the NetWare protocols and maintaining the network's shared data on one or more disk drives. File servers generally allow users on other PCs to access application software or data files. The file server may transfer files to the client PC or, if security allows, alter files as requested by the user. It also maintains information on NetWare's authorized users, thus providing some security. In some cases it also may act as a bridge or router to another network.

There are two types of file servers: a dedicated file server and a nondedicated file server. The **dedicated file server** runs NetWare only and does not run other software, such as Windows applications. The **nondedicated file server** can run both applications and NetWare. The latter is useful in small networks because it allows the server to also act as a client, thus adding one to the number of clients. In large networks one extra client is less significant, and a dedicated server handles the larger

---

*The Arcnet is a token-passing protocol that uses a star topology. It is not a formally defined standard, but it has hundreds of thousands of users and has been in use for over 20 years.

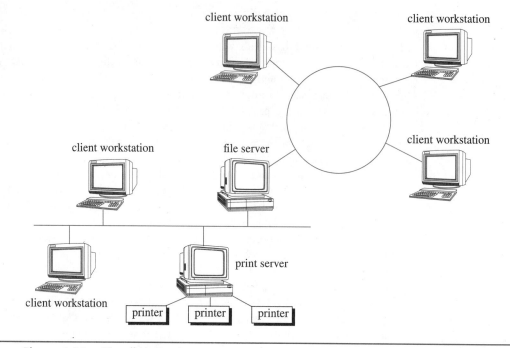

Figure 6.38   Novell Network

number of requests more efficiently. Also, security is usually more of a concern and providing a sharp distinction between client and server hardware aids security efforts.

Another PC may be designated as a **print server.** Its job is to allow users to access shared printers. A print server manages both requests and printers. It analyzes a print request and determines the type of printer (i.e., what format or model) on which it should be printed. It then stores requests in a queue to await the printer. In general, one print server can manage several printers. Conversely, several print servers may have access to a common printer. Consequently, NetWare protocols must allow print servers to access common files. The print server also allows users to examine the queues, request status on queue entries, and even delete them.

While these are perhaps the most visible servers, there are others. A **message server** will transfer email messages between a client PC and a user's mailbox. A **database server** is common in a client/server database system. We will discuss client/server systems in Chapter 7, but essentially it is a mode of operation in which an activity involves processing both at the user and application ends. For example, a typical scenario has a user making a request for a database search. Software at the user end (**client software**) may accept a user request and format it into a standard form required by the database system. The request is then sent to the database server, which performs the search and returns the results to the user. Client software may then intercept the response and display the results in a specific format requested by the users.

The actual number of clients and servers in a NetWare environment varies in practice. Depending on the licensing agreement, the file server can handle up to 250 different clients. It also has a theoretical capacity to manage up to 4 gigabytes of main memory and up to 32 terabytes (trillion bytes) of disk space with up to 100,000 open files.

RUNNING NOVELL NETWARE

To run Novell NetWare, one PC must be designated as a file server. Its configuration must meet minimum criteria regarding disk space, internal memory, and other hardware features. Specifics, of course, vary with the implementation; Reference [Ra94a] discusses configuration requirements further. The server manages the software and data that network users need. It also maintains information on authorized network users and what privileges they have regarding data access.

An important feature of NetWare is its collection of **NetWare Loadable Modules (NLMs),** which add functionality to the operating system. Essentially, they are separate processes designed to run concurrently with NetWare. Each NLM has a specific purpose; the modular design allows users to insert or delete different NLMs to best meet their needs. Typical NLMs allow the installation of print servers, utilities to recover damaged files on a file server, drivers for different types of disk drives, and modules that communicate with protocols such as TCP/IP, AppleTalk, and IPX/SPX (discussed later). The NLMs provide greater functionality by allowing diversity among the types of network devices and protocols.

There are four primary categories of NLMs:

- **Disk drivers.** These are needed to provide access to the **partitions** (logical subdivisions of a disk) on the server's disk drives.

- **LAN drivers.** Since servers must have access to the network, they require a NIC to be installed. A LAN driver is the program designed to operate with the NIC.

- **Name space.** Many systems still run with the DOS/Windows 3.1 requirement that file names be restricted to eight characters plus an extension. Fortunately other systems such as Windows 95, NT, UNIX, and Macintosh have much more liberal file naming requirements. Name space NLMs provide the support necessary to provide compatibility with these systems.

- **General Purpose.** These NLMs provide additional capabilities to monitor disk and memory usage, check disk areas for errors, support CD-ROM hardware, check hardware status, or to remotely access the NetWare server console.

Reference [Si97] provides a fairly detailed description of NLMs and gives some examples of what is required to load and use them.

Each client workstation runs its own operating system as well as a NetWare **shell** (also called a **requester**). If the workstation runs DOS or Windows 3.1, the shell is also called a **virtual loadable module.** More recent systems such as Windows NT or Windows 95 have a requester as part of the software. The NetWare shell is a command interpreter that accepts input from the workstation (Figure 6.39). It

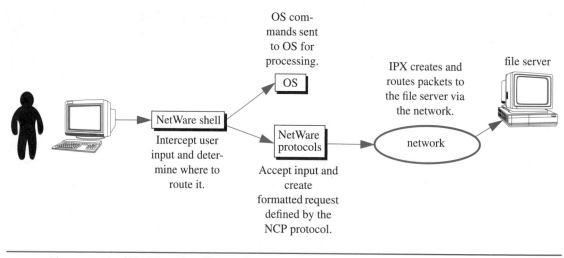

Figure 6.39   NetWare Handling User Requests

analyzes the request and determines whether the operating system or NetWare should handle it. If it is destined for the operating system (OS), the requester passes it on and does not involve the network or any NetWare software.

If the user input is destined for NetWare service, the shell creates and formats a request according to the definitions of the **NetWare core protocol (NCP).** NCP defines the types of requests that can be made and how the server responds to the request it eventually receives. Once the request has been properly formatted according to NCP, the shell then gives it to the **Internetwork Packet Exchange (IPX),** a protocol used to establish and maintain connections between network devices. IPX determines source and destination addresses and stores them in a packet along with the request. When the server receives the packet, it extracts the data, determines the request as defined by NCP, and responds accordingly. IPX does not guarantee packet delivery. Another protocol, **Sequenced Packet Exchange (SPX),** monitors packet transmissions to ensure proper delivery. Similar to the flow control protocols of Chapter 5, SPX sends and receives acknowledgments. If it does not receive an expected acknowledgment it will call on IPX to resend the packet.

All packets must eventually pass through a NIC and onto the actual network. A **network driver** is the interface that ensures that packets are sent according to the network protocol. It is important to realize that network protocols differ from NetWare protocols. NetWare defines the rules and formats to respond to clients' requests. The network protocol, such as token ring or Ethernet, defines how the packets are actually transmitted. Using a network driver builds flexibility into the system and allows IPX to send packets over a variety of different networks.

To give the system even more flexibility, Novell has added another component to its protocol called the **Open Data-link Interface (ODI).** It allows greater interconnectivity among devices and networks running different protocols by providing multiple network connections through a single NIC. ODI contains a **link support**

layer (LSL) that allows the client to run multiple protocols. LSL acts as an interface between those protocols and the NIC. It translates protocol-specific details into a standard form defined by ODI and passes them onto the NIC. To make this work, NIC vendors use LSL specifications to design NICs compatible with NetWare client programs.

What does this mean to the workstation user? The bottom line is that a user can connect to different networks without installing different NICs or rebooting the workstation to load the proper network drivers. The advantage, of course, is added flexibility. Also, future network expansion is simplified because additional network connections can be made without purchasing new hardware. We all know the advantage of fewer purchases!

SECURITY AND INTEGRITY

NetWare provides security in several ways. The first and most obvious is to require users to enter an account number and a password to gain access to NetWare's file system. The account number and password are checked against those maintained by NetWare. If there is no match, the user is not allowed to log in. NetWare stores passwords in encrypted form to provide additional protection. If someone were to gain unauthorized access to the password file, all the intruder would see is encrypted passwords.

NetWare 4.0 features additional security by providing authentication using a private/public key cryptographic system. When a user logs in, NetWare sends the client software an encrypted private key. All subsequent NetWare requests from that user contain a signature created from that key that a server can authenticate. The intent, as described in Section 4.6, is to foil someone who penetrated the first level of security and began submitting requests that appeared to come from an authorized user.

If the user does log in successfully, that does not mean he or she has automatic access to all of NetWare's files. NetWare can grant specific rights that allow a user or group of users to access specific directories and files on a server. These are called **trustee rights;** the user or group is called a **trustee.** NetWare 3.11 maintains trustee rights for each server and stores them in a file called a **bindery.** Each server has its own bindery. Since there are often several file servers and users can potentially log in to each one, there can be duplication among the binderies.

Netware 4.0 takes a different approach by using a **NetWare Directory Service (NDS),** which is based on the X.500 standard.[*] Rather than storing specific information on specific servers, it uses a **distributed database.** That is, pertinent information for tracking authorized users and maintaining security is distributed across all file servers. Instead of connecting to a specific server, the user logs into "the system" and is not aware of which server provides needed files. This appoach adds flexibility by making server locations transparent to the users and allows better cross-referencing among files from different servers.

---

[*]We discuss the X.500 standard in Chapter 8.

Regardless of version, the trustee rights specify who can access which files or directories. NetWare provides GRANT and REVOKE commands to assign or remove trustee rights. Each command specifies a file or directory and a user or group of users. Examples of trustee rights are listed here.

- **Read.** Open and read a file or execute a program.
- **Write.** Open and write to a file.
- **Create.** Create a file or subdirectory.
- **Erase.** Delete any file or subdirectory.
- **Modify.** Rename a directory or file and/or change its attributes. Typical attributes include whether the file may be copied, deleted, shared, renamed, or opened as read only. It does not allow the right to change a file's contents.
- **File Scan.** Get a list of directory files.
- **Access Control.** Change the trustee rights for a file or directory and change the inherited rights mask associated with each file or directory when it is created. By default, when a trustee is given rights to a directory, the trustee also has rights to the files and subdirectories in it. However, the inherited rights mask associated with a file or directory may override the default.
- **Supervisory.** Provide all trustee rights to the file or directory and any subdirectories in the directory.

When applied to files, most of the above rights are rather straightforward. But suppose a right is applied to a directory. Does that mean the same right applies to all files in that directory? What if that directory contains subdirectories? Do the same rights apply to all files in those subdirectories as well? What about subdirectories several levels below? The answer to all of these question is, in general, yes. A right applied to a directory applies to any file reachable through that directory. This is an **inherited right.** Inherited rights simplify the assignment of trustee rights. Suppose a user needs read access to everything in a particular directory. One way is to assign a read right to each file in that directory separately, then to each file in each subdirectory, and so on until all files in all subdirectories have been included. Naturally, this would be awkward to say the least (we'll avoid the temptation to say the most). By using inherited rights, the user automatically gets read access to all files in a directory to which they have read access.

Now let's consider another problem (Figure 6.40). Suppose that read access to directory *A* is applied to a group of people. Based on what we have said, all will have read access to subdirectories *X*, *Y*, and *Z*. Suppose the group is large and only the group leader should have access to subdirectory *Z*. One approach is to grant read access of directory *A* to the group as a whole, but then individually revoke read access to subdirectory *Z* for each member except the leader. Again, the number of actions necessary to perform this can be awkward.

To simplify matters, NetWare provides an **Inherited Rights Filter (IRF),** which can be applied to any directory. Some call it an **inherited rights mask.** The IRF will block specific rights from cascading down into a particular subdirectory.

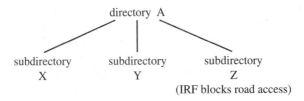

directory A

subdirectory   subdirectory   subdirectory
X   Y   Z
                                  (IRF blocks road access)

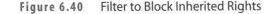

Figure 6.40   Filter to Block Inherited Rights

For example, suppose subdirectory Z had an IRF that filtered out read access. Then no one in the group would have an inherited right to read anything in subdirectory Z. This still doesn't solve our problem since we want the group leader to have read access to Z. However, this can be done by specifically granting read access to that individual.

In the first case, the default allowed everyone read access to Z and it had to be removed explicitly for each member except the leader. In the second case, the default allowed no one read access to Z. However, the leader could be granted read privilege explicitly, thus overriding the default. The second case provides an easier way of assigning the desired rights correctly.

In addition to providing security, NetWare protects the integrity of information when related updates must be made to several files. For example, suppose a company database maintains a list of its sales personnel and customers. Each salesperson's record contains a reference to one or more customers for which he or she is responsible (Figure 6.41a). If the company loses a customer, not only is the customer's

Figure 6.41   Maintaining Consistent Files in NetWare

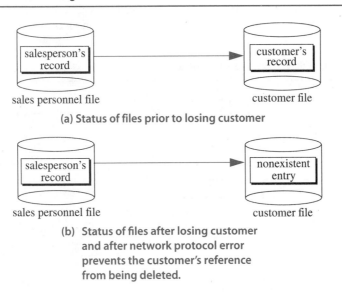

salesperson's record → customer's record

sales personnel file   customer file

(a) Status of files prior to losing customer

salesperson's record → nonexistent entry

sales personnel file   customer file

(b) Status of files after losing customer and after network protocol error prevents the customer's reference from being deleted.

record deleted from the database but any references to it from the salesperson's file also must be deleted. If the customer record was deleted and a network protocol error then prevented the reference to it from being deleted (Figure 6.41b), the database would be inconsistent. To prevent this situation, NetWare provides a **transaction tracking system (TTS)** that allows multiple updates to files to be regarded as a single transaction. TTS performs all of the updates or none at all. If it performed some of the updates and a protocol error prevented the others from being completed, TTS would restore the affected records to their pretransaction values.

Hardware failures can be devastating, as anyone who has ever experienced a head crash (contact between the disk head and disk) knows. Eventually, all disk drives will fail. In some cases, only the drive mechanism fails, allowing the disk to be removed and inserted in another drive. In other cases, the disk's directory is damaged but special utilities can often recover the data on it. If the cause is a head crash, however, the disk surface may be destroyed, making any recovery impossible.

NetWare provides two ways of reducing such problems (Figure 6.42). Both make duplicate copies of updated data by copying it onto different disks, but they differ in how that is done. **Disk duplexing** uses two different controllers connected to the server. When the server must make a change, both controllers write the updated data to their respective disks. With **disk mirroring,** one controller writes the information on two different disks. Disk duplexing is faster because two controllers are doing the work of one. It is also more reliable. If one controller fails, the other can proceed with required changes. On the other hand, disk mirroring provides a more economical approach.

SELECTED NOVELL COMMANDS

Perhaps nothing gives a user a better feel for how software works than a description of the commands he or she uses to interact with it. For this reason we provide a brief description of some of NetWare's more common commands. This is not a complete

Figure 6.42   Disk Mirroring and Duplexing

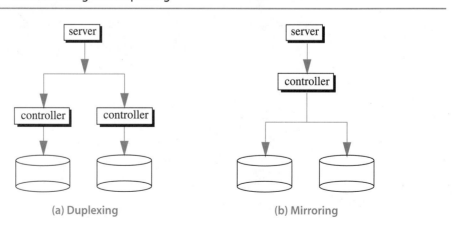

(a) Duplexing   (b) Mirroring

list, but you may find such a list in any NetWare manual or in References [Ra94a], [Ra94b], [Ra94c], or [Si97]. We divide NetWare commands into two types. **Client commands** are those that may be entered from any client or the server. **Server commands,** or console commands, define high-priority requests typically made by the LAN manager and are entered only from the server's console.

Client Commands

- ATTACH allows a user to connect to a different file server. The command must specify the server's name and the user's ID and password.
- LISTDIR provides a list of the subdirectories within the given directory.
- LOGIN/LOGOUT allows a user to log in or log out of the network. The LOGIN command must specify the user's ID and if needed the file server's name. The LOGOUT command may also specify a file server's name if the user wants to log out from just that server. If no parameter is specified, NetWare logs the user out of all servers.
- MAP assigns a client's drive letter (DOS prompt) to a directory path on one of the file server's volumes.
- NCOPY copies files.
- NPRINT allows a user to print a file. Parameters include which printer, server, or queue is requested; the option of deleting the file after printing; the number of copies to print; and whether a banner page should be printed.
- RIGHTS allows the user to examine the current trustee rights.
- SETPASS allows a user to set a password.
- SEND allows a user to send a one-line message to one or more users logged on to the network.
- SLIST displays a list of all file servers connected to the network.
- TLIST displays trustee information.
- WHOAMI displays information regarding the currently logged-in user. It includes the file server name, user name, and login time. If there are multiple servers, a display is provided for each one to which the user is connected.

Server Commands

- BROADCAST sends a message to all users. This can be used to request all users to log off if a manager must bring a server offline.
- DISABLE LOGIN/ENABLE LOGIN prevents or allows users to log in to a server.
- PRINTER provides information about any printers attached to the server. It includes the printer ID, print queues, and printer status.
- PRINTER ADD allows the person entering the command to add new queues and their priorities to the printer.
- QUEUE provides a list of all print queues.

LOGIN SCRIPTS

One of a network manager's most important functions is to make sure network users have easy access to what they need. The manager must understand that many users are not network literate and do not need to be. Users accessing Lotus Notes or Microsoft's Access have their own needs and deadlines and may not want to bother with network-specific details or learn NetWare commands to get what they need. Consequently, the network manager must have some way to make network operations transparent to the user.

A common approach is to create **login scripts,** a collection of commands that are automatically executed each time a user logs into the system. They are similar to MS-DOS's AUTOEXEC.BAT and VMS'S LOGIN.COM files. There are two types of login scripts. The **system login script** defines commands that are executed for each user logging in to the system. Examples include assigning a client's drive letter to a specific directory, displaying messages, and loading specific files onto the client workstation. The **user login script** contains commands needed only by a specific user.[*] We will provide a short overview of some scripting capabilities, but refer you to References [Ra94a] and [Si97] for more complete coverage.

Figure 6.43 shows an example of a system login script. Line 1 prevents the user from interrupting login script execution by entering a Ctrl-C or Ctrl-Break sequence, and line 2 suppresses the display of drive maps. Line 3 displays a message that each user logging in to the system will see. The message is in a file named WELCOME.MSG which the network manager can use to send messages to any user logging in. This is useful to inform users of any anticipated down times, new network features, or anything of general interest such as who won the weekend football pool. The file containing the message is in a directory named PUBLIC, which, in turn, lies in a volume named SYS. PUBLIC is a public-access directory containing NetWare utilities. The **volume** is another name for a disk partition ("SYS" is the usual name). In general, a file is specified by volume name, directory name, and file name. In some cases the directory is actually a directory path with the format "dir1/dir2/dir3 . . .," where dir3 is a subdirectory of dir2 and dir2 is a subdirectory of dir1.

Lines 4 and 5 establish search drives and assign them to specific directories. **Search drives** define the directories that the operating system searches automatically when the user requests a file not in the current directory. Designated by S1, S2, S3, etc., each drive assignment corresponds to drive letters Z, Y, X, etc. Up to 16 search drives may be defined. Directories assigned to the search drives have the format "Volume:directory-path." Thus, line 4 maps drive letter Z to the

---

[*]NetWare 4.0 has four types of scripts. Instead of the system login script, there is a container login script and a profile login script. There is also a default login script for those who have no user login script. Together, they provide a little more flexibility regarding which scripts are executed for which groups of users. Our goal here is to provide an overview of scripting, and the differences are not significant. If you are interested, you might look at Reference [Si97].

```
1    BREAK OFF
2    MAP DISPLAY OFF
3    FDISPLAY SYS:PUBLIC/WELCOME.MSG
4    MAP S1:=SYS:SOFTWARE/PCAPPS
5    MAP S2:=SYS:SOFTWARE/WEBAPPS
6    IF MEMBER OF "COMPSCI" THEN
7      MAP S3:=SYS:SOFTWARE/LANGUAGE
8      #CAPTURE Q=CS_HPPL5 NB NFF
9    END
10   IF MEMBER OF "STATS" THEN
11     MAP S3:=SYS:SOFTWARE/STATLAB
12     #CAPTURE Q=STAT_LASER NB NFF
13   END
14   IF DAY_OF_WEEK = "MONDAY" THEN
15     FDISPLAY SYS:PUBLIC/MONDAY.MSG
16     FIRE PHASERS 5 TIMES
17   END
18   MAP H:=SYS:USERS/%LOGIN_NAME
19   DRIVE H:
```

Figure 6.43   System Login Script

SOFTWARE/PCAPPS directory in the SYS volume and line 5 maps driver letter Y to the SOFTWARE/WEBAPPS directory in the same volume. The directory names, of course, are site dependent.

Lines 6 through 17 show how NetWare can define the working environment for different user groups. In general the network manager can set up a collection of groups, each containing users with similar needs. In our example, we assume there are two groups named COMPSCI and STATS that correspond to people whose area of expertise is in computer science or statistics. When logging in, the system script can check to which group the user belongs using an IF-THEN command statement. The script IF statement is just like the IF statement in your favorite language. It tests a condition and, if true, executes specified statements.

Conditions can take several forms in a NetWare script, but line 6 checks whether the current user is a member of the COMPSCI group. If so, line 7 maps search drive S3 (actually, drive X) to the SOFTWARE/LANGUAGE directory set up for that group. Presumably, it contains language compilers for which no other user has a need. Lines 10 and 11 check whether the user is a member of the STATS group and, if so, assigns search drive S3 to an entirely different directory containing some statistical software. Thus, a user in either group has search drive S3 locating software or tools relevant to his or her needs (Figure 6.44).

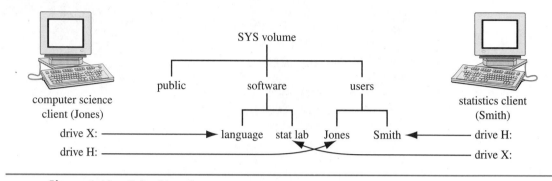

Figure 6.44 Drive Mappings

The #CAPTURE commands in lines 8 and 12 set up printing for each user.[*] We are assuming that because users are in different groups they will likely print to two different networked printers. This is not unusual since different groups are often located in different areas. The CAPTURE commands tell NetWare to intercept any print output either type of user generates and route it to a specified printer queue associated with a printer. The option Q=CS_HPPL5 in line 8 simply specifies a queue name defined by the network administrator, as does Q=STAT_LASER in line 12. The other options, NB and NFF, provide additional information about a print job. In each case, printed output should have no banner page (NB) and has form feed disabled (NFF). The END in lines 9 and 13 indicates the end of the conditionally executed statements.

Line 14 is an example of another condition that a script can check. It checks whether the current day is Monday. If it is, line 15 displays a message, perhaps trying to cheer you up after a long weekend or to depress you by listing all of the mandatory staff meetings you must attend during the upcoming week. In the event that Monday morning blues still find you half asleep, line 16 produces sounds (reminiscent of those in science fiction movies) designed to get your attention. This is for real! The statement FIRE PHASER n TIMES really does produce a sequence of sounds, with *n* specifying how many.

Finally, lines 18 and 19 set drive H to a user's private directory. Like most systems, each user has space in which to store files and programs that is accessible using their login name. The private directories are actually subdirectories of the USERS directory in the SYS volume. The percent sign (%) prior to LOGIN_NAME means that the user's actual login name should be used as a subdirectory of USERS. For example, if SMITH and JONES were two separate login names, then Figure 6.44 shows the assignment of drive letter H for each.

---

[*] The pound sign (#) prior to CAPTURE is there because CAPTURE is actually a NetWare program as opposed to a script statement. The pound sign is the symbol specified when running a program defined outside the scope of the scripting language.

User login scripts have the same format as system login scripts, so we'll not go through another example. User scripts can map additional search drives according to individual user's needs. They can display personalized messages to create a more friendly working environment. They also can contain references to executable files that can display menus and request user input. This is especially useful for those who simply want to log in to the network and see their options displayed in menu form. It is the network manager's responsibility to see that all users get what they need and can see their options in a format best suited to those needs. When there are many users with a variety of needs, this is not an easy task.

6.7   SUMMARY

A major focus of this chapter has been local area networks, or LANs. The IEEE has defined three very different LAN standards. They are 802.3 CSMA/CD (Ethernet), 802.4 token bus, and 802.5 token ring. Table 6.9 summarizes the major features of each.

Table 6.9   Summary of LAN Standards

	ETHERNET	TOKEN RING	TOKEN BUS
Maximum delay before sending	None	Bounded, depending on distance spanned and number of stations. However, if priorities are used, a low priority station may have no maximum delay.	Bounded, depending on distance spanned and number of stations.
Physical topology	Linear	Ring	Linear
Logical topology	None	Ring	Ring
Contention	Random chance	By token	By token
Adding stations	A new station can be added almost anywhere on the cable at any time.	Must be inserted between two specified stations.	Distributed algorithms are needed to add new stations.
Performance	Stations often send immediately under light loads, but heavy traffic can reduce the effective data rate to near 0.	Stations must wait for the token even if no other station is sending. Under heavy loads, token passing provides fair access to all stations.	Stations must wait for the token even if no other station is sending. Under heavy loads, token passing provides fair access to all stations.
Maintenance	No central maintenance.	A designated monitor station performs maintenance.	Distributed algorithms provide maintenance.

ISO also has a standard called Fiber Distributed Data Interface (FDDI). Developed at a time when existing LAN standards were relatively slow, FDDI had potential for becoming the primary network model for 100 Mbps communications. However, the evolution of existing IEEE LANs to 100 Mbps capabilities along with their already widespread use has allowed Ethernets and token rings to maintain their important niche in the LAN market.

Regardless of the LAN standard, there is an upper limit on the number of stations it can handle effectively and the amount of security it can provide. As the need to connect workstations and provide additional security grows, multiple LANs often are connected with bridges. Stations connected to a single LAN can communicate independently of those in a connected LAN. This independence is efficient and provides security. Stations on different LANs can still communicate when necessary, however. This puts a burden on bridge design because the bridge must know when to transfer a frame from one LAN to another. Furthermore, if a bridge connects several LANs it must know over which LAN it should send frames.

Section 6.5 discussed three approaches to connecting LANS. Fixed-routing bridges must be programmed with each station's location relative to the bridge. Each bridge stores that information in routing tables and routes frames accordingly. Transparent bridges also use routing tables, but they are not programmed. Instead, they learn of a station's location by monitoring the data frames. Source-routing bridges put the burden of routing on the sending station, which must determine a route and put it in a frame. The bridges then transmit frames depending on their routing information.

No network can function without a significant amount of software to handle communications. Many proprietary packages exist, but a commonly used one is Novell NetWare. Originally designed to connect primarily PCs and printers, it now connects a wide variety of equipment running different protocols. NetWare requires one or more servers to provide other PCs (clients) with application programs or data files. The LAN manager typically designs scripts for the system and the users to make sure the users attach to the proper servers and get what they need without having to learn many network commands. The trend with the latest version is to create a more open system in which client information is stored in a distributed database. This approach further insulates the client from network details. The bottom line, of course, is to make more services available with a minimum amount of hassle for the user.

Review Questions

1. Distinguish between a local area network and a wide area network.

2. List typical LAN topologies.

3. What is a segment?

4. What are the two major divisions of the data link layers, and what are their major functions?

5. What is a transceiver?

6. Are the following statements TRUE or FALSE? Why?

   a. Ethernet is a seven-layer protocol similar to the OSI model.

   b. StarLAN is a physical star topology that behaves like a bus topology.

   c. A high percent utilization for a common bus network is an indication that the network is performing efficiently and meeting the needs of its users.

   d. The pad field in an Ethernet frame is optional.

   e. In a token ring network, stations take turns sending frames in order of their arrangement on the ring.

   f. All three LAN protocols allow stations to be prioritized.

   g. Token ring has no central control.

   h. Any station can raise or lower the ring priority in a token ring.

   i. In a token bus LAN the stations' logical order is independent of their physical order.

   j. The biggest problem in routing frames from one LAN protocol to another is reformatting the frames to maintain consistency with the LAN's protocol.

7. Describe each of the 802.3 cable specifications.

8. What is a T-connector used for?

9. Why are repeaters necessary in some networks?

10. Why does an Ethernet frame have a maximum size? Minimum size?

11. What purpose does the token serve in a token ring network?

12. Discuss the content and purpose of each field in the token format (token ring network).

13. What is a non-data-J and non-data-K signal?

14. What is a stacking station?

15. What is a monitor station?

16. Describe the purpose of each of the following token ring control frames:

    a. Active monitor present frame

    b. Beacon frame

    c. Claim token frame

    d.   Purge frame

    e.   Standby monitor present frame

    f.   Duplicate address test frame

17.   What is the Fiber Distributed Data Interface (FDDI)?

18.   What is a 4 of 5 code?

19.   Distinguish between a slotted ring and a token ring.

20.   What is an orphan frame?

21.   Distinguish between a token bus and token ring LAN.

22.   Describe the purpose of each of the following token bus control frames:

    a.   Claim token frame

    b.   Resolve contention frame

    c.   Set successor frame

    d.   Solicit successor 1 frame

    e.   Solicit successor 2 frame

    f.   Who follows frame

23.   Distinguish between a token-holding timer and a token-rotation timer.

24.   Describe how a token bus deals with a lost token.

25.   Why does a token bus require a complex initialization procedure?

26.   How does a station remove itself from a token bus network?

27.   Distinguish between a repeater and a bridge.

28.   List major reasons for using bridges between two LANs.

29.   What is a routing table?

30.   Distinguish between a fixed-routing bridge and a transparent bridge.

31.   What is the flooding algorithm and what purpose does it serve?

32.   What problem can flooding cause when there is a loop in a LAN topology?

33.   What is a spanning tree within the context of an interconnection of LANs?

34.   What is a root bridge?

35.   What is a bridge's root port?

36.   What purpose does a LAN's designated bridge serve?

37.   What is a source-routing bridge?

38. What is a bridge protocol data unit?

39. Distinguish between an all-routes broadcast frame and a single-route broadcast frame.

40. What is the purpose of Novell NetWare?

41. What is a file server?

42. Distinguish between a dedicated and a nondedicated file server.

43. What are trustee rights?

44. Distinguish between disk duplexing and disk mirroring.

45. Distinguish between client commands and server commands.

46. What is a login script?

Exercises

1. What is the maximum theoretical percent utilization in a 10 Mbps 802.3 LAN (10Base5 cable) with 128 stations connected to five 500-meter segments if the frame size is 128 bytes? 1024 bytes?

2. Consider the LAN specifications from Exercise 1. What is the longest time a station might need to detect a collision? If the LAN were just a single 2500-meter segment? Repeat the same calculations as in Exercise 1.

3. How many bits can occupy a 500-meter ring containing 50 equally spaced stations (assuming each has a one-bit delay)? Assume a data rate of 4 Mbps. What about a data rate of 16 Mbps?

4. Why do we seemingly complicate the token ring protocol by routing each frame bit or token bit as soon as it is received? Why not just receive all the bits for a token, examine them, and then pass them all to the next station?

5. Consider a 200-meter 4 Mbps token ring containing 20 stations, each transmitting with equal priority. Suppose no station is allowed to transmit more than 5000 data octets before giving up the token. Once a station gives up the token, how long will it take (in the worst case) for that station to get the token again?

6. In the discussion on reserving tokens we stated that the station that raises a token's priority has the responsibility to lower it later. Why lower it at all? Why not leave the priority as it is?

7. Finish Table 6.2 to the point at which all stations have sent their frames and a token with priority 0 is back on the ring.

8. Repeat the example described by Figure 6.14 and Table 6.2 assuming the token is traveling in a clockwise direction.

9. If a token ring is prioritized what is the longest time a station may have to wait before it can claim a token?

10. In our discussion of SMP frames, each station receiving one repeated it and later sent its own. Why not have each station that receives an SMP frame drain it from the ring and send its own immediately? That way each station would know its upstream neighbor in the time it takes for one SMP frame to circulate the ring.

11. Consider the algorithm of Figure 6.13. Discuss the effects of removing code associated with each of the following conditions.

    a. Condition 2

    b. Condition 4

    c. Condition 7

12. Why does the token bus protocol use two solicit successor frames instead of just one?

13. Suppose the following stations are trying to get into a token bus network.

    Station V: address = 0011010010
    Station W: address = 0011100110
    Station X: address = 0001100110
    Station Y: address = 0011011000
    Station Z: address = 0011001110

    Suppose station B is station A's successor and that A sends a solicit successor 1 frame. Describe the events that eventually allow the first station into the ring. Which station gets in? Assume A's address is 0011100000 and B's address is 0011000001.

14. Using multiple tokens in a ring can improve performance, but the same is not true for the token bus. Why?

15. Pseudocode the logic a station uses to claim a token using the claim token frame.

16. Assume the following:

    • There are four stations on a token bus, which circulate the token in the order *A-B-C-D*.
    • THT = 6 and TRT = 32 for each station.
    • Each station has an unending stream of frames in each class to send.
    • The token has just arrived at *A*.

    Describe which frames are sent using the priority mechanism discussed in Section 6.4.

17. Consider an interconnection strategy among LANs in which the most frequently communicating LANs are connected over the fewest bridges. Assume the following LAN pairs must be no more than the specified number of bridges apart. Design an interconnection that uses the fewest number of bridges.

   - One bridge apart: L1 and L5; L2 and L3; L2 and L4
   - Two (or fewer) bridges apart: L1 and L3; L2 and L5; L1 and L2

18. Build routing tables for the following bridges.

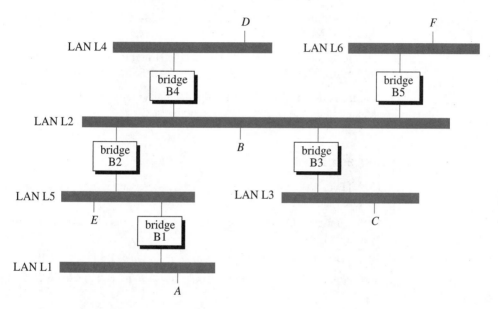

19. Consider the LANs of Figure 6.27 and assume all the routing tables are empty initially. Assume the following events occur in the order listed. Over what LANs are the specified frames transmitted? Show the routing table entries of each bridge after all frames have been sent.

   a. *A* sends a frame to *F.*

   b. *E* sends a frame to *A.*

   c. *D* sends a frame to *E.*

   d. *C* sends a frame to *B.*

20. List all routes between *A* and *B* in Figure 6.31. Ignore any route in which a frame goes through the same bridge twice. If we do not ignore those routes how many are there?

21. Suppose bridge B1 in Figure 6.31 fails. Execute the spanning tree algorithm and show the new root bridge, cheapest bridge ports, designated bridges, and the resulting enabled bridge connections.

22. Assume the internetwork of Figure 6.31 is changed so that all listed costs are equal. Assuming that the cost of a transmission between two distinct LANs is now the number of bridges through which it must travel, determine the spanning tree.

23. Suppose *A* sends an all-routes broadcast frame to *B* in Figure 6.31. How many copies of it does *B* receive?

24. Modify the system login script from Figure 6.43 to account for the following changes:

   a. Define another search drive and assign it to the MENUS1 subdirectory in the APP directory of the SYS volume.

   b. Define a working group called ACCTING1 and for any user in it, map drive G to the ACCTING1 subdirectory in the USERS directory on the SYS volume.

   c. For users in the ACCTING1 group, display a message in the file MSG1.MSG located in the same ACCTING1 subdirectory.

REFERENCES

1. [Be92] Bertsekas, D. and R. Gallager. *Data Networks,* 2nd ed. Englewood Cliffs, NJ: Prentice Hall, 1992.

2. [Bo94] Boisseau, M., M. Demange, and J-M. Munier. *High Speed Networks.* New York: Wiley, 1994.

3. [Dr95] Drozdek, A. and D. Simon. *Data Structures in C.* Boston: PWS, 1995.

4. [Jo96] Johnson, H. *Fast Ethernet: Dawn of a New Network.* Englewood Cliffs, NJ: Prentice Hall, 1996.

5. [Ll96] Lloyd-Evans, R. *Wide Area Network Performance and Optimization.* Reading, MA: Addison Wesley, 1996.

6. [Lo97] Lounsbury, A. "Gigabit Ethernet: The Difference Is in the Details." *Data Communications,* vol. 26, no. 6 (May 1997), 75–80.

7. [Mo89] Moshos, G. *Data Communications: Principles and Problems.* St. Paul, MN: West, 1989.

8. [Pa95] Parsons, T. *Introduction to Algorithms in Pascal.* New York: Wiley, 1995.

9. [Ra94a] Rains, A. and M. Palmer. *Local Area Networking with Novell Software.* Danvers, MA: Boyd & Fraser, 1994.

10. [Ra94b] Ramos, E., A. Schroeder, and A. Beheler. *Data Communications and Networking Fundamentals Using Novell NetWare (3.11).* New York: Macmillan, 1994.

11. [Ra94c] Ramos, E., A. Schroeder, and A. Beheler. *Networking Using Novell Netware (3.11).* New York: Macmillan, 1994.

12. [Ro97] Roberts, E. "Gigabit Ethernet: Fat Pipe or Bomb." *Data Communications,* vol. 26, no. 6 (May 1997), 58–73.

13. [Si97] Simpson, T. *Hands-On Netware: A Guide to NetWare 4.1 with Projects.* Cambridge, MA: Course Technology, 1997.

14. [St90] Stallings, W. *Handbook of Computer Communications Standards,* Vol. 2, 2nd ed. Indianapolis, IN: Howard Sams, 1990.

15. [St93] Stallings, W. *Local and Metropolitan Area Networks,* 4th ed. New York: Macmillan, 1993.

16. [St94] Stallings, W. *Data and Computer Communications,* 4th ed. New York: Macmillan, 1994.

17. [Wa91] Walrand, J. *Communications Networks: A First Course.* Boston: Irwin, 1991.

18. [Wa96] Walrand, J. and P. Varaiya. *High Performance Communications Networks.* San Francisco: Morgan Kaufmann, 1996.

CHAPTER 7

WIDE AREA NETWORKING

Information can tell us everything. It has all the answers. But they are answers to questions we have not asked, and which doubtless don't even arise.
—**Jean Baudrillard,** French semiologist

7.1 INTRODUCTION

Local area networks (LANs), discussed in Chapter 6, typically cover small geographic areas. They are designed around relatively simple bus or ring topologies. Some networks, however, called **wide area networks (WANs),** cover much larger areas, sometimes spanning several continents. In those cases, the LAN protocols are inappropriate and new ones must be defined.

Consider again the analogy of a highway system. Many cities have a single major freeway through the center (common bus) or a bypass circling them (ring). If the city is not large, this design handles most highway traffic reasonably well. But what about larger areas such as states or entire countries? It would be unreasonable to have an interstate system consisting of a single highway through America's heartland or circling the country along the coastal areas and the Canadian and Mexican borders. Instead, a complex connection strategy links major highways; bypasses; and state, county, and city roads. It is not reasonable to categorize this type of system as a bus, ring, or even a combination of two. It is much more complex.

Like a national highway system, the topologies of wide area networks are complex, usually somewhere between a simple bus or ring structure and a fully connected one. With more complex topologies come more complex protocols. Collision detection is no longer a viable way to control traffic over so many paths. Similarly, token passing will not work on such a grand scale.

In addition to geographic distance and complexity, there are other differences between LANs and WANs. For example, typical LAN uses include file transfer, electronic mail, and file servers. People use WANs for electronic mail and file transfer, but also for remote logins, an application in which a user in one location logs in to a computer at another. WAN protocols must distinguish among various applications.

Another difference is in routing. Section 6.5 discussed some approaches to routing in LAN interconnections. The more complex WAN topologies require more complex routing strategies. The fact that there are many ways to go from one point to another by itself makes the situation more complex. Anyone who has ever planned a long trip with a detailed map knows the problem of choosing the best route.

To add to the complexity, sometimes a link in a chosen route experiences a failure. What does the network protocol do with all the data traveling that route? In some cases, a route may prove so popular that too much data travels over it. The result is congestion and sometimes failure. Can network protocols avoid such situations? If they can't, what can they do to minimize their effects? To return to our highway analogy, these problems are similar to major road construction preventing traffic flow or excessive traffic on the road to a popular vacation spot during a major holiday. Most of us know these problems well and understand that little can be done short of staying home.

When data is delayed due to failures and congestion it must be stored somewhere while WAN protocols decide what to do with it. Network nodes must be equipped with software and buffers to do this—the equivalent of roadside motels for data.

Management is another problem. LANs are controlled and managed by a single organization or department. If a problem occurs, users know who to call. Some WANs, such as the Internet, have evolved due mainly to voluntary efforts of universities and government agencies. Consequently, there is no central authority responsible for fixing problems or updating protocols so that they do not happen again. Such a network's operations depend on the cooperation of the organizations that use it.

Many WANs evolved by connecting existing networks. Because these networks often used different equipment and different protocols, connecting them was a problem. **Protocol converters,** which define the logic that translates one protocol to another, were used to establish connections.

Chapter 6 discussed some LAN protocol converters called repeaters and bridges. With these methods, the incompatibilities occur at a low level. For example, repeaters, an OSI layer 1 connection, deal primarily with the electrical (or optical) interface (Figure 7.1a), converting one type of signal to another or simply regenerating it. Bridges that work at OSI layer 2 (Figure 7.1b) are needed when frames have different formats or when some logical separation among LANs is needed.

WANs provide a greater variety of networks and incompatibilities. Frame sizes may limit the types of data that can travel among networks. Sometimes frames must be divided to maintain compliance with another network's protocol. Perhaps two networks use different routing strategies. Layer 2 logic cannot deal with these incompatibilities. In such cases, a **router,** a connection at OSI layer 3 (Figure 7.1c), is used to handle the differences. A router knows the differences in the lower three layers of both network protocols and translates between them.

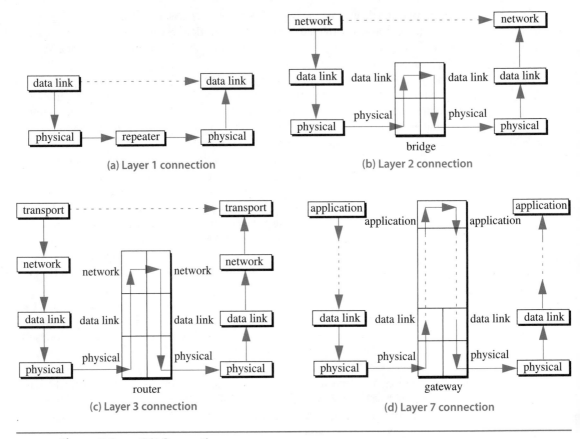

Figure 7.1   OSI Connections

In theory, two different networks may differ at any of the OSI layers. The logic required to connect them becomes more complex as the number of layers where they differ increases. In the extreme case, there may be total incompatibility (up through layer 7). For example, they may use different codes, encryption techniques, or compression techniques. They may use different rules for establishing and maintaining connections. In such cases, a connection at layer 7 called a **gateway** (Figure 7.1d) converts between protocols.

This chapter discusses some of the issues of WAN design and protocols. For example, Section 7.2 discusses routing, the logic required by network nodes to make sure information gets to its destination. It will present and compare a few common strategies and will address problems, such as congestion, caused by poor routing decisions. Section 7.3 discusses a popular WAN called a packet-switched network, one that divides all its information into packets and transmits them individually. This section also discusses the ITU X.25 protocol, which is commonly used to connect to packet-switched networks.

Section 7.4 presents the Internet Protocol. Actually, there are two Internet protocols. One is an ISO standard and is part of the network layer in the OSI model; we will not discuss this protocol. The other is based on an Internet protocol developed by the U.S. Defense Advanced Research Projects Agency (DARPA). It has been used in the network layer of the ARPANET and is most often used with the Transmission Control Protocol (TCP), a transport protocol discussed in Section 7.5. Together they are known as TCP/IP and form the layer 3 and layer 4 protocols used to connect commercial, research, military, and educational networks. The combined network is accessible to professionals worldwide and is known as the **Internet.**

In Section 7.6 we discuss Internet programming through the introduction of a UNIX construct called a socket. We will introduce the client/server paradigm for programming and give a working example of how to use sockets to implement a simple file transfer protocol between two computers assuming only that there is an Internet connection between them.

7.2   NETWORK ROUTING

Most people are familiar with the general concept of routing. Essentially it means that if you want to go from point A to point B you have to determine a way to get there. For example, if you live in Winona, Minnesota, and want to drive to Charleston, South Carolina, for your vacation, you will probably spend some time studying road maps to determine the best way to get there. Similarly, if you want to transfer information between computers in those two locations that are connected via a WAN, network protocols must determine how to get it there.

When LANs are organized around a single bus or ring, routing is not a problem. If they are connected with bridges, the bridges make the routing decisions (as explained in Section 6.5). The topologies are not very complex, and the bridges do the routing rather easily.

Figure 7.2 shows a more general network topology. Some stations often communicate directly with more stations than do others. Presumably they represent locations in heavily populated areas or locations with a high volume of information traffic. The stations with fewer connections might have fewer needs or correspond to more remote sites. For example, nodes A and B might represent sites in major metropolitan areas, and nodes X and Y may correspond to locations in remote parts of the country.

Suppose one station wants to communicate with another to which it is not connected directly. Network protocols must find a path that connects them. To make matters more complex, there may be many paths. For example, suppose X sends something to Y in Figure 7.2. Two possible paths are X-A-B-C-D-Y and X-A-Z-D-Y. Which is better? The answer typically depends on a comparison of the costs and the time required to send the information over each path.

The comparison is not always straightforward. In Figure 7.2 you might think that the path through A, Z, and D is better because it is shorter than the other alternative. Shorter is not always better, however, as anyone traveling by car knows. Many

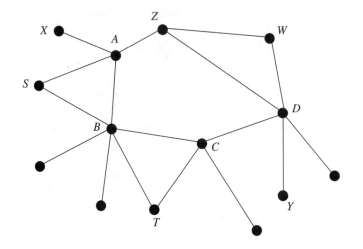

Figure 7.2   Generalized Network Topology

people will choose to drive a longer distance if it means using a road that has more lanes, is in better condition, or has more rest stops than a shorter alternative. Even though they drive farther they may reach their destination more quickly and with less difficulty.

ROUTING TABLES

Similar to the bridges shown in Section 6.5, network nodes may use **routing tables.** Like those in Section 6.5, routing tables here do not normally specify the entire route. Instead they specify the next node in a route to a specified destination and the cost to get there. For example, consider the network in Figure 7.3, where a cost is associated with the connection between two adjacent nodes. Suppose we want to find the cheapest route, the one that minimizes the sum of the costs of the connections between adjacent nodes in the route. For example, there are several routes from

Figure 7.3   Network and Associated Connection Costs

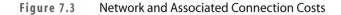

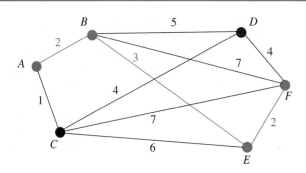

A to *F*, but the cheapest one goes from *A* to *B* (cost of 2), *B* to *E* (cost of 3), and *E* to *F* (cost of 2) for a total route cost of 7.

Figure 7.4 shows partial routing tables of nodes *A*, *B*, and *E*. (We will discuss how these tables are created shortly.) Node *A*'s table indicates that anything destined for node *B*, *E*, or *F* should be sent directly to *B*, where *B*'s routing table will indicate the next node in the cheapest route. Similarly, anything destined for *C* or *D* should be sent to node *C*. From there, *C*'s routing table indicates the next step.

To illustrate, suppose an application at node *A* wants to send data to node *F*. Logic at *A* looks for an entry in its routing table with destination *F*. The entry states that node *B* is the successor on the route, and the network protocol sends the data to *B*. Logic at *B* examines its routing table looking for an entry corresponding to destination *F*. The table's third entry indicates the data should go to node *E* next. Finally, the routing table at node *E* indicates that *F* is the next node on the route.

TYPES OF ROUTING

Who defines the routing tables and how? The process by which a routing table is defined is called a **routing algorithm.** There are several basic types, and we will discuss four of them: centralized routing, distributed routing, static routing, and adaptive routing. Then we will discuss in detail some specific routing algorithms.

Centralized Routing   **Centralized routing** means that all interconnection information is generated and maintained at a single central location. That location then broadcasts this information to all network nodes so that each may define its own routing tables. One way to maintain routing information centrally is a **routing matrix.** It consists of a row and column for each node in the network. A row corresponds to a source node, and a column to a destination node. The entry in the position specified by the row and column indicates the first node in the route from the source to the destination. From this entry the entire route can be extracted.

Figure 7.5 shows a routing matrix for the network in Figure 7.3. As before, the routes selected are the cheapest ones. In the case where two routes both have the

Figure 7.4   Partial Routing Tables for Nodes *A*, *B*, and *E*

DESTINATION	NEXT NODE	COST
B	*B*	2
C	*C*	1
D	*C*	5
E	*B*	5
F	*B*	7

(a) Partial routing table for node A

DESTINATION	NEXT NODE	COST
D	*D*	5
E	*E*	3
F	*E*	5

(b) Partial routing table for node B

DESTINATION	NEXT NODE	COST
F	*F*	2

(c) Partial routing table for node E

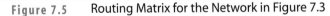

	A	B	C	D	E	F
A	—	B	C	C	B	B
B	A	—	A	D	E	E
C	A	A	—	D	E	F
D	C	B	C	—	F	F
E	B	B	C	F	—	F
F	E	E	C	D	E	—

Source Node (label at left, spanning rows)

Figure 7.5   Routing Matrix for the Network in Figure 7.3

cheapest cost, one is chosen arbitrarily. Consider again the route from *A* to *F*. According to the matrix's first row and sixth column, node *B* is the first one in the cheapest route. The next node is determined by considering the route from *B* to *F*. Examining the second row and sixth column indicates that node *E* is next. Finally, the node following *E* (node *F*) is found in the fifth row and sixth column. Thus, the route is from *A* to *B* to *E* to *F*.

Creating a routing table for a network node requires the row from the matrix corresponding to the node. For example, node *A*'s routing table in Figure 7.4 (minus the cost[*]) is the same as row 1 of the matrix. Similar statements can be made for the other nodes.

Distributed Routing   **Distributed routing** means there is no central control. Each node must determine and maintain its routing information independently. It usually does this by knowing who its neighbors are, calculating the cost to get there, and determining the cost for a neighbor to send data to specific destinations. Each neighbor, in turn, does the same thing. From that information each node can derive its own routing table. This method is more complex than centralized routing because it requires each node to communicate with each of its neighbors independently.

It is difficult to appreciate the complexity of this approach because examples typically show a global view of a network with its connections and their costs. This overview can bias the way we see the strategy unless we constantly remind ourselves that one node's knowledge of the entire network is very limited. To illustrate, consider the network shown in Figure 7.6. Assume that each node initially knows only the cost to its neighbor; later it can add to its information base anything its neighbors tell it. For example, *A* initially knows only that it can send something to *B* (cost = 1) or to *D* (cost = 2). It has no knowledge whatsoever that nodes *C* and *E* even exist. Other nodes have similar knowledge (or lack of it). However, if neighboring nodes communicate, *A* learns the identity of *B*'s and *D*'s neighbors and soon

---

[*]We did not include costs in the routing matrix, but it is a simple matter to do so by storing the cost with each node in the matrix.

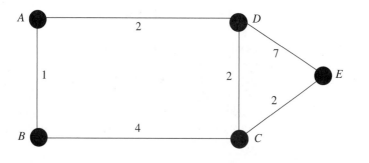

Figure 7.6   Network Example for Distributed Routing

learns of nodes C and E. By learning of B's and D's costs to get there, and knowing the cost to get to B and D, node A can calculate the cost to get to C and E. By periodically exchanging information about neighboring nodes, each one learns the identity of others in the network and the cheapest paths to them. Shortly we will discuss a specific distributed algorithm to do this.

Static Routing   **Static routing** means that once a node determines its routing table, the node does not change it. In other words, the cheapest path is not dependent on time. There is an underlying assumption that the conditions that led to the table's definition have not changed. This is sometimes a valid assumption because costs often depend on distances and the data rates between intermediate nodes. Except for major equipment upgrades and moving of equipment, these parameters do not change.

Adaptive Routing   Static routing works well as long as network conditions do not change. In some networks, however, this is a bad assumption. For example, if the cost of each link depends on network traffic, it is time dependent. Consider the problem of sending packets from node A to node E in the network of Figure 7.6. The optimal route is A-D-C-E. Suppose that after node A transmits the packet to node D, the D-C link and the D-E link costs each increases to 10 because of a surge of heavy traffic. The cheapest route from A is now A-B-C-E, and the route on which the packet embarked initially is now very expensive. In this case it would actually be cheaper to send the packet back to A and start over again. An **adaptive routing** strategy allows a network node to respond to such changes and update its routing tables accordingly.

There are pitfalls to this system. For example, suppose that in our current example D does send the packet back to A and then the cost of the A-B link increases to 10. The logical choice would be to send the packet back to D. You can now see the problem: Conceivably, the packet could shuttle back and forth among several nodes, never making any progress toward its eventual destination. One technique to avoid this maintains a counter in the packet header that is incremented on each transmission. If the count exceeds some value, the packet is removed from the network. In such cases the routing logic will not guarantee delivery of the packets. However, there is usually a flow control protocol running at a higher layer which will time out and resend the packet.

In general, adaptive routing is difficult to implement efficiently. Nodes can keep up with changing conditions only by getting reports from other nodes about link costs. These reports add to network traffic and, in turn, contribute more to the changing conditions. They also take time, so that by the time a node learns of a changing condition, that condition may no longer be in effect.

Table 7.1 gives a brief summary and comparison of the four types of routing.

DIJKSTRA'S ALGORITHM

Dijkstra's algorithm, sometimes called the **shortest path algorithm** or **forward search algorithm,** is a centralized, static algorithm, although it can be made adaptive by executing it periodically. It also requires that a node executing it have information regarding link costs among the network nodes. Several networks such as ARPANET and Tymnet II use this algorithm.

Each node executes Dijkstra's algorithm to determine the cheapest route to each network node. In cases where a route cost is simply the number of intermediate nodes, the cheapest route is also the shortest one. The algorithm is an iterative one, building a set of nodes, one by one, with each iteration. Each node in the set has the property that the cheapest route to it from the given node is known.

Table 7.1 Types of Routing

ROUTING TYPE	ADVANTAGES	DISADVANTAGES
Centralized routing	Simple method because one location assumes routing control.	The failure of the central location or any links connected to it has a severe effect on providing routing information to network nodes.
Distributed routing	Failure of a node or link has a small effect in providing accurate routing information.	Exchange of information is more complex. May also take longer for a node to learn of conditions in remote locations.
Static routing	Simple method because nodes do not have to execute routing algorithms repeatedly.	Insensitive to changing conditions. A good route may turn into a very bad one.
Adaptive routing	Provides the most current information regarding link costs.	High overhead because nodes must maintain current information. Transmitting information regarding changing conditions adds to network traffic.

Figure 7.7 shows an outline of the algorithm. Initially, it defines a set S consisting of just one node, A, the node executing the algorithm. It then defines a function where, for each node X, Cost(X) = the cost of the cheapest route from A to X for which intermediate nodes are in S. Initially, since S contains only node A, Cost(X) is the cost of a direct link from A to X. If there is no such link, Cost(X) is assigned an arbitrarily large number. The function Prior(X) in the algorithm contains the node preceding X in the cheapest route.

The algorithm contains a loop. With each pass it determines a set W consisting of all nodes not in S but with a direct link to something in S (Figure 7.8). It chooses one node X in W for which Cost(X) $\leq$ Cost(Y) for any other node Y in W. It then adds X to set S and updates the cost function Cost(V) for every V not yet in S. It compares the current Cost(V) with Cost(X) plus the cost of any direct link from X to V. If the latter value is smaller, the algorithm redefines Cost(V) to be that value. The intent is to determine whether the addition of X to S allows a cheaper route from A to V through nodes in S.

The correctness of the algorithm is not obvious, and proof that it is correct exceeds the goals of this text. For a more formal treatment, see Reference [Ah83]. We will, however, apply this algorithm to the example network of Figure 7.9. Table 7.2 shows the values the algorithm generates when applied to this network. In step 1, the set S contains only the source node A. The only nodes connected to A are B and C, and the costs of those edges are 2 and 1, respectively. Consequently, Cost(B) = 2 and Cost(C) = 1. Initial values for Cost(D), Cost(E), and Cost(F) are arbitrarily large and are designated by ∞. Also, Prior(B) = A and Prior(C) = A. Since the algorithm has not yet found any routes to D, E, and F, the Prior function is undefined at those nodes.

As we enter the loop, the set W contains nodes B and C, because they are the only ones connected to A. Next, since Cost(C) < Cost(B), we choose $X = C$ and add it to S. The last line in the loop now requires that we examine Cost(V) for each V not

---

Figure 7.7   Dijkstra's Algorithm

```
Define S as a set of nodes. Initially S contains node A.

Define Cost(X) as the cost of the cheapest route from A to X using only nodes from S
    (X excepted). Initially, Cost(X) is the cost of the link from A to X. If no such
    link exists, then Cost(X) is an arbitrarily large value (larger than any possible
    route cost).   For those nodes linked to A define Prior(X) = A.

do {
    Determine the set of nodes not in S, but connected to a node in S. Call this set W.

    Choose a node X in W for which Cost(X) is a minimum. Add X to the set S.

    For each V not in S, define Cost(V) = minimum {Cost(V), Cost(X)+cost of link
        connecting X to V}. If Cost(V) is changed define Prior(V) = X.

    }
while not all nodes in S.
```

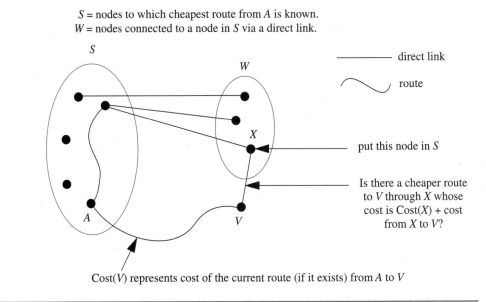

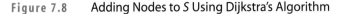

Cost(V) represents cost of the current route (if it exists) from A to V

Figure 7.8   Adding Nodes to S Using Dijkstra's Algorithm

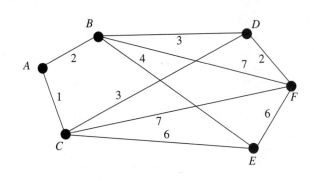

Figure 7.9   Network and Associated Connection Costs

yet in S. This consists of nodes B, D, E, and F. Since the cost function represents the cheapest path from A through nodes in S, we must ask whether the additional node in S provides a cheaper route. In other words, consider any node V not in S. If Cost(C) plus the cost of the direct link connecting C to V is less than Cost(V), then the route from A to C followed by the link from C to V represents a cheaper route. Table 7.3 shows the necessary comparisons for each node V not in S. For nodes D, E, and F, the latter values are smaller, and node C is established as their prior node. The second row of Table 7.2 reflects these changes.

The second pass through the loop proceeds similarly. Node B is added to S because Cost(B) is smallest among nodes outside of S. Furthermore, the inclusion of

Table 7.2   Values Defined by Dijkstra's Algorithm for the Network in Figure 7.9

| | | | | COST FUNCTION FOR | | | | | PRIOR FUNCTION FOR | | | | |
STEP	S	W	X	B	C	D	E	F	B	C	D	E	F
1	{A}	{B, C}	C	2	1	∞	∞	∞	A	A	—	—	—
2	{A, C}	{B, D, E, F}	B	2	1	4	7	8	A	A	C	C	C
3	{A, B, C}	{D, E, F}	D	2	1	4	6	8	A	A	C	B	C
4	{A, B, C, D}	{E, F}	E	2	1	4	6	6	A	A	C	B	D
5	{A, B, C, D, E}	{F}	F	2	1	4	6	6	A	A	C	B	D

Table 7.3   Cost Comparisons for Dijkstra's Algorithm

V	COST(V)	COST(C) + COST OF LINK CONNECTING C TO V
B	2	No link from C to V
D	∞	1 + 3 = 4
E	∞	1 + 6 = 7
F	∞	1 + 7 = 8

B in S provides a cheaper route to E (through nodes in S). Row 3 of Table 7.2 shows how the entries under E change. Node B is the new prior node for E, and Cost(E) is now 6. As an exercise, you should follow the algorithm and verify that rows 4 and 5 in Table 7.2 are correct. When the algorithm finishes, the table's last row shows that the cheapest routes to B, C, D, E, and F cost 2, 1, 4, 6, and 6, respectively.

The Prior function can be used to recover the actual route. For example, if you want the actual route from A to F, Prior(F) = D specifies that D precedes F on that route. Prior(D) = C specifies that C precedes D, and Prior(C) = A means A precedes C. Thus, the cheapest route from A to F is A-C-D-F.

BELLMAN-FORD ALGORITHM

Dijkstra's algorithm produced the cheapest path by working forward from a given source. Another approach is to work backward from a desired destination. The **Bellman-Ford algorithm,** sometimes called the **backward search algorithm** or the **distance-vector algorithm,** does this. A distributed version of it is used in the Canadian DATAPAC network, Tymnet I, and the original ARPANET ([Sp91], [St94]).

It is based on the following principle. Let Cost(A, Z) be the cost of the cheapest route from node A to Z. Suppose A has a direct connection to nodes B, C, . . . , D (Figure 7.10). Then

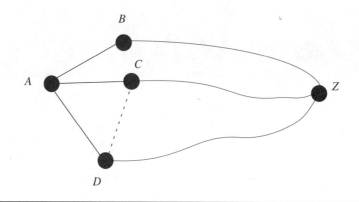

Figure 7.10   Cheapest Route from *A* to *Z*

$$\text{Cost}(A, Z) = \text{smallest of} \begin{cases} \text{cost of link from } A \text{ to } B + \text{cost of cheapest route} \\ \text{from } B \text{ to } Z \\[1em] \text{cost of link from } A \text{ to } C + \text{cost of cheapest route} \\ \text{from } C \text{ to } Z \\[0.5em] \qquad\qquad\qquad\qquad\qquad\qquad\quad \vdots \\[0.5em] \text{cost of link from } A \text{ to } D + \text{cost of cheapest route} \\ \text{from } D \text{ to } Z \end{cases}$$

According to this principle, node *A* can determine the cheapest route to *Z* as long as *A* knows the cost to each neighbor and each neighbor knows the cheapest route to *Z*. Node *A* then can perform the preceding calculation and determine the cheapest route. But how does each neighbor know the cheapest route to *Z*? The answer is in how the algorithm works. There are both centralized and distributed versions of the algorithm. Having already discussed a centralized algorithm, we will present the distributed version.

As mentioned previously, each node knows only the cost to each neighbor and any information the neighbor can provide. Thus, in the distributed algorithm each node broadcasts what it knows to each of its neighbors. Each node receives new information and updates its routing tables accordingly. As the neighbors continue to broadcast the information periodically, information about each of the network nodes and connections eventually propagates throughout the network. Information coming in to nodes may allow them to discover new nodes and new cheapest paths to other nodes.

To illustrate, we apply the algorithm to the network in Figure 7.11. Each node maintains information on the cheapest route to other nodes. It contains the route's cost and the first node on that route. Initially, each node knows only the cost to get to its neighbor. Table 7.4a shows how this information is stored. Each row corresponds to a source and each column to a destination. Each table entry contains the first node on the route and the route's cost. In Table 7.4a the first node on a route is always the

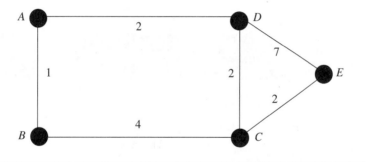

Figure 7.11   Network for the Bellman-Ford Algorithm

same as the node in the column heading because no routes other than those to neighbors are known yet. This situation will change as the algorithm proceeds, however.

Keep in mind that although this table lists a row and column for each node, each node knows only what is in a row corresponding to it. For example, A knows only that the costs to B and D are 1 and 2, respectively; B knows only that the costs to A and C are 1 and 4, respectively; and so on. Some nodes may not even know of others' existence. For example, A does not know nodes C and E exist. B does not know nodes D and E exist; and so on. This is indicated by *Unknown* in the table.

Figure 7.12 contains a pseudocoded version of the algorithm.[*] Initially, a node stores information about routes to its neighbors in its routing table. The first while loop indicates that the algorithm continually monitors information coming in from its neighbors. Inside the loop a node receives information from each of its neighbors.[†] From each neighbor it learns of nodes to which the neighbor has access and the costs of the associated routes. For each node Z to which a neighbor N has access there are two possibilities:

1. The current node has no previous knowledge of Z. The current node inserts the entry (N, current cost to $N + N$'s cost to Z) in its routing table. The current node now knows of a route to Z via N.

2. The current node already has a route to Z. The current node compares the cost of that route with the cost of going to N plus N's cost to Z. If the latter value is smaller the current node has found a cheaper route to Z. It replaces its current cost with the cheaper one and specifies N as the new first node along a route to Z.

Table 7.4b shows how each node's information changes as each of its neighbors tells it what it knows. B tells A it has access to C with a cost of 4. Since A knows it already has access to B with a cost of 1, it concludes it now has access to C with a cost of 5 (cost to B plus cost from B to C). Similarly, D also tells A it has access to C but with a cost of 2. Node A now concludes that it has access to C via D with a total cost of 4. Since this is cheaper than going through B, it inserts the entry (D, 4) in its routing table (Table 7.4b). D also tells A that it has access to E with a cost of 7. Since

Table 7.4 Three Iterations of the Bell-Ford Algorithm

		DESTINATION				
		A	B	C	D	E
Source	A	—	(B, 1)	Unknown	(D, 2)	Unknown
	B	(A, 1)	—	(C, 4)	Unknown	Unknown
	C	Unknown	(B, 4)	—	(D, 2)	(E, 2)
	D	(A, 2)	Unknown	(C, 2)	—	(E, 7)
	E	Unknown	Unknown	(C, 2)	(D, 7)	—

(a) First Iteration

		DESTINATION				
		A	B	C	D	E
Source	A	—	(B, 1)	(D, 4)	(D, 2)	(D, 9)
	B	(A, 1)	—	(C, 4)	(A, 3)	(C, 6)
	C	(D, 4)	(B, 4)	—	(D, 2)	(E, 2)
	D	(A, 2)	(A, 3)	(C, 2)	—	(C, 4)
	E	(D, 9)	(C, 6)	(C, 2)	(C, 4)	—

(b) Second Iteration

		DESTINATION				
		A	B	C	D	E
Source	A	—	(B, 1)	(D, 4)	(D, 2)	(D, 6)
	B	(A, 1)	—	(C, 4)	(A, 3)	(C, 6)
	C	(D, 4)	(B, 4)	—	(D, 2)	(E, 2)
	D	(A, 2)	(A, 3)	(C, 2)	—	(C, 4)
	E	(C, 6)	(C, 6)	(C, 2)	(C, 4)	—

(c) Third Iteration

A knows it has access to *D* with a cost of 2 it concludes it has access to *E* with a cost of 7 + 2 = 9. It then stores the entry (*D*, 9) in the routing table.

From our view of the network, we know there is a route from *A* to *E* through *D* and *C* that has a cost of only 6. But remember that we have a unique perspective using information that *A* does not yet have. Consequently, *A* does not yet know of this route. Don't let our view bias your interpretation of the algorithm.

Continuing in this way, *B* receives information from *A* and *C* about routes to other nodes.[*] The information from node *A* tells *B* there is a route to *D* with a cost of 3. Similarly, the information from *C* tells *B* there is another route to *D*

```
For each neighbor insert the entry (neighboring node, link cost) in the current
    routing table.
while network protocols baffle me do
for each neighboring node N do
{
    receive information from N's routing table;
    for each node Z in N's routing table do
        if Z is not in the current routing table
            insert the pair (N, current cost to N + N's cost to Z) in it;
        else
            if the current cost to N + N's cost to Z < current cost to Z
                replace the current cost to Z with the current cost to N + N's cost to Z and
                specify N as the new first node along a route to Z;
}
```

Figure 7.12   Bellman-Ford Algorithm

with a cost of 6 and a route to E with a cost of 6. Assimilating this information and choosing the cheapest routes, row 2 of Table 7.4b shows B's new routing information.

After each node has heard from each neighbor once, Table 7.4b shows each node's routing table. At this point each node knows the best way to get to each neighbor and to each of its neighbor's neighbors. However, it may not yet know of any optimal routes requiring three or more links. Thus, each node goes through another round of gathering information from each neighbor and determining whether there are better routes. For example, A knows from Table 7.4b that the cheapest route to E is via D for a total cost of 9. However, when A hears from D again it learns that D can now get to E with a cost of 4. Therefore, since the link cost from A to D is 2, A now concludes it can get to E via D with a total cost of 6. You should follow all the steps of the algorithm in Figure 7.12 and verify the entries in Table 7.4b and 7.4c.

---

[*] This algorithm is not complete because there are cases in which it will fail. However, our intent now is to illustrate the concept of backward learning in order to find shorter paths. We will examine shortcomings of this version later.

[†] Although the algorithm depicts an orderly sequence of receptions from each neighbor, it will almost certainly not happen this way. The actual reception of information depends on many real-time events and is very unpredictable. Our main goal is to describe *how* a node responds to that information, so the algorithm serves our purposes.

[*] Exactly what B receives from A depends on whether A sent information before or after it received information from D. Since we cannot guarantee the timing, we will assume that each node sends what it has at the beginning of each step.

Problems with Bellman-Ford Algorithm   As long as each node continually applies the algorithm, it responds to decreases in route costs anywhere in the network. Depending on the network topology, however, it takes a little time to react to such changes. The reason is that if a link cost decreases between two nodes, only their immediate neighbors learn of it during one pass of the algorithm. Nodes two links away require up to two passes of the algorithm to learn of the changes, nodes three links away require up to three passes, and so on. In general, the time required to receive news of changing costs is proportional to the number of intermediate nodes.

However, there is a more serious problem. What happens if the cost of a link between two nodes increases? Worse yet, what happens if a link between two nodes fails? This latter case can be considered as an increase of cost to infinity. Let's take a look at an example. Row 2 in Table 7.4c indicates that the cheapest route from B to E is through C at a cost of 6. This is true partly because the cost of the C-E link is 2. What if it increased to 22? The algorithm, as described, will not change B's routing table because it only makes changes when shorter routes are found.

Fortunately, this problem has an easy solution. Unfortunately, the solution can have side effects in certain cases. In general, suppose X is a node and N is the first node on a route that X considers the cheapest to node D.

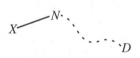

The algorithm already provides for the case where X hears from another neighbor of a cheaper route. However, suppose X hears from N that the latter's cost to D has increased. Since N was the first node on X's cheapest route to D, X must update its routing table and increase the cost of the route to D through N. It is a simple matter to modify the algorithm to do this.

For example (referring again to Table 7.4c), if the C-E link increased to 22 (an increase of 20), C tells B of the increase. B's response is to modify its routing table, changing the entry corresponding to E from $(C, 6)$ to $(C, 26)$. Node B now thinks the cheapest route to E is through C at a cost of 26. (Similar changes will occur at the other nodes as well.) This, of course, is incorrect, but a couple more iterations of the algorithm will establish cheaper routes through the D-E link and the routing tables will then reflect the realities of the link costs.

This seems like a reasonable solution, but consider the following scenario:

- Assume a subset of Figure 7.11 consisting *only* of the A-B, B-C, and C-E links.
- After a couple iterations of the algorithm, C's cheapest route to E costs 2, B's cheapest route to E costs 6, and A's cheapest route to E costs 7.
- The C-E link fails (i.e., the cost of the C-E link is now ∞).

Node C sees the failure and updates its routing table to specify a cost of ∞ to reach E. Furthermore, C passes this information to B, which changes its table to indicate that the route to E through C now costs ∞. Unfortunately, B hears from A of a route to E that costs 7.[*] B has no idea that the route from A comes right back to B. Consequently, since the cost of the B-A link is 1, B now updates its table to indicate that the cheapest route to E goes through A at a cost of 8 (1 to get to A plus 7 for the cost of A's route to E). Now, the following can occur:

1. A hears from B that its cheapest route to E costs 8. Consequently, A updates its routing table to indicate its cheapest route to E goes through B at a cost of 9 (1 to get to B plus 8 for the cost of B's route to E).

2. B hears from A and increases the cost of its route through A to 10.

3. A responds and increases its cost through B to 11.

4. The loop continues ad infinitum.

As A and B continue exchanging routing information their costs continue to escalate, neither aware that the only link to E is gone. From our bird's eye view of the network, this is ludicrous. However, each node knows only what its neighbors tell it and this situation can occur.

This is called the **count-to-infinity problem** and can be solved by defining some threshold value. If route costs to a node go above the threshold value, then replace the cost with ∞, making the node unreachable. The problem is that the threshold must be large enough so as not to be confused with a legitimate large cost. In that case, the number of iterations needed to reach the threshold increases. As a result, the algorithm takes a much longer time to respond correctly to the problem.

You might think the above problem could have been avoided entirely if A had simply not sent information to B for routes that go through B. That is, why should A tell B of a route to E that goes through B? It doesn't make sense. This brings us to another variation on the algorithm called **split horizon.** It is a simple modification of the information sent to a neighboring node. In general, suppose node X knows of a route to D through a neighbor N. The split horizon rule dictates that X tells N that its cost to D is ∞. (This way N won't try to get to D through X and follow a route leading right back to N.) If this were implemented in the example above, A would have told B that its cost to E is ∞ (because A's route goes through B). Since B already knew the cost to E through C was ∞, B would realize that E is unreachable. In the next step A would have realized the same.

While it solves the problem described here, there is still no guarantee this method will work in all cases. For example, again consider the network of Figure 7.11 but assume the D-E link is not present. That is, all routes to E go through the C-E link and the routing tables reflect that. In addition,

- D's route to E goes through C first.
- B's route to E goes through C first.
- A's route to E goes through D first.

---

[*]This depends on timing. If A had heard first from B that the cost to E is ∞, then A would see the cost to E as ∞. The point is, we don't know what will happen first and must consider all possibilities.

Suppose the *C-E* link fails at some point. *C* will see the cost to *E* as ∞. Furthermore, *C* will not try to go through *B* or *D* since both tell *C* the cost to *E* is ∞ (split horizon rule). Unfortunately, *A* and *B* might exchange messages (split horizon won't stop them from exchanging information), causing *A* to think there is a route to *E* through *B*. *B* will think there is a route to *E* through *A*. Now the split horizon rule no longer applies to *B* giving information to *C*. Consequently, *B* tells *C* of a route to *E*. *C* now thinks it can get to *E* through *B*.

At this point what happens becomes rather muddled since so much depends on timing. The bottom line is that the loop in the network causes *A*, *B*, *C*, and *D* to exchange messages, giving the impression of a variety of paths to *E* opening and closing. They begin acting senile, continually changing where they should go to get to *E*. This instability will continue, with costs escalating. If a threshold value is used, the loop would eventually stop. Still, it would take some time.

LINK STATE ROUTING

The problems we have outlined occurred because nodes were trying to exchange information about how to get to a specific destination. The nice thing about Dijkstra's algorithm is that each node executes it locally to make its own choice. The drawback is the need for a node to have information about the network's topology and link costs. If a node could get this information then it could use Dijkstra's (or any other) algorithm. The **link state routing protocol** is designed to do just that.

Link state routing is similar to Bellman-Ford routing in one regard: Each node communicates what it knows to its neighbors. It differs in what information it exchanges. Link state routing is designed around the following ideas:

- A node gathers information on the status of each link to each neighbor. For example, important information might include the bit rate of that link, the delay time in sending packets over that link, the number of packets queued for transmission, and the reliability of that link. These are all things that might determine the cost of a link.

- A node builds a **link state packet** for each link. The packet identifies the two nodes connected by that link and contains the information it has collected. The node then sends each packet to each neighbor.

- A node receiving link state packets forwards them to all of its neighbors (with the usual exception of the neighbor from which it received the packet).

- As link state packets are exchanged among nodes, each node eventually learns about the network topology and the cost and status of links between network nodes. Consequently, it can execute a cheapest route algorithm such as Dijkstra's algorithm (using itself as the source) to determine its own route (or at least the first node on that route) to a given destination. It can then build a routing table according to that information.

Like Bellman-Ford routing, this approach can take advantage of both decreasing and increasing network costs as long as each node periodically builds and sends link state packets with current information. It can also react to link failures. Furthermore, problems like the ones described previously don't occur. If a link fails, all nodes eventually hear about it via the link state packets. Consequently, they can determine new routes that avoid the absent link.

However, this doesn't mean the protocol is without problems. For example, if the network has loops, link state packets can circulate through the network forever as nodes continue to exchange them. Not only would this add to network traffic, but there would also be a problem distinguishing an old link state packet from a more recent one. A solution to this problem is to install a counter in each packet. The counter is a positive number put in the packet when it is created. Each time a node forwards a packet to a neighbor, it decrements the counter. Eventually, the counter reaches 0 and the receiving node discards it.

Another problem is that there can still be a period of time between a link failure and a remote node finding out about it. During that time packets can be routed incorrectly, which can cause delays (or even failures) in packets arriving at their destination.

As we can see, routing in a dynamic environment can be troublesome. The bad things we have described probably won't happen, but unfortunate timing can make them happen. Consequently, what you have are approaches that work most of the time but may fail every once in a while. Anyone with experience in debugging programs knows these are the toughest and nastiest problems to find. In fact, we will see later that Internet routing won't even guarantee delivery of packets. If a packet doesn't seem to be making progress the Internet Protocol will simply throw it away. We'll discuss the Internet Protocol in Section 7.4.

HIERARCHICAL ROUTING

The routing approaches discussed so far have one thing in common: They are designed to give each node proper routing information. Sometimes, however, there are too many nodes to provide each one with routing information efficiently. Treating each node as an equal participant in a large network generates too much information to share and send throughout the network. An alternative is to have some nodes do the routing for others. A common approach is **hierarchical routing.** It has the following features:

- All nodes are divided into groups called **domains.** We can consider a domain to be a separate and independent network.

- Routes between two nodes in a common domain are determined using the domain's or network's protocols.

- Each domain has one or more specially designated nodes called **routers** (sometimes called **gateways**) that determine routes between domains. Effectively the routers themselves form a network.

- If a domain is large it may consist of multiple subdomains, each of which contains its own router. They determine the routes between subdomains of the same domain.

Suppose node X wants to send a packet to node Y. If they are in the same domain the route can be determined using any of the previously discussed techniques. On the other hand, suppose they are in different domains (Figure 7.13). Node X sends the packet to router A within its domain. Node A then has the responsibility of determining the best route to node Y's domain (domain 2) and sending the packet. Since node B is a router for domain 2, it receives the packet and then sends it to node Y. This approach applies for any pair of nodes from domains 1 and 2. Effectively, A is performing necessary routing on behalf of any node in its domain, thus reducing the total number of nodes that must perform such tasks.

We can represent the domain concept using a hierarchical structure (Figure 7.14). All domains correspond to second-level tree nodes under a common root.[*] All network nodes within a domain correspond to third-level tree nodes under the domain. If the domain contains subdomains they also are third-level tree nodes, and any network nodes in them are at the fourth level under the appropriate subdomain.

In general, network routers are defined partly by the hierarchy. Thus, suppose Z in Figure 7.13 wants to send a packet to X. Since Z is in subdomain 1, it sends the packet to W, the router for Z's subdomain. In turn, W routes across subdomains to C, the router for domain 3. C then routes across domains to A, which finally sends the packet to X.

So far we have omitted one detail. For hierarchical routing to work, the sending node specifies the destination's address, including its domain and any subdomains. By including the address, each router determines whether the destination is in the current domain (or subdomain). If it is, the router can deliver the packet. If not, the

Figure 7.13   Domains in Hierarchical Routing

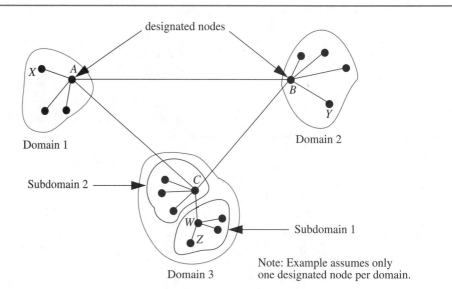

Note: Example assumes only one designated node per domain.

---

[*]Don't think of the root as an actual network node. It simply means all its dependents (domains) are connected.

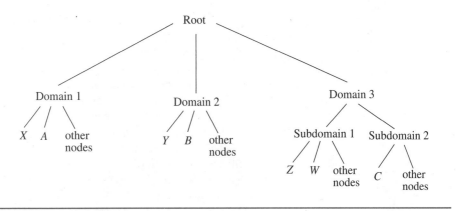

Figure 7.14   Hierarchical Arrangement of Domain Nodes

router must determine the domain to which the packet must go. This is similar to sending letters via the postal system using the typical address format,

Name

Street address

City, State, Zip code

Postal workers in Hartford, Connecticut, don't care if a letter is addressed to Jane Smith at 123 Main Street unless the city and state are also specified as Hartford, Connecticut. If the city and state are different, the Hartford postal workers' routing responsibility is to make sure the letter is sent to the appropriate city, where that city's postal workers deliver letters according to address and name. Similarly, a network node specifies an address as a sequence of domain and subdomain specifiers. For example, in Figure 7.13 node X might send a packet to node Z by addressing it to Z.subdomain-1.domain-3.

The Internet is a network that uses hierarchies in its addressing scheme. The hierarchy reflects the fact that the Internet is actually a collection of networks, each with its own set of protocols. Universities, companies, and government agencies typically have a network connecting their computers. These networks, in turn, may also be part of the Internet.

An **Internet address** is a 32-bit number represented as a sequence of four 8-bit numbers separated by dots. For example, the author's Internet address is 143.200.128.3, where each of the four numbers has an 8-bit representation. Each Internet address may also be interpreted as having two parts: an Internet Protocol (IP) network address assigned to a site network and an address for a local device (i.e., a PC) on that network. The address given is an example of a Class B address,[*]

---

[*]The Internet Protocol also defines Class A addresses (8-bit network address and 24-bit local identifier) and Class C addresses (24-bit network address and 8-bit local identifier). There are even Class D and E addresses, but we'll discuss that in Section 7.4.

meaning the first 16 bits (143.200) designate the IP network address and the other 16 bits (128.3) designate a computer.

During routing of packets, a router first examines the IP network address. If the packet is destined for another site it is routed based solely on that IP network address. Otherwise, the router examines the local part of the address and extracts, if necessary, the physical address identifier. After that it queues the packet for delivery to its destination along the proper physical network. From there, lower-layer network protocols handle delivery according to the type of network. This process is basically a two-level hierarchical routing technique. There are a few things that need further description; we will deal with them when we discuss the Internet in Section 7.4.

Some sites may have a single IP network address assigned to them but actually have multiple physical on-site networks called **subnets.** A single IP network address allows the site to expand and develop network applications independent of its connection to the Internet. For example, local management might use part of the 16-bit local ID (perhaps the first few bits) to designate a particular subnet. This creates a three-level address hierarchy, with the first two octets designating an IP network, the next few bits designating a subnet, and the remaining bits designating the actual destination on that subnet.

ROUTING INFORMATION PROTOCOL

As we have already stated, large networks can, in general, be viewed as a collection of domains. Some prefer the term *autonomous system* to domain to reflect the fact that they can operate independently. In such networks we can define two main categories of routing strategies: interior and exterior protocols.[*] **Interior protocols** control routing among routers within an autonomous system. **Exterior protocols** control routing among routers from different autonomous systems.

One example of an interior protocol long used in the Internet is the **Routing Information Protocol (RIP).** RIP is the protocol used by the routed[†] program developed at the University of California at Berkeley to perform routing on their local networks. Routers that connect multiple networks use RIP to let each other know the shortest route to a specified network. Typically they use a **hop count,** the number of intermediate routers, to measure distance. For example, Figure 7.15 shows several networks connected by routers. The hop count from network N1 to N2 is 1, and the hop count from N1 to N4 is 2, using the shortest route. None of the routers knows that yet, however. The algorithm starts when each router sends a message along each of its networks. This message indicates that all of the networks to which the router is connected can be reached in one hop. When routers on that network get the message, they know which networks they can reach using two hops.

---

[*]These go by different names depending on who you read. For example, interior protocols may also be called interior gateway protocols, interior router protocols, or intradomain protocols. Exterior protocols also may be called exterior gateway protocols, exterior router protocols, or interdomain protocols.

[†]Routed is pronounced route-d and was named using UNIX naming conventions.

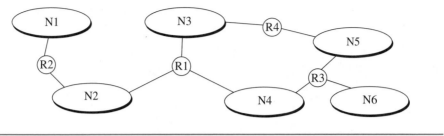

Figure 7.15 Routers Connecting Networks

They store this information in their routing tables and periodically broadcast it over the networks. By repeatedly receiving information, storing it, and broadcasting it, each router eventually knows the smallest number of hops to a given network.

Let's see how this would work on the network of Figure 7.15. Using RIP, the following events can occur:

1. R2 sends a message along N2 that it can get to N1 in one hop. (It also sends a message along N1 that it can get to N2 in one hop.)

2. Because R1 is connected to N2, it now knows it can get to N1 in two hops and stores that fact in its routing table. Subsequently, R1 broadcasts the following over N4: It can get to N2 and N3 in one hop and to N1 in two hops. (It also broadcasts similar information over N3 and N2.)

3. R3 receives and stores the information it received over N4 and broadcasts the following over N5: It can get to N4 and N6 in one hop, N2 and N3 in two hops, and N1 in three hops. It also will broadcast similar information over N4 and N6.

At this point some of the broadcast information becomes redundant. For example, because of R3's broadcast over N5, R4 learns it can get to N2 in three hops. Of course, if it previously received R1's broadcast over N3 it already knows it can get to N2 in two hops. In this case it does not store the most recent information.

What happens if a router or network along a route fails? For example, R4 knows it can get to N2 in two hops, but what if network N3 fails? When a router stores routing information it also starts a timer. When the timer expires it marks the route as invalid. It depends on new routing information to reestablish a route. Of course, the routers must cooperate by sending routing information on a regular basis (typically every 30 seconds). Thus, if N3 failed, events 1 to 3 would still occur (except those involving N3). This time when R4 learns that it can get to N2 in three hops it stores that fact because there is no alternative.

OPEN SHORTEST PATH FIRST

Another example of an interior routing scheme is **Open Shortest Path First (OSPF).** The "open" means that the algorithm is nonproprietary, that is, not owned by any company. Essentially, OSPF is a form of link state routing with a few additional features to jazz it up:

- OSPF includes the ability to authenticate messages.
- It provides for additional hierarchies. As explained previously, a domain may consist of subdomains.
- It can utilize multiple routes to a given destination. This is useful especially for heavily traveled routes. Sending all packets through the same route, even if it is "best," can cause congestion. Using backup routes can increase overall performance. This is called **load balancing** and is a little like being forewarned of a major traffic jam on an interstate highway. You might want to get off and travel some smaller country roads for a while.
- It can use several factors in defining link states. Examples factors include the link's length, bit rate, delay, and dollar cost.
- It can better respond to the needs of the user. For example, a user might want to send a small message quickly. Since the packet is small, a high bit rate isn't critical but following links with little or no delay is. On the other hand, a user might want to transfer a large file, which might be best done via links that support very high bit rates.

BORDER GATEWAY PROTOCOL

The **Border Gateway Protocol (BGP)** is an example of an exterior protocol. It shares some common features with distance-vector routing. One major difference is that instead of sharing the cost of a route to a particular destination, it shares the actual route specified as a sequence of domains or Autonomous systems. There are several reasons for specifying actual routes instead of just the first link on a cheapest route. One is that exterior protocols such as BGP are often more concerned with just getting to a destination as opposed to finding the best or cheapest way. Since routes inevitably go through one or more autonomous systems and each system may define link costs differently, comparing route costs through different systems may be meaningless. As a result, the very concept of a "best route" may have no meaning to an exterior protocol.

Another reason for sharing actual routes is that there may be other factors besides cost involved in finding a route. Each router might implement specific policies or constraints that any route must satisfy. This is especially important for global connections such as found in the Internet. For example, a router in some country may have an explicit policy to avoid any route that passes through an unfriendly country. Similarly, a company router might have a policy to avoid any route going through a competitor.

Routers can exchange packets of information much as they do with link state routing. This gives them a list of possible routes to a specific destination. Each of the routes can be explicitly examined to identify any that may violate a stated policy. Any such routes are purged from the router and will not be considered.

SUMMARY OF ROUTING TECHNIQUES

Table 7.5 provides a brief summary of the general routing strategies discussed. They are by no means the only ones, but along with the routing strategies involving LAN bridges in Section 6.5, they represent a significant number of the strategies in use today. For more information on different strategies, Reference [Ta96] has an extensive list. In addition, References [Co94] and [Co95] devote a lot of attention to routing in the Internet.

CONGESTION AND DEADLOCK

As networks grow larger and accommodate more nodes, routing strategies must deal with an ever-increasing number of packets. The increased demand can put network operations in peril. What happens when one or more network links fail? What happens if the number of packets that must be transmitted exceeds the network's ability to do so? A potentially serious consequence is **congestion,** or the excessive buildup of packets at one or more network nodes.

Once again we can draw on the useful analogy of traffic control in an urban area. Highways and roads must be designed with the anticipated amount of traffic in

Table 7.5   Summary of Routing Strategies

METHOD	COMMENTS
Dijkstra's algorithm	Forward learning algorithm that can be implemented as a central routing strategy. It can also be used with link state routing.
Bellman-Ford algorithm	Backward learning algorithm. Nodes learn from each neighbor the cheapest route to a node and the first node on that route. Used in the Internet or in any large network where changing link conditions require nodes to update their routing tables.
Link state routing	Nodes collaborate by exchanging link state packets providing status information on adjacent links. A node can collect all the packets it receives and determine the network topology. Then it can execute its own shortest route algorithm.
Hierarchical algorithm	Method of dividing nodes into domains or autonomous systems. Interior protocols do routing within a system, whereas exterior protocols find routes across different systems. Used in the Internet or in any network where there is a large number of nodes, making it impractical for each to run the same routing strategy.
RIP	An interior routing protocol used to track the fewest number of hops to a given network. Developed by UC-Berkeley for its local networks and used in the Internet.
OSPF	An interior routing protocol similar to link state routing but that provides additional features for better performance and flexibility.
BGP	An exterior protocol that allows routers to implement specific policies or constraints that a route must meet. Routers exchange actual routes to a destination instead of just costs and the first link in a route.

mind. Anyone who has driven in an urban area knows the problem. During rush hour the amount of traffic is excessive and a highway's ability to handle it diminishes. An accident or road construction can put several lanes or an entire stretch of highway out of commission. In either case traffic slows (or stops completely), causing terrible congestion. People in their cars can't reach their destinations. The transportation system has lost its usefulness temporarily.

Similarly, congestion in a network reduces its usefulness. Packets experience longer delays and network users see the network as unresponsive and unable to meet their needs. What can network protocols do in such cases? One option is to do nothing and let congestion disappear naturally. Even in rush hour traffic people eventually get home and the congestion disappears. However, this is not a practical solution for networks. (Many people probably feel it's not a practical solution to highway congestion either.) For one thing, users expect better service, and it should be provided. Second, the congestion might not disappear because it can have a compounding effect. Congestion at a node hampers the node's ability to receive packets from other nodes. Consequently, those nodes can't get rid of their packets as quickly, and incoming packets begin to accumulate there as well. This can have a chain reaction effect in which all nodes begin to experience congestion, making the problem worse.

There are several ways to handle congestion:

- **Packet elimination.** If an excessive buildup of packets occurs at a node, eliminate some of them. This reduces the number of outstanding packets waiting for transmission and reduces the network load. The drawback, of course, is that the destroyed packets do not reach their destinations. The problem of lost packets was discussed in Section 5.3. Presumably the sending node's protocol eventually will determine that a packet never reached its destination and will resend it. If the congestion was due to a heavy burst of traffic it may have subsided somewhat when the packet is sent the next time. Destroying packets sounds drastic, but if the congestion is sporadic the network protocols can handle it well and the inconvenience to the unlucky user whose packets are destroyed is minimal. We do not, however, recommend this approach for automobile traffic congestion.

- **Flow control.** As Chapter 5 discussed, flow control protocols are designed to control the number of packets sent. However, they are not a true congestion control approach. The problem is that flow control limits the number of packets between two points, whereas congestion often involves packets coming into a node from many sources. Thus, even if nodes regulate the number of packets they send, congestion still can occur if too many nodes are sending them.

  You might respond by suggesting that each node regulate its traffic so that even if every node is sending, the total number of packets would still be manageable. The problem is that if many nodes are not sending they are underutilizing the network. Again, you might respond by suggesting that each node reduce its outflow only if it detects other nodes sending. In a large network, however, this is not practical. Many nodes won't even see the packets sent by others. Furthermore, establishing some communication protocol among them would add to the network traffic and compound the problem we are trying to solve.

- **Buffer allocation.** This approach can be used with virtual circuits. Recall from Section 1.4 that a **virtual circuit** is an established route between network nodes that is determined before any data packets are actually sent. Once a route is established, protocols at a node on that route can reserve buffers specifically for the virtual circuit. Effectively, the establishment of a virtual circuit notifies participating nodes that packets will be forthcoming and that they should plan for them. If other requests for virtual circuit establishment come to that node it can reject them if insufficient buffer space is available. Network protocols then would have to find a different route for the circuit or notify the source that the request for a virtual circuit has been denied. Section 7.3 discusses virtual circuits further.

- **Choke packets.** This approach provides a more dynamic way to deal with congestion. Each node monitors the activity on its outgoing links, tracking the utilization of each. If the utilization of the lines is small the danger of congestion is low. However, an increasing utilization means a larger number of packets are being sent. If the utilization of any line exceeds some specified criterion, the node's protocol responds by putting itself into a special warning state. When in the warning state, the node will respond by sending a special **choke packet** in response to any incoming packet destined for the outgoing line. The choke packet goes to the source of the incoming packet. When the source receives the choke packet it responds by reducing the number of packets it is sending for a specified period of time.

    After the period expires, one of two things can happen. If no additional choke packets arrive, the node can increase the packet transmission rate to its original value. If more choke packets continue to arrive, it will reduce the packet transmission rate even further. By reducing the incoming traffic the original node has a chance to let the utilization of its outgoing lines drop below the threshold to an acceptable level.

In the worst case, congestion can become so severe that nothing moves. Figure 7.16 illustrates this problem. Three nodes, A, B, and C, have reached the point where their buffers are full and cannot accept any more packets. A's packets are all destined for B which cannot receive any packets because its buffers are full. Thus A cannot send until B sends some of its packets and releases buffer space. B's packets are destined for C, whose buffers are also full. C's packets are destined for A, whose buffers are full. In other words, A is waiting for B's buffers to clear; B is waiting for C's buffers to clear, and C is waiting for A's buffers to clear. This situation, in which all nodes are waiting for an event that won't occur, is called **deadlock** (also called **deadly embrace** or **lock-up**).

The case just described is an example of a **store-and-forward deadlock,** so named because nodes store packets while waiting to forward them. Figure 7.17 illustrates another type, **reassembly deadlock.** In this example, the node uses common buffers for incoming packets from different sources (A and B). It also uses a selective

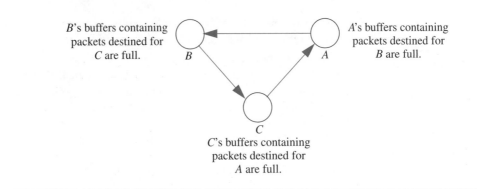

B's buffers containing
packets destined for
C are full.

A's buffers containing
packets destined for
B are full.

C's buffers containing
packets destined for
A are full.

Figure 7.16 Store-and-Forward Deadlock

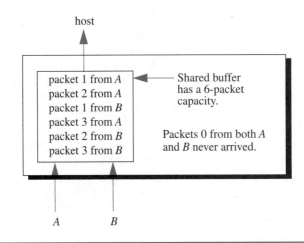

host

| packet 1 from A |
| packet 2 from A |
| packet 1 from B |
| packet 3 from A |
| packet 2 from B |
| packet 3 from B |

Shared buffer
has a 6-packet
capacity.

Packets 0 from both A
and B never arrived.

A   B

Figure 7.17 Reassembly Deadlock

repeat sliding window protocol for receiving packets from A and B destined for the node's host. Recall that the selective repeat protocol allows packets to arrive out of order. The receiver then reassembles them before sending them to the host.

In our example, A and B both sent a packet 0, neither of which arrived. However, subsequent packets numbered 1 through 3 from both A and B have arrived. If we assume the buffers are filled, the node cannot accept any more packets. Because both packet 0s are missing, however, the node cannot reassemble them and deliver them in order to the host. Moreover, the node will not accept either packet 0 even if it does arrive. Consequently, the node is placed in a state in which it can neither take action nor respond to an event that would allow it to take action. It is deadlocked.

Reassembly deadlock can be prevented through a handshake establishing a connection between the sending and receiving nodes. The handshake can establish the window size and the receiver can reserve sufficient space and use it only for that connection. Store-and-forward deadlock is a bit more problematic. It can be reduced or even eliminated by using sufficient buffer space, but the problem is knowing just how much buffer space to reserve, especially in datagram services in which packets come and go randomly.

One approach to deadlock is to let it happen and then deal with it. When deadlock occurs the typical response is to discard some packets and release the buffer space. The discarded packets, of course, never reach their destination. This is the price to be paid for breaking the deadlock. Presumably, communication protocols will determine that the packets never arrived and will send them again later. If deadlock occurs rarely, this may be the best way to deal with it.

On the other hand, for a network more susceptible to deadlock it may be less costly to take steps to prevent it from happening or at least decrease its probability of occurrence. Any of the previously mentioned congestion control techniques will decrease the chances of deadlock, but there is still no guarantee deadlock will not occur. Another approach, presented in Reference [Me80], maintains the number of hops (nodes through which a packet travels) in each packet. When a host first inserts a packet into the network the hop count is 0. As the packet travels through the network each node increments the hop count by one. In addition, each node divides its buffers into distinct groups, each one corresponding to a hop count from 0 up to the maximum expected hops. The node then stores an incoming packet into a buffer depending on the number of hops in the packet, but only if a buffer is available. If not, the packet waits at the preceding node until it is available. Figure 7.18 shows how it works. A host submits a packet initially and the host's node stores the packet in buffer 0. The next node to receive the packet stores it in buffer 1, the next one in buffer 2, and so on.

This method prevents deadlock because a packet always goes to (or waits for) a higher numbered buffer. Another way to state it is that a packet in one buffer will never wait for a lower or equal numbered buffer. Because of this the circular wait condition of Figure 7.16 can never occur. The argument against this approach is that

Figure 7.18   Storing Packets Depending on Hop Count

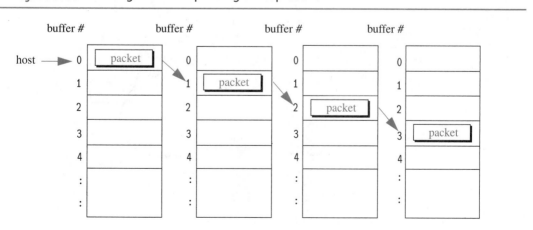

buffers may be underutilized. Preassigning a packet to a buffer prevents its transmission whenever that buffer is occupied; however, if it is the only buffer occupied, the others go unused.

7.3 PUBLIC DATA NETWORKS: THE X SERIES PROTOCOLS

In the 1970s many European countries began to develop **public data networks** (networks available to anyone with a need for network services). The problems they faced were different from those in the United States. In the United States, public networks could be developed in large part by leasing existing telephone lines. In Europe this could not be done easily due to problems inherent in traversing communications systems across international boundaries. Thus, instead of developing separate and incompatible standards European countries worked under the auspices of ITU to develop a single standard. The result is the public data network service interface referred to as the **X series** of protocols. This section discusses four common protocols: X.25, X.3, X.28, and X.29.

Public data networks are commonly **packet-switched networks,** represented by the ubiquitous network cloud shown in Figure 7.19. They operate by transporting packets submitted at one part of the "cloud" and routing them to their destinations. Typically, switching logic (circuits) at nodes in the network make routing decisions. The previous section focused on this aspect of networks, so we will not discuss it further here. Instead we take the perspective of someone interacting with the network. Packets enter from point *A* and exit at points *B, C,* or *D*. We do not necessarily know (or care) how they get there. Our main focus is to define the logical connection between the source and the destination.

Figure 7.19   Packet-Switched Network

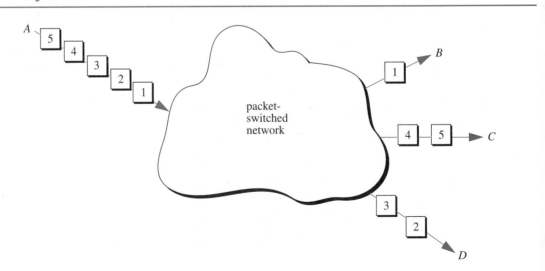

Packet-Switched Network Modes

Virtual Circuits   Packet-switched networks typically operate in one of two modes. The first is by a virtual circuit between two points. It is somewhat analogous to creating a telephone connection between two people. A device connected to the network requests a connection to a device somewhere else. This request is routed through network nodes, establishing a path between the caller and destination. All subsequent packets sent by the caller follow that same path. (We will discuss the actual process of calling and establishing the connection later in this section.)

The connection is not a physical one, however. The connections between nodes are not dedicated solely to one virtual circuit. In fact, a node and its connection to a neighbor may participate in several virtual circuits. Figure 7.20 shows two overlapping virtual circuits. *A* and *B* have both requested and established connections to *C* and *D*, respectively. The paths begin at different locations but overlap at nodes *X* and *Y*. *X* handles packets corresponding to either virtual circuit and routes them to *Y*. *Y*, in turn, routes packets differently depending on the virtual circuit on which they arrive.

Because virtual circuit paths can overlap, each node must be able to determine the virtual circuit corresponding to an incoming packet. As the initial connection request goes through each node, the node assigns a virtual circuit number to it, determines the next node to which it sends the request, and makes an entry in its routing table. The routing table contains each virtual circuit number and the next node along the corresponding path.

Note that each node assigns virtual circuit numbers independently, so one virtual circuit may be identified by different numbers at different nodes. Consequently, each node informs the circuit's preceding node of the virtual circuit number it uses for incoming packets. This allows a preceding node to know the virtual circuit number assigned by the next node and to store it in the packet. Thus, incoming packets contain the number of the virtual circuit coming in to the node. The node's routing logic accesses the routing table entry corresponding to it and sends it to the

Figure 7.20   Overlapping Virtual Circuits

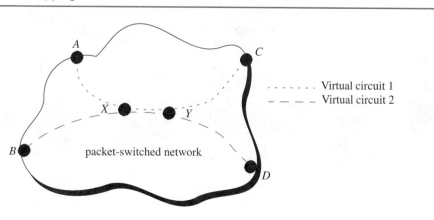

next node. If the next part of the virtual circuit has a different number, the node stores it in the packet as well. For example, Figure 7.21 shows a packet traversing each of the virtual circuits of Figure 7.20. The virtual circuit between *A* and *C* is assigned the numbers 1 (by *X*), 5 (by *Y*), and 3 (by *C*). The circuit between *B* and *D* is assigned the numbers 2 (by *X*), 3 (by *Y*), and 1 (by *D*).

Table 7.6 shows what the relevant entries of *X*'s and *Y*'s routing tables look like. A packet coming in to *X* from *A* contains the virtual circuit number 1. *X*'s routing table indicates that the next node is *Y* and that it uses 5 as the virtual circuit number. Consequently, *X* stores 5 into the packet and sends it to *Y*. A packet entering *Y* from *X* will contain a virtual circuit number of 5 or 3. If it is 5, *Y*'s routing table indicates *C* as the next node and an outgoing virtual circuit number of 3. If it is 3, *D* is the next node and the outgoing virtual circuit number is 1.

Datagram Service   One advantage of virtual circuits is that routing decisions are made just once for each circuit, eliminating the need to make such decisions for each packet. Your first thought might be that this is particularly beneficial when many packets are sent. The opposite may be true, however, because many packets usually means more time has elapsed since the circuit was established. Consequently, the conditions that may have made the current path a good one may no longer be true.

Figure 7.21   Sending Packets along a Virtual Circuit

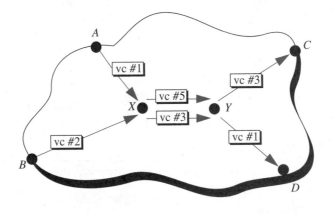

Table 7.6   Routing Tables for Nodes *X* and *Y* from Figure 7.20

ROUTING TABLE FOR *X*			ROUTING TABLE FOR *Y*		
INCOMING VC NUMBER	OUTGOING VC NUMBER	NEXT NODE	INCOMING VC NUMBER	OUTGOING VC NUMBER	NEXT NODE
1	5	*Y*	5	3	*C*
2	3	*Y*	3	1	*D*

That is, conditions may have changed so that the current path takes longer. The result, in that case, is reduced efficiency.

Another option is a **datagram service.** With it each packet contains the source and destination addresses. As packets enter the network, nodes apply routing logic to each packet separately. Presumably, this allows each node to route depending on the most current information it has regarding potential paths. Figure 7.22 shows datagrams traversing the network. Packets 1 through 3 enter at *A* and *A* routes them to *X*. Just after packet 3 enters the network, *A* gets new routing information that indicates *Y* is now a better choice for packets destined for *D*. Consequently, it routes packets 4 and 5 to *Y*.

In theory, all packets may travel different routes and take advantage of the best routes currently available. A disadvantage is that there is no guarantee that packets will arrive at *D* in the same order they were sent. Consequently, more complex logic is required to reassemble packets at their destination (recall the selective repeat protocol of Section 5.3). Table 7.7 lists some other advantages and disadvantages of the virtual circuit and the datagram service.

X.25 PUBLIC DATA NETWORK INTERFACE STANDARD

An important part of working with public data networks is their interface. One widely used interface is the ITU **X.25 standard.** Many people use the term *X.25 network*, causing some to believe mistakenly that X.25 defines the network protocols. It does not. X.25 defines the protocol between a DTE and a DCE connected to a public data network (Figure 7.23). We note that early versions focused mainly on the asymmetric DTE-DCE relationship. Recent versions have recognized the need for peer-to-peer communications between two DTEs. Consequently, X.25 can be used strictly as a user-to-network interface or as a user-to-user connection across a public data network. The latter use partially explains why some people refer to public data networks as X.25 networks. The term is technically incorrect, but to those for whom

Figure 7.22   Datagram Service

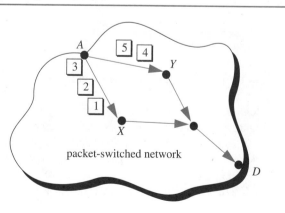

packet-switched network

Table 7.7   Comparison of Virtual Circuits and Datagrams

VIRTUAL CIRCUIT	DATAGRAM
Helps prevent congestion. Since a node knows it is part of a virtual circuit it can reserve space for the anticipated arrival of packets.	Unexpected packets make congestion control more difficult.
If a virtual circuit is open too long, the current path may not be the best given current network conditions.	Nodes route each packet using the most current information about the network.
A routing decision is made just once for each set of packets sent along the virtual circuit.	Separate routing decisions are made for each packet.
Packets arrive in the order they were sent.	Packets can arrive out of order requiring the destination to order them.
A node failure breaks the virtual circuit connection, causing a loss of packets.	If a node fails packets can be routed around it.

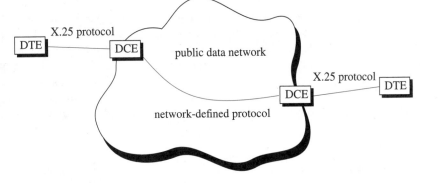

Figure 7.23   X.25 Public Data Network Interface

X.25 defines the communication protocol via the network, the misnomer is understandable.

   X.25 defines a synchronous transmission analogous to the three lowest layers of the OSI (Figure 7.24). The network layer receives user data and puts it into an X.25 packet. The X.25 packet is passed to the data link layer, where it is embedded in a LAPB frame (Section 5.5 discussed LAPB). The physical layer then transmits the LAPB frame using the X.21 protocol discussed in Section 3.2. Alternatively, X.25 may use the X.21bis standard, which was designed as an interim standard to connect

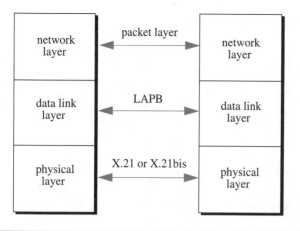

Figure 7.24   X.25 Protocol Layers

V series modems with packet-switched networks. The X.21 standard was supposed to replace it, but, as with many plans, it did not happen. A more extensive treatment of X.21bis is found in Reference [Bl91]. In some cases, X.25 may even use the EIA 232 protocol.

Accomplishing all of this requires intelligent DTEs capable of creating packets and implementing the protocols. One problem that sometimes occurs is that DTEs correspond to asynchronous terminals, which lack the intelligence to do this. We will treat this case later. Since we have already discussed the two lower layers, we will focus here on the network layer's packet protocol.

Packet Format   The first step is defining the packet format. As with previous protocols, formats vary depending on the type of packet. Figure 7.25 shows two primary formats. The relevant packet fields are as follows:

- **Flags.** The first four bits define the **general format indicator (GFI)** and, to some extent, define the packet format. For example, two of the bits specify whether 3-bit or 7-bit numbers are used for sequencing and acknowledging. Another bit, called the **D bit,** specifies how to interpret acknowledgments. If the D bit is 0, acknowledgments come from the DCE. If the D bit is 1, they come from the remote DTE. In effect, the D bit determines whether flow control is being managed for a local DTE-DCE connection or for a logical connection with the remote DTE.

- **Logical group number** and **logical channel number.** Together they define a 12-bit number for a virtual circuit the DTE has established. This allows the DTE to establish up to 4096 virtual circuits.

- **Control** (data packet). Contains either 3-bit or 7-bit sequence and acknowledgment numbers used for flow control. X.25 flow control uses windows and is not

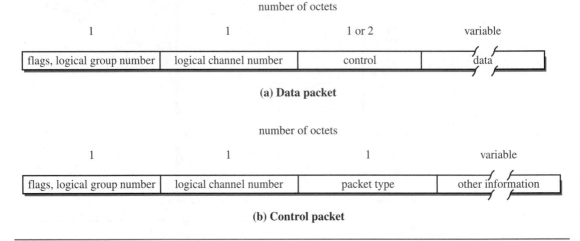

number of octets

1	1	1 or 2	variable
flags, logical group number	logical channel number	control	data

(a) Data packet

number of octets

1	1	1	variable
flags, logical group number	logical channel number	packet type	other information

(b) Control packet

Figure 7.25   X.25 Packet Formats

significantly different from flow control protocols discussed previously. This field also contains a bit set in the last of a series of packets to indicate the end of a packet stream.

- **Data** (data packet). Self-explanatory.
- **Packet type** (control packet). There are several packet types, defined in Table 7.8.

Virtual Calls   X.25 provides two types of virtual circuits between DTEs. A **permanent virtual circuit** is similar to leasing a telephone line: Either DTE can send data without the overhead of making and establishing a call. It is particularly useful when a high volume of data is transferred. A **virtual call,** the second type, requires a call connection protocol to be performed prior to any data transfer.

Figure 7.26 shows the call connection and termination process between two DTEs. (For brevity, we have not shown the DCEs or the network, but don't forget they are there.) The DTE wanting to make a call constructs a **call request packet** containing the virtual call (or logical channel) number and sends it via its DCE and the network. When the receiving DCE gets the packet it assigns a virtual call number to the request and delivers the packet to the receiving DTE. Note that there is no requirement that the channel numbers be the same at each end. As described previously, they are defined dynamically. If that DTE is willing and able to accept the call, it sends a **call accepted packet.** Once the first DTE receives the call accepted packet the virtual call is established.

Next, the DTEs exchange data and acknowledgment packets in a full-duplex mode, using a flow control similar to that used in HDLC[*] (Section 5.5). When

---

[*]There are some differences between HDLC and X.25 flow control, but they are not significant at this level of discussion.

Table 7.8   X.25 Packet Types

TYPE	FUNCTION
Call request	When a DTE wants to establish a connection (call another DTE) it sends a call request packet.
Call accepted	If the called DTE accepts the call, it acknowledges it by returning a call accepted (or call confirmation) packet.
Data	Used to transfer high-level protocol data between the DTEs. There are typically up to 128 bytes of data, but handshake protocols may agree to transfer up to 4096 bytes in a packet.
Clear request	Sent by a node wanting to terminate a virtual circuit. It can also be used by a DTE not wanting to accept a call. A receiving DTE sees it as a clear indication packet.
Clear confirmation	Sent in response to a clear request packet.
Diagnostic	If a DCE receives a packet containing erroneous codes it may send a diagnostic packet to the DTE, thus indicating a problem.
Receive ready	A DTE sends a receive ready packet to acknowledge a data packet and to indicate it is able to accept more data packets. It defines network-level flow control and is similar to that in HDLC (Section 5.5).
Receive not ready	A DTE sends a receive not ready packet to acknowledge a data packet and to indicate it cannot accept more data packets until further notice.
Reject	A DTE sends a reject packet when it does not accept an incoming data packet.
Reset request	If a protocol error (such as congestion, loss of packet, or failure of a node along the virtual circuit) occurs, a DTE can start over by sending a reset request packet. It eliminates any outstanding packets, recovers buffer space, and reinitializes the sending and receiving packet counts to 0. It does not establish a new virtual circuit between the DTEs; it just reinitializes the current one. In the case of a failed node the two DCEs may have to recreate the virtual circuit. This process is transparent to the DTEs.
Reset confirmation	Sent to acknowledge a reset request packet.
Restart request	In the event of a more serious error such as DTE failure or loss of a network connection, a DTE can clear all its virtual circuits with a restart request packet. It has the same effect as sending a clear request packet along all current virtual circuits.
Restart confirmation	Sent to acknowledge a restart request packet.
Interrupt	Transmission of data packets is subject to flow protocols at the LAPB level. The interrupt packet corresponds to a high-priority packet that bypasses the lower-level flow control constraints. For example, it would not be rejected at the remote DTE due to a full receiving window. It can carry at most 32 bytes of data and is used when data absolutely must get to the remote DTE (sort of like an X.25 Federal Express). Useful if the sending DTE is a terminal and its user has pressed the break key or has entered a control sequence to terminate an activity.
Interrupt confirmation	A DTE receiving an interrupt packet sends an interrupt confirmation packet in response. X.25 does not allow more than one outstanding interrupt. Thus, once a DTE sends one it cannot send another until it receives a confirmation.

either DTE decides to end the connection (DTE *A* in Figure 7.26), it creates and sends a **clear request packet.** The local DCE responds by doing two things. First, it sends the clear request packet to the remote DTE. Second, it responds to its local DTE by sending it a **clear confirmation packet.** As far as the local DTE is concerned, the virtual call is terminated and the logical channel number is available for future calls. Eventually, the remote DTE receives the clear request packet. It sees it as a clear indication packet and responds by sending a clear confirmation packet to its DCE. That DCE also clears the channel number, making it available for other calls.

Although X.25 is popular, perhaps more so in Europe, it has its critics. For example, one of the strongest criticisms is that X.25-based protocols provide only a connection-oriented service. Another is that its network layer (layer 3) is incomplete and actually contains features found in higher-layer protocols. For example, the OSI layer 3 provides routing capability, but the X.25 layer 3 has no such capability. Furthermore, X.25 provides for some connection-oriented features with the remote DTE. Since end-to-end connections are more typical in layer 4 protocols, some see this as a blending of two layers into one, thus blurring the distinction between layers as defined by OSI.

Triple-X Standard for Non-X.25 Devices

One disadvantage of the X.25 protocol is the need for DTEs that support it. In other words, it requires a computer, workstation, or other intelligent device capable of creating and interpreting X.25 packets. These categories leave out the almost countless

Figure 7.26   Virtual Call

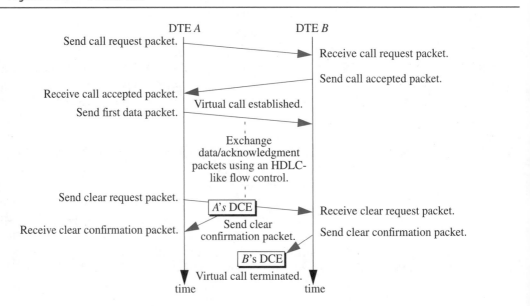

number of dumb terminals or character-oriented devices still in use. How can they communicate with devices that support X.25? One approach is to purchase X.25-supported devices and replace the non-X.25 devices. For anyone who must manage a budget, however, this may not be a practical solution.

Fortunately, another solution does exist: a set of protocols defined by the ITU. They are the **X.3 packet assembler/disassembler (PAD), X.28 PAD-terminal interface,** and **X.29 PAD-host interface** (Figure 7.27). The PAD replaces the DCE as a network interface. It accepts characters from character-oriented devices and assembles them into packets before sending them onto the network. Similarly, it can receive packets from the network, disassemble them, and transmit the data as a character stream to the terminal. The X.28 protocol defines a set of commands that the terminal and PAD use to exchange information. Similarly, X.29 defines a communication protocol between the PAD and the remote host.

X.3 Packet Assembler/Disassembler   A PAD works with **dumb terminals,** that is, those with no local computing ability. Dumb terminals are little more than electronic typewriters that transfer characters to and from the network. One problem is that many of them work in unique ways. A simple example is the deletion of characters. Most of us are poor typists who make many mistakes, but we usually can correct them by backspacing and deleting unwanted characters. The trouble is that on some terminals you backspace by typing the backspace key. On others you use the Delete key, an arrow key (←), a backslash key (\ ), or a combination of keys (for example, Ctrl-D or Alt-F). It is like trying to find the windshield wiper, light, and door controls on a car. Somewhere fiends spend their time thinking up new places to put controls and new ways to turn them on or off. Does this unmarked button turn on the lights, open the trunk, lock the doors, or eject you from the seat through the sun roof? All you can do is press it and hope for the best.

Figure 7.27   Triple-X Protocols

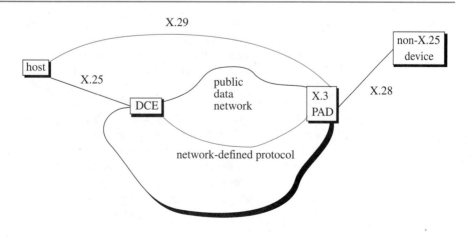

The PAD accepts keystrokes used by a particular terminal and translates them into a standard form. For example, suppose two people are using an editor over a network. A person at one terminal may press a left-arrow key, whereas a person at another terminal may press the backspace key for the same function. The PAD translates each into the command required by the editor. The editor does not know that two different characters were typed. Similarly, the users do not know their entries were translated. In general, a PAD does not route each typed character individually to the network. Instead, it buffers them. At some point, it assembles them into an X.25 packet and transmits it along the network. This is why we use the name "packet assembler."

When data arrives from the network, the process works in reverse. The PAD accepts a packet and disassembles it. It translates control characters into the proper form for a particular terminal. One technique involves creating a network virtual terminal (see Section 8.1). The OSI application layer contains software that translates control sequences into standard forms. It converts terminal-specific commands from the user into a form the text editor can understand. Similarly, the text editor can issue cursor movement commands without regard for the type of terminal. The application layer converts them to control a particular type of terminal.

PADs do more than interpret control sequences from terminals and put them into packets. There are 22 parameters that define how a PAD communicates with a DTE. Table 7.9 describes each of them.

X.28 and X.29 Protocols   The PAD is the heart of the communications protocol between character-oriented DTEs and remote hosts over an X.25 network. In addition to assembling and disassembling packets, its parameters specify how and when to perform certain functions. In order to provide flexibility we must have the capability to request that it perform those functions and to alter its parameters. Two other protocols, X.28 and X.29, define how to do this.

The X.28 protocol defines the communication between the PAD and the character-oriented device. X.28 specifies commands that the terminal can give to the PAD and specifies the responses the PAD returns. For example, a user can enter a command to request a virtual call to a remote host (Figure 7.28a). The command then goes to the PAD, which must create an X.25 call request packet and send it over the network. When the call accepted packet returns (Figure 7.28b), the PAD returns an acknowledgment to the user. Other commands include those to clear or reset a virtual call or to send an interrupt packet. In these cases, the PAD responds by acknowledging receipt of the command. X.28 commands also allow the terminal to request the current PAD parameter values or to define new ones.

The X.29 protocol defines how the PAD and a remote host communicate and specifies allowable commands and acknowledgments. Using X.29, the remote host can change PAD parameters. For example, PAD parameter 2 specifies whether user-entered characters are echoed back to the terminal. This is useful except when a user is entering a password as part of a login. Thus, when a remote host is ready to accept a password it can send a command to the PAD changing parameter 2 to suppress echoing. After the password has been entered the remote host resets the parameter to resume echoing.

Table 7.9   PAD Parameters

X.3 PARAMETER REFERENCE NUMBER	DESCRIPTION
1. PAD recall	Escape from data transfer mode to command mode in order to send PAD commands.
2. Echo	Controls the echo of characters sent by the terminal.
3. Data forwarding	Defines the characters to be interpreted by the PAD as a signal to forward data; indication to complete assembly and forward a complete packet.
4. Idle timer delay	Selects a time interval between successive characters of terminal activity as a signal to forward data.
5. Ancillary device control	Allows the PAD to control the flow of terminal data using X-ON/X-OFF characters.
6. Control of PAD service signals	Allows the terminal to receive PAD messages.
7. Operation of the PAD on receipt of breaking signal from DTE	Defines PAD action when a break signal is received from the terminal.
8. Discard output	Controls the discarding of data pending output to a terminal.
9. Padding after carriage	Control PAD insertion of padding characters after a carriage return is sent to the terminal.
10. Line folding	Specifies whether the PAD should fold the output line to the terminal; predetermined number of characters per line.
11. Binary speed of DTE	Indicates the speed of the terminal; cannot be changed by DTE.
12. Flow control of the PAD	Allows the terminal to flow control data being transmitted by the PAD.
13. Line feed insertion	Controls PAD insertion of line feed after a carriage return is sent to the terminal.
14. Line feed padding	Controls PAD insertion of padding characters after a line feed is sent to the terminal.
15. Editing	Controls whether editing by PAD is available during data transfer mode (parameters 16, 17, and 18).
16. Character delete	Selects character used to signal character delete.
17. Line delete	Selects character used to signal line delete.
18. Line display	Selects character used to signal line display.
19. Editing PAD service signals	Controls the format of the editing PAD service signals.
20. Echo mask	Selects the characters that are not echoed to the terminal when echo (parameter 2) is enabled.
21. Parity treatment	Controls the checking and generation of parity on characters from and to the terminal.
22. Page wait	Specifies the number of lines to be displayed at one time.

*Source: U. Black, *The X Series Recommendations*, McGraw-Hill, Inc., 1991. Reprinted with permission.

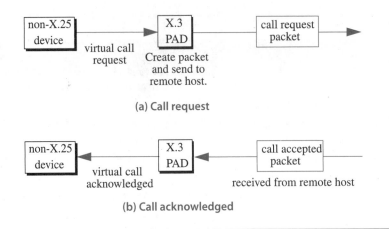

(a) Call request

(b) Call acknowledged

Figure 7.28   PAD Responding to Virtual Call Requests

The X.29 protocol is particularly useful when the user has no knowledge of the PAD or network. The user simply wants to use the terminal to connect to a remote device for some service. He or she does not want to worry about specific terminal characteristics (such as those described previously) or about setting PAD parameters. This way the remote host can instruct the PAD to set its parameters accordingly and allow the user to focus on the reason for the remote connection in the first place.

7.4   INTERNET PROTOCOLS

Probably the best-known wide area network actually consists of many networks and is collectively called **the Internet.** Its history dates back to the late 1960s, when the Advanced Research Projects Agency (ARPA) of the U.S. Department of Defense (DoD) began funding universities and private organizations for the purpose of developing communications systems. The research eventually led to the development of ARPANET, a small experimental network that demonstrated the feasibility of connecting different computers by a packet-switching network. It has since grown and evolved into the Internet and connects thousands of universities, private institutions, and government agencies worldwide.

Many use the term *internet* to refer to any collection of connected networks. The network that resulted from the ARPA project is commonly referred to as the Internet (with a capital I). The Internet consists of thousands of separate networks. It services people in probably every corner of the industrialized world, not to mention some remote areas as well. It is difficult to know just how many people use the Internet, but with networks existing in virtually every private and public organization and the proliferation of Internet service providers, they easily number in the tens of millions and quite possibly, hundreds of millions world-wide. This section and the next will present an overview of both IP and TCP. However, there are books devoted solely to these topics and the interested reader is encouraged to consult references such as [Co94], [Co95], and [Mi96].

OVERVIEW OF TCP/IP

The Internet connects many networks, each of which runs a protocol known as **TCP/IP.** TCP (Transmission Control Protocol) and IP (Internet Protocol) correspond roughly to layers 4 and 3 of the OSI model, respectively, although they are not part of the OSI model. They were developed along with the ARPA project and have become DoD standards. TCP/IP is probably the most widely implemented protocol in the world and runs on almost anything from PCs to supercomputers.

The TCP/IP pair of protocols is part of a protocol collection called the **TCP/IP protocol suite** (Figure 7.29). TCP provides connection-oriented services for higher-layer applications and relies on IP to route packets through the network in order to make those connections. These applications, in turn, provide specific services for Internet users. For example, **SMTP (Simple Mail Transfer Protocol)** defines the protocol used for the delivery of mail messages over the Internet. The **TELNET** protocol allows users to log in to remote computers via the Internet. **FTP (File Transfer Protocol)** allows Internet users to transfer files from remote computers. DNS (Domain Name System) provides a mapping of host names to addresses. We will discuss these protocols later.

TCP is a connection-oriented transport protocol designed to provide reliable communications over different network architectures. Its predecessor in the original ARPANET was NCP (Network Control Protocol), which was designed to run on top of a reliable network. ARPANET was sufficiently reliable, but as it evolved into an internetwork reliability was lost. Consequently, the transport protocol was forced to evolve as well. NCP, redesigned to run over unreliable networks, became TCP. **UDP (User Datagram Protocol)** provides a connectionless mode of communication over dissimilar networks. UDP and TCP provide the transport user with the two typical modes of communication. We will discuss both TCP and UDP in more detail in the next section.

The Internet Protocol is a layer 3 protocol designed to provide a packet delivery service between two sites. It is commonly, but not exclusively, used with TCP.

Figure 7.29   Internet Protocols

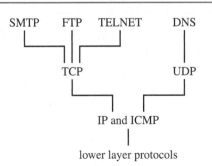

Figure 7.30 shows how it works with TCP. Suppose two sites (*A* and *B*) need a connection-oriented service requiring the transmission of some data. Common examples are email and file transfers. TCP provides the reliable connection independent of the network architectures in between the two, and IP does the work of routing packets through different networks. It's a little like making a telephone call. At one level, you simply dial and someone at the other end answers (you hope). You have made a connection. Furthermore, you have no knowledge of how that connection was made or how many telephone switches your call may have been routed through. That's handled by the telephone companies involved. Figure 7.30 shows a possible Internet connection between *A* and *B*.

To begin, the TCP at site *A* creates a TCP segment[*] containing the user's data and "sends" the segment to site *B*. If all goes well *B* will acknowledge what it receives. From TCP's point of view it has made a direct connection with *B* (dotted line). IP, however, intercepts the segment and creates an **IP packet** (whose format we discuss shortly) containing the TCP segment. Perhaps site *A* is a company computer and the packet needs to get to a router over a token ring LAN. In that case, data link protocols create a token ring frame, put the IP packet in the frame's data field, and send it to the router via the token ring network. The lower-layer protocols really do not know they are transporting an IP packet and frankly do not care. They just perform their tasks as specified in the previous chapter, delivering whatever data they have.

When the frame arrives at the router, its data link layer extracts the IP packet from the token ring frame and gives it to the router's IP. IP examines the address in

Figure 7.30 IP Transmitting Packets over Different Networks

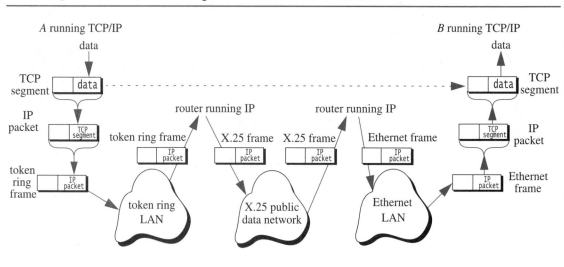

---

[*] A **TCP segment,** similar to a packet, contains data and other overhead information. We discuss its format in Section 7.5.

the packet and determines via routing tables that it should go to another router over an X.25 public data network. The router's lower layers of X.25 embed the IP packet into an X.25 packet and send it over the public data network.

The second router must also make a routing decision. In this case, it decides that the intended recipient is connected to an Ethernet network to which it has access. Consequently, the router's data link layer for that LAN creates an Ethernet frame, stores the IP packet in it, and sends it over the Ethernet. Eventually the Ethernet frame reaches its destination, where the Ethernet data link protocols extract the data (IP packet) and give it to the IP at site *B*. The IP interprets the packet and gives the TCP segment to TCP, which eventually extracts the data and gives it to *B*. This simple description serves to show IP's role in routing packets over dissimilar networks.

INTERNET ADDRESSING

Since routing is an important part of the Internet protocol, it is important to understand what an Internet address looks like and how a router interprets it. To many email users an Internet address has the form

user@host.department.institution.domain

However, this is not an actual Internet address. It is a text representation identifying a user at some host computer connected to the Internet. The characters prior to the @ represent the user and those after are the text representation (**text address**) of some host computer. The periods in the text address separate its components. The first part (the name immediately to the right of the @) generally specifies a host computer at a particular site. The rightmost name refers to an Internet domain. A word of caution is needed here! In this context, a **domain** is a collection of sites of a particular type. They are different from the domains described in the previous section and do not have any geographic significance. That is, two sites in the same domain may be in the same city or they may be a thousand miles apart. These domains are used primarily for administration and organizing text addresses for eventual translation to an Internet address. As such, they are not used for routing. Table 7.10 lists some common domain names and the types of sites to which each corresponds.

The other parts of the text address can be almost anything, depending on a particular site. Typically the names identify an organization, a department, or a specific computer. For example, uwgb.edu specifies the University of Wisconsin-Green Bay in the educational domain and nasa.gov indicates the National Aeronautics and Space Administration in the government domain. If the institution is large enough it may be divided into departments (more subdomains) and host computers within each department. For example, the author's full email address is shayw@gbms01.uwgb.edu. If we were large enough to warrant separate network connections in different departments, a department identifier could be inserted between "gbms01" and "uwgb." When the site is small, there may be a default computer used to receive all incoming messages to obviate the need to specify the computer. In our case, a computer named "gbms01" is the default, which allows the author's email address to be listed as Shayw@uwgb.edu.

Table 7.10 Internet Domains

DOMAIN	MEANING
com	Commercial institution
edu	Educational institution
int	International organizations
gov	Government agency
mil	Military
net	Network service providers
org	Nonprofit organizations
country code	For example, jp for Japan or nl for the Netherlands

So, how does this relate to an actual Internet address? As the previous section mentioned, the Internet is a collection of independent networks, each of which may contain many computers. Consequently, each computer can be identified by specifying two things: the participating network and a local address distinguishing it from other computers on that network. When an organization wants to get its network connected to the Internet it applies to the **Network Information Center** (also called **InterNIC**), a collaborative activity among AT&T, the National Science Foundation, and Network Solutions, Inc. The application specifies the text address the organization wishes to use. If the text address duplicates no others currently being used and the application is accepted, the InterNIC assigns a unique network number to that organization's network.[*] Local management can then allocate local addresses to machines on their network. Together, the network number and local address define a 32-bit **Internet address** for a machine.

There are several different classifications of an Internet address, which depend largely on the size of the organization's network (Table 7.11). A **Class A** network uses an 8-bit network number whose first bit is always 0. The remaining 24 bits are assigned locally. Class A addresses are used only for very large networks. For example, the ARPANET has a network number of 10 (binary 0000 1010). With a 24-bit local identifier, a Class A network can support up to $2^{24} = 16,777,216$ different nodes. However, with 7 variable bits in the network number there can be no more than $2^7 = 128$ different Class A networks. **Class B** addresses use 16 bits for both the network number (the first two bits are always 10) and the local identifier. Such networks are still fairly large (up to 65,536 nodes) but nowhere near the Class A capacity. Finally, **Class C** addresses are for relatively small networks. They use 24 bits for the network number (the first three bits are always 110) and 8 bits for the local identifier.

---

[*]We have oversimplified the application and acceptance process. The Web site www.internic.net provides an overview of that process.

Table 7.11 Internet Address Classifications

CLASSIFICATION	32-BIT ADDRESS (n'S REPRESENT BITS IN THE NETWORK NUMBER; x'S REPRESENT BITS IN THE LOCAL IDENTIFIER)				NUMBER OF POSSIBLE NETWORKS	MAXIMUM NUMBER OF NETWORK NODES
	BYTE 1	BYTE 2	BYTE 3	BYTE 4		
Class A	0nnnnnnn	xxxxxxxx	xxxxxxxx	xxxxxxxx	$2^7 = 128$	$2^{24} = 16,777,216$
Class B	10nnnnnn	nnnnnnnn	xxxxxxxx	xxxxxxxx	$2^{14} = 16,384$	$2^{16} = 65,536$
Class C	110nnnnn	nnnnnnnn	nnnnnnnn	xxxxxxxx	$2^{21} = 2,097,152$	$2^8 = 256$
Class D	1110 followed by a 28-bit multicast address					
Class E	1111; reserved for future use					

A **Class D** address is used for multicasting. That is, one **multicast address** defines a group of host computers. If, for example, an email is sent to a multicast address then every host computer in that group gets the email. It is a bit easier than explicitly sending the email to each member of that group separately.

DOMAIN NAME SYSTEM

Now that we have described both the text form of an address and the 32-bit address, the next logical question is, How does one transform to the other? Each site runs a protocol that accesses a distributed database called the **Domain Name System (DNS).** The operative words here are *distributed* and *database*. As a database, DNS contains copies of text addresses and their associated 32-bit addresses. For example, the DNS contains the text address gbms01.uwgb.edu with its associated Internet address of 143.200.128.3.

DNS, however, is not stored in any one location. To do so would be to invite disaster should that site fail. Besides, one site would never be able to handle the hordes of requests for address translation from sites throughout the world. Instead, DNS is distributed among a collection of **DNS servers** scattered throughout the Internet. In general, a server is one-half of a client/server model.[*] When a host computer needs an address translation, it calls on one or more of the servers to look for the specified text address and return the Internet address. In fact, if you have access to a UNIX system you can test DNS translation using the utility nslookup. For example, entering the command nslookup gbms01.uwgb.edu returns the 32-bit address 143.200.128.3. Try it on some other text addresses.

It sounds simple enough and, yes, we did oversimplify. Still, the basic idea of address lookup is correct. The difficult part is in the implementation and in managing

---

[*]We will discuss the client/server model in Section 7.6. For now, just think of it as a model in which two different programs can run concurrently and exchange requests and responses over a network connection.

the millions of addresses among the servers and providing a quick translation of a text address. This is where the domain concept comes in. We can view DNS as a hierarchical arrangement of text addresses organized first by the domain name. Figure 7.31 shows how some text addresses are organized (space limitations dictate that we do not try to list all Internet addresses).

At the top level the hierarchy is organized by domain. For example, all "edu" institutions are grouped, as are "com" institutions, and so on. Still the edu domain is rather large, so a second-level hierarchy organizes subgroups. Universities such as UWGB (University of Wisconsin-Green Bay), UWM (University of Wisconsin-Milwaukee), MIT, and so forth are grouped under the edu domain. Similarly, there are other subgroupings under the com, org, and other domains. There may be additional hierarchies depending on whether large institutions are divided further into departments.

Now, just because we stated that text addresses are organized in a hierarchy does not mean they are stored that way. Storing and organizing are not the same. We have already mentioned the existence of servers scattered throughout the Internet and that no one server contains all of the information in DNS. The information represented by the hierarchy of Figure 7.31 is divided into **zones,** each of which is a hierarchy of one or more nodes. Furthermore, no two zones overlap. Each zone corresponds to at least two servers (primary and backups), each of which has the responsibility of managing information in that part of the hierarchy. Consequently, the hierarchy is perhaps more accurately applied to an organization of servers.

When a host needs an address translation it sends a request to a local name server. If the local server can provide the translation it does so. If not then the request is sent to one of the DNS servers represented at the top of the hierarchy. For example, text addresses that end in *com* and *edu* go to different servers. If that server has access to the information represented by the text address specified, it returns the Internet address; if not, the server knows of another server that should be able to provide more information.

Figure 7.32 shows how this works for one case. This figure shows one small fictitious branch coming off the com domain. The ACME company maintains two networks, one each for the products and personnel departments. The products department, in turn, consists of research and development and sales divisions. Circles around the nodes define zones.

Figure 7.31   DNS Hierarchy

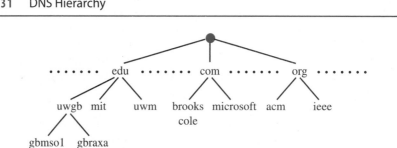

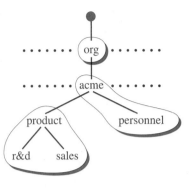

Figure 7.32   Zones in a DNS Hierarchy

Suppose an outsider specifies the text address hercules.products.acme.com. "hercules" is a computer in the research and development division of the products department of the ACME company. The server for the com domain cannot be expected to know the full address of every host computer in every commercial network (there are just too many). However, the "acme" part of the text address tells the server that another server at the ACME site can provide more information. The text address is then sent to the ACME site.

A possible scenario is that the personnel department is fairly small but the products department is larger; consequently, management at ACME decided to use a separate server for their products network. Perhaps the network managers at the products department simply did not want to bother with the personnel network. In any event, the server in the ACME zone still cannot resolve the full address because the text address indicates a zone for which it is not responsible. Note that if the text address contained "personnel.acme.com" then it could because both the ACME and personnel nodes are in the same zone. However, since the products node is in a different zone, a request is sent to another server in the products zone. At that point, the remaining part of the text address is the responsibility of that server, which accesses and returns the corresponding Internet address.

Through a sequence of exchanges among various servers, a text address can be translated into a 32-bit Internet address. For further study, one could investigate the actual protocols to do that, including the formats and types of exchanges among various servers. References [Ta96] and [Pe96] provide some of that information.

IP PACKETS

Having provided the basics of Internet terminology and operation we can now discuss the packet format and some specific features of the Internet Protocol. An IP packet is similar in many ways to the packet and frame formats previously discussed. Still, there are some unique features that warrant discussion. Figure 7.33 shows the contents of an IP packet.

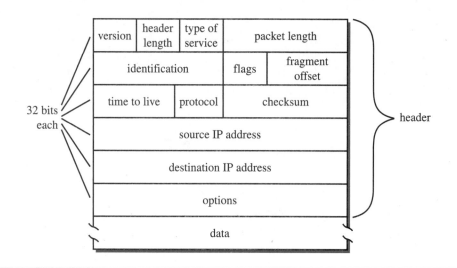

Figure 7.33 Internet Packet

The following list explains the IP packet fields:

- **Version.** Specifies the version of IP that created the packet. This allows different versions of IP to work together.

- **Header length.** Specifies the number of 32-bit words in the **packet header** (the fields preceding the data).

- **Type of service.** Specifies transport-layer requests regarding handling of the packet. This field allows four request options: precedence, low delay, high throughput, and high reliability. A 3-bit **precedence** field allows packets to be prioritized (0 for low and 7 for high priority). Protocols would allow high-priority (or precedence) packets to be transmitted before low-priority ones. This would be especially useful for exchanging control packets indicating status. It also could be used to execute distributed congestion control algorithms without being affected by the congestion it is trying to control (similar to a police vehicle making its way through a heavily congested traffic area to get to an accident so they can get traffic moving again.) Currently, most routers ignore service type, but its implementation allows for changes in newer versions.

  A transport protocol can request a **low-delay** transmission, useful when the transport user has logged into a remote computer and wants quick responses. IP protocols at various routers then can route the packets (containing user requests or remote system responses) over less-congested networks, thus reducing response time. On the other hand, a user may be using a file transfer protocol to get a large file. In this case choosing networks with a high bit rate may be more important than quick responses. Putting a **high-throughput** request in the packet causes the router's IP to look for high-speed networks over which to route a packet. Finally, the **high-reliability** request specifies that the packet be delivered reliably. While IP is not designed to provide error-free service, it can look for networks that have a track record of providing more reliable service and make routing choices accordingly.

- **Packet length.** Specifies the length of the entire IP packet. It is a 16-bit field, thus providing a maximum length of 65,535 octets.

- **Identification, flags, fragment offset.** These three fields are used in fragmentation (discussed shortly).

- **Time to live.** A station sending a packet into the Internet for the first time sets the time-to-live field to specify the maximum time the packet can remain in the Internet. When another router receives the packet it decrements the time-to-live field by the amount of time the packet spent in the router and sends the packet to the next router. If the time-to-live field reaches 0 or less the router discards the packet and sends an error message to the sending station. This step guarantees that routing or congestion problems do not cause packets to circulate endlessly within the Internet.

- **Protocol.** Specifies the higher-layer protocol using IP. It allows the destination IP to give the data to the appropriate entity at its end. For example, if the IP packet contains a TCP segment the protocol value is 6. Packets containing UDP or ICMP segments have protocol values of 17 or 1, respectively.

- **Checksum.** Used for error detection of packet headers. Since the data corresponds to a TCP or other protocol segment it has its own error detection, which is done at a higher layer. Thus, IP needs to worry only about detecting errors in the header. An advantage of this is that error checking fewer bits allows each router to service the packet more quickly. To calculate the checksum, the header is interpreted as a sequence of 16-bit integers. The values are added using 1's complement arithmetic and the result is complemented and stored in the checksum field. On the receiving end, the checksum is recalculated from the arriving information. If it disagrees with the value stored in the checksum field, the receiver knows an error has affected the header. Note that the checksum must be recalculated with each transmission because the header changes (i.e., the time-to-live field changes).

- **Source IP address and destination IP address.** These fields contain the addresses of the sending and receiving sites.

- **Options.** This field is not required in every packet but can be used to request special treatment for the packet. It consists of a series of entries, each corresponding to a requested option.

  The **record route option** traces the route a packet takes. The sending station reserves space for a list of IP addresses in the options field. Each router routing the packet inserts its own address in the list (space permitting), thus allowing the receiving station to determine which ones handled the packet.

  The **timestamp option** is similar to the record route option. In addition to storing its address, each router stores the time at which it routed the packet.

  The **source route option** allows the sender to specify the route to be taken by storing a sequence of IP addresses in the options field. Each router uses this information instead of its own routing tables. This is not the normal mode of routing because it requires knowledge of the physical topology. It can be useful if network administrators suspect there is a problem with a router and want to test a specific route.

The **loose source route** option does not provide the exact route but does provide a list of routers through which the packet must travel.

The **security option** can list certain routers or locations that should be avoided during routing.

More extensive discussions of these options and their execution are found in Reference[Co95].

* **Data.** Contains the data provided by the next-higher layer.

FRAGMENTATION

One of the problems the Internet Protocol faces is that different network architectures allow different maximum frame sizes (also called **maximum transfer units** or **MTUs**). If the IP packet length is smaller than each MTU encountered in a path there is no problem, but if an MTU is smaller the packet is divided into smaller units called **fragments.** The fragments travel to their eventual destination (possibly over different routes), where they must be reassembled. For fragmentation to work, the destination IP must be able to distinguish fragments from unfragmented packets and recognize which fragments correspond to the same packet, in which order they must be reassembled, and how many fragments are contained in each packet. The identification, flags, and fragment offset fields provide that information.

Suppose a router receives a packet and determines it must travel over a network with an MTU smaller than the packet length. It divides the packet into fragments, each containing part of the packet's data. Furthermore, each fragment has a **fragment header** almost identical to the packet header to allow for subsequent routing. Many fields in the fragment header perform the same roles as their counterparts in the packet header. The following fields are relevant to the current discussion:

* The router puts the packet's identification value into each fragment's **identification field.**
* The **flag field** contains a **more fragments bit (mfb).** The router sets the mfb bit in each fragment except the last one. There is also a **do not fragment bit** that, if set, does not allow fragmentation. If a router receives such a packet, it discards the packet and sends an error message to the sending station. The sending station uses the message to determine threshold values at which fragmentation occurs. That is, if the current packet size is too large, the sender could repeat with smaller packet sizes to eventually determine when fragmentation occurs.
* Since a fragment contains part of a packet's data, the router also determines the offset in the packet's data field from where the data was extracted and stores it in the **fragment offset field.** It measures offsets in units of eight bytes each. Thus, offset 1 corresponds to byte number 8, offset 2 to byte 16, and so on.

Figure 7.34 shows a packet being divided into three fragments. It assumes the network has an MTU that allows no more than 1400 bytes of data. Consequently, the router divides an incoming packet with 4000 data bytes into three fragments. Each of the first two fragments has 1400 data bytes. The first one's fragment offset field is 0, indicating its data begins at offset 0 in the packet. The second one's fragment offset field is 175, indicating its data begins at byte 1400 (8×175) of the packet. The third has 1200 bytes of data and an offset of 350. The mfb bits in the first two fragments are 1, indicating that each is a fragment and that more fragments exist. The last fragment's mfb is 0, indicating that it is the last fragment. The fact that it is a fragment at all is deduced from the value in the offset field.

When the destination IP sees two different fragments with the same identification, source, and destination address, it knows they came from the same packet. It reassembles all such packets ordered by the values in their respective offset fields. It recognizes the last fragment as the one with the mfb equal to 0 and a nonzero offset. As part of the reassembly process it also sets a **reassembly timer** on receipt of the first fragment. If it does not receive all the fragments before the timer expires it assumes that one or more were lost. In that case, it discards the currently held fragments and sends an error message to the sending station. The result is that it gets all the fragments or none at all.

IP ROUTING

Much of the groundwork has been set to discuss routing in the Internet. In fact, most of the ideas have already been presented. IP routing is based on routing tables stored

Figure 7.34   Packet Fragmentation

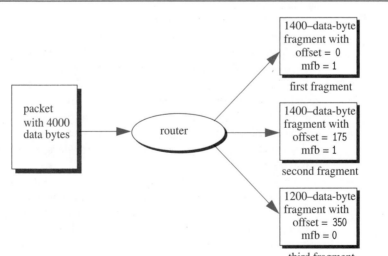

Fragments all have the same identification,
source, and destination fields.

at routers and the interpretation of IP addresses. Previous sections have already dealt with these topics, and we will not reproduce those discussions here. Still, there are a couple of routing details that should be addressed while we are on the topic of the Internet. Recall from earlier discussions that, to an Internet user, an email address may have the form

user@host.department.institution.domain

Domain name servers translate the characters after the @ to a 32-bit number that is typically expressed as a sequence of four 8-bit numbers separated by decimal points (dotted notation). For example, the IP address of the host computer specified in shayw@gbms01.uwgb.edu corresponds to the 32-bit number 10001111-11001000-10000000-00000011 or, using the equivalent dotted notation, 143.200.128.3.

One issue we have not dealt with yet is the distinction between an IP address and a physical address. A unique 32-bit IP address is assigned to each computer on the Internet. Its **physical address** is the one used by the underlying physical network. For example, stations connected to an Ethernet sense addresses stored in IEEE 802.3 frames to determine which ones are destined for it. However, these addresses are Ethernet addresses (48-bit numbers assigned to the network interface card). They have local significance but none on a global IP scale. How will such a station recognize a packet containing an IP address?

The answer is that it doesn't. Recall from Figure 7.30 that IP packets (IP address and all) are stored in frames if they travel through a LAN. Frames contain addresses depending on the data link control protocols. Within a LAN the frame's address specifies the frame's destination. If the frame goes to a router the IP there extracts the packet, examines the address, and determines where to send it next. On the other hand, if the router must send the packet to a PC on an attached LAN it must put the packet into a LAN frame and send it. The next question must be, If the packet is embedded in a LAN frame what physical address is used? In other words, how does the router determine the physical address given the IP address? There are several ways, depending on specifics of the lower layers.

When a router receives an IP packet there are two possibilities. Either the packet's destination is attached to a network to which the router is also attached, or it is not. The router recognizes the first case because the first part of each IP address specifies the network where the destination exists. If it recognizes the network as one to which it is attached it knows it can send the packet directly to its destination. This is called **direct routing.** It puts the destination's physical address in the frame and sends it. So again the question arises: How does the router determine the physical address given the IP address?

One approach, **dynamic binding** (also called **address resolution protocol**), has the router transmit a broadcast request frame containing an IP address to all stations on the LAN. The broadcast requests that the station with that IP address respond with its physical address. That station sends its physical address back to the router and the router stores it and the IP address in a local cache. It then sends the frame to the appropriate station using the physical address it just retrieved. By storing the IP and physical address in a local cache the router can avoid another broadcast request if it must send another packet to the same station. At least that is true for a while because the cache is purged periodically. The reason for the purging is to make sure the cache is current and contains correct information. Of course, a logical question is, How can information become incorrect? Isn't the physical address for a computer constant? The answer is no. If an Ethernet card in a PC failed then a new one would need to be installed. Since each physical card has a unique address, any information relating the PC's IP address and old physical address is now incorrect.

Next, suppose the destination is not reachable directly through one of the router's networks. In that case the router uses hierarchical routing as discussed in Section 7.2 to determine another router and send the packet there. The packet then travels from router to router until it reaches one connected to the destination's actual network and proceeds as just described.

Let's go through an example and put this all together. The following steps summarize a router's actions:

1. Receive an IP packet and extract the IP address.

2. If the packet's source route option is marked, route the packet according to the route indicated. Skip the remaining steps.

3. Determine the network number contained in the IP address.

4. Does the network number match any network to which the router is connected?

5. If yes, determine the physical address of the destination (either by cache lookup or dynamic binding) and send a frame containing the IP packet to that destination.

6. If no, find the network number in the routing table and forward the packet to the specified router.

7. If, for some reason, the network is not in the routing table, forward the packet to a default router.

Assume the example topology of Figure 7.35. Router 1 is connected to a network whose number is 143.200 (i.e., every node on that network has an IP address of 143.200.x.y). Similarly, router 2 is connected to a network whose number is 143.100. Suppose router 1 receives a packet with an IP address of 143.200.10.5. It examines the network number 143.200 and knows it can deliver the packet to the destination directly. It sends a broadcast request frame containing the number 143.200.10.5. Since it is a broadcast frame each station on the LAN gets it, but only station *A* responds by returning a frame to the router containing *A*'s physical address. The router then stores the IP packet into a frame containing *A*'s physical address and sends it.

On the other hand, suppose router 1 receives a packet containing address 143.100.20.4. Router 1 knows it is not connected to network 143.100 and that it must route the packet to another router. It examines its routing table and finds it should forward the packet to router 2. When router 2 gets the packet it performs tasks similar to those we just described for router 1. Of course the packet may have traveled through several routers, but the steps are all similar to those we have just outlined.

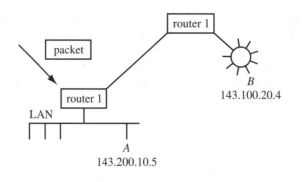

Figure 7.35 IP Routing

INTERNET CONTROL MESSAGE PROTOCOL

Because IP does not provide a guarantee of reliable service, the **Internet Control Message Protocol (ICMP)** is a protocol used for reporting errors and for providing routers updates on conditions that can develop in the Internet. ICMP sends messages by encapsulating them in IP packets and setting the header's protocol field to 1.

The following list explains some typical control messages sent by ICMP.

- **Destination unreachable.** As we have stated previously, IP cannot guarantee delivery of a packet. The destination may not exist or it may be down, the sender may have made a source route request that cannot be carried out, or a packet with its do not fragment bit set may be too large to be encapsulated into a frame. In such cases the router detecting the error sends an ICMP packet to the original sender. It contains the entire IP header of the undeliverable packet and the first 64 bits of its data, thus allowing the sender to recognize which packet was undeliverable.

- **Echo request.** ICMP uses this packet to determine whether a particular destination is reachable. For example, if *A* wants to know whether *B* is reachable it sends an echo request packet addressed to *B*. If *B* receives the packet it responds by sending an echo reply packet back to *A*. The echo reply packet will return any data placed in the echo request packet. This may be simpler than committing a protocol to sending a whole series of packets to a destination only to find out it is unreachable.

- **Echo reply.** Sent in response to an echo request.

- **Parameter problem.** Suppose an IP packet contains an error or an illegal value in one of its header fields. A router discovering the error sends a parameter problem packet back to the source. This packet contains the IP header in question and a pointer to the header field that is in error.

- **Redirect.** Suppose a host station sends a packet to a router and the router knows the packet could have been delivered faster via some other router. To facilitate future routing the router sends a redirect packet back to the host. It informs the

host where the other router is and that it should send future packets with the
same destination to it. This allows the host to update its routing tables dynamically and to take advantage of changing conditions in the network. The redirect
packet is not used for router-to-router route updates because IP packets contain
the source address but not the address of the most recent router that had it.
When a router receives a packet from another router it does not know which one
sent it.

- **Source quench.** If a router is receiving too many packets from a host it can
  send a message requesting a reduction in the rate at which packets are sent.

- **Time exceeded.** A time exceeded packet is sent when the time-to-live field in
  an IP packet reaches 0 or when the reassembly timer (set on receiving a packet's
  first fragment) expires. In either case, the packet or any unassembled fragments
  are dropped from the network. The guilty router then sends a time exceeded
  packet to the source indicating its packets were not delivered.

- **Timestamp request and reply.** Timestamp packets allow a host to estimate
  the time required for a round trip between it and another host. A host creates
  and sends a timestamp request packet containing the time of transmission
  (original timestamp). When the receiving host gets the packet it creates a
  timestamp reply packet that contains the original timestamp, the time at
  which the receiving host got the packet (receive timestamp), and the time at
  which the receiving host sends the reply (transmit timestamp). When the original sender receives the reply it records the time it arrived. The difference
  between the arrival time and the original timestamp is the time required for
  the round trip. By calculating the difference between the receive timestamp
  and transmit timestamp the host also can determine how long the other host
  took to respond once it got the request. By subtracting this from the round-trip
  time the host can also estimate the transit time for both the request and the
  reply. Timestamp packets allow the host to estimate the network's efficiency
  in delivering packets.

- **Address mask request and reply.** The previous section mentioned subnets as a
  way of assigning multiple physical networks the same IP network number. By
  using a few additional bits of the local ID part of an IP address, subnet numbers
  may be assigned to different physical networks. For example, a Class B site can
  manage eight separate physical networks by using 3 bits from the local ID to
  specify the physical network. These bits, together with the 16-bit IP network
  number, form the subnet number. To extract a subnet number from an IP
  address, an internal router uses a **subnet address mask** and performs a bitwise
  logical AND operation between it and the actual IP address. For example, suppose a host in the previously mentioned Class B site has an IP address of
  143.200.123.78. What is the subnet number? In this case the address mask is
  255.255.224.0 or 11111111.11111111.11100000.00000000 (note the nineteen
  1s because of the 16-bit IP network number and the 3 bits from the local ID).
  Next, do a bitwise logical AND between the mask and the IP address. The result
  is the 19-bit subnet number (followed by thirteen 0s), in this case 143.200.96.0.

A host can send an address mask request packet to a router to determine the address mask for the network to which it is attached. The router can respond with the reply.

- **Information request and reply.** These messages were originally designed to let a host determine its IP address when it starts up. Other protocols typically do this now and these two control messages have become obsolete.

IPv6

As we indicated at the beginning of this section, the Internet Protocol began evolving in the late 1960s. In the field of computing that's analogous to the Stone Age. The Internet Protocol has certainly evolved, but there are signs that it is aging and won't provide what is needed in the 21st century.

IP Address Depletion   One serious problem facing the Internet is address depletion, or an insufficient number of addresses to serve global needs. Since Internet addresses are 32 bits there are only a finite number of addresses available. Your first reaction might be as follows: 32 bits allows a total of 2^{32} or about 4.3 billion different address. Yes, the world has more people than that but on a global scale the majority still are not Internet users. Therefore the problem isn't severe. That rationale is incorrect, and here's why.

As we described previously, there are different classes of Internet addresses. Suppose a medium-size organization applies for and gets a Class B network. Perhaps the organization has 500 people, so 500 different addresses are used. By defining a Class B network, local management has the ability to assign $2^{16} = 65,536$ different local identifiers (recall Table 7.11). Since there only 500 users, about 65,000 Internet addresses go unused. Since they all correspond to the same Class B network number they cannot be reclaimed by any other organization. What this particular organization does not use is lost to the general Internet population.

A logical response might be to suggest a couple of Class C networks instead of a Class B network. Since Class C networks have 256 local identifiers for each network, it would be more efficient to assign Class C networks. In the previous example, two Class C networks would accommodate up to 512 Internet users. If there are 500 users, only 12 addresses go unallocated.

There are a couple of problems with this approach. The biggest is planning for growth. There isn't a network manager worth his or her salt that wouldn't plan for future growth in a company network. Suppose the company applies to InterNIC and gets a Class C network. If the network grows beyond 256 users it will have to apply for another Class C network. In fact, for every increment of 256 users a new application must be filed. The additional paperwork, headaches, and delays is certainly counterproductive. With a Class B network, growth up to 65,536 users can be accommodated without the formality of applications and approval processes (except the first one, of course). From the network manager's perspective this is a far simpler scenario.

Another problem is the additional routing table information. Recall that the section on hierarchical routing discussed the difference between interior and exterior routing. In the Internet, exterior routing is based on network numbers. Using Class C networks means assigning more networks. More networks means more network numbers for routers to track. Consequently, performance of exterior routing protocols suffers. Use of Class B networks simplifies the external routing. There will be more subnets with this scheme, but they will be distributed over many hierarchical domains. As a result, the number of subnets within a domain is still quite manageable.

The bottom line is that, for many, Class B addresses are more desirable to allow growth within an organization. Since the goal of any network is to provide a service to its users, it makes sense to use Class B networks where appropriate, even if doing so wastes addresses. Consequently, IP must evolve to deal with address depletion.

Other IP Shortcomings   The original purpose of the Internet was to connect computers and exchange data. Consequently, protocols were developed to accomplish this primary goal. The problem is that connecting computers will not be the only goal of a global network in the future and therefore different protocols must emerge to meet these new goals. Just as the personal computer was the phenomenon of the 1980s, multimedia and video applications are and will be the phenomena of the 1990s and the early 21st century. Entertainment and digital technology continue to blend together to create new demands on global networks. Pay per view service is already available on cable systems, and video on demand is probably not far away. In limited applications it is already here. Growing numbers of people are already enjoying real-time video games over the Internet.

Mobility is another development. In the current Internet the vast majority of host computers never change locations. They may move from one office to another, but that's a problem for local management. From the Internet Protocol's perspective they remain in fixed locations. However, this is changing. Mobile computers and satellite technology are providing the means for any two devices to communicate from anywhere in the world. The protocols must develop to allow millions of pairs of devices to make connections from arbitrary locations.

Some see current technologies such as cell phones, pagers, and portable computers eventually merging into a personal communication device that serves a variety of needs. Making telephone calls or being paged are obvious ones, but many see the day when such a device can do many other tasks. Homes may be equipped with computerized devices with which you can communicate. If you are getting home later than you planned you might use a personal communication device to turn on the lights at home or start the oven. A sensor system might send a signal to you if you left without locking all the doors or turning off the lights, which, of course, you could correct using the same system. You'll be able to plug the device into a portable computer and download files from any other remote computer to which you have access, all without benefit of a telephone. You might even use the system to feed your cyberpet that you left at home. All of these applications will require site-independent communications.

Security is another issue. The Internet Protocol isn't particularly secure. This is why passwords, authentication techniques, and firewalls are so important to many applications. People recognize that packets arriving on the Internet can come from virtually anywhere and that strong measures are necessary to protect their resources. The past years have seen enough examples of fraud and hacking into private computers to suggest that security will always be a concern.

Despite all of this, there is one overriding goal when developing any new protocols: the ability to coexist with current systems. The biggest impediment to any emerging technology in computing is making sure it runs concurrently with existing technologies. Then over a period of years applications can gradually migrate from the old to the new. On a global scale there is just no other way.

People have been thinking about these ideas for many years and the concepts are certainly not new. In 1991, the Internet Engineering Task Force (IETF) began looking at the issue of changing the existing IP and creating a next-generation IP informally referred to as **IPng (IP Next Generation).** In an attempt to get the computing community involved, they invited various professionals (researchers, manufacturers, vendors, programmers, etc.) to submit proposals. An appointed committee called the IPng directorate evaluated the proposals and rejected many because they served special interests or were just too complex. However, one proposal included a design called Simple Internet Protocol (SIP) [De93], which was extended to use ideas described in other proposals. The resulting protocol was named **Simple Internet Protocol Plus (SIPP).**

In 1994 the IETF met in Toronto and, based on the recommendations of the IPng directorate, selected SIPP as the basis for the next-generation Internet Protocol, which would be formally known as **IPv6 (IP version 6).** Later in the year the Internet Engineering Steering Group approved it and the following year entered the protocols into the IETF standard process. We will provide an outline of IPv6; the reader is encouraged to locate References [Hi96], [St96], [Br95], and [Co95] for additional detail.

Packet Headers   We begin discussion of IPv6 by examining the packet header format. This provides a framework in which to explain some the options IPv6 provides and how they differ from the current version of the Internet Protocol (IPv4). Figure 7.36 shows the IPv6 packet header. On comparison with the IPv4 packet of Figure 7.33, two things are immediately evident. The addresses have more bits and the header format has fewer options. The latter may seem to contradict the goal of providing additional capabilities, but it doesn't, as we will soon see.

The **version field** has four bits and identifies which version of IP this packet represents (4 for the current IP and 6 for the new one).

The **priority field** also has four bits and is particularly useful in congestion control. The concept of priority is simple: Higher values indicate more important packets. It is how priorities are used that is significant. We have already discussed congestion and some ways to deal with it. IPv6 recognizes that delays in some applications such as email are often not noticeable, whereas delays in others such as multimedia applications render viewing next to impossible. The trick is identifying which packets correspond to which applications.

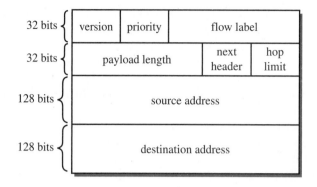

Figure 7.36   IPv6 Packet Header

A site sending out IP packets can use this field to indicate importance relative to other packets the site sends. Priority values between 0 and 7, inclusive, correspond to packets that the site may hold a little longer in response to congestion. IPv6 recommends values depending on the application. For example, email has a priority of 2, FTP and HTTP (Hypertext Transfer Protocol of the World Wide Web) have a priority of 4, Telnet (remote login protocol) has a priority of 6, and SNMP has a priority of 7. As you can see, the higher values correspond to applications for which delays are typically more noticeable. Values above 7 correspond to real-time or multimedia applications, cases where delays range from very inconvenient to unacceptable. For example, downloading sound or video files for real-time viewing requires little or no delay. (Of course, if delays could somehow be synchronized with your need for snack breaks then they could be tolerated.)

The 24-bit **flow label field** is used in conjunction with the priority field. Specifics as to exactly how this field will be used have not been finalized as of this writing, but the idea is to identify packets that require "special handling" by routers. Normal handling requires routers to search routing tables before forwarding packets. Since tables change over time, packets with the same destination can travel different routes.

IPv6 defines a **flow** as a sequence of packets sent by a source to a single destination in response to some application. If they are packets designed to provide real-time viewing at the destination, special handling might mean to route them all the same way (and quickly) to guarantee they arrive in order. In fact, it is much like a virtual circuit. To set up a flow, the source generates a random nonzero number and stores it in the flow label field of each packet in that flow. A router applies a hash function to that flow number to calculate a location that contains information on how the packet should be handled. Instructions on the special handling would be set up prior to the flow. The router uses a hash function because it is generally the quickest way to find something. Random numbers are used because they result in fewer collisions when subjected to hash functions. Often, the bottom line is for the router to get the packet out as quick as possible.

The 16-bit **payload length field** is the number of bytes in the packet minus 40. Since the header is 40 bytes, this field specifies how many significant bytes follow it. Do not interpret this to mean the payload length is the number of data bytes. If there were just one header that would be true, but other headers may follow the first one.

This brings us to the 8-bit **next header field,** an important distinction from IPv4. The current IPv4 packet header contains an options and protocol field to indicate when routers should take different actions. Because different options are embedded in that field, each router has to parse through each packet header (specifically, the option field) to determine whether there are options that will affect its decisions. This means additional logic and time at each router. Consequently this slows the routing process.

To allow the existence of different options, IPv6 implements several **extension headers,** which are essentially additional headers between the header of Figure 7.36 and the packet's payload (data). The next header field of each header specifies the type of extension that follows (if any). If there are none, then like the protocol field of the IPv4 header, it specifies the transport protocol (e.g., TCP or UDP) using IPv6. Perhaps the most significant aspect of this arrangement is that some of the extension headers will be ignored by routers. Routers will therefore be able to forward packets more quickly.

At present there are six types of extension headers:

- **Authentication header.** This provides for packet authentication, something not present in IPv4.

- **Destination options header.** This provides information for the destination. It's not used yet but allows for the future development of any options that only the destination needs to know.

- **Fragmentation header.** This header provides information in the event that packet fragments must be reassembled. It is somewhat like the fragmentation and reassembly process of IPv4. There is a significant departure from IPv4 fragmentation, however. Intermediate IPv4 routers were able to fragment an incoming packet if it was too large. IPv6 will not fragment a packet at an intermediate router. This is important because it simplifies the router logic and contributes to more efficient and quicker routing. Of course, a logical question to ask is, What happens if a router gets a packet that is too big to send over the next network? In this case, the router just throws the packet away and sends a message (via ICMP) back to the source. That message indicates that the packet was too big and specifies the maximum allowable size. The source will fragment the packet and send the fragments. The destination will reassemble them.

- **Hop-by-hop header.** This header, if present, must be examined by each router. The idea is to specify any information that each router should have. This header is largely undeveloped but there is an option for allowing packets that exceed 64 KB in size (normally, the default maximum size is 64 KB). This can be useful for supercomputers that transfer huge amounts of information over the Internet.

- **Routing header.** This provides additional routing information such as IPv4's loose route option. That is, this extension header will contain the 128-bit addresses of routers through which this packet must travel.

- **Security header.** This indicates that the packet's payload has been encrypted. In theory, any encryption algorithm can be used, but a form of DES is the default.

Finally, the **hop limit field** is essentially the same as the time-to-live field in the IPv4 packet.

IPv6 Addressing   The last two fields in an IPv6 packet header are the source and destination addresses, which are self-explanatory. What is not self-explanatory are the types of addresses IPv6 defines and some issues surrounding compatibility with IPv4 addressing. The most obvious difference with IPv4 is that addresses are 128 bits, four times as long as IPv4 addresses. In theory this allows for $2^{128} \approx 10^{40}$ different addresses. One of the problems with exponential notation is that it is often difficult to understand just how large a number is. To help understand how large 2^{128} is, Reference [Hi96] made some calculations. It showed that if all the addresses were spread out evenly across the surface of the entire earth then there would be about 10^{24} addresses for each square meter of the earth's surface, more than enough for each person, earthworm, and insect that populates the planet. (There might even be a few left over for some viruses or bacteria.)

There are three general classifications of addresses: unicast, anycast, and multicast. A **unicast address** specifies a unique interface. There are several types of unicast addresses, and we will discuss them shortly. An **anycast address** specifies a group of interfaces. A packet with an anycast destination address may be delivered to any one in the group (usually the one closest to the source). A **multicast address** also specifies a group, but in this case the packet goes to each interface in the group.

Notation for 128-bit addresses differs from that used in IPv4. Using the current notation in which dots separate three-digit numbers would result in a notation containing 16 three-digit number separated by dots. Naturally, this becomes somewhat unwieldy. Instead, colons will replace dots, and each 16 bits in an address will have a four-digit hexadecimal number notation. An example IPv6 address has the form

7477:0000:0000:0000:0000:0AFF:1BDF:7FFF

Each hexadecimal digit in this representation has a unique 4-bit equivalent. The result is still unwieldy but better than the alternative. For addresses that contain a lot of 0s (and with 2^{128} addresses, a lot of them will), a shorthand notation will be used. Essentially, the 0s will not be listed and a double colon (::) will indicate their presence. The actual number of 0s that are missing is calculated by subtracting the number of hexadecimal digits in the notation from 32, the number of hexadecimal digits needed for a full 128-bit representation. For example, the above address would be written as

7477:: 0AFF:1BDF:7FFF

Since this notation contains 16 digits, we know there must be 16 missing 0s. In cases where the 0 string begins the address, the notation will start with the double colon. In other words, the address

$$0000{:}0000{:}0000{:}0000{:}0AFF{:}1BDF{:}000F{:}0077$$

could also be written as

$$::\ 0AFF{:}1BDF{:}000F{:}0077$$

To further simplify addresses, leading 0s within a 4-digit group need not be listed. This allows us to simplify this address' notation as

$$::AFF{:}1BDF{:}F{:}77$$

Just as IPv4 divided its addresses into Class *A*, *B*, *C*, *D*, and *E*, depending on the leading bits, IPv6 does something similar. There are currently 22 types of addresses, each having a unique bit prefix. The prefixes range from three to ten bits. For example, an address beginning with eight 0s corresponds to an IPv4 address. (Actually, IPv4 addresses begin with many more 0s, but more about that later.) Those beginning with eight 1s are multicast addresses. Those starting with 0000 010 are compatible with Novell's IPX protocol. Most of the predefined prefixes have not been assigned and are being reserved for future growth. This leaves about 85% of the addresses reserved for the future.

Of particular interest are the unicast addresses, which are the most analogous to IPv4 addresses. Figure 7.37 shows the format of a unicast address. Like an IPv4 address, there is an implied hierarchy; it is just more complex. The first three bits of a unicast address are 010. The remaining bits define a five-level hierarchy. The example topology of Figure 7.38 illustrates how the hierarchy can be organized.

In general, a **network service provider** contracts with customers to provide access to the Internet. The customers for a particular provider may all be connected through some regional network spanning a city, county, or several counties, depending on the population base. In some cases, the customers might be large companies or universities that have their own internal hierarchical structure. As Section 7.2 discussed, they may divide their network into subnets, each having a unique identifier. These subnets would then provide eventual access to the people who use the services.

Since there will be many network providers, part of the address of Figure 7.37 will identify the provider. Thus, routing done to find the correct provider is done independent of the provider's customers. The network provider would then assign subscriber IDs to its customers. Some large companies may define their own subnets. Each would have its own subnet number, and the full IPv6 addresses of each

Figure 7.37   Unicast Address Format

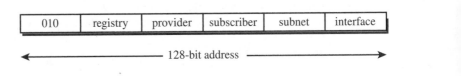

| 010 | registry | provider | subscriber | subnet | interface |

128-bit address

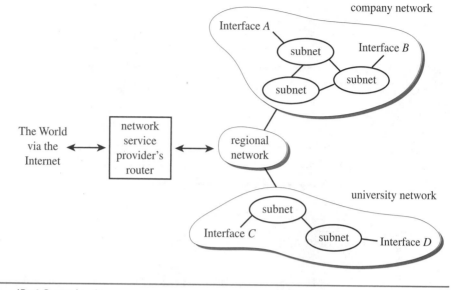

company network

Interface *A*

subnet

Interface *B*

subnet

subnet

The World
via the
Internet

network
service
provider's
router

regional
network

university network

subnet

Interface *C*

subnet

Interface *D*

Figure 7.38   IPv6 Organization

subnet would contain the same subscriber number. Finally, the subnets connect users. Each user on the same subnet has a different interface ID but they all have the same subnet, subscriber, and provider IDs. All of this is really just an extension of the hierarchical routing strategies discussed in Section 7.2.

Finally, the **registry ID** in Figure 7.37 accounts for international or continental borders. A Canadian registry will maintain a list of authorized providers in Canada. Similar registries will exist in the United States, Europe, and so on. Thus, the registry ID is at the top level in the hierarchy and allows for some routing decisions to be made based on geography. This would help packets sent from Canada to the United States to avoid European routers.

Compatibility with IPv4   There are many millions of computers communicating using IPv4. Such a large number prohibits any possibility of converting to IPv6 overnight or during a weekend. The coordination difficulty, inevitable problems, and costs make this scenario impossible. Upgrading the world's computers to IPv6 will require many years because individual sites must define their own timetables for implementation. Consequently, both IPv4 and IPv6 routers must be able to coexist and maintain all necessary connections. IPv6 protocols are designed to recognize IPv4 protocols. On the other hand, IPv4 protocols were designed well before IPv6 and have no knowledge of it. This presents some problems that must be solved.

To help solve these problems the IPv6 address structure allows IPv4 address types. Figure 7.39 shows two ways to put an IPv4 address into an IPv6 address structure. Since the IPv6 addresses are larger than IPv4 ones, it is not terribly difficult to

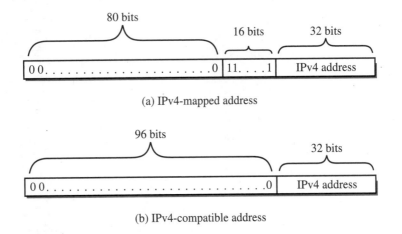

(a) IPv4-mapped address

(b) IPv4-compatible address

Figure 7.39   IPv4 Addresses in an IPv6 Format

find a way to store IPv4 addresses. The tricky part is to make the two protocols work together. Figure 7.39a shows an IPv4-mapped address. Suppose a packet must go through a network of IPv6 routers to get to an IPv4 destination. One option is for the routers to revert to IPv4 whenever the destination is an IPv4 node. Since the purpose of IPv6 was to improve on IPv4, that's not a good option.

If routers run IPv6, how will they know the address is that of an IPv4 node and that they should not interpret it according to the IPv6 hierarchy? Again, this is where the address type comes in. The eighty 0s and sixteen 1s designate an IPv4 address. Consequently, routers interpret addresses according to IPv4 rules as opposed to those suggested by Figure 7.37.

What about the reverse problem? Suppose two IPv6 routers need to exchange packets but the only route is through a network of IPv4 routers (Figure 7.40a). Since IPv6 addresses contain information not storable in an IPv4 packet, we seem to have a real problem here. Fortunately, there is a real solution: **tunneling.** For example, suppose *A*, *B*, *C*, and *D* in Figure 7.40a all speak IPv6 and that *A* wants to send a packet to *D*. Unfortunately, the only way to go from *B* to *C* is through a network of nodes that speak only IPv4. Since *D*'s address is 128 bits, how can we push that packet through a network that has no concept of a 128-bit address?

When *B* gets the IPv6 packet from *A*, it embeds it into an IPv4 packet (Figure 7.40b) containing destination *C*. IPv4 protocols do what is necessary to get the IPv4 packet from *B* to *C*. When *C* gets the packet it extracts the IPv6 packet from the IPv4 packet. IPv6 routing is effectively resumed when *C* sends the packet to *D*. From the perspective of IPv4, routing in this network is no different from what we have discussed before. From the perspective of IPv6, there was a single link from *B* to *C* (i.e., a **tunnel**).

Now, if you are following the details you might have one remaining question: If *C* is an IPv6 router how do we get its address into the IPv4 packet? Again, this is

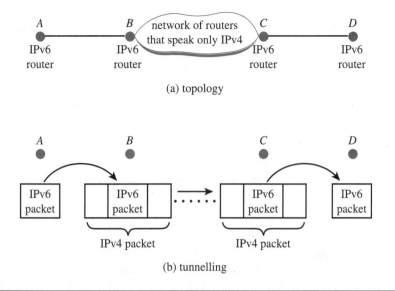

(a) topology

(b) tunnelling

Figure 7.40   Routing IPv6 Packets over IPv4 Networks

part of the transition. Any node that is on either end of a tunnel is assigned an IPv4-compatible address as in Figure 7.39b in addition to its IPv6 address. Consequently, it is easily stored in an IPv4 packet header.

Summary   IPv6 performs the same primary functions as IPv4, providing a connectionless routing capability. However, it has added capabilities such as authentication and encryption not available in IPv4. It also increases the address space dramatically and simplifies the headers to make routing more efficient. There are other factors that also contribute to more efficient routing. Intermediate nodes no longer fragment and reassemble packets. There is no error detection (checksum) capability in IPv6, unlike IPv4, thus relieving routers of another time-consuming task. Removing the checksum is really no loss. Most networks are very reliable. Besides, lower-level data link protocols and, as we'll see, higher-layer protocols have error detection methods.

7.5   TRANSPORT PROTOCOLS

So far we have primarily dealt with network operations. Frame formats, routing, congestion control, and addressing are all essential to allowing one station to talk to another. But *how* they talk with each other is equally important. A **transport protocol** is the lowest-layer protocol that defines what one station can say to another on behalf of the user. The lower three layers define how a network operates; the transport layer is the first to define the end-user protocol.

There are similarities with the data link protocols we discussed previously in that we are focusing on how information is exchanged between two entities. However, data link protocols defined communications between stations with a physical connection. Connection-oriented transport protocols define communications between sites with a logical connection. There are also connectionless transport protocols, but for now we'll just consider a connection-oriented protocol.

The transport layer also provides the "connection" the user perceives. For example, users can log on to computers at remote sites, giving them the impression they are connected. But the connection is not a physical one as exists when connecting wires or making telephone calls. There is not necessarily a dedicated circuit devoted to transmitting information between the user and computer.

The transport layer can provide the perception of a connection by interfacing between the user and network protocols. It is similar to a secretary whose function is to place calls on behalf of an executive. The secretary gets the executive's request, makes the call, and reaches the desired person, thus making the connection. The executive then proceeds to have the conversation independent of any trouble the secretary may have had in finding the desired person, who may have been in an important meeting, out to lunch, or on the racquetball court. When the executive has finished talking, the secretary may end the connection by getting additional important information such as a client's address, phone number, or racquetball court location.

A transport protocol does more than make and break connections, however. The lowest three layers provide the means to connect separate devices, but the transport layer is the lowest layer that actually allows its users to communicate effectively and securely. Some transport layer functions are as follows:

- **Connection management.** This function defines the rules that allow two users to begin talking with one another as if they were connected directly. Defining and setting up the connection is also called **handshaking.**

- **Flow control.** It limits how much information one station can send to another without receiving some acknowledgment. If this sounds familiar, great! You are remembering some of the information from previous chapters. In Chapter 5 we discussed flow control and its relevance to the data link layer. To have flow control again in the transport layer may seem strange at first, but remember that the transport layer must operate independently of the lower layers. Lower layers may allow more or less (or no) flow control. In order to preserve this independence a transport layer may use its own flow control. Thus, it may seem redundant, but independence often introduces redundancy. Furthermore, the transport layer defines flow control between the end users. Data link protocols define flow control between two intermediate, but adjacent, entities.

- **Error detection.** This is another case that seems to duplicate lower-layer features. Some errors, however, escape lower-layer error detection. This statement does seem unusual because it means that even if data link error detection provides reliable transmission along each link there is still no guarantee of error-free transmission between the source and destination. How can this be? Consider the router in Figure 7.41 (taken from Figure 7.30). Suppose it receives

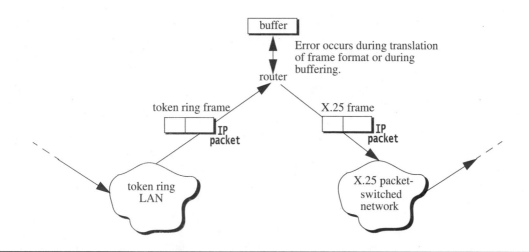

Error occurs during translation
of frame format or during
buffering.

token ring frame

IP
packet

X.25 frame

IP
packet

token ring
LAN

X.25 packet-
switched
network

Figure 7.41   Error Undetected by Lower-Layer Detection Techniques

the IP packet intact, but an error that affects the packet's contents occurs during
reformatting of the frame containing the packet. Any number of software or
hardware errors can cause such a problem. Since the checksum is calculated
after the new frame is created it includes the erroneous data. Strictly speaking, it
is not a transmission error because it occurred while the packet was in the possession of the router. But try telling that to the transport user, who saw his or her
data changed while in transit. A transport-layer error detection mechanism
would detect this error.

- **Response to users' requests.** Examples include sending and receiving data,
  as well as specific requests. For example, a user may request high throughput,
  low delays, or reliable service. As discussed in the previous section, the IP
  can deal with these. The transport layer passes the request from the user to
  the IP.

- **Establishment of connectionless or connection-oriented communication.**

To summarize, a transport protocol must provide reliable communications
between end users. This is especially important because IP does not guarantee reliable service. Transport protocols must provide acknowledgments and timers to
make sure all of a user's data is sent and received. As with error detection, lower-
layer protocols can determine when frames are lost in transit. But again, we want
reliability to exist independent of lower layers. Besides, suppose an intermediate
network node lost a frame after it received and acknowledged it but before it retransmitted the frame. As mentioned earlier, any number of on-site errors could cause
this. Because there was no error in any point-to-point link it would be up to an end-
to-end protocol to detect the error.

Two transport-layer protocols that the DoD designed specifically to run with
its ARPANET IP are the **Transmission Control Protocol (TCP)** and the **User**

Datagram Protocol (UDP). TCP is a connection-oriented protocol that forms the connection management facilities of the Internet. It is the most widely used transport-layer protocol in the world. UDP is a connectionless transport-layer protocol. It is used much less frequently but is still part of the TCP/IP suite. The rest of this section focuses on TCP and discusses UDP. To be complete, we must mention that the ISO also has defined its own layer 4 transport protocol. The Internet and TCP are such dominant forces in defining connections, however, that the DoD TCP is likely to be around for a long time.

TRANSMISSION CONTROL PROTOCOL

TCP provides a connection-oriented user-to-user byte stream service. This means it provides a logical connection between two sites and is capable of transmitting a sequence of bytes between them. It divides a byte steam into a sequence of segments and sends them to the destination via a variation on a sliding window flow control protocol. It provides the initial handshaking by establishing, maintaining, and releasing connections. It handles requests to deliver information to a destination reliably, an important consideration since the lower layer (usually IP) does not guarantee delivery of packets. TCP receives data or requests from its user (Figure 7.42), stores it in a **TCP segment** format, and gives it to the IP. It plays no role in the subsequent routing and transfer of information. The receiver's TCP gets a segment, responds to the information in it, extracts the data, and gives it to the user. From TCP's perspective, there is no network.

TCP Segment   Figure 7.43 shows the contents of a TCP segment. The following list defines the fields.

Figure 7.42   TCP as a User-to-User Service

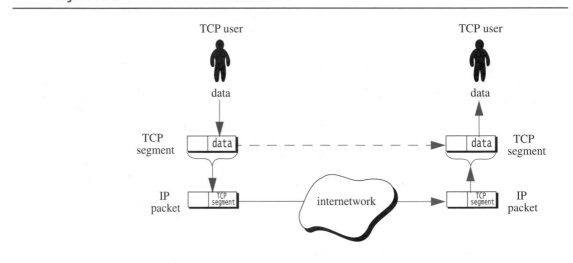

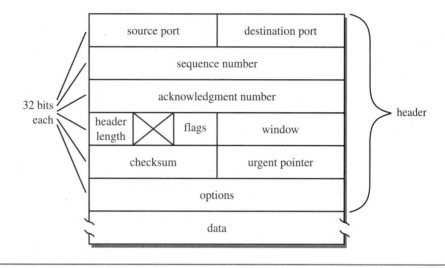

Figure 7.43 TCP Segment

- **Destination port** (16 bits). Identifies the application to which the segment is sent. This is different from the IP address, which specifies an Internet address. Since many applications can run at the same Internet node, this field identifies which one. In the next section we'll see how you can define your own ports to define communications between applications running at different sites. Port numbers below 256 are called **well-known ports** and have been assigned to commonly used applications. For example, port 53 corresponds to a DNS name server and ports 21 and 23 are assigned to FTP and Telnet, respectively.

- **Source port** (16 bits). Specifies the application sending the segment.

- **Sequence number** (32 bits). Each byte in the stream that TCP sends is numbered. For example, if each data segment contained 1000 data bytes, the sequence numbers of the first bytes in consecutive segments would be x, $x +$ 1000, $x + 2000$, and so on, where x is the sequence number of the first byte.[*] If the segment contains data, this field contains the sequence number of the segment's first data byte. In contrast to other protocols that number each packet or frame consecutively, TCP numbers the bytes. TCP also uses this field as part of the initial call connection strategy (discussed shortly). Using 32 bits allows sequence numbers up to about 4 billion. This is significant because the chances for duplicate sequence numbers are all but eliminated. In turn, this relaxes the constraints on window sizes discussed in Chapter 5 that were needed to avoid protocol errors.

---

[*]The initial sequence number is not necessarily 1 and is negotiated when the connection is established. We discuss this under connection management.

- **Acknowledgment number** (32 bits). Contains the byte sequence number the receiving TCP entity expects to receive. Effectively, it acknowledges receiving all bytes prior to the one specified. This is similar to acknowledgments discussed in Sections 5.2 and 5.3 except that here the protocol is acknowledging bytes, not packets.

- **Header length** (4 bits). Specifies the size of the TCP header as a multiple of four bytes. Header length can vary due to the variable-length options field, discussed shortly, and this field allows the receiving TCP protocol to know where the data starts.

- **Flags** (6 bits). The flag field specifies when other fields contain meaningful data or specify certain control functions. For example, two of the flags, **ACK** and **URG** (sounds like prehistoric sibling names), specify whether the acknowledgment and urgent pointer fields (discussed shortly) contain meaningful data. Four other flags are as follows:

  FIN (finish): Indicates the last TCP data segment.

  PSH (push): Ordinarily, TCP decides when a segment contains enough data to warrant its transmission. In some cases an application can force TCP to send a segment earlier by issuing a push command. For example, an interactive application might issue a push after a user has entered a line from a keyboard. This provides a better and smoother response than allowing TCP to buffer several lines of input before sending any of them. When TCP receives a push command it sets the PSH field in the segment. When the PSH field is set in an incoming segment, the receiving TCP entity makes the segment's contents available to its application immediately. If the application is for displaying incoming data on a video screen, this mechanism provides a quick and smooth display.

  RST (reset): Indication from the sending entity that the receiving entity should break the transport connection. Used when an abnormal condition occurs, it allows both entities to terminate the connection, stop the flow of data, and release buffer space associated with the connection.

  SYN (synchronize): Used in the initial connection setup, it allows the two entities to synchronize (agree on) initial sequence numbers (discussed shortly).

- **Window** (16 bits). This field tells the TCP entity that receives this segment how many more data bytes it can send beyond those that have already been acknowledged. As we will discuss shortly, this corresponds roughly to the window size of a sliding window protocol (Sections 5.2 and 5.3). It differs from protocols we have discussed in that a TCP entity receiving a byte stream can use this field to change the side of the window on the sending end.

- **Checksum** (16 bits). Used for transport-layer error detection. The checksum algorithm interprets the contents of the TCP segment as a sequence of 16-bit integers and sums them. This is not as strong an error detection algorithm as others we have discussed in Chapter 4 and has generated some criticism.

- **Urgent pointer** (16 bits). If the URG bit is set, the segment contains urgent data, meaning the receiving TCP entity must deliver it to the higher layers as quickly as possible. Urgent data is at the beginning of the segment, and the urgent pointer points to the first byte following the urgent data. This allows the receiving entity to distinguish urgent data from nonurgent data. Some have criticized the urgent field as a weak implementation of urgency. True, the urgent field generates special handling once the segment has been received, but it does not affect the flow control responsible for getting the segment there in the first place. It's a little like standing in a long line at a bank teller's window and then demanding to speak to the president once you get to the teller's window.

- **Options** (variable size). One option allows a TCP entity to specify the maximum segment size it will receive from the other entity. This value typically is specified during the initial connection setup. It is an important option because TCP may connect two computers with very different capabilities. Successful communication requires that each be aware of any limitations (such as buffer size) the other has. For example, a large IBM mainframe would not want to overwhelm a small PC with segments that are too large. The PC would establish the maximum segment it can receive when it establishes the connection. Because the header size is a multiple of four bytes, the option field is padded to make sure the header ends on a 32-bit boundary.

    Another option allows the TCP entities to agree on a 32-bit window field instead of a 16-bit one. This is particularly useful when high bandwidth lines are used to transfer large files. A 16-bit window never allows a sending protocol to have a window larger than $2^{16} = 64$ KB. This is no longer considered a very large file.

- **Data** (variable size). User-supplied data.

TCP Connection Management   **Connection management** is the process of establishing, maintaining, and ending a connection. But what exactly is a connection? As indicated previously, a connection is more virtual than physical. (Isn't everything these days?) Basically, two TCP entities agree to exchange TCP segments and establish some parameters describing the segment exchange. Typical parameters describe the sequence numbers used for bytes and the number of bytes an entity can receive. The entities then send each other segments and do error checking, acknowledging, and flow control as if they were connected directly, leaving transmission details to the lower layers.

To begin, the two entities must agree to establish a connection. Initially, this seems straightforward: One entity makes a request to connect and the other says OK. This is a two-way handshake, discussed in Section 1.4. We also mentioned that it can cause problems if the first request is delayed and subsequently shows up at a much later time, thus causing an unintentional second connection. We responded by discussing a three-way handshake, in which one entity makes a connection request, the second acknowledges the request, and the first acknowledges the acknowledgment. This might be a good time to review that section if some of the details are not clear.

More is involved than simply sending connection requests and acknowledgments. We mentioned earlier that TCP treats data as a sequence of bytes to be divided and sent in segments. Rather than numbering each segment, TCP stores the sequence number of the first data byte in the sequence field of a segment. The sequence field is a 32-bit field, thus allowing sequence numbers over 1 billion. To avoid the problems associated with a two-way handshake, the three-way handshake establishes the initial sequence numbers each TCP entity uses. The following steps of the three-way handshake are illustrated in Figure 7.44:

1. TCP entity A transmits a TCP segment requesting a connection (time t_1). It sets the SYN flag to indicate the segment represents a connection request and defines the sequence field to be x. It may determine x using a timer or counter. Each new request is accompanied by different and larger (modulo 2^{32}) initial sequence numbers.

2. TCP entity B transmits a TCP segment acknowledging both the request and the sequence number (time t_2). It does this by setting the SYN flag and defining the acknowledgment field = $x + 1$ and the sequence field = y. B determines y in much the same way A determines x.

3. TCP entity A acknowledges the acknowledgment (time t_3). The next segment it sends contains sequence field = $x + 1$ and acknowledgment field = $y + 1$.

After the three segments have been sent and received, each entity knows what initial sequence number the other is using and, by way of the acknowledgment field, has

Figure 7.44 Three-Way Handshake Protocol

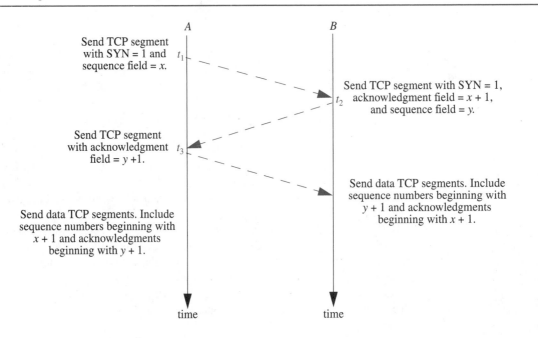

told the other what it is expecting. Subsequent data segments contain increasing (modulo 2^{32}) sequence numbers, where each increment is equal to the number of data bytes in the previous segment. We will elaborate shortly when we discuss flow control.

Terminating connections is similar to establishing them. TCP provides full-duplex communication, however, so one entity wanting to disconnect does not necessarily mean the other is ready. Basically, both parties must agree to disconnect before doing so. Consequently, another three-way handshake protocol is used to terminate a connection (Figure 7.45):

1. TCP entity A gets a CLOSE request from its application (time t_1). It responds by sending a TCP segment with the FIN flag set and sequence field $= x$. The FIN flag indicates there is no more data and that the current segment represents a disconnect request. The parameter x represents the current sequence count the TCP entity had been maintaining.

2. TCP entity B receives the segment (time t_2). It responds by notifying its application of the request to disconnect, effectively telling it no more data is on the way. It also sends a TCP segment back to A acknowledging receipt of the request. Meanwhile B's application could continue to send data or simply prepare to issue its own disconnect request.

3. TCP entity B gets a CLOSE request from its application (time t_3). It sends a TCP segment to A with the FIN flag set and acknowledgment field $= x + 1$.

4. When TCP entity A receives the acknowledgment (time t_4), it sends an acknowledgment and disconnects. When the acknowledgment arrives at B (time t_5), it also disconnects.

Figure 7.45   TCP Disconnect Protocol

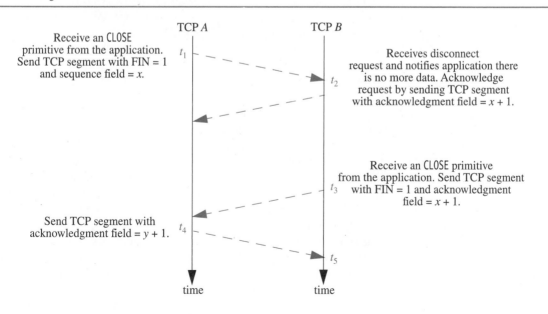

TCP A TCP B

Receive an CLOSE primitive from the application. Send TCP segment with FIN = 1 and sequence field = x. t_1

Receives disconnect request and notifies application there is no more data. Acknowledge request by sending TCP segment with acknowledgment field = $x + 1$. t_2

Receive an CLOSE primitive from the application. Send TCP segment with FIN = 1 and acknowledgment field = $x + 1$. t_3

Send TCP segment with acknowledgment field = $y + 1$. t_4

t_5

time   time

Flow Control   Once the initial connection is made the two TCP entities can exchange segments using full-duplex communication, buffering both the segments they send and those they receive. The TCP entity buffers segments it sends because there is no guarantee the segment will arrive. Therefore it may have to retransmit it. It buffers the ones it receives because there is no guarantee segments arrive in order. Remember, this is a logical connection as opposed to a physical one and any number of problems in a lower layer can cause delivery problems. Effectively the entities exchange segments using a variation of the sliding window protocols discussed in Chapter 5. We will not repeat a detailed discussion of flow control, but we do focus on a couple of differences between TCP flow control and the flow control discussed in Chapter 5:

- Here, the sequence number refers to byte sequences instead of packet (or segment) sequences.

- Each entity can alter the size of the other's sending window dynamically using the segment's window field.

Each entity implements flow control using a **credit mechanism,** also called a **window advertisement. A credit,** stored in the segment's window field, specifies the maximum number of bytes the entity sending this segment can receive and buffer from the other entity. This number is in addition to those already received and buffered (but not yet taken by a higher layer). The TCP entity getting this segment uses the credit to determine how many more bytes it can send before it must wait for an acknowledgment or for the credit to increase.

Figure 7.46 shows an example of this mechanism. We assume that the two entities have already negotiated the initial connection, initial sequence numbers, and credits using the three-way handshake. TCP entities A and B have initial sequence numbers 100 and 700, respectively. We also assume that each segment contains 100 bytes of data and that each entity can buffer up to 200 bytes. That is, each has a credit of 200. Entity A starts by sending two segments, one with sequence number (s) 101 and the other with sequence number 201. The acknowledgments (a) indicate what A is expecting from B. To simplify this example we will show only the credit values in packets that B sends to A.

After sending the second frame, A has used up its credit and must wait (time t_1). Later it receives a segment from B containing a sequence number equal to 701 and an acknowledgment equal to 301. This means B has received bytes sequenced up to 300 and is expecting byte number 301 next. The segment also contains a credit (c) of 0 because the two segments that B has received are still in B's buffers. In short, B has no room for new segments and indicates this using a credit of 0. Consequently, A must still wait. At time t_2, B delivers the first segment it received to a higher layer, thus freeing up 100 bytes of buffer space. The second segment is still there, so that buffer space is still not available. However, let's assume that at this point B has also been able to increase its total buffer space to 300 bytes. Since the second segment containing the 100 bytes is still in the buffer, B now has 200 bytes of buffer space available. In the next segment it sends to A it specifies an acknowledgment of 301 and a credit of 200.

After a while A receives that segment from B. Consequently, A sends two more segments, but at time t_3 must wait again for another acknowledgment. To simplify,

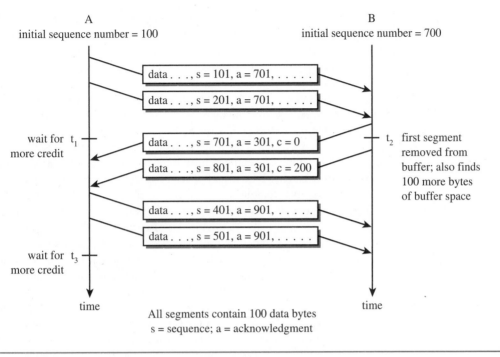

A
initial sequence number = 100

B
initial sequence number = 700

data . . ., s = 101, a = 701, ...

data . . ., s = 201, a = 701, ...

wait for t_1
more credit

data . . ., s = 701, a = 301, c = 0

t_2 first segment
removed from
buffer; also finds
100 more bytes
of buffer space

data . . ., s = 801, a = 301, c = 200

data . . ., s = 401, a = 901, ...

data . . ., s = 501, a = 901, ...

wait for t_3
more credit

time

time

All segments contain 100 data bytes
s = sequence; a = acknowledgment

Figure 7.46 Flow Control Using a Credit Mechanism

this example showed only credits that *B* sent to *A* and how *A* was affected by them. However, be assured that credit limits apply to *B* also.

The main advantage of the credit mechanism is that it allows the protocol to be more robust. Rather than living with a fixed window size the TCP entities can take advantage of changing conditions. If there is little activity at a particular site, the TCP entity may acknowledge a segment with an increased credit to make better use of otherwise unused buffer space. On the other hand, if there is a lot of activity with other connections, it may send a segment reducing the credit to keep incoming information at a manageable level.

Congestion Control   The flow control method of the previous section seems to provide for an efficient and smooth exchange of segments. However, other problems can occur that this method does not solve. To illustrate, the previous discussion showed that the window sizes (credits) were adjusted based only on what *A* or *B* can handle. It did not take into account what might happen in between. For example, suppose both *A* and *B* are connected to fast T-1 links and can send segments very rapidly. What happens if the only route connecting *A* and *B* goes through a link capable of just 64 Kbps? It's a little like connecting two 3-lane high-speed freeways with a 30-mph local road. The highways have a large traffic capacity but the local road does not. The result is congestion and long backups at the exit ramps.

It's important to realize that just because a receiving entity can handle a certain number of packets does not mean the route to it can handle the same number. You may recall that the section on IP discussed some approaches to congestion, but they generally deal with IP packets that are already in the network. A logical enhancement to congestion solutions would be to refine the TCP protocols to limit the amount of traffic that gets onto the network in the first place. To some extent flow control does that but, again, it really only responds to what the receiver is capable of getting, not what is happening in between.

To enhance congestion control mechanisms, Jacobson [Ja88] described a refinement to TCP that allows a sending entity to respond to congested links and to alter the number of segments it can send. Currently, all TCP implementations are supposed to support this technique.

To facilitate our discussion we again use an example where TCP entity *A* has established a connection with TCP entity *B*. Also, we'll focus the discussion on the transmission from *A* to *B*, but be assured it works the same way for transmissions in the reverse direction. To implement this technique *A* maintains a **congestion window** that specifies the number of bytes it thinks it can send without causing or adding to congestion (we'll see soon how it determines this). If the congestion window's capacity is larger than *A*'s credit (*B*'s capacity for receiving segments) then *A* will still not send more than the credit allows. In effect there is no change from previous discussions.

However, if the congestion window's capacity is smaller, then *A* uses that value instead of the credit to determine how many segments to send before waiting for an acknowledgment. At all times, *A* defines its sending window to be the smaller of the congestion window size and the credit specified by *B*. It then uses flow control protocols to send segments and receive acknowledgments.

At this point there are two logical questions. How can *A* determine when congestion exists? How does *A* respond to congestion? The answer to the first question is in the timeout mechanism. Suppose *A* sends as many segments as its sending window allows and a timeout occurs before an acknowledgment arrives. In theory, a timeout might happen if the segment was damaged and never reached its destination. In practice, many network links are optical fiber, which is very reliable; damaged packets occur rarely in these cases. Consequently a timeout usually means that the segment was delayed somewhere due to congestion. Thus, *A* interprets a timeout as the presence of congestion.

The normal response to timeouts is to resend the segments, but all this does is add to the congestion and make it worse. The approach taken here is to reduce the size of the congestion window by half, recalculate the sending window as described previously, and resend only the number of segments that the recalculated sending window allows. If another timeout occurs, the size of the congestion window is again cut in half. As long as timeouts occur the congestion window is repeatedly reduced by half to a minimum value equivalent to one segment. If at some point the segments in the reduced window are all acknowledged then the protocol will stop reducing the congestion window's size. By following this protocol, *A* rather quickly reduces the amount of information it enters into the network. This should give the Internet Protocols time to respond and alleviate the congestion.

Next, suppose *A*'s sending window size is much smaller than the credit sent by *B*. If congestion is alleviated *A* will have a sending window whose size was determined by conditions that no longer exist. The protocol is able to respond by increasing the window size to take advantage of the uncongested links.

To do this, whenever all of the segments in the sending window have been acknowledged and no timeouts have occurred, *A* will increase its congestion window by the equivalent of one segment and again recalculate the sending window size. Consequently, in the absence of timeouts *A* can send increasing numbers of segments, up to what *B* can receive, and more fully utilize the network's capacity. This pattern of reducing and increasing the congestion window continues as long as the connection is maintained.

You might have noticed that *A* will reduce the congestion window much more quickly than it will increase it. Largely, this reflects a philosophy that dictates that solutions to congestion must be implemented quickly since people are affected by it. On the other hand, a lack of timeouts may not mean that congestion has been eliminated. More than likely it just reflects the fact that congestion is perhaps a little less severe. Consequently the protocol implements a more conservative approach when trying to increase the traffic. There's little point to quickly increasing the number of segments only to have congestion return.

The only remaining task is to describe how the protocol defines the congestion window initially. Actually, it works much like the recovery period after congestion, with some minor changes. Initially, the congestion window size is defined as the equivalent of one segment. If *A* sends one segment and gets an acknowledgment, the protocol doubles the congestion window size to the equivalent of two segments. If those segments are acknowledged, the protocol again doubles the size to four segments. In the absence of any timeouts the congestion window size is repeatedly doubled until the credit value is reached. If at some point a timeout does occur, the protocol establishes the size as that used prior to when the timeout occurred.

As you can see, the protocol tries to increase the congestion window much more quickly in this case than it does after detecting congestion. This is logical as the protocol assumes that initially there is no congestion and tries to establish an exchange rate fairly quickly. Oddly enough this startup procedure is called a **slow start.** The name is not in relation to the procedure followed after congestion is detected; instead, it is a slow start relative to standard flow control, in which there is no congestion window. In the latter case *A* would simply send as many packets as *B* has indicated it can receive without any regard for how the intermediate links can handle the sudden burst in traffic.

TCP Primitives   Up to now we have concentrated on the concepts behind TCP and have not addressed the interface between TCP and the application that uses it. Unlike previous topics we have discussed, there is no formal standard on how to use TCP. (Of course, given the abundance of standards this is not necessarily a disadvantage.) For example, TCP documentation specifies several primitive operations to open and close connections, send and receive data, request and report status, and so on.

TCP performs many tasks and, to a certain degree, acts independently. Still, we should not lose sight of the fact that it is a middle-level protocol and must communicate with the next higher level protocol. In the OSI model this would be the session layer, but in practice could actually be a presentation or application layer. In any case, the TCP protocol allows for communication between TCP and that layer (which we call the TCP user). As with most protocols, TCP defines requests that its user may direct to TCP and responses that TCP can return. Table 7.12 lists primitives[*] with a brief description of each. In the Type column, *Request* means a user-to-TCP request, and *Indication* or *Confirm* means a TCP-to-user response.

Table 7.12   TCP Primitives

NAME	TYPE	DESCRIPTION
ABORT	Request	Close the connection because of error.
ACTIVE-OPEN	Request	Initiate a connection.
ACTIVE-OPEN-W/DATA	Request	Initiate a connection and include data with the request.
ALLOCATE	Request	Increase buffer space for incoming data.
CLOSE	Request	Close the connection normally.
CLOSING	Indication	Tells TCP user that the remote TCP entity has issued a CLOSE.
DELIVER	Indication	Tells TCP user that data has arrived.
ERROR	Indication	Indicates an error has occurred.
FULL-PASSIVE-OPEN	Request	Tells the TCP entity the user is able to accept connection requests from a specified remote site.
OPEN-FAILURE	Confirm	Tells TCP user the previous ACTIVE-OPEN request failed.
OPEN-ID	Confirm	Provides the name associated with the connection requested by the ACTIVE-OPEN request. Requires acceptance of the request by the remote site.
OPEN-SUCCESS	Confirm	Tells TCP user the previous ACTIVE-OPEN request succeeded.
SEND	Request	Request to send data over the connection.
STATUS	Request	Requests connection status.
STATUS-RESPONSE	Confirm	Responds to STATUS request with connection status.
TERMINATE	Confirm	Tells the TCP user the connection has ended.
UNSPECIFIED-PASSIVE-OPEN	Request	Tells the TCP entity the user is able to accept connection requests from any remote site.

---

[*]Because so many network applications run under the UNIX operating system, a separate set of primitives called Berkeley sockets was designed to be used in a UNIX environment. We discuss sockets and socket programming in Section 7.6.

USER DATAGRAM PROTOCOL

We have spent most of this section on the Internet's TCP, but don't assume it is the only transport protocol in use. Although it is the most commonly used protocol, others warrant mention. One of these is the User Datagram Protocol (UDP), a connectionless transport-layer protocol. It is less complex than TCP, as indicated by the format of a UDP segment (Figure 7.47). It contains very little overhead, which suggests limited abilities. The segment includes the usual source and destination addresses, the segment length, and a checksum for error detection. Because it is connectionless there is no handshake to establish a connection. When UDP has data to send, it creates a UDP segment and gives it to the IP for delivery. At the receiving end, UDP gets the data from IP and does an error check. If there is no error, UDP passes the data to its user; if there is an error, UDP discards the data. There is no formal mechanism for acknowledging errors or a provision for flow control or segment sequencing. It is little more than an interface between a higher layer and IP. If interested, Reference [Co95] discusses the protocol in more detail.

OSI TRANSPORT PROTOCOLS

The ISO has also defined several transport protocol standards for its OSI model. In fact, there are five classes, labeled **TP*i*** (i = 0, 1, 2, 3, or 4), of transport services in the OSI model. Classes 0 through 3 are designed to work with networks that provide error-free service (unlike IP). They provide no error control and provide mainly connection and disconnection services. Their differences are relatively minor. For example, TP2 and TP3 can multiplex two or more transport connections over the same network connection. TP0 and TP1 do not. TP1 and TP3 allow the connected transport entities to be resynchronized in the event of network errors or congestion problems. Thus, they provide segment sequencing, whereas TP0 and TP2 do not. TP3, but not TP1, provides flow control. Additional information on these protocols can be found in References [Sp91], [St94], [Ta96], and [Qu90].

TP4 is designed to run on top of unreliable network services such as IP and is similar to TCP. Because of its similarity we do not go into detail but will outline some of the more important differences. One difference is in the terminology. For

Figure 7.47   UDP Segment

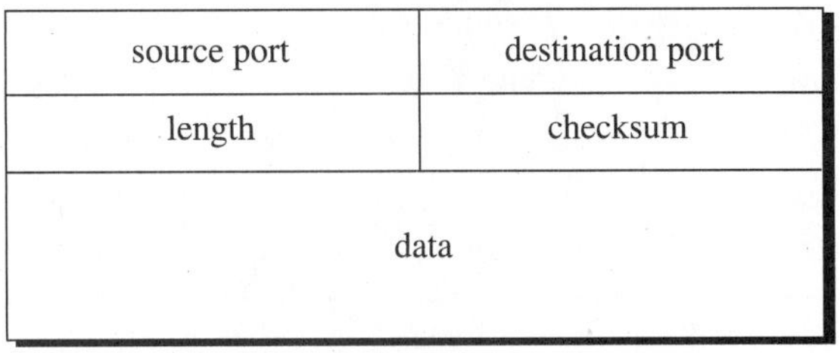

source port	destination port
length	checksum
data	

example, OSI uses the phrase **transport protocol data units (TPDUs)** to refer to the transport segments. Other areas of difference are as follows.

- **Segment types.** TP4 allows 10 different TPDU types (Table 7.13) for different functions. Each type is designated by a field in the TPDU header. This allows TP4 headers to be smaller because the header needs to contain only what is necessary for a particular function. On the other hand, the single-segment format makes TCP simpler.

- **Important data.** TCP uses urgent pointers to locate important data in the TCP segment. TP4's approach is to send important data in an ED TPDU ahead of any waiting DT TPDUs. An arriving ED TPDU alerts the receiving TP4 entity that the TPDU's contents should be processed quickly.

- **Graceful close.** As discussed earlier, the TCP disconnect protocol calls for both TCP entities to exchange disconnect requests and confirmations. This way if one entity receives a disconnect request but still has data to send, it may do so. TP4 does not provide this graceful close. If a station receives a disconnect request (DR TPDU) it sends a disconnect confirmation (DC TPDU) and informs the TP4 user. If TP4 still has data to send, it discards the data segments and the data is lost. In fairness to the OSI model, the data is not permanently lost because the session layer deals with the problem. However, some people have criticized the relegating of the solution to a higher layer.

- **Piggybacked acknowledgments.** TP4 does not provide for piggybacked acknowledgments, as does TCP, but instead uses AK TPDUs to acknowledge receipt of data (or an EA TPDU if acknowledging expedited data). However, TP4 does allow the concatenation of a DT and AK TPDU into a single network protocol packet. The effect is the same as piggybacking and the distinction with TCP is primarily a matter of semantics.

Table 7.13   TP4 TPDU Types

TPDU TYPE	FUNCTION
CR	Connection request
CC	Connection confirmation
DR	Disconnect request
DC	Disconnect confirmation
DT	Data
ED	Expedited data
AK	Acknowledgment
EA	Expedited data acknowledgment
ER	Error
RJ	Rejection

- **Sequencing.** TP4 sequences by numbering the segments, as opposed to the byte-oriented approach of TCP. DT TPDUs normally contain an 8-bit sequence field (although 32-bit fields are an option) that contains the TPDU number.

- **Flow control.** TP4 can use a credit mechanism much like TCP. However, it may also use no flow control and rely on flow control procedures at lower layers. Sending an ED TPDU affects flow control in two ways. First, the sending TP4 entity cannot have more than one ED TPDU outstanding. That is, it must receive an EA TPDU before it can send another ED TPDU. Second, a TP4 entity sends an ED TPDU ahead of any waiting DT TPDUs. The entity may send the waiting TPDUs afterward but cannot generate and send any new DT TPDUs until the expedited data is acknowledged. This is a bit unusual, but the idea is to expedite data transfer. Although TP4 can send an ED TPDU before other DT TPDUs, it cannot guarantee it will arrive first. Consequently, TP4 really has no facility to speed up data delivery. Instead, it suspends sending new TPDUs in the hope that the absence of traffic will help the ED TPDU arrive faster.

7.6   SOCKET PROGRAMMING

Because so many network applications run under the UNIX operating system, in particular Berkeley UNIX, a separate set of TCP primitives was designed to be used by UNIX systems. Through these primitives, UNIX applications running on different computers connected to the Internet can communicate using a mechanism called a socket. The primary goal of this section is to provide a minimal but very functional client/server model. This means we will show you how to develop two distinct programs that can talk to each other. The only assumption is that they run on two different UNIX systems with Internet access. Specifically, we will develop two programs that implement a file transfer protocol. One program will read text from a file, divide it into packets, and send them to the other program using a socket connection. The second program will accept the packets one at a time and build a file from their contents. Furthermore, these programs will run concurrently and asynchronously.

To keep this section concise and focused we will provide only the necessary socket details for this application and will not build a lot of options into the programs. We will also not attempt to provide an exhaustive treatment of all socket commands and all the environments in which they can be used. At this level, these are just not important because our goal is to provide functionality. As such, we will develop an actual working client/server application and you can build from there. If you have a UNIX that supports Berkeley sockets (and most do) you should be able to run the programs we present with little or no modification. We will assume basic knowledge of UNIX and the C programming language. There are many ways to expand on what we will do, and anyone interested in a detailed description of sockets, their commands, and various options should consult References [Co96] and [Co97].

SOCKETS

The **socket** is a UNIX construct and is the basis for UNIX network I/O. At a superficial level it is similar to UNIX pipes and files. A UNIX application creates a socket when it needs a connection to a network. It then establishes a connection to a remote application via the socket and communicates with it by reading data from the socket and writing data to it.

Figure 7.48 illustrates the idea. A local program can direct information through a socket into the network. Once there, network protocols (which we don't worry about at this level) guide the information through the network, where it is accessed by a remote program. Similarly, the remote program can put information into its socket. From there, it goes through the network and ends up back at the local program. By defining the rules through which the local and remote programs exchange information we can, in fact, define our own protocol.

CLIENT/SERVER MODEL

Before we try to define any kind of protocol we begin by describing a fundamental model behind most network protocols, the **client/server model.** The essence of the client/server model (Figure 7.49) involves two distinct programs, usually running on different machines at different locations. The machines have network connections. Whether the network is a local area network, a wide area network, or something in between is not a concern at this point. The fundamental concept is the same either way.

Essentially both the client and server act out certain roles. The **server** is there to provide services and respond to requests coming in from client programs. A typical example is to provide access to files located on the remote machine. A user runs the **client** program on a local machine and, through it, makes various requests. Following our example, a user may request access to one or more files located on a different (remote) machine. Thus, a typical exchange might look something like this:

Figure 7.48   Socket Connection to a Network

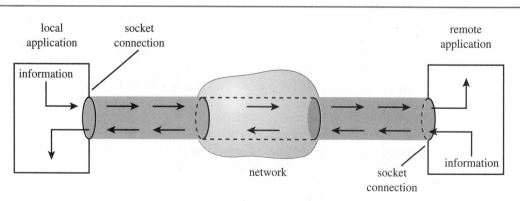

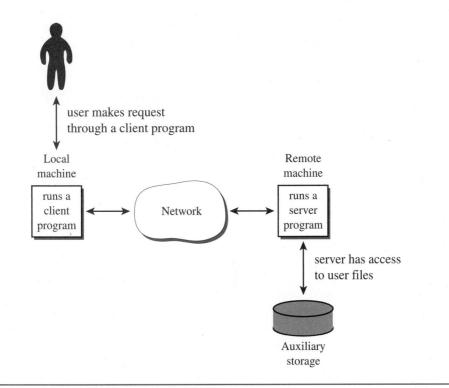

Figure 7.49   Client/Server Model

1. User requests a file.
2. Client sends request to the server on behalf of the user.
3. Server receives a request from a client and analyzes it.
4. Server copies a file from its auxiliary storage.
5. Server transmits contents of the file back to the client.
6. Client gets file's contents from the server and makes it accessible to the user.

In general, one server may provide service to many clients. Thus, another design issue, particularly for the server, is how the server can handle multiple client requests efficiently. We'll discuss that a bit later; for now we need to worry about how a server handles requests from one client.

SOCKET DATA STRUCTURES

When we eventually discuss some of the socket calls, we will have to describe the parameters passed to them. Some of these parameters have types that are designed specifically for network communications. Therefore, we begin by discussing different data structures required by socket calls. Each of these structures is located in a UNIX header file. We will specify which header files are required later.

The first structure we need is

```
struct sockaddr_in {
    u_short sin_family;
    u_short sin_port;
    struct in_addr sin_addr;
    char sin_zero[8]
}
```

where

```
struct in_addr {
    u_int s_addr
}
```

Essentially this is a 16-byte structure that contains a socket address (a combined IP address and port number; we are assuming a TCP/IP network). Table 7.14 specifies what the fields represent.

The next structure is

```
struct hostent {
    char *h_name;
    char **h_alias;
    int h_addrtype;
    int h_length;
    char **h_addr_list
}
```

Table 7.15 defines the fields of the hostent structure.

Table 7.14   Fields of the sockaddr_in Structure

FIELD	MEANING
sin_family	This 16-bit integer specifies which protocols will be used to implement the socket connection. In general, sockets can be used with more than just TCP/IP networks, but that's not something we'll discuss here.
sin_port	This 16-bit field specifies a port number identifying an application (recall the definition of port number when we discussed the TCP header).
s_addr	32-bit Internet address (assumes that sin_family specifies the TCP/IP protocol).
sin_zero	Unused. Contains all zeros.

Table 7.15   Fields of the hostent Structure

FIELD	MEANING
h_name	Null-terminated character string for the text address of a host computer.
h_alias	List of alternative names for the host (not important here).
h_addrtype	Type of address (specifies an Internet address in our example).
h_length	Address length.
h_addr_list	List of additional addresses for the host (not important here).

SOCKET COMMANDS

There are many different socket-related commands. Table 7.16 lists those we need for our example and provides a short description of each.[*]

CLIENT/SERVER EXAMPLE

We are now ready to write a client/server protocol used to transfer a file. The first step is to outline the socket-related calls in each of the client and server programs. This helps us understand their purpose without being burdened with a lot of details. Figure 7.50 shows both a client and server. Keep in mind that both run concurrently on different machines. The only assumption we are making is that both have Internet connections.

The figure shows that the first thing both the client and server do is create a socket with the socket command. After that the client calls gethostbyname to determine the IP address associated with the text address of the remote host running the server. Once the IP address is known, the client connects to the server. At this point the client is able to exchange messages with the server using send and recv commands. We will have to define the rules governing the exchange and determining when the exchange is done. The last thing the client does is close the socket and quit.

The server, upon creating a socket, must get the name of the host on which it is running (call to gethostname). It then uses the host name and calls gethostbyname to get relevant information about it (i.e., its IP address) and stores it in a hostent structure (not shown yet). It then calls bind to associate an IP address and port number with the socket and begins listening for any incoming calls. When a call arrives, the server accepts the call and the socket connection with a client is made. At that point it follows the same protocol the client uses to exchange a series of messages. When it is done it closes the socket and quits.

---

[*]Again, we've made no attempt to be complete because our primary goal is to provide what is necessary for our application.

Table 7.16   Summary of Required Socket Commands

COMMAND	MEANING
socket(int domain, int mode, int protocol)	Creates a socket. The first parameter specifies which domain is used. For example, the symbolic constant AF_INET specifies the Internet domain. AF_UNIX specifies a UNIX domain. The second parameter specifies a mode of communication. For example, the symbolic constant SOCK_STREAM indicates we will use connection-oriented byte streams. SOCK_DGRAM means a connectionless datagram mode of communication. The third parameter specifies a protocol or, if 0, allows the system to rely on a default (in this case, TCP/IP). If this command is successful, it returns an integer (descriptor) of the socket to be used in subsequent commands. At this point the socket is little more than an index to a UNIX kernel descriptor table. More is needed to establish an actual connection.
gethostbyname(char *hostname)	Returns a pointer to a hostent structure containing relevant information about the host specified by the text address in hostname.
gethostname(char *hostname, int length)	Puts the character string for the text address of the current host computer into the hostname variable. The second parameter represents the number of available bytes in hostname.
connect(int s, struct sockaddr_in *sa, int size)	Requests a connection with a remote socket. The call must specify the local socket identifier (s) and a structure containing the remote socket address (*sa). This call is needed when a connection-oriented service is required. The third parameter just specifies the size of the *sa structure. As a function it returns the status of the request.
bind(int s, struct sockaddr_in *sa, int length)	Assigns an address and port number (inside *sa) to the socket s. The server will issue this command to make itself accessible to remote clients that connect to this socket.
listen(int s, int n)	Used by a connection-oriented server that responds to requests from remote clients. It indicates that the server is ready for connection requests and listens for them over the socket s. It then puts them into a queue for subsequent processing. The second parameter (n) specifies the number of requests that can be queued. If a request comes in while the queue is full, the server rejects it.
accept(int s, struct sockaddr_in *sa, int length)	Allows the server to accept a connection request over the socket s. When accepted, the IP address of the client making the request will be stored in the structure *sa. In addition, this function actually creates and returns a new socket with all of the same properties as s. The reason for this is that usually, after a server accepts a call, it forks a child subprocess, which uses the new socket to communicate with the client. Meanwhile the parent continues to listen over the old socket for any new requests. We'll see how this works in our example later.
send(int s, char *buffer, int length, int flags)	Sends data through a socket s. The location and length of the data correspond to parameters buffer and length, respectively. It does not specify the destination because a previous connect or accept command established who is on the other end of the socket. The flags parameter is not important here.

(continues)

Table 7.16   *(continued)*

COMMAND	MEANING

recv(int s,
     char *buffer,
     int length,
     int flags)
	Receives data from a socket and stores it in the specified buffer. The length parameter specifies the buffer's length. As with send, the flags parameter is not important here.

close(int s);	Closes the specified socket.

Figure 7.50   Outline of Client and Server Using Socket-Related Commands

CLIENT	SERVER
socket (creates socket)	socket (creates socket)
:	:
:	:
gethostbyname (maps remote host name to an IP address)	gethostname (gets local host's name)
	gethostbyname (maps the name to an IP address)
:	:
:	:
connect (issues a connection request to a specified server on the remote host)	:
	bind (specifies IP address and port number)
:	:
:	:
:	listen (puts socket in passive mode; server is ready to accept requests)
:	:
:	:
:	accept (accepts a connection request)
:	:
:	:
:	
exchange information via send and recv commands	exchange information via send and recv commands
:	:
:	:
close (terminates connection)	close (terminates current connection)

Certainly there are details to fill in, but it helps to understand the framework in which we describe them. Therefore, before you continue you should make sure you at least understand the reasons for these socket-related calls and the basic organization of client and server programs. The next step is to provide details for working client and server programs. Figures 7.51 and 7.52 contain source code for them. You can copy and run them according to the following rules (assuming they are run under UNIX):

- Compile the server and run it first. The server must be running so that the client has someone to call.

- The port number of the server is 50000. We used a very large number so as not to conflict with any other port numbers that may be in use. You are free to use other port numbers but you should avoid those already in use.

- Compile the client and assume the executable file is named myftp. Run the client by entering the command myftp text-address-of-host. For example, if the text address of the host computer is hercules.uwgb.edu, then you run the client by typing myftp hercules.uwgb.edu.

- The server will transfer a predetermined file to the client. That is, the server chooses the file name.

- The client will ask you what name you would like to give to the file that it gets from the server.

- The server reads the text file, divides it into packets, and sends them to the client in groups of five. After every fifth packet the server waits for an acknowledgment from the client.

- The client responds accordingly, receiving the packets and extracting file data from them. It stores the data from each packet in a text file. After the last packet arrives the file transfer is complete. The client also sends an acknowledgment after the receipt of every fifth packet.

- There is no error detection, and flow control is restricted to what we have just described.

We now begin a description of the client and server. For the most part, we will limit the discussion to logic related to the sockets and leave it to the reader to study the details related to the C language. Comments in the source code should help, and we will provide some general descriptions related to tasks that are primarily C oriented.

Client Source Code   The beginning of the client (Figure 7.51) contains header files that you must include. They contain definitions for the socket-related calls and for the data structures we have described. We have defined a fairly simple protocol packet. The first thing it contains is a servicetype field indicating different types of packets. In this example, there are only two packet types: data and ack (for acknowledgment). It also contains a sequence number, a field indicating how many data bytes it contains, a

```
/***********************************/
/*           CLIENT            */
/*           CLIENT            */
/*           CLIENT            */
/***********************************/
/* This program is designed as a client that will call on a server running on another machine. The assumed
   protocol is TCP/IP and connections are via the Internet */

#define PACKETSIZE 20
#include <sys/types.h>
#include <stdio.h>
#include <sys/socket.h>
#include <netinet/in.h>
#include <netdb.h>

#define PORTNUM 50000

typedef enum {data, ack} servicetype;

/* transmission unit for this program's protocol */
typedef struct
{
  servicetype service;                    /* type of packet */
  int    sequence;                        /* packet's sequence number */
  int    datasize;                        /* amount of data (in bytes) in packet */
  int    last;                            /* last packet indicator */
  char   data[PACKETSIZE];                /* holds data */
  int    checksum;                        /* for error detection */
} PACKET;

/*******************************************/
/* open a file and return its identifier   */
/*******************************************/
FILE * openfile( )
{
  char * filename;
  FILE * fid;

  printf("This program will copy a file from a remote server\n");
  printf("Enter the name under which the file should be saved>");
  filename = (char *) malloc(30);
  scanf("%s", filename);
```

Figure 7.51   Client Program *(continues on next page)*

```
  if ((fid = fopen(filename, "w")) == NULL)
  {
    printf("error opening file\n");
    exit (1);
  }
  free(filename);
  return fid;
}


/********************/
/* create a socket   */
/********************/
int opensocket( )
{
  int s;

  if ((s = socket (AF_INET, SOCK_STREAM, 0)) < 0)
  {
    perror ("socket error");
    exit (1);
  }
  return s;
}


/************************************************************/
/* get remote host information and connect to remote server  */
/************************************************************/
void makeconnection(int argc, char *argv[ ], int s)
{
  struct hostent * ph;                      /* holds remote host name and address information */
  struct sockaddr_in sa;                    /* holds IP address and protocol port */

  memset(&sa,0,sizeof(sa));                  /* zero out the sa structure */
  if (argc !=2)                              /* Be sure the command to run the client contains the remote
                                                host's text address */
  {
    printf ("Error in command line\n");
    exit (1);
  }
  if ((ph = gethostbyname (argv[1])) == NULL)  /* get relevant information about the remote host */
  {
    printf("error in gethostbyname\n");
    exit(1);
```

Figure 7.51   *(continued)*

```
    }
                                        /* Store remote host's IP address, server's port number,
                                           protocol type into sa structure */
    memcpy((char*) &sa.sin_addr, ph->h_addr, ph->h_length);
    sa.sin_port = htons ((u_short) PORTNUM);    /* specify port number of remote server */
    sa.sin_family = ph->h_addrtype;
    if (connect (s, &sa, sizeof (sa)) < 0)      /* connect to remote server */
    {
        perror ("connect error");
        exit (1);
    }
}

/***********************************************************/
/* get a file from the remote server in fixed-size packets */
/***********************************************************/
void getfile(FILE * fid, int s)
{
    PACKET * packet;                            /* protocol packet */
    int i;

    packet = (PACKET *) malloc (sizeof(*packet));
    do
    {
        if (recv(s, packet, sizeof(*packet), 0) <= 0)   /* get packet from remote server */
        {
            printf("error reading\n");
            exit(1);
        }
        printf("Received packet %4d: %s\n", packet->sequence, packet->data);
        for (i=0;i < packet->datasize; i++)             /* Store packet's contents into text file */
            putc (packet->data[i], fid);
        if (packet->sequence % 5 == 4)                  /* If this was the 5th packet, send an acknowledgment */
        {
            printf("acknowledging 5th packet-Press enter to continuen");
            getchar();
            packet->service = ack;
            if (send(s, packet, sizeof *packet, 0) <= 0)   /* Send the acknowledgment */
            {
                printf("ERROR in send\n");
                exit(1);
            }
        }
```

Figure 7.51   *(continued)*

```
    } while (!packet->last);          /* Continue repeating the above until the last packet is
                                         received */

    fclose(fid);
}

void main (int argc,char *argv[])
{
    int s;
    FILE * fid;

    fid = openfile();
    s = opensocket();
    makeconnection(argc, argv, s);
    getfile(fid, s);
    close(s);
}
```

Figure 7.51   *(concluded)*

field indicating which packet is the last in a stream, and a checksum field (which we don't use here). For simplicity, these fields are type int. Finally, the remaining field is an array with a storage capacity of 20 bytes, representing the data in the packet.

A cursory examination of the client shows it has four C functions: openfile, opensocket, makeconnection, and getfile. The function openfile prompts the user to enter a name under which the client will store the transferred file. Once the user enters the name, the function opens it in write mode. If all goes well the function returns the file identifier. The second function, opensocket, creates a socket. It contains a provision to exit the program if the socket call fails. If successful the function returns the socket identifier.

The function makeconnection gets remote host information and connects to the server running on it associated with the specified port number. Remember, we are assuming that the user enters the text address of the remote host when typing the name of an executable client (e.g., myftp hercules.uwgb.edu). As such, the text string hercules.uwgb.edu is stored in the main function parameter argv[1], and the other main function parameter, argc, has a value of 2. The function calls gethostbyname to put relevant remote host information into the hostent structure located via the pointer variable ph. Then it moves other relevant information such as the server's port number into the socket address structure specified by the variable sa.[*] Once variable sa con-

---

[*]The code contains a reference to a function htons (host to network short). When dealing with different machines, an incompatibility in the way integers are stored may occur. Some machines store the most significant bits in bytes with a larger address (little endian), whereas some store the most significant bits in bytes with a smaller address (big endian). The htons operator makes sure that the network correctly interprets data defined in your program.

tains necessary information, the function calls the function connect, thereby sending a connection request to the server.

The last function is the most complex because it contains the rules governing the file transfer. Yet, mercifully, it is simpler than many other protocols we have described. We are truly beginning to see the advantages of layering now. As mentioned previously, the protocol requires the client to receive five packets, extract their contents, and write them to a file. After receiving every fifth packet, the client creates a packet of type ack (acknowledgment) and sends it back to the server. It continues doing this until it receives a packet for which packet->last is 1. The function has a few printf and getchar commands that serve no purpose other than to let the person running it see what is happening. After the last packet arrives, the client closes the file. It then returns to the main program, where it closes the socket and quits. The file has been transferred.

Server Source Code   The server program (Figure 7.52) is a little more complex since it has more to do. Like the client, it must include all necessary headers and define a compatible packet structure. It contains six functions: gethoststuff, openfile, opensocket, bindnlisten, acceptconn, and sendfile. Its main part also is a little more complex, so let's start there. Since this server is strictly for testing, we have designed it to accept precisely three calls and do the same thing each time. This can test its ability to respond to different clients concurrently. Each time it accepts a connection request, it returns a new socket (sd) with all the same properties as socket s. The server then forks a new child process to handle the details of the file transfer using the socket sd. It is imperative to understand the UNIX fork command to see how this works; you should consult a UNIX book and study it if you are not familiar with it.

To summarize, the fork command creates a separate child process that executes the code immediately after the line "if (fork()==0)". This section of code closes the socket s (since this is the socket that the parent uses, the child has no need for it), calls on functions to open a file and return its identifier, and do the file transfer, and quits. Remember, it is the child that quits; the parent process is still running and able to accept more calls. In this case the parent executes the line after the else that closes the socket returned by the accept call (variable sd). Since this is the socket that the child uses, the parent has no need for it.

The previously mentioned functions perform tasks indicative of their names. The first function, gethoststuff, gets information relevant to the host on which the server is running (for portability the server code should make no assumptions about the host on which it is running). It also stores necessary information in the socket address structure sa and returns a copy of it. Function openfile opens a specified text file (we are assuming a file named test.dat) for read access and returns the file identifier. This, as you probably guessed, is the file that the server will transfer. The function opensocket creates a socket and returns its identifier. It has a provision to exit if, for some reason, the socket cannot be created. The bindnlisten function assigns the address and port number to the socket and puts the server into a listen mode.

At some point a connection request arrives (as a result of the client's call to connect). When it arrives, the server accepts the connection. The accept call creates a

```
/**********************************/
/*            SERVER           */
/*            SERVER           */
/*            SERVER           */
/**********************************/
/* This program is designed to act as a server that will accept calls from a client written on another machine.
   The assumed protocol is TCP/IP and connections are via the Internet */


#define PACKETSIZE 20
#include <sys/types.h>
#include <sys/socket.h>
#include <netinet/in.h>
#include <netdb.h>
#include <stdio.h>
#include <sys/param.h>

#define PORTNUM 50000

typedef enum {data, ack} servicetype;
/* transmission unit for this program's protocol */
typedef struct
{
  servicetype service;                      /* type of packet */
  int   sequence;                           /* packet's sequence number */
  int   datasize;                           /* amount of data (in bytes) in packet */
  int   last;                               /* last packet indicator */
  char  data[PACKETSIZE];                   /* holds data */
  int   checksum;                           /* for error detection */
} PACKET;


/*************************************************/
/* get host info for eventual socket connection */
/*************************************************/
struct sockaddr_in gethoststuff()
{
  struct sockaddr_in sa;                    /* holds IP address and protocol port */
  struct hostent * ph;                      /* holds host name and address info */
  char myname[MAXHOSTNAMELEN+1];            /* host name */

  gethostname(myname, MAXHOSTNAMELEN);      /* Get name of host on which this server is
                                               running */

  printf("host name is %s\n", myname);
  if ((ph = gethostbyname(myname)) == NULL) /* Get relevant information about the host */
```

Figure 7.52   Server Program *(continues on next page)*

```
{
    printf("gethostbyname failed\n");
    exit(1);
}
memset(&sa, 0, sizeof(struct sockaddr_in));
```
                                                    /* Put protocol family type and port number into sa
                                                       structure */
```
    sa.sin_family = ph->h_addrtype;
    sa.sin_port = htons(PORTNUM);
    return sa;
}


/****************************************/
/* Open a file and return its identifier */
/****************************************/
FILE * openfile()
{
    FILE * fid;
    char * filename = "test.dat";

    if (( fid=fopen(filename, "r")) == NULL)
    {
        printf("error opening file\n");
        exit(1);
    }
    return fid;
}


/******************/
/* Create a socket */
/******************/
int opensocket()
{
    int s;

    if (( s = socket (AF_INET, SOCK_STREAM, 0)) < 0)    /* Create a socket */
    {
        perror ("socket error");
        exit (1);
    }
    return s;
}
```

Figure 7.52   *(continued)*

```
/*****************************************/
/* Bind and listen for a socket connection*/
/*****************************************/
void bindnlisten (int s, struct sockaddr_in sa)
{
  if (bind (s, &sa, sizeof (sa)) < 0)            /* Assign IP address and port number with socket s */
  {
    perror ("bind error");
    exit (1);
  }
  listen (s,5);                                  /* Listen for incoming client calls */
}


/*****************************/
/* Accept a socket connection */
/*****************************/
int acceptconn(int s)
{
  int sd;
  struct sockaddr_in sa;
  unsigned int sasize;

  sasize = sizeof(sa);
  if ((sd = accept (s, &sa, &sasize)) < 0)       /* Accept a connection */
  {
    perror ("accept error");
    exit (1);
  }
  printf("connection accepted from: %u\n", sa.sin_addr.s_addr);
  return sd;
}


/***********************************************************/
/* Send the contents of a file using fixed-size packets */
/* Wait for an acknowledgment after every 5th one       */
/***********************************************************/
void sendfile(FILE * fid, int sd)
{
  PACKET * packet;                               /* protocol packet */
  int i,
  count = 0;                                     /* packet count */
  char c;
```

Figure 7.52   (continued)

```
packet = (PACKET *) malloc (sizeof *packet);
packet->last=0;
c=getc(fid);
do
{
  for (i=0; i<PACKETSIZE && c != EOF; i++,c=getc(fid))   /* Put file data into packet */
    packet->data[i] = c;
  packet->datasize = i;
  if (c==EOF)
    packet->last=1;
  packet->sequence = count++;
  packet->service = data;
  printf("Sending packet %4d: %s\n", packet->sequence, packet->data);
  if (send(sd, packet, sizeof (*packet), 0) <= 0)        /* Send packet to client */
  {
    printf("error in writing to socket\n");
    exit(1);
  }
  if (count % 5 == 0)                                    /* After the 5th packet wait for an
                                                            acknowledgment */

  {
    if (recv(sd, packet, sizeof *packet, 0) < 0)
    {
      printf("socket read failed\n");
      exit(1);
    }
    printf("Receiving acknowledgment \n");
  }
  } while (c != EOF);                                    /* Stop when end of file is
                                                            reached */

  printf("file transfer done\n");
  free(packet);
}

int main (int argc, char *argv[])
{
  int s;                          /* identifies a socket */
  int sd;                         /* identifies connection to socket */
  struct sockaddr_in sa;          /* holds IP address and protocol port */
  int i;                          /* temp variable */
  FILE * fid;                     /* file identifier */

  sa = gethoststuff();
  s = opensocket();
```

Figure 7.52   *(continued)*

```
    bindnlisten(s, sa);
    for (i=0;i<3;i++)                          /* This test server will accept three calls from
                                                  clients before it quits */
    {
        sd=acceptconn(s);                      /* call function to accept call. The new socket is
                                                  sd */
        if (fork()==0)/* Create child process to do file transfer */
        {
            close(s);                          /* Close socket s. Child does not need it since it
                                                  uses socket sd */

            printf("beginning file transfer\n");
            fid=openfile();
            sendfile(fid,sd);
            fclose(fid);
            close(sd);
            exit (1);
        }
        else
            close(sd);                         /* Close socket sd. Parent does not need it. */
    }
    printf("press enter to quit\n");
    getchar();
    close(s);
}
```

Figure 7.52   *(concluded)*

new socket whose identifier is returned and associated with variable sd. As previously mentioned, this socket has all the same properties as socket s. When control returns to the main program, the server forks, thus creating a child that uses sd and closes s. The parent closes sd and returns to the top of the loop to accept another call when it comes in over s.

Finally, the function sendfile reads 20 characters at a time from the text file and deposits them into packets. It sends five packets at a time before it waits for an acknowledgment from the client. As with the client, there are printf statements that are there to let you see what is happening as the program runs. Eventually, the end of the file is reached and the function stops creating packets. At that point, the file transfer is complete.

7.7   SUMMARY

This chapter covered wide area networks and some of the common protocols that make them work. Specifically, we covered four aspects of wide area network operations: routing strategies; the X series of protocols for public data networks; network-layer protocols, including the Internet Protocol; and transport-layer protocols, including TCP. We capped the section with a discussion of socket programming and client/server models.

Routing strategies deal with how packets are transferred between two sites. We discussed four basic routing types:

1. *Centralized:* Routing information is maintained in a central location.
2. *Distributed:* Routing information is distributed among the nodes.
3. *Static:* Routing information does not change even with varying network conditions.
4. *Adaptive:* Changing network conditions alter routing information.

One way to manage routing information is to use routing tables that specify where to forward incoming packets. Maintaining them depends on the routing algorithms used. We discussed a few approaches, such as the following:

- Dijkstra's algorithm, a centralized algorithm designed to determine the cheapest path between two nodes.
- The Bellman-Ford algorithm, a distributed approach by which each node communicates information on reachable nodes to each of its neighbors.
- Link state routing, in which nodes collaborate by exchanging link state packets that provide status information on adjacent links. A node can collect all the packets it gets and determine the network topology. Then it can execute its own shortest route algorithm
- Hierarchical routing, in which nodes are divided into groups (domains), each of which has its own routing protocol.
- The Routing Information Protocol, used for interdomain communication in which designated domain nodes exchange information with each other regarding reachable networks and the number of hops required to get there.
- Open Shortest Path First Protocol, an interior routing protocol similar to link state routing but which provides additional features to provide better performance and flexibility.
- Border Gateway Protocol, an exterior protocol that allows routers to implement specific policies or constraints that a route must meet. Routers exchange actual routes to a destination instead of just costs and the first link in a route.

Finally, we discussed two problems that can occur during routing. Congestion develops when a node receives more packets than it can handle efficiently, thus causing an increase in the time required to forward them. Deadlock occurs when there is a circular list of nodes, each of which cannot forward any frames to the next one in the list.

Next we discussed packet-switched networks and two modes of operations. In a datagram service all packets are transmitted independently. In a virtual call service two stations must establish a connection during which a logical circuit (path) is defined. All subsequent packets transmitted follow that path. A popular standard for communicating with public data networks is the X.25 standard. It corresponds to the lower three protocol layers for communication between a DTE and network DCE. It defines packet format, connection establishment and termination, and the exchange of data packets.

For sites that do not have X.25 devices to communicate with a public data network, other protocols make communication possible. The X.3 packet assembler/ disassembler (PAD) replaces the DCE as a network interface. The PAD then communicates with a non-X.25 device using the X.28 standard protocol and with a remote host using the X.29 standard protocol.

Another common layer 3 protocol is the DoD's Internet Protocol (IP), used in the Internet. It allows the transfer of data over dissimilar networks and makes the differences transparent to higher-layer protocols. IP defines packet format, routing options, types of service, and ways to deal with fragmented packets too large to travel some networks. It uses hierarchical routing, thus requiring addresses to be specified using a dotted notation. The one thing that IP does not do is guarantee delivery of its packets. Consequently, another protocol, the Internet Control Message Protocol (ICMP), does error reporting and provides routers with updates on conditions that develop in the Internet. It defines different control and error messages and transmits them via the IP.

Due to the tremendous growth of users, new technologies, and applications such as the World Wide Web, multimedia applications, videoconferencing, and mobile computing, the current IP is showing its age. A next generation of the IP (IPng or Ipv6) has been proposed. It provides a much larger address space that allows, in theory, up to 2^{128} unique addresses. It has also redefined some of the Internet protocols to make routing much more efficient, a necessary criterion for video and other real-time applications. It will likely take years to incorporate the new IP into a worldwide network, and there are provisions that allow it to run alongside IPv4 until that happens.

Transport protocols are the lowest-layer protocols that deal with end-user communication and work independently of network operations. A common protocol used in the Internet is the Transmission Control Protocol (TCP), a connection-oriented protocol. Some of the primary functions are connection management, flow control, and error detection. Effectively, TCP guarantees the reliable exchange of information. Some unique aspects of TCP are

- Definition of a single-segment format for both data and control.
- A three-way handshake that requires not only an acknowledgment of a connection request but an acknowledgment of the acknowledgment.
- A credit mechanism for flow control similar to sliding window protocols.

There are no formal standards for interfacing with TCP at a higher layer, but there are two common approaches. One is to use TCP primitive operations that define the request/confirmation exchange between TCP and its users. The other is the socket interface used by many UNIX-based systems.

The ISO also has defined several transport protocols: TP0, TP1, TP2, TP3, and TP4. They differ in part in the type of networks over which they run. TP4 is the most similar to TCP, but with several important differences: It defines multiple segment formats for greater flexibility, uses a different disconnect strategy, handles important data differently, and has a different flow control.

Sockets are a construct that allow client/server models between programs running on different computers connected by the Internet. A client application can connect to a server if it knows the Internet address of the server's location and the server's port number. The client can then send requests to the server. The server can accept connections from a variety of clients and respond accordingly. Many Internet applications follow this model. The application presented in Section 7.6 represented a simple file transfer protocol. The client connected to a server, requested the transfer of a specified file, and received the file's contents through a stream of packets. The server complemented the client's actions by reading the file, dividing it up into small pieces that it stored into a series of packets, and sending the packets to the client. All client/server communications were done via the socket.

Review Questions

1. What is a protocol converter?

2. At what OSI layers can protocol converters exist? List common ones and their names.

3. To what layer does TCP/IP correspond?

4. What is a routing table?

5. List the four major routing classifications and state what is characteristic of each.

6. Are the following statements TRUE or FALSE? Why?

   a. Distributed routing requires routing tables at each node.

   b. Adaptive routing allows a node to update its routing tables.

   c. The shortest path and the cheapest path are generally the same.

   d. Hierarchical routing organizes all network nodes into a tree structure.

   e. Congestion means that all of a network's paths have become clogged with traffic.

   f. Congestion does not always lead to deadlock.

   g. The X.25 protocol defines packet-switched network operations.

   h. Distinct virtual circuits may overlap.

   i. A datagram service will not deliver packets in the correct order.

   j. The triple-X protocols are typically used where there is not an X.25 device.

   k. The Internet Protocol provides reliable delivery of packets.

   l. TCP provides reliable delivery of packets.

7. Distinguish between a forward search and a backward search algorithm.

8. What is hierarchical routing?

9. Why does link state routing overcome the problem described for the Bellman-Ford algorithm?

10. Distinguish between interior and exterior protocols.

11. What is the purpose of using names and symbols in Internet addressing rather than the assigned numerical addresses?

12. What is a domain name server?

13. List common Internet domains.

14. What do nodes that use the Routing Information Protocol maintain in their routing tables?

15. Distinguish between network congestion and deadlock.

16. List some ways to deal with congestion.

17. What are the two types of deadlock?

18. Why does assigning packets to specific buffers, as shown in Figure 7.18, prevent store-and-forward deadlock?

19. What is a virtual circuit?

20. What is a packet-switched network?

21. Why can't each node in a virtual circuit use the same number to identify the circuit?

22. What is a datagram service?

23. What does the X.25 standard define?

24. List the X.25 packet types related to call establishment.

25. How does a permanent virtual circuit differ from a virtual circuit?

26. What is a packet assembler/disassembler?

27. List the main functions of the triple-X protocols X.3, X.28, and X.29.

28. Why is IP packet fragmenting sometimes necessary?

29. List some major functions of IP.

30. What is the time-to-live field in an IP packet?

31. What is a maximum transfer unit? How does it affect the Internet Protocol?

32. Distinguish between an Internet address and a physical address.

33. What is dynamic binding?

34. What is the Internet Control Message Protocol used for?

35. List typical control messages defined by ICMP.

36. How does IPv4 fragmentation differ from IPv6 fragmentation?

37. What is tunneling?

38. List several factors that contribute to IPv6's ability to route more quickly.

39. Why did IPv6 eliminate the checksum in the packet header?

40. What is a timestamp request?

41. What is a handshake?

42. What is an urgent pointer?

43. Distinguish between a two-way and a three-way handshake.

44. What is a TCP credit?

45. List TCP primitives related to connection management.

46. What is a UNIX socket?

47. What is the User Datagram Protocol?

48. List and distinguish the five OSI transport-protocol standards.

Exercises

1. How many distinct routes are there from X to Y in the network of Figure 7.2?

2. Define the routing tables for all the nodes in the network in Figure 7.3.

3. Create a routing matrix for the following network. In cases where two routes have the cheapest cost, choose the one containing the fewest nodes. If both criteria are the same then choose one arbitrarily.

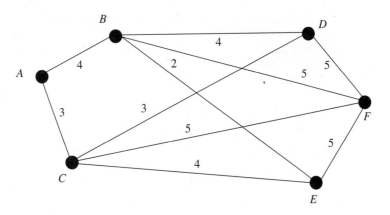

4. Apply Dijkstra's cheapest path algorithm to the following network. Create a table similar to Table 7.2 showing pertinent values at each step of the algorithm.

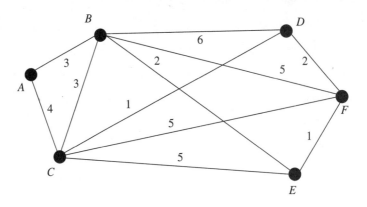

5. Design an algorithm that, when run after Dijkstra's algorithm, will list all nodes on the cheapest path to a given destination.

6. Using terminology from Dijkstra's algorithm, prove that whenever the Cost(V) function is changed, it still represents the cheapest route from A to V via nodes in S.

7. The premise of the Bellman-Ford algorithm is that if Cost(A, Z) is the cost of the cheapest route from node A to Z and A has a direct connection to nodes B, C, and D then

$$\text{Cost}(A, Z) = \text{smallest of} \begin{cases} \text{cost of link from } A \text{ to } B + \text{cost of cheapest route} \\ \text{from } B \text{ to } Z \\ \\ \text{cost of link from } A \text{ to } C + \text{cost of cheapest route} \\ \text{from } C \text{ to } Z \\ \quad\vdots \\ \text{cost of link from } A \text{ to } D + \text{cost of cheapest route} \\ \text{from } D \text{ to } Z \end{cases}$$

Why is this premise valid? That is, prove this assertion.

8. Create tables similar to Tables 7.4a through 7.4c by applying the Bellman-Ford algorithm to the following network.

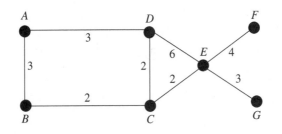

9. How is the Routing Information Protocol similar to the Bellman-Ford algorithm?

10. Consider Figure 7.21. Suppose A establishes a virtual circuit to D, and B establishes a virtual circuit to C. If both virtual circuits go through X and Y, what would X's and Y's routing tables look like?

11. Suppose a router at A in the figure shown here receives an IP packet containing 4000 data bytes, fragments the packet, and routes the fragments to B via network 1. B in turn routes all the fragments except the second one to C via network 3. However, it fragments the second one and sends the fragments to C via network 2. Show the fragments that C receives and specify relevant values in the fragment headers.

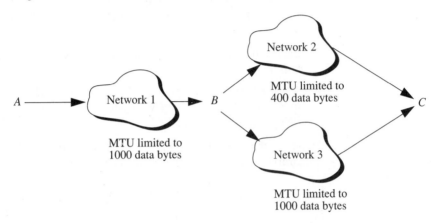

12. In IP fragmentation, why is the identification field in the fragment header necessary? Why can't the destination simply use the source address to determine related packets and reassemble them according to the offset field values?

13. What does the routing table for router G look like for the internetwork below? For each network, specify the address of a router to which a packet must be sent. In the

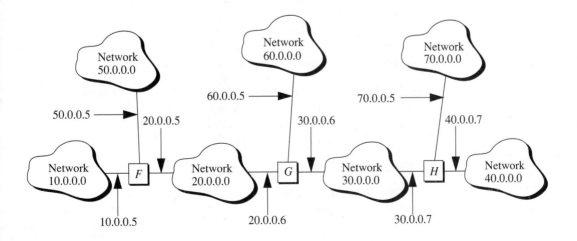

case of a direct connection indicate that the packet must be delivered directly to its destination.

14. In the previous exercise, what do the routing tables for *F* and *H* look like?

15. Why don't TCP segments contain the number of data bytes each one has? How is the receiving TCP entity supposed to know how many data bytes to extract from a segment?

16. Assume the following:

    - TCP entities *A* and *B* have initial sequence numbers 400 and 900, respectively.
    - Each segment contains 100 data bytes, and each has an initial credit of 200 bytes.
    - Each entity delivers a segment as soon as it receives it, thus freeing up the buffer space.
    - *A* is capable (flow control permitting) of sending TCP segments at intervals of time *T* (starting at *T* = 0); *B* is capable of sending its segments at intervals of time 3*T* (starting at time 1.5*T*).

    Assuming the transmission time between *A* and *B* is negligible, sketch a diagram similar to Figure 7.46 showing the segment exchange up to time 12*T*.

17. Repeat Exercise 16 assuming *A*'s credit increases to 300 after it receives the second segment from *B*.

18. Consider TCP's flow control logic, discussed in Section 7.5. Since an entity uses the credit field to determine when it can send new segments, what is the purpose of the acknowledgment? In other words, what would happen if we eliminated the acknowledgment field from the segment?

19. Modify the file transfer protocol of Section 7.6 by implementing an error detection mechanism such as a checksum. You can simulate errors by having the server periodically damage a packet immediately prior to sending it over the socket. For example, it might call a random number generator and, based on the number returned, might zero out a packet's bytes. If you would like more random-looking errors, you might have the server add a random number to a random byte in the packet.

20. Use sockets to implement a talk protocol between a client and server program. The protocol would allow a half-duplex mode of communication in which client and server exchange messages defined by what the user types at the keyboard. You will have to figure out who starts "talking" and how to end the conversation.

21. Modify the protocol of Section 7.6 by adding any or all of the following:

    - The client should ask its user the name of the file on the remote host. The client then sends that name to the server over the socket connection.

- Create a disconnect packet and have the client and server disconnect only after the client sends the server a disconnect packet and the server acknowledges it.

- Build a menu option into the client allowing the user to choose whether the client should request a file transfer or a talk protocol as in Exercise 20.

- Have the client and server both send a file to each other concurrently.

- Alter the server so that it receives a single packet after accepting a connection. The packet will specify whether the server executes a file transfer or a talk protocol with the client. Of course, the client must send such a packet.

- Design the server so that it is capable of transferring a file to one client while, at the same time, it is engaged in a talk protocol with another. It will have to fork child processes to respond to the requests.

REFERENCES

1. [Ah83] Aho, A., J. Hopcroft, and J. Ullman. *Data Structures and Algorithms.* Reading, MA: Addison-Wesley, 1983.

2. [Bl91] Black, U. *The X Series Recommendations.* New York: McGraw-Hill, 1991.

3. [Br95] Bradner, B. and A. Mankin. "The Recommendation for the IP Next Generation Protocol." RFC 1752, January 1995.

4. [Co94] Comer, D. E. and D. Stevens. *Internetworking with TCP/IP.* Vol. II, *Design, Implementation, and Internals,* 2nd ed. Englewood Cliffs, NJ: Prentice-Hall, 1994.

5. [Co95] Comer, D. E. *Internetworking with TCP/IP.* Vol. I, *Principles, Protocols, and Architecture,* 3rd ed. Englewood Cliffs, NJ: Prentice-Hall, 1995.

6. [Co96] Comer, D. E. and D. Stevens. *Internetworking with TCP/IP.* Vol. III, *Client-Server Programming and Applications for the BSD Socket Version,* 2nd ed. Englewood Cliffs, NJ: Prentice-Hall, 1996.

7. [Co97] Comer, D. E. and D. Stevens. *Internetworking with TCP/IP.* Vol. III, *Client-Server Programming and Applications-Windows Sockets Version,* Englewood Cliffs, NJ: Prentice-Hall, 1997.

8. [De93] Deering, S. "SIP: Simple Internet Protocol." *IEEE Network Magazine,* vol. 7, no. 3 (May/June 1993), 16–28.

9. [Hi96] Hinden, R. "IP Next Generation Overview." *Communications of the ACM,* vol. 39, no. 6 (June 1996), 61–71.

10. [Ja88] Jacobson, V. "Congestion Avoidance and Control." *Proceedings of SIGCOMM Symposium,* August 1988, 314–329.

11. [Me80] Merlin, P. M. and P. J. Schweitzer. "Deadlock Avoidance in Store-and-Forward Networks I: Store-and-Forward Deadlock." *IEEE Transactions on Communications,* vol. COM-28 (March 1980), 345–354.

12. [Mi96] Miller, M. *Troubleshooting TCP/IP,* 2nd ed. New York: M&T Books, 1996.

13. [Pe96] Peterson, L. and B. Davie. *Computer Networks: A Systems Approach.* San Francisco: Morgan Kaufmann, 1996.

14. [Qu90] Quarterman, J. *The Matrix: Computer Networks and Conferencing Systems Worldwide.* Bedford, MA: Digital Press, 1990.

15. [Sp91] Spragins, J. D., J. L. Hammond, and K. Pawlikowski. *Telecommunications Protocols and Design.* Reading, MA: Addison-Wesley, 1991.

16. [St94] Stallings, W. *Data and Computer Communications,* 4th ed. New York: Macmillan, 1994.

17. [St96] Stallings, W. "IPv6: The New Internet Protocol." *IEEE Communications Magazine,* vol. 34, no. 7(1996), 96–108.

18. [Ta96] Tanenbaum, A. S. *Computer Networks,* 3rd ed. Englewood Cliffs, NJ: Prentice-Hall, 1996.

CHAPTER 8

ADDITIONAL NETWORK PROTOCOLS

Among all the world's races, some obscure Bedouin
tribes possibly apart, Americans are the most prone to
misinformation. This is not the consequence of any
special preference for mendacity, although at the higher
levels of their public administration that tendency is
impressive. It is rather that so much of what they
themselves believe is wrong.
—**John Kenneth Galbraith,** U.S. economist

8.1 INTERNET APPLICATIONS

Since TCP/IP is such a widely used protocol it seems logical to discuss some applications that run on TCP/IP networks. Probably the most well-known ones are Telnet, FTP, email, and, of course, the World Wide Web. Internet applications involve interaction between programs running on different computers on the network (i.e., a client/server model). We have dealt with clients and servers in Sections 6.6 and 7.6 and we won't repeat the discussion here. Still, it helps to remember that all of the protocols we will discuss require cooperation between two programs on different machines running a common protocol.

VIRTUAL TERMINAL

Networks provide communication between many types of equipment and software. One significant problem is that software is often written with specific equipment in mind. Full-screen text editors are examples. The editor displays text on a screen and allows the user to move the cursor and make changes. But the displayed number of rows and columns varies from one terminal type to another. Commands to move the cursor, delete, and insert text require control sequences that often vary by terminal type. Perhaps you have noticed that different terminals have different keyboards. Some sequences are not even available on some models.

Other examples include software that depends on screen formats for input. Often layouts provide a simple, uncluttered view of a user's options. Spacing, tabs, and highlighting help the user work with the software. But, again, such features are terminal dependent. In some cases the screen layout is even dependent on the font used and its size. It would be nice if programs could access a full range of screen-oriented functions, regardless of the terminal. But how can we achieve this?

Translation problems also apply to **smart terminals** that have local computing power. This is a typical approach in a client/server model in which computing power is provided in two locations, the user site and the remote site. A user runs a remote application (server program) that provides information to the user. The user then can make changes locally (using client software). For example, suppose that accounting software on a server can display a full screen of tax information from a remote database. An accountant can examine the information and determine its validity. Using the client, he or she can correct mistakes or make updates locally. The client's processor makes all the changes, and the server has no knowledge of them. When the changes are complete, the accountant sends the information to the server, which stores it in the remote database.

This approach has a major advantage: It does not require any communication during editing, thus reducing the network workload. Only the final version is transmitted. The problem is that client configurations vary considerably. How can we allow different ones to access common software?

One approach uses a **virtual terminal protocol.** A **virtual terminal** is a data structure maintained by either the application software or a local terminal. Its contents represent the state of the terminal. For example, they may include the current cursor position, reverse video indicator, cursor shape, number of rows and columns, and color. Both the user and the application can reference this structure. The application writes to the virtual terminal without worrying about terminal-specific matters. Virtual terminal software does the required translation, and the data is displayed. When a user enters data, the process works in reverse. Virtual terminal protocols define the format of the data structure, software converts user input to a standard form, and the application then reads the standard "screen."

Virtual terminals may contain more data than the screen can display. This is especially useful when scrolling. For example, suppose the virtual terminal can store 200 lines in a buffer but only 24 can appear on the screen at a time. Information in the virtual terminal will specify the first and last lines of displayed data (Figure 8.1). The displayed data is the **window** and is marked by **window delimiters.** If the user enters a scroll command, the virtual terminal software simply changes the window delimiters. The result is that different text lines are displayed on the terminal.

TELNET

One example of a network virtual terminal protocol is **Telnet.** It was designed for the ARPANET and is one of the protocols in the TCP/IP suite. Perhaps most people know Telnet as the application that allows remote logins.

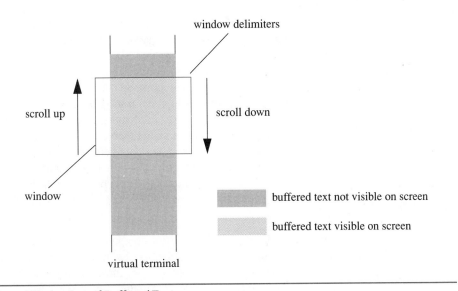

Figure 8.1   Windowing of Buffered Text

To the user, a **remote login** appears to be no different than a login to a local computer (Figure 8.2a). However, Figure 8.2b reflects the situation more accurately. A user works at a PC (or is connected to another computer) that runs protocols to connect to a network. The protocols establish a connection over the network to a remote computer. The user and remote computer exchange commands and data

Figure 8.2   Remote Connection

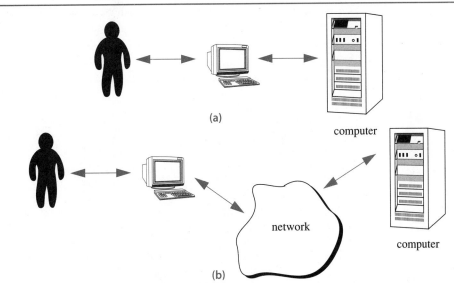

using protocols such as those discussed in Chapter 7. The user is working at a higher layer, however, so this is all transparent and appears much like a local login. The only difference may be slight delays between responses, especially if the remote computer is far away or network traffic is heavy.

Telnet works in a client/server mode (Figure 8.3). That is, a PC (or other computer) runs Telnet (client) locally and transmits data between the user and network protocols. It also can format and send specific commands, some of which we will describe shortly. The remote computer (server) also runs its version of Telnet. It performs similar functions, exchanging data between network protocols and the operating system and interpreting user-transmitted commands.

A user typically uses Telnet in a couple of ways. One is to log in to a local computer, wait for a system prompt (">" in our example), and enter the command

> `> Telnet text-address`

The text address specifies the host computer to which the user wants to connect. Telnet then calls on the transport protocol to negotiate and establish a connection with the remote site. Once connected, the user must log in to the remote site by specifying the account number and password. Another way to use Telnet is to enter the command Telnet without a text address. The local system will respond with a Telnet prompt (Telnet >). If you are running on a graphical user interface (GUI), there is typically a Telnet icon you can access. Either way you can enter Telnet commands (or select them from a menu). For example, you can connect to the remote site by entering a connect or open command (depending on the local system) specifying the text address.

Once connected, Telnet works in the background completely transparent to the user. However, the user can escape from the remote login to give subsequent commands to Telnet. This is normally done by entering a control sequence such as Ctrl-]. This returns the Telnet prompt to the user but does not break the remote connection.

Table 8.1 shows some of the Telnet commands. Each command is coded and sent as an eight-bit number. To distinguish a command from data that may have the same eight-bit value, each command is preceded by the eight-bit IAC code

Figure 8.3   Telnet Client/Server Relation

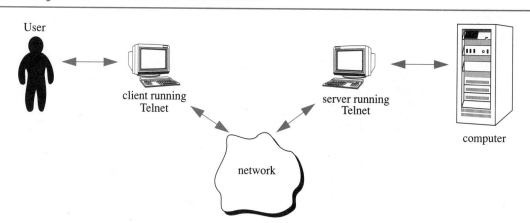

Table 8.1   Telnet Commands

COMMAND	ASCII VALUE	DESCRIPTION
Abort output (AO)	245	Terminates the output of a process initiated on the remote host while allowing the process to continue running. Can be used when the remote host does not recognize the Ctrl-O command.
Are you there (AYT)	246	Asks the remote host whether it is running.
Break (BRK)	243	Terminates the process on the remote machine, a useful feature if the process is stuck in a loop or is generating more output than you care to have, such as the text for a political speech.
Do	253	Part of a negotiation that allows the client and server to agree on an option or set of parameters (discussed shortly). Can indicate a request for the other site to use a particular option. May also be a response to a Will command, indicating that it will do the requested option.
Don't	254	A response to a Will command, indicating that it will not do the requested option.
Erase character (EC)	247	Erases the most recent character entered on the remote host. Useful if the remote does not recognize your backspace or Delete key.
Erase line (EL)	248	Erases the most recent line entered on the remote host.
Go ahead (GA)	249	Used when the remote host and user synchronize their exchanges, it tells the remote host it can send.
Interpret as command (IAC)	255	Instructs the receiving Telnet to interpret the next byte as a command.
Interrupt process (IP)	244	Terminates the process on the remote machine.
No operation (NOP)	241	Sends a no-operation command to the remote host. Technically a NOP does nothing, but it can be used to determine whether the connection exists. If the connection is broken and you send a NOP, you will get an error message.
Subnegotiation begin (SB)	250	The starting delimiter for a sequence of Telnet commands.
Subnegotiation end (SE)	240	The ending delimiter for a sequence of Telnet commands.
Will	251	It can indicate a request that the other site use a particular option. It can also be a response to a Do command, indicating that it will do the requested option.
Won't	252	A response to a Do command, indicating that it will not do the requested option.

(11111111). Consequently, receipt of this code tells Telnet to interpret the next byte as a command. In the event the IAC code appears in data, Telnet performs byte stuffing, inserting an extra IAC code in the stream, to distinguish data from command. In some cases Telnet may send a sequence of commands. In this case the IAC code is followed by the SB code (see Table 8.1) the list of coded commands, and finally the SE code. That is, SB and SE delimit the list of commands transmitted in one stream.

Let's give an example showing how a command may be sent. Suppose you have logged in to a remote host and are about to get a directory listing by entering the command dir, but you inadvertently entered dirr. Your usual response is to backspace or enter the Delete key to eliminate the second r. But what if the remote host does not recognize those keys? One option[*] is to proceed as follows:

```
>dirr <CTRL]>
Telnet>send EC
press enter key
get a directory listing
```

The first line shows the system prompt (>) followed by the incorrectly entered command (dirr). If the user has discovered the typing error, he or she can respond by entering the Ctrl-] sequence. This causes the user to escape to Telnet, where he or she can enter send EC (second line). This causes the EC command to be sent, effectively erasing the second r in line 1. In line 3 the user presses the Enter key and gets the directory listing.

The number of Telnet options is extensive, and options vary depending on the software and hardware you run. There is usually a help facility that gives you information about them. Consequently, we do not attempt a complete description of them. Instead we list a few of the more common options in Table 8.2. The options have codes that are specified during the option negotiation phase. The best way to get detailed knowledge of how to use Telnet is through the documentation provided with your system.

FILE TRANSFERS

One of the most common network applications is file transfer. It has many uses. People working on group projects or doing related research often must share files. The ability to access and transfer files is essential for information sharing. Instructors create files for students to use in programming assignments. Applications such as airline reservations and electronic banking also require the access and transfer of at least part of a file. Finally, probably no one even knows the number of files being downloaded from various sites on the Web.

Logistics play an important role in file transfer. In some cases, a collection of files may be stored and maintained on different computers. This is a **distributed file system.** In other cases, all files are in one place, and a **file server** manages them. In any case, when a user wants to transfer a file he or she makes a request to the appropriate application. It, in turn, observes the network's file transfer protocols. What must the protocol handle?

---

[*]This example was done by telneting from a digital UNIX version 3.2 system to a DEC ALPHA OPENVMS version 6.2 system and may differ depending on the system on which you run.

Table 8.2   Telnet Options

OPTION	MEANING
autoflush	When enabled and an interrupt character is sent, any data in the display buffers is flushed and the display terminated. Otherwise the display continues until the buffer is empty.
autosynch	When enabled, the interrupt character is sent as urgent data. Otherwise it is sent in sequence with any other characters.
binary transmission	End-of-line characters are not mapped to the ASCII control characters <CR> and <LF>. This is necessary when transmitting binary data.
crlf	Causes the client to put the ASCII control characters <CR> and <LF> at the end of each line it sends. This is needed if the remote system expects these characters at the end of each line.
crmod	Causes the client to make sure that each line the user receives ends with the ASCII control characters <CR> and <LF>. This causes received lines to scroll upward on the screen.
local characters	Determines whether control sequences are interpreted by the client or the remote server.
terminal-type	Specifies information regarding the type of terminal and its characteristics. This is necessary for programs such as full-screen text editors that utilize cursor positions.

The first consideration is the file structure, which varies. For example, some files consist of a simple sequence of bytes. Others are **flat files** consisting of a linear sequence of records. **Hashed files** allow random access to a record through a key field value. **Hierarchical files** may organize all occurrences of a key field in a tree structure.[*] These differences pose a problem when transferring files.

One way to simplify transfers between incompatible systems is to define a **virtual file structure,** one supported by the network for the purpose of file transfer. Figure 8.4 shows the transfer process. User *A* wants to transfer a file to user *B*, but they work on computers that support different file systems. User *A*'s file must be translated into a network-defined structure. The file transfer protocol then handles the actual transfer, and the file finally is converted to a structure supported by user *B*'s computer.

A virtual file must preserve the essential ingredients of a file. For example, it must contain the file's name, attributes, and coded information on the actual structure to allow for proper translation. Of course, it must also contain the data.

---

[*]Be sure to distinguish between a file's structure and its implementation. For example, a file may be hierarchical, but there are many implementations of a hierarchical structure.

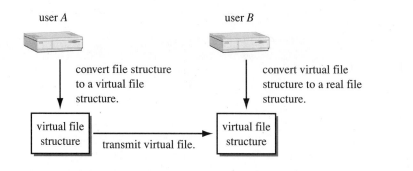

Figure 8.4   File Transfer between Computers Supporting Different File Structures

Another issue in file transfer is accessibility. A file transfer system should not honor every request. It must consider protection. Is the file read-only? Can the user update the file or execute its contents? For that matter is the requester allowed access at all? Law enforcement and defense agencies would not want a system that allows access to all of their files. Multiple accesses to files also must be considered. Are they allowed? Passwords, locks, and keys are used for file protection and concurrency control.

FTP   One common file transfer protocol is called just that—**File Transfer Protocol,** or **FTP** (no kudos for imagination here). It is another protocol in the TCP/IP suite and is built on the same client/server paradigm as Telnet. A user, interacting with a local FTP program, connects to a remote site also running FTP. As with Telnet this can be done in a couple of ways. First is to simply enter the command[*]

ftp *text-address*

which will establish a connection to the specified remote computer, much as Telnet does. The second way is to enter

ftp

and wait for the prompt ftp>. Next the user enters

ftp> open *text-address*

to establish the connection. Sometimes connect is used instead of open. Once connected, the user is asked to enter a user identification followed by a password. On entering the appropriate identification and password the user then can peruse subdirectories, get directory lists, and get copies of files.

Many sites make files available to the general Internet community. This means a user can access them without having an account on that machine. When a user connects to the site he or she usually enters "anonymous" for the account name and

---

[*]As with Telnet, FTP can be run from a GUI that allows you to choose menu options from a list. We'll proceed as if you were entering your own commands. It works the same either way.

either "guest" or his or her email address as the password. The latter is to track use of accesses. This application is often called **anonymous FTP.**

On the surface, FTP looks just like Telnet: Both allow a user to establish a remote connection. The difference is that Telnet allows a legitimate login, whereas FTP primarily provides access to certain files and directories.

Once the FTP connection is established, the user sees the prompt FTP>. At that point he or she has many choices. As before, we do not try to cover all the commands; instead we summarize some of the most commonly used ones in Table 8.3.

Table 8.3   FTP Commands

COMMAND	MEANING
cd	Changes the working directory on the remote host.
close	Closes the FTP connection.
dir or ls	Provides a directory listing of the current working directory.
get	Copies the specified file from the remote host to the local system. The local file receives the same name as the one on the remote host. In the event there is incompatibility between naming conventions or the user simply wishes to give the transferred file a different name, he or she can specify a second parameter indicating a local file name.
glob	Acts as a toggle allowing or disallowing the use of wildcard characters. For example, if * is a wildcard character and its use is allowed then mget *.TXT would get all files with a TXT extension.
help	Displays a list of all client FTP commands.
mget	Copies multiple files from the remote host to the local system.
mput	Copies multiple files from the local system to the remote host, contingent on the remote host allowing the creation of new files.
put	Copies a specified file from the local system to the remote host if allowed by the remote host.
pwd	Displays the current working directory on the remote host.
quit	Quits FTP.
remotehelp	Displays a list of all server FTP commands.
struct	Specifies the file's structure. Some options are unstructured and random access.
type	Allows the user to specify the file type. Types ASCII and binary (sometimes called image) are most common. With ASCII files some control bytes may be changed to maintain readability on a different system. Binary files are transmitted with no changes in the contents. Other file types are EBCDIC and logical byte. EBCDIC is common on IBM mainframes, and logical byte corresponds to systems with a byte size different than eight bits.

The user can get information on the commands by typing help or a question mark (?). Probably the most commonly used commands are cd to change the working directory in the remote host and get, which copies a file from the remote to the local site.

Anonymous FTP allows files and technical reports to be made available to the general Internet community. Just what is available depends on what the remote site has put in the anonymous FTP account. There are thousands of FTP sites, and their contents may change often, so we make no attempt to list them. We will, however, present an example showing how to use FTP to get access to a wide range of network- and communications-related information through a series of documents called the **request for comments (RFC) series.** These are research notes that are available in electronic or printed form. They cover a wide range of topics such as Internet protocols, network management and administration, email, network standards, and much more.

Table 8.4 lists some of the repositories for RFC documents. The first column indicates the site to which you must connect via FTP and the second specifies the subdirectory containing RFC files. RFCs are numbered and have the form RFC xxxx, where the designation "xxxx" is a four-digit number. We will not even think about providing a list of RFCs since it would require about 40 pages to do so. Table 8.5 lists a few RFCs that relate to topics covered in this book. Reference [Co95] contains an extensive list of RFCs.

Most of the RFC repository sites maintain an RFC list in a file that can be accessed using FTP or email. Figure 8.5 shows how this was done in one instance. Boldface characters represent those typed by the user and plain characters correspond to FTP responses. Line 1 shows the ftp command to connect to the remote site ds.internic.net. Line 20 corresponds to the login request and the entry for the anonymous login. Line 22 requests the password, which in this case is the author's email address. As with most systems, the password was not echoed and is shown here only to illustrate the interaction. Line 28 changes the working directory to the rfc subdirectory of the current directory. It is the subdirectory containing RFC documents. Finally, line 30 requests that a copy of a file named rfc-index.txt be transferred to the local site. This file contains a list of all RFCs available in that repository as well as the topics covered. The copied file also will be named rfc-index.txt. The remaining lines indicate the status of the file transfer as it occurs.

Table 8.4 RFC Repositories

LOCATION	SUBDIRECTORY CONTAINING RFCs
ds.internic.net	rfc
nic.ddn.mil (DDN MILNET users)	rfc
nisc.jvnc.net	rfc
venera.isi.edu	in-notes
wuarchive.wustl.edu	doc/rfc
src.doc.ic.ac.uk	rfc

Table 8.5 RFC Documents

RFC NUMBER	TOPIC
1105, 1266, 1265	Border Gateway Protocol (BGP)
1591, 1101	Domain Name System (DNS)
114, 172, 265, 354, 542, 765, 959	File Transfer Protocol (FTP)
777, 792	Internet Control Message Protocol (ICMP)
791, 760	Internet Protocol (IP)
1577	Internet Protocol over ATM
1752, 1726	IPng
1007, 1008	ISO transport protocol
1370, 1246, 1245	Open Shortest Path First protocol (OSPF)
1387, 1388, 1721, 1723, 1058	Routing Information Protocol (RIP)
788, 821	Simple Mail Transfer Protocol (SMTP)
1067, 1098, 1157	Simple Network Management Protocol (SNMP)
764, 854	Telnet protocol specification
793, 761, 675	Transmission Control Protocol (TCP)
1103, 1188, 1390	Transmitting IP datagrams over Fiber Distributed Data Interface (FDDI)
1042	Transmitting IP datagrams over IEEE 802 networks
877	Transmitting IP datagrams over public data networks
1738	Uniform Resource Locators (URLs) in the WWW
768	User Datagram Protocol (UDP)
874	X.25 critique
822, 987, 1616	X.400 email standard
1279, 1309	X.500 directory services

If you want a copy of a particular RFC, the usual way is to enter

```
get rfcxxxx.txt
```

where "xxxx" represents the four-digit RFC number. If you do this, be forewarned; some of them are large files.

The hosts in Table 8.4 are not the only sites accessible via FTP, and RFCs are not the only files of interest. Thousands of FTP sites are available, and various Internet sites boast of information related to anything from aardvark anatomy to zymurgy. With this many sites, it can be difficult to know the useful ones and what they contain. Usually, people learn of sites through professional contacts, professional literature, Web surfing, or word of mouth.

```
1    /usr/users/shayw-$>ftp ds.internic.net
2    Connected to ds.internic.net.
3    220- InterNIC Directory and Database Services
4    220-
5    220-
6    220-Welcome to InterNIC Directory and Database Services provided by AT&T.
7    220-These services are partially supported through a cooperative agreement
8    220-with the National Science Foundation.
9    220-
10   220-Your comments and suggestions for improvement are welcome, and can be
11   220-mailed to admin@ds.internic.net.
12   :
13   :
14   display message not relevant to our discussion
15   :
16   :
17   220-
18   220- ****************************
19   220 ds2 FTP server (Version 4.105 Fri Jan 5 14:34:54 EST 1996) ready.
20   Name (ds.internic.net:shayw): anonymous
21   331 Guest login ok, send your email address as password.
22   Password: shayw@uwgb.edu
23   230- Guest login ok, access restrictions apply.
24   230- Local time is: Wed Aug 6 16:17:05 1997
25   230
26   Remote system type is UNIX.
27   Using binary mode to transfer files.
28   ftp> cd rfc
29   250 CWD command successful.
30   ftp> get rfc-index.txt
31   200 PORT command successful.
32   150 Opening BINARY mode data connection for rfc-index.txt (299856 bytes).
33   226 Transfer complete.
34   299856 bytes received in 3.6 seconds (82 Kbytes/s)
35   ftp> quit
36   221 Goodbye.
37   /usr/users/shayw-$>
```

Figure 8.5   Figure 8.5 Sample Use of FTP to Transfer a File

Trivial File Transfer Protocol   Although FTP provides a wide range of options for the TCP/IP suite, such as multiple file types, compression, and multiple TCP connections, many applications, such as LAN applications, do not need a full range of services. In these cases a simpler file transfer protocol, the **Trivial File Transfer Protocol (TFTP),** will do the job. One difference between FTP and TFTP is that the latter does not use a reliable transport service. Instead, it runs on top of an unreliable one such as UDP. TFTP uses acknowledgments and timeouts to make sure all pieces of a file arrive.

Like other protocols, TFTP defines the communication rules between a client and a server. It defines five packet types to do this:

- **Read request.** A request to read a file from a server.
- **Write request.** A request to write a file to the server.
- **Data.** A 512-byte (or less) block containing part of the file to be transferred. Blocks are numbered starting at 1.
- **Acknowledgment.** Acknowledges receipt of a data packet.
- **Error.** Communicates an error message.

When a client wishes to transfer a file it sends either a read request or write request packet, depending on which way the file transfer is to occur. The file then is transferred in 512-byte pieces using a stop and wait protocol. Only the last block may contain fewer than 512 bytes.

SIMPLE MAIL TRANSFER PROTOCOL

Certainly one of the most common uses of networks is electronic mail, the ability to send a message or file to a specific user at a local or remote site. Typically, you send a message by specifying the email address of the recipient. The usual address format is name@host-text-address. The message is buffered at the destination site and is accessible only by the intended user.

There are some similarities with file transfer protocols. For example, both use a client and server to negotiate transfer of data. However, email typically sends the file to a specified user, in whose account the message is buffered. Also, the email client and server work in the background. For example, if you get a file using FTP, you typically wait until the file arrives before doing another task. If you send (or receive) a file using email you can do other tasks while the client and server perform the mail delivery in the background. In the case of receiving mail you need not even be logged on. You will be notified of new mail the next time you log in to the system.

The standard mail protocol in the TCP/IP suite is the **Simple Mail Transfer Protocol (SMTP).** It runs above TCP/IP and below any local mail service. Its primary responsibility is to make sure mail is transferred between different hosts. By contrast, the local service is responsible for distributing mail to specific recipients.

Figure 8.6 shows the interaction between local mail, SMTP, and TCP. When a user sends mail, the local mail facility determines whether the address is local or requires a connection to a remote site. In the latter case, the local mail facility stores the mail (much as you would put a letter in a mailbox), where it waits for the client SMTP. When the client SMTP delivers the mail, it first calls TCP to establish a connection with the remote site. When the connection is made, the client and server SMTPs exchange packets and eventually deliver the mail. At the remote end the local mail facility gets the mail and delivers it to the intended recipient.

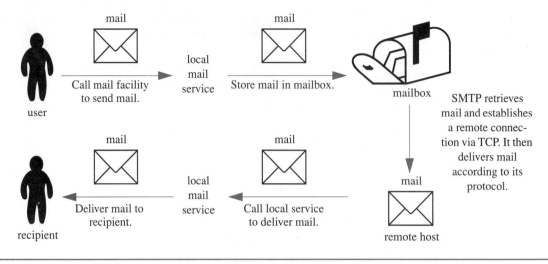

Figure 8.6   SMTP Interacting with Local Mail and TCP

Figure 8.7 shows the packet exchange between the client and server. The packets are also called SMTP **protocol data units (PDUs)** or simply **commands.** When the TCP connection is made the server sends a 220 PDU indicating it is ready to receive mail. The number 220 serves to identify the type of packet. Afterward, the client and server exchange the identities of their respective sites. Next, the client sends a MAIL FROM PDU indicating there is mail and identifying the sender. If the server is willing to accept mail from that sender it responds with a 250 OK PDU.

The server then sends one or more RCPT TO PDUs specifying the intended recipients to determine whether the recipients are there before sending the mail. For each recipient, the server responds with a 250 OK PDU (recipient exists) or a 550 recipient not here PDU. After the recipients have all been identified, the client sends a DATA PDU indicating it will begin mail transmission. The server's response is a 354 start mail PDU, which gives the OK to start sending and specifies a sequence the client should use to mark the mail's end. In this case the sequence is <CR> <LF> . <CR> <LF>.[*] The client sends the mail in fixed-size PDUs, placing this sequence at the mail's end. When the server gets the last PDU, it acknowledges receipt of the mail with another 250 OK PDU. Finally, the client and server exchange PDUs indicating they are ceasing mail delivery, and TCP releases the connection.

This description has outlined the basic functionality of SMTP and has not gone into the details of PDU format or issues such as forwarding mail or responding to nonexistent addresses. More information on SMTP can be found in References [Co95] and [Ru89] and in RFC documents 788 and 821.

---

[*]This is the same as carriage return, line feed, period, carriage return, line feed. This sequence cannot appear in the body of the mail because SMTP disallows sending mail containing a single period on a separate line.

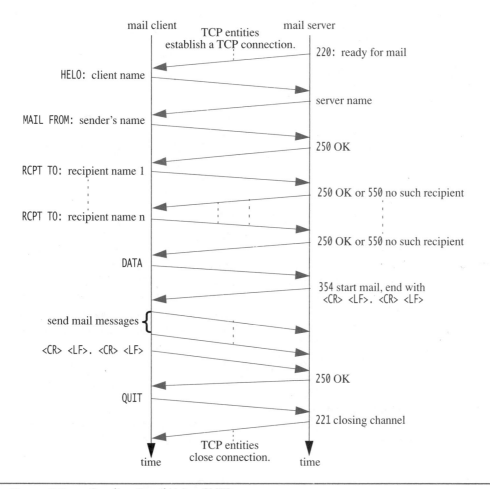

Figure 8.7   Sending Email Using SMTP

SIMPLE NETWORK MANAGEMENT PROTOCOL

The **Simple Network Management Protocol (SNMP)** is a management protocol designed to make sure network protocols and devices not only work but work well. It allows managers to locate problems and make adjustments by exchanging a sequence of commands between a client and a server. Unlike previous applications, it runs on top of UDP instead of TCP. Still, because it is an important part of Internet management it warrants a discussion.

Figure 8.8 shows the SNMP architecture. A network manager runs a management client program at a site that communicates with a management server program at another site. Typically the server programs are run on remote hosts and especially network routers. Both management programs use commands defined by the SNMP protocol. Primarily the commands define how to request information from a server and send information to a server or client.

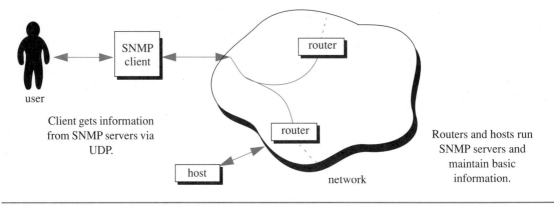

user

Client gets information
from SNMP servers via
UDP.

Routers and hosts run
SNMP servers and
maintain basic
information.

network

Figure 8.8 SNMP Architecture

SNMP has several goals (described in RFC 1157). The first is to simplify SNMP functions to reduce support costs and make SNMP easier to use. Second, it must be extensible to accommodate future updates in network operations and management. Third, the protocol must be independent of design specifics of hosts or routers. The result is an application-layer protocol that interfaces with transport services.

Because SNMP is a management application it must know what processes it is to manage and how to refer to them. The routers and hosts that SNMP manages are called **objects.** An object has a formal definition according to **ASN.1 (Abstract Syntax Notation 1),** a formal language designed expressly for the definition of PDU formats and objects. A formal treatment of the objects and ASN.1 is far beyond the scope of this text, but you can find some additional information in References [Co95], [Co94], and [Ro96].

Management Information Base   Each object's server maintains a database of information that describes its characteristics and activities. Because there are different object types, a standard defines precisely what should be maintained. This standard, the **management information base (MIB)** was defined by the group that proposed SNMP. There are eight categories of information specified by MIB. As before, a complete description of each one is very detailed, and References [Co95], [Co94], and [Ro96] have more information. Here we will specify each of the categories and some examples of the information they contain.

- **System.** Describes the host or router operating system and contains information such as when the server was booted, a description of the device it runs on, device location, and a contact person.

- **Interface.** Describes each network interface and contains items such as MTU (see Section 7.4) size, transmission rate, number of packets discarded for various reasons, number of octets transmitted and received, number of interfaces, and an interface description.

- **Address translation.** Contains a table used to change an IP address into a network-specific one.

- **IP.** Describes information specific to the Internet Protocol. Examples of information maintained include default time-to-live value for IP packets, number of datagrams eliminated for various reasons, number of datagrams forwarded and delivered to the transport protocol and received from the data link protocol, number of fragments created, number of datagrams reassembled, and routing tables.

- **ICMP.** Describes information specific to the ICMP protocol. Primarily it contains many counters tracking the numbers of each type of control message (Section 7.4) sent by ICMP.

- **TCP.** Among the items it contains are timeout lengths, number of connections, number of segments sent and received, maximum number of simultaneous connections, IP address of each entity using TCP and the IP address of the remote connection, and number of failed connection attempts.

- **UDP.** Among the items it contains are the number of datagrams delivered, discarded, or received and the IP addresses of entities using UDP.

- **EGP (Exterior Gateway Protocol).** This is a protocol to exchange routing information between two autonomous networks in an internet. As with other categories, the MIB maintains counters tracking the number of EGP messages sent and received.

SNMP Commands   The management programs that use SNMP run asynchronously. That is, they send out requests but can do other things while waiting for responses. Generally the requests, or PDUs, request information from a server, send information to a remote management program, or respond to special conditions. SNMP defines five PDU formats:

1. **GetRequest.** This command causes a GetRequest PDU[*] to be sent containing a command code, object name, and specification of an MIB variable. The receiving entity responds by sending a GetResponse PDU containing values of the variable requested or an error code in the event of an error.

2. **GetNextRequest.** This command is similar to GetRequest except that the request is for values of variables that "follow" the ones specified in the PDU. The notion of following is based on a lexicographic order determined by the MIB design. This is especially useful for traversing tables maintained by the management server.

3. **GetResponse.** A PDU sent in response to a previously received GetRequest PDU. It contains values requested or error codes.

---

[*]The specific PDU format and mechanism for identifying MIB variables is rather complex. References [Co95] and [Ro96] contain fairly detailed discussions.

4. **SetRequest.** This command allows the manager to update values of MIB variables maintained by remote management programs and to remotely alter the characteristics of a particular object, which, in turn, can affect network operations. The format does not violate any security measures that prevent unauthorized updates.

5. **Trap.** This PDU is sent from a server to the manager when specific conditions or events have occurred. It allows the manager to stay abreast of changes in the operating environment. Some of the trap PDUs and their events are listed here:

   a. **Coldstart trap.** The management program has been reinitialized with potential changes in the object's characteristics.

   b. **Warmstart trap.** Reinitialization has occurred, but no characteristics have been altered.

   c. **Linkdown trap.** A communications link has failed.

   d. **Linkup trap.** A previously failed communication has been restored.

   e. **EgpNeighborLoss trap.** The station has lost contact with an EGP peer neighbor.

   f. **Authentication failure trap.** An SNMP PDU that failed an authentication check has been received.

A newer version of SNMP, **SNMP 2,** was designed to overcome some of the perceived weaknesses of SNMP. For example, one of the criticisms of SNMP is that, because of its simple command format, communication requires a large number of packets. SNMP 2 provides more messaging options, thus allowing the clients and hosts to communicate more efficiently. SNMP 2 also provides more security than the original SNMP through its implementation of message authentication and DES encryption. A third enhancement is increased flexibility to allow SNMP 2 to run on top of multiple protocols such as AppleTalk, IPX, and OSI. These issues and others are discussed in more detail in References [St96], [Ro96], and [Ro95].

As with just about any protocol, SNMP and SNMP 2 are not the only management protocols. The ISO management protocol is the **Common Management Information Protocol (CMIP).** When used over a TCP connection, CMIP is known as **CMOT (CMIP over TCP).** CMIP is more complex than SNMP and is reputed to be more suitable for larger networks. References [St96], [St94], [Ro95], and [Ro96] are textbooks devoted completely to network management.

8.2   WORLD WIDE WEB

Almost certainly, the most significant development to occur since this book's first edition is the **World Wide Web (WWW).** Protocols such as Telnet, FTP, and email have drawn the Internet community together and have made enormous amounts of information available. However, the development of the Web has, among other things, made the information much easier to reach. Whether for serious research or simply for fun and games, millions of people have discovered how much the Web has to offer. They have also discovered frustration and delays as the number of Web sites has grown exponentially. This growth has not only caused vast amounts of traffic throughout the Internet, resulting in delays, but also often hindered the task of finding useful information because of the sheer volume of information.

There is so much that can be said about the Web that, as with other topics we have discussed, entire books have been written on the subject. They range from listing various sites through discussions of Web protocols to helping you develop your own Web page. Without question the Web is an important topic in this field and should be discussed. The problem is deciding what to discuss. We believe an important goal is to blend some theory with application. This contributes to your overall knowledge base and provides some useful skills as well. Toward this end the goals of this section are as follows:

- An overview of the WWW and its fundamental operational concept.

- An overview of the HTML language used to create a Web page. We will not attempt to discuss all of HTML but will describe enough to generate a minimally functional Web page.

- An integration of programming into Web page development. This is what we are really aiming for and the previous items serve as short-term goals needed to do this. We will deal with a client/server model again and will describe how to incorporate programming into both the client and server side of the protocols. Specifically, we will introduce JavaScript and CGI (Common Gateway Interface) programming and conclude with another working example representative of many applications on the Web. Again, we cannot provide all details of either but we can show you enough to get you started on your own Web programming.

WEB PAGE ACCESS

We will assume the reader has had some Web experience, at least to the extent of accessing various sites and following (clicking on) links to other sites. Indeed, the ease with which anyone can use the Web has been both an enormous advantage and (to some) a disadvantage. We begin by describing the underlying actions that occur when surfing through the Web.

Fundamental to Web operations is **HTTP (Hypertext Transfer Protocol),** a client/server protocol designed to allow the exchange of information over the Web. HTTP defines the types of requests that a browser can make and the types of responses a server returns. Through HTTP, a user can retrieve Web pages from remote servers or store pages on the server if he or she has appropriate access. HTTP also provides the ability to append new information to pages or to delete them altogether. We will focus strictly on the retrieval aspect.

Figure 8.9 shows the basic concepts involved. A user at a PC runs a **browser.** Common browsers at the time of this writing are Netscape and Internet Explorer. There is also a text-oriented browser called Lynx. The browser runs on the client side

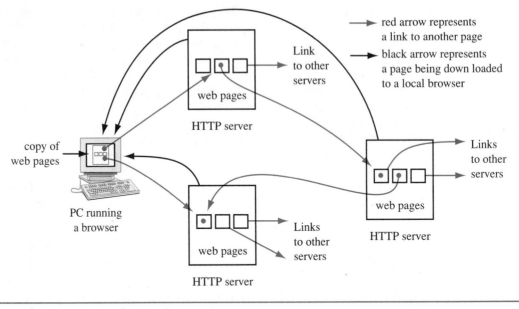

Figure 8.9 Web Overview

and has the ability to display the contents of a Web page.[*] We'll discuss what a Web page looks like shortly, but for now just assume it is a document (file) that presents information to the user. In addition each Web page has **links** (references) to other Web pages. These pages are stored in auxiliary storage accessible by remote HTTP servers.

A user can follow a link by placing the mouse cursor over some designated text or picture and clicking the mouse button. At that point the local HTTP client sends a request to a remote HTTP server for a specified Web page. The server responds by transferring that page back to the client, where it eventually replaces the old page on the screen (although the old page is usually buffered in case the user wants to return to it). The user can again follow a link from this new page and call up yet another Web page. Another remote HTTP server responds the same way and transfers the requested Web page back to the browser. The user can repeat this process as often as needed. Links can connect documents stored at HTTP servers located all over the world, and with a click of a mouse button a document is transferred to your local PC.

Of course we have oversimplified things. Perhaps, more correctly stated, we have assumed the existence of TCP, IP, and data link protocols to handle the details of the actual transfer. Thus, from a certain perspective it is that simple. Once again, we see the benefits of layered protocols because the tasks at higher layers are much simpler to describe if we assume lower layers exist.

---

[*] A Web page is perhaps more accurately called an *HTML document,* but we'll discuss that later.

At the heart of all of this is the answer to a question: How does a browser know where to look for a requested page? Every page accessible via the Web must be uniquely named to avoid confusion. To accomplish this, three things are necessary: the page's location, a name unique to that location, and the protocol needed to access that page. Collectively, these three items define the **Uniform Resource Locator (URL)** of the page, which has the form

protocol://site-address/name

For example, you can access the author's Web page (also called the home page) via the URL

http://www.uwgb.edu/~shayw

The protocol is HTTP[*] and the site address is www.uwgb.edu. The last part, ~shayw, is an indirect reference to a specific file. The string "shayw" represents an account on the host computer www.uwgb.edu. The tilde (~) prior to the account name indicates a file named index.htm in a subdirectory named www in the account shayw. This is a conventional way to access a person's home page without worrying about naming conventions on the host computer. An alternative would have been to specify explicitly the sequence of subdirectories, ending with the actual file, but that is more difficult. Also, by using the tilde prior to an account name we can maintain consistency among all who create a home page on the host computer. Of course, if you wanted to access a different file then you would have to indicate it explicitly. For example, the syllabus for our computer networks course is in a file named syll358.htm in the author's www subdirectory. You could go directly to that page using

http://www.uwgb.edu/~shayw/syll358.htm

Of course, making a list of all pages you might want to access and referencing them explicitly is awkward. An alternative to specifying a page directly is to follow a link to it from an entry on another Web page. That's a relatively straightforward thing to do but first we need to describe how to present the contents of a Web page to someone running a browser.

HYPERTEXT MARKUP LANGUAGE

The next logical step is to describe how to set up a Web page and how to include links in it. The language that allows you to do this is the **Hypertext Markup Language (HTML).** Basically, a user creates a file (usually with a .HTM or .HTML extension) containing HTML elements. This file (also called an **HTML document**), defines how a Web page appears on a browser. (We will ignore the case of text-only browsers here). However, before we provide a short overview to HTML, the first thing we need to know is just what can be in an HTML document.

---

[*]The HTTP protocol is not the only prefix possible in a URL. One can also specify other protocols such as FTP, Telnet, and email.

When viewing a Web page through a browser, a user can see the following types of content:

- Straight text.
- Graphic or animated images.
- A link to another HTML document. Typically, links are represented by under-lined text that has a different color or by an image. By moving the mouse cursor over the text or image and clicking the mouse button, a new HTML document is downloaded and appears on the browser's screen.

In general, HTML can provide some pretty sophisticated-looking pages with fancy formats and color-coordinated backgrounds and images. Because the author has no talent with color coordination (his wife can testify to that), we'll just concentrate on some basic functionality. We'll leave it to the imagination of the reader to generate creative Web pages. We also will make no attempt to be complete in our description of HTML, but we will describe some of the more common elements of it. There are an almost uncountable number of HTML books on the market that can provide all the information you need.

HTML uses **tags** to indicate what you want to include in an HTML document and how you want to display it. They are typically written as

<tag options> . . . some stuff in between . . . </tag>

Some tags require both a beginning and ending delimiter. Both contain the tag iden-tifier, but the ending delimiter also contains the character /. These delimiters tell the browser what to do with the stuff in between. In some cases options specified in the beginning delimiter provide additional information.

Figure 8.10 shows a sample HTML document and some typical tags that allow the viewer to see three things: a graphic image, some basic text, and links to other documents. Figure 8.11 shows the actual displayed page. The first and last lines of Figure 8.10 correspond to the HTML tag (<html> and </html>) and indicate that everything in between should be interpreted according to HTML rules. Each HTML document has a **head** and a **body.** The tags <head> and </head> delimit the head, and the tags <body> and </body> delimit the body. The head can contain several things, one of which is a title (delimiters <title> and </title>). The browser takes text that is between the title tags and displays it at the top of the window. Can you see the phrase "The Title Goes Here" in Figure 8.11?

The body is where all of the text information, graphic images, and hypertext links will eventually go. For example, to display an image you must first create an image and store it in a file. The HTML **image tag** (<img>) specifies that file, and the image is displayed when viewing the document. The option in the image tag of Figure 8.10 specifies the file as "logo.gif." The image in Figure 8.11, which is our university's logo, was created previously and stored in that file. The center tag delimiters (<center> and </center>) on either side of the image tag cause the image to be centered on the screen. If the center tag delimiters were not present, the image in Figure 8.11 would have appeared on the left side of the screen. The body contains a couple tags (<hr>) that insert a horizontal rule. Figure 8.11 shows three dim hori-

```
<html>
<head>
<title>The Title Goes Here</title>
</head>
<body>
<center><img src = "logo.gif"></center>
<hr>
<center> <h1>Links to Courses </h1> </center>
This is a short paragraph containing links to three courses. Each can be accessed by clicking
on the course number. The first one is titled<B> Numerical Analysis</B> and has a course
number of <A HREF = "http://www.uwgb.edu./~shayw/syll350.htm">266-350</A>. The second course
is titled <B>Data Structures</B> and has a course number
<A HREF = "http://www.uwgb.edu./~shayw/syll351.htm">266-351</A>. Finally the third course is
titled <B> Data Communications and Computer Networks</B> and has a course number
<A HREF = "http://www.uwgb.edu./~shayw/syll358.htm">266-358</A>.
<hr>
If you have any comments or questions you can send them to <A HREF="mailto:shayw@uwgb.edu">
Bill Shay</A> at the University of Wisconsin-Green Bay
<hr>
</body>
</html>
```

Figure 8.10   Figure 8.10 Sample HTML Document

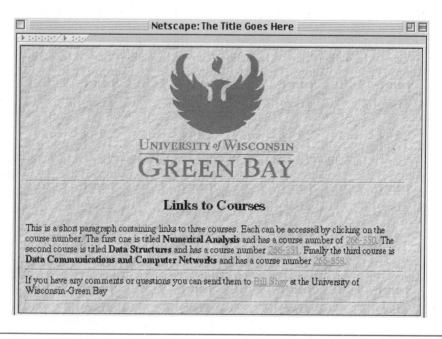

Figure 8.11   View of HTML Document in Figure 8.10

zontal lines that are used as separators. This is a common visual aid to help separate different parts of a display.

Most of the rest of the body contains text, which appears in Figure 8.11. There are, however, some differences in the way the text is displayed. Some text has a larger typeface, some is in boldface, and some is underlined (which actually corresponds to links). Again, HTML tags make the difference. The header tag delimiters (<h1> and </h1>) define a level 1 header. They cause any text between them to be displayed in a larger typeface. There are also tags corresponding to <h2>, <h3>, <h4>, <h5>, and <h6>, which have a similar effect except the type sizes vary. Tag <h1> defines the largest and tag <h6> the smallest. Also, any text between the bold tags (<B> and </B>) appears in boldface.

The most important tags for our purpose are the **anchor tags** (<A> and </A>), for these define actions the user can choose with a simple click of a mouse button. Anchor tag delimiters have several forms and uses. One possibility is an anchor of the form

<A HREF=url> *clickable text* </A>

These delimiters serve two functions. The first is to display **clickable text.**[*] This means that you can move the mouse cursor over that text and click a mouse button to retrieve a remote document. The second is to define the URL of that document. For example, Figure 8.10 has the following embedded in the body:

<A HREF = "http://www.uwgb.edu./~shayw/syll350.htm">266-350</A>

The HREF option defines the URL of a document stored in the author's Web directory. The clickable text in this case is "266-350." Figure 8.11 shows that text as underlined. The user could move the mouse cursor over it, click a button, and retrieve the desired document, in this case a file named syll350.htm in the author's Web directory.

Anchors can also be used to initiate actions besides those used to retrieve an HTML document. Toward the end of Figure 8.10 there is another anchor,

<A HREF="mailto:shayw@uwgb.edu">Bill Shay</A>

In this case, the clickable text corresponds to the author's name. The HREF option identifies a mail server program. When activated, a form appears that allows the user to enter an email message to be sent to the email address specified (in this case, shayw@uwgb.edu). The form also includes a Send button that, when clicked, sends the message.

Table 8.6 contains some other commonly used HTML tags and a brief description of what they do. There are many more tags and many other options to the tags we list. The interested reader can consult any HTML book on the market.

HTML FORMS

As we stated previously, a major goal of this section is to introduce the reader to Web programming, or the ability for a client or server to take certain actions beyond those specified by HTML. We begin by discussing an HTML **form.** You can also think of it

---

[*] An image tag can be used instead of text, creating a clickable image.

Table 8.6   Some HTML Tags

TAGS	MEANING
\<A\> . . . \</A\>	Anchor. Displays the text located between the delimiters. If there is an image tag between the delimiters then it is displayed. The anchor also has an option to specify a URL to which a link is made if the user moves the mouse cursor to the text or image and clicks the mouse button.
\<B\> . . . \</B\>	Boldface. Text between the delimiters is displayed in boldface.
\<body\> . . . \</body\>	Delimits the body of an HTML document.
\<br\>	Line break. Inserts a line break in the Web page. That is, anything after \<br\> appears beginning on the next line.
\<center\> . . . \</center\>	Centers the text located between the delimiters.
\<font\> . . . \</font\>	Options affect the color and size of any text between the delimiters.
\<form\> . . . \</form\>	Creates and displays a form that allows a user to enter information into specified locations on the form. The form can then be submitted for some action to occur. In some cases the form is also used to display results obtained from the information that was entered.
\<h1\> . . . \</h1\>	Displays the text located between the delimiters in a large typesize. There are also tags for \<h2\>, \<h3\>, \<h4\>, \<h5\>, and \<h6\>, each of which defines a different size for the text.
\<head\> . . . \</head\>	Delimits the head of an HTML document.
\<HR\>	Displays a horizontal rule, a line used to visually separate parts of a Web page.
\<html\> . . . \</html\>	Indicates that everything between the delimiters is to be interpreted according to HTML language rules.
\<I\> . . . \</I\>	Displays the text located between the delimiter in italics.
\<img\>	Specifies a file containing a graphic image or animation that is displayed when viewing the Web page.
\<input\>	Used with a form, it allows a user to enter information.
\<li\>	Indicates a list element in a list.
\<option\> . . . \</option\>	Used to provide options in a pop-up menu.
\<P\> . . . \</P\>	Indicates the start of a new paragraph in the Web page.
\<script\> . . . \</script\>	Delimits script language code for client-side programming.
\<select\> . . . \</select\>	Allows user to select among a list of options in a pop-up menu.
\<table\> . . . \</table\>	Defines a table to be displayed on the Web page.
\<title\> . . . \</title\>	Defines the title of an HTML document.
\<ul\> . . . \</ul\>	Defines an unordered list of elements.

as a template for the entering and display of information. Forms are quite common, especially when conducting Internet searches via search engines such as AltaVista, Lycos, or Yahoo. Prior to requesting a search the user enters keywords or phrases into a form. The user can click on a Clear button to erase anything he has typed or on a

Submit or Search button to submit the information to the search engine. Depending on the search engine, the user may also be able to select various options that affect the search results, such as looking specifically for sound or graphic image files.

Submitting forms often requires actions from both the client and server. For example, perhaps your local pizza parlor has a Web page allowing you to order a pizza. You might fill out a form containing your name, address, telephone number, pizza ingredients, and so forth. When the form is submitted the server should respond with the cost and perhaps an estimated delivery time. The client might also take some action such as verifying certain information on the form. For example, if someone orders a large pizza with mushroom, pepperoni, and earth worms the client might recognize one of these as not a viable topping. The idea is to identify certain requests as nonsense before going through all the trouble of submitting the form to the server. In general, this is more efficient because it prevents the Web software from submitting requests that cannot possibly be satisfied.

We begin the discussion of forms by giving an example of a form that can be handled entirely by the client. Figure 8.12 shows a form that allows a user to enter a series of numbers and to calculate any of the largest, smallest, and sum of the numbers. There are some restrictions, as explained in the form's instructions, and eliminating them makes nice assignments. The form contains the following elements:

- Text providing instructions on what to do and how to do it.
- Space (text box) allowing the user to enter a series of numbers.
- Spaces allowing the display of the largest, smallest, or sum of the entered numbers.

Figure 8.12   HTML Form for Statistical Calculations

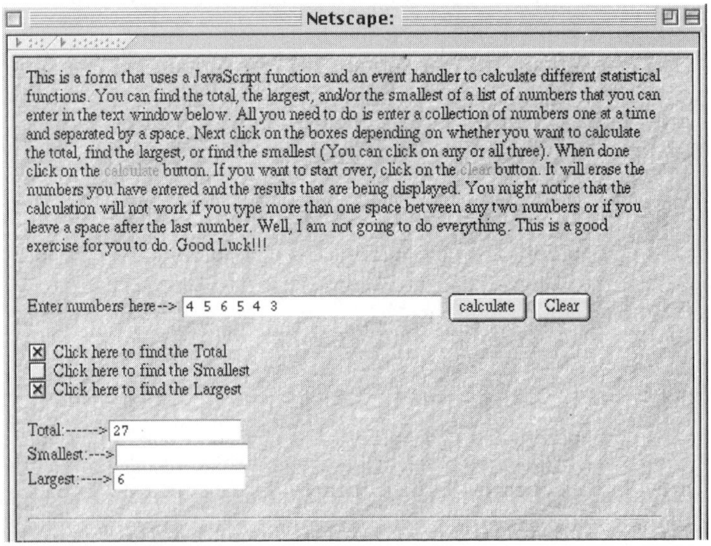

- Checkboxes allowing the user to determine which of the calculations he or she wants displayed.
- Buttons that cause an action to occur. Possible actions are to make the desired calculations or to clear (erase) all the entered numbers. The latter option exists in case the user made an error and needs to reenter a new set of numbers.

Initially, the form's spaces are blank. Figure 8.12 shows the results after the user has done the following:

1. Entered the numbers 4, 5, 6, 5, 4, and 3.
2. Clicked the checkboxes to calculate the total and largest of the entered numbers.
3. Clicked on the Calculate button.

Performing these actions cause the 27 and 6 to be displayed in the Total and Largest boxes, respectively. If the user clicked on the Clear button, all of the numbers in Figure 8.12 would disappear. The user could then enter a new collection of numbers and get new results.

If the user does as instructed, the results are returned. But what if the user does not do as instructed? Anyone who has programmed for others knows that one of the most difficult aspects of programming is responding to things the user is not sup- posed to do. For example, what if the user enters numbers but does not select any of the three checkboxes before clicking on the Calculate button? What if the user clicks on the Calculate button but has not yet entered any numbers?

Figure 8.13 indicates possible responses to each of these. Figure 8.13a shows a window that appears if the user clicks the Calculate button without having checked any of the boxes. Figure 8.13b shows a window that appears if the user clicks the Calculate button without having entered any numbers. In either case, the user would click on the OK button and try again to use the form correctly.

All of the actions described here must be programmed by the person setting up the Web page and can be handled through the use of scripts and a scripting language. A **script** is essentially a program that is automatically executed in response to another action. The **scripting language** is, of course, the language used to write the script. What we need to do next is describe how each of the above can be set up in an HTML document.

Figure 8.13   Responses to Unexpected User Actions

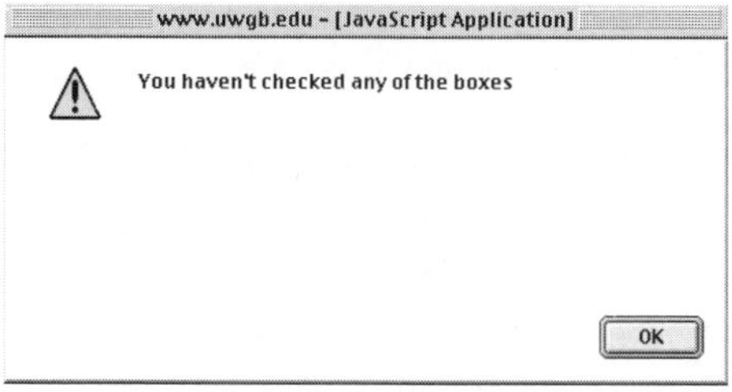

(a) User did not check any boxes

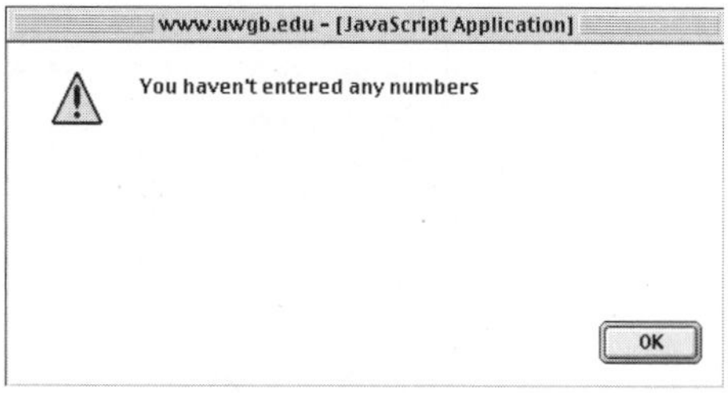

(b) User did not enter any numbers

The first step is to show how to define a form and how to use it for both input and output. Figure 8.14 shows HTML commands that define the form of Figure 8.12. The first half of the form simply contains the text providing user instructions, as shown in Figure 8.12. Within the text are two font tags with a color option specifying the 24-bit color value (8 bits for each of red, green, and blue) of the delimited text. In this case the color value of ff0000 means there is only a red component, so the delimited text (in this case, the words calculate and clear) appears on a Web browser in red.

The lines following the instructions contain **input tags** that define how information is entered into the form. Each box, button, or checkbox of Figure 8.12 is defined by one input tag. Note that each input tag has several options. The options are as follows:

- **Type = "text".** This is for free-form input and output. It causes a text box to be displayed in which a user can type anything he or she wants. As we will see, a client script can also use this type to display information. In Figure 8.12, the numbers the user enters and the eventual results all correspond to this type.

- **Type = "checkbox".** This allows the user to move the mouse cursor over a box and select it by clicking the mouse button. When selected, an X is displayed (see Figure 8.12). The user may select as many checkboxes as he or she wants.

Figure 8.14 HTML Commands to Define the Form of Figure 8.12

```
<form>
This is a form that uses a JavaScript function and an event handler to calculate
different statistical functions. You can find the total, the largest, and/or the
smallest of a list of numbers that you can enter in the text window below. All you
need to do is enter a collection of numbers one at a time and separated by a space.
Next click on the boxes depending on whether you want to calculate the total, find the
largest, or find the smallest. (You can click on any or all three).
When done click on the <FONT COLOR="ff0000">calculate </FONT>button. If you want to
start over, click on the <FONT COLOR="ff0000">clear </FONT>button. It will erase the
numbers you have entered and the results that are being displayed. You might notice
that the calculation will not work if you type more than one space between any two
numbers or if you leave a space after the last number. Well, I am not going to do
everything. This is a good exercise for you to do. Good Luck!!!<BR><BR><BR>
<left> Enter numbers here--> <Input type="text" Name="expr" size=30>
<Input Type="button" Value="calculate" Onclick="compute(this.form)">
<Input Type="reset" Value="Clear"><BR><BR></left>
<Input Type="checkbox" Name="gettotal">Click here to find the Total<BR>
<Input Type="checkbox" Name="getmin" >Click here to find the Smallest<BR>
<Input Type="checkbox" Name="getmax">Click here to find the Largest<BR><BR>
Total:------><Input Type="text" name="total" size=15><BR>
Smallest:---><Input Type="text" name="min" size=15><BR>
Largest:----><Input Type="text" name="max" size=15><BR>
</Form>
```

- **Type = "reset"**. This option results in the display of a button that, when clicked, erases all information the user may have entered into the form. The input boxes are either cleared or restored to any default values that may have been set up when the form was defined.

- **Type = "button"**. This creates a button that, when clicked, will cause some action to occur. We'll soon see how to specify what the action is.

- **Name = "*some_name*"**. This assigns a name to the input area (box, button, or checkbox). The name is not visible to the user but, as we will see later, a scripting language can use these names when examining user input.

- **Value = "*some_value*"**. In general the value option depends on the input type. Here we have used it only with input types "button" and "reset." As Figure 8.12 shows, the string that is assigned to the value is the string that appears on the form's button.

- **Size = *number*.** When used with a text box, this option specifies the size of the box (measured in numbers of characters).

- **Onclick = "*some_action*"**. This is an example of an **event handler,** or the specification of some action whenever some event occurs. When applied to a button, this option specifies a script that is automatically executed whenever the button is clicked (the event). Presumably the script will intercept the form and all it contains and perform some action.

JAVASCRIPT AND CLIENT-SIDE PROGRAMMING

The final step is to explain how to write a script that responds to the form of Figure 8.12. Specifically, we need a script to do the following when the user clicks on the Calculate button:

- Determine a value for each checkbox that was selected and place the result in the appropriate text box.

- Generate an alert box (an error message) if the user did not select any checkboxes.

- Generate an alert box if the user did not type any numbers.

Figure 8.15 contains JavaScript code that does this. We will not assume any familiarity with JavaScript, but we will assume that the reader has knowledge of the C language and understands at least the basic concepts of object-oriented programming and object hierarchies. Furthermore, we will not attempt to provide any details of JavaScript beyond those which we need here.

Before we begin, there are several things to note relevant to the code in Figure 8.15:

- JavaScript code is delimited with <script> and </script> tags.

- The code resides in the head of the HTML document.

- The code contains five functions: compute, MakeArray, dototal, domin, and domax. As specified by the OnClick event handler in Figure 8.14, control will go first to the function compute, which will coordinate the actions the script must take.

```javascript
<Script language = javascript>

function MakeArray(form)
{
  var ind1=0;
  var ind2=0;
  var blank=" ";
  var i = 0;

  while ( (ind2=form.expr.value.indexOf(blank, ind1)) != -1)
    {
    this[++i]= parseInt(form.expr.value.substring(ind1, ind2));
    ind1=ind2+1
    }
  this[++i]=parseInt(form.expr.value.substring(ind1,form.expr.value.length));
  this.length=i;
}

function dototal(myarray, form)
{
  var sum=0;
  for (var i=1; i<=myarray.length; i++)
    sum = sum + myarray[i];
  form.total.value=sum;
}

function domin(myarray, form)
{
  var temp=myarray[1];

  for (var i=2; i<=myarray.length; i++)
    if (myarray[i] < temp)
      temp = myarray[i];
  form.min.value=temp;
}
```

Figure 8.15 JavaScript Code for Client-side Programming *(continues on next page)*

```
function domax(myarray, form)
{
  var temp=myarray[1];

  for (var i=2; i<=myarray.length; i++)
    if (myarray[i] > temp)
      temp = myarray[i];
  form.max.value=temp;
}

function compute(form)
{
  var myarray;

  if (form.expr.value.length==0)
    alert("You haven't entered any numbers")
  else
  if ( !form.gettotal.checked && !form.getmin.checked && !form.getmax.checked )
    alert("You haven't checked any of the boxes")
  else
  {
    myarray = new MakeArray(form);
    if (form.gettotal.checked)
      dototal(myarray, form);
    if (form.getmin.checked)
      domin(myarray, form);
    if (form.getmax.checked)
      domax(myarray, form);
  }
}

</script>
```

Figure 8.15   *(continued)*

- The numbers the user enters exist as a string expression. The JavaScript code must parse this string, locate the numbers, and store them into an array.
- JavaScript is an object-oriented language with a complex object hierarchy. We will not describe the entire hierarchy, but it is important to understand at least that part of the hierarchy relevant to the code in Figure 8.15.

Figure 8.16 shows the hierarchy that we need. JavaScript sees the form with which we are working as an object. The form is also a property of a **document object** (think of it as our HTML document). In general a document can have many forms. The form, in turn, also has properties, listed on the third level of the hierarchy in Figure 8.16. Each one corresponds to an input tag defined in the form of Figure 8.14. In fact, if you compare the name options of those tags and the names in Figure 8.16, you'll find they are the same. As we will soon discover, this will allow the script to access objects associated with those tags. There is more to Figure 8.16, but we'll describe it as the need arises.

Recall from Figure 8.14 that the input tag of type "button" has another option of the form Onclick="compute(this.form)". When the user clicks on that button, control goes to the JavaScript function named compute. Furthermore, the current form object, along with all of its properties and methods, is passed to the function. The keyword this is commonly used in JavaScript to refer to a current object. Of course, *current* depends on the context in which it is used. In this case, this.form refers to the current form (the one in Figure 8.14) in the current HTML document.

Once control passes to the function compute, the function's parameter allows JavaScript code to access all information about the form through the object named form. The first thing that compute checks is whether the user has entered any numbers in the form. Recall from Figure 8.14 that the form contains an input tag of type "text" that has a name of expr. This is where user input goes, and expr is also a property of the object form (see Figure 8.16). Furthermore, the object hierarchy also shows that expr has a value property. It represents the actual string entered through the expr text box. Last, since each string has a length representing the number of characters in it, value has a property named length. If the user enters no characters, the string's length is 0. Consequently, JavaScript checks this condition by comparing form.expr.value.length with 0 (note that the dotted expression corresponds to a sequence of properties defined by the object hierarchy in Figure 8.16). If it is a match, JavaScript calls an alert function, passing the string "you haven't entered any

Figure 8.16   JavaScript Object Hierarchy Relevant to Figure 8.15

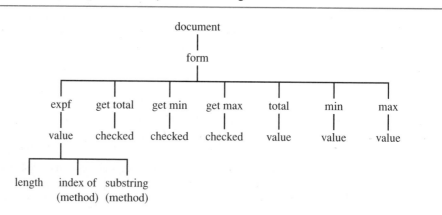

numbers". The alert function causes a window like that in Figure 8.13b to appear. Of course, if the length is not 0 that step is skipped and no alert box appears. Note that a non-zero length does not mean the user has actually entered numbers. It means only that the user has typed something. This script does not check the string for non-numeric characters. We leave it as an exercise to expand error-checking capabilities.

Next, JavaScript must determine whether any of the checkboxes were selected. Again it uses the object hierarchy to do this. There are three checkboxes named gettotal, getmin, and getmax, and each is a property of the object form. Because each is defined as type "checkbox", each has a property called checked. If the user moves the mouse cursor over a checkbox and clicks a mouse button, the corresponding checked property is set to true. Consequently, each checked property is either true or false according to whether the corresponding checkbox was selected by the user. The second if statement in compute compares the checked property of each checkbox and, if all are false, displays another alert box.

If at least one checkbox is selected, control passes to the last else clause. The first line,

myarray = new MakeArray(form)

calls a function that parses the user-entered string, and stores all the numbers in the array named myarray. (We'll see how that works shortly.) The remaining three if statements again determine which checkboxes were selected. For each one that was selected, JavaScript calls a function to do the designated task. For example, the function dototal sums up the values in the array myarray using a variable sum. The last line in dototal stores the sum in form.total.value. This latter expression follows the object hierarchy and assigns the sum as the value of a text box named total. Because of this, the actual sum appears in that box on the form, as shown in Figure 8.12.

The functions domin and domax determine the smallest and largest values in myarray, respectively. They assign the results in a manner similar to that in dototal.

The last piece of the puzzle is to describe how JavaScript extracts the numbers from the user-entered text string. A full understanding of how this happens is probably not possible without a more complete description of JavaScript and its objects and types. We will outline the main ideas and leave it to the reader to consult a textbook on JavaScript for further details on their implementation.

Essentially, the line (from the function compute)

myarray=new MakeArray(form)

calls on a function MakeArray, which creates and returns an array object containing the needed numbers. Within that function JavaScript code assumes the numbers are stored in a text string with a single blank space separating each number. As before, JavaScript refers to the string using the object notation form.expr.value. It then calls on a method form.expr.value.indexOf(blank, ind1), which returns the first index (or subscript) of the first blank character located past position ind1. Initially, ind1 is 0, so the first call to this method finds the index of the first blank in the string. As the loop is executed, Figure 8.17 shows how ind1 and ind2 relate to the text string. In general, they delimit the characters representing one of the numbers entered by the user. The two index values are used in a substring method that extracts a substring consisting

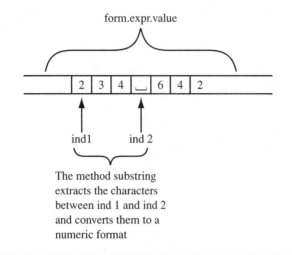

form.expr.value

The method substring extracts the characters between ind 1 and ind 2 and converts them to a numeric format

Figure 8.17 Extracting Numbers from a Text String

of characters between them. Finally, JavaScript uses the function parseInt to convert that substring into a numeric format.

As JavaScript goes through the loop, it stores converted substrings into an array object named this. As mentioned before, this is a keyword used to refer to a calling object. In this case the function MakeArray acts much like a constructor for the array object myarray. Consequently, used in this context this actually corresponds to the object array myarray.

Common Gateway Interface and Server-side Programming

The last topic in this section addresses server-side programming. For example, during your hours of Web surfing you may have wondered how a search engine works. You know it accepts one or more keywords you give it and that something at another site looks up possible references and sends them back to you. Our task here is to describe how this works and to write a search engine stub. As with previous topics, there are several ways to do server side programming. Again, however, we will focus on one particular, but fairly standard, technique. Those interested in alternatives should consult a book on HTML programming or on Web development.

We already know that an HTTP server can do some simple tasks, such as sending a requested document back to an HTTP client. However, some activities, such as those found in search engines, require more complexity than HTTP servers are equipped to handle. In such cases the HTTP server relies on a **gateway program** to handle additional logic. Gateway programs may be written in languages such as C or even shell scripts such as a Bourne shell script in UNIX. Our task here is to introduce the **Common Gateway Interface (CGI),** which allows a server to communicate with a gateway program. Once done, it is a small step to writing your own gateway programs. We will conclude with a working example.

There are three questions we need to answer:

1. How does a gateway program get information from a client?
2. How does the gateway program do its task?
3. How does the gateway program send information back to the client?

The answer to the first item lies in the HTML form. Figure 8.18 shows a simple interface to a search engine, which we will simulate. It contains just the functional parts necessary to request a search: some simple instructions, a text box in which to enter your search words, a button to clear what you have typed, and a button to initiate the search.

Figure 8.19 shows the HTML code to generate this form. It is similar to the HTML code of Figure 8.14 except for two things we have not presented before. First, the input type of "submit" causes a button to appear on the form. Clicking that button causes the form, and information entered in it, to be submitted. Second, the options in the <form> tag indicate how the information is passed (method="get")[*] and

Figure 8.18   Interface Form to a Search Engine

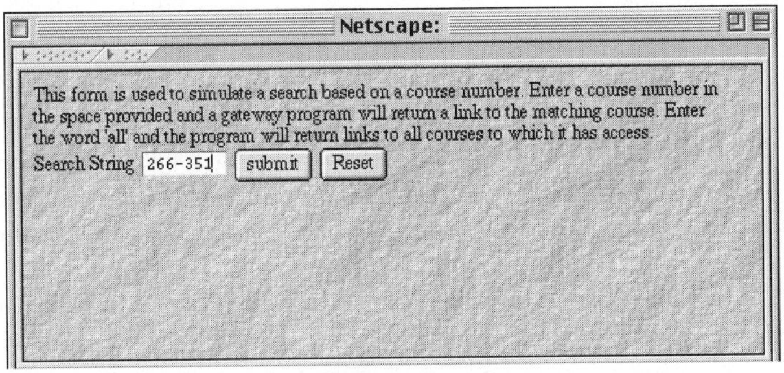

Figure 8.19   HTML Code for the Form of Figure 8.18

```
<form method="get" action="http://www.uwgb.edu/htbin/cgi.exe">
This form is used to simulate a search based on a course number. Enter a course number
in the space provided and a gateway program will return a link to the matching course
syllabus. Enter the word all and the program will return links to all courses to
which it has access.
<BR><BR>
Search String <Input Type="Text" Name="srch" size=8>
<Input Type="submit" Value = "submit">
<Input Type="reset">
</form>
```

---

[*]The get method is one way to send information to a gateway program. For alternatives consult a text on HTML or CGI programming.

the URL of the executable file that is the gateway program (action="http://www.uwgb.edu/htbin/cgi.exe").[*] The latter option indicates that the gateway program is in a file named cgi.exe in a system directory named htbin. Generally, network administrators require that gateway programs reside in a specific directory. For security reasons, they want to avoid defining protection limits that allow anyone off site to run programs in arbitrary accounts.

When a form is submitted using a get method, the HTTP client passes information as a string. The string consists of the referenced URL and a list of name/value pairs, each having the form "*name=value*." There is typically one name/value pair for each input item used to enter information. The name is that defined in the HTML code and the value is whatever the user has indicated. A question mark character (?) separates the name/value pairs from each other and from the URL. For example, suppose the user entered "266-351" in the above form, as shown in Figure 8.18. The HTTP client sends a character string of the form

http://www.uwgb.edu/htbin/cgi.exe?srch=266-351

Since there is only one input box in which to enter information, the string consists only of the URL and one name/value pair, srch=266-351.

Because the action option specified a gateway program named cgi.exe, the HTTP server passes the string to it. The gateway program must access that string and extract the necessary information. To do this, the CGI uses environment variables accessible by the gateway program. There are several different environment variables, but the one of concern here is query_string.

Figure 8.20 shows a gateway program written in C that does a "search" for whatever the user enters in our form. Examination of the gateway program reveals that this is really just a stub designed to test whether it can get the correct information from the environment variable and return the appropriate information to the user. The program contains an array of structures hard-coded into it containing the information being sought. Each structure consists of a course number (e.g., "266-351"), a URL, and a course title. This program will extract a course number from the query_string environment variable, search the array for a matching number, and return both the course name and URL to the client. Through the returned URL, the user sees a reference to the selected course.

For example, if the user entered "266-351" as Figure 8.18 shows, then the response returned would be as shown in Figure 8.21. The search results form echoes the string the user entered and below it displays a link represented by a course name. Using this form, the user can click on that name to follow the link. In effect we have mimicked exactly what a search engine does. There is a provision in our gateway program to return all URLs if the user enters the search string "all" instead of a course number. This was done to test whether the gateway program could return multiple links.

The only step left is to describe how the gateway program of Figure 8.20 generated the results in Figure 8.21. Most of the program is understandable to someone

---

[*]This references a gateway program at the author's site. Attempts at setting up your own gateway programs must be cleared with network personnel at the intended site.

```
#include <string.h>
#include <stdio.h>
#include <stdlib.h>
#include "cgilib.h"

// int cgi_show_env();

void listmatches();

// structure type subject to search
typedef struct {
    char cnum[32];
    char url[50];
    char cname[32];
} entry;

void main(int argc, char *argv[])
{
  // list of elements subject to search
  entry mystuff[25]=
    { "266-350", "http:// www.uwgb.edu/~shayw/syll350.htm", "Numerical Analysis",
      "266-351", "http:// www.uwgb.edu/~shayw/syll351.htm", "Data Structures",
      "266-358", "http:// www.uwgb.edu/~shayw/syll358.htm", "Computer Networks",
    };

  int i;
  int status;
  char * srchstring; // search string passed over from html form

  status = cgi_init(argc, argv);
  srchstring = cgi_info("QUERY_STRING"); // gets search string from environment variable
  if (srchstring = strchr(srchstring, '='))
    srchstring++;
  listmatches(mystuff, srchstring);
}

void listmatches(entry mystuff[25], char * srchstring)
{
  int i;

  cgi_printf("Content-type: text/html\n\n");
  cgi_printf("<html>\n");
```

Figure 8.20   C Code for Server Side CGI Programming *(continues on next page)*

```
cgi_printf("<body>\n");
cgi_printf("<h1>Search results</h1>\n");
cgi_printf("<h3>This is a list of links based on your search of</h3>");
cgi_printf("<h2>%s</h2></Center>\n\n\n", srchstring);
cgi-printf("<img src=http://www.uwgb.edu/~shayw/cool_fli.gif>
for (i=0;i<=2;i++)
{
  if (strstr(mystuff[i].cnum, srchstring)||strstr(srchstring, "all") )
    {
      cgi_printf("<A href=%s> %s </A>\n<BR>",
        mystuff[i].url, mystuff[i].cname);
    }
}
cgi_printf("</body>\n");
cgi_printf("</html>\n");
}
```

Figure 8.20   *(concluded)*

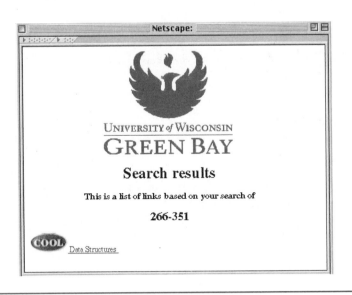

Figure 8.21   Results of Search

with a knowledge of C, so we will focus on parts that relate strictly to the exchange of information with the client. As previously stated, the first thing the gateway program must do is get the query string. It does this through the statement

```
srchstring = cgi_info("QUERY_STRING");
```

which puts the string into the C variable srchstring. In this example we are assuming that the form allows only one input box and that the user has entered only a single search phrase (either a course number or the word all). This simplifies the program logic; we leave it as an exercise to expand on this program. Since the search string has the form

url?srch=phrase

the program need only locate the "=" to find the phrase for which it must search. It uses the C string function strchr to locate the "=" and redefines the variable srchstring to locate the phrase. Finally, it calls on the function listmatches passing over the phrase.

This function employs a standard linear search of an array to look for the phrase and display the results. The difference is the presence of a collection of cgi_printf statements. These statements are very much like C's printf statements, with one fundamental difference. The printf statement sends output to a standard output device. The cgi_printf statement sends output to a document that will be interpreted as an HTML document. Examination of these statements reveals that they are producing HTML code.

Inside the loop, the program looks for a match between the phrase and the course numbers of each array item. When one is found, the statement

```
cgi_printf("<A href=%s> %s </A>\n<BR>", mystuff[i].url, mystuff[i].cname);
```

sends both the URL and name associated with the matching record to an HTML document. Note that they are contained in an anchor tag. When the program finishes, the HTTP server sends this document back to the client, where the document is displayed according to the rules of HTML. The result is that the user sees the appropriate name, which is actually a clickable reference corresponding to the URL returned. The search is complete and the user clicks on the name to follow the reference.

If the user had entered "all" instead of a course number, he or she would have seen references to all of the URLs listed in the array structure.

8.3   ELECTRONIC MAIL: X.400 AND X.500 STANDARDS

Once again we visit the topic of electronic mail (email), not because we like being redundant but because the SMTP of Section 8.1 is not the only email protocol. An entire series of standards developed by ITU-T describes the transfer and delivery of mail. Recall that electronic mail allows users to exchange messages. The sender enters a message and an identifier of the intended recipient. The message is then deposited in that person's "mailbox." The recipient can check the mailbox and display messages at any time.

Figure 8.22 shows how electronic mail works from the user's perspective. The electronic mail service is an application with which a user interacts. Sending mail means interacting with an electronic mail application that accepts mail and deposits it in local storage near the intended recipient. The recipient then can display the messages at his or her convenience.

Displaying messages is only a small part of the email service. For example, if a user is on vacation for several weeks, messages may accumulate. Rather than going

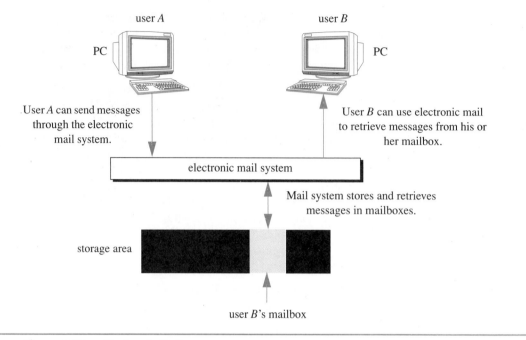

Figure 8.22 Electronic Mail

through them sequentially, the user can request a list of them. The list reports attributes such as the size of each message and who sent it. It also displays a short comment describing the message. The comment could be "critical information about your future at this company" or "junk mail." The sender must include the comment because the electronic mail system has no idea what the message says. The list also may specify whether the message is new or has been answered or forwarded. So when you see 50 new "critical" messages from your boss, you might consider answering them before perusing your junk mail!

X.400 MAIL STANDARDS

Due to the popularity of email, the ITU-T issued its own standards for email in 1984. They are referred to collectively as the **X.400 family** of standards, and they operate at the OSI application layer. X.400 also forms the foundation of the ISO email system, MOTIS, and is the ISO analog to TCP/IP's SMTP. It is based on a model for message handling systems illustrated by Figure 8.23. The model has four main parts: **user agent (UA), message transfer agent (MTA), message handling system (MHS),** and **message transfer system (MTS).**

Superficially, the user agent interacts with the user and essentially defines what the user can do. The MTAs define a collection of nodes that execute a protocol to

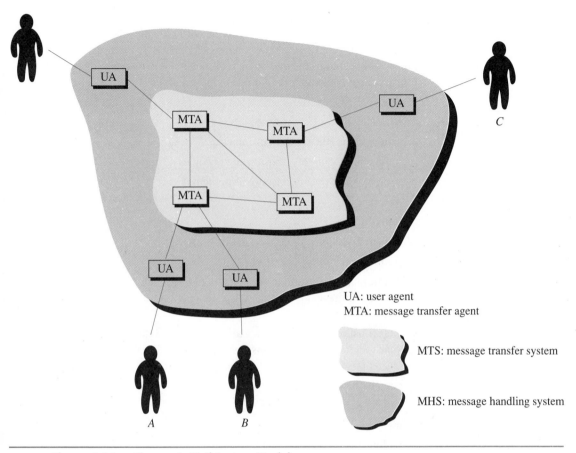

UA: user agent
MTA: message transfer agent

MTS: message transfer system

MHS: message handling system

Figure 8.23   Electronic Mail System Model

ensure proper routing of mail. They form the backbone of the mail system, and their physical connections vary. They play a role similar to that of routers in internetworks but operate at a higher OSI layer. Collectively the MTAs form the message transfer system. The MTAs and UAs form the message handling system, which ensures the eventual delivery of mail. Let's now examine each component in greater detail.

User Agent   The UA is the user interface. It has two main functions. First, it routes messages between the user and the local MTA, allowing the user to send and receive mail. Second, it manages the **message store (MS),** which, as you probably suspect, is used to store messages. The UA performs its functions at the request of the user and, to the user at least, defines the system's capabilities. The following list includes some of the UA's functions.

- Send mail. The UA accepts a message and address from a user and gives it to the MTA for delivery. The UA will invoke an editor to allow the user to write a message or it will simply send the contents of a previously constructed file (which presumably contains the message). It also appends a **header** (Figure 8.24) to the user message containing the following information:

  a. sender

  b. recipients

  c. cc recipients (those who get copies)

  d. blind copy recipients (those who get copies secretly)

  e. subject (short note describing its contents)

  f. message ID

  g. reply-by date

  h. sensitivity (degree of confidentiality)

  i. priority

  This information is useful to the receiving UA for delivering the message to the appropriate users and for displaying a summary of all mail messages in a user's mailbox.

- Display a list of mail messages. This is similar to a directory list in a computer account that lists all files. In this case, the UA provides a list of all messages for the current user. Each entry in the list typically contains the following items:

  a. source of the message

  b. subject field

  c. message size

  d. various indicators indicating whether the message has been read, deleted, answered, or forwarded to another user

  e. message ID

  f. date received

- Display the contents of a message on the computer or workstation screen.

Figure 8.24   Messages, Headers, and Envelopes

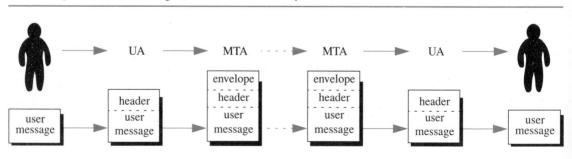

- Reply. The UA allows the user to respond to a currently displayed message by invoking an editor through which the user can construct a response. When the user is finished, the UA automatically sends the response to the source of the previously displayed message.

- Forward the current message to one or more specified recipients.

- Extract the message and store it in a file. This is convenient if you want to save a message, print it, or make it available to others without explicitly forwarding it to them.

- Delete unwanted messages. Note that messages are not always physically deleted but rather are marked for deletion. Then another command such as a purge deletes all files marked for deletion. This allows accidentally deleted messages to be recovered.

- Undelete a message. Removes the deletion mark mentioned previously.

Message Transfer Agent   The MTA is software running on a dedicated workstation or computer and is part of the email system's backbone. Each MTA communicates with one or more UAs and other MTAs. Its basic function is to accept mail from a UA or another MTA, examine it, and route it. For example, when it receives mail from a UA it verifies the format of the mail. If it is not correct it informs the UA an error has occurred so the sender can be notified. If it is correct there are two possibilities. First, the recipient is reachable via another UA to which the MTA is connected. An example is user A sending mail to user B in Figure 8.23. In this case the MTA gives the mail to the appropriate UA for delivery. Second, the UA that will deliver the mail is connected to another MTA. Here user A may have sent mail to user C in Figure 8.23. In this case the mail must be routed to another MTA. Collectively the MTAs execute a routing strategy that sends the mail through one or more MTAs until it reaches the desired one. Then the mail is sent to the appropriate UA for delivery.

Recall that the UA appends a header to a message sent from the user. If the MTA must route the mail to another MTA it also appends additional bytes to the message and header. These additional bytes are called the **envelope** (Figure 8.24).This is similar to the terminology used by the postal system. Letters are inserted into envelopes that contain the necessary information for delivery or return. The envelope is used by the MTAs for routing, error checking, and verification. The following are some of the fields in the envelope:

- Destination address

- Sender address for possible acknowledgment or return

- Mail identification number

- Priority. As with regular mail, higher priorities may hasten delivery (at increased cost, of course) or may bring out the worst in the system, like putting "Fragile" on a package.

- Deferred date. A user may specify that delivery must occur after a given date.

- Delivery date. A user may specify that delivery must occur before a given date. (Good luck!)
- Field specifying whether a message should be returned if it cannot be delivered
- Bytes for error detection
- Encryption information, such as the location of a key
- Digital signatures. This field can provide authentication of the sender. For example, recall the encryption method from Section 4.6. This is useful if a sender later denies transmitting something, or at least "cannot recall" sending it. (It's amazing what people may forget in front of investigating committees, court-martials, tribunals, the press, or other unfriendly questioners.) Digital signatures also can be used to verify receipt of a message.

Message Transfer System   The MTAs are physically connected in ways similar to the network topologies discussed earlier. They need not be part of the same computer system. Collectively they form the message transfer system (MTS). Mail travels through MTAs depending on its source and destination, somewhat like files under FTP or mail under SMTP. X.400, however, operates on a **store-and-forward** concept. Each MTA runs the X.400 protocols transferring the message in its entirety from one MTA to the next. That is, each entire message is stored at each MTA between the originator and recipient.

This system differs from previous protocols in which individual packets or datagrams are stored at intermediate nodes but are assembled at the destination. This is not to say that X.400 messages are not divided into smaller packets at lower levels, but it does mean that each MTA node runs protocols up to the application layer and that messages are stored intact at each MTA (Figure 8.25). This approach may seem less efficient than simply reassembling them at the destination, but it is useful when the mail must go through networks running dissimilar network and transport layers. Protocols such as FTP and SMTP assume similar transport protocols (TCP).

Message Handling System   The MHS, the most extensive part of the mail model, contains all the MTAs and UAs. It also includes specifications on, among other things, interaction between two UAs, two MTAs, and a UA and MTA. About the only thing not included is the interface between the UA and user.

The MHS can handle three types of protocol data units (PDUs): messages, probes, and reports. A **message** contains the user information, header, and envelope. A **probe** consists of an envelope only, a seemingly strange thing to have. Its purpose is to determine whether a specific destination is reachable without actually sending anything (perhaps similar to sending an empty envelope through the mail to see if a destination exists before shipping a warehouse full of furniture). The **report** (also called **reply**) is a response sent to the source of a previous message specifying whether it has been received.

ITU-T has defined several standards for MHS operations. Some of those standards, which constitute the X.400 family, are summarized in Table 8.7.

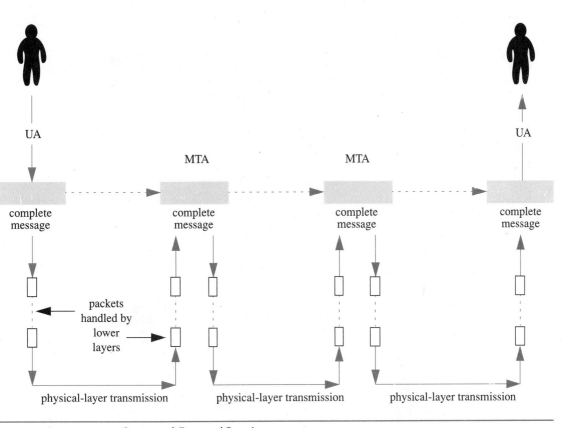

Figure 8.25   Store-and-Forward Routing

MHS is defined in part by a series of protocols (called the **P protocols**) that define communication between various components. As we have discussed many times throughout this book, protocols are used to define the interaction between two distinct entities. The MHS is no exception. Figure 8.26 shows some of the protocols and the agents that communicate using them.

The **P1 protocol (message transfer protocol)** defines communication between two MTAs. The first MTA creates the envelope according to P1 specifications, and subsequent MTAs interpret the envelope's contents. P1 treats the message and header as data and makes no attempt to interpret anything in them. The **P2 protocol,** sometimes called the **interpersonal messaging (IPM) protocol,** deals with the header and body of a message and defines the exchange between two UAs. The sending UA creates the header, and the receiving UA interprets its contents.

When the UA and MTA reside in the same system they typically communicate using proprietary software. However, sometimes they may run remotely (in separate locations). For example, a UA may be in a PC, with the MTA accessed via a dialup line or an X.25 connection. In such cases another ITU-T protocol, the **P3 protocol** or **submission and delivery protocol,** defines the interaction between them. Finally,

Table 8.7   Some of the X.400 Family of Protocols

STANDARD	FUNCTION	MEANING
X.400	System service and overview	Describes MHS services, interactions among various components of the MHS, protocol layering, and naming and address conventions.
X.402	MHS architecture	Describes MHS architecture and rules for naming and addressing.
X.403	Testing	Describes testing requirements, timers, procedures, and protocol data units.
X.408	Code conversion	Specifies rules for converting between different codes and formats.
X.411	MTS overview	Describes how MTS works.
X.413	Message store	Defines the message store (MS).
X.419	MHS protocols	Describes MHS protocols P1, P3, and P7 defining communication among MTA components.
X.420	Interpersonal messaging	Describes both interpersonal messaging and the P2 protocol.

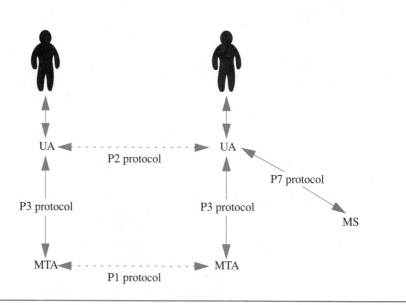

Figure 8.26   P Protocols

when a user wants to access mailed messages he or she does so through the UA. The UA, in turn, accesses the message store (MS), the place where messages are stored. The **P7 protocol** defines the interaction between the UA and MS.

These descriptions give you a basic outline of the structure of an X.400 mail system and introduce you to some of the terminology. The entire protocol contains vast amounts of information and could fill a textbook. It you are interested in more detailed discussions, Reference [Bl91] has them.

An X.400 system can provide the typical operations of sending and receiving mail as well as many more services, such as those in the following list (actually specified by the X.401 protocol):

- **Alternate recipient allowed** lets the originating UA specify an alternate recipient in case the intended recipient cannot be found. In this case the mail goes to the alternate.

- **Authorizing users indication** allows the originator to specify who authorized the mail being sent.

- **Blind copy recipient** indication lets the originating UA cc (send copies of the mail to others). The difference between this and the normal cc function is that the blind recipients are not identified to those receiving the mail.

- **Cross referencing indication** specifies other mail related to the current message.

- **Deferred delivery service** lets the originator specify a time and date after which the mail should be delivered. The mail should not be delivered before that date.

- **Deferred delivery cancellation** lets the originating UA cancel a deferred delivery message.

- **Delivery notification** provides an acknowledgment to the originating UA when the mail has been delivered. Note that it does not mean the recipient has actually read the mail, just that the mail has been delivered.

- **Expiry date indication** allows the originator to specify to the recipient a time and date after which the message is invalid. MHS does not specify what happens when the time has passed.

- **Grade of delivery service** lets the sending UA specify whether the mail should be sent on an urgent, normal, or nonurgent basis. This is similar to the different classes of delivery defined by the postal system.

- **Hold for delivery service** lets a UA request that the MTS hold mail destined for it. This is useful when the UA is not available to receive mail. It is similar to an individual requesting that the post office hold all incoming mail while he or she is on vacation.

- **Latest delivery service** allows the originating UA to specify a time before which the mail must be delivered. This is useful when it absolutely, positively has to be there by a certain time.

- **Multidestination delivery service** allows mail to be sent to multiple recipients.

- **Nondelivery notification** allows the originating UA to be notified when mail was not delivered properly.

- **Probe service** lets a UA determine whether mail can be delivered to an address without actually sending any mail.

- **Proof of delivery service** allows the authentication of the recipients of a message and its contents using digital signature encryption techniques.

- **Proof of submission service** provides proof that a message has been submitted to the MTS for delivery.

- **Redirection of incoming messages** service allows a UA to redirect all incoming messages to another UA. This is similar to routing all your new work to a colleague while you are on vacation.

- **Reply request indication** requests that the recipient reply to the message.

- **Return of content service** provides for mail to be returned in the event it is not delivered.

- **Stored message deletion service** allows a UA to remove mail from its MS. It's like throwing away your unwanted mail.

- **Stored message listing service** provides a list of messages in the MS.

- **Stored message fetching service** lets the UA retrieve specific mail from the MS.

There are many more services available, but many are less common than those above. If you are interested, References [Bl91] and [St97] contain an extensive list of services.

X.500 DIRECTORY SERVICE

One significant design aspect of any mail system is **addressing,** the method of identifying any one of the potential recipients. One approach to addressing is the domain system discussed in Sections 7.2 and 7.4, familiar to anyone using email over the Internet. However, the growth of the Internet has created a serious address depletion problem for IPv4, causing some to worry that soon there will be more users than allowable addresses. Since the ITU-T recommendations are made with the intention of connecting the entire population of the industrialized world, ITU-T standards take a different approach to addressing.

As we know, email systems allow users to send messages to others, but there is always one stipulation: the email address must be provided. Therefore, another important issue is the **mail directory** or **directory service** (Ref. [We13]), which provides the address of an individual given that he or she is unambiguously identified. It is similar to the telephone system: You can call almost anywhere in the world, but you must know the number first. If you don't know the number, resources such as telephone books or directory assistance can help, but even they are restrictive. Telephone books can be up to a year out of date. Using directory assistance requires that you first know the area code in which the desired person resides. Then you dial the directory assistance for that code and specify the name of the person you want to call. Typically you must also specify the person's address. Dialing directory assistance for the 312 area code (Chicago area) and asking for John Smith's number will not be very productive.

After developing the X.400 standards the ITU-T wanted to define standards for a directory with functions similar to those of the telephone directory. The result is the **X.500 directory service standard,** which has several important features:

- **Distributed directory.** The actual directory would be distributed across many sites throughout the world. It appears as a single centralized directory to each user (Figure 8.27), but it is located and maintained at physically separate sites. This is unlike the telephone system, in which a user has to call a different directory assistance depending on the area code.

- **Hierarchical structure.** This is similar to the telephone system, in which the area code defines a geographic region. Even within the region telephones with the same three-digit prefix tend to be from the same area of town. It is unlike the Internet system, however. No, we haven't forgotten that we described the Domain Name System of the Internet as a hierarchical organization, but it is more logical than physical. For example, two sites with the same .edu domain name can reside in the same city or at opposite ends of the United States. Don't conclude from this that there is no directory service for the Internet. The Network Information Center (NIC) maintains a WHOIS database with a query facility that allows users to search the database.

- **Consistency.** Some call it a **homogeneous name space.** Basically it means that all users see the same information presented the same way. On a global scale this is a daunting requirement. Telephone numbers in the United States all have the same format, but the format changes for international calls. Similarly, Internet addresses have the same format, but address formats of non-Internet sites differ.

- **Address lookup service.** Again, it is similar to the telephone service but more general. The user could get an address by specifying a variety of items that uniquely identify a person, for example, the person's name, where he or she works, the department he or she is in, or his or her telephone extension. Services also include abilities similar to those provided by the yellow pages. A user could get a range of addresses for businesses providing a particular type of service or addresses within a particular department in a large company.

Figure 8.27   Distributed Directory

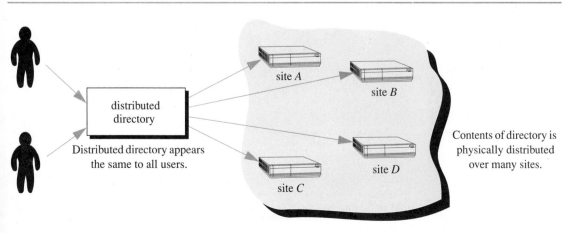

The structure of the X.500 directory is primarily a distributed hierarchy. That is, it has a logical hierarchical structure (tree), but parts of the tree are maintained at different sites. Collectively, all of the information in the directory is called the **directory information base (DIB).** The DIB consists of entries each of which contains information about a real-world entity such as a country, company, department, or person. The entries are organized in hierarchical fashion and form the **directory information tree (DIT).** The distributed aspect means that different branches of the tree are maintained by different organizations, but collectively the hierarchy is maintained. Each entry contains attributes describing the object it represents. Therefore, to specify an object represented in the DIB a user must uniquely identify attributes of the entries leading to it.

Figure 8.28 shows an example DIT. Here second-level nodes correspond to countries, third-level nodes to organizations within a country, fourth-level nodes to departments within an organization, and fifth-level nodes to a person within a department. The information shown means that Mary Smith works as a senior engineer in the engineering department at the ACME corporation in the United States. Thus, if someone wanted to send email to Mary Smith he would specify the following:

$$C = US, \qquad O = ACME, \qquad D = engineering, \qquad N = Mary\ Smith$$

This format represents a keyword approach to referencing directory information, using *C* for country, *O* for organization, *D* for department, and *N* for name. The

Figure 8.28 Directory Information Tree

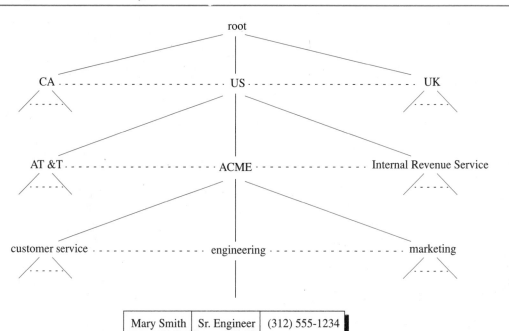

keywords and attributes define a path from the tree's root to the desired entry. If there were several Mary Smiths working in the same department, the format would require additional attributes specifying the proper Mary Smith. These could include Mary Smith's title, telephone number, or postal address. Somewhere there must be an attribute distinguishing the two Mary Smiths. (Either that, or Mary Smith has a clone.)

It is worth mentioning that X.500 uses object-oriented terminology to describe its DIT. Each DIT node corresponds to an object and belongs to an object class. All entries in an object class have the same attributes and the same parent in the DIT (Figure 8.29). Furthermore, an object class inherits the attributes from the object class of its parent and forms a subclass. Consequently, the attribute list that defines a DIT entry also defines the path from the root to that entry. One main advantage of using objects and object classes is the ability to create new classes by extending or modifying other classes. This is one of the prime motivators of the object-oriented paradigm in many fields of computer science.

Two more important components of the X.500 model are the **directory user agent (DUA)** and **directory system agent (DSA)** (Figure 8.30). They play roles

Figure 8.29   Object Class

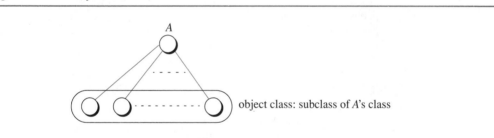

Figure 8.30   Directory Structure

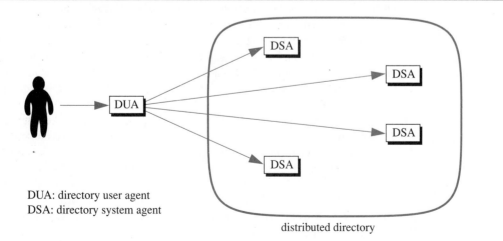

DUA: directory user agent
DSA: directory system agent

distributed directory

similar to the UA and MTA in the X.400 model. A network user typically makes a request through some application that interfaces with the DUA. The DUA, in turn, interacts with the distributed directory to provide whatever service the user requested. Typical services are finding the email address of a user, changing someone's address, or inserting and deleting addresses. Remember, however, that the directory is distributed over many sites (potentially hundreds) and that each site contains part of the directory managed by the DSA at that site. Thus the DUA, through network protocols, accesses the proper DSA in response to the user's request.

SUMMARY

This section on X.400 and X.500 standards cannot begin to fully describe the complexity of managing and transmitting information on a global scale. In fact, you should not think of these standards as finished products. Much developmental work is still being done, and X.400 is not without its detractors. Some cite its "lackluster performance as a platform for LAN applications" as a shortcoming. It also has stiff competition from other mail services such as SMTP and Novell's Message Handling Service (MHS). Even so, companies such as AT&T, IBM, Sun Microsystems, and Digital Equipment Corporation are supporting numerous X.400 products. Many believe these standards will form the foundation for future gateways that will be able to interpret a wide array of business documents and applications and pave the way for a truly global communications system.

8.4 INTEGRATED SERVICES DIGITAL NETWORK

Over 100 years ago people began stringing wires between houses and towns so they could communicate by telephone. Since then the telephone network has evolved into a global communications system using every communications medium we have described in this book. There is one more feature that distinguishes the telephone system from other networks we have discussed: It has a large analog component. We haven't forgotten that optical fibers and digital switching devices have introduced significant amounts of digital technology into the network. Telephones, however, are still analog devices transmitting analog signals to the local exchange office. This part of the telephone network is often called the **local loop** or the **last mile.** (The latter phrase refers to the largest impediment to an all-digital system.)

Initially, the analog system was a logical choice because the telephone was designed to transmit a person's voice. Since then the two fields of communications and computer science have been merging. Computers are critical to communications systems, and communications systems are commonly used to connect computers. Consequently, the ITU-T is developing a standard for a global digital communications system called the **Integrated Services Digital Network (ISDN).** If fully implemented, it would allow the complete integration of both voice and nonvoice (e.g., data, fax, video) transmission within a single system. We will discuss the numerous advantages of such a system shortly.

Figure 8.31 shows the functionality of ISDN's **basic rate.** It provides three separate channels: two **B channels** transmitting at 64 Kbps and one **D channel** transmitting at 16 Kbps. It is often referred to as **2B+D.** The B channels transmit pure data such as pulse code modulated (PCM) voice data or data generated by other devices such as a PC. The D channel is used for control and for some low-speed applications such as **telemetry** (remote reading of meters) or alarm systems. The three channels are time-division multiplexed onto a **bit pipe** providing the actual bit transmission.

ITU-T also has developed a North American standard for a **primary rate** of 23B+D (23 B channels and one D channel), which fits nicely onto the T-1 carrier system. It also has a European standard of 30B+D, which fits onto their 2.048 Mbps channel. The additional data channels provide the capacity for more data from different sources.

Oddly enough, the biggest impediments to eventually implementing a global digital communications system are not the technical problems (but do not underestimate them). The main problems are logistical and economical. One significant problem is convincing telephone users that they will benefit from ISDN and that the conversion costs will be justified. Most people use their telephone systems for one thing: reaching out and talking with friends and neighbors. They don't care whether their voice is carried via analog or digital signals. On the other hand, the advantages of the ISDN basic service providing two data channels are easily articulated. For

Figure 8.31   ISDN Basic Service

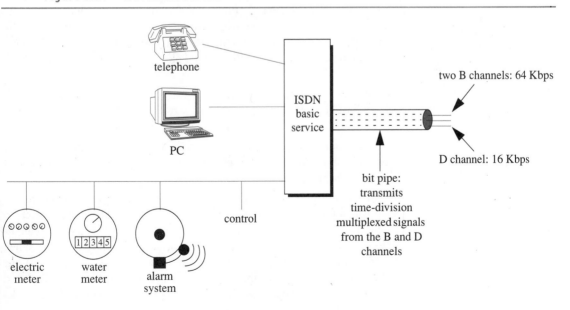

example, parents would no longer be stuck when their son or daughter monopolizes the line, because they would have a second line. (Of course, if they have two children they might still be out of luck.)

ISDN Services

This section lists some of the services that an all-digital system would provide. Some of them are already implemented in many parts of the world on a regional or company-wide basis. The eventual goal is to make them available to everyone. Furthermore, an all-digital system would facilitate the implementation of services. Many of them, for example, would require an on-site video screen and some of the text-processing ability of a PC.

- One of the B channels could be used to send messages electronically. They could be routed depending on the recipient's telephone number and stored in a local repository near the recipient for eventual access.

- Telephone numbers of incoming calls could be displayed even before the telephone is answered. Remember, digital systems mean that both outgoing data and incoming signals are digitized. The source number could be encoded in the received signals. This feature would allow you to decide whether you want to answer the telephone and would deter obscene or crank phone calls. It also would facilitate the identification of incoming calls to a 911 emergency system, a particular advantage if the caller is incoherent or a very small child. The downside of this ability is that it defeats the purpose of unlisted numbers. Thus, provisions must be available to turn off the display of such numbers.

- Telephone numbers of incoming calls could also be used as keys to database records. This has applications for professionals who deal with clients or patients (doctors, lawyers, brokers, insurance agents, and so on). Software could use the incoming source number to access the client's record and to display pertinent information on a screen. This feature would allow the professional to answer questions quickly and efficiently.

- Voice mail service similar to the service already provided by answering machines would allow callers to leave messages. The difference is that messages would be recorded and stored in a local repository.

- Fax transmission service would allow faxing of documents or video screens. In one possible application, photographs taken at automatic bank machines could be faxed to a bank for security.

- Every month utility companies send employees to neighborhood homes to read electric, gas, and water meters. ISDN telemetry service would allow the meters to be connected to the company and monthly readings accessed via a simple call. In addition, sensors could be placed in a home to detect fires or illegal entries. When they are activated, telephone calls could be made automatically to the nearest fire or police station. At the station the number of the incoming call could be displayed or used to access a database providing the address from which the call was made.

- Videotex, interactive access to remote databases, would allow access to, for example, directory databases providing telephone listings such as those currently found in telephone books. Users could access library databases and query what they have in their collections and access encyclopedias or public records to get information on a particular topic.

- Users could transfer money between bank accounts, shop by entering product codes and credit card numbers, and pay off credit balances by transferring money from their bank accounts—all by telephone.

- Multiple B channels would allow some of these activities to be done simultaneously. If a family member were currently using the telephone to talk to a friend, another person could use the other channel to perform another activity.

The potential applications are staggering. Unfortunately, so are the potential abuses. Having so much information available by a simple phone call will require enormous security efforts. It also raises important social and ethical issues. How much information should be available? How do you prevent it from falling into the wrong hands? Could telemetry be extended to monitor (and perhaps control) other events in the home? Capabilities already allow electric companies to remotely turn off power to air conditioners (with the customer's permission) during peak usage times. Could (should) this power be extended to control energy use during an energy crisis? (Who defines when a crisis exists?) These are topics of which any serious student of communications should be aware.

ISDN ARCHITECTURE

An ISDN should work with a large variety of users and equipment, especially if it is to be integrated into an office environment. This includes both equipment designed with ISDN in mind and current equipment whose design predates ISDN and has little in common with it. To help in the design of connection strategies and the standardization of interfaces, ITU-T has divided the equipment into **functional groups.** Devices within a group provide specific capabilities. ITU-T has also defined **reference points** used to separate these groups, a useful aid to standardizing interfaces. Together they help categorize basic connection strategies and provide a basis on which to design more complex architectures. The following list describes the primary functional group designations.

- **NT1 (network termination 1).** Nonintelligent devices concerned with physical and electrical characteristics of the signals. They primarily perform OSI layer 1 functions such as synchronizing and timing. NT1 devices typically form the boundary between a user's site and the ISDN central office. The central office, in turn, functions much as the telephone system's central office, providing access to other sites.

- **NT2 (network termination 2).** Intelligent devices capable of performing functions specified in OSI layers 2 and 3. Among this group's functions are switching, concentration, and multiplexing. A common NT2 device is a digital PBX. It can be used to connect a user's equipment together or to an NT1 to provide access to the ISDN central office.

- **NT12.** Combination of NT1 and NT2 into a single device.

- **TE1 (terminal equipment 1).** ISDN devices such as an ISDN terminal, digital telephone, or computer with an ISDN-compatible interface. Such devices typically connect directly to a network termination device.

- **TE2 (terminal equipment 2).** Non-ISDN devices, including printers, PCs, analog telephones, or anything that has a non-ISDN interface such as RS.232 or X.21.

- **TA (terminal adapter).** Device designed to be used with TE2 equipment to convert their signals to an ISDN-compatible format. The purpose is to integrate non-ISDN devices into an ISDN network.

Figure 8.32 shows typical functional groups and how they can be connected. To standardize the interfaces ITU-T has defined reference points between the groups. Although the connections shown are rather simple, they can be combined into much larger and more complex ones. However, the reference points will always divide the functional groups as shown. There are four reference points:

1. **Reference point R** separates TE2 equipment from the TA (Figure 8.32a). Point R can correspond to several different interfaces according to the TE2's standard.

2. **Reference point S** separates NT2 equipment from ISDN devices (Figure 8.32a,b). It supports a 2B+D channel and has a bit rate of 192 Kbps.[*] Effectively, it separates devices dedicated to user functions from devices devoted to communications functions.

3. **Reference point T** is the access point to the customer's site (Figure 8.32a,c). Generally, it separates the customer's equipment from the network provider's equipment. Typically, if T is an interface between an NT1 and either terminal equipment or adapter it corresponds to a 2B+D channel. If it lies between two NT devices it corresponds to a 23B+D channel.

4. **Reference point U** defines the connection between an NT1 and the ISDN central office (Figure 8.32d). Communication between different sites can go through one or more **signal transfer points** (a type of routing device) and are handled by a protocol known as Signaling System no. 7 (described shortly).

---

[*]The bit rates from the two B channels and the D channel add up to 144 Kbps. Additional overhead bits push the bit rate up to 192 Kbps, as we will show soon.

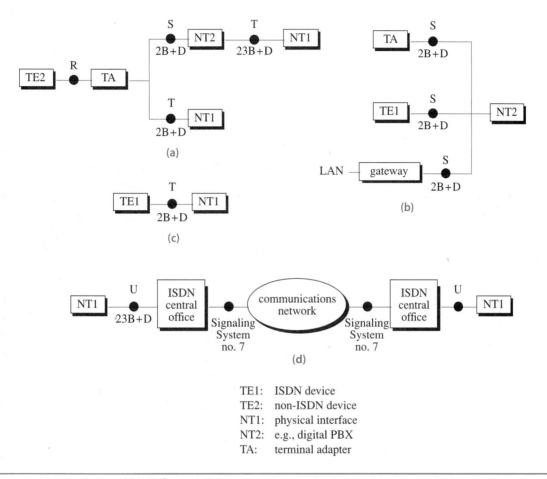

Figure 8.32   ISDN Reference Points

PROTOCOLS

On the surface ISDN is similar to the current telephone system. To establish a connection to another site the user performs some control functions. In the conventional telephone system this means dialing a number; in ISDN it means sending control packets. The telephone uses **in-band signaling**; that is, the tones generated by pressing buttons are sent over the same channel that will later carry your voice. ISDN control information is sent over the D channel. Since this is a different channel from the ones used to carry your voice or data, it is called **out-of-band signaling.** A significant aspect of out-of-band signaling is that after a connection is made for a B channel the D channel can be used for another purpose. Activities such as telemetry or another call request can be made in parallel with the B channel's transmissions. Another significant aspect is that B channels transmit data (or digital voice) only. That is, ISDN does not specify the content of a B channel and treats all bits as pure data. If two users communicate over the B channel using a particular protocol such as packet switching, they must specify the packet formats and transmit them over the B channel. However, the actual packet format, including headers and control information, is transparent to ISDN.

Several types of connections can be made over a B channel. First is a **circuit switched connection** similar to that within the telephone system. All signaling and control information exchange occurs over the D channel. A second connection is a **virtual circuit** over a packet-switched network. Again, all control information to establish the call and define the virtual circuit is done over the D channel. The third connection type is similar to a leased line service. The connection is ever present and does not require call establishment prior to sending data.

The D channel is another story. It carries control information such as call establishment or termination, the type of call, and the B channel assigned to that call. Consequently, protocols must be defined to control transmission over the D channel. Before we discuss them, however, we will describe the physical transmission of the B and D channels.

A complete description of protocols that form the foundation of ISDN would easily fill at least one book (see References [St95], [Ho95], [Ca98], and [Gr90]). Our approach, then, is to provide an introduction to some of the pertinent protocols and leave it to the reader to see these references if interested in more detail. Relevant to ISDN, ITU-T has developed two separate series of recommendations called the I series and Q series documents. The **I series,** I.100 to I.605, first issued in 1984 and updated in 1988 and 1992, consists of over 60 separate documents and describes topics such as ISDN network architecture, reference configurations, routing principles, and the user–network interface. We will describe a couple of these protocols shortly.

The **Q series,** Q.700 to Q.795, describes a layered protocol known as **Signaling System no. 7 (SS7).** First issued in 1980, SS7 defines a standard that provides functionality in an **integrated digital network (IDN).** Note the use of the term *IDN* as opposed to *ISDN*. An IDN represents an outgrowth of the old analog telephone system, in which signal transmission and switching were handled separately. With the ability to put all the transmissions in a digital form, the two functions have been integrated. An ISDN will use an IDN but includes the ability to integrate digitized voice with many other types of digital data onto the digital links.

Signaling System No. 7   SS7 is a four-layer protocol (Figure 8.33). The bottom three layers make up the **message transfer part (MTP)** and perform functions similar to the X.25 protocol. Unlike X.25, however, SS7 is concerned with internal network functions such as routing and reliability. For example, it provides for the reliable transport of messages using a connectionless mode of transfer. The fourth layer, the **user part,** contains specifications for call control, message formats, various applications, and maintenance.

The lowest layer, the **signaling data link** (ITU-T document Q.702) provides all the physical and electrical specifications and provides a 64 Kbps full-duplex transmission. The second layer, the **signaling link layer** (Q.703), provides reliable com-

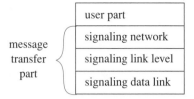

message transfer part	user part
	signaling network
	signaling link level
	signaling data link

Figure 8.33   Signaling System No. 7

munications between two consecutive points in the network. As with other layer 2 protocols, it defines the frame format and provides error checking and flow control. It is similar to HDLC, and another discussion is not useful here.

The third layer, the **signaling network layer** (Q.704), provides reliable message transfer between two signaling points (end points). It performs two major functions: routing and management. For example, it determines whether to transfer a message to another network node or to deliver it to the fourth layer (user part). In the former case, it must determine the next node. In the latter case, it must determine which user part gets the message. Management functions include the exchange of information among nodes regarding routes, error and congestion recovery, and rerouting.

The user part actually consists of a **telephone user part (TUP)** and an **ISDN user part (ISUP).** The TUP, described by documents Q.721 to Q.725, describes the establishment of circuit-switched connections for telephone calls, including types of control messages and their format. Example messages include those that specify charges for a call, an indication that a call has been answered, or a message that a circuit has been released due to an error.

The ISUP, documents Q.761 to Q.766, performs similar functions but is designed to be a service for ISDN users as opposed to telephone users. Some examples of ISUP messages are described in the following list:[*]

- **Initial address message (IAM).** A message sent in the forward direction to initiate seizure of an outgoing circuit and to transmit number and other information relating to the routing and handling of a call.

- **Subsequent address message (SAM).** A message that may be sent in the forward direction after an initial address message, to convey additional called party number information.

- **Information request message (INR).** A message sent by an exchange to request information in association with a call.

- **Information message (INF).** A message sent to convey information in association with a call requested in an INR message.

---

[*]J. Griffith, *ISDN Explained,* ©1990, pp. 34–35. Reprinted by permission of John Wiley & Sons, New York.

- **Address complete message (ACM).** A message sent in the backward direction indicating that all the address signals required for routing the call to the called party have been received.

- **Call progress message (CPG).** A message sent in the backward direction indicating that an event has occurred during call setup that should be relayed to the calling party.

- **Answer message (ANM).** A message sent in the backward direction indicating that the call has been answered. This message is used in conjunction with charging information in order to (1) start metering the charge to the calling customer, and (2) start measuring call duration for international accounting purposes.

- **Facility request message (FAR).** A message sent from an exchange to another exchange to request activation of a facility.

- **Facility accepted message (FAA).** A message sent in response to a facility request message indicating that the requested facility has been invoked.

- **Facility reject message (FRJ).** A message sent in response to a facility request message to indicate that the facility request has been rejected.

- **User-to-user information message (USR).** A message to be used for the transport of user-to-user independent of call-control messages.

- **Call modification request message (CMR).** A message sent in either direction indicating a calling or called party request to modify the characteristics of an established call (for example, a change from data to voice).

- **Call modification completed message (CMC).** A message sent in response to a call modification request message indicating that the requested call modification (for example, from voice to data) has been completed.

- **Call modification reject message (CMRJ).** A message sent in response to a call modification request message indicating that the request has been rejected.

- **Release message (REL).** A message sent in either direction to indicate that the circuit is being released because of the reason (cause) supplied and is ready to be put into the IDLE state on receipt of the release complete message. In case the call was forwarded or is to be rerouted, the appropriate indicator is carried in the message together with the redirection address and the redirecting address.

- **Release complete message (RLC).** A message sent in either direction in response to the receipt of a release message, or if appropriate, to a reset circuit message, when the circuit concerned has been brought into the IDLE condition.

This list merely scratches the surface of SS7. If you would like to read more about SS7, consult any of References [Gr90], [Bl97], [Sc86], and [Ap86].

ISDN Protocols   There are over 60 documents in the ITU-T I series describing ISDN standards. Our approach is to introduce you to the user–network interface recommendations describing a three-layer protocol. The first layer (I.430) describes the physical bit stream for the ISDN basic service. There is a similar description (I.431) for the primary service. [Gr90]

The physical-layer bit stream for the basic service corresponds to that at reference points S or T (Figure 8.32). Figure 8.34 shows how the basic service 2B+D channel is multiplexed over the bit pipe. Before we describe it we note several important facts:

1. The frame format for frames going from a TE to an NT differs from those going in the reverse direction. We will explain these differences shortly.

2. Communications between a TE and an NT are full duplex so that frames going in opposite directions do not collide.

3. The word *frame* carries a slightly different meaning than that used many times before. Its format is not defined by a layer 2 (or higher) protocol. Instead, it simply defines how bits from the two logical B and D channels are multiplexed into a single physical transmission stream.[*]

Each frame contains 48 bits and is sent every 250 μsec, resulting in a bit rate of 192 Kbps. Each frame also contains two 8-bit fields from each of the B channels (labeled B1 and B2). A service using the B channel deposits 16 bits into the appropriate fields in each frame. The 16 bits sent every 250 μsec result in a data rate of 64 Kbps for each B channel. Four D bits are stored separately in each frame (labeled

Figure 8.34 ISDN Physical Frame Format

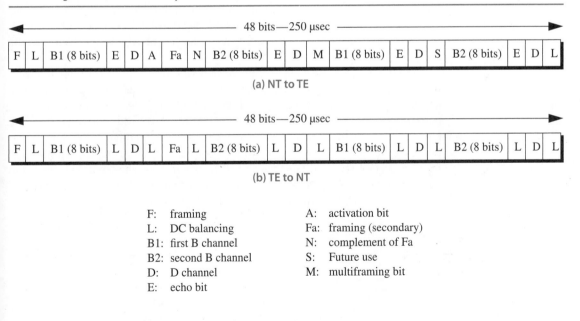

(a) NT to TE

(b) TE to NT

F:	framing	A:	activation bit
L:	DC balancing	Fa:	framing (secondary)
B1:	first B channel	N:	complement of Fa
B2:	second B channel	S:	Future use
D:	D channel	M:	multiframing bit
E:	echo bit		

---

[*]An analogous format exists for a 23B+D channel. For further details see References [St95] and [Gr90].

D), resulting in a data rate of 16 Kbps for the D channel. This means that when a TE has a packet of information to send over the D channel it does so 4 bits at a time.

The remaining bits are for some low-level control functions. As we describe them it is worth noting that ISDN uses a **pseudoternary coding** or **alternate mark inversion** technique in which a 1 bit is represented by zero volts and a 0 bit is represented by either a positive or a negative signal. Furthermore, each 0 bit has polarity opposite that of the most recent 0. This forces the signal representing a string of 0s to alternate between positive and negative.

The **F bit** is a framing bit, a positive signal indicating the beginning of the frame. The **L bit** is a DC balancing bit. After the F bit it is a negative signal. Together they provide timing and synchronization of the incoming frame. The remaining L bits are set to 0 if the number of preceding 0s is odd and set to 1 otherwise. This is a means of providing electrically balanced signals.

The **E bit** is an echo bit, and there is one for each D bit. In general, the NT uses it to echo back each D bit it receives. In cases where several TEs are connected to an NT via a single physical bus (Figure 8.35), the E bit also is used as a primitive form of contention for the D channel. When a TE has nothing to send on the D channel, it transmits a steady stream of 1s. Consequently, if none of the TEs is using the D channel, the NT receives all 1s in the D bit positions and echoes them back. Thus, by checking the returning E bits a TE can detect an idle D channel.

When a TE wants to send something on the D channel, it monitors the returning E bits. If it contains 0s the TE knows that some other TE is using the D channel and waits. If the returning E bits are all 1s either the D channel is idle or another TE is transmitting a data stream consisting of all 1s along it. However, a higher-layer protocol performs bit stuffing to limit the number of consecutive 1s that can be sent, so if a TE detects a number of 1s exceeding this value it concludes the D channel is idle and starts sending.

The problem is that another TE might start sending along the D channel as well. However, the mechanism used and the fact that they compete for space in the same physical frame guarantees that one will be successful. To see how this works, suppose the leftmost TE of Figure 8.35 sent a D bit equal to 1 (no signal). Suppose the physical frame reaches the next TE, which then deposits a 0 (high or low signal) into the D bit position. The effect is that the 1 from the first TE is replaced with the 0 from the second TE. Both TEs (and any others that may also be sending) listen to the returning E bits. If a TE detects an E bit different from the D bit it sent, it concludes that some other TE has grabbed the D channel and temporarily abandons its attempt

Figure 8.35   Multiple TEs Connected to an NT via a Single Bus

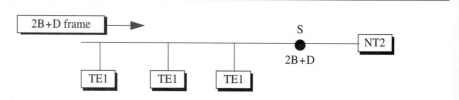

at getting the D channel. If the TE sees its own D bits echoed back as E bits it continues sending along the D channel. Another contributing factor is that there is a 10-bit delay time between sending a D bit and receiving the corresponding E bit. Thus, because the D bits are more than 10 bits apart in the physical frame the determination is made before the second D bit is sent. If the first and subsequent D bit from two TEs are the same, both continue sending until there is eventually a difference. At that point the unsuccessful TE stops transmitting.

Of the remaining physical frame bits, the **A bit** is an activation bit and can be used to activate a TE. The **Fa** and **M bits** are used for multiframing, which allows the addition of another channel (Q channel). The **S** and **N bits** are reserved for future use.

The ISDN layer 2 protocol, defined by I.440 and I.441, is known as **link access protocol for channel D (LAP-D).** If you have an absolutely fantastic memory you might recall its mention in Section 5.5. It is very similar to HDLC, and there is very little to say that has not already been said.

The layer 3 protocol, defined by I.450 and I.451, includes the types and formats of ISDN messages sent over the D channel, protocols for establishing and clearing calls, management functions, and facility support. We will discuss ISDN messages and call control here.

Figure 8.36 shows the ISDN message format. The **protocol discriminator** allows the D channel to send messages from multiple protocols by identifying a protocol corresponding to a message. Currently the protocol discriminator can specify X.25 messages or the user–network call-control messages that we will describe shortly. However, the ability exists to include other layer 3 protocols in the future.

The **call reference field** specifies the call to which the message refers. This is necessary because the D channel is used to set up and clear calls from many other channels. Without it there is no way to specify to which call a control refers. The four-bit field preceding the call reference specifies the number of octets in the call reference field. This is needed because the basic and primary services have different call reference lengths. The message type field is self-explanatory. The I.451

Figure 8.36   ISDN Layer 3 Message Format

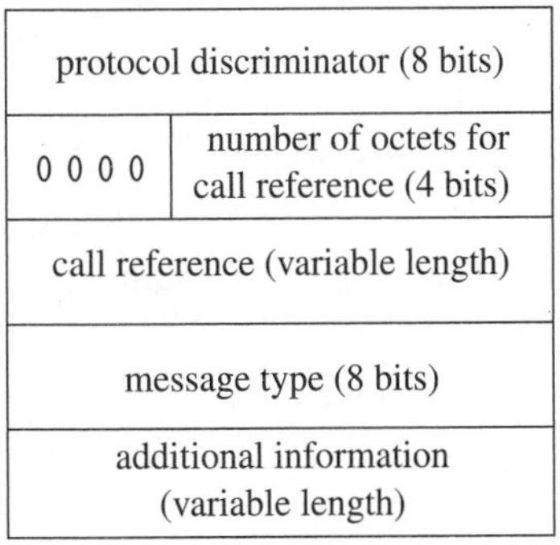

protocol discriminator (8 bits)	
0 0 0 0	number of octets for call reference (4 bits)
call reference (variable length)	
message type (8 bits)	
additional information (variable length)	

recommendation specifies about 30 different types of messages, some of which are listed in Table 8.8.

The remaining field's content and format depends on the message type and provides additional information. It contains information similar to that in other message types we have seen before, such as source and destination address. It can also specify a B channel, redirection addresses, reasons for specific messages, and call status.

Call Setup   Setting up a call is not terribly different (at this level of discussion) from other initialization procedures we have discussed in this book. Figure 8.37 shows the exchange of messages during a typical setup. While going through this example keep in mind that each TE is operating on behalf of a user. If it helps to

Table 8.8   Some ISDN Layer 3 Messages

CALL	MEANING
Call establishment	
Alert	Sent to calling TE indicating that the called TE has alerted its user to an incoming call.
Call proceeding	Sent by the network indicating the call request is in progress.
Connect	Sent to calling TE indicating a call has been accepted.
Connect ack.	Sent by calling TE indicating receipt of the connect message.
Setup	Sent by the calling TE requesting call establishment.
Setup ack.	Sent by the network to the calling TE indicating a previous setup message has been sent. It also requests that the calling TE send more information to process the call request.
Call information	
Resume	Resume a suspended call.
Resume ack.	Previously suspended call has been resumed.
Resume reject	Previously suspended call could not be resumed.
Suspend	Request suspension of call.
Suspend ack.	Call has been suspended.
Suspend reject	Call has not been suspended.
User information	Used to transfer information between two TEs.
Call clearing	
Disconnect	Request to disconnect the call. It should be followed by a request to release the B channel.
Release	Request to release a B channel. It is issued after a user "hangs up."
Release complete	Indicates the B channel is released.

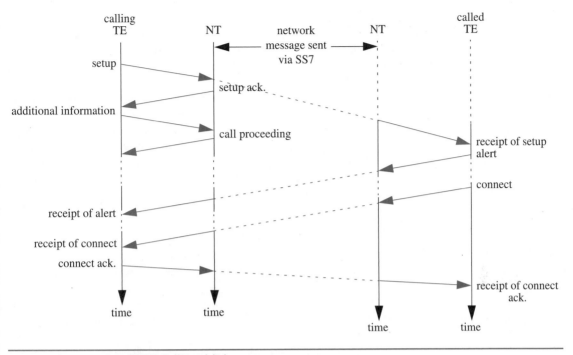

Figure 8.37   ISDN Call Establishment

think of the user as someone making a telephone call over a circuit-switched network, go ahead.

When a user wants to place a call he makes a request to the TE. The telephone analogy would be pushing buttons to specify a number. The TE responds by sending a setup message to the NT. The setup message contains information such as the source and destination addresses, channel, whether the source address should be forwarded, or who will be charged for the call. When the network gets the setup message, it routes it according to the SS7 protocols, thus determining a route to the other end. It also sends a setup acknowledge message back to the TE. The latter informs the TE that the call request has been forwarded and requests more information from the TE if the setup message contained insufficient information.

Once the network has the information it needs, it sends a call proceeding message back to the TE. Meanwhile, if all goes well the setup message travels through the network and reaches the destination TE. The destination TE then does two things. It sends an alert message back to the caller indicating it has received the setup message, and it notifies its user of the incoming call. In the case of a telephone call it does this by generating the familiar ringing sound. When the alert message returns to the calling TE the caller also hears the ringing sound.

When the user being called answers, the called TE sends a connect message back to the caller. Once the calling TE receives it, the ringing on its end stops and the TE responds with a connect acknowledgment. The exchange of the connect and connect acknowledgment messages identifies and confirms the B channel to be used and begins the time during which a charge will accrue. Each TE then routes the PCM-coded voice into the proper B channel, as described in the discussion on Figure 8.34, and the conversation begins.

A call ends when one TE sends a disconnect message to the network, typically after the user hangs up. The network routes the message over the network and sends a release message back to the TE. The TE then sends a release complete message back to the network, clearing the B channel at that end. When the disconnect message arrives at the other end, the network and TE there also exchange release and release complete messages. This procedure clears the B channel at that end also.

BROADBAND ISDN

The digital nature of ISDN is attractive, but some have criticized the establishment of a 64 Kbps data rate for B channels. Indeed, in an era of 100 Mbps rates for LANs and rates in the gigabit range for optical fiber, ISDN's 64 Kbps pales by comparison. In response, ITU-T has been developing a new set of documents describing **broadband ISDN (B-ISDN).** The intent is to use current high-bandwidth technologies to provide services requiring a high transfer rate.

Several services could be provided by a B-ISDN. Videoconferencing and video telephones are two. Current ISDN standards could provide videophone service, but only for small screens. For larger screens with a high-quality video image, higher data rates are needed. Another example is pay television, similar to what already exists in many hotels. From your television you choose what you want to watch from a library of movies. At the end of the billing period you are charged depending on your choices.

One of the issues surrounding B-ISDN is the method of transfer. ISDN services use preallocated positions in the layer 1 frames for the channels (recall Figure 8.34). This approach, also called **synchronous transfer mode (STM),** is essentially time-division multiplexing. The disadvantage of it is that unassigned channels result in wasted bandwidth. Could other channels use the unassigned bandwidth to increase their own rates?

Another approach uses **Asynchronous Transfer Mode (ATM),** a new technology that has received much attention in recent years. ATM is a very fast packet switched protocol using small fixed-size packets (called **cells**) optimized for multimedia use. It establishes logical connections similar to X.25, but the small fixed-size packets allow packets to be created and routed using underlying hardware. In addition, rather than preassigning slots for a channel's cells they are allocated to applications needing them. The advantage is that otherwise empty slots can be used. The disadvantage is the extra complexity and the fact that each slot requires a header. For example, the header would define a virtual circuit so that ATM packets could be routed quickly. These problems have been addressed, and some are predicting that ATM is the technology of the future. We will discuss ATM in the next section.

8.5   ASYNCHRONOUS TRANSFER MODE

The impact that the Internet has had on our society is almost beyond measure. It has, without doubt, revolutionized how we communicate with others, seek and organize information, spend our free time, and, in general, how we do our jobs. The 1980s and 1990s have seen tremendous growth in the Internet, with some estimates having it double in size every 18 months. The Internet is very good at what it was designed to do: provide the means necessary to share vast amounts of information among many diverse systems. However, some have raised questions about its ability to meet the needs of the future. We have already discussed the aging aspects of the Internet Protocol and the development of IPv6 to meet those needs. Developers of IPv6 worked very hard to overcome the aging IP and prepare for the global communications network of the 21st century. Key design issues of IPv6 were developed specifically to increase the speed with which IP packets can be routed through the Internet.

However, the 1990s have seen tremendous growth in video and voice communications. For such applications some claim that IPv6 will still not be adequate. The reader should be aware that we do not refer to situations that allow a user to access a video file (remember MPEG?) and run it locally. The video applications we speak of here refer to the ability to view video in a real-time mode.

One example is video on demand, in which a customer can request a movie from a provider at an arbitrary time. The provider maintains a digitized copy of the movie and transmits it to the customer, who watches as it is being transferred. Another example is videoconferencing. Imagine sitting at a PC whose screen is divided into several windows, each containing the image of another individual. Each of them has the same capability. You can speak into a microphone and each person can see you and hear your words as you speak them. Likewise, you can see them and hear their words. Except for the small images on the screen it is as if you were all in the same room participating in the conversation. (An additional advantage may be to call on a local program to draw mustaches and Groucho Marx eyebrows on whomever tends to monopolize the conversation.)

Such applications require more than the rapid delivery of the digitized voices and images. They require delivery with real-time constraints, that is, a consistent and predictable flow of information. There must be little, if any, noticeable delay, for such delays cause pauses in the sentences or a video effect similar to that in movies from the turn of the century (20th century, that is), where the video images really looked like a sequence of still pictures. Some have argued that IP will not be able to meet these constraints and that a different technology, **Asynchronous Transfer Mode (ATM),** is where the future of audio and video applications lies.

To the user ATM is designed to resemble the circuit-switching technology of telephone systems in that everything appears to work in real time. However, ATM represents a complete departure from such circuit-switching technology. For example, it maintains the capability of routing individual packets of data. The following items describe the primary attributes of an ATM network and, at a glance, help you see some of the differences of ATM compared with IP and with circuit-switching networks.

- Connection oriented.
- Packet switching.
- Fixed-size packets called cells.
- High-speed, low-delay transmission of cells.
- Cells will not arrive out of order.
- Speeds of 155.5 Mbps (this is the data rate necessary for full-motion video) or 622 Mbps (four 155.5 Mbps channels) over SONET (defined later). As the technology evolves, the future no doubt will see gigabit per second rates.
- Designed in large part for real-time video and voice applications.
- Heavily promoted by telephone companies.
- Technology used by B-ISDN.

In general, ATM works by initially setting up a connection between two sites during which a virtual circuit between them is established. In ATM terminology this is called **signaling.** It is based on the ITU-T protocol Q.2931, which itself is a subset of Q.931. The virtual circuit corresponds to a specific path determined during signaling, and all cells sent through the virtual circuit follow the same path. When the transmissions are complete, ATM protocols include a disconnect phase.

Much of this may sound similar to topics we have discussed previously, especially X.25. The differences, of course, are in the details and operations. This section will provide an overview of ATM, how some of the benefits are realized, some techniques for switching (routing) of cells, cell definition, virtual circuits, connection management, and a discussion of the layered reference model. Once again, this is a topic that can fill a book and has. Our main goal is to provide the reader with a fundamental understanding of just what ATM is and how it differs from other protocols. Of course, the interested reader is encouraged to seek out additional details in References [Bl95] and [On95].

BENEFITS OF SMALL FIXED-SIZE CELLS

One of the key aspects of ATM is that it transmits all information in 53-byte cells (48 bytes of data plus 5 header bytes, whose format we'll describe later). This raises a couple of logical questions. What is so special about transmitting information in fixed-size cells, and why is the size set at 48 bytes of data? The answer to the second question is, Because those involved in developing the protocol wanted something else. As silly as that sounds, the size actually is the result of compromise, a solution in which no one gets what they actually want.

When ATM was in the early stages of development, its committee sought a cell size that would meet several constraints. For example, it had to work well with existing equipment. Cells also had to be small enough so they could pass through intermediate switches quickly and keep internal queues small. The size also had to be small enough to implement error correction techniques efficiently. The committee had a European faction that promoted the use of 32-byte payloads. European countries are relatively small, and a 32-byte payload could be implemented without their telephone companies having to install echo cancellers (circuits that remove signals that echo back from their destination). U.S. telephone companies had been installing echo cancellers anyway and preferred a larger 64-byte payload to decrease the header-to-cell size ratio. Japan also favored the 64-byte payload. The solution was to take a numerical average of the proposed sizes of 32 and 64 bytes; the 48-byte payload was the result.

There are several advantages of transmitting information in small fixed-size packets. First, it is simpler. Programmers learn this fundamental fact early. Writing programs that manipulate fixed-size record structures is easier than writing ones that deal with variable-size structures. There are just fewer checks to make. This, of course, simplifies both the hardware and software required to do the job and also keeps the costs lower.

A second advantage of having small cells is that one cell won't occupy an outgoing link for lengthy periods. For example, suppose a switch just began forwarding a cell when another high-priority cell arrives. High priority typically means it can move to the front of an outgoing queue but it won't interrupt transmission of a cell already in progress. Consequently, it must wait for the transmission to be complete. If that cell is large, then the time the high-priority cell must wait is longer. A smaller cell means the high-priority cell gets out quicker.

Another reason a switch can get small cells through more quickly is the ability to overlap input and output operations. To see how this works, first understand that a cell typically arrives in its entirety and is buffered before being forwarded. If a cell contains a 1000-byte payload, then all 1000 bytes must be received and buffered before the first byte can be sent through an outgoing link. Figure 8.38 illustrates. Figure 8.38a shows a timeline during which the incoming bytes from a large cell are received. The first bytes are not forwarded until time t_1, after all bytes have arrived. Figure 8.38b shows what happens if a large cell is divided among smaller 48-byte cells. In this case the first cell can be forwarded as soon as it arrives at time t_0 (much earlier than time t_1) because it does not have to wait for all the other cells to arrive. During the timeline of Figure 8.38b, information is being received and forwarded simultaneously, thus increasing the rate at which cells are forwarded toward their final destination.

There are other benefits. For example, because information gets forwarded more quickly, less of it is maintained in the switch, which, in turn, contributes to smaller outgoing queues. The result is that the payload spends less time sitting in buffers. Another benefit is that bytes arrive at a more consistent rate at the final destination as opposed to a burstier arrival pattern in which many bytes arrive quickly in one large cell followed by longer wait times between cells. This is especially important in video and voice applications for which data must arrive quickly and consistently.

One last benefit is that small fixed-size cells facilitate designing switches capable of forwarding multiple packets concurrently. This is especially useful because it reduces times when one cell must wait for another cell to be forwarded. How this works is difficult to understand until we have described some switching technologies, so we defer this discussion until a bit later.

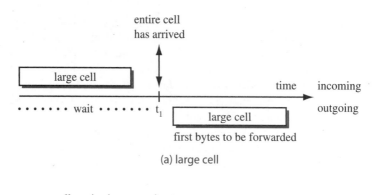

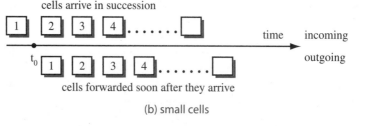

Figure 8.38 Overlapping Cell Input and Output

OVERVIEW OF ATM NETWORK

We begin by outlining what an ATM network looks like and discussing some of its components. Figure 8.39 shows that an ATM network consists of **ATM switches.** Generally, the ATM switch[*] is analogous to the IP router in that it's responsible for receiving incoming cells and forwarding them outward along the correct link. ATM switches have links to one another, forming a network with a variety of paths. Each switch, in turn, can connect to a variety of user-oriented devices such as a computer, television, video camera, or local area network. The figure doesn't show it, but each user device needs an interface card that speaks ATM.

There are two types of links in an ATM network. The **Network–Network Interface (NNI)** connects two ATM switches, and the **User–Network Interface (UNI)** connects the switch to a user device. There are some differences between the links; for example, how they interpret cells. We'll deal with that shortly. For now we just present them for reference.

---

[*]The difference between a switch and router is not well defined. Some user the term *router* when referring to the Internet and its ability to connect a variety of different technologies. Others use the term *switch* when referring to a collection of homogeneous links connecting similar technologies. This suggests that the difference is whether the device can connect different technologies. However, vendors are advertising switches that are more versatile in their ability to connect different technologies, which blurs this distinction. In other cases *switch* refers to a multiport bridge operating at OSI layer 2, in contrast to a *bridge*, which was originally designed to connect just two LANs. The bottom line is that at this level whatever distinction there may be is not important.

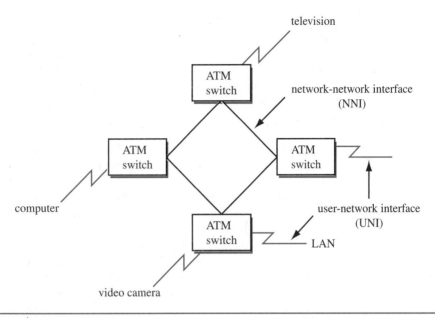

Figure 8.39 ATM Network

SWITCHING

As stated previously, ATM communication is connection oriented. When a site has information to send to another, it requests a connection by sending a message. The message passes through various switches, setting up a virtual path as it does so. In contrast to IP, subsequent data cells contain a **virtual path ID,** which the switch uses to route the cell through outgoing links. The switch maintains a table in which each entry contains two pairs: an input port/virtual path ID and an output port/virtual path ID. When a cell arrives over a particular input port, the switch uses that port identifier and the virtual path ID in the cell to locate a table entry. It changes the cell's virtual path ID to the one paired with the associated output port and sends the cell through that port. For example, suppose a table entry contained the following:

INPUT PORT	VIRTUAL PATH ID	OUTPUT PORT	VIRTUAL PATH ID
:	:	:	:
:	:	:	:
C	5	F	8
:	:	:	:
:	:	:	:

Then a cell containing a virtual path ID of 5 arriving on port C is forwarded over port F with its virtual path ID changed to 8.

The process is really very similar to that described at the beginning of Section 7.3 and there is little point in elaborating again. The only difference of note is in terminology. X.25 uses a virtual circuit ID in its packets, whereas ATM cells contain virtual path IDs. At this level they play the same role. However, we will see later that ATM also defines a virtual circuit in addition to the virtual path and we will also see how they differ.

Banyan Switches   Using routing tables this way can forward cells very quickly, especially if the table entries are hashed on the incoming port identifier and virtual path ID. Paths are established and released simply by inserting and deleting new entries into the table.

There are other techniques used to provide switching functions in high-speed networks, some of which can make use of switching several cells concurrently. One example is a **Banyan switch.** A Banyan switch has an equal number of input and output lines (typically equal to a power of 2). Inside the switch there are multiple stages. The number of stages is related to the number of output lines. For example, if there are 2^k output lines then there are k stages in the switch.

Each cell is associated with a **bit string** (also called a **switching string**) of length k, and each bit in the string takes the cell from one stage to the next. This bit string might be in the cell or it might be stored in a table along with a virtual path ID. Its location is not important to the discussion here.

Figure 8.40 shows a Banyan switch with eight inputs and outputs and three stages between them. A cell can enter any one of the eight inputs and pass to one of four switching elements (first stage). Based on the first bit of the switching string, the cell follows one of two possible outputs into one of four elements at the second stage. There, switching logic examines the second bit of the switching string and

Figure 8.40   Banyan Switch

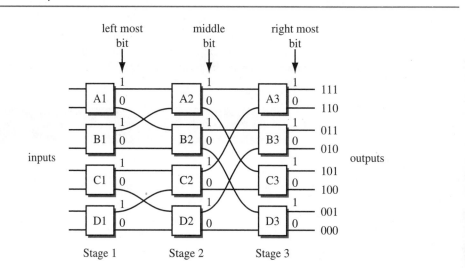

passes the cell along one of two possible outputs into the third stage. The process is repeated once more using the remaining bit, and the cell is finally forwarded through one of the switch's outputs.

Each output in Figure 8.40 is labeled with a unique three-bit string that defines the output line over which the cell is forwarded. There are a couple of interesting things about this switch. First, the output depends only on the switching string and is independent of the input line over which a cell arrives. For example, Figure 8.40 highlights three possible paths corresponding to a cell with switching string 100. Cells entering elements A1 and B1 get passed to A2 in the second stage. From there both would go to C3. The cell entering D1 passes to C2 and then to C3. As you can see, each starts at a different element at the first stage but ends up at the output corresponding to 100.

Another interesting feature is that switching logic can handle multiple cells concurrently. For example, one cell with switching string 100 passes through A1, A2, and C3. Suppose another cell with switching string 110 arrives at D1. It would pass through D1, C2, and A3. Since the two cells involve different elements the routing can be done concurrently. In other words, one cell does not have to wait for another. This is a particularly important feature because it allows a switch to forward more cells and hence reduce waiting time, a desirable trait for real-time video or voice.

On the other hand, suppose a cell with switching string 100 arrives at A1 and another with string 101 arrives at B1. Each has different inputs and outputs but both must pass through A2. If they arrive at the same time there will be a collision. The important thing here is that the switch may be able to handle two cells concurrently, but there is no guarantee. In the event there is a collision, each switching element must have the ability to decide which cell to pass first and to put the other one in a queue for subsequent passing.

There are other switching technologies in addition to Banyan switches. One example is a **cross-bar switch** with n inputs and outputs. The inputs are typically displayed as a series of horizontal lines, and the outputs as a series of vertical lines. Each input line crosses all n output lines, and each output line crosses all n input lines. Each crossing corresponds to a switching element that can switch a cell from an input to an output line. A disadvantage is that there are n^2 switching elements, a lot for a switch.

There is also a **knockout switch,** which is a form of cross-bar switch. The problem with the cross-bar switch is that two cells destined for the same output at the same time will collide. In addition, the cells may arrive on different input lines and go through different switches to get to the desired output, making it more difficult to handle the collision. With the knockout switch each output has an **arbiter** that is connected to every input line. If two cells from different inputs are destined for the same output, the cross-bar switch part routes them to the arbiter, which then handles the collision by queuing one and sending the other.

REFERENCE MODEL

ATM is actually part of the B-ISDN specification as defined by ITU-T; Figure 8.41 shows the layered reference model. Our approach here is to give a brief overview of the model first and follow up with a more detailed discussion of relevant topics. The

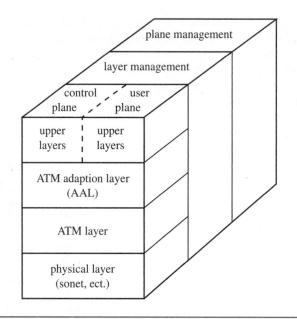

Figure 8.41   ATM/B-ISDN Reference Model

first thing you might notice about this model when compared with others is the three-dimensional look to it. That's because the combined ATM/B-ISDN model specifies both user-oriented and management functions. For example, the **control plane** specifies how connections are made and released. The **user plane** specifies the transport of data and related issues such as flow control and error detection and correction. Behind the scenes the **layer management** provides management functions. One of its responsibilities is to provide operations, administration, and maintenance (OAM) services through information packets that switches exchange to keep the system running effectively. Management services may also be provided by SNMP or CMIP. Finally, **plane management** makes sure the various planes coordinate their activities properly.

At the bottom of the model the **physical layer** specifies the physical characteristics of transmission. Although ATM does not specify rules for physical transmission, it was originally designed with the intention of running over **SONET (Synchronous Optical Network).** Originally proposed by Bellcore (Bell Communications Research), SONET is an optical network using time division multiplexing to accommodate simultaneous channels. Controlled by a clock, it transmits bits at rates ranging from about 155.5 Mbps to in excess of 2 Gbps. It defines the way in which telephone companies transmit their data over optical networks. Besides SONET, ATM can also run on top of FDDI, T-1 and T-3 systems, both shielded and unshielded twisted pair, and even wireless media [Va97].

Above the physical layer is the **ATM layer.** It performs activities similar to those found in OSI layers 2 and 3. For example, it defines the cell format and how to respond to information found in the header. It also is responsible for setting up and releasing connections and establishing both virtual circuits and virtual paths (a distinction we will make shortly). Finally, it also performs congestion control.

The **ATM adaptation layer (AAL)** provides the interface between applications and the ATM layer and is divided into two sublayers: the segmentation and reassembly sublayer (lower sublayer) and the convergence sublayer. The **convergence sublayer** provides the interface for a variety of applications to use ATM. What it does depends on the application and the type of traffic it generates. In fact, later we will see that there are several versions of AAL depending on whether the traffic is uncompressed video, compressed video, or a variety of other types. The **segmentation and reassembly sublayer** stores information from higher layers into ATM cells and may add its own header to the payload. On the receiving end, it extracts the payload from each cell and reassembles them into an information stream for the application to process.

CELL DEFINITION

This is a good time to provide some details about how ATM works, and a logical place to start is by defining the ATM cell and describing how ATM handles its contents. As previously mentioned, an ATM cell has 53 bytes, 48 of which are the cell's payload. This leaves just 5 bytes for the cell header. Figure 8.42 outlines what they are as they pass through a Network–Network Interface (NNI). For cells that travel through the User–Network Interface (UNI) there is a slightly different interpretation of the header's contents. In the latter case, the first four bits define a **generic flow control (GFC) field,** leaving just 8 bits for the virtual path identifier. However, once the cell enters the network switches may write over the GFC field using a 12-bit virtual path ID.

The GFC is designed to control the flow of traffic from a device into the ATM network (but not in the reverse direction). There are essentially two classes of connections, controlled and uncontrolled, which are either part of the configuration or negotiated during the establishment of a connection. When a connection is **controlled** the network provides information to the user regarding how many cells it can send. It's a bit like the credit mechanism used for flow control in TCP. On **uncontrolled** connections the network simply enables or disables the sending of cells. When enabled, the user device is free to send cells until the network disables it. It's a bit like an X-ON/X-OFF form of flow control.

Figure 8.42 ATM Cell Header (NNI)

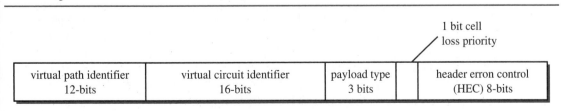

The small number of header bytes is one contributing factor to ATM's speed: there are fewer things to check in each cell when it arrives at a switch. Let's now examine each field separately.

Header Error Control   The **header error control (HEC) field** is somewhat self-explanatory: It provides for error checking. However, there are a few noteworthy items. First is that it only provides error checking for the other four header bytes, leaving the payload unprotected. This, of course, makes error checking, and consequently cell delivery, much faster. (Remember, speed is essential in an ATM network.) Of course, leaving the payload unprotected might at first seem a problem, but, for a couple of reasons, it is not. One is that ATM was designed to run on top of optical fiber systems, which are very reliable. Consequently, the odds of errors occurring are very small. Even if they did occur they could be detected at a higher layer if necessary. Another reason is that many applications involve video or audio. Consequently, an error in a frame that will be displayed for a small fraction of a second will not be noticeable or, at worst, might correspond to a barely perceptible flicker. Would it make sense to wait for a retransmission of such a frame? The answer is no. However, protecting the header is crucial because it contains the virtual path and circuit identifiers that determine where the cell goes.

Another noteworthy item is that the error checking is an adaptive technique based on the CRC method. It can detect over 90% of multiple-bit errors and can even correct single-bit errors. The latter is particularly significant because a study by AT&T and Bellcore published in 1989 [AT89] showed that over 99.5% of errors in optical fiber systems are actually single-bit errors.

The HEC field also performs another unrelated function. Recall discussions in Section 5.5 of data link protocols in which frames contained special bit patterns that designated the frame's beginning. ATM defines no such pattern, so a logical question to ask is, How can low-level protocols detect the beginning of a cell? This depends in part on the physical layer. For example, SONET encapsulates ATM cells in an envelope (similar to previous protocols in which a packet was encapsulated in a frame, except that several cells can be in an envelope). Information in the envelope locates the start of the first ATM cell.

However, not all physical layers will provide such an envelope. In fact, with a synchronous medium, cells must be transmitted in a regular pattern defined by a clock. There is no envelope or special bit patterns to locate the start of a cell. They simply arrive at regular intervals and the receiving device must be able to determine where cell boundaries are. Recognizing where cell boundaries are as a synchronous bit pattern arrives is called **framing.** For example, consider a sequence of ATM cells, each containing information from a video camera. The receiving device must synchronize by locating cell boundaries in order to provide proper viewing.

Although there is no particular bit pattern to identify the start of an ATM cell, one technique uses the fact that every undamaged header has something in common: Applying the error-checking method using the 40-bit string that defines the header generates a value consistent with the last 8 bits in that string. Consequently, one technique to locate the cell boundary is as follows:

1. Apply the error-checking method using 40 consecutive bits. If it does not generate a result consistent with the last 8 bits, shift one bit and try again (Figure 8.43).

2. Repeat the above step until a consistent result is found. This indicates that these 40 bits could be a legitimate header. However, random chance could cause a consistent result to be found among 40 other bits (a false header).

3. Once a potential header is found, skip the next 48 bytes (payload) and apply the same technique using the subsequent 40 bits. We are assuming that legitimate headers are each separated by 48 bytes. If the technique does not produce a consistent result, then the previous result was an accident and we must start over.

4. Suppose we find several 40-bit strings, each separated by 48 bytes from an adjacent one, that all generate a consistent HEC value. Then there is a high probability that they are all legitimate headers. In that case, framing has been achieved and the receiving device is now synchronized with incoming cells.

The above technique looks complex, but use of circular shift registers similar to those in Section 4.3 can implement it efficiently. Also, there is the issue of how many consecutive potential headers we should find before we conclude the device is synchronized. Since the HEC field is just 8 bits, the probability of locating a false header is $1/2^8 = 1/256$ for a given 40-bit string. The probability of locating two consecutive false headers is $1/(256)^2$. In general, the probability of locating n false headers is $1/(256)^n$. Larger values of n take more time but will be less likely to synchronize incorrectly. In fact, if n is just 4 the probability of synchronizing incorrectly is 1 out of about 4.3 billion.

Cell Loss Priority   The **cell loss priority (CLP) bit** indicates a cell's priority level. Whenever congestion occurs, ATM has the option of deleting cells in order to relieve it. It chooses cells with a CLP value of 1 first. It is up to the application to determine which cells are not critical. For example, MPEG-compressed video images use differences between frames and actual compressed frames (recall the difference between I-frames and P-frames from Section 3.5) in its transmitted images. If those frames that represent small differences were deleted the overall effect on viewing is likely to be negligible. Consequently, the applications might set the CLP bit for the cells containing those frames to 1.

Figure 8.43   Looking for a Cell Boundary

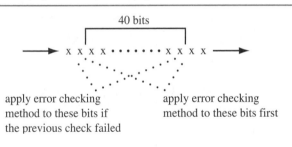

Payload Type The **payload type field** provides some specific information about the cell. The leftmost bit specifies whether the payload is user data or OAM information. Switches can exchange OAM messages to provide status checks and keep the system running smoothly. The second bit indicates whether the cell has passed through any congested switches. This lets the receiver know of any congestion problems developing along a particular path. In some cases the third bit can be used to indicate the last in a sequence of ATM cells.

VIRTUAL CIRCUITS AND PATHS

Prior to this point we have not made any distinction between a virtual circuit and virtual path. This changes with ATM, as Figure 8.44 shows. Conceptually, a **virtual circuit** represents a logical connection between two end points. For example, in Figure 8.44 there is a logical connection between *A* and *X*, *B* and *Y*, and *C* and *Z*. However, each connection corresponds to the same **path.**

Each cell contains a 12-bit **virtual circuit ID** (8 bits across the UNI) and a 16-bit **virtual path ID.** Thus, from a user's perspective each connection can be defined by a 24-bit connection identifier that consists of two parts: the circuit ID (8 bits) and path ID (16 bits). It's analogous to Internet addressing, where we indicated that a 32-bit address consisted of a network ID and a host ID. The advantage was that internal routing mechanisms could route based solely on the network ID. The host

Figure 8.44 Virtual Circuits and Virtual Paths

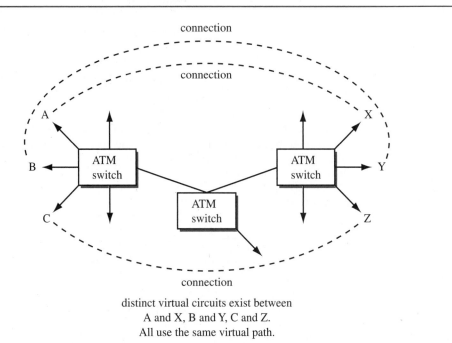

distinct virtual circuits exist between
A and X, B and Y, C and Z.
All use the same virtual path.

ID wasn't used until the packet reached the destination network and could be sent directly to the host.

Likewise, ATM switches forward cells based solely on the 16-bit virtual path ID. Making decisions based on a 16-bit number instead of a full 28-bit identifier (remember that when a cell enters the network the circuit ID expands to 12 bits) allows switching to occur more quickly. Again, this is a major goal of ATM. Using 16-bit numbers instead of 28-bit numbers also keeps internal switching tables smaller (a maximum of 2^{16} entries as opposed to 2^{28} entries). The circuit ID is needed only when the cell arrives at the last ATM switch, which must forward the cell directly to the user.

Another advantage of using both circuit and path IDs is realized if there is a problem in a link. For example, suppose a hundred connections have been established that all use the same path. If a problem develops along the path, a new one must be found. If switching were based on a 28-bit number, then the internal tables for each new switch in the alternate route would require a new entry for each connection. In this case a hundred changes to each table would be made. However, since switching is based on just the path ID and all connections use the same path, each table requires just one change to accommodate all the connections. Clearly, this is a lot quicker.

CONNECTION MANAGEMENT

There are two types of connections: a **permanent virtual circuit** and a **switched virtual circuit.** The permanent circuit is analogous to a leased telephone line, and the switched circuit must be established using a connection protocol. The connection protocol is based on algorithms in ITU-T Q.2931 (itself a subset of Q.931). On the surface, establishing an ATM connection follows procedures similar to those of establishing connections in other protocols we have discussed. One side initiates a call request specifying some of the attributes desired of the connection and waits for an acknowledgment. The control plane is responsible for setting up the connection.

Figure 8.45 outlines the connection setup logic when *A* requests a connection to *B*. There are four different message types used in setting a connection; the steps below show how they are used.

1. On behalf of *A* the control plane sends a **setup message** to *B* across the UNI. This message contains information relevant to the requested connection. For example, it contains *B*'s address and some other items that we'll describe shortly.

2. The switch receiving the setup message does two things. First it sends a **call proceeding message** back to *A* informing it that the request has been received and is in progress. This message also contains the virtual circuit and path IDs to be used once the connection is established. Second, the switch forwards the setup message toward *B*.

3. The setup message travels through the network across various NNIs toward *B* using whatever routing algorithm is implemented (ATM does not specify what it is). The route eventually chosen defines the virtual path and circuit. As a setup message progresses through switches, each switch responds by returning a call

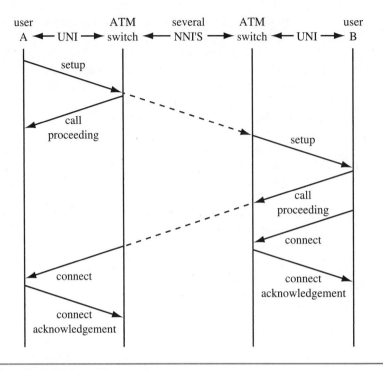

Figure 8.45   Establishing a Connection

proceeding message to the switch that sent the setup. Consequently, each switch that will eventually be part of the virtual path is aware that a connection is in progress.

4. Eventually *B* gets the setup message. *B* can respond immediately with a **connect** or, if it expects a delay, it can return a call proceeding message. Eventually, if all goes well, *B* sends the connect message over the UNI to a switch. The switch returns a **connect acknowledgment message.** *B* is now free to start sending information to *A*. The connect message travels back to *A* through the same switches (in reverse order) that the connect message traveled. Each switch responds by forwarding it and returning a connect acknowledgment. As each switch gets the connect, it knows it is part of a virtual path and makes an entry associated with the path ID into its tables. It is now prepared to route subsequent cells along the proper path.

5. Eventually the connect gets to *A* and it responds with a connect acknowledgment. *A* is now free to send information to *B*.

Releasing a connection proceeds similarly. Either side can initiate a release by sending a **release message.** It travels through the virtual path, with each switch returning a **release complete message.** The switches use this to remove path information from their tables and forward the release to the next switch along the path.

Connection Parameters   Earlier we stated that the setup message contains information relevant to the requested connection. In general it specifies the quality of service and type of traffic it expects. For example, a request for video on demand has different expectations than a connection to be used for a file transfer. This is important information to have in the setup message because one of ATM's goals is to maintain a desired quality of service.

When a setup message enters the network, each switch must decide whether it can be part of the requested path without adversely affecting the quality of service for existing paths. You can only have so many video-on-demand paths going through a switch. The switch may proceed as above or reject the setup request. This is where much of the complexity lies. Potentially many possible paths must be investigated before one is found that will provide the needed quality of service. Of course, it is also possible that no such path will be found. The objective is to avoid establishing paths that will have a negative impact on existing users, including the one trying to establish the connection. Effectively this method guarantees users a certain quality of service and is also a form of congestion control.

We have used the phrase *quality of service* rather generally. Listed here are some specific items that a setup message might contain.

- **B-ISDN service class.** B-ISDN defines four classes. **Class A** traffic requires a constant bit rate and strict synchronization between the sender and receiver. This is needed for uncompressed video or audio transfer where the images are to be recorded, transmitted, and then viewed (or heard) as they are received. **Class B** allows a variable bit rate but still requires that the sender and receiver be synchronized. This is typical of compressed video, in which bit rates differ depending on how much compression is being done. However, synchronization is still necessary because it is still being viewed in real time. **Class C** is for connection-oriented traffic with no timing constraints. **Class D** is a connectionless service with no timing constraints. The latter two are for the more mundane applications such as file or data transfers that have no real-time constraints.

- **Peak cell rate.** The maximum rate at which cells will be sent.

- **Sustainable cell rate.** An upper bound on the average rate of cell transfer defined over a period of time. The peak cell rate may be higher for short periods, but for an extended period the rate should not exceed what is specified here.

- **Time.** Parameter used to determine the maximum sustainable cell rate.

- **Minimum cell rate.** Specifies the lowest rate at which cells must be received. Anything below that rate is considered unacceptable.

- **AAL version.** We will discuss this topic next.

ADAPTATION LAYERS

We close the section on ATM by describing the **ATM adaptation layer (AAL).** Figure 8.46 shows that it is the interface between higher layers and the ATM layer and consists of two sublayers: the **segmentation and reassembly sublayer (SAR)**

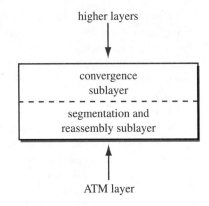

Figure 8.46 AAL Sublayers

and the **convergence sublayer (CS).** The convergence sublayer's responsibilities depend on the type of information the applications at higher levels generate.

Figure 8.47 shows general actions taken by the convergence and SAR sublayers. We intend this to be an overview; there are different types of AAL that may or may not do some of these tasks. We will worry about those differences shortly. Generally, some application at a higher layer generates data, which we view as a byte stream. The convergence sublayer extracts some of those bytes and adds a header and trailer to create its own CS packet. The SAR sublayer gets the CS packet

Figure 8.47 General AAL Activities

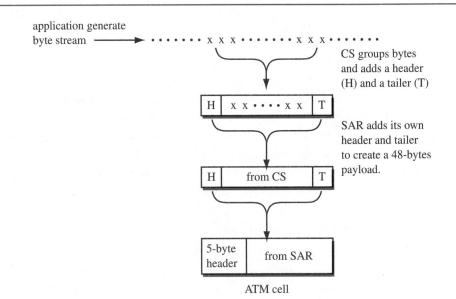

and adds its own header and trailer to create a 48-byte payload that then gets stored into an ATM cell. The figure seems to indicate that the convergence and SAR sublayers do the same things in that they add headers and trailers to data received from a higher layer. Well, that is true, but the difference lies in what those headers and trailers contain. However, to make that distinction requires that we introduce the different AAL types.

AAL types differ primarily in the classes of traffic they will handle. **AAL 1** deals with Class A traffic, and **AAL 2** with Class B traffic. The pattern seems to suggest that AAL 3 and AAL 4 deal with Class C and D traffic. To some extent that was true, because ITU-T did develop an AAL 3 and AAL 4. However, as development progressed it became apparent that there were no significant differences so they elected to combine them. One might think the result would be labeled AAL $3\frac{1}{2}$ but in fact it is called **AAL 3/4.** After AAL 3/4 was developed, some were concerned about what they perceived as inefficiencies. Consequently, **AAL 5** was developed as a successor to AAL 3/4. We won't worry about AAL 3, AAL 4, or AAL 3/4. Reference [Bl 95] discusses all the AAL versions. We will, however, outline AAL 1, AAL 2, and AAL 5.

AAL 1   Figure 8.48 outlines how Class A traffic is handled. A video application generates a real-time uncompressed byte stream. AAL 1 captures 46 or 47 bytes at a time and puts them in an AAL 1 packet. A difference with Figure 8.47 is that only the SAR sublayer creates a header, which is either 1 or 2 bytes long. From there each packet becomes the payload of an ATM cell, which is then transmitted toward its destination.

Figure 8.49a shows the format of an AAL 1 packet. The first bit indicates whether an optional second header byte is present. This header byte, if present, is used when the payload field is not full and locates the data within the payload field.

Figure 8.48   Sending Class A Traffic

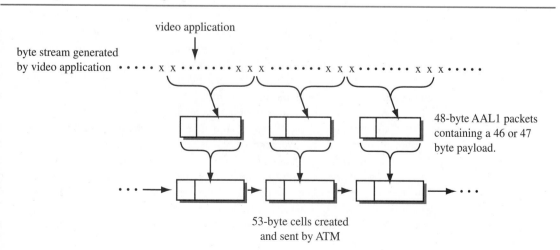

byte stream generated by video application

video application

48-byte AAL1 packets containing a 46 or 47 byte payload.

53-byte cells created and sent by ATM

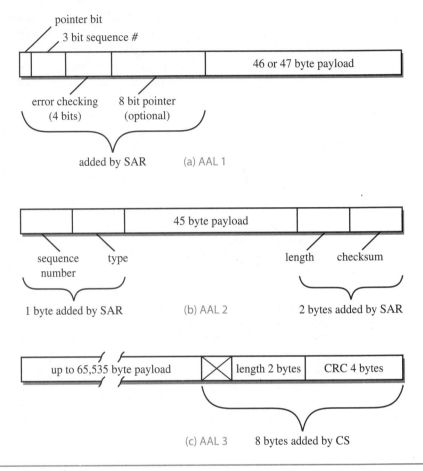

Figure 8.49   AAL Packet Types

This method can be used in cases where filling the payload field to capacity takes more time than the application can tolerate. By only partially filling the payload field, the information can be passed to the ATM cell and eventually sent more quickly. This may be necessary to maintain the constant bit rate required by Class A traffic. An implication of this is that the convergence sublayer must be synchronized with a clock to deliver the correct amount of data to the SAR sublayer on a timely basis.

Of the remaining seven bits of the first header byte, three are used for a sequence number. The convergence sublayer provides the sequence number, and the SAR sublayer creates the header in which to store it. This allows the receiving CS to detect a loss of information or a misinserted cell. Either of these can occur if an undetected error occurs in the path ID of the cell en route to a destination. The cell could be misdirected to an incorrect location, which would see this error as a misinserted cell. The correct destination would see a gap in arriving sequence numbers that constitutes a loss of information. Any misinserted cells are ignored (imagine seeing bogus images during a touchdown in the last seconds of the Superbowl). If the receiver detects a loss, it notifies the sender but does not request a retransmission. Remember, we are assuming this is a real-time video or audio application and therefore resending images or sounds serves no useful purpose. The viewer will have to be content with seeing a flicker in the image or hearing a blip in the sound (assuming the loss is even noticeable).

The remaining four bits are used for error checking the three-bit sequence field. Provided by the SAR sublayer, three of the four bits correspond to a CRC for the three sequence number bits, and the fourth bit establishes parity for the combined sequence number and CRC bits. The parity bit provides an extra measure of protection. In fact, it can correct single-bit errors and detect double-bit errors. Interestingly the packet's payload is not protected. However, as stated before, ATM generally runs on reliable media. Even if loss does occur it may not be noticeable. Also, checking only the sequence field requires less time and helps contribute to timely deliveries of real-time packets.

AAL 2   Figure 8.49b shows the format of an AAL 2 packet. Like AAL 1, only the SAR sublayer adds anything to the payload. In this case it adds both a header (one byte) and a tailer (two bytes). The header's sequence number has the same purpose as the sequence number in an AAL 1 packet. The **type field** reflects the variable bit rate nature of Class B traffic. With Class A traffic, data was strictly a bit stream with no need for message boundaries. Images are displayed as the data that represents them is received. Because Class B traffic includes compressed images, message boundaries are needed to help identify new frames (recall MPEG discussions on sending frames or differences between frames). The type field helps identify message boundaries by indicating when a cell corresponds to the first, last, or intermediate cell of a message.

The **length field** specifies the number of data bytes in the payload. Finally, the **checksum field** provides error checking of the entire packet. AAL 2 is still in the process of development, so there are aspects that are not fully explained yet. For example, the size of the overhead fields has not yet been specified. In addition, there have been suggestions that the type field may also contain timing information relevant to audio or video data.

AAL 5   We conclude our discussion of ATM with an outline of AAL 5, whose packet format is described by Figure 8.49c. Perhaps the first thing you will notice is that AAL 5 packets can be considerably larger than other AAL packets. This is partly because AAL 5 was not designed with real-time video or voice in mind, thus the need for small packets is not so critical. Another difference is that the convergence sublayer adds overhead to the payload instead of the SAR sublayer. Figure 8.50 shows basic steps in sending a potentially large data block. An application generates a block of data and gives it to the CS, which adds an 8-byte tailer and passes the packet to the SAR sublayer. The SAR sublayer divides the packet into 48-byte

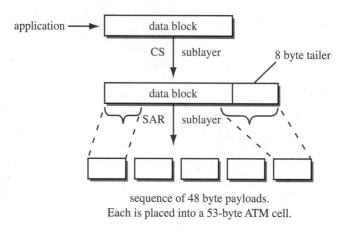

application ⟶ data block

CS | sublayer

8 byte tailer

data block

SAR | sublayer

sequence of 48 byte payloads.
Each is placed into a 53-byte ATM cell.

Figure 8.50　AAL 5 Dividing a Data Block into ATM Cells

payloads, each of which is placed into an ATM cell. On the receiving end the steps are reversed.

Note that Figure 8.50 suggests that the size of the entire packet (data block plus trailer) is a multiple of 48 bytes. Since the amount of data can vary, the data block may actually be padded with anywhere between 1 and 47 extra bytes. The number is chosen to make the packet's size a multiple of 48.

The tailer contains just two items of note. First is a 32-bit CRC field providing error checking on the entire packet. Here is another indication that this format was not designed for real-time audio or video: Using a 32-bit CRC on potentially many thousands of bytes would take too long. The second field specifies the number of bytes in the payload field.

Because the application runs on top of ATM the data is still divided into small cells. However, an important aspect is that this division is done at a different layer. In AAL 1 and AAL 2, data was divided into small packets early so that they could be processed and sent as quickly as possible. Here the convergence sublayer deals with a potentially large block and creates the tailer for it. Due to the block's size this will take longer, which would be unacceptable for Class A or Class B traffic. However, for Class C or Class D traffic such delays are not a problem.

Service-Specific Connection-Oriented Protocol　The AAL protocols we have described deal primarily with data transfer. We have not yet discussed a protocol used primarily for providing a reliable connection. Early developers of ATM recognized that error detection and recovery would be needed for signaling and for certain data applications. Toward this end AAL was divided into two parts: a common part and a service-specific part. AAL 5 is an example of a common part. Two additional protocols, the **Service-Specific Coordination Function (SSCF)** and the **Service-Specific Connection-Oriented Protocol (SSCOP)** constitute the service-specific part. SSCOP and SSCF lie between AAL 5 and a higher-layer signaling protocol such as Q.2931, with SSCF providing the interface between SSCOP and Q.2931. Together, SSCF and SSCOP are also called the **signaling ATM adaptation layer (SAAL).**

SSCOP is a synchronous bit-oriented protocol whose main functions include flow control and actions to be taken when errors are detected. It uses a form of selective repeat sliding window protocol in which the window sizes can be adjusted dynamically and missing frames can be requested and transmitted explicitly.

The signaling layer (i.e., Q.2931) communicates with SSCOP through the SSCF. The SSCOP creates specific packets, which it sends to the peer SSCOP entity at the other end. The receiving SSCOP extracts information from these packets and, through its SSCF, passes them on to the signaling layer there. SSCOP packets are variable length, with a maximum size of 64 Kbytes.

The following lists most of the SSCOP packet types:

- **Begin** and **begin acknowledgment** packets are used to establish and acknowledge the establishment of an SSCOP connection.

- **End** and **end acknowledgment** packets are used to release and acknowledge the release of an SSCOP connection.

- **Reject** packets are used to reject connection requests by a peer SSCOP entity.

- **Resynchronize** and **resynchronize acknowledgment** packets are used to reestablish connections and connection parameters in the event that a connection fails.

- **Sequenced data packets** contain user information. The packet uses 24-bit packet sequence numbers, which, if you recall the discussion on sliding window protocols, allows for potentially large windows. That is significant because small windows can limit the protocol's throughput.

- **Poll packets** are used to request the status of the receiver. SSCOP does not rely on a timer to resend packets that never arrived. This reduces its dependence on timer implementation. Instead it uses the poll packet, which contains the successor of the sequence number of the last transmitted packet. This packet also requests that the receiver reply with its status. On receiving the poll packet, the receiver can tell if any previously sent packets have not arrived.

- **Stat packets** are sent by a receiver in response to a poll packet. The stat packet contains the limiting sequence number of the receiver window, the sequence number of the next expected packet, and sequence numbers of any missing packets. On receipt of the stat packet the sender knows how many more packets it can send without overflowing the receiver window and which packets have not arrived. It can respond accordingly.

- An **unsolicited status packet** is essentially the same as a status packet except that it is not sent in response to a poll packet.

To be sure, there is more to SSCOP. The reader is encouraged to consult References [On95] and [He95] for additional details on SSCOP and related issues.

8.6   SYSTEMS NETWORK ARCHITECTURE

The last protocol we will discuss is IBM's **Systems Network Architecture (SNA).** SNA is of interest because it predates OSI; it was first released in 1974. In addition, it is probably the most widely used proprietary network architecture. Originally it was designed to connect a single host with terminals, but was updated in 1976 to allow multiple hosts to communicate. In 1985 another update included the support of LANs and arbitrary topologies.

Figure 8.51 shows the layered structure of SNA. It shows seven layers, but be warned that some references present SNA as a six- or even a five-layer protocol. The discrepancies occur because some people do not consider the lowest or highest layers to be part of SNA. In some of the older versions the upper two layers were considered one. At this level of discussion the number of layers is not important, as we are not going to present a detailed discussion of the questionable layers anyway. On the surface SNA resembles the OSI model. That is not surprising, because both are designed to connect a variety of devices.

One difference between SNA and OSI is that each OSI layer has its own header that it appends to data received from the next-higher layer. This does not occur in SNA. As with OSI, two SNA users communicate, with the layers providing specified tasks in the presentation and transmission of the data. Figure 8.52 illustrates the process. At the highest layer the user data is divided into one or more **request/response units (RUs).** Each layer passes the RU down to a lower one, with some of them adding extra headers. Transmission control adds an RU header, path control adds a transmission header, and data link control adds a link header. Some references show a function header added at the second-highest layer, but others consider it as part of the RU, as we have done here. Finally, the lowest layer transmits the RU and the appended headers as a bit stream.

In this last section we will summarize each of the layers and introduce some of the IBM terminology used in an SNA environment.

Figure 8.51   SNA Seven-Layer Protocol

transaction services
presentation services
data flow control
transmission control
path control
data link control
physical link control

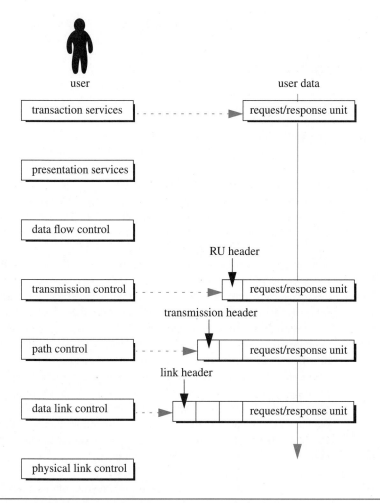

Figure 8.52   Packaging Data in SNA

LOWER LAYERS

Physical Link Control   The **physical link control layer** provides the physical and electrical specifications. It allows a variety of communication modes, including cable, optical fiber, and satellites. In some cases, it also allows multiple and distinct connections between two points, which lets the user specify a particular type of transmission, similar to the service type provided by the Internet Protocol (Section 7.4). This layer also can be used to divide data from a long stream into separate units and transmit them separately. Typical transmissions use serial links, although parallel transmission can be used between a mainframe and a front-end processor (a special processor designed to handle requests on behalf of the mainframe).

Data Link Control   SNA's **data link control layer** uses Synchronous Data Link Control (SDLC), the protocol on which HDLC is based. The two are very similar. Since we discussed HDLC in Section 5.5, we will not repeat the discussion for SDLC. Reference [Me88] discusses SDLC in detail.

PATH CONTROL

The **path control layer,** like OSI's network layer, determines paths and makes routing decisions. One difference is that the paths are all virtual paths that are determined during the connection establishment phase by a higher layer. SNA does not provide a connectionless mode of transfer.

Describing path control requires the use of several SNA-related terms and an understanding of its components. In general we use the word *node* to represent an entity in the network. An SNA node is a device capable of executing SNA protocols and storing data. It can be almost anything, including a terminal, device controller, workstation, mainframe, or front-end processor. SNA distinguishes between two types, a **peripheral node,** which has limited processing capabilities and includes devices such as terminals, printers, and controllers; and a **subarea node,**. which has more extensive capabilities and includes mainframes and communications processors.

Figure 8.53 shows how the two types of nodes typically are arranged and helps explain some other distinguishing features. SNA divides its network into domains, or subareas, each containing one subarea node and many peripheral nodes. The subarea nodes from all of the subareas communicate and are capable of routing information to one another using the full range of SNA protocols. They form the network's backbone. Peripheral nodes in a subarea typically communicate directly only with the subarea node. If they want to communicate with a peripheral node in another subarea they must use intermediate subarea nodes. As a result, subarea nodes are sometimes called **boundary nodes.**

Network Addressable Units   Each node also contains several **network addressable units (NAUs).** As the name implies, an NAU is an entity having its own unique SNA address. Primarily an NAU is a software construct capable of executing SNA protocols on the node. In effect it defines the network access point for a user (Figure 8.54) or other application. In some cases an NAU is created when a user logs on to a system for the purpose of network access. In other cases an NAU is always present within the node for management, administration, or testing purposes. In all cases, NAUs correspond to the entities among which SNA connections are established for the eventual exchange of RUs.

Each NAU's address contains two parts, the **subarea address** and the **element address.** Together they define the subarea and NAU within the subarea. The element address of an NAU is unique within its subarea. The subarea nodes route RUs along the backbone using only the subarea address.

Three types of NAUs are logical unit, physical unit, and system service control point. The **logical unit (LU)** defines the access point for an SNA user. It can also be called the **user port.** There is one LU for each session,[*] and it performs necessary functions for a user to communicate with another. The following list gives brief descriptions of the several types of LUs. If you are interested in a more detailed description of LUs, Reference [Me88] provides it.

Figure 8.53   SNA Node Arrangement

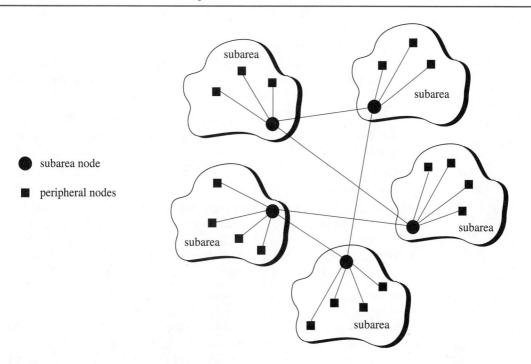

Figure 8.54   Network Access via NAU

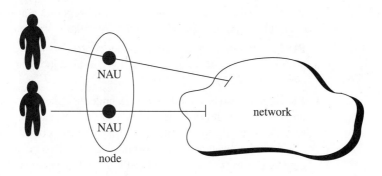

---

[*] A **session,** created by higher layers, is analogous to the TCP connection discussed in Section 7.5. We will discuss the SNA session in more detail later, but for now just think of it as a connection through which two NAUs communicate.

- **LU 0** corresponds to sessions that use SNA transmission and data flow control layers. The higher layers are not part of the SNA architecture and are often specific to a particular device or user. Typically this would be used for devices that have their own proprietary high-layer protocols.

- **LU 1** corresponds to sessions involving certain types of terminals, printers, or storage devices. Typically, these devices send and receive data streams corresponding to the SNA character string codes, an EBCDIC-based code defining specific control and data characters.

- **LU 2** corresponds to sessions involving another type of device called a **3270 terminal.** These terminals support the 3270 data stream, an old format used to define data and how it is to be presented on the screen.

- **LU 3** is similar to LU 2 but corresponds to printers instead of terminals.

- **LU 4** corresponds to sessions between two terminals or between a terminal and a host.

- **LU 6** allows sessions between any two applications running on different mainframes.

- **LU 6.2** (also called **advanced program-to-program communication** or **APPC**) supports a session between any two applications running on one of many types of devices (hosts, PCs, minicomputers). It is predicted to be the only LU used in the future and is designed for a truly distributed environment (some view LU 6.2 as a bona fide distributed operating system).

A **physical unit (PU)** is used for administration and testing functions. It generally manages a node's resources and performs control functions necessary to set up sessions and move information between the node and the network during the connection setup phase. It is responsible for activating or deactivating the node with regard to network access, and there is one PU for each node. As with LUs, there are several types of PUs. They are defined by the type of node in which they reside.

- **PU 1** is used in simple terminal nodes and supports non-SNA low-level protocols. It has limited capabilities and is essentially obsolete.

- **PU 2** is used in devices such as cluster controllers (devices that allow several terminals to connect to a common link), remote job entry stations, or printers connected to a host.

- **PU 2.1** may also be called a network node, peripheral node, or advanced cluster controller node. It is used in a variety of devices, such as PCs or minicomputers such as Systems /36 and /38. PU 2.1 is significant because prior to its introduction hosts were needed to route traffic between two peer nodes that were not connected directly. The advent of PU 2.1 allowed a distributed environment using LU 6.2.

- **PU 4** is used in a communication controller or front-end processor.

- **PU 5** is used in host computers.

The last type of NAU, the **system service control point (SSCP)**, is part of an IBM protocol called **Virtual Telecommunications Access Method (VTAM).** It has a much broader responsibility than either the LU or the PU. Whereas the LU and PU have responsibility for a particular node or device, the SSCP has responsibility for an entire domain or, in the absence of multiple domains, the entire SNA network. It does this in part by communicating with the various PUs within its domain. SSCP resides on a host, and its primary functions involve management of all communications within its subarea, network startup, session establishment, control of domain resources, maintenance, and error recovery.

With all the new and different terms being introduced, you may be having difficulty keeping them straight. Figure 8.55 attempts to help by showing some typical components, their connections in an SNA subarea, and where the various NAUs reside. It shows two terminal controllers, one with three active users at their respective terminals and the other with none. Consequently the first controller has three LUs (one for each user) and the other has none. Each of the terminals contains a PU of type 1. The terminal controllers contain type 2 PUs, the communications controller has a type 4 PU, and the host has a type 5 PU. The communication controller and host here do not show an LU because the users' needs are met at the terminal controller. Certainly a variety of other configurations can exist, and Reference [Sh90] shows some of them.

Virtual Route Control   One of the path control layer's main functions is the establishment of a path between two NAUs. It contains three components: the virtual route control, the explicit route control, and transmission group control.

Because all SNA communications are connection oriented, they require the establishment of a **virtual route** (similar to the virtual circuit of Section 7.3) before the exchange of user data. The **virtual route control** component does this by defining the logical connection between two NAUs. As with other networks we have discussed, no one component knows the route, and the route is transparent to the

Figure 8.55   Relationship among NAUs in an SNA Network

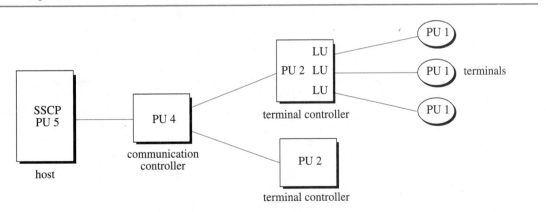

user. If the route crosses domain boundaries, routing tables at a subarea node transfer information to the next subarea node along the virtual route.

Each routing table entry contains a destination subarea address, a route number, and the location of the next node along the specified route to the specified address. The NAU's destination address and the route number to it are stored in a message's transmission header. On arrival, a subarea node looks for the subarea address and route number and compares them with its routing table's entries. From there it determines the next subarea node and stores the message in a queue to await transmission to it. In the event the message has arrived at the proper subarea, the node examines the element address and routes the message to the appropriate NAU.

Another virtual route control function is **pacing** (flow control). Pacing limits the number of **path information units (PIUs)** a node can send. As you probably guessed from the context, a PIU is the unit of information exchanged by the path control layers. Pacing uses a variation of a sliding window protocol, defining the maximum number of PIUs a node can send before it gets a response. The first PIU sent by a node contains a **virtual route pacing request indicator,** a request to the destination node to send a response called the **virtual route pacing response.**

There are now two possibilities. First is that the source node receives the response before it has sent all the PIUs in its window. In this case the source will begin sending PIUs from the next window after it sends all the PIUs in the current window. It assumes that since the destination responded so quickly it has the capacity to accept even more packets. (It's a lot like trying to please your boss by showing how much work you can get done. The more work you do, the more free time you are assumed to have. Therefore, you must not be busy enough.)

Suppose, on the other hand, the response does not arrive before the node sends the last PIU in the window. The node then puts a **virtual route pacing count indicator** in that last PIU. It is a signal to the destination that the source did not receive the response before sending the last PIU in the window. It is also a request that the destination send the response earlier if at all possible so the sending node can avoid waiting. In this case, the sending node increases its window by one (unless restricted by a maximum window size) and, when the response does arrive, resumes with the new and slightly larger window. The reason for the larger window is an attempt by the sender to increase its efficiency by waiting less. In the case in which the response arrives promptly there is no point in increasing the window because the sender does not wait anyway.

The pacing technique also can respond to congestion. If a node along a route is congested, it sets a **change window indicator** in the PIUs that it handles. When those PIUs reach their destination, the node sets a **change window reply indicator** in the virtual route pacing response it sends back to the source. When the source receives the response it decreases the window size by one (subject to a default minimum). This is a slow response to congestion, and there are more aspects to flow control at this level than presented here. As before, we refer the interested reader to References [Me88] and [Sp91] for further details.

Explicit Route Control   The path control layer's **explicit route control** sublayer allows a user to specify a **class of service (COS).** The COS allows a user to specify a high priority, a quick response, a secure line, a lower cost, or a higher throughput. This is similar to the Internet's type of service option in Section 7.4. Since SNA allows multiple connections between two subarea nodes (Figure 8.56), the COS partly determines which one to use. For example, a high-throughput COS is better served by an optical fiber link, but a coaxial connection might be chosen for a low-cost COS. A quick-response request would avoid a satellite link. The explicit route includes the virtual route further qualified by the actual transmission links between subarea nodes.

Transmission Group Control   The last component of path control is the **transmission group control.** A **transmission group** consists of one or more parallel transmission lines between two nodes that all can be assigned to the same explicit route. The purpose is to transmit different parts of user data in parallel to increase the overall transmission rate. Figure 8.57 shows an example. Two users at remote sites establish a connection and appear to communicate at a 50 Mbps rate. Unknown to each of them, the path control layers defined an explicit path with a three-line transmission group. One line has a 10 Mbps rate and the other two have 20 Mbps rates. Assuming everything works correctly and that information is transmitted over all three lines simultaneously, the perceived rate of transfer is 50 Mbps.

The transmission group control also can increase the data rate using **blocking** when there is only one transmission link available. It combines several PIUs into a single but larger unit called the **basic transmission unit (BTU).** It then sends the BTU to the next-lower layer for transmission as a single unit. The receiving path

Figure 8.56   Explicit Routes between Two Subarea Nodes

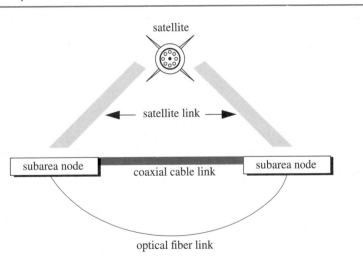

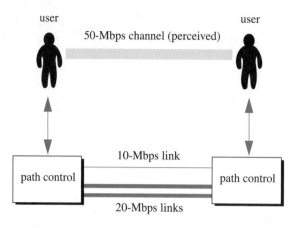

Figure 8.57   Gaining Bandwidth via Multiple Links

control layer extracts the PIUs from the BTU. Blocking several PIUs reduces the overhead bits required in sending otherwise separate units. It also eliminates the time between sending separate PIUs because they are sent together. You might review Section 5.2, which addressed the issue of effective data rates as a function of overhead, frame size, and overall bit rate.

TRANSMISSION CONTROL

The **transmission control layer** is analogous to the OSI transport layer. It is an end-to-end protocol defining a logical connection (**session**) between two NAUs (Figure 8.58). Despite the similar terminology, the SNA session is more like the OSI transport connection than the OSI session. Once established, the session allows the two NAUs to communicate on a level transparent to the underlying network structure. The transmission control layer has two main components, the session control and the connection point manager.

Figure 8.58   Transmission Control Session between Two NAUs

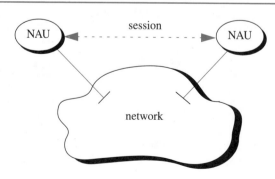

Session Control   The **session control** has the responsibility for starting, maintaining, and ending sessions. Perhaps the logical place to start is to identify the five different session types.

The first session type (LU-LU) connects two LUs and handles the actual data transfer between two users. The second (PU-PU) is used to transfer network control information between adjacent PUs. The third (SSCP-SSCP) is used in multidomain networks. It is necessary for any communications between NAUs in different domains. The fourth (SSCP-PU) establishes communication between an SSCP and each PU in its domain. As stated previously, SSCP-PU communication is necessary for maintenance, error recovery, and control of domain resources. The last session type (SSCP-LU) defines a connection between the SSCP and each LU in its domain. Such sessions are a prerequisite for the LU to be involved in any other activity.

Session establishment is not a simple task, and the approach varies depending on the NAU types and whether they reside in the same or different domains. We will describe one example of establishing a session between two LUs in different domains (Figure 8.59). References [Sp91] and [Me88] provide details on other session types. During this discussion we assume that all necessary SSCP-LU, SSCP-PU, and SSCP-SSCP sessions already exist. As stated earlier, they are necessary before LUs can establish sessions with each other.

Similar to previous protocols, there are different types of **BIUs (basic information units)** conveying different information. Session establishment defines the BIUs exchanged and the various responses to them. Suppose, in our example, LU *A* requests that a session be established with LU *B*. LU *A* might correspond to a user at a workstation trying to access a file server represented by LU *B*. When the user at *A* enters the command to request access, the session control protocol goes into action.

Figure 8.60 outlines the series of BIUs the NAUs exchange. First, LU *A* indicates that it wants a session by sending an **INITSELF** request to the SSCP in its domain. LU *A* has no idea whether LU *B* is in its domain or not, so the SSCP will make that determination. The request also identifies the LU making the request and to whom the request is made. The SSCP in domain *A* gets the request and determines whether LU *B* is in its domain or another one. In this case, LU *B* is in another domain, adding complexity to the request. Now SSCP *A* must communicate with SSCP *B* and get it involved in the session establishment.

Figure 8.59   Configuration for Example Session Establishment

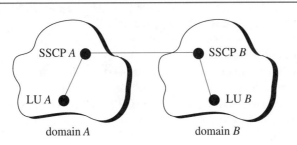

domain *A*   domain *B*

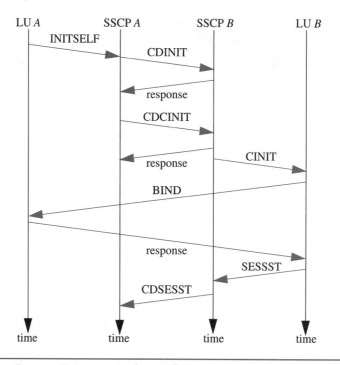

Consequently, SSCP *A* sends a **CDINIT (cross-domain initialize)** request to SSCP *B*. This is a preliminary indication to SSCP *B* that an LU from domain *A* wants a session with an LU in domain *B*. If SSCP *B* agrees to help in the session establishment (specified in the response), SSCP *A* follows with a **CDCINIT (cross-domain control initialize)** request. This request contains all the details regarding the proposed session and provides information about the LU making the request. It may seem strange to do this with two separate requests, but it is common to make a request and get agreement before providing all the information. It's a bit like a student approaching an instructor and saying "May I ask a question?" before actually asking it.

When SSCP *B* gets the information in the CDCINIT request, it responds to SSCP *A* and then sends a **CINIT (control initiate)** request to LU *B*. It tells LU *B* that LU *A* wants a session and requests that LU *B* send a **BIND** command all the way back to LU *A*. The BIND command actually initiates the session establishment and also contains some session parameters that *B* suggests (we will see some examples when we discuss the higher layers). When LU *A* gets the BIND, if it agrees with the controlling parameters it sends a response back to LU *B*. As far as LU *A* and LU *B* are concerned, the session is now established. The only task left is to inform the SSCPs that it is established. LU *B* sends SSCP *B* a **SESSST (session started)** message and SSCP *B* sends a **CDSESSST (cross-domain session started)** message to SSCP *A*.

We know that much of this reads like an excursion through a large bowl of alphabet soup. SNA, along with much of the IBM industry, is loaded with acronyms. If necessary you should read the section a second or even third time, take two aspirins, and call an IBM representative in the morning.

Connection Point Manager The **connection point manager's (CPMGR)** main function is to provide support for data flow over a session. It has several specific responsibilities, among them being the following:

- **Message sequencing.** As in previous protocols, messages are sequenced to make sure they arrive in order. It also uses message numbers to relate responses to previous requests.

- **Message buffering.** It maintains queues for incoming and outgoing messages.

- **Expedited messages.** Similar to the urgent indicator in TCP (Section 7.5), it allows certain "important" messages to be sent ahead of others following the normal sequence.

- **Pacing.** We haven't forgotten that we said that pacing is a function of the virtual route control sublayer. In that case, pacing refers to the traffic over a particular virtual route. However, a virtual route (or part of one) may support multiple sessions. In this case, pacing refers strictly to the flow rate between the two session partners. The pacing algorithm is basically the same as that used by virtual route control, except in this case the window size is fixed.

- **Encryption.** During session establishment the BIND message specifies whether none, some, or all messages will be encrypted. The CPMGR uses the DES algorithm to encrypt messages.

DATA FLOW CONTROL

The fifth layer in SNA is the **data flow control** layer, whose functions are similar to the OSI session layer (Section 1.4). It is perhaps the lowest layer to provide services directly to the user. Despite the name, it has nothing to do with flow control as we have defined it. That is primarily a function of the lower layers. Responsibilities of this layer include the following:

- **Specifying send/receive modes.** Specified in the BIND command, this function allows the LUs to exchange data using a half-duplex transfer mode, a useful feature if buffers must be shared by incoming and outgoing messages. There are two types of half-duplex modes: half-duplex flip-flop and half-duplex contention. **Half-duplex flip-flop** requires that the two LUs take turns sending, with the BIND command specifying who goes first. When the sending LU has finished sending, it sets a bit (**change direction indicator**) in the last RU and enters a receive mode. When the receiving LU detects the indicator, it enters the send mode. It is similar to passing a token back and forth. In this way they continue to take turns being in the sending and receiving modes.

With **half-duplex contention** mode, either station can enter a send mode and transmit. However, if both do so at the same time a contention results. To address this, one of the LUs is designated a contention winner (by the BIND command) during session establishment. It is a bit like determining who is going to win before playing the game. When contention happens the winner rejects incoming messages and sends a reject response to the loser. The loser then must exit the send mode, dequeue the messages it sent, receive the incoming messages, and try sending later.

- **Chaining.** Chaining is a way of defining a sequence of RUs going in one direction (a **chain**) that must be processed together. Chain indicators in the RU headers indicate the beginning and end of a chain. The idea is that a particular request might be made using several RUs. With chaining, the protocols could recover from an error by restarting the activity from the beginning of the chain. For example, suppose a small file was being transferred as a chain of RUs to a file server. If the drive failed and destroyed the information already written, the protocols could recover, start from the beginning of the chain, and write all the information to a backup device.

  There are three types of chains: no-response chain, exception-response chain, and definite-response chain. The **no-response chain** means that no response is required for any RU in the chain. The **exception-response chain** requires a response only in the event of an error detected in one of the chain's RUs. The **definite-response chain** requires a response whether the chain was received intact or not.

- **Bracketing.** Chains can be generalized into **brackets** (Figure 8.61), providing another level for organizing RUs. A bracket typically corresponds to a **transaction,** a user-defined unit of work that might actually consist of several request/response exchanges. A typical example is a database query, in which you enter a primary key, retrieve the information (and consequently lock the record), make

Figure 8.61   Relationship between Chaining and Bracketing

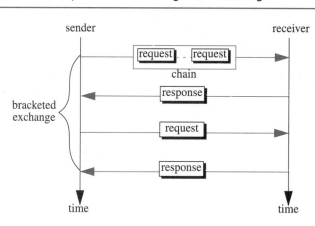

updates, and store the result. An application layer could define these activities as a single transaction, thus causing all the associated RUs to be bracketed. The idea is to avoid a situation in which an error occurs after retrieving the record, thus severing the connection and leaving the record locked. With bracketing, the protocols would process all of the RUs or none at all. If an error occurred in the middle it would restart from the beginning of the bracket.

- **Defining request/response modes.** We stated earlier that there are two types of RUs, a request and a response. Generally a response will follow a request, but there are exceptions. Flags in an RU header can specify three types of responses: do not respond, respond only if an error occurs, respond always. Four request/response modes define the relationship between a request and a response.

  In **immediate request mode,** if a sender sends a request (or a chain) requiring a definite response it may not send another until it receives the response. This rule does not apply to requests requiring exception responses or none at all. In other words, several of those requests can be pending. **Delayed request mode** allows the sender to have several requests requiring definite responses pending (there is an analogy here with the unrestricted and stop and wait flow control protocols if you think of responses as similar to acknowledgments). **Immediate response mode** requires the receiver to return responses in the same order the associated requests arrived. **Delayed response mode** allows them to be returned in any order. These modes largely define how much synchronization you want between the requests and responses.

The data flow control layer primarily provides a service for the layer above it, the presentation services. That is, the previous functions typically apply to RUs that data flow control receives from presentation services. However, in some cases the data flow control layers on each end can define and exchange their own RUs. For example, one end can stop the flow of incoming messages temporarily by sending a QUIESCE AT END OF CHAIN command. The other end will finish with its current chain but will send nothing more until it receives a RELEASE QUIESCE command.

An NAU also can prepare for session termination by sending a SHUTDOWN command to begin the session termination procedures at the transmission control layer. The other end will send any outstanding responses and then send a SHUTDOWN COMPLETE command, thus terminating the session. For information and other examples of RUs that data flow control can exchange, we refer you to Reference [Me88].

HIGHER LAYERS

Earlier we stated that references vary regarding the number of layers they attribute to SNA. In part this is due to developments within the SNA architecture itself. For example, in earlier versions of SNA there was one layer (**function management layer**) above the data flow control layer. With the development and release of LU 6.2, that layer was divided into the presentation services and transaction services layers (Figure 8.51).

We do not want to enter into discussions involving details that vary according to versions and the impact that LU 6.2 had on SNA. We do feel, however, that it is important to understand that such differences exist and to have a general idea of the impact of LU 6.2. Therefore, our approach here is to finish up this section, chapter, and book with brief summaries of these last two layers and refer you to more extensive readings.

At this level of discussion the **presentation services layer** is similar to the OSI presentation layer. It provides format translation to account for differences in the internal representation of data or in the control characters used to display data on a screen or print it. It also provides compression to increase transmission efficiency. A notable difference from OSI is encryption, a responsibility of the transmission control layer instead of the presentation services layer.

The **transaction services layer** allows an operator to configure the network by adding or removing communication links. It also allows the gathering and display of network usage statistics, a useful feature in planning for future expansion or reconfiguration. This can include tracking various performance measures and providing accounting services to charge users for using the network. Applications also exist to provide testing and to help track down and isolate network errors. In some cases the network can diagnose what went wrong and either provide a solution or bypass the problem until it can be fixed. The earlier versions of SNA had these services in the function management layer (also called NAU services layer). Reference [Me88] has an entire chapter devoted to these topics.

Finally, we mention LU 6.2 again because it has had a significant impact on the SNA architecture and its abilities. Prior to it, communicating entities were always involved in a master/slave relationship (a typical terminal-to-host connection). The slave entity had less processing power and had to make requests to the master regarding establishing and defining the protocols. With the advent of workstations and distributed computing environments, however, the need grew for more peer-to-peer sessions. This means that either end has significant computing power and can take the initiative in establishing sessions or making other requests. It also eliminates the need to exchange data in predefined formats and allows a two-way interactive ability between programs running on very different processors. We said it before but it bears repeating: LU 6.2 goes a long way toward making the underlying architecture completely transparent to the end user and providing distributed computing capabilities. The downside (and there is always a downside) is that it is expensive and may not be the best choice for environments that do not need a distributed environment. References [Sh90] and [Me88] provide some different viewpoints on LU 6.2, how it works, and its role in future systems.

As with many protocols, there is some disagreement as to whether SNA will eventually be superseded by other protocols such as OSI or even TCP/IP. Some feel that TCP/IP is better designed for decentralized computing environments. IBM, of course, is not going to sit on its reputation and has developed its **Advanced Peer-to-Peer Networking (APPN).** Derived from SNA, it allows a wide variety of computers to communicate across many different types of networks (including LANs and WANs). Some believe it will outperform current versions of TCP/IP and OSI protocols and will be in demand for a variety of applications from low-speed transport to multimedia applications. Yet others believe that TCP/IP still provides more flexibility and service to a greater variety of platforms. Regardless of the diverse views of many professionals, one thing is certain: There will continue to be many approaches to meeting network needs. Understanding them and their differences will challenge us well into the 21st century.

Review Questions

1. Distinguish between a smart terminal and a virtual terminal.

2. Describe the client/server mode of computing.

3. What is Telnet?

4. Distinguish between a remote login and a conventional login.

5. What is a virtual file structure?

6. Are the following statements TRUE or FALSE? Why?

    a. Telnet allows you to log in to any account on a remote machine as long as it is reachable via a network connection.

    b. TCP and IP are OSI model layer 3 and layer 4 protocols.

    c. Sending mail over the Internet does not require a connection.

    d. Each message sent via the X.400 protocol is stored in its entirety at each intermediate X.400 node.

    e. Two user agents at the same site can communicate directly under the X.400 protocol.

    f. The all-digital capability of ISDN would provide immediate advantages to everyone who uses it.

    g. SNA pacing is the same as a sliding window protocol.

7. How does anonymous FTP differ from FTP?

8. What is an RFC?

9. Distinguish between TFTP and FTP.

10. What is SMTP?

11. Why are TCP and IP at different layers in the protocol hierarchy?

12. What is SNMP?

13. What is SNMP's management information base?

14. What is the External Gateway Protocol?

15. What is the Hypertext Markup Language?

16. What is a Common Gateway Interface script?

17. What is the reason for having programming capabilities on both the client and server ends for Web page development?

18. Distinguish among a coldstart trap, warmstart trap, and linkdown trap.

19. Why are there two standards for email, namely SMTP and X.400?

20. Distinguish between an X.400 user agent and a message transfer agent.

21. List four functions of X.400's user agent that you think would be most useful to you.

22. What does the message transfer agent put in a message's envelope?

23. How does a store-and-forward protocol differ from previous protocols such as a packet-switched protocol?

24. Distinguish among an MHS probe, message, and report.

25. Distinguish among MHS's P1, P2, and P3 protocols.

26. List four MHS services you think would be most useful to you.

27. Distinguish between the X.400 and X.500 protocol families.

28. What is a directory service?

29. Distinguish between X.500's directory information base and directory information tree.

30. Distinguish between a directory user agent and a directory system agent.

31. What is ISDN?

32. Distinguish between ISDN's basic and primary services.

33. List four ISDN services you think would be most useful to you.

34. List and summarize the four primary functional groups in ISDN.

35. List and summarize the four reference points in ISDN.

36. What is the difference between out-of-band and in-band signaling?

37. What is Signaling System no. 7?

38. What is pseudoternary coding?

39. What is broadband ISDN?

40. Why do some predict that ATM is the protocol of the future?

41. What is the purpose of having several AAL layers?

42. Distinguish among Class A, B, C, and D traffic on an ATM network.

43. Why are ATM cells 53 bytes long?

44. List some advantages of using small fixed-length cells in ATM.

45. What is the difference between a virtual path and a virtual circuit in ATM, and why is there a distinction?

46. What is the advantage of using a Banyan switch rather than a common routing table?

47. Why does the header error control field in an ATM cell header check only the header and leave the payload unprotected?

48. Describe how the header error control field can also be used to locate an ATM cell's boundary.

49. List some items an ATM setup message might contain.

50. Why is it acceptable for AAL 5 packets to contain variable-length and potentially large payloads, whereas it is unacceptable for AAL 1 and AAL 2?

51. What is SNA?

52. List each of SNA's seven layers and give a brief description of its functions.

53. Distinguish between an SNA subarea node and peripheral node.

54. What is a network addressable unit?

55. Distinguish between an SNA logical unit and a physical unit.

56. How does the virtual route control change the size of an NAU's window?

57. Why is pacing done at both the path control layer and the transmission control layer?

58. What is the path control's transmission group?

59. Distinguish between explicit route control and virtual route control.

60. List and summarize the five types of SNA sessions.

61. What is a connection point manager?

62. List the major functions of SNA's data flow control layer.

63. Distinguish between the data flow control's chain and bracket.

Exercises

1. Do a remote login to some account and experiment with the Telnet commands. For example, you can do the following:

   - Type a large file, escape to Telnet, and abort the output.
   - Determine the response to the AYT command.
   - Send EC commands to erase characters in an incorrectly typed command.

- Run a long program, escape to Telnet, and interrupt the process.
- Send an EL command to erase an incorrectly typed line.

If you do not have access to an account on a remote machine you can log in to your own account and access your account a second time via Telnet. It's a little like calling yourself on the telephone, but it works and allows you to become familiar with Telnet. (You will have to determine whether your site allows multiple logins to one account.)

2. Connect to a remote site via anonymous FTP, transfer a small file to your account, and write a short summary of the file's contents.

3. Send someone you know an email message over the Internet. If you don't know anyone at a remote site who has access to the Internet, send an Internet mail message to someone locally; to the author of this text, indicating your opinion of the text; or to yourself. (As in Exercise 1, this is a little like sending yourself a letter but, again, it helps you get familiar with Internet email.)

4. If you haven't already done so, create a Web page containing at least some text and links to remote URLs. You decide what to put in the page.

5. Modify the JavaScript code of Figure 8.15 so that the user may insert an arbitrary number of spaces between the numbers he or she enters.

6. Create an HTML form that allows a user to enter the dimensions of a rectangle and uses a script to return the rectangle's area. The script should determine whether the dimensions are positive and, if they are not, generate an alert box.

7. Repeat Exercise 6 but include checkboxes to indicate whether the user wants the area or perimeter (or both) of the rectangle. The script must make sure the user selects at least one option.

8. Modify the gateway program of Figure 8.20 to allow multiple entries to be made on the form of Figure 8.18. The gateway program should return references matching any one of the numbers entered in the text box.

9. Suppose Mary Smith's (from Figure 8.28) husband is a marketing analyst in the same company. How would someone send him email using the X.500 directory service?

10. Suppose each of the TE1s in the following figure tries sending something to the NT2 at the same time.

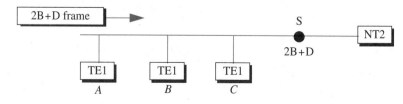

Suppose also that each is trying to send the following over the D channel.

- *A* sends 10011101.
- *B* sends 10001100.
- *C* sends 10011001.

Which TE1 wins the contention?

11. ISDN's B channel capacities were designed with the intention of transmitting voice. Section 2.4 showed that to capture most of a voice's characteristics, 8-bit samples taken at a frequency of 8000 samples per second is sufficient and requires a bit rate of 64,000 bps. However, some encoding techniques actually allow voice data to be transmitted using 32,000 bps, and others will likely allow 16,000 bps to be sufficient. What effect will this have on the ISDN standard?

12. Draw a diagram similar to that of Figure 8.37 showing the ISDN disconnect procedure.

13. Describe a scenario in which four cells can be routed through the Banyan switch of Figure 8.40 simultaneously with no collisions.

REFERENCES

1. [Ap86] Appenzeller, H. R. "Signaling System No. 7, ISDN User Part." *IEEE Journal on Selected Areas in Communication,* vol. SAC-4, no. 3 (May 1986), 366–371.

2. [At89] AT&T and Bellcore. "Observations of Error Characteristics of Fiber Optic Transmission Systems." *CCITT SG XVIII*, San Diego, CA, January, 1989.

3. [Bl91] Black, U. *The X Series Recommendations.* New York: McGraw-Hill, 1991.

4. [Bl95] Black, U. *ATM: Foundation for Broadband Networks.* Englewood Cliffs, NJ: Prentice-Hall, 1995.

5. [Bl97] Black, U. *Emerging Communications Technologies.* Englewood Cliffs, NJ: Prentice-Hall, 1997.

6. [Ca98] Catanzaro, B. *Step-by-Step ISDN: The Internet Connection Handbook.* Englewood Cliffs, NJ: Prentice-Hall, 1998.

7. [Co94] Comer, D. E., and D. Stevens. *Internetworking with TCP/IP.* Vol. II; *Design, Implementation, and Internals.* 2nd ed. Englewood Cliffs, NJ: Prentice-Hall, 1994.

8. [Co95] Comer, D. E. *Internetworking with TCP/IP.* Vol. I; *Principles, Protocols, and Architecture.* 3rd ed. Englewood Cliffs, NJ: Prentice-Hall, 1995.

9. [Gr90] Griffiths, J. M. *ISDN Explained.* New York: Wiley, 1990.

10. [Ho95] Hopkins, G. *The ISDN Literacy Book.* Reading, MA: Addison-Wesley, 1995.

11. [He95] Henderson, T. "Design Principles and Performance Analysis of SSCOP: A New ATM Adaptation Layer Protocol." *Computer Communications Review,* vol. 25, no. 2 (April 1995), 47–59.

12. [Me88] Meijer, A. *Systems Network Architecture: A Tutorial.* New York: Wiley, 1988.

13. [On95] Onvural R. *Asynchronous Transfer Mode Networks: Performance Issues,* 2nd ed. Norwood, MA: Artech House, 1995.

14. [Ro95] Rose, M. *How to Manage Your Network Using SNMP.* Englewood Cliffs, NJ: Prentice-Hall, 1995.

15. [Ro96] Rose, M. *The Simple Book: An Introduction to Internet Management.* Englewood Cliffs, NJ: Prentice-Hall, 1996.

16. [Ru89] Russel, D. *The Principles of Computer Networking.* Cambridge, England: Cambridge University Press, 1989.

17. [Sc86] Schlanger, G. G. "An Overview of Signaling System No. 7." *IEEE Journal on Selected Areas in Communication,* vol. SAC-4, no. 3 (May 1986), 360–365.

18. [Sh90] Sherman, K. *Data Communications: A User's Guide,* 3rd ed. Englewood Cliffs, NJ: Prentice-Hall, 1990.

19. [Sp91] Spragins, J. D., J. L. Hammond, and K. Pawlikowski. *Telecommunications Protocols and Design.* Reading, MA: Addison-Wesley, 1991.

20. [St94] Stallings, W. *SNMP, SNMPv2, and CMIP: The Practical Guide to Network-Management Standards.* Reading, MA: Addison-Wesley, 1994.

21. [St95] Stallings, W. *ISDN and Broadband ISDN with Frame Relay and ATM,* 3rd ed. Englewood Cliffs, NJ: Prentice-Hall, 1995.

22. [St96] Stallings, W. *SNMP, SNMPv2, and RMON: Practical Network Management,* 2nd ed. Reading, MA: Addison-Wesley, 1996.

23. [St97] Stallings, W. *Data and Computer Communications,* 5th ed. Englewood Cliffs, NJ: Prentice-Hall, 1997.

24. [Va97] Varshney, U., "Supporting Mobility with Wireless ATM." *Computer,* vol. 30, no. 1 (January 1997), 131–133.

25. [We13] Weder, C., J. Reynolds, and S. Heker. "Technical Overview of Directory Services Using the X.500 Protocol." RFC Document 1309.

Glossary

abort	a sudden end to an activity, usually due to some type of error
Abstract Syntax Notation 1 (ASN.1)	formal language designed expressly for the definition of protocol data unit formats and the representation of and operations on distributed information
accept	socket command used by a server to accept a request for a socket connection from a client
access control (token ring)	octet in a token containing priority, reservation, token, and monitor bits
ACK timer	timer used in flow control protocols to determine when to send a separate acknowledgment in the absence of outgoing frames
acknowledgment	indication that a station has received something from another
active monitor present frame	special frame used in the token ring protocol to indicate the presence of an active monitor station
adaptive routing	routing strategy that can respond to changes in a network
address field	field in a frame or packet identifying its sender or receiver
address learning	ability of a LAN bridge to update its routing tables dynamically
address lookup service	ability to get the email address of someone by specifying any of a variety of items that uniquely identify a person
address recognized bit	bit in a token ring frame indicating whether the destination address has been recognized
advanced peer-to-peer networking	an SNA derivative allowing a wide variety of computers to communicate across many types of networks
Advanced Research Projects Agency	agency of the U.S. Department of Defense

Advanced Research Projects Agency Network (ARPANET)	network developed by the Advanced Research Projects Agency that evolved into protocols used in the Internet
all-routes broadcast frame	frame that a bridge will route onto all available LANs
Aloha	word used as a greeting or farewell
Aloha protocol	packet radio protocol in which a station sends a packet and, if it collides with another, will send another after a random amount of time
alternate mark inversion	digital encoding in which a 1 bit is represented by zero volts and a 0 bit is represented alternately by a positive and a negative signal
Amateur Packet Radio Network	packet radio network using TCP/IP and registered with the Internet
American National Standards Institute	private, nongovernmental standards agency whose members are manufacturers, users, and other interested companies
American Standard Code for Information Interchange (ASCII)	seven-bit code that assigns a unique combination to every keyboard character and to some special functions
amplitude	largest magnitude of an analog signal
amplitude modulation (amplitude shift keying)	method of representing bits using analog signals with different magnitudes
analog signal	continuously varying signal
analog-to-digital conversions	process of converting an analog signal to a digital one
anonymous FTP	application allowing remote users access to a set of files at a given site
application layer	seventh and highest layer of the OSI protocol, which works directly with a user or with application programs
Arcnet	token-passing protocol that uses a star topology
asynchronous balanced mode	mode for HDLC in which either station can send data, control information, or commands
asynchronous response mode	mode for HDLC in which a primary station can send data, control information, or commands, and a secondary station can send control information or data only
asynchronous transfer mode (ATM)	very fast packet-switched protocol using small fixed-size packets optimized for multimedia use
asynchronous transmission	transmission mode in which bits are divided into small groups (bytes or octets) and sent independently
ATM adaptation layer (AAL)	component of the ATM protocol that provides the interface between applications and the ATM layer
attenuation	degradation of a signal as it travels along a medium

authentication	verifying the sender of a message or authenticity of a document
autobaud modem	a modem capable of automatically choosing one of several modulation standards
automatic repeat request	error control whereby a station requests the sending station to resend a message if an error occurs
B channel	ISDN channel capable of transmitting at 64 Kbps
backbone	that part of a network comprising the primary transmission paths
backward learning algorithm	routing algorithm in which a node learns from its neighbors the cheapest route to another node
balanced circuit	circuit using two lines carrying equal but opposite signals
bandpass filter	device used to extract individual modulated signals
bandwidth	difference between the highest and lowest frequencies that a medium can transmit
baseband mode	mode in which a cable's bandwidth is devoted to a single stream of data
baud rate	rate at which signal components can change
Baudot code	a five-bit code originally designed for the French telegraph and still used today in telegraph and telex communications
beacon frame	token ring control frame used to inform stations a problem has occurred and the token-passing protocol has stopped
beam shaping	process of allowing a satellite signal to be concentrated in a small area
BEL	an ASCII control character causing a CRT or terminal to emit an audible sound; Also a unit of measurement of signal power relative to noise power.
Bellman-Ford algorithm	a type of backward learning algorithm
binary exponential backoff algorithm	algorithm used to determine when a station should resend a frame after a collision
binary synchronous control (BSC) protocol	byte-oriented data link protocol made popular by IBM
binary-coded decimal (BCD)	a code used in early IBM mainframes
bind	socket command to associate a socket with a text address and port number
bindery	Novell NetWare file containing file access rights for a user or group of users
bit pipe	the actual bit transmission in the ISDN protocol
bit stuffing	the insertion of an extra bit to avoid a long run of the same bit
bit time	time required for one bit to be transmitted
bit-level ciphering	encryption by bit manipulation
bit-oriented protocol	a protocol that treats frames as bit streams
block check character	character used by the BSC protocol for error checking
Border Gateway Protocol	a protocol that allows routers to implement specific policies or constraints that route must meet.

boundary nodes	nodes forming the backbone in the SNA protocol
bridge	an OSI layer 2 connection between two networks
bridge port	bridge to a LAN connection
bridge protocol data units	unit of information exchanged by bridges
bridge routing	the process a bridge uses to determine which frames to forward and where to forward them
broadband mode	mode in which a cable's bandwidth is divided into ranges, each carrying separately coded information
broadcast address	address indicating a frame should be sent to all stations on a network
Brouter	device providing functions at both OSI layer 2 and layer 3
buffering	temporary storage of information
bulletin boards	data banks allowing the exchange of software, files, or other information
burst error	error affecting a large number of bits
bus topology	way of connecting devices so they all communicate via a common cable
byte multiplexer	device that combines bytes from different sources into a common data stream
byte stuffing	insertion of an extra byte to avoid misinterpreting a data byte as a control byte
byte-oriented protocol	protocol that treats frames as byte streams
cable modem	a device designed to connect a computer with a cable service provider's signals
Caesar cipher	simple encryption technique in which a character is replaced by another dependent only on the value of the original character
call confirmation	indication that a call has been accepted
call request	action taken by a device when it wants to establish a connection
Cambridge ring	ring network containing several rotating tokens
Carriage Return	ASCII control character causing a print mechanism or cursor to return to the leftmost print position
Carrier Sense Multiple Access (CSMA)	protocol used to sense whether a medium is busy before attempting to transmit
Carrier Sense Multiple Access with Collision Detection (CSMA/CD)	same as Carrier Sense Multiple Access but also has the ability to detect whether a transmission has collided with another
carrier signal	signal that is modulated by an input signal to create another signal
cell	geographic region having a reception and transmission station to communicate with cellular telephones, also transmission unit defined by ATM protocol.
cellular telephone	portable telephone capable of connecting to the telephone system using radio communications
centralized routing	routing using information that is generated and maintained at a single central location

channel	bandwidth range
channel utilization	measurement specifying percentage of time a channel spends transferring information
Cheapernet	IEEE 802.3 network using 10 BASE 2 cable
checksum	field used for error detection formed by adding bit strings interpreted as integers
choke packet	control packet sent to a station causing it to reduce the number of packets it is transmitting
ciphertext	message that has been encrypted
circuit switching	a connection that is dedicated to the communication between two stations
cladding	part of an optical fiber that is optically less dense than the core, thus causing light to reflect back into the core
claim token frame	token ring control frame used to determine a monitor station
class of service	SNA path control option allowing a user to specify a high priority, quick response, secure line, lower cost, or higher throughput
Clear to Send	RS-232 signal from a DCE giving a DTE permission to send
client	device or program in a client server model that sends requests to a server
client / server model	model of communication between two devices in which each has computing power
clipper chip	controversial encryption device capable of being placed in telephones for the purpose of scrambling conversations
coaxial cable	conductive wire surrounded by an insulating layer, wire mesh, and a protective outer cover
code	association of bit patterns with specific information such as characters or actions
codec	device used to translate an analog signal to a digital equivalent
collision	the result when two or more stations simultaneously send a signal over a medium designed to transmit one signal at a time
collision detection	ability of a station to determine when a collision has occurred
combined station	station that can act as both a primary and a secondary station in the HDLC protocol
Comité Consultatif International de Télégraphique et Téléphonique (CCITT)	former standards organization whose members include various scientific and industrial organizations, telecommunication agencies, telephone authorities, and the ISO; it has been replaced by the ITU-T
common bus topology	way of connecting devices so they all communicate via a common cable
Common Gateway Interface (CGI) program	a server program which can be activated from within an HTML document
Common Management Information Protocol	ISO management protocol
communications subnet	collection of transmission media and switching elements required for routing and data transmission

compact disc	storage medium in which information is stored optically by making very small pits in a reflective material
compression	way to reduce the number of bits during transmission while retaining most or all the meaning of the transmitted message
CompuServe	information service allowing subscribers to access a distributed database
concentrator	intelligent statistical multiplexer that can verify, acknowledge, and compress data
congestion	excessive amount of traffic over a network that causes a degradation of service and response times
connection	mechanism through which two stations exchange information
connection management	protocol used to establish, maintain, and release connections
connection request	request to establish a connection
connection strategy	strategy used to implement a connection
contention	term used when two or more stations want to transmit over a common medium at the same time
contention protocol	technique used to control access to a common medium from multiple entry points
control bits	the part of the data frame used for control functions such as routing and handling
control characters	binary codes that correspond to an action rather than data
control prefix character	special character inserted into a data stream by Kermit to avoid misinterpreting a data character as a control character
control-Q	control character used to tell a device to resume sending
control-S	control character used to tell a device to stop sending
credit	used in flow control, it specifies the number of bytes a TCP entity can receive from another
credit mechanism	method used to implement flow control in TCP
crossbar switch	a switching device that contains switching logic for each pair of input and output lines
crosstalk	interference on a line caused by signals being transmitted along another one
cyclic redundancy check	error detection method based on interpreting bit strings as polynomials with binary coefficients
D channel	ISDN channel typically used for control and low-speed applications
Data Carrier Detected	RS-232 signal indicating that a DCE is receiving a suitable carrier signal
Data Circuit-Terminating Equipment (DCE)	device used as an interface between a DTE and a network
data compression	way to reduce the number of bits during transmission while retaining most or all of the meaning of the transmitted message

Data Encryption Standard (DCE)	encryption technique developed by IBM and adopted as a standard by the U.S. government
Data Link Escape	control character used as a toggle switch causing a device to interpret subsequently received characters differently
data link layer	layer 2 of the OSI protocol
data link protocols	protocols operating at OSI layer 2
data rate	measurement specifying the number of data bits a medium can transmit per unit of time
Data Set Ready	RS-232 signal indicating the DCE has connected to a communications medium
Data Terminal Equipment (DTE)	device connected to a communications medium via a DCE
data terminal ready	RS-232 signal indicating a DTE is ready
datagram	independent transmission unit in a packet-switching network
de facto standards	standards that exist by virtue of their widespread use
deadlock	situation in which stations are waiting for events to occur that cannot happen because of their own current states
deadly embrace	same as deadlock
decibel	measurement related to signal-to-noise ratio
decryption	process of restoring an encrypted message to its original form
demodulation	restoring a signal that has been modulated to its original form
designated bridge	during execution of the spanning tree algorithm for LAN interconnection, a bridge elected to forward frames from a LAN
destination address	address to which a frame or packet is to be delivered
differential encoding	compression technique in which a frame is represented by the difference between it and a preceding frame
Differential Manchester encoding	Manchester encoding technique in which 0 and 1 are distinguished by whether the signal changes at the beginning of a bit interval
differential phase shift keying	distinguishing an analog signal by measuring its phase shift relative to that of a previous signal
Diffie-Hellman key exchange	a method of key distribution that works by having a sender and receiver exchange calculated values from which an encryption key can be computed.
Digital Equipment Corporation	major corporation perhaps best known for manufacture of its VAX and alpha line of computers
Digital Network Architecture	proprietary network protocol developed by the Digital Equipment Corporation
digital signal	square-wave signal taking on only a high or low value
digital signature	method of authentication involving encrypting a message in a way only the sender would know

Dijkstra's algorithm	algorithm used to find the cheapest (shortest) path between two nodes in a graph
discrete cosine transforms	a calculation used in the first of three phases in the JPEG compression scheme that generates a set of spatial frequencies.
directory information base	distributed database containing information in an X.500 directory
directory service	service that provides the email address of an individual given that he or she is unambiguously identified
directory system agent	component of X.500 that manages part of the directory information base at a given site
directory user agent	component of X.500 providing the interface between an application and the distributed information base
disconnect	termination of a connection
disk duplexing	process of using two different controllers to make duplicate copies of data maintained by a file server
disk mirroring	process of using one controller to make duplicate copies of data maintained by a file server by writing it to two different disks
distortion	change in a signal due to electronic noise or interference
distributed directory	directory made up of components residing at different sites
distributed file system	collection of files in which files are maintained by different computers
distributed routing	routing strategy in which each node determines and maintains its routing information independently
do not fragment bit	control bit that disables fragmentation of a packet during its transmission
DoD Internet protocol	network layer protocol adopted by the Department of Defense and used in the Internet
domain	group of nodes in a network
Domain Name System	distributed protocol that translates a symbolic Internet address to a 32-bit numeric address
double bit errors	transmission error affecting two bits
downstream neighbor	neighboring node within a ring in the direction the token travels
downward multiplexing	transport-layer function that takes data from a single source and sends it to separate network nodes
DTE-DCE interface	protocol used to define communication between a DTE and a DCE
duplicate address test frame	token ring control frame used to look for stations with the same address
echo reply	ICMP packet sent in reply to an echo request
echo request	ICMP control packet used to determine whether a particular destination is reachable

effective data rate	measurement specifying the number of actual data bits that can be transmitted per unit of time
eighth-bit prefix character	character used in Kermit to precede some transmitted bytes from a binary file
electrical ground	voltage level with which all signal voltages are compared
Electronic Industries Association	standards agency consisting of members from electronics firms and manufacturers of telecommunications equipment and a member of ANSI
electronic mail (email)	service allowing the sending of files or messages to another site electronically
Electronic Numerical Integrator and Calculator (ENIAC)	first completely electronic computer
electronic telephone directories	online database providing services similar to that of the conventional telephone directories
encryption	rendering of information into a different and unintelligible form
encryption key	data used to encrypt a message
End of Transmission	control character indicating the end of a transmission
End of Transmission Block	control character indicating the end of a block of data
envelope	additional control bytes added to a message by the message transfer agent in the X.400 email standard
erase character	TELNET command to erase the most recent character entered on a remote host
erase line	TELNET command to erase the most recent line entered on a remote host
error	unplanned event affecting accuracy of data or a protocol
error control	specification of how a station checks frames for errors and what it does if it finds them
error correction	process of correcting bits in a frame that were changed during transmission
error detection	process of determining whether bits in a frame have changed during transmission
error recovery	ability of a protocol to recover in the event of a failure in a network or lower-level protocol
Escape	control character causing one or more subsequent characters to be associated with some action
Eskimo pies	warm-weather treat
ether	imaginary substance that many once believed occupied all of outer space
Ethernet	local area network connected using a common bus and using a CSMA/CD contention protocol
even parity	method of error detection in which an extra bit is added whose value is 0 or 1 in order to make the total number of 1 bits in the transmission unit even
expedited messages	SNA mechanism that allows certain messages to be sent ahead of others

expiry date indication	MHS service allowing the sender of a message to specify a time and date after which the message is invalid
explicit route control	sublayer of SNA's path control layer that chooses actual transmission links between subarea nodes
extended binary coded decimal interchange code	eight-bit code for characters and control functions used heavily on IBM mainframes
exterior gateway protocol	SNMP protocol that exchanges routing information between two autonomous networks in an internet
extremely low frequency (ELF)	communication signals with a frequency less than 300 Hz
facsimile (fax) machine	device that scans and digitizes images for transmission over telephone lines
Federal Communications Commission (FCC)	federal agency that regulates and licenses communications
fiber distributed data interface	ANSI standard for a ring network using optical fiber
file server	device responsible for the maintenance and security of a network's files
file transfer protocol	rules for the access and exchange of files between two sites
filter	device that allows signals of a certain frequency to pass
fingerd	UNIX utility that allows users to obtain information about others
finite state machine	formal model describing the set of all possible states and state transitions of a system
fire	activity corresponding to the movement of tokens in a Petri net
fixed routing	routing techniques based on information that does not change except by reprogramming
fixed-routing bridges	bridges that do fixed routing
flags	bit indicators that indicate a function or status
flooding algorithm	routing algorithm that transmits a message to all possible locations
flow control	protocol that regulates the exchange of information between two devices
Form Feed	control character causing a print mechanism or cursor to advance to the beginning of the next form or screen
forwarding database	information used by a device to route frames from one network to another
Fourier series	mathematical formula used to describe an arbitrary periodic signal
fragment	part of a packet formed by fragmentation
fragment header	control information in a fragment
fragment offset field	specifies the offset in a packet's data field from where the fragment's data was extracted

fragmentation	process of dividing a packet into pieces to maintain consistency with a network's protocol
frame	unit of information exchanged by low-level protocols
frame check sequence	field in a frame used for error checking
frame control	field in a token ring frame containing frame type and other control information
frame copied bit	bit indicating whether a token ring frame was copied by its intended destination
frame format	way in which bits are organized in a frame
frame reject	signal that an incoming frame was rejected by the receiving protocol
frame status	field in a token ring frame specifying whether a frame was copied or its destination address was recognized
frame timer	timer used in flow control protocols to determine when to resend a frame if it has not been acknowledged
frequency	rate at which a signal repeats
frequency modulation (frequency shift keying)	method of representing bits using analog signals with different frequencies
frequency-division multiplexing	process of accepting analog signals within distinct bandwidths and combining them into a more complex signal with a larger bandwidth
full duplex	transmission mode in which a device can send and receive simultaneously
fully connected topology	connection strategy in which every device in a network is connected directly to every other one
gateway	OSI layer 7 connection between two networks
generator polynomial	polynomial used as a divisor in the CRC method of error detection
GEnie	information service providing access to on-line databases
geosynchronous orbit	orbit at which a satellite moves at the same speed that the earth rotates, thus appearing stationary to a ground observer
getsockname	UNIX socket command requesting the local address for a socket
getsockopt	UNIX socket command requesting information for a socket
glob	FTP command allowing/disallowing the use of wildcard characters
go ahead	Telnet command telling a remote host it can send
go-back-n protocol	sliding-window flow control protocol in which the receiver must receive frames in order
graded-index multimode fiber	optical fiber whose cladding has a variable refractive index
graph	mathematical model consisting of nodes and edges connecting the nodes

gremlin	mythical creature responsible for all lost frames in a network
group address	address specifying several stations in a predefined group
guard band	unused frequency between two adjacent channels
guest station	secondary station in the HDLC protocol
hacker	person who likes to program just for the sheer enjoyment of doing so
half duplex	transmission mode in which a device must alternate between sending and receiving
Hamming code	error correction method by doing several parity checks in prescribed positions
handshaking	process of defining and setting up a connection
Hayes compatible modem	intelligent modem capable of responding to a certain set of commands
hertz (Hz)	signal measurement specifying the number of cycles per second
hierarchical routing	routing technique in which nodes are divided into groups called domains
high-definition television	television technology providing a much sharper image than conventional television
High-level Data Link Control (HDLC)	data link protocol defined by ISO
hop count	a measurement in a routing technique that counts the number of stations along a route
Horizontal Tab	control character causing a print mechanism or cursor to move horizontally to the next tab setting
horn antenna	device used for microwave transmission
host	a computer attached to a network and capable of running user applications.
Huffman code	frequency-dependent compression technique
hypertext markup language (HTML)	language used to create World Wide Web documents
hypertext transfer protocol (HTTP)	application-layer protocol used in the World Wide Web to access and transfer Web documents
I series	set of documents describing ISDN architecture, configurations, routing principles, and interfaces
IEEE 802 Standards	set of network standards for local and metropolitan area networks
in-band signaling	signaling technique in which the signals are sent in the same channel or bit stream as data
index of refraction	measurement specifying how much light will bend as it travels from one medium to another
information frames	HDLC frames carrying data
infrared light	electromagnetic waves with frequencies just below that of visible light
Institute of Electrical and Electronic Engineers (IEEE)	professional organization that publishes journals, runs conferences, and develops standards

Integrated Services Digital Network (ISDN)	standard for a proposed global digital communications system
intelligent modem	modem capable of responding to a certain set of commands
International Organization for Standardization (ISO)	world-wide organization consisting of standards bodies from many countries
International Telecommunications Union (ITU)	standards organization whose members include various scientific and industrial organizations, telecommunications agencies, telephone authorities, and the ISO; formerly known as (CCITT)
Internet	collection of networks that run the TCP/IP protocol
Internet Control Message Protocol (ICMP)	Internet protocol for error reporting and providing routers updates on conditions that can develop in the Internet
Internet Engineering Task Force (IETF)	an international community whose members include network designers, vendors, and researchers, all of whom have an interest in the stable operation of the Internet and in its evolution
Internet Protocol	network-layer protocol originally developed by the Advanced Research Projects Agency
Internet Protocol version 6 (Ipv6)	an updated version of the current Internet Protocol
Internet worm	famous intrusion into the Internet that clogged systems and forced many to shut down
Internetwork packet exchange (IPX)	protocol used by Novell NetWare to establish and maintain connections between network devices
isochronous transmission	similar to asynchronous transmission, except the time between characters is equal to the amount of time needed to send an integral number of characters
JavaScript	a language used to write client-side scripts for World Wide Web applications
Joint Photographic Experts Group (JPEG)	a group formed as a cooperative effort by the ISO, ITU, and IEC that developed a compression standard, commonly known as JPEG compression, to compress both gray scale and photographic quality color images
Kepler's laws of planetary motion	mathematical models used to describe planetary motion
Kermit	Muppet character and a file transfer protocol
key distribution	problem of sending encryption keys to those receiving encrypted messages
laser	very pure and narrow beam of light
Lempel-Ziv encoding	compression technique that replaces a repeated string with code
light-emitting diode (LED)	device that produces less concentrated light than a laser and is often used as an alternative to a laser in fiber optic communication

Line Feed	control character that causes a print mechanism or cursor to advance to the next line
Link Access Protocols (LAP)	data-link-layer protocol that handles logical links between stations
link state routing	a routing strategy in which routers send and forward packets specifying the status of a link between two specified routers; each router uses the accumulated information to build routing tables
listen	socket command that puts a server in a passive mode allowing it to accept connections
local area network (LAN)	network spanning a relatively small geographic area connecting a variety of devices
local exchange	local office containing switching logic to route telephone calls
local loop	wires connecting telephones to the local exchange office
lock-up	see deadlock
logical link control (LLC)	IEEE standard data link protocol used in local area networks that handles logical links between stations
login scripts	collection of commands (Novell NetWare) that are automatically executed each time a user logs in to the system
longitudinal redundancy check	error detection mechanism done by visualizing a two-dimensional array formed by storing each byte in a frame and then calculating a parity bit for all of the bits in each column
low earth orbit (LEO) satellites	a proposed collection of satellites orbiting at low altitudes used to define a world wide communications network
machine state	collection of values associated with a system at an instant in time
mail directory	service providing the address of an individual given that he or she is unambiguously identified
major synchronization points	error recovery mechanism that divides session-layer transmissions into separate, and recoverable, dialog units
management information base	database used by SNMP that describes routers and hosts
Manchester code	digital encoding scheme in which the digital signal always changes state in the middle of an interval
Manufacturing Automation Protocol	proprietary network protocol for the General Motors Corporation
maximum transfer unit	maximum frame size that can be transferred over a network
medium access control	lower sublayer of the data link protocol that controls access to the transmission medium
medium attachment unit	PC-installable device containing the interfacing electronics and logic necessary to connect to an Ethernet

memory-resident viruses	computer virus that waits in memory for an executable file to be placed there
Menehune	central facility used in the Hawaiian Islands' Aloha (packet radio) system
Merkle's puzzles	method of key distribution in which a receiver randomly chooses one of many transmitted messages to determine the encryption key
message age timer	timer maintained by a bridge specifying a maximum time during which it expects to hear from the root bridge elected by the spanning tree algorithm
message handling system	most extensive part of the X.400 mail system containing all of the message transfer agents and user agents
message sequencing	placing messages in a specified order
message store	place where an X.400 user agent stores its messages
message switching	alternative to packet switching or circuit switching in which a transmitted message is stored at each node, but different messages may travel different routes
message transfer agent	software running on a dedicated computer and part of the X.400 system's backbone whose major function is to accept mail from a user agent or another message transfer agent, examine it, and route it
message transfer part	bottom three layers of Signaling System now 7; performs function similar to X.25
message transfer protocol	defines communication between two X.400 message transfer agents
message transfer system	that part of the X.400 mail system formed by the collection of message transfer agents
microwave transmissions	method of transmission using electromagnetic waves with a frequency below that of infrared light
Military Network	part of the Internet's backbone; connects military establishments throughout the U.S. and in some foreign countries
minor synchronization points	mechanism used to subdivide a session layer's dialog units
modal dispersion	phenomenon resulting from light reflecting at different angles in an optical fiber, causing some of the light to take a bit longer to get to the other end of the fiber
modem	device that converts analog signals to digital ones and vice versa
modem standards	standards defining how to convert between digital and analog signals
modulated signal	result of changing a carrier signal by another input signal
modulation	process of using one signal to change another one
monitor station	token ring station that has some maintenance and control responsibilities
monoalphabetic cipher	primitive encryption technique in which a text character is replaced by another that is chosen dependent only on the character being replaced

more fragments bit	a bit indicator that is set in every fragment of an IP segment except the last one
Morse code	transmission code developed for telegraph systems in which each character is represented by a series of dots and dashes
Moving Pictures Expert Group (MPEG)	often used to refer to a compression method for video files; more accurately, the group that defines standards for video compression
multicast	sending information to a particular group of host computers
multidrop link	HDLC link in which a primary station can communicate with several secondary stations
multiplexer	device combining signals from several inputs and sending them out over a single channel
multipoint link	see *multidrop link*
narrowband radio	transmission using a single radio frequency in order to achieve a higher data rate
National Institute of Standards and Technology (NIST	A standards making agency of the United States Department of Commerce
negative acknowledgment	flow control indication that a frame was not received correctly or was not received at all
neighbor identification procedure	token ring protocol allowing each station to learn the identity of its upstream neighbor
Netscape Navigator	popular browser used to obtain access to documents on the World Wide Web.
NetWare	commercial network operating system released by Novell
NetWare core protocol	procedures that a server uses to respond to a client's request
NetWare Directory Services	distributed database storing lists of NetWare userS, resources, and access rights on all NetWare servers
NetWare loadable modules	collection of software modules that can be used to meet individual users' needs
NetWare shell	NetWare command interpreter that accepts commands entered from a workstation
network	collection of devices running software allowing them to communicate via some transmission medium
network addressable unit	Systems Network Architecture (SNA) entity having its own address
Network Control Protocol	predecessor to TCP in the original ARPANET
network interface card (NIC)	board placed into a PC for the purpose of interfacing with a network
network layer	OSI layer 3 protocol responsible for routing packets through a network
network termination 1	ISDN designation for nonintelligent devices concerned with physical and electrical characteristics of a transmission signal

network termination 2	ISDN designation for intelligent devices capable of performing functions specified in OSI layers 2 and 3
network topology	manner in which network devices are connected physically
network virtual terminal	application-layer software that translates terminal-specific control sequences into standard forms
noise	unwanted signals that interfere with a transmitted signal
noiseless channel	channel impervious to noise
noisy lines	lines having more than a typical amount of noise
nonbroadcast frame	frame destined for a specific destination
non-data-J (also non-data-K)	digital signal that does not conform to any Manchester code for defining bits
nondedicated file server	server that may also run applications
nondelivery notification	X.400 service indicating mail was not delivered properly
Non-persistent CSMA	protocol in which, after a collision has occurred, the station does not monitor the transmission medium, instead waiting for one time slot before checking for activity
nonreturn to zero	digital encoding scheme in which 0s and 1s are represented by specific voltage levels
normal response mode	HDLC mode in which the primary station controls the communication
Novell NetWare	commercial network operating system
null modem	device used to connect two DTEs directly
Nyquist theorem	theoretical result that relates the data rate to a signal's baud rate and the number of signal components
octet	group of eight bits
odd parity	method of error detection in which an extra bit is added whose value is 0 or 1 in order to make the total number of 1 bits in the transmission unit odd
Open Data-link Interface (ODI)	Novell NetWare package allowing multiple protocols to send their packets through a single board and network connection
open system	set of protocols that would allow any two different systems to communicate regardless of their underlying architecture
Open Systems Interconnect (OSI)	protocol standard developed by the International Standards Organization to implement an open system
optical fiber	communications media consisting of a thin strand of glass through which light travels
orphan frame	token ring frame circulating endlessly because no station will remove it from the ring

out-of-band signaling	signaling technique in which the signals are sent in a separate channel or outside the data bit stream
outstanding frames	frames that have been sent but not yet acknowledged by a flow control protocol
P-persistent CSMA	protocol in which, after a collision has occurred, the station monitors the transmission medium and, when it is quiet, transmits with probability p ($0 \leq 2 \ p \ 2 \leq 1$)
pacing	SNA virtual route control function controlling the number of transmission units a node can send
packet	transmission unit for a specified protocol
packet assembler/ disassembler (PAD)	protocol that accepts characters from character-oriented devices and assembles them into X.25 packets; it also accepts X.25 packets from a network, disassembles them, and transmits their data as a character stream to a character-oriented device
packet elimination	congestion control scheme that eliminates some packets if there is an excessive buildup of them at a node
packet header	control information in a packet
packet-switched network	network over which messages are divided into pieces called packets and transmitted separately
parabolic dish reflector	microwave antenna whose dish is parabolic in shape
parallel transmission	transmission mode in which several bits are transmitted simultaneously
parity bit	extra bit in an error detection mechanism whose value is 0 or 1 in order to make the total number of 1 bits in the checked stream either even or odd
path	sequence of nodes in a network through which data must pass as it travels from sender to receiver
path control	layer 3 of the SNA protocol model responsible for determining paths and making routing decisions
Percent utilization	statistical measurement specifying the amount of time on an actual successful transmission as a percent of the total time spent on contending and sending
period	time required for a periodic signal to repeat a pattern once
periodic signal	signal that varies with time but repeats a certain pattern continually
peripheral node	SNA node that has limited processing capabilities
Petri nets	way to model a protocol using a graph to represent states and transitions
phase modulation	method of altering a signal by changing its phase shift
phase shift	horizontal shift in a periodic signal
phase shift keying	see phase modulation
physical layer	OSI layer 1 protocol responsible for defining the electrical and physical properties of the transmission medium
picture element	smallest visible component of an image on a television or video screen

piggyback acknowledgment	technique of sending an acknowledgment within a data frame
pixels	see *picture element*
plaintext	unencrypted message
point-to-point link	HDLC link in which a primary station communicates with one secondary station
poll bit	HDLC flag allowing a primary station to request a response from a secondary station
polyalphabetic cipher	encryption technique in which each occurrence of a text character is replaced by a different character depending on the original character and its position in the message
polymorphic virus	a virus capable of mutating or changing in order to avoid detection when it infects a file
polynomial	mathematical expression formed by adding terms each of which is a constant multiplied by an unknown term raised to a positive integral power
portable telephones	telephones that connect to the telephone system using radio communication
preamble	special bit pattern appearing at the beginning of some frame formats
predecessor	token bus term referring to the station from which a given station receives a token
prefix property	property stating that the bit code for a character never appears as the prefix of another code
presentation layer	OSI layer 6 protocol
presentation services	SNA layer 6 protocol
primary rate	ITU standard for ISDN consisting of 23 B channels and 1 D channel
primary station	type of station designated by HDLC that manages data flow by issuing commands to other stations and acting on their responses
print server	network device that manages a printer and handles print requests
private branch exchange (PBX)	private telephone system
probe service	X.400 service that lets a user agent determine whether mail can be delivered to an address
Project ELF	attempt by the Navy to install a large antenna in the upper peninsula of Michigan for the purpose of submarine communication using extremely low frequency
proof of delivery service	X.400 service allowing the authentication of the recipients of a message
proof of submission service	X.400 service providing proof a message has been submitted to the message transfer system
protocol	set of rules by which two or more devices communicate
protocol converters	logic to convert one protocol to another

pseudoternary coding	see *alternate mark inversion*
public data networks	packet-switched networks managed by a government or public utility
public key cryptosystem	encryption technique for which there is no attempt to protect the identity of the encryption key
pulse amplitude modulation	technique of sampling an analog signal at regular intervals and generating pulses with amplitude equal to that of the sampled signal
pulse code modulation	similar to pulse amplitude modulation, except the amplitude of the pulse must be one of a set of predefined values
pure Aloha	protocol developed at the University of Hawaii for a packet radio system
purge frame	token ring control frame that clears the ring of any extraneous signals
Q series	series of ITU-T documents describing a layered protocol called Signaling System No. 7, a standard providing functionality in integrated digital networks
quadrature amplitude modulation	modulation technique in which bits are assigned to an analog signal dependent on a combination of its amplitude and phase shift
radio	device capable of sending or receiving electromagnetic signals in the 10 KHz to 100,000 MHz range
reassembly deadlock	deadlock caused by running out of buffer space while accepting packets from multiple sources
reassembly timer	timer used by the Internet Protocol specifying the time in which it expects to receive all fragments from a packet
receive not ready	HDLC frame type used to stop the flow of incoming frames
receive ready	HDLC frame type used to indicate a station is ready to receive frames or to acknowledge frames already received
receiving window	flow control parameter specifying which frames can be received
receiving window size	flow control parameter specifying the maximum number of frames a receiving station can hold before passing them to a higher layer
record route option	Internet protocol parameter specifying that the route a packet takes be placed in the packet
recv	UNIX socket command used to receive information via a socket connection.
reference points R, S, T, U	ITU-T-defined reference points used to divide ISDN functional groups
refraction	phenomenon relating to the changing direction of light as it passes from one medium to another
regional center	telephone office covering (typically) a multistate region
relative encoding	see *differential encoding*
remote logins	process of logging in to a computer at a remote site
repeater	OSI layer 1 connection that receives signals and regenerates them before sending them on
reply	message sent in response to another

reply request indication	X.400 service requesting that a recipient reply to a transmitted message
request disconnect	protocol request from a station that a connection be terminated
Request for Comments (RFC)	series of documents containing research notes available via FTP
reservation system	token ring protocol mechanism allowing a station to try to reserve a token on its next pass
resolve contention frame	token bus control frame used in an arbitration protocol when two or more stations attempt to enter the logical ring simultaneously
return of content service	X.400 service providing for mail to be returned in the event it is not delivered
ring indicator	signal from a DCE to DTE indicating the DCE is receiving a ringing signal from the communications channel
ring initialization	token bus protocol that determines the logical order of the stations
ring topology	circular arrangement of devices each capable of communicating directly with its neighbor
root bridge	specially designated bridge determined by the spanning tree algorithm corresponding to the root of the spanning tree
root port	bridge port corresponding to the cheapest path to the root bridge
route	sequence of stations through which a frame must travel from its source to its destination
route designators	sequence of LAN and bridge IDs specifying a path
route discovery	process used by source routing bridges to determine the path to a particular station
route learning	process by which a bridge learns what to put in its routing table
Routed	routing program developed at the University of California at Berkeley to do routing on their local area network
router	OSI layer 3 connection between two networks
routing algorithm	method used to determine a route
routing directory	database used by a bridge or router to decide where to send frames it receives
Routing Information Protocol	routing strategy that uses a hop count to determine the path in a network
routing table	see *routing directory*
RS-232 standard	rules defining communication between a DCE and DTE
RS-422	electrical standard, using balanced circuits, for communication between a DCE and DTE
RS-423	electrical standard, using unbalanced circuits, for communication between a DCE and DTE

RS-449	operational standard, designed to replace RS-232, for communication between a DCE and DTE
run-length encoding	compression technique that replaces a run of bits (or bytes) by the number of bits (or bytes) in the run
run-length encoding prefix	special character used by Kermit to differentiate a data string from a run-length-encoded string
sampling frequency	rate at which analog signals are sampled
satellite	object orbiting the earth
satellite transmission	microwave transmission to or from an orbiting satellite
script	file containing a collection of commands to be executed
search drives	defines the directories that an operating system searches automatically when a user requests a file not in the current directory
secondary station	type of station designated by HDLC that responds to a primary station
security	pertaining to the protection or hiding of information from unauthorized people
segment	a formatted collection of information items for a protocol (usually TCP)
selective reject	HDLC control frame requesting that a particular frame be resent
selective repeat protocol	sliding-window flow control protocol in which the receiver defines a window specifying frames it can receive
self-synchronizing code	digital encoding scheme in which the signal always changes state in the middle of a bit interval
sending window	flow control parameter specifying which frames can be sent
sending window size	flow control parameter specifying the maximum number of frames a sending station can send before receiving acknowledgments
sequence number	number used for ordering frames or packets
serial transmission	mode of transmission in which all bits are sent in sequence
server	network device whose function is to respond to requests from the network users
service classes	mechanism used to prioritize data transmitted over a token bus network
service type	Internet packet field corresponding to transport layer requests regarding handling of the packet
session	logical connection between two end users
session control	component of SNA's transmission control layer
session layer	OSI layer 5 protocol
Shamir's method	method of key distribution such that a specified number of people must be present to determine it
Shift Down/Up	Baudot code control character changing the interpretation of subsequently received characters
Shift In/Out	ASCII-code control character changing the interpretation of subsequently received characters
shift register	part of a circuit used to implement cyclic redundancy checks

shortest path algorithm	logic used to determine the shortest path between two points
signal constellation	diagram using plotted points to define all legitimate signal changes recognized by a modem
signal ground	voltage level against which all other signals are measured
signal speed	speed at which a signal travels through a medium
signaling data link	lowest layer of Signaling System No. 7 providing physical and electrical specifications
signaling link layer	second layer of Signaling System No. 7 providing reliable communications between two adjacent points in the network
signaling network layer	third layer of Signaling System No. 7 providing reliable message transfer between two signaling points
Signaling System No. 7	four-layer protocol that defines a standard for functionality in an integrated digital network
signal-to-noise ratio	measurement used to quantify how much noise there is in the presence of a signal
Simple Mail Transfer Protocol (SMTP)	standard mail protocol in the TCP/IP suite
Simple Network Management Protocol	management protocol designed to make sure network protocols and devices work well
simplex	mode in which communication goes only one way
single-bit error	error affecting just one bit
single-mode fiber	optical fiber with a very small diameter designed to reduce the number of angles at which light reflects off the cladding to one
single-route broadcast frame	frame that is broadcast only through ports that are part of a spanning tree
sliding window protocol	flow control protocol where the sending and receiving stations restrict the frames they can send or receive
slot	time interval of length equal to the time required to transmit one frame
slotted Aloha protocol	Aloha protocol requiring a station to transmit at the beginning of a slot
slotted ring	similar to a token ring but with several rotating tokens
slow start	part of the startup process to the TCP flow control algorithm, in which the sending entity tries to determine how much it can send before congestion causes delays
smart terminals	terminals with computing capability
socket	UNIX construct and a mechanism used to connect to a network
socket commands	commands used to create and manage sockets and to send and receive information via a socket
solicit successor frame	token bus control frame used to invite new stations to join the logical ring

source address	address of a station sending a message
source quench	ICMP control message requesting a reduction in the rate at which packets are sent
source routing bridge	bridge that routes a frame based on the contents of the frame's route designator
spanning tree algorithm	distributed algorithm executed by bridges to determine a connection among all participating LANs that contains no redundant paths
spatial frequencies	values in the JPEG compression scheme that relate directly to how much the pixel values change as a function of their position in a block
split horizon	modification of a routing algorithm in which a node does not send information it received from a neighboring node back to that node
spot beam	type of antenna allowing satellite signals to be broadcast to only a very small area
stacking station	token ring station that has raised the token's priority
standard	agreed-on way of doing something
standby monitor present (SMP) frame	token ring control frame used in the protocol's neighbor identification procedure
star topology	arrangement of devices in which all communication goes through a central computer or switch
starLAN	network that has a star topology but uses a bus protocol
start bit	single bit signal used in asynchronous transmission alerting the receiver that data is arriving
start of frame delimiter	special bit pattern indicating the start of a frame
Start of Text	control character indicating the beginning of a text transmission
state transition	changing of a system from one state to another due to the occurrence of some event
state transition diagram	model of a system depicting all possible states and the events that cause the system to change states
static routing	routing strategy that uses information that does not change with time
statistical multiplexer	time-division multiplexer that creates a variable-sized frame
step-index multimode fiber	optical fiber with a larger diameter allowing several angles at which light reflects off the cladding
stop and wait protocol	protocol in which a sender sends a frame and waits for the acknowledgment to return before sending the next frame
stop bit	single-bit signal used in asynchronous transmission indicating the end of the transmission
store and forward	network protocol for which a message is stored in its entirety at each intermediate node along the path to the destination
store-and-forward deadlock	deadlock caused by a situation in which none in a circular list of nodes can send because the next one's buffers are full

study	the process by which one reads material, lists what one does not understand, rereads the material to gain further insight, makes another list of what one still does not understand, and repeats this process as often as necessary until the list is empty
subarea nodes	see *boundary nodes*
subareas	domains in an SNA network
submission and delivery protocol	protocol defining the interaction between X.400's user agent and message transfer agent
subnegotiation begin	starting delimiter for a sequence of Telnet commands
subnegotiation end	ending delimiter for a sequence of Telnet commands
subnet	an independent physical network that is also a component of a larger network
successor	token bus term referring to the station to which a given station sends a token
supervisory frame	frame used by HDLC to indicate a station's status or to send negative acknowledgments
switch	a device capable of forwarding information packets from one network to another. The term is often applied to cases in which the connected networks have similar technologies.
SYN character	character used in byte-oriented protocols indicating the start of a frame
synchronization points	see *major synchronization points* and *minor synchronization points*
Synchronous Data Link Control (SDLC)	bit-oriented data link protocol developed by IBM and similar to HDLC
Synchronous Optical Network (SONET)	an optical network using time-division multiplexing to accommodate simultaneous channels. Controlled by a clock, it transmits bits at rates ranging from about 155.5 Mbps to in excess of 2 Gbps.
system login script	NetWare term applying to a file containing commands that are executed for each user logging in to the system
Systems Network Architecture (SNA)	IBM's seven-layer communications protocol
T1	a digital carrier service with 24 channels and a bit rate of 1.544 Mbps
teleconferencing	communication system allowing people at different sites to not only hear but see each other as well
telegraph	primitive communication device consisting of a power source, switch, and sensor
telemetry	sensing of status or reading of data at remote sites
telephone	device used for voice communication
Telnet	application-layer virtual terminal protocol allowing remote logins
terminal adapter	device designed to be used with ISDN TE2 equipment to convert their signals to an ISDN-compatible format
terminal equipment 1 (TE1)	ISDN primary functional group designation for ISDN devices

terminal equipment 2 (TE2)	ISDN primary functional group designation for non-ISDN devices
terminators (Schwarzeneggers)	electronic devices placed at the end of a medium preventing any electronic echoing of signals
three-way handshake	mechanism to establish a connection consisting of a connection request, acknowledgment to the request, and an acknowledgment to the acknowledgment
time exceeded	ICMP control message sent to a source station when a packet or unassembled fragments are dropped from the network due to a timer expiration
time to live	Internet Protocol packet field specifying the maximum amount of time the packet can remain in the network
time-division multiplexing	process of accepting digital signals from several sources, storing them in a single frame, and sending the frame over a single channel
timestamp reply	ICMP control message sent in response to a timestamp request
timestamp request	ICMP control message sent to a remote host when a local host wants to estimate the round-trip time between it and the remote host
token	special frame circulating among all devices in a network used to determine when a station can send information over the network
token bus	bus topology network that controls access to the bus by using a token-passing protocol
token passing	process of circulating a token so that when a station captures the token, it may send data
token ring	ring topology network that controls access to the ring by using a token-passing protocol
token-holding timer	token bus timer specifying the maximum time a station may spend sending class 6 frames
token-rotation timer	token bus timer that determines the maximum time for a token to rotate around the logical ring
tone dialing	telephone dialing mechanism in which each digit sends a tone consisting of two frequencies
TPi	one of five classes of transport services in the OSI model
transaction	user-defined unit of work
transaction services	SNA layer 7 protocol
Transaction Tracking System	NetWare service allowing multiple updates to files to be regarded as a single transaction
transceiver	device that clamps onto an Ethernet cable for the purpose of interfacing between a PC and the cable
transceiver cable	cable connecting a transceiver to a PC
transmission control protocol (TCP)	transport protocol used in the Internet
transmission group control	component of SNA's path control layer managing one or more parallel lines between two nodes

transmission rate	measurement specifying the number of bits per second that can be transmitted over a medium
transmit data	RS-232 circuit used to transmit data from the DTE to DCE
transparent bridge	bridge that creates and updates its own routing tables
transparent data	mode of transmission in which a receiving station does not react to the contents of incoming bytes
transport layer	OSI layer 4 protocol responsible for end-to-end communications
transport protocol data unit (TPDU)	transmission unit for the OSI transport protocol
transposition cipher	encryption technique that rearranges the plaintext characters
trunk	high-capacity lines capable of transmitting many telephone conversations simultaneously
trustee rights	rights granted by NetWare to a group of users allowing them to access specific directories and files
twisted pair	communication circuit consisting of two insulated wires twisted around each other
tunneling	embedding of a IPv6 packet inside an IPv4 packet for the purpose of transmitting an IPv6 packet through a collection of routers that are not IPv6 compatible
two-way handshake	mechanism to establish a connection consisting of a connection request and an acknowledgment to the request
ultrahigh frequency	television transmission using electromagnetic waves between 300 MHz and 3 GHz
unbalanced circuit	circuit using one line for signal transmission and a common ground
undetected transmission errors	transmission errors that go unnoticed by the receiving station
Uniform Resource Locator (URL)	A text string specifying an Internet location and a protocol used to access an information document at that location
unrestricted flow control	essentially a lack of flow control; the sending station sends frames and makes no effort to limit the number it sends
upstream neighbor	token passing-term applying to the station from which a token is received
urgent data	data in a TCP segment that must be delivered to higher layers as quickly as possible
urgent pointer	TCP segment field pointing to urgent data
user agent	X.400 mail system component that interacts with the user and essentially defines what the user can do
User Datagram Protocol (UDP)	connectionless transport-layer protocol
user login script	NetWare term applying to a file containing commands that are executed for a specific user logging into the system
verification	process of verifying the sender of a message
very high frequency (VHF)	television transmission using electromagnetic waves between 30 MHz and 300 MHz

very small aperture terminal (VSAT) system	satellite communication system using small antenna dishes
videoconferencing	system allowing people in different locations to see and hear each other in a real-time setting
videotex	interactive access to remote databases
Vigenére cipher	substitution cipher in which the encryption key is a two-dimensional array of characters
virtual circuit (route)	logical connection that is established prior to any packet switched data transfer and for which all packets travel through the same network nodes
virtual route control	SNA path-control-layer function establishing a logical connection between two network addressable units
virtual terminal protocol	protocol defining communication between an application and terminal, independent of terminal characteristics
virus	unauthorized set of instructions that spreads from one computer to another, either through a network or through peripheral transfers
voice mail	system allowing telephone callers to leave messages in a local repository
waveguide	cylindrical tube that is part of a horn antenna
Wide Area Information Server (WAIS)	client/server application in which servers provide access to a variety of databases
wide area network (WAN)	network spanning a large geographic distance, often connecting many smaller networks running a variety of different protocols
window	abstract concept defining a subset of frames for the purpose of flow control between two stations
wire center	central switch providing a physical connection between any two of a group of devices
wireless communications	communication independent of a physical connection
World Wide Web	term applied to the collection of documents, links to other documents, and protocols to access them via the Internet
worm	program that intrudes into a system and has the potential to damage the system's security
X.25 standard	standard for connecting stations to a packet-switched network
X.400 standard	standard defining an electronic mail system
X.500 directory service	standard defining a distributed directory for an electronic mail system
X-OFF	flow control character causing incoming data to stop
X-ON	flow control character causing incoming data to resume

Acronyms

AAL, ATM adaptation layer

ABM, asynchronous balanced mode

ACK, Acknowledgment

AM, amplitude modulation

ANSI, American National Standards Institute

APPC, advanced program-to-program communication

APPN, advanced peer-to-peer networking

ARM, asynchronous response mode

ARPA, Advanced Research Projects Agency

ARQ, automatic repeat request

ASCII, American Standard Code for Information Interchange

ASN.1, Abstract Syntax Notation 1

ATM, Asynchronous Transfer Mode

BCD, binary-coded decimal

BCDIC, binary-coded decimal interchange code

BGP, Border Gateway Protocol

B-ISDN, broadband Integrated Services Digital Network

BSC, binary synchronous communication

CBX, computer branch exchange

CCITT, Comité Consultatif International de Télégraphique et Téléphonique

CDDI, Copper Data Distribution Interface

CGI, Common Gateway Interface

CMIP, Common Management Information Protocol

CMOT, CMIP over TCP

CPMGR, Connection Point Manager

CRC, Cyclic redundancy check

CS, convergence sublayer

CSMA, Carrier Sense Multiple Access

CSMA/CD, Carrier Sense Multiple Access with Collision Detection

DARPA, Defence Advanced Research Projects Agency

DCE, Data Circuit-Terminating Equipment

DCT, discrete cosine transform

DES, Data Encryption Standard

DIB, directory information base

DIT, directory information tree

DLE, data link escape

DNS, Domain Name System

DoD, Department of Defense

DPSK, differential phase shift keying

DSA, directory system agent

DSR, Data Set Ready

DSS, Digital Signature Standard

DTE, Data Terminal Equipment

EBDIC, Extended Binary-Coded Decimal Interchange Code

EGP, External Gateway Protocol

EIA, Electronic Industries Association

ELF, extremely low frequency

ENIAC, Electronic Numerical Integrator and Calculator

ESC, escape

FCC, Federal Communications Commission

FDDI, Fiber Distributed Data Interface

FDM, frequency-division multiplexing

FM, frequency modulation

FSK, frequency shift keying

FTP, File Transfer Protocol

HDLC, High-level Data Link Control

HDTV, high-definition television

HTTP, Hypertext Transfer Protocol

HTML, Hypertext Markup Language

IBM, International Business Machines

ICMP, Internet Control Message Protocol

IDN, integrated digital network

IEC, International Electrotechnical Commission

IEEE, Institute of Electrical and Electronic Engineers

IETF, Internet Engineering Task Force

IP, Internet Protocol

IPv6, Internet Protocol version 6

IPng, Internet Protocol next generation

IPM, interpersonal messaging

IPX, Internetwork Packet Exchange

ISO, International Organization for Standardization

ITU, International Telecommunications Union

JPEG, joint Photographic Experts Group

LAN, local area network

LAP, Link Access Protocol

LED, light-emitting diode

LEO, low earth orbit

LLC, logical link control

LSL, link support layer

MAC, medium access control

MAP, Manufacturing Automation Protocol

MAU, medium attachment unit

MHS, message handling system

MIB, management information base

MILNET, Military Network

MPEG, Moving Pictures Expert Group

MTA, message transfer agent

MTS, message transfer system

MTU, maximum transfer unit

NAK, negative acknowledgment

NAU, network addressable unit

NBS, National Bureau of Standards

NCP, Network Control Protocol

NDS, NetWare Directory Service

NIST, National Institute of Standards and Technology

NLM, NetWare loadable modules

NNI, Network-Network Interface

NRM, normal response mode

NRZ, nonreturn to zero

NSA, National Security Agency

NTSC, National Television Standards Committee

OAM, operations, administration, and maintenance

ODI, Open Data-link Interface

OSI, Open Systems Interconnect

OSPF, Open Shortest Path First

PABX, private automatic branch exchange

PAD, packet assembler/disassembler

PAM, pulse amplitude modulation

PBX, private branch exchange

PCM, pulse code modulation

PDU, protocol data unit

PEM, Privacy Enhanced Mail

PGP, Pretty Good Privacy

PM, phase modulation

PSK, phase shift keying

QAM, quadrature amplitude modulation

RFC, Request for Comments

RIP, Routing Information Protocol

RPC, remote procedure call

RSA algorithm, Rivest, Shamir, Adleman algorithm

SAR, segmentation and reassembly sublayer

SDLC, Synchronous Data Link Control

SMTP, Simple Mail Transfer Protocol

SNA, Systems Network Architecture

SNMP, Simple Network Management Protocol

SONET, Synchronous Optical Network

SPX, Sequenced Packet Exchange protocol

SS7, Signaling System no. 7

SSCF, Service Specific Coordination Function

SSCOP, Service Specific Connection Oriented Protocol

SSCP, system service control point

STM, synchronous transfer mode

TCM, trellis-coded modulation

TCP, Transmission Control Protocol

TCP/IP, Transmission Control Protocol/Internet Protocol

TDM, time-division multiplexing
TFTP, Trivial File Transfer Protocol
TOP, technical and office products
TPDU, transport protocol data unit
TPi, transport protocol i
TRT, token-rotation timer
TTS, Transaction Tracking System

UA, user agent
UDP, User Datagram Protocol
UHF, ultrahigh frequency
UNI, User-Network interface

URL, Uniform Resource Locator
UUCP, UNIX-to-UNIX copy program

VHF, very high frequency
VSAT, very small aperture terminal
VTAM, virtual telecommunications access method

WAIS, Wide Area information Server
WAN, wide area network
WWW, World Wide Web

INDEX